1 MONTH OF
FREE
READING

at

www.ForgottenBooks.com

By purchasing this book you are eligible for one month membership to ForgottenBooks.com, giving you unlimited access to our entire collection of over 1,000,000 titles via our web site and mobile apps.

To claim your free month visit:

www.forgottenbooks.com/free126655

ISBN 978-1-5285-8002-1
PIBN 10126655

REPORTS OF CASES

DECIDED IN

THE SUPREME COURT

OF THE

STATE OF OREGON.

ROBERT G. MORROW,

REPORTER.

VOLUME XXVIII.

SAN FRANCISCO:
BANCROFT-WHITNEY COMPANY,
LAW PUBLISHERS AND LAW BOOKSELLERS.
1896.

OFFICERS

TABLE OF CASES REPORTED.

CASES ARGUED AND DETERMINED

IN THE

SUPREME COURT

OF

OREGON.

Decided at PENDLETON, July 20, 1895.

MAXWELL *v.* BOLLES.

[41 Pac. 661.]

1. ERROR CURED BY SUBSEQUENT EVIDENCE.—Error in admitting evidence of the contents of an instrument without proof of its loss or destruction is cured by subsequent testimony showing the loss.

2. ADMISSION BY PLEADINGS—INCONSISTENT DEFENSES.—Where a defendant denies the execution or delivery of a note, and in a separate defense alleges that the same note was made with a fraudulent intent, the execution of the note is admitted, for the two statements are utterly inconsistent: *Veasey* v. *Humphreys*, 27 Or. 515, cited and approved.

3. CROSS-EXAMINATION.—The right of cross-examination is obviously an important one to an opponent, and the practice should be liberal with the purpose of eliciting all the facts in their true light. So, on an issue as to the consideration for a mortgage, the party attacking the instrument is clearly entitled to cross-examine the mortgagee on the facts and the circumstances surrounding its execution and delivery: *Ah Doon* v. *Smith* 25 Or. 89, and *Sayres* v. *Allen*, 25 Or. 215, approved and followed.

4. TIME WHEN ATTACHMENT LIEN ATTACHES TO CHATTELS.—A writ of attachment creates no lien on personal property until it is actually taken into the custody of the officer if it is capable of manual delivery; and when the property is in several parcels so as to require separate and distinct seizures, the lien as to each attaches only as of the time of its actual

seizure, and does not relate back to the time of the seizure of the first parcel.

APPEAL from Union: MORTON D. CLIFFORD, Judge.

This is an action by Isaac T. Maxwell against J. T. Bolles to recover possession of personal property. The complaint, in substance, alleges that on February twelfth, eighteen hundred and ninety-four, one J. Q. Shirley made, executed, and delivered to the plaintiff his promissory note for the sum of one thousand dollars, due one year after date, and, as security for the payment of the same, gave him a chattel mortgage on thirty-one head of horses, of the value of nine hundred and sixty dollars, which mortgage is conditioned that should the mortgaged property or any part thereof be "taken on attachment or execution, the whole of the principal and interest shall become due and collectible, at the option of the mortgagee or his assigns, and it shall be lawful for such person, his agents or assigns, to take immediate possession of said property, and to sell the same at public sale"; that said mortgage was duly and regularly filed in the office of the county clerk of Union County at nine o'clock a. m. of the twelfth day of February, eighteen hundred and ninety-four, and has ever since been and is still on file in said office; that thereafter, and on the thirteenth of February, the defendant, as sheriff, attached a portion of said mortgaged property under a writ of attachment issued in an action brought by Wright and Davis Brothers against Shirley, and ever since and now wrongfully and unlawfully withholds the possession thereof from the plaintiff; that by reason of said attachment plaintiff became and is entitled to the immediate possession of said property under the terms of his mortgage. The answer specifically denies, on information and belief, the material allegations of the complaint, and affirmatively avers that on February eleventh, eighteen hundred and ninety-four, there was placed in his hands for service two certain writs of attachment issued out of the Circuit Court for Union County, in actions therein pending, in which Wright and Davis Brothers were plaintiffs, and Shirley defendant, commanding and directing him to attach and take into his possession sufficient of the property of Shirley to satisfy the amount named in said writs; that afterwards, and on the twelfth day of February, eighteen hundred and ninety-four, and before the hour of nine o'clock a. m. of said day, under and by virtue of said writs, the defendant attached and took into his possession the personal property in controversy in this action, being the same at the time the property of Shirley and in his possession. And for a further defense he avers, on information and belief, that the promissory note and mortgage set out in the complaint were both voluntarily executed and delivered by Shirley to plaintiff without any consideration, and for the purpose of hindering, delaying, and defrauding the creditors of Shirley, and especially Wright and Davis Brothers, whose action was then pending, and that such note and mortgage were so received and accepted by plaintiff. The reply having put in issue the allegations of the answer, a trial was had, resulting in a verdict and judgment in favor of the plaintiff, and defendant appeals, assigning error in the ruling of the trial court in the admission of evidence and in its instruction to the jury.   REVERSED.

For appellant there was a brief and an oral argument by *Mr. Thos. H. Crawford.*

For respondent there was a brief by *Messrs. J. M. Carroll* and *Rand, Williams and Shinn*, and an oral argument by *Mr. Carroll* and *Mr. J. L. Rand.*

Opinion by MR. CHIEF JUSTICE BEAN.

1. It is claimed that the court erred in allowing the plaintiff to testify as to the existence and contents of the alleged promissory note given him by Shirley without first proving its loss or destruction. It is a rule of universal application that the existence and contents of a written instrument, when material and in issue, cannot be proved by parol without first showing that it is not within the power of the party offering such evidence to produce the writing itself. The instrument sought to be proved is regarded necessarily as the primary or best evidence of its own existence and contents, and, if possible, must be produced. This is but an application of the rule that the best evidence of a disputed fact must be produced of which the nature of the case is susceptible: 1 Greenleaf on Evidence, §§ 82, 84; Rice on Evidence, § 146. But in this case the bill of exceptions shows that the fact was elicited upon cross-examination that the note in question was not in possession of the plaintiff, but had been stolen from him two or three weeks before court convened; so that the error, if any, in admitting evidence of the contents of the writing without first proving its loss, was cured by the subsequent testimony of the defendant.

2. And, besides, it may well be doubted whether the existence or contents of the note was really in issue in the case at all. True, the defendant denied its execution or delivery upon information and belief, but in his answer he affirmatively admits the execu-

tion of both the note and mortgage, but alleges that they were made and received without consideration, and for the purpose of hindering, delaying, and defrauding the creditors of Shirley, and this admission probably rendered proof of their execution and delivery unnecessary: *Veasey* v. *Humphreys,* 27 Or. 515 (41 Pac. 8). From the pleadings it will be observed that the plaintiff claims title and right to the possession of the horses described in the complaint by virtue of a chattel mortgage thereon executed by Shirley on the twelfth day of February, eighteen hundred and ninety-four, which was filed for record at nine o'clock in the morning of said day; while the defendant claims that the writ of attachment under which he justifies was served by taking the property in question into his custody before the mortgage was filed, and that the note and mortgage were given and received for the purpose of hindering, delaying, and defrauding creditors, and especially the said Wright and Davis Brothers; the real questions presented, then, were, *first,* was the chattel mortgage filed before the attachment; and, *second,* if so, was the note and mortgage to plaintiff given and received in good faith to secure a *bona fide* debt?

3. The next error assigned relates to the refusal of the court to compel the plaintiff to answer certain questions on cross-examination. The bill of exceptions discloses that plaintiff testified on his direct examination that the note and mortgage were given for and to secure an indebtedness to him from Shirley for work and labor performed on Shirley's farms prior to February, twelfth, eighteen hundred and ninety-four. On cross-examination he was asked by defendant's counsel the following, among other questions: "Was it for work you done for him just before the note was given?" "For what particular length of time did you

work for Mr. Shirley, and what dates? and between what dates did you work for him for which the thousand-dollar note was given?" "What time in eighteen hundred and eighty-nine did you commence to work for him?" "What were you to receive a month for your work?" "How much did he pay you on your work between these dates over and above the thousand-dollar promissory note?" To each and all of these questions plaintiff by his counsel objected, whereupon the court sustained the objection and excused the witness from answering. One of the most important questions, if not the principal contested question, in the case, was whether there was any consideration for the note and mortgage under which plaintiff claims possession of the property; and, the plaintiff having testified in chief that it was work and labor performed by him for Shirley, it was clearly competent for the defendant on cross-examination to ask him when he commenced work, when he quit, what time he worked between those dates, what wages he was to receive, and how much he had been paid for his work over and above the amount covered by the note. These were all matters of legitimate cross-examination, and went to impeach the consideration of the very instrument under which plaintiff was claiming the right to the possession of the property in question. If the mortgage was without consideration, it was void as to the defendant, and plaintiff could not recover in the action. It was, therefore, of the utmost importance to the defendant that the right to cross-examine the plaintiff upon this matter should not be denied him. The cross-examination of a witness should always be allowed a free range, and it should not be limited to the exact facts stated in the direct examination, but may extend to other matters connected therewith which tend to limit, explain, qualify, or rebut any inference resulting from the direct examination: *Ah Doon v. Smith*, 25 Or. 89 (34 Pac. 1093); *Sayres* v. *Allen*, 25 Or. 215 (35 Pac. 254.) The range and extent of the cross-examination of witnesses is left to the discretion of the trial court, and will be reviewed by an appellate court only in case of an abuse of such discretion, but the bill of exceptions here discloses that defendant was not allowed to cross-examine the plaintiff at all upon the consideration of the note and mortgage, the objections to the questions being that such evidence was immaterial and irrelevant, and the court so ruled. The right to cross-examine the witness was a valuable legal right, of which the defendant could not be justly deprived, and the denial of such right was clearly error.

4. The next question is as to when the attachment under which defendant justifies took effect. The evidence in his behalf tended to show that on Saturday, the tenth day of February, he received the writs of attachment together with a list of the property to be attached, but too late for service on that day. On the following Monday morning, about seven o'clock, his deputy, accompanied by the agent of Shirley who had possession of the property, left Union to go to the Stanton and Jones Ranches, some four or five miles distant, where the horses were, for the purpose of attaching them. While on the way, and before reaching the Stanton Ranch, they met parties driving some of the horses to town, which they proceeded to attach and list. They then went to the Stanton Ranch, and attached and listed some more of the horses, and then went to the Jones Ranch and completed the attachment, getting through about noon, and returning to

Union about two o'clock in the afternoon. The evidence tended to show that a portion of the horses were attached prior to nine o'clock, the date at which the mortgage was filed, and it was admitted that some of them were not attached until after that time. The contention for the defendant is that, in contemplation of law, the attachment dated from the time the officer commenced to take the horses into his custody, and if that was prior to the filing of the mortgage, the attachment took precedence over it, although a part of the horses were not actually seized until after it was filed. But, as we understand the law, a writ of attachment creates no lien on personal property until it is actually taken into the custody of the officer, if it is capable of manual delivery and not in the possession of some third person; and when the property is so situated as to require separate and distinct seizures, the lien as to each attaches only at the time of its actual seizure and taking into custody by the officer: *Kuhn* v. *Graves,* 9 Iowa, 303; *Lott* v. *Roosevelt,* 9 Cowp. 526; *Burhans* v. *Tibbitts,* 7 How. Pr. 77. It is true it is sometimes said that in legal contemplation the law knows no fraction of a day, but common sense and common justice as well require that the exact time may be shown when it will promote substantial justice, and hence, when the statute says that from the date of the attachment the attaching creditor shall be deemed a purchaser in good faith, it simply means from the actual time that the property is attached, and not from the date of the writ or of the day on which the attachment is made. The mortgage of the plaintiff, if otherwise valid, was therefore a prior lien upon all the property therein described which had not been actually seized or attached by the sheriff at the time it was filed, and the defendant is entitled to the possession of such of the horses, if any, as he may have actually attached prior to such filing. The judgment of the court below is reversed and a new trial ordered.

REVERSED.

Decided June 3; rehearing, July 22, 1895.

SCHMIDT v. OREGON GOLD MINING CO.

[40 Pac. 406, 1014.]

1. APPEAL FROM CONSENT DECREE — CODE, § 536. — A decree entered at the request of a party, the other party being present and expressly consenting thereto, cannot be appealed from by either side: *Rader* v. *Barr*, 22 Or. 496, approved and followed. Such a decree will be governed by the provisions of section 536, Hill's Code, although, strictly speaking, it is not a decree given either by confession or for want of an answer.

2. CONSENT DECREE — CONDITIONS BEYOND THE SCOPE OF THE PLEADINGS. — Where the complaint in a suit by a trustee to foreclose the mortgage prays judgment for reasonable attorney fees and for professional services rendered therein, and the parties consent that judgment be rendered in accordance therewith, provisions in the decree that the trustee recover the attorney fees and fees for other professional services in trust for the parties rendering the services are not so entirely without the scope of the pleadings, and the authority of the parties to agree thereto, that the appellate court will declare them void at the instance of the party requesting that such judgment be rendered.

3. CONSENT DECREE — ISSUES MADE BY THE PLEADINGS. — A judgment or decree entered upon the pleadings or after a contest must fall within the issues made by the pleadings, but consent decrees will be valid and binding if they fall within the general scope of the case.

4. POWER OF ATTORNEY — PRESUMPTION — PRACTICE. — The courts must presume, in the absence of a showing to the contrary, that orders and proceedings of attorneys in the conduct of cases are made and conducted under proper authority from their clients, and when it is desired to impeach the acts of attorneys as beyond the terms of their employment, the proper method is to move in the lower court where the facts may be determined by testimony, rather than by an appeal from the objectionable proceeding.

APPEAL from Union: MORTON D. CLIFFORD, Judge.

This suit was instituted to foreclose three several mortgages executed by the Oregon Gold Mining Com-

pany to A. L. Schmidt as trustee to secure the payment of certain bonds of the company, bearing dates
respectively May first and October first, eighteen hundred and eighty-eight, and September first, eighteen
hundred and eighty-nine. Each of said mortgages in
effect provides that in case of default in the conditions
imposed the trustee might foreclose and sell the property described therein, and that out of the proceeds he
should be allowed for attorney's fees such sum as the
court might adjudge reasonable, together with all necessary costs and expenses incurred, including a reasonable compensation to himself for the execution of the
trust. The complaint sets forth by appropriate allegations the legal purport of these promises, and the
prayer, among other things, is "for judgment and decree fixing and determining the amount to which plaintiff is entitled in this suit for reasonable attorney's
fees for foreclosing the said mortgage, and for professional services herein, and declaring the same a lien
upon the said mortgaged property, rights, privileges,
and franchises, and directing payment therefor out of
the proceeds of said mines, and the proceeds arising
from the sale of said mortgaged property." The decree, among other things, contains the following findings and provisions, viz.: "Now at this day this cause
came on to be heard upon the motion of plaintiff for
judgment and decree as prayed for in the complaint
herein, the plaintiff appearing by T. Calvin Hyde and
T. H. Crawford, of counsel, and the defendant by C. A.
Johns and W. F. Butcher of counsel. And it appearing to the court that the referee heretofore appointed
herein by the court to take the testimony in this case,
and to report the same to the court, together with his
findings of fact and conclusions of law thereon, namely,
Charles F. Hyde, an attorney of this court, did, with

the assistance of John Wheeler, Esq., the official stenographer of this court, proceed to and take the testimony in full of the plaintiff in this cause regularly as
in his appointment ordered and directed, at which time
the said defendant notified the plaintiff by and through
its said attorneys that defendant would offer no testimony, but would consent to a judgment and decree as
prayed for in plaintiff's complaint, and that for this
reason no testimony was offered and taken on behalf of
the defendant by said referee in this cause; and it further appearing to the court that the said referee has
filed in court the testimony so taken by him on behalf
of the plaintiff, and the same fully sustains the allegations of plaintiff's complaint, and that said defendant
by his said attorneys in open court here now consents
that a judgment and decree may be here now made
and entered in this cause in favor of said plaintiff,
A. L. Schmidt, trustee, and against the said defendant,
the Oregon Gold Mining Company, as prayed for in
plaintiff's complaint, and that in said judgment and
decree the court shall fix the referee's fees at the sum
of two hundred dollars, the stenographer's fees at the
sum of —— dollars, and the plaintiff's attorneys' fees
at such sum as the court may find reasonable for the
services performed, and that the referee's fees, stenographer's fees, and the plaintiff's attorneys' fees shall
be a preferred lien upon the mortgaged property of
the defendant, and the proceeds thereof, in favor of
the said referee, stenographer, and the plaintiff's said
attorneys, for the respective amounts due each as
found and settled by the parties and the court, and
that they or either of them may have execution therefor against the said mortgaged property." * * *
"18. The court further finds that the sum of five
thousand five hundred and fifty dollars is a reasonable

attorney's fee in this suit for the foreclosure of the said several mortgages and trust deeds, and that of said sum plaintiff's attorney, T. Calvin Hyde, should receive the sum of two thousand seven hundred and fifty dollars, and the plaintiff's attorney, T. H. Crawford, should receive the sum of two thousand seven hundred and fifty dollars, and that said amounts so allowed each of said attorneys should be a preferred lien upon the said mortgaged premises, and upon the funds arising from the sale of the said mortgaged property, for the payment of the same, for the enforcement of which either of said attorneys should have execution. * * * 19. That upon the agreement of the parties herein made in open court, the court finds and fixes the compensation of Charles F. Hyde, referee herein, at the sum of two hundred dollars, and the compensation of the court stenographer, John Wheeler, at the sum of one hundred and fifty dollars, and that the compensation and fees of said referee and stenographer should also be preferred liens upon the said mortgaged property, and the proceeds thereof, for the payment of the same." * * * "It is therefore ordered, considered, adjudged, and decreed, that plaintiff A. L. Schmidt, as trustee for the holders of said bonds, have and recover off and from the defendant * * * the further sum of five thousand five hundred dollars, reasonable attorneys' fees herein, in trust for T. Calvin Hyde and T. H. Crawford, plaintiff's attorneys herein; and for the further sum of two hundred dollars, referee's fees, in trust for Charles F. Hyde, referee herein; and for the further sum of one hundred and fifty dollars, stenographer's fees herein, in trust for John Wheeler, court stenographer, and for the costs and disbursements of this suit. * * * And it is further ordered, adjudged,

and decreed that the judgment herein made and entered for attorneys' fees, stenographer's fees, and costs
and disbursements, be and the same is hereby adjudged and decreed to be a first lien upon all the
property described in said several mortgage deeds,
and the proceeds arising from the sale thereof, * * *
and that the proceeds arising from such sale be applied to the payment of the attorneys' fees decreed in
this suit, the referee's fees, and the stenographer's
fees."

The notice of appeal contains nine assignments of
error, which may be comprised in two as follows:
First, the court erred in finding, adjudging, and decreeing that plaintiff recover off and from defendant five
thousand five hundred dollars attorneys' fees in trust
for T. Calvin Hyde and T. H. Crawford, two hundred
dollars in trust for Charles F. Hyde, referee, and the
further sum of one hundred and fifty dollars in trust
for John Wheeler, stenographer, and that these several sums should be a first and superior lien upon the
property described in the said several mortgages, and
directing the same to be first paid out of the proceeds
thereof; and, *second,* the court erred in not adjudging
and decreeing the amount found to be reasonable as
attorneys' fees to plaintiff, and in not decreeing to
plaintiff a reasonable sum as compensation for services under his trust as such trustee. The appeal is
taken by Messrs. Dolph, Nixon and Dolph, as attorneys
for plaintiff. The defendant made no appearance in
this court, but T. Calvin Hyde and T. H. Crawford, in
their own behalf, and as attorneys for Charles F. Hyde
and John Wheeler, attack the appeal by a motion to
dismiss it, and filed a brief herein. The ground
mainly relied upon for dismissal is that the decree

appealed from was given by consent, and is therefore not appealable.   DISMISSED.

Opposed to the motion was a brief by *Messrs. Dolph, Nixon and Dolph,* and an oral argument by *Mr. Joseph N. Dolph,* making these points:

Under the allegations of the complaint, and the provisions of the mortgages concerning costs and expenses of foreclosure, any allowance for attorneys' fees should have been made to the plaintiff. Messrs. Hyde and Crawford were not the only attorneys employed by the plaintiff. The question for this court to consider is whether the court below erred in attempting, without any allegation in the complaint to give it jurisdiction of the subject-matter, to render a decree in favor of persons not parties to the suit and against a party with whom they had no contract; to make a contract between the plaintiff and his attorneys without the knowledge or consent of the plaintiff; and without allegations as to the value or the character or the extent of the services rendered, and without notice to the plaintiff to adjudicate a claim of plaintiff's attorneys against their client. It would seem as if it were unnecessary to submit arguments to show that such a proceeding is not warranted by law and is without precedent in practice. That a judgment or decree cannot be rendered in an action or suit for or against a person not a party is an elemental principal of law. It would be idle to expect to find a decision directly in point for such a thing as was attempted in this case. It was probably never before attempted by any court. The decree in so far as it purports to be a decree in favor of Messrs. Hyde and Crawford was made without jurisdiction and is void: Freeman on Judgments, § 154, 3d ed.

The statutes of Oregon provide in what cases and to what extent an attorney has a lien for services and in what manner such lien may be secured: Hill's Code, § 1044. Subdivision 4 provides for a lien for attorney's fees, and that such lien shall be subordinate to the rights existing between the parties to the action, suit, or proceeding. As to referee's fees and stenographer's fees all that it is necessary to say is that the Code provides what fees may be taxed in a suit, and the manner of their taxation.

A decree or judgment adjudicating a matter outside the issue raised by the pleadings is an absolute nullity and open to collateral attack: Beach's Modern Equity Practice, § 790; Gibson's Suits in Chancery, § 539; *Jones* v. *Davenport,* 45 N. J. Eq. 77; *Reynolds* v. *Stockton,* 43 N. J. Eq. 211; *Elliott* v. *Pell,* 1 Paige, 263; *Tripp* v. *Vincent,* 8 Barb. Ch. 613; *Goodhue* v. *Churchman,* 1 Barb. Ch. 596.

ON REHEARING.

No case like this one has come under our observation, and we hope for the honor of the legal profession no case like it is to be found in the reported decisions. The court evidently proceeded upon the theory that the provisions of the decree appealed from were adjudications of rights between the parties to the suit, whereas they are solely concerning claims, demands, or rights between the attorneys for plaintiff and the referee and stenographer on one side, and the plaintiff on the other. The supposed consent upon which they are based is the consent of the attorneys for the plaintiff agreeing with themselves for the plaintiff to an adjustment of claims of their own against the plaintiff, and to a decree against the plaintiff in their favor.

There is a salutary principle of law coeval with the history of law itself, and which no court in any civilized country has ever yet failed to apply and enforce, which, even if the matters adjudicated or attempted to be adjudicated had been within the issues made by the pleadings, and the attorneys had been parties to the suit, would have made the transaction wholly void. It is the rule that prohibits all persons having fiduciary relations with others from using their position, power, or authority for their own advantage.

The attorneys for plaintiff instead of taking judgment and decree in favor of the plaintiff, procured a decree which is in legal effect a decree in favor of themselves and against the plaintiff. It is immaterial how this was done. No consent, as we shall presently show, of the attorneys for the plaintiff could authorize such a proceeding. The decree does not provide that the plaintiff shall recover the five thousand five hundred dollars in trust for the attorneys, to be paid after the mortgaged debt is satisfied or *pro rata* with the bondholders or with the other expenses, but to be first paid, even if such payment exhausts the entire proceeds of the property.

Such a judicial proceeding is a scandal upon the administration of justice, and if allowed to stand must weaken the respect for the courts and the confidence of citizens in the security for their rights of property, and prevent the investment in Oregon of capital from other states and from foreign countries. There could be but one greater reproach upon our judicial system and the legal profession, and that would be to have the law deliberately settled by the highest court in the state that the party injured in such a case was precluded by the act of his attorney from having the error corrected and the wrong righted on appeal. It must receive the severest condemnation by every up-right judge and every honorable lawyer. It is not such a transaction as to induce a court of equity to adopt a new principle of equity or to strain the application of an established principle to protect it from judicial investigation, or to prevent the righting of the wrong done. It is entirely immaterial whether the amount decreed to the plaintiff's attorneys was reasonable or unreasonable, so far as the legal questions are concerned. It is a matter of comparative unimportance whether the plaintiff in this particular case shall be robbed or not; but it is of the utmost importance to the profession, to suitors, and to the courts that the legal questions involved should be properly settled. If the attorneys for a plaintiff can by their own act, acting for themselves and at the same time for their client, consent to a decree and bind their client by their consent by which five thousand five hundred dollars of the amount their client is entitled to recover is decreed to them so that the wrong cannot be considered and righted on appeal, there is nothing to prevent them from so binding their client to a decree by which the entire relief the plaintiff is entitled to is decreed to the attorneys instead of to the plaintiff, or by which the plaintiff is decreed to recover the entire relief he is entitled to in trust for the attorneys. There can be no distinction drawn between the two cases.   •

The plaintiff's attorneys had no authority to consent to the provisions of the decree complained of. If upon the face of the decree it is held that the decree appears to have been consented to by the plaintiff's attorneys, and, therefore, by the plaintiff, it is too plain for argument that an attorney at law has

no implied authority to enter a consent decree, by
which a definite fee is given him, and made a first
lien upon the property which is the subject of the
action. The authority of an attorney as an attorney
at law to bind his client has never been extended to
such a case. His authority in the management of a
suit is only to do in behalf of his client all acts in
and out of court, necessary to the prosecution and
management of the suit, and which affect the remedy
only and not the cause of action: *Moulton* v. *Bowker,*
115 Mass. 36 (15 Am. Rep. 72). An attorney is not
dominus litis. His relation with his client is fiduciary:
Hughes v. *Wilson,* 26 N. E. 50. An attorney employed
to foreclose a lien against land has no lien entitling
him to a sale thereof: *McCoy* v. *McCoy,* 15 S. E. 973.
And it has been held that he cannot give up the security of his client without payment or express authority: *Terhune* v. *Colton,* 2 Stock. Ch. 21; *Tankersley* v.
Anderson, 4 Dessaus, 45. Nor to release sureties upon
the claim of his client: *Savings Insurance* v. *Chinn,* 7
Bush (Ky.), 539; *Givens* v. *Brisco,* 3 J. J. Marsh, 529,
532; *Union Bank* v. *Govan,* 10 Sm. and M. 333. Nor to
discharge a lien created by levy of execution: *Banks* v.
Evans, 10 Sm. and M. 35 (58 Am. Dec. 734); *Benedict* v.
Smith, 10 Paige, 126. Nor to release a lien obtained
by judgment, or to discharge any security resulting
from his prosecution of the claim. And an honest belief that he is acting in his client's interest cannot
supply the defect of authority to make such an arrangement: *Wilson* v. *Jennings,* 3 Ohio St. 528. He may
control the manner of conducting a cause, but cannot
waive any substantial acquired right of his client:
Howe v. *Lawrence,* 2 Zab. 99.

It is also held that an attorney cannot release a
third person for the purpose of making him a compe-

tent witness: *Shores* v. *Caswell*, 13 Metc. 413; Succession of Weigel, 18 La. Ann. 49; *Marshall* v. *Nagel*, 1 Bailey, 308. Nor discharge an indorser upon a note committed to him for collection without satisfaction or the express consent of his client: *East River Bank* v. *Kennedy*, 9 Bosw. 543; *Bowne* v. *Hyde*, 6 Barb. 392; *Kellogg* v. *Gilbert*, 10 Johns. 220 (6 Am. Dec. 335); *Simonton* v. *Barrell*, 21 Wend. 362; *York Bank* v. *Appleton*, 17 Me. 55; *Varnum* v. *Bellamy*, 4 McLean, 87. Nor sell or assign a judgment of his client: *Maxwell* v. *Owen*, 7 Coldwell, 630; *Baldwin* v. *Merrill*, 8 Humph. 132; *Campbell's Appeal*, 29 Penn. St. 401 (72 Am. Dec. 641); *Rowland* v. *Slate*, 58 Penn. St. 196. Nor discharge a judgment or execution except upon payment in full: *Beers* v. *Hendrickson*, 45 N. Y. 665; *Lewis* v. *Woodruff*, 15 How. Pr. 539; *Wilson* v. *Wadleigh*, 36 Me. 496; *Harrow* v. *Farrow*, 7 B. Mon. 126 (45 Am. Dec. 60); *Chambers* v. *Miller*, 7 Watts, 63. Nor receive any other thing but lawful money in payment of his client's claim: *Stackhouse* v. *O'Hara*, 14 Penn. St. 88; *Harper* v. *Harvey*, 4 W. Va. 539; *Smock* v. *Dade*, 5 Rand. 639; *Jeter* v. *Haviland*, 24 Ga. 252; *Miller* v. *Edmonston*, 8 Blackf. 291; *Jones* v. *Ransom*, 3 Ind. 827; *Trumbull* v. *Nicholson*, 27 Ill. 149; *Lawson* v. *Bettison*, 7 Eng. 644; *Bailey* v. *Bagley*, 19 La. Ann. 172; *Wright* v. *Dailey*, 26 Texas, 730; *West* v. *Ball*, 12 Ala. 340; *Clark* v. *Kingsland*, 1 Sm. and M. 248. Nor indorse a note left him for collection: *Child* v. *Eureka Powder Works*, 44 N. H. 354. Nor compromise a suit: *Holker* v. *Parker*, 7 Cranch, 436; *Stokely* v. *Robinson*, 34 Penn. St. 315; *Huston* v. *Mitchell*, 14 S. and R. 307 (16 Am. Dec. 506); *Dodds* v. *Dodds*, 9 Penn. St. 315; *Abbe* v. *Rood*, 6 McLean, 106; *Derwort* v. *Loomer*, 21 Conn. 245; *Keller* v. *Scott*, 2 Sm. and M. 81. Nor employ associate counsel, save in the absence of his client: *Briggs* v. *Georgia*, 10 Vt. 68. Nor waive the right of inquisition: *Hadden* v. *Clark*, 2 Gratt. 107. Nor accept service

of summons: *Masterson* v. *LeClaire*, 4 Minn. 163. Nor
consent to a judgment against his client: *People* v. *Lan-
born*, 1 Scam. 123. Nor enter a *retraxit*: *Lambert* v. *Sanford*, 2 Blackf. 137 (18 Am. Dec. 149). Nor make an
agreement for suspension of proceedings upon a judgment: *Pendexter* v. *Vernon*, 9 Humph. 84. Nor discharge
a trustee: *Quarles* v. *Porter*, 12 Mo. 76. Nor give an extension of time upon a debt due to his client: *Lockhart*
v. *Wyatt*, 10 Ala. 231 (44 Am. Dec. 481). Nor transfer
to another the property in a note committed to him for
collection. Nor bind his client by an agreement to re-
fund money overpaid: *Ireland* v. *Todd*, 36 Me. 149; see
Bingham v. *Salene*, 15 Or. 208 (2 Am. St. Rep. 152) cited
in brief of counsel for respondents.

See also section 219, Week's on Attorney at Law,
for a full statement of what the attorney may not do
by virtue of his retainer and without special authority.

The leading case upon the subject of purchases by
persons thus occupying confidential relations towards
the vendor is, probably, *Fox* v. *Mackreath*, 1 Lead. Cas.
in Eq. part 1, White and Tudor (4th Am. ed.), 188,
p. *115· There the court held that a purchase by a
trustee for sale from his *cestui que trust*, although he
may have given an adequate price and gained no advantage, should be set aside at the option of the *cestui
que trust*, unless the connection between them had been
dissolved, and the knowledge of the value of the property acquired by the trustee had been communicated
to the *cestui que trust*. Exhaustive notes are added to
the report of this case by the very able editors, and
most of the cases relating to purchases by persons occupying confidential relations, are reviewed. We have
cited these authorities concerning the powers of an attorney at law to bind his client, and concerning the
relations between attorney and client to show, *first*, that

it was not within the power of plaintiff's attorneys of
their own volition and by their own act, to consent,
so as to bind their client, to a decree by which the re·
lief which the plaintiff was supposed to be entitled to
upon the complaint and upon consent of the defend.
ant should be adjudged and decreed to them, the
plaintiff's attorney, instead of to the plaintiff; *second,* to
show how courts scrutinize the dealings of attorneys
with their clients, and how jealously they protect the
interests of the clients, and that therefore such a de·
cree as the one in this cause will not be held to be a
consent decree.

Upon the authorities above cited we respectfully
contend that the agreement between counsel above
recited was plainly beyond the power of counsel to
make. It introduced new and important rights, and
conferred them upon plaintiff's counsel, entirely un·
known to either party. It materially changed and un·
settled the rights of all the parties, and made them
different from what they were under the mortgage.
It postponed the rights of the plaintiff under the
mortgage, as well as of the bondholders, to the rights
of plaintiff's attorneys, by giving the attorneys a first
lien on the mortgaged property. We submit that the
taking of a decree by plaintiff's attorneys in their
own favor and against their client was clearly not
within their authority, was a violation of their obligations and duty as attorneys at law and as officers of
the court, was a violation of their obligations and
duties to their client, and in violation of the just, long
established, and inflexible rule of law which requires
not only common honesty but the utmost good faith
in dealings of persons holding fiduciary relations with
others and which renders all such transactions as the
one in question void.

Was the decree on its face a consent decree? We believe that the court also erred in holding and deciding that the decree in question purports on its face to be a consent decree, so far, at least, as it relates to the matter of attorney's fees. The only motion made by plaintiff's attorneys or consent by them to the decree, so far as it relates to attorney's fees, is found in these words: "Now at this time this cause came on to be heard, on the motion of plaintiff, for a judgment and decree as prayed for in the complaint herein." The defendant, it is true, consented to several things concerning attorney's fees; but, as we have already stated, the defendant had no interest whatever in and no control whatever over the matter of the claim of the plaintiff's attorneys against the plaintiff for fees and could give no consent whatever which would bind anybody concerning the same. In conclusion, we have not hesitated to discuss freely the nature of the transaction concerning which we complain, and to present as forcibly as possible our reason for claiming that the court erred in dismissing the appeal. We have not examined all the cases in which the question of consent decrees has been discussed; but we repeat that we have not been able to find and we think there cannot be found a reported decision which holds that a decree to be a consent decree must not be between the parties to the suit, and must not be concerning a matter which is within the general scope of the case, that is to say, within the issues made by the pleadings; and we feel certain that no case can be found which holds that an attorney at law, representing his own interests and the interests of his client at the same time, can consent for his client so as to bind him to a decree adjudicating a claim of his own against his client without pleadings and without notice.

We have made and now submit this application to the court, not only because the interests of our client seemed to demand that it should be done, but because we believed the good name and honor of the legal profession required that the transaction in question and the legal questions involved should receive further consideration by the court.

Opinion by MR. JUSTICE WOLVERTON.

1. Section 536 of Hill's Code provides that "any party to a judgment or decree other than a judgment or decree given by confession, or for want of an answer, may appeal therefrom." The decree appealed from, in a strict sense, is neither a decree given by confession nor for want of an answer; but it has been held by this court that by consenting to the rendition of a judgment against himself the defendant, in effect, waives his answer, and thereby leaves no issue in the case to be tried; and that from such a judgment no appeal lies: *Rader* v. *Barr*, 22 Or. 496 (29 Pac. 889). In the present case the decree shows upon its face that the "defendant, by his said attorneys, in open court, here now consents that a judgment and decree may be here now made and entered * * * as prayed for in plaintiff's complaint." What more could plaintiff have obtained in the absence of an answer, or upon defendant's entire default? The recitals in the decree also show that the defendant gave its consent to the fixing of plaintiff's attorneys' fees by the court at such sum as it should find reasonable, and, there being no evidence in the record to guide it in determining what would be reasonable, we conclude that the parties intended that the court should ascertain the amount in its own way, and that they should

be bound by the result. And, further, it is apparent
that the amount of the attorneys' fee which plaintiff
should recover and have entered in the decree as the
finding of the court was a matter not to be determined by the court *in invitum.* The simple fact that
plaintiff did not complain of the court's judgment in
fixing this sum at five thousand five hundred dollars
would indicate that he so understood it, and expected
to be fully bound thereby. All other conditions of
the decree appear to be either deducible directly from
the allegations of the complaint, or were specially
consented to by the defendant. As to the matter of
the referee's and stenographer's fees, the record shows
that they were fixed and entered by the express
agreement of both parties. So we have here a decree
which the plaintiff, through his attorney, specifically
requested the court to make, and to every feature of it
which the defendant has upon the record consented.
True, the record does not show upon its face that the
plaintiff consented to the decree in the form as entered, but it was entered nevertheless at his expressed
request, so that this decree is essentially a consent
decree. The conditions, simply stated, are, the court
is requested by one party to make certain findings,
and to enter a decree thereon with certain definite
conditions. To all this the other party consents, and
the decree is entered. Now the party making the request appeals to this court, and demands that the decree be reversed in part, without even so much as
moving the lower court to modify its findings, or the
decree entered thereon, or calling its attention to errors and irregularities, so that the court could, upon
its own motion, purge the record of its infirmities.
To say the least, this is not fair treatment of the
court below, and in support of its decree this court

will presume the consent of plaintiff to the entry thereof in its present form: Hayne's New Trial and Appeal, § 285, p. 846; *Parker* v. *Altschul,* 60 Cal. 380; *Lesse* v. *Clark,* 28 Cal. 36; *Wilson* v. *Dougherty,* 45 Cal. 35; *Reynolds* v. *Hosmer,* 45 Cal. 627. Consent excuses error, and ends all contention between the parties. It leaves nothing for the court to do but to enter what the parties have agreed upon, and when so entered the parties themselves are concluded. From such a decree there is no appeal: Beach on Modern Equity Practice, § 795; *Armstrong* v. *Cooper,* 11 Ill. 540. Under section 692 of the Revised Statutes of the United States the practice of the national courts is to entertain an appeal from a consent decree; but they will not decide any matters that appear to have been consented to by the parties, and if the errors complained of come within the waiver the decree of the court below will be affirmed: *Pacific Railroad* v. *Ketchum,* 101 U. S. 295. This court, however, is committed to the doctrine that no appeal lies from such a decree: *Rader* v. *Barr,* 22 Or. 496 (29 Pac. 889). For these reasons the appeal must be dismissed.

2. It is further claimed that, notwithstanding the parties may have consented to all the terms and conditions of the decree, yet that those portions thereof wherein it is found and decreed that plaintiff have and recover off and from the defendant two thousand seven hundred and fifty dollars in trust for T. Calvin Hyde, two thousand seven hundred and fifty dollars in trust for T. H. Crawford, two hundred dollars in trust for Charles F. Hyde, and one hundred and fifty dollars in trust for John Wheeler, are entirely without the scope of the complaint, and for that reason void, and therefore reversible upon appeal. Undoubtedly, under

the allegations of the complaint, the plaintiff could recover the fees named. He sues in the capacity of trustee, and whatever he may recover by reason of the decree would be in trust for the bondholders. Now, if, at his own request, the court has decreed that he recover these certain fees in trust for the parties named, who, for all that appears of record, have earned them, when, at the same time, he, as trustee for the bondholders, is under personal obligations to these parties for services rendered in the suit instituted by him, we cannot say that these provisions are so entirely without the scope of the pleadings, and the authority of the parties to agree to under them, as that the court will declare them void at the instance of a party requesting the court to enter just such a decree. We therefore consider the point not well taken.

As to the error assigned because the court did not ascertain and decree to plaintiff a reasonable sum as compensation for services rendered as trustee, if the question was properly here we could not consider it, as no testimony is found in the record upon which to base such a finding and decree.   DISMISSED.

ON REHEARING.
[40 Pac. 1014.]

Opinion by MR. JUSTICE WOLVERTON.

A motion for rehearing having been filed in this case, and with it a vigorous and very able brief by Messrs. Dolph, Nixon and Dolph, of counsel for appellants, we have been impelled to review with much care and pains our former opinion, but with the same result. When the former opinion was rendered we had some misgivings as to whether we were right in hold-

ing that the provisions of the decree concerning attorneys', referee's, and stenogragher's fees were not so
entirely without the scope of the pleadings as to render them void, simply because we had been cited to
no adjudicated cases that seemed to bear directly upon
the question, and were unable to find any at the time
that were in point, but believed the opinion to be
founded upon sound principles of law. Further re-
search has confirmed us in this view. The authorities
will be cited and discussed later on. Counsel do not
controvert the soundness of the decision in *Rader* v.
Barr, 22 Or. 495, (29 Pac. 889,) but contend that it has
no application to the case at bar, and assign as the
sole ground for this contention that the provisions of
the decree to which they take exception are without
the scope of the pleadings. But, conceding the premises to be true, *non constat* that the conclusion contended for would follow. Let us examine the premises, and determine their effect in a case of this nature.

3.   As a general proposition all provisions of a decree outside of the issues raised by the pleadings are
void, but this cannot be predicated of a consent decree.   All the authorities cited by counsel support the
general proposition, but are not applicable to consent
decrees.   Nor is any allusion made in these authorities
to such decrees, except in *Jones* v. *Davenport,* 45 N. J.
Eq. 77 (17 Atl. 570).   This was a suit to set aside a
deed to certain real property as fraudulent and void
as against creditors.   The complaint also contained a
general allegation that a certain one hundred shares
of bank stock had been transferred in fraud of the
creditors.   The lower court by its decree set aside the
deed, but refused to disturb the transfer of bank stock,
for the reason that the allegations of the complaint

were insufficient to show a fraudulent disposition of
such stock. Afterwards an amended decree was entered under the same pleadings, by consent of the parties, as of the date of the original, decreeing that the
transfer of the stock was also fraudulent. Subsequently, however, upon application to the same court,
the decree as so amended was declared to have been
irregularly entered, and for that reason set aside.
Upon appeal to the supreme court VAN FLEET, V. C.,
said of this proceeding: "There can be no doubt that
that decree was an absolute nullity. The principle is
authoritatively settled that a decree or judgment on a
matter outside of the issue raised by the pleadings is
a nullity, and is nowhere entitled to the least respect
as a judicial sentence." But a consent decree is not
in a strict legal sense a "judicial sentence." "It is,"
says Mr. Gibson in his excellent treatise entitled Suits
in Chancery, § 558, "in the nature of a solemn contract, and is, in effect, an admission by the parties
that the decree is a just determination of their rights
upon the real facts of the case, had such been proved.
As a result, such a decree is so binding as to be absolutely conclusive upon the consenting parties, and it
can neither be amended or in any way varied without
a like consent, nor can it be reheard, appealed from,
or reviewed upon a writ of error. The one only way
in which it can be attacked, or impeached, is by an
original bill alleging fraud in securing the consent."

Mr. Beach, in his Modern Equity Practice, § 792,
says: "Parties to a suit have the right to agree to
anything they please in reference to the subject-matter of their litigation, and the court, when applied to,
will ordinarily give effect to their agreement, if it
comes within the general scope of the case made by
the pleadings." See, also, *Pacific Railroad* v. *Ketchum,*

01 U. S. 297. In *Schermerhorn* v. *Mahaffie,* 34 Kan, 108, (8 Pac. 199,) it was held that a decree rendered by consent of the parties was not void as between themselves, because it did not give to each just what the petition called for, and what ought as a matter of right have been given to each of them. Chancellor WALWORTH, in *Bank of Monroe* v. *Widner,* 11 Paige, 533, (43 Am. Dec. 768,) says: "An agreement to refer a suit pending to an arbitrator, and that a judgment shall be entered in the cause in conformity with his decision, will justify the entry of a judgment accordingly, which judgment will be binding upon the par ties, as a judgment by consent." Chief Justice WAITE, in *Pacific Railroad* v. *Ketchum,* 101 U. S. 297, after giving utterance to the language quoted above from Beach's Modern Equity Practice, says: "It is within the power of the parties to this suit to agree that a decree might be entered for a sale of the mortgaged property without any specific finding of the amount due on account of the mortgage debt, or without giving a day of payment. It was also competent for them to agree that if the property was bought at the sale by or for the bondholders, payment of the purchase money might be made by a surrender of the bonds. * * * All these were matters about which the parties might properly agree; and, having agreed, it does not lie with them to complain of what the court has done to give effect to their agreement." *Fletcher* v. *Holmes,* 25 Ind. 458, was a case wherein suit was brought to foreclose a mortgage in which neither the mortgage nor the complaint to foreclose showed any right to a personal decree against the defendant, but he appeared, and with his consent one was rendered. Regarding such decree the court says: "It cannot be doubted that without May's consent such a judgment against him,

upon that complaint, would not have been warranted. We need not say whether or not it would have been void. But he consented to it. Was it then void as against May, because the complaint did not allege sufficient facts to justify it without such consent? We can conceive of no reason why a judgment entered by agreement, by a court of general jurisdiction, having power in a proper case to render such a judgment, and having the parties before it, should not bind those by whose agreement it is entered, notwithstanding the pleadings would not, in a contested case, authorize such a judgment. The object of a complaint is to inform the defendant of the nature of the plaintiff's case. It is for his protection that it is required. If he wishes to waive it, or agrees to the granting of greater relief than could otherwise be given under its averments, without amendment, and such relief is given by his consent, we think that the judgment is not even erroneous, and much less void as to him."

A judgment or decree entered upon the pleadings or after contest must fall within the issues raised by the pleadings, but a consent decree will be valid and binding upon the parties if its provisions fall within the general scope of the case made by the pleadings. This distinction is clear and incisive, and, it will be seen by the foregoing authorities, is recognized both by the text writers and the courts. In a recent case just reported a suit was instituted by the Central Trust Company of New York to foreclose a mortgage given by the Marietta and North Georgia Railway Company, with which was consolidated a creditor's suit by V. E. McBee and others against the trust company and others to restrain the prosecution of the foreclosure suit, and the enforcement of other liens claimed upon the mortgaged property, and praying for a sale, and **payment of** their claims from the proceeds. It was decreed, among other things, "that the counsel representing the claimants in the original bill of *V. E. McBee and Company et al.* v. *Knoxville Southern Railroad Company et al.,* viz., Washburn and Templeton, are entitled to compensation out of the general fund arising from the sale of the road for their services in bringing said sale, and administering the assets of said insolvent railroad company, and a lien is declared upon said fund in their favor." This portion of the decree was approved by the circuit court of appeals of the United States Sixth Circuit. TAFT, J., speaking for the court, says: "The complainants who filed the creditors' bill and brought in all the lien holders did a work in the administration and direction of the assets of the railroad company beneficial to all concerned. For services in filing the bill, therefore, and bringing in all lien claimants, it was not improper for the court to order a fee paid to complainants' counsel out of the fund realized from the sale": See *Central Trust Company* v. *Condon,* 14 C. C. A. 314 (67 Fed. 84, 110). In *Central Railroad* v. *Pettus,* 113 U. S. 124, (5 Sup. Ct. 387,) which was a creditors' suit, it was held that "when an allowance to the complainant is proper on account of the solicitors' fees, it may be made directly to the solicitors themselves, without any application by their immediate client." This doctrine was based upon the authority of *Trustees* v. *Greenough,* 105 U. S. 527. So that we here find authority for entering a decree directly in favor of the attorneys for the plaintiff. These were creditors' bills, it is true, but the decrees were rendered in contested cases, without issues being formed under the pleadings by the attorneys or solicitors as parties litigant. Now, in the light of these authorities, can it be said that the decree here pur-

ports to adjudicate matters outside of and beyond the
general scope and purview of the case made by the
pleadings? As was said in the former opinion, the
plaintiff sues as trustee, each step taken by him was
in the capacity of a trustee, and whatever sum of
money he may realize by a sale under the decree of
the court would come into his hands as trust funds,
to be distributed to the bondholders in just propro-
tion to their several demands. Under the terms of
the mortgage he is entitled to recover a reasonable
attorney's fee, together with his costs and disbursements. Now, if, by his direction, and with the consent of the defendant, it is decreed by the court that
he recover the attorneys', referee's, and stenographers'
fees in trust for the very persons whom he has employed, and who have rendered him services in his
capacity as trustee, there exists no good and sufficient
reason why it should not be binding upon all the
parties interested, and the right to have execution
issue at their instance would not affect its legality.
The decree of the court has, at his instance, only
extended his trusteeship, as regards the funds to
come into his hands, so that he has become trustee
to the use of his attorneys and the officers of the
court, as well as the bondholders, of a fund in which
they are all entitled to share, and whether the property brings a small or large sum cannot change the
situation. Aside from all this, when it is determined
that plaintiff is party to a decree from which there is
no appeal, a determination of this question upon
either contention would still leave this court powerless to relieve him in this proceeding. We still adhere to the opinion, and the reasoning upon which it
is based, that plaintiff is without a remedy by appeal,

and no good results could come of enlarging upon it here.

4. Another question briefly. It is insisted "that an attorney at law has no implied authority to enter a consent decree, or to consent to a decree by which a definite fee is given to him, and made a first lien upon the property which is the subject of the action." Conceding the soundness of this proposition, it is not apparent how it can aid the appellant, in the absence of proof that the act complained of was done without express authority. We cannot say here in this proceeding that Messrs. Crawford and Hyde acted only upon their implied authority from Schmidt. There is not a scintilla of evidence in the record to show whether they acted with or without authority, and, for all that appears, they may have had the most ample and complete power and authority to request, consent to, and have entered just such a decree as was entered, and which the plaintiff now seeks to have reviewed on appeal by this court. In *Pacific Railroad* v. *Ketchum,* 101 U. S. 297, Chief Justice WAITE says: "A solicitor may certainly consent to whatever his client authorizes, and, in this case, it distinctly appears of record that the company assented through its solicitors. This is equivalent to a decree finding by the court as a fact that the solicitor had authority to do what he did, and binds us on appeal so far as the question is one of fact only. The remedy for the fraud or unauthorized conduct of a solicitor, or the officers of a corporation, in such a matter, is by an appropriate proceeding in the court where the consent was received and acted on, and in which proof may be taken and facts ascertained."

The law governing the reciprocal and correlative
duties of attorney and client are well settled, and if
these attorneys have exceeded their authority to the
injury of the appellant he is not without a remedy,
but it is not by an appeal, unless facts accompany
the record to show the dereliction of duty.

A REHEARING IS DENIED.

Argued April 15; decided July 22, 1895; rehearing denied.

FELDMAN *v.* NICOLAI.

[40 Pac. 1011.]

DEBTOR AND CREDITOR — PREFERENCES — FRAUD.— In the absence of an intention to hinder, delay, or defraud other creditors, a debtor may
prefer a particular creditor to the exclusion of others by transferring
his property to him in consideration of the indebtedness;* but where
such creditor is a relative, or a member of the debtor's family, the
transaction will be scrutinized with more than ordinary care: *Jolly* v.
Kyle, 27 Or. 95, cited and approved.

APPEAL from Multnomah: L. B. STEARNS, Judge.

This is a suit by certain judgment creditors of
Adolph Nicolai to set aside two deeds, and subject the
real property therein described to the payment of certain judgments rendered against the grantor. The
facts are that on April first, eighteen hundred and
ninety, the defendants Adolph Nicolai and Karoline,
his wife, for the expressed consideration of eight thousand five hundred dollars, executed to their son-in-law,
the defendant W. W. McGuire, a warranty deed which
purported to convey the following described real property, to wit: Beginning at a point in the north line of

---

*To the same effect see *Marquam* v. *Sengfelder,* 24 Or. 2; *Currie* v. *Bowman,* 25
Or. 365 (44 Am. and Eng. Corp. Cases, 662, with note); and *Jolly* v. *Kyle,* 27 Or. 95,
as applied to individuals. For an application of the right of preference among
creditors of a corporation, see *Sabin* v. *Columbia Fuel Company,* 25 Or. 15.— RE-
PORTER.

block one hundred and ninety-four in the city of Portland, Oregon, which is forty-five feet westward from
the northeast corner of said block, and running thence
southward parallel with Sixth Street ninety-five feet;
thence westerly parallel with Jackson Street fifty-five
feet; thence north parallel with Sixth Street ninety-
five feet, and thence easterly fifty-five feet to the place
of beginning; and on October twentieth of that year
the said Nicolai and wife, for the expressed consideration of one dollar and other good and valuable considerations, executed to their daughter Rosalia McGuire,
wife of the defendant W. W. McGuire, a warranty
deed, subject to certain mortgages, which purported
to convey the following real property: lot one in block
sixteen in Couch's Addition, and the west half of lots
seven and eight in block one hundred and ninety-four
in said city. At the the date of the latter conveyance
the defendant Nicolai was indebted in various amounts
to the several plaintiffs, who thereafter obtained judgments against him upon their respective demands, and
had executions issued thereon, and delivered to the
sheriff of Multnomah County, but that officer, being
unable to find any property of the defendants in the
writs upon which he could levy, returned them wholly
unsatisfied. The plaintiffs uniting their claims in this
suit allege, *inter alia,* that the defendant Nicolai is insolvent and that said deeds were executed without any
consideration and with a fraudulent intent to hinder,
delay, and defraud his creditors, and that they were
accepted by the defendants W. W. and Rosalia Mc-
Guire, with full knowledge and notice of Nicolai's insolvency and intention for the purpose of aiding him
in carrying said intention into effect. The defendants
deny this allegation, and for a further defense allege
that the lots conveyed to Rosalia were subject to two

mortgages securing an indebtedness of sixteen thousand dollars, the payment of which they assumed, and which, together with judgment liens and street assessments against the property, and certain indebtedness due and owing from Nicolai to W. W. McGuire for money paid out, advanced to, and expended for him, and certain of his indebtedness which they assumed and agreed to pay, amounting at the time of the sale and conveyance to thirty thousand dollars, constituted and was a full and adequate consideration therefor, and that they purchased said property in good faith, and paid therefor the consideration aforesaid, without any intention to hinder, delay, or defraud any of the creditors of Nicolai. The court, before the cause was submitted, granted leave to amend the answer by adding an allegation to the effect that the deed from Nicolai to Rosalia McGuire was executed in pursuance of an agreement between herself and husband that she should hold the title to the premises in trust for him. A reply having put in issue the allegations of new matter contained in the answer, a trial was had before the court resulting in a decree confirming the defendants' title to the property and dismissing the suit, from which decree the plaintiffs appeal.

AFFIRMED.

For appellants there was a brief by *Messrs. Watson, Beekman and Watson,* and *George W. P. Joseph,* with an oral argument by *Mr. Edward B. Watson.*

Neither of the answers make out a complete defense to the cause of suit alleged in the complaint. The general denials of want of consideration and of fraudulent intent do not repel the presumption of fraud arising from the specific acts charged in the complaint, which are not denied: Bump on Fraudulent

Conveyances (3d ed.), 559; *Robinson* v. *Stewart*, 10 N. Y. 194.

Neither of the two separate defenses in the answer of W. W. and Rosalia McGuire, show that they were purchasers in good faith and for a valuable consideration: *Webb* v. *Nickerson*, 11 Or. 385; *Weber* v. *Rothchild*, 15 Or. 389, 390 (3 Am. St. Rep. 162); *Hyland* v. *Hyland*, 19 Or. 55, 56; *Boone* v. *Chiles*, 10 Pet. 210, 211.

Parol evidence of the assumption of judgment liens, as part of the consideration for the two deeds, is in conflict with the covenants against incumbrances, and therefore, incompetent: *Estabrook* v. *Smith*, 6 Gray, 579; *Ruggles* v. *Barton*, 16 Gray, 152, 153; *Corbett* v. *Wrenn*, 24 Or. 305 (35 Pac. 660.)

Evidence that W. W. McGuire, alone, purchased the real property conveyed by the two deeds, and assumed the judgment and mortgage liens thereon, as part of the consideration, is in direct conflict with the averments in the answer of himself and Rosalia McGuire of a joint purchase and assumption by them, and therefore irrelevant: *Schooner Hoppet*, 7 Cranch, 394, 395; *Boone* v. *Chiles*, 10 Pet. 211; *Bender* v. *Bender*, 14 Or. 355, 356.

The acceptance of the deed of October twentieth, eighteen hundred and ninety, by Rosalia McGuire, the grantee, containing the recital in the covenant, "except said mortgages which the said grantee hereby assumes and agrees to pay," established a contract between her grantors and herself, and bound her individually to discharge said incumbrances, or answer for any deficiency: *Burr* v. *Beers*, 24 N. Y. 178 (80 Am. Dec. 327); *Thorp* v. *Keokuk Coal Company*, 48 N. Y. 253.

The mere assumption of incumbrances on real property, without an agreement to protect the grantors and the rest of his property therefrom, is not a sufficient consideration for its conveyance, as against other creditors: Bump on Fraudulent Conveyances (3d ed.), 227, 228; *United States* v. *Mertz,* 2 Watts, 406; *Carpenter* v. *Carpenter,* 25 N. J. Eq. 194; *First National Bank* v. *Bertschy,* 52 Wis. 438; *Lyon* v. *Haddock,* 59 Iowa, 682.

A sale is not complete until the consideration has been paid. And if the purchaser has notice of the fraudulent intent of his grantor before payment of the purchase money, it is sufficient: Bump on Fraudulent Conveyances (3d ed.), 203; *Florence Sewing Machine Company* v. *Zeigler,* 58 Ala. 221; *Matson* v. *Melchor,* 42 Mich. 477; *Arnholt* v. *Hartwig,* 78 Mo. 485; *Bush* v. *Collins,* 85 Kan. 535 (11 Pac. 425); *Hunsinger* v. *Haffer,* 110 Ind. 390 (11 N. E. 463.)

Both the deeds from Adolph and Karoline Nicolai to W. W. and Rosalia McGuire, respectively, as well as the two sheriff's deeds to W. W. McGuire for part of the same property, were fraudulent in fact, and void as to the plaintiffs, as shown by the following badges of fraud, appearing from the evidence:—

Transfer of all all Adolph Nicolai's property: Bump on Fradulent Conveyances (3d ed.), 34 and 36; *Twyne's Case,* 1 Smith's Lead. Cas. (6 Am. ed.), 33; *Tubbs* v. *Williams,* 7 Humph. 367; *Bigelow* v. *Doolittle,* 36 Wis. 115; *Lahitle* v. *Fiere,* 42 La. Ann. 864 (8 So. 598); *Nesbitt* v. *Digby,* 13 Ill. 387; *Pervel* v. *Merritt,* 70 Mo. 275.

His heavy indebtedness and great financial embarrassment known to his grantees: Bump on Fraudulent Conveyances (3d ed.), 36 and 37; *Glenn* v. *Glenn,* 17 Iowa, 498; *Crawford* v. *Kirksey,* 50 Ala. 591.

Pendency of actions and suits, and expectation of more, to the knowledge of his grantees: Bump on Fraudulent Conveyances (3d ed.), 37 and 38; *Godfrey* v. *Germain,* 24 Wis. 410; *Reeves* v. *Sherwood,* 45 Ark. 520.

The conveyance of October twentieth, eighteen

hundred and ninety, pending a sixty day's stay of proceedings in plaintiff, Maria Feldman's action, mentioned in the complaint, at his request, and upon his promise to pay on or before the expiration of said period, and to save him costs on entry of judgment; and also pending an order of said circuit court enjoining him from making any transfer of his property, duly made in proceedings supplemental to execution on a judgment in favor of J. C. Rutenic, September twenty-sixth, and personally served September twenty-ninth, eighteen hundred and ninety: *Morris Canal Company* v. *Stearns,* 23 N. J. Eq. 414; *Coleman* v. *Roff,* 45 N. J. Law, 7; *Younger* v. *Massey* S. C., 17 S. E. 711, 712.

Intentional false statements of consideration are conclusive of fraud: Bump on Fraudulent Conveyances (3d ed.), 43; *Barker* v. *French,* 18 Vt. 460; *Tripp* v. *Vincent,* 8 Paige Ch. 178, 179; *Lynde* v. *McGregor,* 13 Allen, 174 (90 Am. Dec. 188); *Hawkins* v. *Alston,* 4 Ired. Eq. 137; *Marriott* v. *Givens,* 8 Ala. 694; *Venable* v. *Bank,* 2 Pet. 112; *Parker* v. *Barker,* 2 Metc. 430.

The indefinite, suspicious, and irreconcilably contradictory evidence introduced by defendants to prove the averred consideration for the two deeds: Bump on Fraudulent Conveyances (3d ed.), 55, 56; *Page* v. *Francis* (Ala.), 11 So. 736, 738; *Hudgins* v. *Kemp,* 20 How. 52, 53; *Marshall* v. *Green,* 24 Ark. 410; *Bouchard* v. *Glacier,* 64 Iowa, 675; *Pickett* v. *Pipkin,* 64 Ala. 520.

W. W. McGuire's resistance to the other judgments claimed to have been assumed, and, when compelled to pay them to save the property, his taking an assignment of each judgment, and keeping it alive instead of cancelling or entering satisfaction of record: Bump on Fraudulent Conveyances (3d ed.), 226; *Webb* v. *Ingham,* 29 W. Va. 389 (1 S. E. 816, 821); *Forstall* v. *Larche,* 39 La. An. 286 (1 So. 650, 651); *Younger* v. *Massey*

(S. C.), 17 S. E. 711, 713, 714; *Starr* v. *Starr*, 1 Ohio, 721; *Oliver* v. *Moore*, 23 Ohio St. 473.

No accounts kept, and few, if any, notes taken, for numerous large loans of money by W. W. McGuire to Adolph Nicolai, none of which were produced in evidence: Bump on Fraudulent Conveyances (3d ed.), 51; *Scoggin* v. *Schloath*, 15 Or. 380, 383-384; *Whelden* v. *Wilson*, 44 Me. 1; *Haney* v. *Nugent*, 13 Wis. 283; *Hubbard* v. *Allen*, 59 Ala. 283; *Hendricks* v. *Robinson*, 2 Johns. Ch. 296-298; *Lehman* v. *Guenhut*, 88 Ala. 478 (7 So. 299, 300).

The facts and circumstances in evidence conclusively established fraud: *Clark* v. *Raymond* (Iowa), 53 N. W. 354-356; *Jackson* v. *Mather*, 7 Cowp. 301; *Switz* v. *Bruce*, 16 Neb. 463; *Fisher* v. *Moog*, 39 Fed. 665-672; *Hildreth* v. *Sands*, 2 Johns. Ch. 35, 43-46; same case on appeal, 14 Johns. 492; *Stoddard* v. *Butler*, 20 Wend. 505, 513-515; *Lyons* v. *Leahy*, 15 Or. 8-15.

For respondents there was a brief by *Messrs. Mitchell, Tanner and Mitchell,* and *Paxton and Beach,* and an oral argument by *Messrs. Albert H. Tanner* and *Ossian Franklin Paxton.*

Where a creditor takes the property of his debtor in payment of his debt, as was the case here according to the averments of the answer, it is not necessary for him to negative notice, for he might take the property in payment of his debt, although he knew the intention of the debtor was to hinder, delay, and defraud other creditors: *Shelby* v. *Boothe*, 73 Mo. 74; *Knower* v. *Central National Bank*, 124 N. Y. 560 (29 Am. St. Rep. 700); *Dudley* v. *Danforth*, 61 N. Y. 626; *Chase* v. *Walters*, 28 Iowa, 460; *Ross* v. *Sedgwick*, 69 Cal. 247; *Levy* v. *Fischel*, 65 Texas, 311; *Brown* v. *Forth*, 7 B. Mon. 357; Bump on Fraudulent Conveyances, 182, 186, 187; *Sabin*

v. *Columbia Fuel Company*, 25 Or. 15 (34 Pac. 692); *Marquam* v. *Sengfelder*, 24 Or. 2; *Warren* v. *Wilder*, 114 N. Y. 209.

Inadequacy of price to be evidence of fraud must have been so clearly and grossly inadequate as to shock the conscience of the court, and indicate that the vendor must have had some fraudulent scheme in mind or he would not have disposed of the property at such a figure: Bump on Fraudulent Conveyances, 43; Wait on Fraudulent Conveyances, § 232.

If the purchaser, though a relative, is an honest creditor and takes the property in payment of a just debt, his title is not invalidated; he cannot be convicted of fraud on any less evidence than any other person: *Silvers* v. *Potter*, 48 N. J. Eq. 539; *Barr* v. *Church*, 82 Wis. 382; *Coley* v. *Coley*, 14 N. J. Eq. 350.

Where a deed alleged to be fraudulent, recites a money consideration, parol evidence is admissible to show that a larger or additional sum was in fact paid or agreed to be paid: *Scoggin* v. *Schloath*, 15 Or. 380, at page 383; *Pomeroy* v. *Bailey*, 43 N. H. 118.

"Badges of fraud," so called, do not constitute fraud in themselves, but are only circumstances from which the court or jury may infer fraud: Wait on Fraudulent Conveyances, § 226. And the unfavorable inferences from these "badges of fraud" may be entirely overcome by evidence showing the honesty and fairness of the transaction.

Opinion by MR. JUSTICE MOORE.

A careful examination of the evidence shows that on April first, eighteen hundred and ninety, the defendant Adolph Nicolai owed various persons about twenty-five thousand dollars, of which sum four thousand four hundred and thirty-seven dollars and fifty-five cents was due the defendant W. W. McGuire, to pay which Nicolai and his wife executed their deed of that date. While there is a controversy about the amount due McGuire at that time, we think the evidence fully shows that it was the sum stated above, and that no actual fraud was intended by either party to the deed, and hence the only question to be considered is whether the grantee paid a full consideration for the premises. The value of the property conveyed is estimated by two witnesses at four thousand dollars, and by three others at four thousand two hundred dollars, four thousand three hundred dollars, and five thousand dollars, respectively. The eight thousand five hundred dollars mentioned in the deed appears to have been adopted by the parties as the amount to be inserted as the consideration therefor before the interest had been computed upon the sum due McGuire, without any intention of defrauding Nicolai's creditors. The right of a debtor to prefer a particular creditor is not prohibited by statute, but where such creditor is a relative or member of the debtor's family the court will examine the evidence relating to the transfer of the debtor's property in satisfaction of the preferred creditor's claim with greater care: *Jolly* v. *Kyle,* 27 Or. 95 (39 Pac. 999). Tested by this rule, we conclude the defendant W. W. McGuire has paid an adequate consideration and clearly established his title to the premises conveyed to him. The evidence also shows that the lots conveyed to Rosalia McGuire were subject to the following liens: Mortgages and interest, sixteen thousand two hundred and thirty dollars; street assessment, one hundred and ninety-one dollars; judgments, three thousand one hundred and fifty-two dollars; and that in consideration of four thousand two hundred and sixty-one dollars and seventy-five cents due from Nicolai to McGuire, and the latter's agreement to assume and pay off said liens, Nicolai and wife, on October twentieth, eighteen hundred and ninety, conveyed the premises to Rosalia in trust for her husband. The plaintiffs dispute an item of two thousand one hundred dollars claimed to have been loaned by McGuire to Nicolai, but McGuire shows from whom he obtained it, and his bookkeeper testifies that he drew a note for this amount which Nicolai signed, and that he saw McGuire pay Nicolai quite a sum of money. We think it clearly appears from the evidence that between April first, and October twentieth, eighteen hundred and ninety, McGuire loaned to and assumed the payment of debts for Nicolai amounting to four thousand two hundred and sixty-one dollars and seventy-five cents. The deed to Rosalia was immediately recorded, and the parties took possession of the premises under it, and, while there are some circumstances connected with the transfer that would seem to indicate fraud, we are convinced from the evidence that no actual fraud was intended, and that the conveyance was made in good faith, and with no intention upon the part of McGuire or his wife to defraud the creditors of Nicolai. The value of the lots conveyed to Rosalia McGuire is estimated at from eighteen thousand five hundred dollars to thirty-six thousand dollars, in which latter sum two witnesses agree, while six others place the value below twenty-three thousand eight hundred and thirty-four dollars, the amount paid and assumed by McGuire. From this evidence we think an adequate consideration was paid, and hence the decree must be affirmed and it is so ordered.   AFFIRMED.

Argued June 18; decided July 22, 1895.

FARMERS' LOAN COMPANY *v.* OREGON PACIFIC RAILROAD COMPANY.

[40 Pac. 1089.]

1. MODIFICATION OF DECREE.—Where the original decree for the sale of a railroad in a foreclosure proceeding directed the property to be sold as an entirety, for cash, and that so much of the price "as is not required to be paid in cash may be paid in receiver's certificates," it is not an essential modification to subsequently provide that the sale shall be made for United States gold coin only, for the failure to provide in the original order the proportion of the price to be paid in cash left the provision for the acceptance of receiver's certificates of no effect, and the entire price would have been required in cash under the original decree.

2. MODIFICATION OF DECREE.—An order directing that all taxes legally due and owing by a corporation up to a certain date shall be paid out of the purchase money realized from a sale under a prior decree of foreclosure of a trust deed upon the property of the corporation, and that all taxes levied against the property after such date shall be paid by the purchaser, does not alter or vary the essential parts of the original decree, which made no provision for the payment of taxes, so as to be in excess of the authority of the court, where the purchaser would be bound by law without an order to that effect to pay taxes accruing after that date.

3. POWER OF COURTS OVER FINAL DECREES.—A court having acquired jurisdiction to enter a final decree undoubtedly possesses the inherent right to subsequently modify both the time and manner of its enforcement, though the essential provisions of final decrees cannot afterward be changed.

4. RATIFICATION OF EXECUTION SALE.—A court has power to ratify the act of an officer in selling property at a time other than that fixed by a decree, where it might, in the first instance, have ordered a sale on that day.

5. EXECUTION SALE—INADEQUATE PRICE.—An inadequacy sufficient to set aside a public sale of property must be so gross as to shock the conscience, where there are no confidential relations existing between the parties, and no proof of fraud. Within the purview of this general rule the sale of the Oregon Pacific Railroad for one hundred thousand dollars, in December, eighteen hundred and ninety-four, was not a sale for such a grossly inadequate price as to require it to be set aside, so far as appears by the record.

Appeal from Benton: J. C. FULLERTON, Judge.

This is an appeal from an order confirming a sale of railway franchises and property on the foreclosure of a mortgage. The facts are that the plaintiff, having commenced a suit against the defendants, the Oregon Pacific Railroad Company and the Willamette Valley and Coast Railroad Company, to foreclose a mortgage given to secure the payment of bonds amounting to fifteen million dollars, a receiver was appointed, and on April twenty-seventh, eighteen hundred and ninety-one, the defendant companies having by their answers admitted the allegations of the complaint and supplement thereto, a decree was rendered as prayed for, wherein the mortgaged property was ordered sold by the sheriff of Benton County to the highest bidder for cash, without appraisement or right of redemption, and said officer was thereby directed to require of the bidder a deposit of not less than five thousand dollars in cash, to be applied in part payment of the purchase price, if the sale should be confirmed. On October twenty-third, eighteen hundred and ninety-one, the court made an order directing an execution to be issued, and instructing the sheriff to accept no bid less than one million dollars; of which sum twenty-five thousand dollars should be deposited before accepting any bid. An execution having been issued, the sheriff, on January twentieth, eighteen hundred and ninety-two, at a sale of the property, accepted the bid of Zephin Job of one million dollars, of which sum twenty-five thousand dollars was deposited with said officer, who reported the sale to the court, whereupon an order was made that upon the payment of nine hundred and seventy-five thousand dollars within thirty days the sale should be

confirmed; but the bidder having failed to make pay
ment of such sum or any part thereof, the court, on
November seventeenth of that year, ordered a resale
of the property, and directed the sheriff to accept no
bid for a less sum than one million two hundred and
fifty thousand dollars, of which two hundred thousand
dollars was required to be deposited before any bid
could be accepted. A second execution having been
issued, the sheriff was unable to sell the property under these terms, and by order of the court returned
the writ. On April tenth, eighteen hundred and
ninety-three, the court again ordered a resale of the
property, and directed the sheriff to require a deposit
of two hundred thousand dollars from the bidder before any bid should be accepted, and on December fifteenth of that year, another writ having been issued,
the sheriff accepted the bid of two hundred thousand
dollars from J. J. Beldon, Henry Martin, F. K. Pendleton, S. S. Hollingsworth, Joseph Wharton, and James
K. Blair; but on the twenty-sixth of that month the
court, upon the officer's return of the writ, refused to
confirm the sale, and made an order setting it aside,
and directing the return of the deposit. On March
second, eighteen hundred and ninety-four, the court,
upon due notice to Zephin Job and the corporation to
whom he had assigned his right of purchase, made
an order setting aside the conditional confirmation of
the sale made upon his bid, directing a resale of the
property to the highest bidder for what it would bring
in cash, and instructing the sheriff to accept no bid
until two hundred thousand dollars had been deposited with him by the bidder. Another execution having been issued, the property was advertised to be
sold on June seventh, eighteen hundred and ninety-
four, but failing to receive any bid therefor, the offi-

cer returned the writ. On October twentieth, eighteen hundred and ninety-four, the court made another
order directing a resale of the property on a day to
be fixed by the sheriff, between the fifteenth and
twenty--econd days of December of that year, and instructing him to accept no bid until one hundred
thousand dollars had been deposited; and a *pluries*
writ having been issued, the said officer, after having
duly advertised the property and received a deposit
of one hundred thousand dollars, accepted a bid for
that amount, and on the twenty-second day of December. eighteen hundred and ninety-four, sold, subject
to confirmation, all the property and franchises of
the defendant companies to E. L. Bonner and A. B.
Hammond for said sum, and, on the twenty-sixth of
said month, returned the writ. On January third,
eighteen hundred and ninety-five, the bidders at said
sale moved for an order of confirmation, while certain
of the appellants, being either general creditors of the
defendant corporations, or holding receiver's certificates. filed objections thereto, and on the nineteenth
of that month other appellants filed objections to the
confirmation. all which having been overruled, the
court made an order confirming said sale, from which
order this appeal is taken.   AFFIRMED.

For appellants there were briefs by *Messrs. Watson
and Elkins, Wallis Nash,* and *Bronaugh, McArthur, Fenton and
Bronaugh,* with oral arguments by *Messrs. Wallis Nash,
H. C. Watson, Earl C. Bronaugh,* and *William D. Fenton.*

The court below had no power to change, modify,
or vary the original decree after the expiration of the
term at which it was rendered: *Sibbald* v. *United States,*
87 U. S. 812; *Bank of United States* v. *Moss,* 47 U. S. 42;

Bronson v. *Schulten,* 104 U. S. 797; *Morgan's Louisiana and Texas Railway, etc., Company* v. *Texas Central Railway Company,* 82 Fed. 525; *Schell* v. *Dodge,* 107 U. S. 601; *Phillips* v. *Negley,* 107 U. S. 1013; *Trustees* v. *Greenough,* 105 U. S. 527; *Hume* v. *Bowie,* 148 U. S. 245; *Brewster* v. *Norfleet,* 22 S. W. 226; *Savannah* v. *Jesup,* 106 U. S. 563; *Miltenberger* v. *Logansport Railway Company,* 106 U. S. 286; *Trullinger* v. *Todd,* 5 Or. 36; *Williams* v. *Morgan,* 111 U. S. 684; *Deering* v. *Quivey,* 26 Or. 556.

Being final the court had no power to modify the decree: *Barrell* v. *Tilton,* 119 U. S. 637; *Huntington* v. *Little Rock Railway Company,* 16 Fed. 706.

In substantial matters it will be seen that the order of October, eighteen hundred and ninety-four, involves wide and substantial departures from the decree of April, eighteen hundred and ninety-one. The original decree looked to a reconstruction or reorganization of the company. It gave powers to holders of receiver's certificates to bid their securities as part of the purchase money at the sale, and to bondholders to bid their bonds and coupons at such rate and percentage as should be returnable to them from the ultimate proceeds of sale, the deposit of five thousand dollars being reserved to be paid in cash. The bondholders and receiver's certificate holders are both eliminated from the order of sale of October twentieth, eighteen hundred and ninety-four, which is to be for cash to the highest bidder; the purchase money, including the deposit of one hundred thousand dollars, being to be paid in cash or its equivalent in certified checks or drafts satisfactory to the sheriff and to the court, and not otherwise. The result of such an order is apparent in a sale of property valued by hostile experts not much more than two years ago at not less than three million dollars for one hundred thousand dollars. That the bondholders had an equitable right to apply their bonds toward the payment of the purchase money, after satisfying the costs and charges of the litigation and trust, was decided in *Duncan* v. *Mobile and Ohio Railway Company*, 3 Woods, 597.

The effect of the provision in the decree of April, eighteen hundred and ninety-one, for the benefit of the bondholders and certificate holders was two fold; it enhanced the value of their securities by permitting their use as cash in the purchase of the road, and also induced a corresponding reduction of the indebtedness of the court, diminished *pro tanto* the amount of cash required to clear off the labor and material indebtedness of the court through its receivers, and forestalled and prevented the litigation between lien holders, certificate holders, preferred creditors, and labor and material claimants, which is inevitable in the proposed distribution of the almost ridiculous sum which will remain from the one hundred thousand dollars, when the costs and expenses of the court, and the amount allowed for taxes, have been first deducted therefrom: *Kneeland* v. *American Loan and Trust Company*, 136 U. S. 89; *Farmers' Loan and Trust Company* v. *Texas Central Railway Company*, 129 U. S. 206; *Jerome* v. *McCarter*, 94 U. S. 734; *Kneeland* v. *Luce*, 141 U. S. 508; *Wallace* v. *Loomis*, 111 U. S. 776; *Kennedy* v. *St. Paul and Pacific Railway Company*, 2 Dill. 448; *Stanton* v. *Alabama and Chattanooga Railway Company*, 2 Woods, 506; *Bank of Montreal* v. *Chicago, Clinton and Western Railway Company*, 48 Iowa, 518; *Coe* v. *New Jersey Midland Railway Company*, 27 N. J. Eq. 37; *Hoover* v. *Montclair, etc., Company*, 29 N. J. Eq. 4; *Meyer* v. *Johnston*, 53 Ala. 237.

Receiver's certificates are the creations of American courts. They are securities sui generis, brought into use by the courts to enable them to preserve property in their custody, and the faith of the court which issues them is pledged for their redemption. The propriety of their issuance has been repeatedly upheld by the United States supreme and circuit courts, as well as by the state courts: *Kneeland* v. *Luce,* 141 U. S. 508; *Jerome* v. *Carter,* 94 U. S. 734; *Wallace* v. *Loomis,* 111 U. S. 776; *Kennedy* v. *St. Paul and Pacific Railroad Company,* 2 Dill. 448; *Stanton* v. *Alabama and Chattanooga Railroad Company,* 2 Woods, 506; *Bank of Montreal* v. *Chicago, Clinton, and Western Railroad Company,* 48 Iowa, 518; *Coe* v. *New Jersey Midland Railway Company,* 27 N. J. Eq. 37; *Hoover* v. *Montclair, etc., Railroad Company,* 29 N. J. Eq. 4; *Meyer* v. *Johnston,* 53 Ala. 237.

It has been recognized in every case which has come under our notice, that it is the duty of the court to keep faith with its creditors, and to retain possession of the property until their debts are paid or provided for. In those cases wherein railroads have been sold for less than sufficient to pay the court's indebtedness, such sales have been confirmed only on one of two conditions, either that the court's creditors have taken part in the sale and purchase, (by virtue of an agreement of reorganization,) or the court has stipulated with the purchasers to assume any balance of the court's indebtedness: *Farmer's Loan and Trust Company* v. *Central Railroad Company,* 17 Fed. 758; *Jessup* v. *Wabash, St. Louis and Pacific Railroad Company,* 44 Fed. 663; *Mercantile Trust Company* v. *Kanawha and Oswego Railway Company,* 50 Fed. 874; *Shaw* v. *Little Rock Railroad Company,* 100 U. S. 605; *Robinson* v. *Philadelphia and Railroad Company,* 28 Fed. 340; *Kitchen* v. *St. Louis Railroad Company,* 69 Mo. 224; *Gates* v. *Boston and New*

York Railroad Company, 53 Conn. 350; *Canada Southern Railway Company* v. *Gebhard,* 109 U. S. 539; *Shaw* v. *Little Rock Railroad Company,* 100 U. S. 612; *Twin Lick Oil Company* v. *Marburg,* 91 U. S. 591.

It was the duty of the court to encourage and effect some plan of reorganization by which the holders of its certificates would have been protected. In the case before the court one plan of reorganization was submitted by the bondholders, acting through a committee, at the close of eighteen hundred and ninety-one. From dissentions among the bondholders apparent in all the subsequent proceedings before the court, and on the abstract of record, the first plan failed after repeated adjournments, and a most serious lapse of time. When this state of affairs was disclosed, the fatal order was made by the court to sell the property for what it would fetch in cash, little foreseeing the catastrophe to which it inevitably led. No provision was made, or suggested, for any of the creditors of the court. Anxiety to get rid as speedily as possible of the burden of the suit and its appendage, the receivership, appears in the repeated efforts at a sale on these terms. The result is seen in the attempted confirmation of a sale of property, reasonably worth three million dollars, even in bad times and under depressed conditions, for one hundred thousand dollars. Examination of the very numerous cases which have come before the courts during the past ten or fifteen years has failed to find one distantly resembling this. The anxiety of the court to protect its creditors should have been still further stimulated by the consideration that the security of these lenders depended solely on its action. If the court fails the certificate holder, and the sale being in other respects legally made, is confirmed without provision for him in one form or another, the balance of authority appears to leave him without remedy. For in such case he is bound by the decree: *Mercantile Trust Company* v. *Kanawha and Oswego Railway Company*, 58 Fed. 6; *Gordon* v. *Newman*, 62 Fed. 689; Beach on Receivers, 332.

The property was sold for such a grossly inadequate price that it clearly shows a want of good faith; indeed, a deliberate attempt to defraud. The property sold comprises a railroad, laid with steel rails of fifty and fifty-six pounds to the yard, operated for one hundred and thirty miles, and with a very large quantity of partially constructed road, which will reduce to a very low figure the cost of completing and opening the next sixty miles through the remaining part of the Cascade Mountains, and to the Des Chutes River; a telegraph line and instruments, operating the one hundred and thirty miles; sixteen locomotive engines, upwards of three hundred freight cars, seven passenger coaches, and four baggage cars and postoffice cars; three river steamboats on the Willamette River, which cost fifty-seven thousand dollars; a valuable tugboat on Yaquina Bay; tools and machinery in the shops at Yaquina, costing about fifteen thousand dollars; a complete engineering outfit of instruments for four or five parties; hoisting engines, and a large quantity of miscellaneous property; usual and adequate office furniture and fittings. So that it is in no sense an exaggerated statement that the court might have sold off movable property to the value of over twice the whole amount of the purchase money bid by Messrs. Bonner and Hammond, and have had enough rolling stock and outfit left to operate the railroad, and have reserved the railroad itself intact. The bare recital of the facts is surely enough. It is submitted that the books may be searched in vain to find—not a parallel—but an instance of "inadequacy of price" even distantly resembling that now before the court: *Hume* v. *United States*, 21 Ct. of Cl. 328; *Boyd* v. *Ellis*, 11 Iowa, 97; *Herron* v. *Herron*, 71 Iowa, 428; *Horsey* v. *Hough*. 38 Md. 130; *Maquisson* v. *Williams*, 111 Ill. 450; *Hoyt* v. *Pawtucket Savings Institution*, 110 Ill. 300; *Latch* v. *Furlong*. 12 Grants Ch. (Ont.), 393; *Vail* v. *Jacobs*, 62 Mo. 130; *Meyer* v. *Jefferson Insurance Company*, 5 Mo. App. 245.

A consensus of decision shows that a sale on the twenty-second of December is not a sale between the fifteenth and twenty-second. Both limits are excluded: *Richardson* v. *Ford*, 14 Ill. 333; *Bunce* v. *Reed*, 16 Barb. (N. Y.), 352; *Fowler* v. *Rigney*, 5 All. Pr. (N. S.), 182; *Atkins* v. *Boylston Insurance Company*, 5 Metc. (Mass.), 439; *Kendall* v. *Kinsley*, 120 Mass. 95; *Cook* v. *Gray*, 6 Ind. 335; *Robinson* v. *Foster*, 12 Iowa, 186.

Messrs. Turner, McClure and Ralston, John R. Bryson, James K. Weatherford, P. H. D'Arcy and Geo. G. Bingham, Percy R. Kelly, and *W. S. McFadden,* were attorneys for respondents, and oral arguments were made by *Messrs. Bryson, Bingham,* and *McFadden.*

The only brief filed for respondents was by *Mr. McFadden,* representing Bonner and Hammond (the purchasers of the road), from which brief a few extracts are here given.

A decree of confirmation cures all irregularities: *Challiss* v. *Wise*, 2 Kan. 193; *Koehler* v. *Ball*, 2 Kan. 160 (83 Am. Dec. 451); *Wills* v. *Chandler*, 2 Fed. 273; *Townsend* v. *Tallant*, 33 Cal. 45 (91 Am. Dec. 617); *O'Brien* v. *Garlin*, 20 Neb. 347; *McCullough* v. *Chapman*, 58 Ala. 325; *Wilkerson* v. *Allen*, 67 Mo. 502; *Neligh* v. *Keen*, 20 N. W. 277; *Leinenweber* v. *Brown*, 24 Or. 548; *McKugha* v. *Hop-*

kins, 26 N. W. 614; *Morrow* v. *Weed*, 4 Iowa, 77 (66 Am. Dec. 122); *Woodhull* v. *Little*, 102 N. Y. 165; *Cooley* v. *Wilson*, 42 Iowa, 428.

Inadequacy of price is not of itself sufficient ground for setting aside a sale. Evidence of irregularity to the injury of the parties interested must be clear and conclusive before a court will interfere and set aside a sale. The mere inadequacy of price is not a sufficient ground to set aside a judicial sale, unless it be so great as to shock the conscience of the court and raise the inference of unfairness, fraud, mistake, or surprise; and a resale will not be ordered, as a general rule, upon an offer to increase the price brought at the sale, without the support of special circumstances: Jones on Corporations, Bonds, and Mortgages (2 ed.), § 662; *Wesson* v. *Chapman*, 76 Hun, 592 (28 N. Y. 192); Freeman on Executions, § 289; *Weaver* v. *Nugent*, 13 Am. St. 792; *Stockmeyer* v. *Tobin*, 139 U. S. 176 at page 196; *Brittin* v. *Handy*, 73 Am. Dec. 497; *Central Transportation Company of New York* v. *Sheffield and Birmingham Coal and Iron Company*, 60 Fed. 9; *Lake Superior Iron Company* v. *Brown, Bonnell and Company*, 44 Fed. 539; *Harris* v. *Ruby*, 38 Fed. 622; *Herman* v. *Copeland*, 17 S. E. 482; *Blackburn* v. *Selma Railway Company*, 3 Fed. 689.

After confirmation a judicial sale will not be set aside except for fraud, surprise, or other cause, for which equity would relieve in case of sale by parties: *Berlin* v. *Melthorn*, 75 Va. 639; *Virginia Fire Insurance Company* v. *Cottell*, 85 Va. 857; *Huston* v. *Aycock*, 73 Am. Dec. 131; *Williamson* v. *Berry*, 8 How. 495; *Brewer* v. *Herbert*, 96 Am. Dec. 582; *Hart* v. *Burch*, 130 Ill. 427; *Morrow* v. *McGreeger*, 49 Ark. 67; *Todd* v. *Gallego Mills Manufacturing Company*, 84 Va. 586; Freeman on Execu-

tions, §§ 305–310; *Karns* v. *Rorer Iron Company* (Va.), 11
S. E. 431; *Page* v. *Kress* (Mich.), 44 N. W. 1052.

The court may ratify various irregularities in the
proceedings, the principle being that a subsequent
ratification is equivalent to a previous authorization:
Allison v. *Allison*, 13 S. E. 549; *Crosby* v. *Kicst*, 135 Ill. 458;
Huckins v. *Kapf*, 14 S. W. 1016; *Stockmerger* v. *Tobin*, 139
U. S. 176; *Wetmore* v. *St. Paul and Pacific Railroad Company*,
3 Fed. 177; *Driscoll* v. *Morris*, 21 S. W. 629; *Max Moran* v.
Clark, 8 Am. St. 66; *Watson* v. *Tromble*, 50 N. W. 331; *State
National Bank* v. *Neel*, 22 Am. St. 185; *Camden* v. *Mayew*,
129 U. S. 73; *Hartley* v. *Roffe*, 12 W. Va. 401; *Leadville
Coal Company* v. *McCreery*, 141 U. S. 475; *Baty* v. *Veon*, 18
W. V. 291; *Wills* v. *Chandler*, 2 Fed. 273; *Jennings* v.
Carson, 4 Cranch, 2; *Trimble* v. *Herold*, 20 W. Va. 602.

The proposition that before a court can make an
order of sale under the authority reserved in an original decree it must notify and have before it the holders of receivers' certificates, and all persons laboring
or furnishing material for the receivership, announced
in appellants brief, is very extraordinary. It is so re-
freshingly new. And, if correct in principal, what a
limitless field for litigation it will open up for the
legal profession. Each little railroad receivership
may count its parties litigant by the thousand and
our transcontinental receiverships theirs by the ten
thousand. What a pageant to the eyes of us worldly-
minded lawyers. Ten thousand suitors in one case
with ten thousand retained lawyers, counselors, and
barristers. What a happy solution of the labor
question. The overcrowded avocations of life will be
relieved. The law will offer untold opportunities.
Courts, officers, sheriffs, bailiffs, clerks, and criers
will increase, and no man need be without an office.
The thoughts of it all makes one almost delirious

with impatience. Surely, if this is not the law, its judicial enactment would greatly subserve the legal profession. Why should we look backward for a precedent? Counsel for appellants rise above the narrow
confines of adjudicated cases, and must the court plod
while they soar?

The authorities cited by counsel to the effect that
a final decree cannot be changed or modified meet our
approval, and we yield ready assent to the proposition. We hold, however, that courts of equity may
reserve the power to control the manner of enforcement of their decrees, and that such power was reserved by the court in this case. The questions
raised and authorities cited in reference to the duties
of the court to protect the holders of receivers' certificates must be viewed and read by the light of the
conditions, surroundings, and history of this case in
order to decide upon their applicability. Abstractly,
the authorities are well enough. The facts and history of the case, however, do not admit of their application.

So far as the suggestion goes that the court continue the receivership until it can itself go out and
effect a reorganization plan and have the same carried out, we confess to an inablty to accede to the
views of appellant's counsel; and the authorities cited
have failed to carry conviction to our minds that such
a plan is feasible or legal. Courts no doubt will, as
stated in some cases cited, recognize equitable and
proper reorganization schemes provided and arranged
for by creditors and bondholders. But a court certainly will not actively promote or arrange reorganization plans. Suppose, however, the court should attempt a thing so utterly absurd, how is it to require
creditors or bondholders to carry it out? It will be

observed that by the terms of the original decree the mortgaged property must be sold as entirety and for cash, and then follows this clause: "So much of the purchase money as is not required to be paid in cash may be paid in receivers' certificates authorized by the court, and in overdue bonds, interest coupons of bonds secured by the mortgage in question, at such rate and percentage as the holder would be entitled to receive in respect of such bonds and coupons out of the purchase money and proceeds of the sale, as the same may be ascertained. If any question should arise as to the rate or amount of such dividend and percentage, or as to the proportion to be paid in cash and the proportion that may be paid in such bonds and coupons, application may be made to the court from time to time at the foot of the decree." What is the clear and obvious meaning of this language in the decree? Does it convey the idea claimed for it by appellant's counsel, that holders of receiver's certificates, or overdue bonds, or interest coupons could, under the decree, bid their securities at the sale? Bid receiver's certificates, or bonds at a judicial sale! Most extraordinary proposition. Suppose the certificates are only worth ten cents on the dollar. Is the holder of them to stand up and bid certificates against a cash bidder? Or, suppose the bonds are entirely worthless, as they are, are bondholders at the sale to have the privilege of bidding these bonds against holders of receiver's certificates which are worth ten cents on the dollar, and even against a cash bidder? If this construction can obtain there is no doubt but what the property will, at a new sale, bring a much better price in bonds and receiver's certificates. The difficulty will be in getting the court's creditors to receive them in payment of the court's debts. It must be apparent, to every one who reads, that the decree contemplated nothing but a cash sale, giving, however, to the purchaser the privilege of using any of these securities in paying the amount of his bid, just so far as such securities would be entitled to participate in the cash realized at such sale. No other construction can be given to the language of the decree without doing violence to its terms, and stultifying the court that rendered it. It seems inexplicable that the proviso as to bonds, certificates, etc., predicated wholly on possible "futures," as to prospective values thereof, as the same may be ascertained in the distant future, poetically styled, "The sweet by and by," should so bewilder the imagination of appellants. Is this court to grasp at phantasies — ethereal essences, fanned into existence by the wand of the versatile counsel who for years has stood over the tomb of the defendant corporations chanting requiems to the glory of the departed? It was Moses, who, at the murmurings of the Israelites, smote Horeb's rock and made water to flow to slake the thirst of the famishing multitude, and the appellants ask the court in some incomprehensible way to resolve itself into a money center and precipitate cash into the pockets of certificate and bondholders. They signally fail to blaze out the highway to the bonanza fields for the court's occupancy.

The circuit court has been weighed down with this receivership and the operating of the defendant companies since the evening of the twenty-eight of October, eighteen hundred and ninety. Even the letters "O. P. R." and "W. V. and C. R." have hung over the court below an ever-present and veritable nightmare. Every conceivable expedient known to the law has been adopted by the court to relieve itself from this

incubus. Five different modifications as to the enforcement of the decree, after much consideration, have
been judicially promulgated to the world to induce bidders to purchase this combined railroad plant. Time
and again have the properties and franchises of these
defunct corporations been duly advertised for public
sale. Printers' ink has been repeatedly spread from
Oregon to New York City, announcing boldly to the
public that the sheriff of Benton County would appear
at the front door of the courthouse and sell at public auction this property under the decree of the
court, and, in at least seven instances, that sheriff,
for want of bidders, was compelled to postpone the
sale from time to time. Since December of eighteen
hundred and ninety-one, these efforts to unload the
court's embargo have been most vigorous and continuous. So much so, that the court seemed resolved
into a kind of perpetual supplicant to the railroad
world at large for assistance out of the operating
dilemma.

Two receivers have been born and have lived and
died during the operating period of this concern, and
the third and last, an example of the survival of the
fittest, has barely survived, and faintly answers to
rollcall. Nor has the court struggled alone and un-
aided in the premises. By no means! Ninety-seven
different attorneys, learned and unlearned, have administered the balm of consolation to the patient in
doses to soothe, if not relieve, at "upset figures."
To keep pace with this moving procession, the court
has been practically in adjourned session for the past
four years. The live coals on the altar of justice
have been constantly fanned to meet the ever-recur-
ring exigencies, superinduced by the "operating process." In a word, the record discloses the fact to be

that the "corpus" has been treated from every conceivable standpoint, allopathic, homeopathic, and eclec-
tic; but all to no purpose.   It was Burke who said
"What shadows we are, and what shadows we pursue," but it has been left to the ingenuity of appellants by long and close contact with a "going concern" to attempt the rare expedient of reducing
shadow to substance, and erecting an ideal super-
structure thereon.   Unfortunately, the blissful dreams
of bountiful rewards as appertains to Oregon Pacific
certificates is not to be realized in this present evil
world.   No judicial power, as now organized, is gifted
with divination, and no earthly tribunal can speak
the dead into life.   Even the roadbed, structures, and
betterments of the defendant companies have reached
the stage of actual decay.   Desolation and ruin are
everywhere manifest from the Yaquina terminus to
Breitenbush in the Cascades.   The court, certificate
holders, and all concerned, are, under the appellants'
contention, reduced to the position of the unfortunate
pitcher, in Sancho Panza's aphorism, viz., "Whether
the pitcher hits the stone, or the stone hits the
pitcher, it goes ill with the pitcher."   Let the certificate holders therefore be content with their present forlorn condition—*la fortune passe partout.*

Opinion by MR. JUSTICE MOORE.

The respondents contend that because the defendant companies have admitted in their answers that
they were insolvent, and that the value of their property and franchises was insufficient to meet the payment of the bonds and overdue interest coupons secured by the mortgage, and because no decree has
been rendered against them for any deficiency after

the sale of their property, and because they have not made any objections to the confirmation of the sale, they have no appealable interest, and are estopped by the order of confirmation; that none of the other appellants ever intervened in the court below, or became parties to the record; that Sanford Bennett, E. C. Mc-Shane, and Bronaugh, McArthur, Fenton, and Bronaugh are the only persons or firms who filed any objections to the confirmation of this sale within the time prescribed by law; that the appellants have no unity of interest, and that Bronaugh, McArthur, Fenton, and Bronaugh have not taken a cross-appeal. Without considering the respondents' objections, but assuming that the appellants are parties to the record and properly before the court, we will examine the case upon the merits as presented by the record.

1. The appellants contend that the amount bid for the property and franchises was so grossly disproportionate to its value as to render the order of confirmation an abuse of discretion, and, while not expecting the court to set the sale aside on account of inadequacy of the price alone, they insist that some excuse should be found for avoiding the effect of the bid in such cases, and suggest as an additional reason therefor that the court had no jurisdiction or authority at a subsequent term to modify or vary the provisions of the original decree; while the respondents, admitting the legal proposition contended for, insist that the subsequent orders of the court did not modify or vary the original decree, but only prescribed the terms of its enforcement, and that the right to do so is inherent in the court, and was specially reserved in the decree. Assuming, for the sake of argument, that the amount bid was inadequate, we will examine the

original decree and the order of the court of October
twentieth, eighteen hundred and ninety-four, with reference to the right of a purchaser to tender in part
payment of the purchase price receivers' certificates
as cash, this being the particular modification of which
the appellants complain. The original decree, after
providing that the mortgaged property should be sold
as an entirety for cash and without appraisement or
right of redemption, further directs that "so much of
the purchase price as is not required to be paid in
cash may be paid in receivers' certificates, and in
bonds, overdue interest coupon bonds, at such rate
and percentage as the holder would be entitled to receive in respect of such bonds and coupons out of the
purchase money and proceeds of sale, as the same
may be ascertained. If any question should arise as
to the sale and amount of such dividend and percentage, or as to the proportion to be paid in cash and
the proportion that may be paid in such bonds and
coupons, application (for that purpose) may be made
to the court from time to time." The sentence last
quoted makes no provision for ascertaining what proportion of the purchase price may be paid in receivers' certificates, but the preceding sentence, having
provided that so much of it as is not required to be
paid in cash may be paid in certificates, bonds, and
coupons, places the certificates in the same class with
the other evidence of indebtedness, and limits the
right of a bidder to tender them in payment of that
part of the purchase price not required by the court
to be paid in cash. It also required a bidder to deposit the sum of five thousand dollars as an earnest
of his good faith and ability to comply with the terms
of his offer to purchase, but it did not prescribe what
sum should be paid in cash, and hence, in the absence

of such a provision, the whole purchase price could be paid only in that manner. If the sale had been made under the original decree, without any application to the court to prescribe what amount of the purchase price should be paid in cash, can it be successfully contended that the purchaser could have tendered either receivers' certificates, bonds, or interest coupons in payment of any part of it? Had the court, on the application of the parties, fixed the amount of the purchase price, less than the whole, which was to have been paid in cash, then the certificates would have been receivable at their face value in liquidation of that part of it not so payable, for the decree made provision for receiving the bonds and coupons only at such rate and percentage as the holders thereof might be entitled to out of the purchase price, and made no reference to the certificates. The order of October twentieth, eighteen hundred and ninety-four, provided that such sale should be made for cash in United States gold coin; and it was contended at the argument that, since the receivers' certificates were not payable in like coin, they could not be received in payment of any part of the purchase price, and hence this order substantially modified the original decree. It is sufficient to say that, had they been payable in United States gold coin, they would not have been receivable in payment of any part of the purchase price until the court had prescribed what part, less than the whole, should be paid in coin.

2. The order of October twentieth, eighteen hundred and ninety-four, also provided that "All taxes legally due and owing by the defendant companies up to the thirty-first day of March, eighteen hundred and ninety-four, shall be paid out of the purchase money

realized from such sale, by and under the order of
this court, and all taxes levied against such properties
and franchises after the thirty-first day of March,
eighteen hundred and ninety-four, shall be borne and
paid by the purchaser or purchasers at such sale."
It is contended that the order providing for the payment of the taxes levied on the property of the defendant companies prior to March thirty-first, eighteen
hundred and ninety-four, substantially modified the
original decree, and prejudged the rights of the lienholders without having given them an opportunity
to question the validity of such taxes; and that the
portion thereof requiring the purchaser to pay the
taxes levied after that date was invalid, and tended to
reduce the amount of the purchaser's bid to the extent of the unascertained tax. We cannot think, from
an examination of the order, that the court intended
thereby to determine the question of priority of right
to the fund which was to be realized from the sale of
the property. The record shows that the counties of
Benton, Lincoln, Linn, and Marion, upon their petitions to the court, obtained an order directing the receiver to pay the taxes due them from the defendant
companies, which, in effect, transferred the rights
which the said counties had in the property situated
within their respective limits to the fund to be realized from its sale, which fund was to be applied to the
payment of these taxes "by and under the order of
the court." The court, in the order complained of,
did not find what amount of tax, if any, was due
either county, or attempt to establish a prior or any
lien in favor of the said counties. It, in effect, provided that the fund realized from the sale should
stand in the place of the property, and, upon settlement, be distributed among those having a prior right

to it. If the counties had no prior lien on the property for the payment of the delinquent taxes, they could have no prior claim on the fund to be realized from its sale. How could the appellants be injured by this order? If any one had cause to complain, it would be the said counties, and particularly so if the fund was insufficient to pay the delinquent taxes, but they have made no objection to the provisions imposed, with which they are presumably satisfied. While the requirement that the purchaser should pay all taxes levied on the property after March thirty-first, eighteen hundred and ninety-four, may have had the effect to reduce the amount of his bid, it was not in our judgment invalid, for if the sale had been consummated prior to the issue of the warrant for the collection of the taxes of that year, and no agreement had been entered into in reference to their payment, it would have been the duty of the purchaser to pay them: Hill's Code, § 2846. The trial court, in fixing the day of sale not later than December twenty-second, was doubtless aware that it would be impossible for the state board of equalization to complete its examination of the county assessment rolls, and certify the result to the several county clerks, in time to have the tax rolls completed and warrants issued for the collection of the taxes until after that date, and we can see no injury resulting from the court's order calling the purchaser's attention to the provisions of the statute in relation to his duty to pay the taxes of eighteen hundred and ninety-four.

3. The court acquired jurisdiction of the subject matter of the suit by virtue of the constitution and statutes of the state, and of the persons of the de-

fendant companies by their several answers admitting
the allegations of the original and supplemental com-
plaints; and the court, having found the amount due
from the defendants to the plaintiff, and that this sum
was secured by a deed of trust, foreclosed the same,
and ordered a sale of the mortgaged property, and,
having had jurisdiction of the subject matter and persons of the defendant companies, its decree was final
and fully supports the sale of the defendants' property, unless it has been modified by the subsequent
orders of the court.   Mr. Beach, in his valuable work
on Modern Equity Practice, (section 905,) in speaking
of the power of a court to control the execution of its
decree, says: "Notwithstanding the general rule that
the court has no power whatever, after final decree,
to amend, modify, or alter the proofs of the decree, it
retains and possesses the power of controlling the
time of its execution."   The authorities cited in support of the text are: *Bound* v. *South Carolina Railway Company,* 55 Fed. 186; *Monkhouse* v. *Corporation,* 17 Ves. 380;
Edwards v. *Cunliffe,* 1 Madd. 287; *Spann* v. *Spann,* 2 Hill's
Ch. Pr. 122.   In the *Bound Case,* 55 Fed. 186, the decree ordered the sale of a railroad to be made on
April eleventh, eighteen hundred and ninety-three,
and, an appeal having been taken in which no super-
sedeas bond was given, the court, on motion, after
adopting the language quoted in the text, postponed
the sale to December twelfth of that year.   In *Monkhouse* v. *Corporation,* 17 Ves. 380, the plaintiff having obtained a decree foreclosing a mortgage, the defendant
moved the court to suspend its execution until six
months after an appeal could be heard, which motion
was allowed upon condition that the defendant pay
the interest and costs, upon plaintiff's undertaking to
repay the same, if the decree should be reversed.   In

Edwards v. *Cunliffe,* 1 Madd. 287, the decree provided
that unless the amount due was paid on December
twenty-third, eighteen hundred and fourteen, the mortgage foreclosure should become absolute, but the mortgagor, being unable to comply with the terms, the
date of payment was, upon motion, extended four
times. So, too, in *Spann* v. *Spann,* 2 Hill's Ch. Pr. 122,
JOHNSON, J. in delivering the opinion of the court
upon this question, said: "But it is equally clear that
the courts, both of law and equity, or a judge or
chancellor at chambers, have the power, and daily
exercise it, of suspending the execution of even final
process on account of subsequent matter which would
render the execution of it oppressive or iniquitous."
These authorities clearly support the text of the
learned author, and conclusively show that, while a
court cannot, by a subsequent order, modify the essential features of a final decree, it does possess the inherent right of changing the time of its execution.
This right being granted, it must, upon principle, be
conceded that a court possesses an equal right to
modify by a subsequent order the manner of the enforcement of its decrees, for it requires no more
power to modify the manner than it does to change
the time of executing them. In *Turner* v. *Indianapolis,
Bloomington, and Western Railway Company,* 8 Bissell, 380,
(Fed. Cas. 14259,) Mr. Justice DRUMMOND, in comment
ing on the modification of a decree by a subsequent
order, said: "The facts were that the original decree
was entered on the eighteenth of July, eighteen hundred and seventy-seven, and the amendment was made
in May, eighteen hundred and seventy-eight. I admit
the rule which denies the power of the court over a
decree after the term when it was rendered. It can
not change or alter the essential parts of the decree.

But what was the order made by the court in May,
eighteen hundred and seventy - eight? It is termed a
further direction for the execution of the decree theretofore entered. The original decree provided that the
property should be sold on a certain number of days'
publication. That was changed by the amendment.
The original decree provided for the distribution of
the funds arising from the sale in a particular manner. That was changed by the amendment of May,
eighteen hundred and seventy-eight. But these things
did not affect the substance of the decree. Of the
right of the court to make that order, I cannot
doubt." This case was appealed to the Supreme
Court of the United States, where Mr. Justice HAR-
LAN, in rendering the decision upon review of the
foregoing objection, with others, said: "We do not
stop to consider whether these objections find any
support in the record, since it is sufficient to say that,
if any such errors exist, they necessarily inhere, some
in the final decree of foreclosure and sale, and others
in the order which preceded it. They cannot be examined upon an appeal merely from the order confirming the report of sale. Our authority extends, as
we have shown, no further than to an examination of
the exceptions filed by appellants to the report of
sale, from the order confirming which this appeal is
taken. And some of these exceptions plainly have
reference, not to the sale itself, but to the final decree of foreclosure; such, for instance, as that the
terms of sale were too onerous; that the property
was sold subject to various claims, the amount of
which was wholly uncertain; and that the court had
no jurisdiction in the case": *Turner* v. *Farmers' Loan
and Trust Company,* 106 U. S. 522 (1 Sup. Ct. 519). The
modifications complained of do not, in our judgment,

alter or vary the essential parts of the original decree, and were such as the court had authority to make in carrying it into execution.

4. We will now examine the objections to the confirmation. It is contended that the court having instructed the sheriff to sell the property between the fifteenth and twenty-second days of December, eighteen hundred and ninety-four, that officer had no license to sell on either of said days, and hence a sale by him on the twenty-second of that month was void. However this may be, the court has ratified the acts of its agent, and confirmed the sale. "The court," says Mr. Freeman in his work on Void Judicial Sales, (section 42,) "may, if it deems best, ratify various irregularities in the proceedings. If the officer changed the terms of the sale, the court may ratify his action, provided the terms, as changed, are such as the court had power to impose in the first instance." The court in such cases may do by indirection what it could do directly, and, since it could have ordered the sale on the day it occurred, it had power to ratify the act of the officer, if it be conceded that he exceeded his authority by selling the property on the day named: *Jacobs' Appeal,* 23 Pa. St. 477; *Emeroy* v. *Vroman,* 19 Wis. *689 (88 Am. Dec. 726); *Thorn* v. *Ingram,* 25 Ark. 58.

5. The most important contention is that the property and franchises offered for sale were of the value of three million dollars; that the rails, rolling stock, and miscellaneous property alone,—not including the land or buildings,—were worth four hundred and fifty thousand dollars; and that the bid of one hundred thousand dollars is so grossly inadequate as to shock the conscience, and raise the inference of unfairness,

fraud, mistake, or surprise. "The uniform current of
the authorities," says the court in *Marlatt* v. *Warwick*, 18
N. J. Eq. 108, "settles that mere inadequacy of price,
where parties stand on an equal footing, and there are
no confidential relations between them, is not of itself
sufficient to set aside a sale, unless the inadequacy is
so gross as to be proof of fraud, or to shock the
judgment and the conscience." In the case at bar it
is not claimed that the parties did not stand on an
equal footing, that there were any confidential relations existing between them, or that there is any proof
of fraud, and hence the inadequacy sufficient to set
aside the sale must be so gross as to shock the conscience. We have examined the transcript before us
in vain to find any evidence of the value of the said
property and franchises. The receiver, upon his appointment, made an inventory of all that came to his
possession, but he does not appraise a single article,
or give the value in gross, except of some unused material on hand. There was no evidence before the
trial court of the value, and it would be extremely
difficult for us to conclude that the bid was inadequate until we have some evidence upon which the
conclusion can be based. It is said that some experts
were appointed by a committee of the bondholders to
examine the property and appraise its value, but we
cannot find that they were ever appointed by or made
a report to the court upon this important subject. It
does appear, however, from the report of J. W. Whalley, Esq., who was appointed referee to take an account of the receipts and expenses of the defendant
companies under the receivers' management, that for
a period of about fourteen months prior to January
first, eighteen hundred and ninety-two, the lines of
railroad and the river and ocean steamers connected

therewith had been operated at a total loss of eighty-seven thousand nine hundred and eighty-three dollars and seventy-five cents, or six thousand two hundred and eighty-four dollars and fifty-five cents per month; that the receiver had prior to said date issued certificates amounting to six hundred and thirty-eight thousand and forty-one dollars and twenty-nine cents, and that the total liabilities on June thirtieth, eighteen hundred and ninety-two, were nine hundred and five thousand four hundred and fourteen dollars and forty cents, less thirty-seven thousand eight hundred and thirty-six dollars and eighty-six cents, which was available in part payment of that amount, thus showing a total indebtedness at that date of eight hundred and sixty-seven thousand five hundred and seventy-eight dollars and fifty-four cents beyond the bonded indebtedness of fifteen million dollars and interest which were secured by the mortgage. How much this debt was increased from June thirtieth, eighteen hundred and ninety-two, at which time the referee made his supplemental report, to December twenty-second, eighteen hundred and ninety-four, when the sale occurred, the record does not show, but it was admitted in argument that an indebtedness of more than one million dollars had been incurred by the receiver since his appointment on October twenty-eighth, eighteen hundred and ninety. Viewed in the light of a business venture, and not considering the amount necessary to be expended for betterments, a property which was operated as a "going concern" at a total loss of more than six thousand dollars per month, does not, it must be conceded, present a very inviting field to capitalists, and while the amount bid for the property may be grossly inadequate, we cannot say that it is so, in the absence of any evidence of its value, and considering that no sum in excess of that amount has been offered by any one. It is indeed unfortunate that the expenses of the management of the property can not be realized from its sale. No one can examine the record before us without being impressed with the conviction that the trial court has labored long and earnestly to accomplish this result, but without success, and to continue the operation of the road under the management of a receiver would result in further expense which must be borne by those who can ill afford to add it to their present losses. The court, hoping the bondholders would by reorganization buy the property and pay off the expense of the receiver's management, fixed a minimum price of one million dollars, and at another time one million two hundred and fifty thousand dollars, but was unable to effect a sale on these terms, and after waiting more than four years for the consummation of its hopes found the illusion dispelled, and the only remedy remaining was to sell the property for what it would bring, which, having been done, amd the sale confirmed by a court that was acquainted with the property and must have known its value, we can, in the absence of any evidence of the value, do nothing more than affirm the decree, which is so ordered.   AFFIRMED.

Argued April 24; decided August 5, 1895.

BALFOUR *v.* BURNETT.
[41 Pac. 1.]

1. WHO ARE "THIRD PERSONS"—EXECUTION SALES—CODE, § 292.—Parties to a decree for the foreclosure of a mortgage, and who are bound thereby, are not "third persons" as to a sale under the decree, within the meaning of Hill's Code, § 292, providing that real property consisting of several lots or parcels shall be sold separately when a portion is claimed by a "third person" who requests that it shall be so sold. Under this section the term "third person" evi-

dently means one who was not a party to the judgment or decree, but who has acquired title to a portion of the judgment debtor's real property subsequent to the rendition of the judgment or decree, and is privy to and bound by it.

2. EXECUTION SALES OF REAL ESTATE — CONFIRMATION — CODE, § 292.— Under the terms of section 292, Hill's Code, the sheriff may sell real property on execution in separate parcels or *en masse*, and after confirmation his action will not be reviewed, unless it is shown that he has abused the discretion confided in him: *Leinenweber* v. *Brown*, 24 Or. 548, and *Bays* v. *Trulson*, 25 Or. 110, approved and followed.

APPEAL from Douglas: J. C. FULLERTON, Judge.

This is an appeal from an order confirming a sale of real property. The facts are that Balfour, Guthrie and Company, having obtained a decree foreclosing a mortgage on certain tracts of contiguous land in Douglas County, caused an execution to be issued against the property adjudged to be sold, directed to the sheriff of said county, who advertised the sale to take place on February twenty-fourth, eighteen hundred and ninety-four, at which time the defendants, Thomas B. Burnett, Jasper Waite, and Shirley Waite. claim ng a portion of said premises, requested the officer to sell the same separately, but, after offering for sale a part of the lands so claimed by them, and failing to receive any bid therefor, the sheriff sold the mortgaged premises *en masse* to the plaintiffs, who, upon the return of the officer, moved the court for an order confirming the sale, to which the said defendants filed objections. These having been overruled, the court made an order confirming the sale, from which the said defendants appeal, and contend that they claimed a portion of the mortgaged premises as "third persons," and, having requested the sheriff to sell the same separately, his failure to do so was an irregularity which should avoid the sale.

AFFIRMED.

Opinion by MR. JUSTICE MOORE.

1. The statute prescribing the manner of sale, so
far as applicable to the case at bar, is as follows:
"When the sale is of real property, and consisting of
several known lots or parcels, they shall be sold separately or otherwise, as is likely to bring the highest
price, or when a portion of such real property is
claimed by a third person, and he requests it to be
sold separately, such portion shall be sold separately":
Hill's Code, § 292. A proper definition of the term
"third person" is important in the determination of
the defendants' right to insist upon a separate sale of
that portion of the mortgaged premises so claimed by
them. Bouvier, in his law dictionary, in defining the
term, says: "But it is difficult to give a very definite
idea of 'third persons,' for sometimes those who are
not parties to the contract, but who represent the
rights of the original parties, as executors, are not
to be considered third persons"; while Anderson, in
his more recent work, referring to the term, says:
"Strangers are 'third persons' generally,—all persons
in the world except parties and privies. For example,
those who are in no way parties to a covenant, nor
bound by it, are said to be strangers to the covenant." The latter definition would seem to make the
term synonymous with strangers, but, since a person
claiming a portion of the premises subject to the lien
of a judgment must be in privity with the judgment
debtor and bound by the judgment, he could not be
a stranger to it, and hence the definition given by
Anderson is not applicable to the term as used in the
statute; for, if the person claiming a portion of the
premises offered for sale were a stranger to the judgment, his property would not be bound by it, and

there would be no necessity to request a separate sale, and any attempt to sell it as the property of the judgment debtor would be restrained upon invoking the equitable powers of the court. In *Leese* v. *Clark*, 20 Cal. 425, the court, interpreting an act of congress which, *inter alia,* provided, "And be it further enacted that the final decrees rendered by the said commissioners or by the district or supreme court of the United States, or any patent to be issued under this act, shall be conclusive between the United States and the claimants only, and shall not effect the interest of third persons," said: "The term 'third persons' refers not to all persons other than the United States and the claimants, but to those who hold independent titles arising previous to the acquisition of the country. The latter class are not barred by the decree and patent, for they do not hold in subordination to the action of the government, nor by any title subsequent, but by title arising anterior to the conquest."

It will be seen that the court in this case limits the term to a particular class, and does not extend it to all persons other than the United States and claimants thereunder, thus conclusively showing that it is not in all casses synonymous with "stranger." The term "third person," as used in the statute under consideration, evidently means one who was not a party to the judgment or decree, but who has acquired a title to a portion of the judgment debtor's real property subsequent to the rendition of the judgement or decree, and is privy to and bound by it. Having obtained his title subsequent to the lien of the judgment, he is entitled, upon request, to have that portion of the debtor's estate claimed by him sold separately, in order that he may redeem it from the sale, but if he has secured a title to all the real property

which the judgment debtor had, or all that was subject to the lien of the judgment, he has put himself
in the place of his grantor, so far as the property is
concerned, and cannot insist upon a separate sale of
any portion of it. In the case at bar the record discloses that the appellants were parties to the decree
and are bound by it, and, applying the interpretation
above given, they are not "third persons" within the
meaning of the statute. Had they desired a separate
sale of that portion of the mortgaged premises so
claimed by them, they had the right to invoke the
aid of the court to adjust their equities, and by a decree prescribe the manner of sale (2 Jones on Mortgages, § 1616); but, failing to apply for this relief
when they were before the court, they cannot now
claim to be "third persons" to the decree, and hence
had no right to insist upon a separate sale.

2.   The statute invests the officer making a sale of
real property in such cases with a discretion which
will not be reviewed except for abuse: *Griswold* v.
Stoughton, 2 Or. 64 (84 Am. Dec. 409); *Dolph* v. *Barney,*
5 Or. 211; *Bank of British Columbia* v. *Paige,* 7 Or. 455;
Leinenweber v. *Brown,* 24 Or. 548 (34 Pac. 475); *Bays* v.
Trulson, 25 Or. 109 (35 Pac. 26). And the sheriff having sold the premises *en masse,* it must be presumed
that the method adopted was the one best calculated
to realize the greatest amount for the property sold.
There being no error in the order confirming the sale,
it follows that it must be affirmed, and it is so ordered.

                                        AFFIRMED.

Decided April 17, 1894; affirmed on rehearing August 5, 1895.

VEDDER *v.* MARION COUNTY.

[36 Pac. 535; 41 Pac. 3.]

1. HIGHWAYS—REPORTS OF VIEWERS—TIME FOR FILING REMONSTRANCES—CODE, § 4065.—Remonstrances to a petition for the vacation of a county road, which are filed when the report of the viewers is first read, are filed in proper time, under section 4065, Hil.'s Code, providing that the county court can acquire no jurisdiction prior to the final reading of the report. This is so regardless of what appeals or other proceedings may have occurred — the question is whether the remonstrances were filed before the court acted on the viewer's report.

2. VACATING AND ESTABLISHING HIGHWAYS.—The establishment of a new county road upon a petition for the establishment of such road, and also for the vacation of an old road, does not operate to vacate the latter, where the new road does not lie within the termini of the old one, and connects with it only at one end.

3. DISCRETION OF COUNTY COURT IN OPENING ROADS—CODE, § 4065—REPORT OF VIEWERS.—A county court has a discretion regarding the opening of roads that is conferred upon it by the express terms of section 4065 of Hill's Code, and, while it cannot open a road over an adverse report of the viewers, it need not follow a favorable report, unless it is satisfied that the proposed road will be of public utility.

4. VACATING AND ESTABLISHING HIGHWAYS.—A petition for the establishment of a road twenty-nine chains long, and for the vacation of another road connecting with the former at one end and forty-two chains long, and diverging from the former at an angle of more than forty-five degrees, and intersecting the same highway more than thirty chains apart, will be considered as two proceedings,—one for the establishment of a road, and the other for another road,—instead of a proceeding for the alteration of a highway merely.

APPEAL from Marion: GEORGE H. BURNETT, Judge.

This is a special proceeding by G. W. Vedder against Marion County to review the action of the county court in the matter of changing the location of a county road in said county. The record shows that, after giving the required notice, the plaintiff and twenty-seven other householders residing in the vicin-

ity of the proposed road filed in said court the following road petition: "To the County Court of the
State of Oregon, for the County of Marion: The un-
dersigned, your petitioners, respectfully ask for the
location and establishment of a county road commencing at the northwest corner of the donation land claim
of W. Eastham, in section twenty-five, in township five
south of range one west, in said county of Marion,
thence north about one hundred and sixteen rods to
the center of the old county road leading from
Shuck's Mill in said Marion County to the town of
Woodburn in said county. Application will also be
made at the same time to said court to vacate all
that portion of the present county road leading from
Shuck's Mill to said town of Woodburn, which is situated between the termini of said proposed road, and
which runs diagonally across the land claims at present owned by G. W. Vedder and Joseph Schaffer, respectively, in said Marion County." Upon the receipt
of said petition the county court appointed viewers
and a surveyor, and, after examining and surveying
the proposed road, the viewers made their report to
the court, in which they recommended that the proposed road be declared a public highway, and that
part of the old road running through the lands of
G. W. Vedder and Joseph Schaffer be vacated. The
surveyor's plat, which forms a part of the viewers' report, shows that a county road extending easterly
from the beginning point of the proposed road is in-
tersected one hundred and twenty roads east of said
beginning point by the old county road proposed to
be vacated, which extends northwesterly across the
lands of Vedder and Schaffer, and which also intersects the proposed road at its termini. On July eighth,
eighteen hundred and ninety-one, at which time the

viewers' report was filed, objections were made to the
sufficiency of the publication of the road notices, and
the court on the next day made an order dismissing
said petition. The plaintiff commenced proceedings to
review the action of the county court, and, at the
hearing thereof, the circuit court gave judgment dismissing the writ, from which he appealed to this
court, where it was reversed: *Vedder* v. *Marion County*,
22 Or. 264 (29 Pac. 619). After the cause was remanded to the county court a large number of householders, some of whom reside in Clackamas County,
remonstrated against the location of the proposed road
and the vaction of the old one, and four others showed
that if the old road should be vacated they would be
deprived of all access to a public road, and filed claims
for damages. The report of the viewers was, on July
seventh, eighteen hundred and ninety-two, read for
the first time, laid on the table for further consideration, and the matter continued to the August term,
when the court, upon motion, ordered the names of the
remonstrators residing in Clackamas County stricken
from the remonstrance. This being done, the court,
treating the respective parts of the petition asking for
the establishment of the new and the vacation of the
old road as separate petitions, and, under a rule interpreting the term "vicinity" to mean a territory within
two miles of a proposed road, and within the same
distance from an established road along its entire
length, when any part of it is proposed to be vacated,
found that it contained a less number than the petition for the new road, but a greater number than the
petition for the vacation, and made an order establishing the new road as prayed for, but refused to
vacate the old one. The plaintiff thereupon commenced this proceeding, and the record of the county

court having been certified to the circuit court, a trial was had resulting in a judgment on the seventeenth day of February, eighteen hundred and ninety-three, dismissing the writ, from which judgment the plaintiff appeals.　　　　　　　　　　　　　　AFFIRMED.

For appellant there were briefs and oral arguments by *Messrs. Bonham and Holmes.*

For respondent there were briefs and oral arguments by *Messrs. D'Arcy and Bingham.*

Opinion by MR. JUSTICE MOORE.

1. The report of the viewers having been filed at the July term, eighteen hundred and ninety-one, of the county court, it is contended that no remonstrance thereto filed after the case was remanded could be properly considered by the court. The record shows that the report of the viewers was read for the first time on July seventh, eighteen hundred and ninety-two, at which time the remonstrances were filed. This recital must overcome the presumption, if any existed, that the report was read before the petition was dismissed by the county court on July ninth, eighteen hundred and ninety-one, and as the court could acquire no jurisdiction to grant the petition prior to the final reading of the viewers' report: *Latimer* v. *Tillamook County,* 22 Or. 291 (29 Pac. 734); it follows that the remonstrances were filed in proper time.

2. It is contended that the establishment of the new road vacated the old one, and that as soon as the new road was opened to public travel the old one thereby became discontinued. In *Commonwealth* v. *Westborough,* 3 Mass. 406, PARSONS, C. J., in discussing this

question, said: "For establishing an alteration in a way is, in law, a discontinuance of the part altered; and the report of the discontinuance, and the acceptance of it, are merely surplusage. On any other principle, the applying for an alteration must be an application for a new way, and not for altering an old one." In *Commonwealth* v. *Cambridge,* 7 Mass. 157, a petition for an alteration of an existing highway had been presented, which was denied, but a new road was established where the alteration was requested. It was held that the alteration of an old way and the establishment of a new one were substantially different; that the adjudication of the court was not of the matters in dispute, and the proceedings were therefore void. The rule is well established that when a petition for the alteration of an existing road has been granted, all parts of the old road embraced within the limits of the alteration are vacated by implication, though no order to that effect be made: *Brooks* v. *Horton,* 68 Cal. 554 (10 Pac. 204); *Hobart* v. *Plymouth County,* 100 Mass. 159; *Heiple* v. *Clackamas County,* 20 Or. 147 (25 Pac. 291). Section 4061, Hill's Code, authorizes county courts to establish, alter, or vacate county roads. In the case at bar the petitioners ask for the location and establishment of a county road. Their application can not be treated as a petition for an alteration unless the legal effect of the vacation of the old and the establishment of the new road is equivalent thereto. If this be the proper construction, then the county court, by refusing to vacate the old had no authority to establish the new road, and its order to that effect would be a nullity: *Commonwealth* v. *Cambridge,* 7 Mass. 157. The road established forms the west line or base of a triangle, and it is sought to vacate the hypothenuse, extending from its northern terminus to a point on an existing county road one hundred and twenty rods east of its southern terminus. If the termini of the road established were within the limits of the old road, there might be some propriety in holding that the petition was for an alteration of an existing road, as the traveling public could as well be accommodated by the new as it had been by the old way, but since the new road does not lie within the termini of the old, and connects with it only at its north end, the county court, in pursuance of a stipulation of the parties and of the character of the pleadings, properly construed the application to be two petitions,—one for the location and establishment of a new road, and the other for the vacation of an old one,—and could therefore grant or deny either, and hence the establishment of the new road did not operate to vacate the old one.

3. It is also contended that, the viewers having recommended the vacation of the old road, the county court was obliged to grant it. Section 4065, Hill's Code, provides that, "the court, being satisfied that such road will be of public utility, the report of the viewers being forwarded thereto, the court shall cause said report, survey, and plat to be recorded, and from thenceforth said road shall be considered a public highway, and the court shall issue an order directing said road to be opened." It is quite probable that the word "favorable" was intended where "forwarded" is used in said section. This construction would preclude the court from establishing a county road in the following instances: (1) When the viewers' report is unfavorable thereto; (2) when a remonstrance with a greater number of qualified remonstrators than there are names on the petition is filed in proper time; and,

(3) when claims for damages are unsettled. This section requires the viewers to make their report on or before the third day of the term of court next after their appointment, and it is made the duty of the county clerk to read said report on two separate days of the meeting thereof. The report of the viewers thus becomes a condition precedent to any action on the part of the court, and, as this requirement appears in the preceding part of the section, it is very apparent that the legislature intended to adopt the word "favorable" when it made use of the word "forwarded." The court would thus be bound by an unfavorable report of the viewers; but must it, when their report is favorable thereto, establish, alter, or vacate the road? The report would certainly be binding upon the court unless it is vested with a discretion by implication, or by the statutory provision that it must be satisfied that the road will be of public utility before it can be established. If the viewers' report be conclusive upon the court, then the petition must be granted, even if the court is not satisfied that the road asked to be established, altered, or vacated is of any utility. In *Commissioners* v. *Bowie*, 34 Ala. 461, the court says: "Upon the question of the expediency of opening or altering a public road, that court exercises a *quasi* legislative authority, and its decision is not revisable. In the exercise of that authority, it does not act alone upon evidence produced according to legal rules, but is guided to some extent, by its knowledge of the geography of the country, the wants and wishes of the people, and the ability of the neighborhood to keep the road in repair." The legislature has delegated to the county court the authority to establish, alter, and vacate county roads, and as the legislature may determine when the necessity for

a public road exists, so the same authority may be exercised by the county court; and if there were no statute vesting it with this discretion, the court, by implication, could exercise such discretion, unless prohibited by statute. Whether a proposed road will subserve the public need or convenience is a question for the legislature, and not for the judiciary: *Sherman* v. *Buick*, 32 Cal. 241 (91 Am. Dec. 577); *Commonwealth* v. *Roxbury*, 8 Mass. 457; and hence the county court, in determining its utility, acts in a legislative capacity. The authority is not only given by implication, but the statute, section 4065, in positive terms grants this power to the county court, and authorizes it to exercise a discretion in the matter; and hence the conclusion reached by the county court upon these legislative questions is not subject to review: *State* v. *Bergen*, 24 N. J. L. 548. The county court, by implication and by statute having authority to disregard the favorable report of the viewers in the matter of the vacation of the road, it follows that the judgment of the circuit court is affirmed.   AFFIRMED.

ON REHEARING.

Opinion by MR. JUSTICE WOLVERTON.

4. The county court has supervision of all county roads. There are three distinct instances in which the jurisdiction of the court may be exercised: *first*, to establish; *second*, to alter; and, *third*, to vacate. These would seem to be the natural subdivisions for the exercise of its powers as touching the establishment and discontinuance of county roads, from a survey of the statute bearing upon the subject. The language of section 4061, Hill's Code, is: "No county road shall be hereafter established, nor shall any such road be al-

tered or vacated, in any county in this state, except
by the authority of the county court of the proper
county"; and of section 4063: "When any petition
shall be presented for the action of the county court
for the laying out, alteration, or vacation of any county
road, it shall be accompanied by satisfactory proof,"
etc. The jurisdiction of the county court is obtained
by petition signed by at least twelve householders of
the county, residing in the vicinity where said road is
to be laid out, altered, or vacated. It is believed that
it is not good practice to combine two of these causes
for calling into requisition the functions of the court.
STRAHAN, J., in a former appeal of this cause, intimated that in a case where the location of the new
road would virtually supersede the old, or render it
useless or unnecessary, there could be no objection to
combining an application for the location with one for
vacation in the same proceeding, but if there should
appear to be no connection or relation whatever between the two, no doubt then existed but the better
practice would be to prosecute them by separate proceedings: 22 Or. 270 (29 Pac. 619). The reasons for
this are substantial. Suppose a petition be filed for
the establishment of two distinct and detached pieces
of road, separated one from the other by two miles at
the nearest point. The householders residing within
the vicinity of one may not all reside in the vicinity
of the other, and hence those residing without the
vicinity of one and within the vicinity of the other
could not be legal petitioners for both roads. The
same may be said of a petition to establish one road
and to vacate another where relatively situated as in
the supposed case of a petition for two distinct and
detached roads. The application of this principle pro-
motes a construction of the statute which would seem

to be more in consonance with its spirit, as it tends to
prevent the combination of different localities to the
injury of some other.   It might be possible to vacate
a road or a portion thereof by combining it with the
location of another, whereas a petition to vacate singly
would fail, and *vice versa.*   The power to make alterations in county roads is simply the power to make
changes therein.   Where an alteration is made, if the
route of a road is deflected, the new road takes the
place of the old.   Whenever it in effect supersedes the
latter, and renders it useless or unnecessary, the old
road is thereby discontinued as a necessary consequence of the establishment of a different route: *Brook*
v. *Horton,* 68 Cal. 554 (10 Pac. 204); *Hobart* v. *Plymouth*
County, 100 Mass. 159; *Heiple* v. *Clackamas County,* 20 Or.
149 (25 Pac. 291); *Bliss* v. *Deerfield,* 13 Pick. 107; *Goodwin*
v. *Inhabitants of Marblehead,* 1 Allen, 37; *Commonwealth* v.
Inhabitants of Westborough, 3 Mass. 406; *Bowley* v. *Walker,*
8 Allen, 21.

The petition, which is the foundation for the proceedings in the county court, is as follows: "The un-
dersigned, your petitioners, respectfully ask for the
location and establishment of a county road commencing at the northwest corner of the donation land claim
of W. Eastham, in section twenty-five, township five
south, range one west, in said county of Marion, thence
north about one hundred and sixty rods to the center
of the old county road leading from Shuck's Mill in
said Marion County to the town of Woodburn in said
county.   Application will also be made at the same
time to said court to vacate all that portion of the
present county road from Shuck's Mill to said town of
Woodburn, which is situated between the termini of
said proposed road, and which runs diagonally across
the land claims at present owned by G. W. Vedder

and Joseph Shafer, respectively." Since this cause was remanded upon the former appeal the county court has treated the application as if two petitions were presented, one for the establishment of a county road and the other for the vacation of a portion of a county road already established. The counsel for both petitioners and remonstrators have likewise so treated the petition, and the whole cause has been tried out in said court upon the theory that two petitions were before it distinct and disconnected one from the other. It was evidently the intention of the petitioners to institute but one proceeding, and to maintain it as such, but since the decision of this court upon the former appeal the parties and the court below, as well as the county court, have treated it otherwise. The report of the viewers and the survey show that the road proposed to be established begins at the northwest corner of W. Eastham's donation land claim, and runs thence north twenty-eight and eighty-three hundredths chains to its intersection with the Shuck's Mill and Woodburn Road, and the portion of the road proposed to be vacated begins at a point thirty and nine hundredths chains east of the northwest corner of said Eastham's land claim, in the center of the Shuck's Mill and Gervais Road, and runs in a north-westerly course to the northern terminus of the proposed new road.. There is a county road now opened and established between the termini of the road to be vacated and the one to be established. It is now contended upon the rehearing that the petition was in effect for an alteration in a county road, and that it should be so considered and treated; that, while it prays for the location of one road, and the vacation of another, yet, by reason of the proximity of the two roads, and the relation they sustain to each other,

it is in effect a prayer for an alteration only. If this
contention is sound the cause ought to go back to the
court below for another hearing; if otherwise, not.

It may be observed that the south termini of the
road to be vacated and the road to be established are
three eighths of a mile apart, and that each intersects
what is known as the Shuck's Mill and Gervais Road,
this latter road forming the base of a right angle triangle, of which the new road would be the perpendic-
ular and the one to be vacated the hypothenuse. It is
also apparent that householders residing to the east
and just within the vicinity of the southern terminus of
the road sought to be vacated would not be within the
vicinity of the road sought to be established, and the
same would be true on the other hand of householders residing to the west and just within the vicinity
of the southern terminus of the road to be established.
They would not be within the vicinity of the road to be
vacated. Thus, it will be seen that all the parties to
the petition and remonstrance herein might not have
the statutory qualifications to prosecute or contest the
establishment of one or the vacation of the other road,
taken singly. This is a strong circumstance showing
why it would be better to prosecute such proceedings
singly, but it is perhaps not conclusive. Neither is
the circumstance that the termini of the two ways are
not the same conclusive that the proceeding is not for
an alteration. In *Hobart* v. *Plymouth County,* 100 Mass.
159, a petition was filed representing that the highway was narrow and crooked, praying that it might
be widened, straightened, and newly located, and such
parts discontinued as might be rendered unnecessary
by such location; the county commissioners voted to
widen the highway to a certain point, thence to locate a new highway to a point on the line of the old

one, and from thence to widen it further along in the
same general direction. Another public way entered
the old way between the said points. It was held
that the change in the way between said points was,
in legal effect, only an alteration of the old location,
and that a discontinuance of so much of the old way
as was not included in the new location, nor necessary
for the travel of the connecting way, resulted from
such alteration. In *Commonwealth* v. *Boston and Albany
Railroad Company,* 150 Mass. 174, (22 N. E. 913,) a county
road entering another at right angles was deflected at
a point some twenty-eight rods from the point of intersection, and entered the old road about the same
distance north of the old intersection, and it was held
by the court that the portion of the road between the
point of deflection and its first terminus was thereby
vacated. The new road was forty rods and eight links
in length. In determining the matter the court said:
"There is nothing in the language of the petition or
of the adjudication to suggest that anything else was
contemplated than a substitution of a new piece of
road for an old one in the same general line of travel."
It was further observed that the distance to be traveled to a certain point was slightly increased, but that
the commissioners had provided for such a use by
making the road six rods wide at its junction, thus
cutting off the corner towards such point. From this,
and the obligations the town would be under to maintain both roads if allowed to stand, the court concluded that the commissioners intended to and did
actually discontinue that portion of the old road between the point of deflection and the old intersection.
The sides of the triangle formed by the new and the
old ways are about one fourth the length of those
formed by the roads in the case at bar. *Commonwealth*

v. *Cambridge,* 7 Mass. 157, is a case wherein the petition
prayed for an alteration, and stated that the existing
road might with greater convenience be turned or altered in two places, in the direction therein de cribed.
The lower court adjudged that one of the alterations
be made, but that the existing road should not be discontinued. The court on appeal says: "The jurisdiction given to the court is to lay out new county roads,
or to turn or alter old roads, on application made to the
court. * * * The matter in dispute was whether
an existing road should be partially altered, or not;
the adjudication was against the alteration prayed for,
but in favor of a new road, where the alteration was
requested, a new road then not being prayed for. In
form, therefore, it appears that the adjudication was
not of the matter in dispute. Whether it was or was
not substantially, deserves consideration. So far as
an alteration is a charge upon the town it is reasonable they should prefer the alteration to a new road,
because in this last case the old road remains a subject of repair, while the new road requires also to be
made and repaired. But where there is an alteration,
the part of the old road that is discontinued ceases to
be a charge upon the inhabitants. It may, therefore,
be well supposed that when an alteration is prayed
for, it may not be opposed by a town; but their agents
may unite with the petitioners in requesting it, while
they would earnestly oppose a new road. With respect to individuals whose interest may be affected,
they may not oppose a new road, because the old road
remains for them to pass, while they might resist an
alteration, as discontinuing an old road convenient to
them. * * * We are obliged to conclude that the
alteration of an old way, and the establishment of a

new one, are substantially different, and differently affect the opposing parties."

These considerations have cogent application to the case in hand. The petition here is in form for the establishment of a new road and the vacation of an old one, but is it in substance a petition for an alteration? and can it be treated in that light in consideration of the relation which the old road bears to the new, their respective lengths, and their connections with other public roads of the county? The proposed new road is twenty-eight and eighty-three hundreths chains in length, and the road required to be vacated forty one and ninety-five hundreths. They diverge one from the other at an angle of more than forty-five degrees, and intersect the same public road on the south thirty and nine hundreths chains apart. The road to be vacated constitutes a part of what is known as the Shuck's Mill and Woodburn Road, the base of the triangle serving as a part of the Shuck's Mill and Gervais Road. The new way increases the distance to Shuck's Mill from Woodburn almost nineteen chains. Under these conditions it cannot be said that the new supersedes the old and renders it unnecessary. The respective lengths of the two roads are so great and their divergence so marked as to dispel the idea that the one is to supersede the other, or that the location of the one will render the other unnecessary. These conditions being wanting, the petition cannot be considered as substantially one for an alteration only. The county court properly considered the petition as the commencement of two proceedings, the one for a location and the other for a vacation of a county road. The former opinion of the court is therefore adhered to.   AFFIRMED.

Mr. Chief Justice BEAN (dissenting). I am unable to agree with my brethren in this case. In my opinion the petition in question is in effect an application for the alteration of an existing county road, and should have been so treated by the county court.

Argued July 25; decided August 5, 1895.

BUSH *v.* MITCHELL.
[41 Pac. 155.]

ACCEPTING PART OF A JUDGMENT AS A WAIVER OF RIGHT TO APPEAL.—In actions at law the entire case is either affirmed or reversed, so that an appeal cannot be taken from a part of a judgment, and the balance of it be accepted (*Portland Construction Company* v. *O'Neill,* 24 Or. 54, cited); thus, where a judgment went for plaintiff for the amount of a note, but the court refused to allow any attorney's fee, the plaintiff cannot accept the money adjudged to him on the note, and then appeal from the refusal to allow the attorney's fee, for if the case is reversed for one purpose it is for all purposes, and the question of the amount due on the note must be tried again.

APPEAL from Marion: GEORGE H. BURNETT, Judge.

This is a motion to dismiss an appeal. The facts are that on February twenty-fourth, eighteen hundred and ninety-four, the plaintiff, having commenced an action against the defendants, obtained a judgment therein for twenty-four thousand five hundred and fifty-six dollars and fifty cents, the amount due on a promissory note, containing a provision for reasonable attorney's fees in case "suit" was instituted for its collection. The complaint in said action, in addition to the usual averments, also alleged that one thousand two hundred dollars was a reasonable sum as attorney's fees, all which having been put in issue by the answer, the plaintiff at the trial offered evidence tending to prove the said allegation, to the in-

troduction of which the defendants objected because
the proceeding was an action at law and the note provided for an attorney's fee in case of a suit, and, their
objection having been sustained, an exception was
saved. On May twenty-eighth, eighteen hundred and
ninety-four, the judgment, interest, and costs amounted
to twenty-three thousand three hundred and eighteen
dollars and eighty cents, and the defendants, claiming
to have a cross-demand for two thousand nine hundred
and thirty-eight dollars and eighty-three cents, which
they desired to offset, paid to the plaintiff, who received and receipted for the same, the sum of twenty-
two thousand three hundred and seventy-nine dollars and ninety-seven cents on account of the judgment. On August twenty-fourth, eighteen hundred
and ninety-four, the plaintiff served and filed a notice
of appeal, and gave an undertaking therefor, and the
transcript having been filed in this court, the defendants moved to dismiss the attempted appeal, and contend that the plaintiff, having accepted a part of the
judgment, has waived his right of appeal; while the
plaintiff insists that the claim for attorney's fees and
the demand for the amount due on the note are severable, and that, if the error complained of be manifest, the judgment should be reversed and the cause
remanded to try the claim for attorney's fee only.

DISMISSED.

Mr. Ossian Franklin Paxton, for the motion.

Messrs. H. J. Bigger and *Tilmon Ford, contra.*

PER CURIAM. The rule is universal that a party
will not, without the consent of his adversary, be permitted to split up his demand and maintain separate

actions on the several parts: *Little* v. *City of Portland*, 26
Or. 235 (37 Pac. 911). So, too, it is equally well settled that a party will not be permitted to maintain sep
arate appeals from parts of a judgment or decree:
Elliott on Appellate Procedure, § 18. "There is a
class of cases," says the same learned author, (Elliott
on Appellate Procedure, § 99,) "which apparently form
an exception to the general rule that an appeal will
not lie from part of a case, but the cases forming this
class will be found on investigation to be apparent
rather than actual exceptions. The class to which we
refer is composed of cases wherein an issue, distinct,
entire, and complete, is formed between some of the
parties, and upon which issue a final judgment is
given affecting only the interests and rights of the
parties to that issue." In prescribing the form of a
notice of appeal, the statute provides that "such notice
shall state the appellant appeals from the judgment
or decree of the circuit court, or some specified part
thereof, and in case the judgment be one rendered in
an action at law, shall specify the grounds of error,
with reasonable certainty, upon which the appellant
intends to rely upon the appeal": Hill's Code, § 537,
subdivision 1. It also provides that "upon an appeal,
the appellate court may affirm, reverse, or modify the
judgment or decree appealed from, in the respect mentioned in the notice, and not otherwise, as to any or
all of the parties joining in the appeal, and may include in such decision any or all of the parties not
joining in the appeal, except a codefendant of the appellant against whom a several judgment or decree
might have been given in the court below; and may,
if necessary and proper, order a new trial": Hill's
Code, § 544. The section of the statute last quoted,
when interpreted by the apparent exception to the

general rule applicable to appeals, (Elliott on Appellate Procedure, § 99,) would seem to refer to some of the parties between whom a distinct issue is formed, and who would be permitted to appeal from so much of the judgment or decree given in the whole case as may determine such particular issue. For example: the parties to a foreclosure proceeding who seek to establish among themselves a priority of lien. From the example given it can readily be seen that, under the statute, separate appeals may be maintained from distinct parts of a decree in equity, but it may well be doubted if such appeals lie from judgments in actions at law.

THAYER, J., in construing these sections of the statute, says: ''These two provisions, taken together, seem to restrict the review to the part of the decree specified in the notice, although the latter portion of section 533 of the Code, (Hill's Code, § 543,) provides that, upon an appeal from a decree given in any court, the suit shall be tried anew upon the transcript and evidence accompanying it. This would seem to imply that the whole case would be before the appellate court for trial *de novo*, though it might be sufficient answer to repel the inference that an appeal from a part of a decree is not 'an appeal from a decree,' within the meaning of the above provision; that said provision was only intended to apply to an appeal from an entire decree. Still, I think a more satisfactory construction can be given to the provision, and make it harmonize with the view I have indicated, by construing the several provisions together, and giving effect to all of them. Under such construction the conclusion would necessarily follow that the trial of the suit anew would be confined to a trial of the case affecting the part of the decree specified in the notice

of appeal": *Shook* v. *Colohan*, 12 Or. 242 (6 Pac. 503).
The case of *Inverarity* v. *Stowell*, 10 Or. 261, was a controversy between a mortgagee and subsequent lien
claimants, and it was there held that the decree, as to
the lien claimants, being severable, the plaintiff could
appeal from that part of it. "The party appealing,"
says Wade, C. J., in *Barkley* v. *Logan*, 2 Mont. 296, in
construing a similar statute, "must bring the whole
decree before the appellate court, otherwise it has no
jurisdiction to hear the case, and may specify in his
notice of appeal the portion of the decree he wishes
to reverse. He cannot sever the decree, and leave
that portion of it favorable to himself in force in the
district court, and appeal from that portion adverse to
him." So, too, in *Portland Construction Company* v. *O'Neill*,
24 Or. 58, (32 Pac. 764,) it was held that the appellant
could not have a decree in the lower court for a given
amount and here for an additional sum. An appeal
from a part of a decree must necessarily bring to the
appellate court the whole decree, and while the part
appealed from may be affirmed, modified, or reversed,
the portion not reviewed will be affirmed. The whole
cause being tried here *de novo,* a complete decree must
be rendered in this court. In actions at law this court
can review judgments only as to questions of law appearing upon the record, and when error is discovered
the cause must be remanded to the court below for
further proceedings. The reversal of a judgment necessarily opens it, and if opened for one it must be for
all purpose, otherwise litigation would be interminable,
and actions tried and appeals taken piecemeal,—a result which would be contrary to the policy of the law.
Appeals in actions at law must bring up for review
the issues tried in the court below, and the answer in
the case at bar having denied all the material allega-

tions of the complaint, the judgment rendered thereon
is not severable, and the plaintiff's acceptance of a
part of its fruits is an acquiescence therein which
bars his right of appeal: *Moore* v. *Floyd,* 4 Or. 260; *Portland Construction Company* v. *O'Neill,* 24 Or. 54 (32 Pac.
764); *Ehrman* v. *Astoria Railway Company,* 26 Or. 377 (38
Pac. 306); *Lyons* v. *Bain,* 1 Wash. Ter. 482; 2 Beach
on Modern Equity Practice, § 926; 2 Endlich on Pleading and Practice, 174, and notes. It follows that the
appeal must be dismissed, and it is so ordered.

DISMISSED.

Argued July 29; decided August 5, 1895.

Re DEKUM'S ESTATE.
[11 Pac. 159]

EXECUTORS AND ADMINISTRATORS—ALLOWANCE TO WIDOW.—The fact that
a widow, prior to the obtaining by executors of an order of court for
a monthly allowance, agreed, for a valuable consideration, that it
should be in lieu of dower, does not justify the executors in refusing
to pay such monthly allowance, except on condition that she receipts for the same as in lieu of dower, where the order contains
no provision that it shall be so received.

APPEAL from Multnomah: E. D. SHATTUCK, Judge.

This is an appeal from a decree of the Circuit
Court affirming an order of the County Court of Multnomah County. The facts are that on October nineteenth, eighteen hundred and ninety-four, Frank Dekum
died testate in said county, and, his last will having
been admitted to probate, Edward Dekum and Adolph
Dekum, who were named therein as executors thereof,
duly qualified as such, and, on November sixteenth of
that year, filed in said county court their petition,
from which it appears that an inventory had been
taken, and that the appraised value of the estate, over

26 OR.—7.

and above all probable indebtedness, amounted to five hundred and forty-eight thousand and eighty-two dollars; that the net monthly income therefrom, after paying expenses, taxes, and interest, was about one thousand dollars; that the deceased had devised and bequeathed all his property exempt from execution to his children; and upon this showing prayed for an order directing them to pay to Phœbe M. Dekum, widow of the deceased, such sum as the court should find her entitled to receive for her support from the estate, pending the administration thereof. On the twenty-seventh of that month an order was made directing them to pay her three hundred dollars per month for that purpose for the term of one year from the death of her husband, or until the further order of the court. The executors paid the monthly installment which became due November nineteenth, but, having made default in the payment of the allowance for the following month, upon the petition of the widow they were cited to appear and show why they had not complied with the terms of the order. To this petition they filed an answer, alleging, in substance, that they were ready and willing and offered to pay her the allowance awarded upon receiving from her a receipt showing that she accepted the same in lieu of her dower interest in the estate for the month ending December nineteenth, eighteen hundred and ninety-four; that the petition for her allowance and the order made thereon were prepared and obtained by them in pursuance of an express agreement with the widow that the monthly allowance was to be paid her in lieu of any and all dower or claim of dower during the continuance of such allowance. This answer was, upon motion, struck out, and an order made requiring the executors forthwith to pay to the widow

the installment due December nineteenth, eighteen
hundred and ninety-four, from which order the executors appealed to the circuit court of said county, and,
being there affirmed, they appeal to this court.

AFFIRMED.

For appellants there was an oral argument by *Mr.
Milton W. Smith.*

For respondent there was an oral argument by *Mr.
Seneca Smith.*

PER CURIAM. The property of the estate exempt
from execution having been devised and bequeathed
by the testator to his children, and the estate being
sufficient to satisfy all the debts and liabilities of the
deceased, and pay the expenses of the administration,
together with such allowance, the right of the county
court to make the order cannot be successfully controverted: Hill's Code. § 1128.* But it is contended
that the court erred in striking out the executors'
answer to the widow's petition. The order requiring
the executors to pay the allowance contains no proviso or condition that the amount awarded to the
widow for her support should be received by her in
lieu of dower. If, upon sufficient consideration, she
made the agreement alleged in their answer, the
proper time to plead it, if available as a defense, is
when she makes a claim of dower during any portion
of the time embraced in the order making the allowance. Under such circustances the widow was entitled to the monthly installment upon giving an ordi-

---

*Hill's Code, § 1128, authorizes the court, when the property of a decedent
exempt from execution is insufficient to support the widow for one year after
filing of the inventory, to order the executors or administrators to make her an
allowance, provided it is probable that the other estate is sufficient to pay all the
liabilities of the estate and costs of administration in addition to such allowance.

nary receipt therefor, and, not having made any claim of dower, the answer of the executors to her petition was frivolous, and in striking it out the county court committed no error.   AFFIRMED.

Argued July 22; decided October 28, 1895.

STATE *v.* GEE.
[42 Pac. 7.]

FORGERY — ROAD SUPERVISOR'S "CERTIFICATE"— CODE, § 1808.— An instrument denominated a "time check," purporting to be approved by a road supervisor, and indicating that the person to whom it appears to have been issued had performed certain work on a certain public road, the value thereof being a stated amount, is a "certificate" that may be the subject of forgery, within the meaning of section 1808 of Hill's Code, which denounces the forging of any "certificate" of any public officer, in relation to any matter wherein such certificate may be received as legal evidence, and of section 4085, which requires road supervisors to "certify" to the county court their accounts for labor and material used on the public roads.

The defendant, David L. Gee, was indicted for knowingly uttering and publishing a certain forged and counterfeit writing, in form and similitude of the certificate described in the indictment. It is charged, in substance, that pursuant to section 4085 of Hill's Code, as amended by the act of February twentieth, eighteen hundred and ninety-three (Session Laws, 1893, p. 60), the County Court of Multnomah County, on January seventeenth, eighteen hundred and ninety-four, levied a tax of one mill upon all taxable property within the county, which was collected and kept as a separate fund, known as the "road fund," to be used for the purpose of laying out, opening, making, and repairing county roads. Here follow allegations showing the establishment of road district number six, the apportionment of certain road funds to the district, and the appointment and qualification of John

Conley as supervisor thereof. The indictment then
continues: "That by virtue of such office as supervisor it became and was the duty of him, the said
John Conley, to direct and supervise the expenditure
of said moneys as aforesaid appropriated to said road
district number six pursuant to law, by the County
Court of Multnomah County, for making and repairing county roads in his said road district, and to employ laborers to perform such work and labor as he
deemed proper in making and repairing county roads
in said district, and to issue certificates, to persons so
performing labor and furnishing materials in making
and repairing county roads in his said district under
and by his direction and supervision, of the amount of
labor so performed or materials furnished, and the
compensation to be paid therefor; that the certificate
so issued by him, the said John Conley, as supervisor
aforesaid, entitled the holder thereof to recover from
said Multnomah County the amount of money named
in said certificate to be due the person therein named
for labor performed as aforesaid, and created, when
approved by the County Court of said Multnomah
County, an indebtedness from the said county of Multnomah to the person named in said certificate of the
amount of money therein named and certified to by
the said John Conley, supervisor as aforesaid, to be
due the said person for labor performed upon the
county road in said road district number six." Then
follows a description of the certificate and the formal
charging part of the indictment. A copy of the certificate is contained in the indictment, and is as follows:—

"$91.00.

No. 5196.

Name, MILES STANLEY.

TIME CHECK FOR THE MONTH OF DECEMBER, EIGHTEEN HUNDRED AND NINETY-FOUR, DISTRICT NUMBER SIX.

	1	2	3	4	5	6	7	8	9	10	11	12	13	14	15	16	17	18	19	20	21	22	23	24	25	26	27	28	29	30	31	Total hours.	Rate per hour.	Amount.
Team and driver	10	10	10	10	10	10	10	10		10		10	10	10	10		10	10		10	10		10	10	10	10	10	10		10	10	260	.35	$91 00
Man																																		

"Multnomah County, Oregon, December 31, 1894.

"Multnomah County, Oregon, pay to the order of Miles Stanley the sum of ninety-one dollars, in full for twenty-six days' work on Sandy Road.

"Approved: JOHN CONLEY,
"Supervisor.

_____ Foreman."

A demurrer to this indictment was argued to and sustained by the trial court, from which the state appeals under the provisions of the act of February twentieth, eighteen hundred and ninety-three (Session Laws, 1893, p. 60).   AFFIRMED.

Opinion by MR. JUSTICE WOLVERTON.

The only theory upon which this case can proceed is that the law has provided for an official certificate or return of a road supervisor, which may be received by the county court as legal evidence of the facts certified to, and has further prescribed a penalty for forging or counterfeiting the same, and for uttering such certificate so forged or counterfeited with intent to defraud. The indictment is drawn under section 1808, Hill's Code of Oregon which provides that "If any person shall, with intent to injure or defraud any one, falsely make, alter, forge, or counterfeit any public record whatever, or any certificate, return, or attestation, of any clerk, notary public, or other public officer, in relation to any matter wherein such certificate, return, or attestation may be received as legal evidence, or any note, certificate, or other evidence of debt issued by any officer of this state, or any county, town, or other municipal or public corporation therein, authorized to issue the same, or any contract, charter, letters patent, deed, lease, bill of sale, will, testament, bond, writing obligatory, undertaking, letter of attorney, policy of insurance, bill of lading, bill of exchange, promissory note, evidence of debt, or any acceptance of a bill of exchange, indorsement, or assignment of a promissory note, or any warrant, order, or check, or money, or other property, or any acquittance or discharge for money or other property, or

any plat, draft, or survey of land; or shall, with such
intent, knowingly utter or publish as true and genuine
any such 'false, altered, forged, or counterfeited record,
writing, instrument, or matter whatever, such person,
upon conviction thereof, shall," etc. Section 4085,
Hill's Code, upon which the indictment is partly based
provides, among other things, that: "Such county court
shall apportion the taxes so collected among the several road districts in the county. * * * the county
clerk shall thereupon notify the road supervisor in
each of the road districts in his county of the amount
of the road fund set apart for the use of his road
district for opening, making, and repairing county
roads, and building bridges in his road district; and
such supervisor shall direct and supervise the expenditure of such amount of the road fund so set apart
for the purpose herein named, and certify his accounts
for labor performed or material furnished to the
county court; and if the county court approve the
same, it shall order warrants on the county treasurer
in favor of the person performing such labor or furnishing such material, payable out of the fund to the
credit of such road district until such fund is exhausted."

By this act the county court is made the auditing
board, and the funds set apart to the different road
districts are disbursed under its supervision. The supervisor whose duty it is to direct and supervise the
expenditures, is required to certify to the county court
his accounts for labor performed or material furnished. These certified accounts constitute the vouch-
ers upon which the court acts, and upon which it
bases its orders for drawing warrants against the
particular fund. The orders must require the warrants to be drawn in favor of the person or persons

performing labor or furnishing material. No especial
method is prescribed for the supervisor in keeping
his accounts, nor is he directed or required to certify
them to the county court in any particular form; so
that any intelligible form of account which indicates
with reasonable fullness the amount, nature, and kind
of work done or material furnished, with the date and
name of the person doing or furnishing the same, the
value thereof, and the number of the road district,
would be sufficient. So, with the certificate, any form
which informs or assures the county court that the
account in question is the account of the supervisor
is sufficient. To "certify" means simply "to testify in
writing"; "to make a declaration in writing"—Webster. It is not even necessary that the word "certify" or "certified" be used in the certificate, but it is
sufficient if the required statutory fact be made known
in writing under the hand of the officer: *State* v.
Schwin, 65 Wis. 213 (26 N. W. 568). It would be the
duty of the county court to recognize and act upon
any form of certificate which is legally sufficient under the statute, and which would operate under the
law as a supervisor's certified account of labor expended or material furnished for the use of the road
district. The legal efficacy of such a certificate consists, not in its potency, if genuine, in creating a demand against the county, but in its capability of being
utilized as legal evidence of the facts stated therein;
and the test here is, not as is the case ordinarily,
whether the certificate presents upon its face or
through allegations in aid of it a suable demand, but
whether the instrument is such an one that, if genuine, the county court must consider it as legal evidence of the amount and kind of labor done and
performed or material furnished in the matter of de-

termining whether or not it shall "order warrants on
the county treasurer." If the official certificate, return,
or attestation is sufficient for this purpose, it is the
subject of forgery under the statute; otherwise, not.

Now, the account and certificate relied upon consists of an instrument denominated "Time check for
the month of December, eighteen hundred and ninety-
four, district number six," underneath which are written
the words, "Approved: John Conley, supervisor." The
so-called "time check" indicates with reasonable de-
finiteness and certainty that Miles Stanley served time,
or performed two hundred and sixty hours work with
team and driver, in the month of December, eighteen
hundrd and ninety-four, for district number six, the
value being specified at ninety-one dollars. This is an
intelligible and sufficiently definite account of labor
done and performed. It requires no stretch of the imagination to understand from it that Miles Stanley did
and performed, with team and driver, within or for
district number six, two hundred and sixty hours'
labor during the month of December, eighteen hundred and ninety-four, for which he should receive
ninety-one dollars; so that the account itself is sufficient. But, has it been sufficiently certified to the
county court to entitle it to be considered evidence of
the fact that Miles Stanley performed labor as shown
by the account? The word "approved," written be-
neath the account, with the signature of the supervisor subscribed in his official capacity, is, as we think,
a sufficient official certification of the account. It identifies the account as that of the supervisor, and is
equivalent to making it "O K" or "correct," which is
usually recognized as a certification in ordinary business affairs. The fact that what purports to be an
order drawn upon Multnomah County intervenes be-

tween the account and the word "approved" does not change the effect of the certificate. Apparently, it was intended that this order should be signed by somebody as foreman, but, with or without the order, the account may be said to have been certified to the county court by the supervisor. The order unsigned by the foreman can have no effect in any event, whether it be considered approved by the supervisor or not. It cannot reasonably be considered as the supervisor's order as it does not so purport to be. The instrument, if considered genuine, was therefore the subject of forgery.

The indictment, however, is deemed faulty and insufficient. It is alleged, among other things, that it was the duty of the supervisor "to issue certificates to persons performing labor and furnishing material," etc., and "that the certificate so issued by him, the said John Conley, as supervisor aforesaid, entitled the holder thereof to receive from said Multnomah County the amount of money named in the certificate," etc., and the charging part of the indictment proceeds upon the idea that this certificate is of such a nature that, if genuine, it would create a demand against the county. We have seen that such is not the case. The instrument set forth by copy, instead of "purporting to be a certificate entitling the holder thereof to the payment of the compensation therein named by Multnomah County, for work and labor performed upon a county road in road district number six in said Multnomah County and State of Oregon," and "purporting to entitle one Miles Stanley to the payment of ninety-one dollars by the said Multnomah County and State of Oregon," simply purports to be an account with one Miles Stanley for two hundred and sixty hours work and labor with man and team, done and performed at thirty-five cents per hour in district number six, certified by the said John Conley, supervisor, which certified account was receivable by the County Court of Multnomah County, Oregon, as legal evidence that such work and labor had been done and performed in said district number six by the said Miles Stanley. These facts should have been appropriately alleged in the indictment: *State* v. *Johnson,* 26 Iowa, 407 (96 Am. Dec. 158). If it is true that the county court has adopted this form of certificate, or has been accustomed to receive the same as legal evidence of the facts it purports to certify, this is a matter of proof, and it is unnecessary to allege it in the indictment: *Commonwealth* v. *Costello,* 120 Mass. 369; *Horton* v. *State,* 32 Texas, 82; *People* v. *Bibby,* 91 Cal. 470 (27 Pac. 781). The official certificate must of itself be legally competent as evidence; if otherwise, it cannot be aided by the allegation of extrinsic facts: *Commonwealth* v. *Costello,* 120 Mass. 369; *Raymond* v. *People,* 2 Colo. App. 329 (30 Pac. 504); *People* v. *Heed,* 1 Idaho, 531; *State* v. *Briggs,* 34 Vt. 501; *Cunningham* v. *People,* 4 Hun, 455; *People* v. *Harrison,* 8 Barb. 560; *Fadner* v. *People,* 33 Hun, 240. These considerations make it incumbent upon us to affirm the judgment of the court below, and it is so ordered.

AFFIRMED.

Argued July 22; decided October 28, 1895.

CLOSE *v.* CLOSE.

[42 Pac. 128]

DISMISSING APPEAL— FILING ABSTRACT—RULES OF COURT.—An appeal will be dismissed where appellant fails to serve and file the abstract of the record required by the rules of the court, (Rules 4 and 9, 24 Or. 595- 597,) though part of the record has been lost, no effort having been made within a reasonable time to supply the missing papers: *Wolf* v. *Smith,* 6 Or. 74, approved and followed.

APPEAL from Clackamas: T. A. McBRIDE, Judge.

Suit by Lizzie E. Close against David H. Close, in which there was a decree for plaintiff. Defendant appealed, but, having failed to file the printed abstract of the record required by Rules 4 and 9 of the court, (24 Or. 595–597,) the respondent moved to dismiss the appeal.　　　DISMISSED.

Mr. C. D. Latourette, for the motion.

Mr. Harvey E. Cross, contra.

PER CURIAM. This is a motion to dismiss the appeal because the abstract of the record required by the rules of this court has not been served or filed. The defendant undertakes to excuse his failure in this regard on the ground that the evidence taken in the court below and upon which the decree was based has been lost or misplaced. There is no rule requiring the evidence to be printed in the abstract, and, besides, it is the duty of the appellant to bring into this court a perfect record, and if any part thereof has been lost or mislaid it must be supplied in the court below, and if not so supplied within a reasonable time the appeal will be dismissed: *Wolf* v. *Smith,* 6 Or. 74; *Buckman* v. *Whitney,* 28 Cal. 555; *Boyd* v. *Burrell,* 60 Cal. 280. The transcript was filed on March fifth, eighteen hundred and ninety-five, and the lost record has not been supplied, nor has there been any effort made in that direction so far as we have been advised. The appeal must therefore be dismissed, and it is so ordered.　　　DISMISSED.

Argued July 22; decided October 7, 1895.

JACKSON COUNTY *v.* BLOOMER.
[41 Pac. 930.]

NOTICE OF APPEAL—SERVICE ON ADVERSE PARTY—CODE, § 537.—Where a treasurer and his bondsmen are jointly sued on his official bond, and the former suffers a default, but the sureties make a successful defense on the merits of the case, the treasurer is "an adverse party" within the meaning of section 537 of Hill's Code, and must be served with the notice of appeal, for the decision of the appellate court affects the principal just as it does his sureties: *Hamilton* v. *Blair*, 23 Or. 64; *The Victorian*, 24 Or. 121; *Moody* v. *Miller*, 24 Or. 179, cited and approved.

Appeal from Jackson: HIERO K. HANNA, Judge.

This is an action brought by the County of Jackson against George E. Bloomer and the sureties on his bond as treasurer of such county, to recover for his alleged defalcation as such official. The complaint, *inter alia*, alleges the qualification of Bloomer by giving the bond in suit, and that between the dates mentioned in the complaint he, as such treasurer, collected and received something over seven thousand eight hundred dollars belonging to the county, which, in breach of his trust, and in violation of the conditions of his undertaking, he failed and neglected to account for or pay over. Bloomer, although served with summons, made default, and the sureties answered jointly, denying the defalcation alleged in the complaint, and upon the issues thus made the cause was tried, and a judgment rendered in their favor on the merits. From this judgment the plaintiff appealed, without serving a notice on Bloomer. For this reason the respondents move to dismiss the appeal, claiming that Bloomer is an adverse party to the appellant, and should have been served with notice.   DISMISSED.

For the motion there were oral arguments by *Mr. Elward B. Watson,* and briefs by *Messrs. Paine P. Prim and S..n, William M. Colvig,* and *Watson, Beekman and Watson,* urging these points.

All parties to a judgment or decree whose interests may be substantially affected by the adjudication of the appellate court must be included in the appeal, and must be served with notice; without all such parties before it the appellate court has no jurisdiction: *Lilienthal* v. *Caravita,* 15 Or. 339; *Hamilton* v. *Blair,* 23 Or. 64; *The Victorian,* 24 Or. 121. Bloomer being a joint defendant in said action on a joint bond in which he is the principal whose defalcation is sought to be established by said action, evidently has an interest in relation to said judgment against appellant which is in conflict with the modification or reversal sought by the appeal. Such is evidently true, for while said judgment remains unreversed no other action can be maintained against him for the alleged defalcation. And the fact that Bloomer, whose interests are adverse to appellant, has made default, does not preclude the necessity of serving him with notice of appeal: *Moody* v. *Miller,* 24 Or. 179.

Judgment on the merits on an obligation which is joint only, must be joint, against or for all the defendants served. This was the rule at common law, and our statute has not changed it: Freeman on Judgments (3d ed.), 43; *Jaques* v. *Greenwood,* 1 Abb. Pr. 230; *Mandeville* v. *Riggs,* 2 Pet. 482; *Van Ness* v. *Corkins,* 12 Wis. 186; *People* v. *Organ,* 27 Ill. 27; *Rooker* v. *Wise,* 14 Ind. 276. And default of one joint defendant does not alter the rule: *Rich* v. *Husson,* 4 Sandf. (N. Y.), 115. Bloomer's default merely gave the court jurisdiction to enter a joint judgment against or for himself and

the sureties, in accordance with the joint obligations
of the bond set out in the complaint. If the complaint had not stated any cause of action, he could
have appealed from any judgment against him, either
joint or several, notwithstanding his default: *Madison
County Supervisors* v. *Smith*, 95 Ill. 328. And where, as
here, the complaint states no separate cause of action,
Bloomer could have appealed and procured the reversal of any separate judgment against himself on
the merits, although in default: *Waugh* v. *Suter*, 3 Ill.
App. 271.

The successful defense on the merits by the sureties inured to Bloomer's benefit, and, although in
default, entitled him to be discharged also: Freeman on Judgments (3d ed.), §§ 161, 266; *Benton* v. *Gregory*, 8 Ark. 177; *State* v. *Williams*, 17 Ark. 371; *State* v.
Gibson, 21 Ark. 140; *Champlin* v. *Tilley*, 3 Day (Conn.), 303;
Morrison v. *Stoner*, 7 Iowa, 498; *Adderton* v. *Collier*, 32 Mo.
507; *State* v. *Ford*, 8 Humph. (Tenn.), 489; *Girardin* v.
Dean, 49 Texas, 243; *Pfaw* v. *Lorain*, 1 Cin. (Ohio), 720;
Phillips v. *Wheeler*, 6 Thomp. and C. (N. Y.), 300; *French*
v. *Neal*, 24 Pick. 55.

Judgment of dismissal as to one cotrustee is a bar
to any further prosecution of the cause of suit against
the other: *Zorn* v. *Lamar*, 71 Ga. 84, 85. Judgment on
the merits puts an end to the claim or demand sued
on, and is conclusive both as to parties and privies:
Cromwell v. *County of Sacramento*, 94 U. S. 351. Judgment
against sureties on the merits precludes their principal, who was not served, from afterwards recovering
expenses which should have been credited on the debt
secured by the bond: *Wandling* v. *Straw*, 25 W. Va. 692.

A party served, who is aggrieved or benefited by
the judgment on the merits, has a right to appeal, or
be served with the notice of appeal, whether named

in the formal judgment or not; and is an adverse party under our statute: *State* v. *Judge, etc.*, 29 La. Ann. 397; *Williams* v. *Morgan*, 111 U. S. 684. It is sufficient if his interest appears from the whole record. The findings of fact and conclusion of law are in Bloomer's favor on the merits, and entitled him to a formal judgment. It was the duty of the clerk to enter judgment in favor of all the defendants in accordance with the decision: 1 Hill's Code, §§ 219, 265.

Bloomer has an interest in maintaining the decision and judgment, since he appeared on the record, and is a necessary party to the appeal: *Traders' Bank* v. *Belden*, 5 Wash. 777; *Hendrickson* v. *Sullivan*, 28 Neb. 329; *Curtin* v. *Atkinson*, 29 Neb. 612; *Senter* v. *De Bernal*, 38 Cal. 637. As he was served and brought within the jurisdiction of the court below, he is entitled to his day in this court, and the sureties are just as much entitled to have him brought in, as into the court below.

The transcript does not sustain the claim of appellant's counsel in their "additional brief," page 3, that the case was "abandoned" as to Bloomer. The journal entry of the trial recites the appearance of appellant and the sureties, by their respective attorneys, and that defendant Bloomer "comes not but makes default." And the district attorney and his associates in the trial of the case certainly did not think so when they caused the summons to be published to him, and his property to be attached, and filed the proof and returns in the cause before proceeding to the trial, as the amended transcript shows, nor at the time they prepared their first brief in opposition to the motion to dismiss, on page 5, of which they say: "We submit that Bloomer occupies such a position that plaintiff might, if it desired to do so, even now, ask for default to be entered against him in the lower court, and for judgment against him for failure to answer." The circuit court had jurisdiction of Bloomer, as the amended record will show.

But appellant, having assumed the performance of the duty it owed the sureties of making their principal a party and subjecting his property within the state towards the satisfaction of any judgment that might be rendered, and led both the court and sureties to believe that it had done so before proceding to trial, is estopped to allege defects in either proceeding. It cannot be allowed a benefit arising from its own default. The recital in the journal entry of the trial that defendant Bloomer "comes not but makes default," if it does not in itself amount to an adjudication that he had been served and made default, points very strongly in that direction, and confirms the presumption that the court did have jurisdiction. Bloomer only could raise the objection to want of jurisdiction, and he could do so only by appeal. There is nothing to prevent his taking the benefits of such a record against the appellant which is responsible for it, and his consent is presumed. The judgment order authorized by section 157 is a conclusive adjudication as to the validity of the attachment. How can appellant allege its own wrong, if there were any, in obtaining the attachment, to avoid its effect in a controversy with either Bloomer or his sureties? An attachment is, under our system, a provisional remedy only, and not the commencement of an action, and defendant can waive any right to complain of irregularity in its issuance or levy, and does waive it by failing to attack it in any manner sanctioned by the Code or general practice.

Contra there were oral arguments by *Messrs. Henry L. Benson*, district attorney, and *Lionel R. Webster*, with briefs by *Messrs. Benson*, and *Charles Wesley Kahler*, urging these points.

Parties to an action need not be notified of an appeal unless they are parties to the judgment from which the appeal is taken: Elliot's Appellate Procedure, § 153; *Kennedy* v. *Divine*, 77 Ind. 492; *Koons* v. *Mellet*, 23 N. E. 96; *Dittenhœffer* v. *Cœur d'Alene Clothing Company*, 30 Pac. 661. Bloomer never appeared in this action, and when judgment was entered it was in favor of only the sureties for their costs.

Every Oregon case cited in favor of this motion is one in which the notice had not been served on some party who had appeared in the proceeding, and was actually a party to the final adjudication. Moreover, they were all equity cases. Several times our court quotes with approval this language from *Senter* v. *De-Bernal*, 38 Cal. 637: "But he is required to notify all other parties who are interested in opposing the relief which he seeks by his appeal, if they have formally appeared in the action in the court below, or his appeal as to those not served will prove ineffectual; and also, as to those served, if the relief sought is of such a character that it cannot be granted as to the latter without being granted as to the former also." Applying this test to the case at bar, it will be observed that it is an action on a joint and several bond, to which the defendant Bloomer was not a necessary party in the first instance; that he never put in any appearance in the court below; that no default was taken against him, and that there is no judgment as to him. How, then, can it be said that any judgment

against the defendant's sureties can materially affect
his rights?

But it is contended by counsel for respondents that
"while the judgment remains unreversed no other action can be maintained against him for the alleged defalcation. We submit that Bloomer occupies such a
position that plaintiff might, if it desired to do so,
even now, ask for default to be entered against him
in the lower court, and for judgment against him for
failure to answer, and that such procedure is not affected by any judgment as to the other defendants.
It will thus be seen that all the cases cited for this
motion are essentially different from the case at bar
in all the particulars that would give them any logical
bearing here. In this case Bloomer was not a necessary party, and it was a matter of indifference to him
whether the sureties were held liable on his bond or
not. If they succeeded in evading payment, that of
itself neither hurt nor helped him; if he had been
regularly served, had made default, and thereby admitted the allegations of the complaint to be true,
he would have admitted all that anybody has ever
claimed in this case. The purpose of this appeal is
not to enlarge his liabilty beyond what would thus
have been admitted. It is claimed by respondents that
Bloomer filed no answer but made default. That
would not have entitled him to notice of this appeal,
but the fact is that Bloomer was never served with
summons in this case, and therefore never made default in the technical sense of that term. "Bloomer
absconded and left the state and has ever since remained away from this state," is the uncontradicted
allegation of the complaint. The whole record shows
that the lower court never had jurisdiction of Bloomer,
and neither rendered nor attempted to render any judg-

ment against him. The defendant Bloomer has no
substantial interest in the result of this appeal because (1) he was not a necessary party in the first
instance; (2) he has never appeared herein; and, (3)
he is not a party to the judgment appealed from, and
cannot be favorably or otherwise affected by the result
of this appeal.

Opinion by MR. CHIEF JUSTICE BEAN.

The rule is well settled in this state that every
party to a litigation whose interests in relation to the
judgment or decree appealed from is in conflict with
the modification or reversal sought by the appeal is
an "adverse party" within the meaning of section 537
of Hill's Code, and must be served with the notice of
appeal; and if such party is not served the appeal
must be dismissed. And the fact that a party whose
interests are adverse to the appellant, has made default, does not preclude the necessity of serving such
notice of appeal upon him: *The Victorian,* 24 Or. 121
(41 Am. St. 838, 32 Pac. 1040); *Moody* v. *Miller,* 24 Or.
179 (33 Pac. 402); *Hamilton* v. *Blair,* 23 Or. 64 (31 Pac.
197). If, then, Bloomer has an interest in sustaining
the judgment from which this appeal is taken, he is
an adverse party to the appellant, and the failure to
serve him with notice of the appeal is fatal, and the
appeal should be dismissed. Now, the undertaking on
which this action was brought is a joint obligation of
Bloomer and the sureties, in so far, at least, as that
all are liable or none, and, therefore, although he
made default, the defense successfully made by the
other defendants, going as it did to the merits and
showing that the plaintiff had no right of action
against any of the defendants, inures to his benefit,

and prevents the entry of judgment against him on his default. The rule on this question is thus clearly stated by Mr. Black in section 209 of his work on Judgments: "In an action of contract against several defendants, if one of them suffers default, and another, under the general issue, sets up and maintains a defense which negatives the plaintiff's right to recover against either of the defendants, and shows that he has no cause of action, the plaintiff will not be entitled to judgment against the one who was defaulted, but, on the contrary, the successful defense will inure to the latter's benefit, and judgment must be rendered for both the defendants." And to this effect are the authorities: *French* v. *Neal*, 24 Pick. 55; *State* v. *Gibson*, 21 Ark. 140; *Morrison* v. *Stoner*, 7 Iowa, 493; *Adderton* v. *Collier*, 32 Mo. 507; *Waugh* v. *Suter*, 3 Ill. App. 271; *Stapp* v. *Davis*, 78 Ind. 128. From this it seems manifest that Bloomer's interests would be materially affected by the reversal of this judgment, for the reason that it appears from the record as it now stands that plaintiff has no right of action against him or his sureties for a breach of the conditions of his undertaking on account of any of the matters or things alleged in the complaint, and so long as the judgment stands unreversed it is in effect a judgment in his favor, and prevents the entry of a judgment on his default. He is, therefore, vitally interested in sustaining the judgment as it now stands, and consequently is an adverse party to this appeal.

It was suggested by plaintiff's attorneys that Bloomer was not a necessary party to this action, and was never in fact legally served with summons, but these questions are hardly open to the plaintiff here. Whether he was a necessary party or not, the plaintiff saw fit to make him a party, caused a writ of attachment to issue and be levied upon his property, obtained an order for the publication of summons, caused the summons to be published directed to him, and an alleged proof of such publication to be made, and the record shows that all the defendants appeared and demurred to the original complaint, and that when the cause came on for trial Bloomer "made default." Under these circumstances the court will not, at plaintiff's suggestion, critically examine the procedure by which it sought and claimed to have obtained jurisdiction of Bloomer, for the purpose of avoiding the effect of a failure to serve him with a notice of appeal. The motion will be allowed.   DISMISSED.

Argued July 29; decided October 7, 1895; rehearing denied.

BISHOP v. BAISLEY.
[41 Pac. 937.]

1. PLEADING FORFEITURE OF MINING CLAIM.—The defense of a forfeiture of a mining claim through failure to perform the required work thereon is an affirmative defense, and must be specially pleaded where an opportunity is offered for so doing; and the burden of proof is always on the party claiming the forfeiture.

2. AMENDMENT OF PLEADINGS TO CONFORM TO PROOFS—DISCRETION OF COURT.—It is not an abuse of discretion by the trial court to permit at the trial an amendment setting up new defenses based on evidence that was objected to when offered, where the case is sent back to the referee to take such additional testimony as may be offered on the new issues*: Mendenhall v. Harrisburg Water Company, 27 Or. 38, distinguished.

3. PLEADING FORFEITURE IN TERMS.—In pleading under the Code it is only necessary to accurately and concisely state the facts relied upon, and therefore a plea of forfeiture of a mining claim need not aver

*In Cook v. Croisan, 25 Or. 475, it was held reversible error to refuse at the trial, and after counsel had commenced their argument, an amendment to the answer based on evidence that had been received without objection. This, however, was a law action, and the issue raised by the proposed amendment was material and one on which both sides had offered testimony without objection. This case is distinguished in the Mendenhall Case, 27 Or. 38.—REPORTER.

specially that in consequence of the facts set forth "the claim was forfeited."

4. Mines—What is not Annual Work.—Picking rock from the walls of a shaft or outcropping of a ledge, in small quantities, from day to day, and testing it, in order to find a paying vein, cannot be credited as part of the one hundred dollars' worth of "work and improvements" required by Revised Statutes of United States, § 2324, as amended by Supplement to the Revised Statutes of United States, p. 276, to be made by a locator on his claim within one year from the date of his location.

5. Kind of Assessment Work Required.—The requirement that a certain amount of labor or improvement shall be done or made on a mining claim each year in order to hold it is for the double purpose of insuring good faith in the claimant, and of requiring him to show a really valuable mine before claiming a patent; from which it follows that the kind of work required by the statute (United States Revised Statutes, § 2324, as amended,) is work tending to develop and exhibit the value of the mine rather than work expended in discovery or preliminary exploration.

6. Forfeited Claim—Resuming Work.—Where a mining claim has been forfeited by the locator, his afterward going onto the claim with tools, securing samples of the ore, and testing and assaying it is not a resumption of work, within the meaning of section 2324 of the Revised Statutes of the United States as amended in January, eighteen hundred and eighty, providing that a forfeited or abandoned mining claim may be relocated, provided the original claimant has not "resumed work" before the attempted relocation.

7. Equity Jurisdiction—Injunction Against Trespass.—Equity will interfere by injunction to restrain a continuing trespass on a mining claim by the removal of valuable ores, and to compel an accounting for injuries already inflicted, at the suit of one claiming to be the owner of the realty, though out of possession, where a law action is pending to determine the title, and, if a strong showing is made, the trespass will be enjoined even where no law action has yet been commenced. Ordinarily, the injunction will be only temporary pending the trial of the title, but if the plaintiff presents a *prima facie* possessory title that is not seriously disputed, equity will settle the entire controversy without waiting for any proceedings at law.

Appeal from Baker: Robert Eakin, Judge.

This suit was brought by Philip R. Bishop against James L. Baisley and others to restrain trespass upon a mining claim, and to recover damages for the injurious use of it by the defendants. The plaintiff, after showing his citizenship, alleges, in substance, that he is now and was at all times mentioned in his complaint the owner by reason of location and possession under the general mining laws of the United States of a certain quartz mining claim situated in Baker County, Oregon, generally known and designated as the White Pigeon Quartz Claim (then follows a description of the claim by metes and bounds); that on or about the first day of May, eighteen hundred and ninety-three, while he was such owner and in possession of said mining claim, the defendants wrongfully entered and trespassed thereon, and dug a shaft many feet deep upon the vein therein, and at said time, and at various and divers times since, took out, carried away, and converted to their own use, large quantities of very rich gold-bearing quartz, claiming the right so to do, thereby destroying the substance of said mine and depreciating the value thereof, and that they threatened to continue and were continuing said trespass and waste to the irreparable injury of the premises; that the defendants extracted gold from said mine to the value of thirty thousand dollars; that plaintiff has been greatly hindered in the possession and working of said claim to his damage in the sum of fifty thousand dollars; and that he has no plain, speedy, or adequate remedy at law. The relief asked is a decree perpetually enjoining defendants from further trespassing upon said claim, or interfering with plaintiff's possession; that defendants account to plaintiff for the gold extracted by them, and for damages in the sum of fifty thousand dollars. The answer puts in issue every material allegation of the complaint, except the citizenship of defendants, and for a further defense alleges, in substance, that at all the times therein stated the premises therein described were vacant public lands of the United States, chiefly valuable for the mineral they contained, and were subject to location as mineral lands; that on the first day of May, eighteen hundred and ninety-three, defendant J. L. Baisley made a good and valid location of the "Mabel" quartz claim, in Baker County, Oregon. (Here follows a description of the claim and other allegations as to the manner of its location.) Continuing, the answer shows, substantially, that ever since May first, eighteen hundred and ninety-three, defendants have been and now are the owners of said claim by virtue of location and occupancy, and have at all times been and now are in the open, notorious, exclusive, and actual possession thereof, claiming title thereto. The reply denies specifically the material allegations of the answer, and, further replying thereto, alleges, in substance: That about December twelfth, eighteen hundred and ninety-two, defendants applied to and obtained plaintiff's permission to enter upon the said "White Pigeon" claim, and to prospect the quartz ledge thereon, and that their entry upon said claim was made under said license, with full knowledge of plaintiff's claim and right of possession, and in subordination thereto; that while so in possession they wrongfully and fraudulently attempted to make the alleged location of the Mabel Claim,—which covers plaintiff's claim for a distance of one thousand two hundred and sixty feet from the northeast line thereof,—with intent to defraud plaintiff of his rights; and that by reason of the premises the defendants are estopped from contesting the right of plaintiff to the ownership and possession of said "White Pigeon" mining claim.

Upon the issues being thus joined, a referee was appointed by the court to take the testimony, and to report his findings of fact and conclusions of law. In due time all the testimony which the parties had to offer was taken, and on June twenty-fifth, eighteen hundred and ninety-four, the referee reported the same, together with his findings of fact and law, which were favorable to plaintiff. On the same day defendants filed a motion for leave to file an amended answer, which was allowed by the court over plaintiff's protest. Defendants thereupon filed an amended answer similar to the first, except that the defendants set up therein the location of an additional claim on May first, eighteen hundred and ninety-three, designated as the "Queen of the West," which covers the remaining two hundred and forty feet of the "White Pigeon" not covered by the "Mabel," and, by way of a further defense, allege, in substance, that neither the plaintiff nor any of his grantors or predecessors in interest did or performed, or caused to be done or performed, any work, labor, or improvements, of any kind, nature, or description, upon or for the use or benefit of said alleged "White Pigeon" claim, under or by virtue of said alleged location of plaintiff; and that plaintiff and his grantors wholly failed and neglected to represent said claim after the date of said alleged location in any manner or form whatever, or to the value of anything. The plaintiff by his amended reply put in issue all these and other allegations of the amended answer, and the court thereupon referred the case back to the referee to take such further testimony as the parties had to offer. Other testimony was accordingly taken, mainly upon the question as to whether plaintiff had performed one hundred dollars' worth of assessment work prior to January first, eighteen hundred and ninety-three. Whereupon the referee reported the case back with his findings again in favor of plaintiff. Exceptions and objections were filed to the report by both parties. The defendants, excepting only to the amount of damages found, moved the court for a confirmation of the report as to all the other findings. The court thereupon modified the findings of the referee, and rendered a decree for the defendants, from which plaintiff appeals. The testimony necessary to a full understanding of the case is noted in the opinion.   AFFIRMED.

For appellant there was a brief and an oral argument by *Messrs. J. H. and R. J. Slater.*

For respondents there was a brief and an oral argument by *Mr. Charles A. Johns.*

Opinion by MR. JUSTICE WOLVERTON.

There is no doubt that the plaintiff and one C. J. Finn made a sufficient and valid location of the White Pigeon Claim, November twenty-fifth, eighteen hundred and ninety-one. This is the finding of both the referee and the court below, and is borne out by the testimony. On October twenty-fourth, eighteen hundred and ninety-two, Finn sold and conveyed his interest in the claim to plaintiff, and thereupon plaintiff became the sole owner thereof. The fact that J. L. Baisley made a sufficient and valid location of the Mabel Claim, and S. B. Baisley of the Queen of the West, on or about the twelfth day of May, eighteen hundred and ninety-two, is also placed beyond dispute by the testimony, provided the lands and premises occupied by them were at that time open for location and occupancy by the public. The Mabel Claim is identical with the White Pigeon for a distance of one thousand two hundred and sixty feet southwestward from its northeast line, and the Queen of the West covers the rest of it. The question then is, which of the-e parties has the better title to the premises occupied by the White Pigeon Claim? It is claimed by defendants that plaintiff forfeited his claim by not representing it as required by law,—that is to say, by failing to perform work and labor thereon in prospecting and developing it to the amount of one hundred dollars prior to January first, eighteen hundred and ninety-three, and, therefore, that it was open to exploration and location at the time defendants made their location of the Mabel and Queen of the West claims, and con-e-quently their locations were valid, and that their title and right of posession is superior to plaintiff's. Under the United States statutes governing the location of mines, and the acquirements of patents therefor, the locator has one year from the first day of January succeeding the date of his location in which to perform his first annual work: United States Revised Statutes, § 2324, as amended January twenty-second, eighteen hundred and eighty, (Supplement to Revised Statutes, 276). The plaintiff, therefore, had until January first, eighteen hundred and ninety-three, in which to perform his annual labor upon the White Pigeon. If he failed to perform the required amount of labor prior to the last named date, the claim would thereafter be open for relocation by any person competent under the statute. But if, having failed in performing his annual labor, he resumed and performed work thereafter to the extent required by law, his rights after resumption would have been the same as if no default had occurred: *Belk* v. *Meagher,* 104 U. S. 282; *Honaker* v. *Martin,* 11 Mont. 91 (27 Pac. 397). But whether, after having resumed, and while in the actual possession, performing labor, and prior to the full per-

formance of the amount required by law, the claim
would be open to relocation, the authorities are divided. See *Belcher Consolidated Mining Company* v. *Deferrari,*
62 Cal. 160, and *Honaker* v. *Martin,* 11 Mont. 91 (27 Pac.
397). The facts here do not present such a case. It
is, however, plain that if plaintiff had performed one
hundred dollars' worth of work on his claim prior to
the date of the alleged location by defendants of their
claims, as he insists that he has done, the territory
covered by the White Pigeon was not open for relocation, and hence their locations could not be valid.
But, aside from the question of work, plaintiff claims:
First, that before defendants can avail themselves of
a forfeiture, they must plead it; *second,* that the court
erred in allowing defendants to file their amended
answer by which they attempt to allege a forfeiture;
third, that if the court rightfully allowed the amended
answer to be filed, then the forfeiture is insufficiently
alleged; and, *fourth,* that forfeiture was not shown by
the testimony. Of these in their order.

1. A mining claim subsequent to a valid location
is property in the highest sense of the term. It may
be bought and sold, and will pass by descent. It carries with it the "exclusive right of possession and enjoyment of all the surface included within the lines"
of location. The right is a valuable one, and is protected by law. It continues until there shall be a failure to represent the claim; that is, to do the requisite
amount of work within the prescribed time. The right
of possession and enjoyment acquired by location is
kept alive by the representation prescribed by law,
but, when not thus kept alive, the right is forfeited,
and the claim is thereafter open for relocation. In order, therefore, to secure a valid location, it must be

established that rights acquired under a prior one upon the same claim have been forfeited. The affirmative of this proposition is always cast upon the party seeking to establish it, and hence, under the rules of pleading, it must be specially pleaded, where opportunity is offered, before a party can be heard to support it with evidence: *Renshaw* v. *Switzer*, 6 Mont. 464 (13 Pac. 127); *Hammer* v. *Garfield Mining Company*, 130 U. S. 291 (9 Sup. Ct. 548); *Belk* v. *Meagher*, 104 U. S. 279; *Morenhaut* v. *Wilson*, 52 Cal. 263; *Wulff* v. *Manuel*, 9 Mont. 276 (23 Pac. 723); *Quigley* v. *Gillett*, 101 Cal. 462 (35 Pac. 1040); *Mattingly* v. *Lewisohn*, 13 Mont. 508 (35 Pac. 114). Furthermore, ''a forfeiture cannot be established except upon clear and convincing proof of the failure of the former owner to have the work performed, or to have improvements made, to the amount required by law": *Hammer* v. *Garfield Mining Company*, 130 U. S. 291 (9 Sup. Ct. 548).

2. Plaintiff contends that as objection had been interposed to all the evidence offered by defendants to show that plaintiff had not done or performed one hundred dollars' worth of labor upon the White Pigeon Claim, as required by law, for the purpose of establishing a forfeiture on the part of the plaintiff, and that as plaintiff had not offered his full evidence in refutation of the claim of forfeiture, all which was shown by affidavit, the court erred in allowing defendants' motion for leave to file the amended answer. The rule is well established that a party is not entitled to have his pleadings amended to conform to the proof where objection was made to the introduction of evidence to cover which the amendment is desired: *Mendenhall* v. *Harrisburg Water Company*, 27 Or. 38 (39 Pac. 899); *Beard* v. *Tilghman*, 20 N. Y. Supp. 736. But the

court below met this objection by referring the cause
back to the referee, with directions to allow the parties to introduce other evidence touching the additional questions raised by the amended pleadings, so
that the cause might be tried fully upon its merits.
This, we think, was within the sound discretion of the
court, and in furtherance of justice. Courts are always solicitous to reach the merits of every cause,
and to that end are liberal in allowing amendments.
There was no error in allowing the motion.

3. The ground of the next contention is that the
amended answer, after stating the facts relied upon as
constituting the forfeiture of plaintiff's claim, fails to
state "that thereby the claim was forfeited," citing
Gelston v. *Hoyt,* 16 U. S. (3 Wheat.), 247. This was a
case of seizure of a ship and cargo for a supposed
forfeiture, and, under the common-law form of pleading then in use, it was held that, after stating the
facts, it was necessary to aver "that thereby the
property became and was actually forfeited, and was
seized as forfeited." Under our practice these technical forms of pleading are abolished, and it is now
only necessary to set forth the facts constituting the
cause of action or defense concisely without unnecessary repetition. Not having been tested by a demurrer, the allegations of forfeiture are sufficient after
trial.

4. Has a forfeiture of the White Pigeon Claim by
plaintiff been established by the testimony? Numerous witnesses were produced, and testified relative to
the labor done upon the claim prior to January first,
eighteen hundred and ninety-three, and, while they
differed widely as regards the established value of the

work observed by them as having been done in the years eighteen hundred and ninety-one and eighteen hundred and ninety-two, they substantially agreed as to its amount and extent. Many years prior to the location of the White Pigeon there had been sunk on the ledge three different shafts. Some witnesses say two, but there were undoubtedly three. The larger one is sometimes called an incline. The shafts ranged from two to eight feet in depth and were of different relative dimensions. The witnesses gathered their information by passing over the claim; some casually, and some for the express purpose of ascertaining what work had been done. They all describe a new cut at the southwest corner of the claim. Some think it was within the boundary, and others say it was outside, but it is immaterial to this inquiry whether it was within or beyond the boundary. This cut was evidently made with the purpose of tunneling into the hillside, and thereby striking the ledge at some distance under the surface. It was from twenty to twenty-five feet long, three to four feet wide, and, in the face of the cut, or at its deepest point, four or five feet deep. They testify also to some fresh work that had been done in one of the old shafts. This is as far as they all agree. One of the witnesses, C. M. Foster, in rebuttal, recalled having seen a cut spoken of as a "crosscut" running across the ledge, presumably for the purpose of exposing it. The dimensions of this cut are given by the plaintiff as from eight to ten feet long, probably sixteen inches wide, and about twelve inches deep. A witness or two relates having seen some small prospect holes, two or three in number, sunk in the earth at a point where the ledge is broken off and lost sight of, probably for the purpose

28 Or.—9.

of finding the ledge again. This is a synopsis of all
the work observed by the defendants' witnesses, which
had been done in the years eighteen hundred and
ninety-one and eighteen hundred and ninety-two, after
the date of the location of the White Pigeon. It was
comparatively easy to distinguish the new work from
that done in sinking the shafts years prior, from the
action and indications left by the elements upon the
exposures made by. the excavations. Many of these
witnesses were practical miners, and knew the value
of mining labor, and their estimate of the value of the
labor thus expended ranged from nine to thirty dollars — none placing it higher than the latter sum.

Of the testimony offered to overcome this showing,
that of plaintiff in his own behalf is the strongest, and
is practically all that he has offered upon the question, except as he is corroborated by other witnesses.
The work on the cut at the southwest corner of the
claim was done by Howard, Heffrom, and Ellis, under
his directions, for which work he paid Howard ten
dollars. Howard describes how it was done, and gives
the time expended in doing it. He says he worked
two and one half days, four hours counting as a day's
work. Heffrom and Ellis each worked an hour and a
half, and Bishop worked the same time. Bishop testifies that he, himself, put in about twenty days on the
claim, one of which is the one and one half hour's
work referred to by Howard. He says: "My work
consisted in crosscutting the ledge, sinking holes,
prospecting croppings, and working the croppings by
hand and mortar, and reducing the ore to pulp with
water and quicksilver, using acids, and separating the
gold from the quicksilver after working it." On cross-
examination he describes minutely what work he did
and how. He lived at Baker City, and generally went

from his home to the mine, a distance of twelve miles,
and back again each day he worked upon it. Speaking of the first and second days that he was there, he
says: "I prospected the ledge, the croppings." "Prospected by breaking the rock off the ledge, and sampling it." "I worked along the ledge there, picking
and hunting for free gold rock, knowing that she carried free gold." "That was all I done these trips."
Of the third time, he says: "I started to do surface
work—that is, top work—where there was no ledge on
the break of the hill, westerly from the old shaft,
where the ledge is broken off, and no one has found
it." "There were several holes there that I dug at
that time; I cannot tell how many." Also, "worked on
the ledge matter." "I picked rock, examined it, and
prospected for the gold streak that I knew was there."
In regard to the fourth trip in April, eighteen hundred
and ninety-two, the former being along in March, he
says: "I prospected around on that trip on the mine,
east of the old shaft on the westerly end." "Removed
no dirt at that time." "Removed some rock; yes."
The trace left was "by the ledge being disturbed by
breaking it." The fifth time, "broke off rock; put it
in a mortar; panned it out with a gold pan." "I
worked a little in the old shaft and hole number two;
from the old shaft with a pick and shovel." The sixth
trip, "I run a crosscut at that time." "I removed
some dirt, not a great deal, away from the hanging
wall on the southwest, westerly from the old prospect
shaft." The seventh trip, "I cleared away around the
ledge; took off rock; sampled it; marked it, and worked
in hole number two with pick and shovel; threw out
some dirt at that time; sampled it, and brought them
to town." Eighth trip, "I worked on this slope westerly to see if I could find the ledge where the break

was, near the old prospect shaft, with the intention, if I could find it, of running a tunnel, and sinking and clearing out the old prospect shaft." "Prospected around with the pick some. I would break off portions of the ledge matter with my pick, and would break the rock with the eye of the pick, or a small hammer I had with me. I would take my glass and examine the rock, and if it did not suit me I would leave that portion of the ledge and go to another portion. I was hunting the pay chute. The reason I was hunting the pay chute was, I found a piece of rock three inches long and one half inch wide, and about one half an inch deep that had free gold in it." The ninth trip, "I picked down the rock in small pieces; marked them, and cut into the ledge quite a little piece." "I took some samples out of the old shaft number one, marked them and the part of the ledge they came from, and brought them out and took them back with me." Without following this testimony further in detail, suffice it to say that the foregoing fully illustrates the nature of the work done by plantiff for which he claims twenty days.

When asked to "give the number, size, and dimensions of any and all new holes and crosscuts, which were made on the claim after its location, up to January first, eighteen hundred and ninety-three," he replied: "On the westerly slope of the White Pigeon, westerly of the old shaft, there is a crosscut in the hill crosscutting the ledge, I should judge perhaps fifteen feet or more; it would be about two feet to thirty inches wide, twenty-four inches deep; and several holes,—I don't recollect. how many,—in the vicinity of where this crosscut is, would average about three feet, I should judge, in length, and about two in depth. There is a great number of these, I don't recollect how many; sunk several of them to try and find the ledge running parallel with the main White Pigeon. which I think would average two or three feet, and about twenty inches or two feet in depth. There was a hole, number three, an old shaft to the best of my recollection, about four feet long, about thirty inches wide, and about two feet deep. I enlarged hole number two by working, I should judge, about one third. The old shaft, I have made that larger. I should judge, about one foot. The length on one side was ten feet. I had work done on the tunnel site in the fall of eighteen hundred and ninety-two, about twenty feet long, four feet wide, and about four and one half or five feet deep at the big end." He further testifies that C. J. Finn rendered him a statement of thirteen days' work that he did upon the claim, but he has no personal knowledge of his having done any work, except that he saw Finn at the mine one day in June, eighteen hundred and ninety-two, and at that time he was prospecting the ledge for ore samples, some of which he produced. He further states that he spent eight days at home testing the samples of rock which he had taken from the mine, and had some twelve assays made of them, and that it was worth one dollar and fifty cents each to make such assays. All this work, he says, would "exceed one hundred dollars in value." The fact was established that miners' labor was worth from three to three and one half dollars per day. It may be conceded that if the nature of the work done and performed by the plaintiff fills the measure of work required to be done annually on all unpatented claims, he has complied with the law, but, if it does not, that he has fallen short of it. A summary of the value of the labor performed will, therefore, be unnecessary whether classed as assessment work or not.

5.   Section 2324, Revised Statutes of the United States, requires that on each claim located after the tenth day of May, eighteen hundred and seventy-two, and until a patent has been issued therefor, not less than one hundred dollars' worth of labor shall be performed or improvements made during each year. The time in which the first annual labor after location is required to be performed has been noted. Mr. Justice MILLER, in *Chambers* v. *Harrington*, 111 U. S. 353, (4 Sup. Ct. 428,) after explaining the reasons for the adoption of this statute, says: "Clearly the purpose was the same as in the matter of similar regulations by the miners, namely, to require every person who asserted an exclusive right to his discovery or claim to expend something of labor or value on it, as evidence of his good faith, and to show that he was not acting on the principle of the dog in the manger." WADE, C. J., in *Remington* v. *Baudit*, 6 Mont. 141, (9 Pac. 819,) says: "The purpose of requiring one hundred dollars' worth of work or improvements on a mining claim each year is to so develop the mine as that a patent may issue for the claim. It is not the policy of the government to issue patents for the mineral lands until there has been a discovery, and sufficient work done upon the claim to demonstrate its value. * * * A liberal construction should be given the mining act of eighteen hundred and seventy-two, but it should not be so liberal as to authorize a claim to be held without representation, or a patent to be procured before any work had been done on the claim." This language is quoted with approval in *Honaker* v. *Martin*, 11 Mont. 91, (27 Pac. 898,) a later case from the same

state. Before patent can issue, the claimant is required to file with the register a certificate of the United States surveyor-general showing that five hundred dollars' worth of labor or improvements has been done or made by himself or grantors: United States Revised Statutes, § 2325. So that it is apparent the statute touching the location and acquirement of mining claims was enacted to subserve two purposes, namely, to insure good faith in the locator or claimant, and to require of him that he exhibit a claim, which, by reason of its development or the improvements made thereon or for its benefit, is of some value; and it was assumed by congress that five hundred dollars worth of labor or improvements would demonstrate its value as a mine. As to the nature of the labor or improvements, the statute would seem to require that the labor be performed or the improvements made for the development of the claim; that is, to facilitate the extraction of the metals it may contain: *Smelting Company* v. *Kemp*, 104 U. S. 636; *Remington* v. *Baudit*, 6 Mont. 141 (9 Pac. 819).

But it is insisted that whatever labor is performed for the purpose of prospecting a mine, fills the requirements of the statute, and in support of this position counsel cites *United States* v. *Iron Silver Mining Company,* 24 Fed. 568, and *Book* v. *Justice Mining Company*, 58 Fed. 107. In the former of these cases language is employed which would seem to indicate that the term "prospecting" was used in its broadest sense. It is there said that "work done for the purpose of discovering mineral, whatever the particular form or character of the deposit which is the object of the search, is within the spirit of the statute." It is disclosed, however, by the opinion, that labor was claimed for digging prospect holes on a placer mine, evidently in

trying to find veins, leads, and lodes, and it was contended that no work in that direction and for that
purpose ought to be counted in an application for a
patent to placer mining ground; and it was with reference to this state of facts that BREWER, J., with some
hesitancy, used the language above quoted. The latter case simply announces the well-settled doctrine
that "labor and improvements, within the meaning of
the statute, are deemed to be done upon the location
when the labor is performed or improvements made
for the express purpose of working, prospecting, or
developing the ground embraced in the location," and
was said with reference to a tunnel commenced outside of the mining claim in dispute and intended for
its development as well as other contiguous claims.
The word "prospecting," when used with reference to
annual labor to be expended upon a mining claim, is
incapable of so broad a signification as is claimed for
it. It is not used in the sense of "exploration and
discovery," which is necesssary before a valid location
can be made, but rather in the sense of "development
and demonstration," that the value of the ledge may be
determined, as distinguished from the ascertainment
of its existence.

6.   Now the question recurs whether picking rock
from the walls of a shaft or from the side or outcrop-
pings of a ledge, in small quantities, from day to day,
making tests for the purpose of sampling it, breaking
and examining it under a glass, crushing it in a mortar and panning it out, and carrying it away and making assays of it in attempting to find the "pay chute,"
as it is termed, is such as the law will permit the
claimant to be credited with upon his account for annual labor performed? Such labor does not add to

the value of the claim, nor does it tend to the development of the mine. Five hundred dollars' worth of labor of this nature could easily be expended, and yet the surveyor-general would not be able to certify from an inspection of the mine that it had been done. On the contrary, on applying the test of reasonable value, he would find it far short of this amount: *Mattingly* v. *Lewisohn,* 13 Mont. 508 (35 Pac. 114); *Du Prat* v. *James,* 65 Cal. 555 (15 Morrison's Min. Rep. 344; 4 Pac. 562). Such work naturally leads one to question the good faith of the claimant, and to doubt his purpose to represent the claim except upon finding the "pay chute." This class of labor is not such as the statute contemplated, and will not avail the plaintiff; and it is apparent that without it he has failed in performing the one hundred dollars' worth of labor or improvements required by law. The actual work that he did which can avail him consists in the cut at the southwest corner of the claim, which cost him ten dollars; the crosscut made by him in one day for the purpose of exposing the ledge; several prospect holes that he sunk for the same purpose, which could be done within five days as the outside limit; and an enlargement of one or two of the old shafts. The court below very properly found that the assessment work did not exceed fifty dollars. The claim was therefore open to reëntry on January first, eighteen hundred and ninety-three; and, unless plaintiff had resumed work thereafter as required by law,* it was likewise open at the time defendants relocated it. Plaintiff, in April, eighteen hundred and ninety-three, entered one of the old shafts

---

* Revised Statutes of United States, ¿2324, as amended by Supplement to the Revised Statutes, p. 276, declares a mining claim forfeited by failing to put one hundred dollars' worth of work and improvements thereon during any year prior to the issue of a patent, and allows a relocation by another person, provided the original locators "have not resumed work."

and spent an hour or so with pick and hammer in securing samples of the ore, and it is claimed for this
that it was a resumption of work, but this is not a
resumption under any of the authorities: *Honaker* v.
Martin, 11 Mont. 91 (27 Pac. 398). It was further contended that defendants' entry was under a license from
the plaintiff, but it is sufficient to say that this contention is not established by the evidence.

7. This disposes of the case with the exception of
a question which is made as to the jurisdiction of a
court of equity to take cognizance of the matter in
issue, the possession and title being in dispute. It is
clear from the testimony that at the commencement of
the suit the plaintiff was absolutely out, and the defendants were in full possession of the claim. The
inquiry has heretofore proceeded upon the assumption
that the court had jurisdiction to determine all matters connected with the suit. We will now consider
the contention of the respective parties upon this
proposition. This may be termed a suit to enjoin a
trespass, and for an account. It falls within the category of remedies which are of purely equitable cognizance. The trespass, threatened or actual, is the element which in proper cases lays the foundation for
equitable interference; it is the primary "cause of
suit." The power to assess damages is incidental, and
does not exist as an equitable remedy, except in connection with the injunction to restrain the trespass,
and is sustained upon the principle that, as a general
rule, a court of equity having acquired jurisdiction for
one purpose, will retain it for all, and proceed to the
adjudication of legal as well as equitable rights, with
a view to the administration of full relief: *Fleischner* v.
Citizens' Investment Company, 25 Or. 130 (35 Pac. 174).

And upon the further ground of preventing a multiplicity of suits, Chancellor KENT, in *Livingston* v. *Livingston*, 6 Johns. Ch. 417, (10 Am. Dec. 354,) says: "This
protection is now granted in the case of timber, coals,
lead ore, quarries," etc., and quotes from Lord ELDON
in *Thomas* v. *Oakley*, 18 Ves. 184, as follows: "The present established course was to sustain the bill for the
purpose of injunction, connecting it with the account
in both cases (waste and trespass), and not to put
the plaintiff to come here for an injunction, and to go
to law for damages." Mr. Daniels says: "The account
depends entirely upon the injunction; it is incidental
to, and consequential upon it; and if a person is entitled to the one, he is entitled to the other also, on
the principle of preventing a multiplicity of suits; for,
otherwise, he would be obliged to bring his action at
law as well as in equity,—his action by way of satisfaction; his bill by way of prevention": 2 Daniel on
Chancery Pleading and Practice, *1634· Courts of
equity will enjoin a trespass only when there exists
some equitable ground for interference, as where there
is danger of irreparable mischief, or that the value of
the inheritance is put in jeopardy by a continuance of
the trespass, or when it becomes necessary to prevent
a multiplicity of suits; the primary purpose of the
suit is to quiet the possession. In ordinary trespass,
or where the law affords an adequate remedy, equity
refuses to interfere: *Bracken* v. *Preston*, 1 Pinney, 584
(44 Am. Dec. 420). The law is very old which permits
the use of an injunction in restraint of waste. Lord
ELDON says there is a writ at common law after action to restrain waste: *Smith* v. *Collyer,* 8 Ves. Jr. 90.
An injunction for this purpose was and is now allowed a party out of possession against one in possession of lands to restrain irremediable damage to the in-

heritance, but the parties must be privies in title or estate, such as landlord and tenant, mortgagor and mortgagee, or tenant of a particular estate and remainderman, and the injunction will be allowed in all cases where an action will lie to recover possession of lands wasted or damages for the waste: *Chapman* v. *Toy Long*, 4 Sawy. 33 (Fed. Cas. No. 2610); and 3 Pomeroy's Equity, § 1348. But the remedy which permits an injunction against a trespass is of more recent origin, and was first granted by Lord Thurlow late in the eighteenth century. Lord Eldon relates the instance, of which he had a note, the case in which the order was made being now known as the "Flamang Case," as follows: "There was a demise of close A. to a tenant for life; the lessor being landlord of an adjoining close B. The tenant dug a mine in the former close. That was waste from the privity. But when we asked an injunction against his digging in the other close, though a continuation of the working in the former close, Lord Thurlow hesitated much; but did at last grant the injunction—*first,* from the irreparable ruin of the property as a mine; *secondly,* it was a species of trade; and, *thirdly,* upon the principle of this court enjoining in matter of trespass where irreparable damage is the consequence": *Hanson* v. *Gardiner,* 7 Ves. Jr. 307. See also *Mitchell* v. *Dors,* 6 Ves. Jr. 147. Since the time of Lords Therlow and Eldon the remedy against trespass by injunction has become well established, and is now constantly brought into requisition. But, contrary to the injunction against waste, it is allowed a party in possession against a stranger whose entry is unlawful: 1 Spelling's Extraordinary Relief, § 336.

It is said that injunctions are now granted much more liberally than formerly, and that the tendency is to break through the old distinction existing between waste and trespass: *Chapman* v. *Toy Long,* 4 Sawy. 33 (Fed. Cas. No. 2610); *Lowndes* v. *Bettle,* 33 Law Jour. (Eq.), 541. The authorities, however, when closely observed, would seem to indicate that the distinction which has been broken through is mostly the distinction which formerly existed in granting the injunction in one instance while refusing it in the other. The same conditions which lay the foundation for or that will support an injunction in case of waste will not suffice as against trespass. The material and vital distinction regards the possession of the relative parties litigant. In case of waste the privity existing between the parties will always enable the plaintiff, while out of possession, to maintain the suit; while, without the privity of estate or title as in case of trespass, posses- sion, or, what is tantamount thereto, the adjudicated or admitted right of possession, or an action pending therefor, is necessary to justify the interference of a court of equity: 1 Spelling's Extraordinary Relief, § 368. DEADY, J., in *Chapman* v. *Toy Long,* 4 Sawy. 33 (Fed. Cas. No. 2610,) states the rule broadly. He says: "It is also insisted that the complainants must first obtain possession of the premises by an action at law before a court of equity will interfere to restrain the defendants from committing the threatened tres- passes. * * * Wherever a trespass is attended with irreparable mischief, or a multiplicity of suits, or vexa- tious litigation, the remedy by injunction will be ap- plied the same as if it were a technical waste." That was a suit for injunction with an account against some Chinamen who were in possession of a placer mine, and who were disqualified from locating and acquir- ing title to mines from the government. The plaintiff had made location, and, without acquiring possession,

had entered suit. The court, however, awarded only
a temporary injunction. The result of this case is
approved by Mr. Justice Field in *Erhardt* v. *Boaro,*
113 U. S. 539, (5 Sup. Ct. 565,) without adopting
the reasoning. He says: "The authority of the court
is exercised in such cases through its preventive
writ, to preserve the property from destruction pending legal proceedings for the determination of the
title." The doctrine of the latter case is that injunction will issue at the suit of a person out of possession to restrain irremediable mischief going to the
destruction of the substance of the estate, where the
title is being litigated on the law side of the court.
But we are now dealing with a suit for an injunction,
coupled with an account for damages. It is sought to
make the injunction perpetual, and at the same time
recover damages for injuries sustained. The suit, in
its object and purposes, is essentially different from
one wherein a temporary or preliminary injunction
only is sought to restrain injurious acts, irreparable in
their nature, pending an action at law to determine
adverse title or the right of possession. The latter is
ancillary in its nature to the action at law, and in aid
of it, that the plaintiff may reap the full benefit of his
judgment when duly obtained; while, upon the other
hand, as we shall finally see, the action at law is in
some measure auxiliary to a suit for peremptory injunction coupled with an account.

It is a well settled rule of law that where the title
is seriously in dispute the court will not entertain the
injunction, except it be preliminary in its nature, and
for temporary purposes only, to abide the adjudication
of title by an action at law, where the estate is legal
and not equitable. A peremptory or perpetual injunction is never granted in such cases, as that would be

to try the title in a court of equity, where the remedy is purely legal: *Clayton* v. *Shoemaker*, 67 Md. 219 (9 Atl. 635); *Old Telegraph Mining Company* v. *Central Smelting Company*, 7 Morrison's Min. Rep. 556; *Stevens* v. *Williams*, 5 Morrison's Min. Rep. 452. Equity will not try title to real property where the party invoking its ·aid has ample facilities and is in a position to settle the question at law; in other words, where he has an adequate remedy at law. The underlying reason for remitting a suitor to a court of law is that the right of trial by jury may not be denied any person under the pretence of equitable cognizance. So it is that in a suit to restrain a trespass, if the relief sought is a peremptory and permanent injunction, which would in effect estop subsequent adjudication as to title, the plaintiff must possess and show such a title, as against the defendant, as will protect him in the possession. A mere *prima facie* title, possessory in its nature, if not disputed, is sufficient: Spelling's Extraordinary Relief, § 365. But whatever this title may be, if seriously questioned, so that the validity thereof, whether possessory or otherwise, becomes one of the primary issues in the case, then a court of equity will refuse the relief, at least to the extent of making the writ peremptory until the title is settled at law. The rule of practice is well spoken by WHEELER, J., in *Burnley* v. *Cook*, 13 Texas 589 (65 Am. Dec. 79). He says: "In all cases where the right is doubtful, the court will direct a trial, and in the mean time, if there be danger of irreparable mischief, or if there is any other good cause of granting a temporary injunction, it will be ordered, so as to restrain all injurious proceedings; and when the plaintiff's right is fully established a perpetual injunction will be decreed." RUFFIN, C. J., in *Irwin* v. *Davidson*, 3 Iredell on Equity, 317, says: "But it is plain that the jurisdiction to restrain trespasses, like that to restrain nuisances, is not an original jurisdiction of the court of equity, which enables this court, under the semblance of preventing an irreparable injury to a legal estate. to take a jurisdiction of deciding exclusively upon the legal title itself. Therefore, in such case, the plaintiff ought to establish his title at law. or show a good reason for not doing so; and, if he will not, this court cannot undertake, against a defendant's answer. to try the questions of title and trespass and nuisance; * * * and that the court of equity should only grant the injunction where the plaintiff is endeavoring to establish his title at law, and until he should have had a reasonable time allowed for that purpose." It is observed in *Stevens* v. *Williams,* 5 Morrison's Min. Rep 453, that, "regularly the law action should be brought before application is made for an injunction. and that fact should be averred in the bill; but, where that has been omitted through mistake or inadvertence. the rule has been so far relaxed as to admit of the bringing of such suit after the filing of the bill, the plaintiff being put upon terms of commencing the suit within a short time and prosecuting it with diligence." In *Clayton* v. *Shoemaker,* 67 Md. 219, (9 Atl. 635,) it is held that in a case of controversy concerning the legal title the injunction will issue temporarily. so as to retain a *statu quo* condition until the legal title is determined, and if the result is favorable to petitioners then the injunction should be made perpetual. That was a case of continuing trespass.

From these authorities we get the principle and the rule of procedure. A court of equity, always solicitous that there should not be a failure of justice, will make its relief effective so that if, when the legal title and right of possession is settled, the prelimi-

nary injunction does not answer the purposes of the
suit, a peremptory injunction will issue, and such
other and further relief will be granted as is consistent with equity. The injunctive jurisdiction of courts
of equity will be freely exercised to prevent trespass
upon mines, as the digging and removing ores therefrom, and extracting and disposing of their products,
reaches to the very substance and value of the estate, and goes to the destruction of the very essence
thereof. A continued trespass of such a character
would almost inevitably lead to a multiplicity of actions for damages: 2 Beach on Injunctions, § 1155. The
general rule requiring the plaintiff to come with an
uncontroverted legal title extends also to trespass
against mines, but is relaxed somewhat in the case
of irreparable injury going to the very substance of
the estate: 10 Am. and Eng. Ency. of Law, 883;
United States v. *Parrott,* 1 McAllister, 271 (Fed. Cas.
No. 15998). LORD, C. J., in *Allen* v. *Dunlap,* 24 Or. 232,
(32 Pac. 675,) says: "The general rule that a court of
equity will refuse to take jurisdiction and award even
a temporary injunction in cases of a mere trespass, is
conceded; but there is an established exception in
cases of mines, timber, and the like, in which an injunction will be granted to restrain the commission of
acts by which the substance of an estate is injured,
destroyed, or carried away. In such cases, the injury
being irreparable, or difficult of ascertainment in damages, the remedy at law is inadequate." It has been
held in this state that ejectment will not lie to recover
a quartz mine located under the laws of the United
States prior to the entire compliance with the requirements thereof entitling the locator or owner to a patent, but that, the right being possessory only, an ac-

tion may be maintained in the justice's court for the
recovery of the mine, and that that is the proper forum
in which to determine such right: *Duffy* v. *Mix*, 24 Or.
265 (33 Pac. 807). A possessory action establishes the
only title extant when it establishes the right of possession. Now, the jurisdiction of a justice's court, as
regards a question of damages, extends in amount to
two hundred and fifty dollars only, if, indeed, any
damages could be recovered at all in an action for the
recovery of the possession of a mining claim. But if
ejectment would lie, it is problematical whether damages for withholding it would be adequate, because of
the difficulty of its ascertainment. Besides, damages
could only be recovered to the date of the commencement of the action, while equity with its injunctive
powers will afford full relief. Hence plaintiff is required to go to the justice's court for his possession,
and to the circuit court for his damages, and if this
does not prove effective he must come here to a court
of equity for his injunction, thus entailing a multiplicity of actions which it is the province of equity to
prevent. So that here, owing to the peculiar state of
the law, we find additional reason for the interposition
of a court of equity by injunction; and therefore,
where an action has been commenced or is pending
in a justice's court to determine the possessory title
to a mine, by a party out of possession, and damage
is being done going to the impairment or destruction
of the substance of the estate, the plaintiff in the action is entitled to an injunction, with an account, in a
suit instituted for that purpose. An injunction will
issue temporarily, however, to abide the result of the
action; and should the action result favorably to plaintiff, it will be made permanent, with an award of damages commensurate with the injuries sustained. Even

where no action has been commenced, in a strong
case, the injunction will issue, but the court will direct
a speedy trial at law to determine the title and right
of possession where controverted by the defendant,
and the peremptory character of the injunction will
be made to depend upon the result of the law action:
1 Spelling's Extraordinary Relief, § 367. From the
testimony adduced at the trial it is apparent that
plaintiff has not made such a case as would entitle
him to even a temporary injunction to abide the action to determine the right of possession. The decree
of the court below is therefore affirmed.

AFFIRMED.

Argued July 30; decided October 14, 1895; rehearing denied.

STATE *v.* BROWN.

[41 Pac. 1042.]

1. DISQUALIFICATION OF GRAND JUROR[*]—CODE, § 947, SUBDIVISION 4—
"CAUSE" DEFINED.—Hill's Code, § 947, providing that it shall be a
sufficient cause of challenge to any juror called "to be sworn in any
cause" that he has served as a juror within a year, does not apply to
grand jurors, for a "cause" within the meaning of that section is a
civil or criminal action at issue and ready for trial in a circuit court
of Oregon, and grand jurors are not required to try such matters.

2. ACTUAL BIAS OF JUROR—DISCRETION OF COURT—CODE, § 187.—Under
Hill's Code, § 187, providing that the fact that a juror has formed an
opinion as to the merits of a case is not sufficient to sustain a challenge unless the court is satisfied from all the circumstances that
the juror cannot disregard such opinion and try the case impartially,
a clear abuse of discretion in allowing one to act as juror who has
stated that he has formed an opinion must be shown to procure a
reversal of the judgment on that ground, and in this case the facts
set forth do not disclose any such conduct by the trial court: *State
v. Saunders*, 14 Or. 300; *Kumli v. Southern Pacific Company*, 21 Or. 505,
cited and approved.

[*]The qualification of grand jurors is the subject of a very interesting and
exhaustive note to the Iowa case of *State v. Russell*, 28 L. R. A. 195. There is also
a monograph on the competency of grand jurors, the grounds on which they may
be challenged, and the organization and duties of grand juries with the Pennsylvania case of *Commonwealth v. Green*, 12 Am. St. 900. See, also, note to *Commonwealth v. Woodward*, 34 Am. St. 304.—REPORTER.

3. RES GESTÆ.*— The remarks and statements made by a defendant as he was hurrying from the scene of his crime, and immediately after its commission, are admissible as part of the res gestæ; as, for example, evidence that defendant ran away from the place of the shooting, with a pistol in his hand, shouting, "I am the toughest son of a bitch that ever struck this town," is competent on the question of malice, for it is closely connected with the principal event, and tends to show the state of the defendant's mind.

4. IMPEACHMENT—FOUNDATION.—A witness on a trial for murder may be impeached by members of the grand jury as to the testimony given by her before such jury where the proper foundation has been laid.†

5. EXPERT WITNESS.—A nonexpert witness may properly testify as to whether a person seemed excited or otherwise at a specified time.

6. IMPEACHING EVIDENCE — PRESUMPTION.— The necessary preliminary questions to render an impeaching question proper will be presumed to have been asked and answered where the record does not purport to contain all the evidence.

7. CRIMINAL LAW—FAILURE TO ASK INSTRUCTIONS.— Failure of the court to instruct the jury not to be influenced in their verdict by any applause made by the audience in approval of the remarks of the prosecuting attorney is not cause for reversal, where no such instruction was asked, and the court promptly disapproved such applause.

8. INSTRUCTION — USURPING PROVINCE OF JURY — CODE, § 200.— An instruction on a murder trial that there is evidence "to the effect" or "tending to show" a certain fact, and allowing the jury, if they find it to be a fact, to consider it in determining the degree of defendant's guilt, does not, as being a presentation of facts by the court, violate Hill's Code, § 200, prohibiting the court from presenting the facts of a case to the jury, especially where the jury are also in-

---

*How soon after the main event declarations must be made in order to constitute part of the res gestæ in criminal cases, is considered in a note in 19 L. R. A. 737-745. The subject is also discussed in Lewis v. State, 25 Am. St. Rep. 730, and Johnson v. State, 28 Am. St. Rep. 930.—REPORTER.

†The passage in appellant's brief on this point is as follows: "No proper foundation was laid to permit said grand jurors to testify that the witness was not excited when testifying before them, and if such foundation had been laid, it was an immaterial matter, and a witness cannot be impeached on immaterial issues. A witness cannot be impeached by contradictory evidence or inconsistent statements on immaterial and irrelevant matters, nor in any case without the proper foundation is laid by calling the witness' attention to time, place, and circumstances: Winn v. State, 28 S. W. 807; Blough v. Parry, 40 N. E. 70." It will be seen that this case is not an authority for calling grand jurors as impeaching witnesses. That question was, however, fully argued and explicitly decided in State v. Moran, 15 Or. 262.—REPORTER.

structe ! that they are the exclusive judges of all the facts in the case, as well as the weight of evidence and credibility of the witnesses.

9. INSTRUCTIONS NEED NOT BE DUPLICATED.—A requested instruction that has been already given in another paragraph need not be given again.

10. ERROR NOT PRESUMED.—An instruction will be presumed on appeal to have been properly refused where the record does not purport to contain all the evidence.

APPEAL from Douglas: J. C. FULLERTON, Judge.

The defendant Samuel G. Brown having been indicted, tried for, and convicted of, the crime of murder in the first degree, by shooting and killing William Alfred Kincaid, in Douglas County, moved for a new trial, which was denied, and he was sentenced to be hanged. From this judgment he appeals, and assigns as error the denial of a motion to set aside the indictment; the refusal to sustain challenges submitted to trial jurors; the admission of improper evidence; and the giving and refusal of certain instructions. The record discloses that the defendant at the proper time submitted a motion to set aside the indictment for the reason that it had not been found as required by law, and filed therewith the following affidavit: "I, A. M. Crawford, being duly sworn say I am attorney for Samuel G. Brown, the above named defendant, and that Theodore Andrews, who is now a member of the grand jury which found the indictment in this case against said defendant Samuel G. Brown, has been summoned and served as a juror in a cause tried in this court within less than one year prior to the finding of the indictment against said Samuel G. Brown, and is, and was when this indictment was found not competent to act as a juror." In disposing of this motion the following order was made: "And the court, after hearing the arguments of counsel and being fully

advised in the premises, overrules and denies said motion," to which ruling an exception was saved. It is
contended 'on behalf of the defendant that the grand
juror was incompetent, and, having challenged his competency and submitted evidence showing the want
thereof, the court erred in not setting aside the indictment; while in behalf of the state it is insisted
that his competency was a question of fact to be tried
by the court, and as the record is silent as to the
means adopted to reach the conclusion announced, it
cannot be ascertained whether the court found the
statement's contained in the affidavit untrue, or the
motion insufficient in law.   AFFIRMED.

For appellant there was a brief and an oral argument by *Messrs. William R. Willis* and *A. M. Crawford.*

For the state there were briefs and oral arguments
by *Messrs. Cicero M. Idleman,* attorney-general, *L. Loughary,*
and *George M. Brown,* district attorney.

Opinion by MR. JUSTICE MOORE.

1. Without attempting to discuss the proposition
contended for, but treating the facts stated in the affidavit as admitted, we shall examine the grand juror's
competency as a question of law. In the formation
of the grand jury, the statute, in general terms, provides that from a list containing the names of two
hundred persons made from the last preceding assessment roll of the county by the county court, denominated the jury list, (Hill's Code, §§ 952–956,) thirty-one
names shall be drawn, (section 958,) from which number so selected and in attendance upon the circuit
court the names of seven shall be drawn to act as
grand jurors (section 943); and it is made the duty

of the court, before accepting a person so drawn as a grand juror, to be satisfied that he is duly qualified to act as such (section 1233); and no challenge is allowed to the panel from which the grand jury is drawn, nor to an individual juror, unless when so made by the court for want of qualification (section 1234). Section 947, Hill's Code, provides that "a person is not competent to act as a juror unless he be: 1. A citizen of the United States; 2. A male inhabitant of the county in which he is returned, and who has been an inhabitant thereof for the year next preceding the time he is drawn or called; 3. Over twenty-one years of age; 4. In the possession of his natural faculties and of sound mind. Nor is any person competent to act as a juror who has been convicted of any felony, or a misdemeanor involving moral turpitude. No person shall be summoned as a juror in any circuit court more than once in one year, and it shall be sufficient cause of challenge to any juror called to be sworn in any cause that he has been summoned and attended said court as a juror at any term of said court held within one year prior to the time of such challenge, or that he has been summoned from the bystanders or body of the county and has served as a juror in any cause upon such summons within one year prior to the time of such challenge." The correct interpretation of this section must be decisive of the alleged error of which the defendant complains. The object of the legislative assembly in the passage of the latter part of this section was manifestly twofold: *First,* to relieve a person from performing more than his share of jury duty; and, *second,* to prevent persons who make a business of sitting on juries, known as professionals, from being called to act as jurors in any cause before the circuit court at intervals of less than

one year. The affidavit in support of the motion fails
to show that Andrews did not possess all the qualifications prescribed by the statute, or that he had ever
been convicted of any felony or misdemeanor involving moral turpitude; so that if he was disqualified to
act as a grand juror, his incompetency must have existed by reason of the latter clause of the section
under consideration. The phrase, "in any cause," as
used in this section, evidently means a civil or criminal action at issue and ready for trial in a circuit
court of this state, and a person "called" to serve as
a juror in any such cause would be subject to challenge if he had served as a juror in said court in the
trial of any action within one year prior thereto, or
had been summoned and attended as a juror within
the same period, and a challenge upon that ground
must be held sufficient: *Wiscman* v. *Bruns*, 36 Neb. 467
(54 N. W. 858). But this provision cannot apply to
one who has been drawn as a grand juror, because
neither his duty nor oath requires him to be sworn
"in any cause," nor is he required to try an issue of
fact before the circuit court. The portion of the section above quoted providing that no person shall be
summoned as a juror in any circuit court more than
once in one year furnishes an exemption which would
doubtless entitle the person drawn as a grand juror
to be excused from serving as such upon his own application showing prior service within the year, if
made before being sworn; but, as we view the statute,
such prior service cannot be made a ground of challenge against him as a grand juror. Nor is this conclusion in contravention of the spirit or purpose of
the statute, which is intended to provide impartial and
disinterested jurors for the trial of causes; for a
grand juror, otherwise qualified, may have a bias for

or prejudice against a person charged with the commission of a crime, and might have entertained and
freely expressed an opinion concerning the guilt or
innocence of the accused, and yet, under our statute,
neither his bias, prejudice, nor opinion would be a
ground of challenge even by the court when impanel-
ing the grand jury. The enumeration of the persons
who, under the statute, are incompetent, and the in-
sertion of the phrase "in any cause," lead us to believe
that the challenge prescribed on account of the prior
service of a juror is limited to persons called to be
sworn as trial jurors, and has no application to members of the grand jury.

2. The court having denied challenges for actual
bias submitted by the defendant to James Byron, John
Price, L. Ash, John Hancock, L. L. Hurd, J. A. McCal-
lister, J. B. Caulfield, and L. L. Marsters, who were
called as grand jurors, he peremptorily challenged the
first four, thereby exhausting his right to that class of
challenges; and the others having been impaneled, it
is contended that the court erred in denying the said
challenges for cause. The evidence of the qualification of these persons to act as jurors having been
taken before the court and incorporated in the bill of
exceptions, renders an examination of it necessary.
James Byron on his *voir dire* said he had heard what
purported to be a statement of the facts in the case,
which he believed to be true; and from this he had
formed an opinion as to the guilt or innocence of the
accused; that if the facts were as he had heard them,
he had a rather decided opinion, which it would require some evidence, at least, to remove; but when
asked by the court if he thought he could lay aside
any opinion he might have, and decide the case upon

the evidence produced at the trial, and the law as
given him by the court, he answered, "Yes, sir." The
questions propounded to the persons so challenged,
and their answers thereto, are almost identical with
the questions put to and the answers made by Mr.
Byron, except that each had derived his information
from the newspaper accounts of the homicide, J. B.
Caulfield and L. L. Marsters adding that they had
heard others express opinions in reference to the
merits of the case. Section 187, Hill's Code, provides
that on the trial of a challenge for actual bias, "although it should appear that a juror challenged has
formed or expressed an opinion upon the merits of
the cause from what he may have heard or read, such
opinion shall not of itself be sufficient to sustain the
challenge, but the court must be satisfied from all the
circumstances that the juror cannot disregard such
opinion, and try the issue impartially."

In *State* v. *Saunders,* 14 Or. 300, (12 Pac. 441,)
THAYER, J., in speaking of the effect produced upon
persons called to act as jurors by what they had read
or heard of the merits of a case, said: "This depends
much upon the credulity of the persons, and the te-
nacity with which they adhere to preconceived notions,"
so that, if it were not for what was elsewhere said in
the opinion, the inference would follow that if a person
never believed anything he read or heard, or was incapable of retaining an opinion, he would be a competent juror, notwithstanding he had at one time formed
or expressed an opinion concerning the merits of the
case. But further on in the opinion the learned justice
said: "The point to be determined is whether there
exists such a state of mind upon the part of the juror,
in reference to the party challenging, that he cannot
try the case impartially and without prejudice to the

party's substantial rights; and this, the statute says, must be determined by the exercise of a sound discretion. The evidence in this case upon the question of the qualification of the jurors challenged showed that they had, to some extent, formed an opinion as to the guilt or innocence of the accused, which they said would require evidence to remove, but thought they could try the case impartially. The trial judge heard their testimony, had an opportunity to observe their manner, and deemed them qualified to sit in the case. Unless, therefore, we conclude there has been an abuse of discretion, we have no right to interfere in the decision upon that point. It was a question of fact to be determined. The impression or opinion the juror had formed was from newspaper accounts and general rumor, and the circuit court had a better understanding of the extent of the opinion than we can obtain from the bill of exceptions. This court ought not to reverse a judgment upon such grounds, unless the evidence of the juror's incompetency is pretty clear and certain, at least, shows some cogent circumstances against it, circumstances of a nature calculated to impress upon the mind of the juror a conviction, such as having heard the testimony in the case, read a detailed statement of it, or been told it by some one claiming to know." In *Kumli* v. *Southern Pacific Company,* 21 Or. 505, (28 Pac. 637,) BEAN, J., in discussing this question, said: "It is ordinarily more safe and just to the juror and the cause of truth to trust to the impression made upon the trial court, which heard his testimony, and noticed his manner and appearance while under examination, subject to the scrutiny of counsel, than to any written or reported statement of his testimony. His tone, temperament and personal peculiarities, as exhibited on his examination, and

which do not appear in the written report of his testimony, are important factors in determining his competency as a juror. If a person called as a juror on
his examination, when challenged, discloses that he
has a fixed and definite opinion in the case, on the
merits, and nothing further is shown, the court ought,
as a matter of law, to reject him as incompetent.
Such a juror necessarily does not stand indifferent
between the parties; and it matters little from what
source he received the information upon which his
opinion is based. If, however, he has no fixed belief
or prejudice, and is able to say he can fairly try the
case on the evidence, freed from the influence of such
opinion or impression, his competency becomes a question for the trial court, in the exercise of a sound
discretion, and its findings ought not to be set aside
by an appellate court unless the error is manifest."

When a crime has been committed, the local newspapers usually publish an account of it, and sometimes
express opinions concerning the guilt or innocence of
the person supposed to be the author of it; and the
accounts being read by subscribers to these publica-
tions, produce upon their minds impressions which are
in proportion to the confidence reposed in the newspaper giving them circulation. No person of average
intelligence can read such an account in his local newspaper without being more or less influenced by its perusal. From his home paper and his associates with
whom he discusses the history of a crime he forms an
opinion which is predicated upon the assumption that
the information obtained is true, and it may be safe to
say that the person, who, after having read or heard
an account of the commission of a crime in his neighborhood, has not formed an opinion concerning the
guilt or innocence of the person accused of it, might

with propriety be challenged for incompetency. The fact that he entertains such an opinion does not, under our statute, necessarily render him incompetent to try *the* accused as a juror. His mind may be so constituted that he will be able to eliminate the information he has received, together with the impressions and opinions derived therefrom, and impartially determine the fact in issue. If he can do this he is competent; and it is the duty of the court, when a person is called to act as a juror and challenged for actual bias, to interrogate him and ascertain the condition of his mind, and from the facts elicited determine his competency. The decision must necessarily depend largely upon what he says, but it is not always a safe guide, for his answers may show and he may think he is competent, when, in fact, he is not. Nor will he be allowed to judge his own competency. While he is willing to trust himself, the court should not be willing to trust him, unless it is satisfied he can lay aside his information, impressions, and opinions, and fairly and impartially hear and decide. His intelligence, manner, tone, and bearing manifested during the examination, are elements which enter into and form a part of the evidence from which the court determines his competency; and where he is in possession of the facts, knows them to be such, and upon them has formed an opinion, the challenge for actual bias ought to be sustained, for every person accused of a crime is presumed innocent. But where a juror is in possession of the facts, and from them has formed an opinion in advance of the trial, it necessarily reverses this presumption, and compels the defendant to establish his innocence, instead of requiring the state to maintain its charge against him. There are, in an issue raised by a challenge for actual bias, many elements

connected with the examination and settlement of the
question which cannot, from their very nature, be made
or become a part of the bill of exceptions, and hence
the trial court must be presumed, in the exercise of a
sound discretion, to have done its full duty; and, having done so, its judgment should not be reviewed, unless such discretion has been abused. An examination
of the evidence offered upon the challenges submitted
fails to disclose any abuse of this discretion.

3. Robert Dear was called as a witness on behalf
of the state, and, (after testifying that he was not acquainted with the defendant, that he saw him on the
day of the homicide about two or three minutes after
it occurred, that he was running up the street with his
pistol in his hand, waving it around,) was asked, and,
over the defendant's objection and exception, was permitted to aswer the following question: "What did he
say?" To which he answered, "He said, 'I am the
toughest son of a bitch that ever struck this town.'"
T. L. Kimball, another witness on behalf of the state,
said that he was not acquainted with the defendant;
that on the afternoon of August thirteenth, eighteen
hundred and ninety-four, he was in Oakland and saw
the defendant near the depot hotel, and, being asked
what the defendant said at that time, was permitted to
answer the question, over the defendant's objection and
exception, which he did as follows: "He came up the
street waving the pistol, with his finger on the trig-
ger, and he was talking, and all I heard him say, as
he passed the hotel, was 'the toughest son of a bitch.'
That is all I heard him say." It is contended that the
aswers to these questions were inadmissible, and
tended to prejudice the minds of the jurors. The
question here presented is whether the statements of

the defendant, made after the homicide, were admissible as a part of the *res gestæ*. This species of evidence
is not admissible, as a general rule, unless it grows
out of the principal transaction, illustrates its character, and is contemporaneous with it: 1 Greenleaf on
Evidence, § 108. "*Res gestæ*," says Dr. Wharton in his
work on Criminal Evidence, § 262, "are events speaking for themselves through the instructive words and
acts of participants, not the words and acts of participants when narrating the events." The authors of the
American Decisions, in their notes to *People* v. *Vernon*,
95 Am. Dec. 49, upon this subject, say: "Where the
state of a person's mind, his sentiments, or disposition
at a certain time is the subject of inquiry, his statements and declarations at that period are admissible."
The indictment charged malice, and hence the condition of the defendant's mind at the moment of the
homicide was an issue in the case, and any evidence
which tended to show the state of his mind with reference to the deceased at that time was admissible.

In *McManus* v. *State*, 36 Ala. 285, the evidence showed
that the defendant had an altercation with the deceased, resulting in a fight, in which the defendant
threw a piece of a brick at the deceased, hitting him
on the head, from the effects of which he died. About
half an hour after the blow had been given, and after
the fight was entirely over, the defendant, with a pistol in his hand, went to the place where the deceased
was, and said that "he had come to kill the damned
old rascal " meaning the deceased. An exception having been saved to the introduction of this statement
in evidence, the court, in rendering its decision upon
the question, said: "The circuit court did not err in
admitting evidence against the prisoner of his acts,
declarations, and conduct, when he returned, a half-

hour after the blow was stricken, to the scene of the
engagement. The indictment was for murder, and
such declarations and menacing acts tended to show
the hostile feelings of the accused towards the deceased. Armed as he was with a deadly weapon, and
threatening to take the life of the man he had just
before assaulted with great violence, this, in the absence of sufficient provocation, was a circumstance for
the jury to weigh in determining whether he had not
acted with a formed design to take life. It tended to
repel the idea that the fatal blow had been struck in a
sudden transport of passion,—pending the *furor brevis,*
---which, in a proper case, will mitigate homicide to
manslaughter." In *Clampit* v. *State,* 9 Tex. App. 27, the
proof showed that the deceased, having been wounded
by the defendant, was taken to the home of a witness,
who on the succeeding night heard some one near the
house say: "I wish I had a double-barreled shotgun;
I would turn both barrels loose in that room," and
looking out saw the defendant. This evidence having
been admitted, over the defendant's objection, it was
held to be competent as tending to show malice, the
court saying: "With reference to the testimony objected to and set out in the bill of exceptions, we are
of opinion, in view of the other evidence, that the
testimony was admissible, as tending to show the malice of the defendant towards the deceased. It was
properly allowed to go to the jury for that purpose."
In these cases the statements of the accused, though
made some time after the assaults, clearly tended to
show malice towards the persons injured by them;
but in the case at bar, while the statement of the defendant may not have referred to the deceased, it was
so clearly connected with the homicide as to be, in our
judgment, admissible as a part of the *res gestœ,* and

tended to show such a state of mind at that moment
as would authorize the jury to infer the presence or
absence of malice towards the deceased.

4. Hattie Mattoon, a witness on behalf of the defendant, testified that on the day of the homicide the
defendant was drunk; and that when a witness before
the grand jury, in the examination of this case, she
was excited; whereupon the question was asked her,
"Didn't you testify in the grand jury room before the
grand jury on the third day of December, eighteen
hundred and ninety-four, that he was sober at the
time of the killing?" and she answered, "No, sir; I
did not." Question—"Didn't you testify in the grand
jury room, in the presence of the grand jurors, on
the third day of December, eighteen hundred and
ninety-four, that Brown was not drunk?" Answer—
"No, sir." The several members of the grand jury
were called as witnesses for the state, and, over the
defendant's objection, were permitted to testify that
when Hattie Mattoon was before them as a witness
she did not appear to be excited, and that she there
said the defendant was not drunk on the day of the
homicide. It is contended that the court erred in permitting the grand jurors to testify, but the foundation
having been laid by calling her attention to the time,
place, circumstances, and persons present, and her denial of the statements there made, rendered the evidence competent for the purpose of contradicting her,
and the condition of her mind when a witness before
the grand jury being a subject of inquiry, there was
no error in permitting the jurors to testify upon that
question.

28 OR.—11.

5. A witness, without being an expert, may be asked whether a person appeared excited or otherwise at a given time: Rogers on Expert Testimony, § 3.

6. W. C. Underwood, as a witness for the state, testified that he was present at the coroner's inquest held over the body of Alfred Kincaid, when Hattie Mattoon was there as a witness, and he was permitted to answer the following question: "What, if anything, did Hattie Mattoon say about stretching her testimony in order to benefit the defendant Samuel G. Brown?" to which he responded by saying: "She said that she would stretch her testimony, or color it in any way, so as to help Mr. Brown." The defendant insists that the court erred in permitting this question to be answered. The record before us does not show that any foundation was laid for asking this impeaching question, but it does not purport to contain all the evidence, and hence it must be presumed that the proper preliminary questions were asked and answered before the witness was permitted to answer it.

7. The district attorney, during the closing argument, offered to read to the jury the evidence as transcribed by the reporter, which the court denied, but permitted him, over the defendant's objection, to refresh his memory therefrom, when he remarked: "I am going to refresh my memory," at which remark the audience applauded, whereupon the court ordered the bailiffs to either keep order or clear the courtroom. The defendant assigns as error the failure of the court to instruct the jury that they should not be influenced in their verdict by any applause made by the audience in approval of the remarks of the dis-

trict attorney in his closing argument. No request was made by the defendant for such instruction, and while it is very unfortunate that the solemnity of any judicial proceeding should be interrupted by applause, and particularly so in a trial of this character, the court very promptly set its mark of disapproval thereon, and would, without doubt, have given the instruction had it been requested.

8. Exceptions were taken to the following instructions: "30. There has been some evidence to the effect that it was the defendant who sent for the deceased, and not the mother of the deceased. If you find from the evidence that such is the fact, you have a right to consider that in connection with the evidence which tends to show that the deceased was shot by the defendant soon after he reached the spot near the house where the defendant was standing when the deceased reached there, as tending to show the purpose for which the defendant sent for the deceased, and also in determining whether the act of killing was done with premeditation and deliberation." "31. There is some evidence tending to show that the defendant, a short time before the killing, and after he had some trouble with the mother of the deceased at her home where the killing is alleged to have occurred, went out in the town of Oakland and endeavored to borrow a pistol from several parties, and to one or more of them he stated that he had some difficulty with the Deardorff family, or something to that effect; and there is evidence tending to show that after he failed to borrow a pistol he purchased one and had the same loaded; this purchase was made, according to the evidence, only a short time before the killing is alleged to have occurred;

this fact, if you find it to be a fact, you have a right to consider in connection with the circumstances and the time of the alleged killing, in determining the degree of the crime under the instructions I have heretofore given you, if you find from the evidence that a crime was committed." It is contended that these instructions are in violation of section 200, Hill's Code, which provides that "In charging the jury, the court shall state to them all matters of law which it thinks necessary for their information in giving their verdict, but it shall not present the facts of the case, but shall inform the jury that they are the exclusive judges of all questions of fact." The record shows that the court in another instruction said to the jury: "You are the exclusive judges of all the facts in the case, as well as the weight of the evidence, and the credibility of the witnesses," and having so instructed it cannot be justly said that the court presented the facts of the case to the jury.

In *People v. Vasquez,* 49 Cal. 560, the trial court, in charging the jury, stated that "Testimony has been introduced before you tending to show that the defendant Vasquez, and others, were engaged in the robbery of one Snyder, at Tres Pinos; and while so engaged, and in the furtherance of the common purpose of Vasquez and his associates to accomplish this robbery, the deceased was slain by the defendant, or by some of the parties with whom he was then engaged in the robbery." An exception to the instruction having been taken, it was contended that it was an expression of the opinion of the judge as to the effect of the evidence adduced at the trial, but the court, in rendering the opinion, say: "The instruction is not subject to that objection. It does not charge the jury with respect to the weight or effect of the evidence, nor as to what facts are thereby established. An instruction is not pertinent nor in any sense proper unless given in view of the evidence, as tending or not tending to prove some fact in issue; and it could not be erroneous for the court to state to the jury correctly, as was done in this case, the state of the evidence in respect to which the instructions were given." The court in the instructions complained of did not assume even that the facts had been established. It stated that evidence had been introduced tending to show that certain facts existed, but, in the first instruction, said: "If you find from the evidence that such is the fact," and in the second, "this fact, if you find it to be a fact," thus leaving to the jury the determination of the particular facts, besides charging them generally upon the duty of ascertaining each fact in issue.

It is also contended that the court erred in refusing to give at the request of the defendant the following instructions: 1. "To constitute murder in the first degree there must be some other proof of malice than the mere proof of killing, unless the killing was effected in the commission or attempt to commit a felony; and premeditation and deliberation when necessary to constitute murder in the first degree, and it is necessary, except the killing was effected in the commission or attempt to commit a felony, must be proven by poisoning, lying in wait, or some other proof that the design was formed and matured in cool blood, and not hastily upon the occasion, and if there is a reasonable doubt in your mind that the intent was so formed you cannot find murder in the first degree." 2. "If you find from the evidence that the accused acted in the shooting from fear of great bodily injury to himself, and not from premeditated design to kill, then you cannot find the defendant guilty of murder in any

degree." 3. "If you find from the evidence that the
accused did the shooting in the belief that it was necessary to preserve his life, or to save himself from
suffering great bodily harm from the deceased, and
that he had reasonable grounds for such belief, then
the accused is justified in the killing and you cannot
find him guilty of any crime under the indictment."
4. "If you find from the evidence that the defendant
bought a pistol a short time before the killing, and
that the defendant had no trouble or quarrel with the
deceased, the fact that defendant bought said pistol is
no proof of malice." 5. "I instruct you that in this
case the evidence is not sufficient to warrant a conviction of murder in the first degree." The tenth instruction given by the court is as follows: "The law provides that there shall be some other evidence of malice than the mere proof of killing to constitute murder
in the first degree, unless the killing was effected in
the commission or attempt to commit a felony. And
deliberation and premeditation, when necessary to constitute murder in the first degree, shall be evidenced
by poisoning, lying in wait, or some other proof that
the design was formed and matured in cool blood."
It will be observed that this instruction differs from
the first request, in that it omits the words, "and not
hastily upon the occasion," but in the eighth instruction the court defined this clause by saying: "No
particular time is necessary within which to form the
design, but in order to constitute deliberation the design to do the act charged must exist in the mind of
the party charged with its commission." The court
in the second instruction defined a reasonable doubt,
and, after referring to the defendant's plea, said: "By
this plea of not guilty on the part of the defendant
the burden is placed on the State of Oregon to prove

every material allegation in this indictment to your satisfaction, beyond a reasonable doubt."

In *State* v. *Morey,* 25 Or. 241, (35 Pac. 655, 36 Pac. 245,) it was held that an instruction similar to the eighth correctly interpreted the law. From the second, eighth, and tenth instructions above set out it clearly appears that the defendent's first request has been substantially complied with. A part of the twenty-seventh instruction is as follows: "And if you find any evidence to the effect that the deceased made any demonstrations toward the defendant, from which the defendant had reasonable grounds to believe, acting as a reasonable and prudent man, that his life was in imminent danger, or that he was in danger of great bodily harm at the hands of the deceased, then the defendant would be justified in defending himself, and if necessary would have the right to take the life of the deceased to preserve his own life, or to prevent great bodily harm to himself." This instruction substantially embraces the propositions of law contained in the second and third requests. The fourth request is fully covered by the thirty-first instruction given above.

10. In considering the fifth request, it is sufficient to say that the record does not purport to contain all the evidence, and hence it must be presumed the court properly denied it. The bill of exceptions contains other alleged errors which we have examined, and having considered those presented by the defendant's brief and relied upon in the argument, we feel that he has had an impartial trial in the manner prescribed by law, and there being no error in the record the judgment is affirmed. AFFIRMED.

Argued October 16; decided November 4, 1895.

SUGAR PINE LUMBER CO. *v.* GARRETT.

[42 Pac. 129]

1. WAIVER OF OBJECTION TO DEPOSITION.—An objection that the certificate to a deposition did not show that the deposition was taken by the person to whom the commission was addressed, nor.in the official capacity designated therein, must be taken by motion to suppress before the trial is begun, otherwise it will be considered waived under the rule that objections to depositions for defects that may be remedied by retaking cannot be made at the trial.

2. SECONDARY EVIDENCE.—A letter-press or other copy of a letter is admissible to prove the contents of the original, where the latter is proven to have been mailed, postage prepaid, directed to the adverse party at his usual postoffice address, and a notice has been given to the latter to produce the original, but he had failed to do so, and there is evidence that such copy is identical with and in every respect an exact copy of the original letter.

3. NOTICE TO PRODUCE PAPERS—NONJUDICIAL DAY.—A notice to produce papers at a trial is good though given on a nonjudicial day, and, in the absence of any showing to the contrary, one day's notice may be considered sufficient.

4. COSTS ON APPEAL—DISCRETION OF COURT—CODE, ? 552.—Where a judgment is modified on appeal to the circuit court, the question of costs is in the sound discretion of that court, and its decision will be disturbed only in case of abuse.

5. MILEAGE FOR WITNESSES.—A party is entitled to recover mileage for the number of miles actually traveled by each witness within this state: *Crawford* v. *Abraham*, 2 Or. 167, approved and followed.

APPEAL from Multnomah: E. D. SHATTUCK, Judge.

This action was originally commenced in a justice's court to recover an alleged balance of two hundred and twenty-four dollars and twenty cents for certain lumber and building material sold and delivered by the Sugar Pine Door and Lumber Company to William Garrett and Company. A trial in the justice's court resulted in a judgment in favor of plaintiff for the amount demanded. From this judgment the defend-

ants appealed to the circuit court, where the cause
was tried anew, and judgment rendered in favor of
the plaintiff for the sum of one hundred and seventy-
nine dollars and ninety cents, from which the defendants appeal to this court.   AFFIRMED.

For appellants there was a brief and an oral argument by *Messrs. Granville G. Ames,* and *Emmet B. Williams.*

For respondent there was a brief and an oral argument by *Mr. Albert H. Tanner.*

1. As a defense to the action the defendants
pleaded in their answer that the Pacific Builders'
Supply Company was the agent of the plaintiff, and
had the exclusive right and authority to sell the out-
put of its mill in Multnomah County, and receive
payment therefor; that they purchased the lumber and
material in question from such company, and paid it
for the same prior to the commencement of this action. Except as to some matters of costs and disbursements, the errors assigned are directed to the
rulings of the court having reference to this question
of payment. The purchase of the lumber and the
payment to the supply company were both admitted,
and the only contested question on the trial was as
to its authority to receive the payment. It is not
claimed, as we understand the record, that the original
appointment of the supply company as plaintiff's
agent for the sale of lumber authorized it to receive
payment from purchasers; but defendants sought to
show that by the general course of dealing said company was held out to them by the plaintiff as having
such authority, and gave evidence tending to that effect. The plaintiff, to rebut this evidence, and to

show that any authority which the supply company
had to receive money for it from the defendants was
revoked prior to the payment, and that it had notified
defendants in writing not to make any payments to
the supply company, offered to read in evidence the
deposition of one E. N. Grant, its former bookkeeper,
taken at Los Angeles, California, on a commission issued in pursuance of a stipulation of the parties. The
defendants objected to the reading of this deposition,
on the ground that the commission was issued to
C. C. Davis, a notary public, while the certificate attached to the deposition showed that it was taken before Charles C. Davis, commissioner, and did not show
that he was a notary public or the party to whom the
commission was issued. This objection was overruled,
and such ruling is assigned as error. In our opinion,
the objection came too late; it did not go to the rele-
vancy or materiality of the testimony, or the competency of the witness, but to defects which could have
been remedied by retaking the deposition or by an
amendment to the certificate. In such case the objection to a deposition should be taken by a motion to
suppress, or by some other appropriate proceeding
prior to the trial. "A party should not be permitted
to lie by," says SHERWOOD, J., "and lull his adversary
into a sense of security by failure to file any motion
to suppress his depositions, thus induce him to announce himself ready for trial, and then count on
springing the question of some informality on him,
for the first time, when he offers to read those depositions in evidence": *Delventhal* v. *Jones*, 53 Mo. 460.   And
in *Doane* v. *Glenn*, 88 U. S. (21 Wall. 33), it was held
that an objection to a deposition on account of defects
which might have been obviated by retaking it cannot
be made on the trial, but must be noted when the de-

position is taken, or presented afterwards by motion
to suppress before the trial is begun. In this case the
court said: "The party taking a deposition is entitled
to have the question of its admissibility settled in advance. Good faith and due diligence are required on
both sides. When such objections, under the circumstances of this case, are withheld until the trial is in
progress, they must be regarded as waived, and the
deposition should be admitted in evidence. This is
demanded by the interests of justice. It is necessary
to prevent surprise and the sacrifice of substantial
rights. It subjects the other party to no hardship.
All that is expected of him is proper frankness." To
the same effect is Weeks on Depositions, § 440; 5 Am.
and Eng. Ency. of Law, 610, and authorities there
cited: *Howard* v. *Stilwell and Bierce Manufacturing Company*,
139 U. S, 199 (11 Sup. Ct. 500); *American Publishing Company* v. *C. E. Mayne Company*, 9 Utah, 318 (34 Pac. 247);
Hill v. *Smith*, 6 Tex. Civ. App. 312 (25 S. W. 1079). It
is true some authorities from California, cited by defendants, hold otherwise, but on principle as well as
authority we are of the opinion that the rule as above
stated is not only sound, but eminently fair and just.

2. Objection is also made to the ruling of the
court permitting the plaintiff to prove the contents of
a letter from itself to defendants by a copy thereof attached to Grant's deposition, and by a press copy in
plaintiff's letter-book, in which letter defendant's were
notified to remit direct to plaintiff, and not through
the supply company. Before this evidence was admitted, it was shown that the original had been mailed
at Grants Pass, postage prepaid, directed to the defendants at their usual postoffice address; that a notice
had been given them on January first, eighteen hun-

dred and ninety-four, the day before the trial, to produce the original; that they had failed to do so, and
that the copy attached to Grant's deposition and the
letter-press copy were identical in every respect, and
exact copies of the original letter. Under these circumstances we think the evidence was properly admitted. It was the best evidence plaintiff could produce as to the contents of the letter.

3.   The court below held that sufficient notice had
been given defendants to produce the original. There
is nothing here to indicate that such ruling was erro
neous, and we are not advised of any rule of law which
would render such a notice insufficient because it was
given on a nonjudical day, except as it might affect
the question of reasonable time.

4.   Nor was there any error in allowing plaintiff
judgment for costs. Where a judgment is modified on
appeal to the circuit court, the question of costs is in
the sound discretion of that court, and its decision will
only be disturbed here in case of the abuse of such
discretion: Hill's Code, § 552.

5.   The allowance of mileage to the witness Kinney
was in accordance with the rule announced by this
court in *Crawford* v. *Abraham,* 2 Or. 163, which, so far as
we are informed, has been uniformly approved and
followed ever since it was announced in that case.
The facts are that this witness traveled a total distance of five hundred and thirty-eight miles for the
sole purpose of testifying in this case, and he was allowed fifty-three dollars and eighty cents therefor.
There was no error in submitting to the jury the
question as to the right of the supply company to

receive payment on sales made by it for plaintiff. Its authority depended upon controverted questions of fact growing out of the manner in which it had been held out to the defendants by the plaintiff, and these questions could only be determined by the jury.

AFFIRMED.

Decided October 21, 1895.

HIBERNIAN BENEVOLENT SOCIETY *v.* KELLY.

[42 Pac. 3; 30 L. R. A. 167.]

1. WHAT IS A CHARITABLE INSTITUTION*—CONSTITUTION, ARTICLE IX, § 1--CODE, § 2732, SUBDIVISION 3.—To constitute a benevolent corporation a "charitable" one within the meaning of article IX, § 1 of the state contitution, and section 2732, Hill's Code, exempting from taxation certain property of "charitable institutions," it is not necessary that its benefits be extended to needy persons generally without regard to the relation the recipient may bear to the society or to dues or fees paid; but it is still "charitable" though it restricts its benefactions to its own members and their families.

2. WHAT PROPERTY OF CHARITABLE INSTITUTIONS IS EXEMPT FROM TAXATION—CODE, § 2732, SUBDIVISION 3.—Under subdivision 3 of section 2732, Hill's Code, which provides that "such real estate belonging to charitable institutions as shall be actually occupied for the purposes for which they were incorporated" shall be exempt from taxation, a building owned by a charitable institution, only part of which is occupied for the purposes of the institution, is not exempt, though the revenues derived from the use of the remainder of the building are devoted to the objects of the institution; under this section the test of the exemption is the use of the property itself, and not the

---

*Many examples of what have been held to be charities are cited and discussed in the following cases and the notes appended to them: *Fire Insurance Patrol* v. *Boyd* (Pa.), 1 L. R. A. 417, 6 Am. St. 745; *Coltman* v. *Grace* (N. Y.), 3 L. R. A. 147; *Bullard* v. *Chandler* (Mass.), 5 L. R. A. 106; *Pennoyer* v. *Wadhams,* 20 Or. 274, 11 L. R. A. 210; *Crearer* v. *Williams* (Ill.), 21 L. R. A. 454; *Sears* v. *Chapman* (Mass.), 35 Am. St. 502. In the case of *Philadelphia* v. *Masonic Home,* 160 Pa. St. 572, (23 L. R. A. 545, 40 Am. St. 736,) it was held that a home open only to aged and indigent members of the Masonic order is not a "purely public" charity within the meaning of those words in a constitutional provision for exempting property from taxation. For a collection of cases deciding what are not public charities, see note to *Stratton* v. *Physio-Medical Institute* (Mass.), 5 L. R. A. 87.—REPORTER.

application of the income derived from it.* In such cases the assessor should so value the property that the tax will really be paid by the unexempt part, though the assessment may run against it all.

3. ESTOPPEL AGAINST TAXATION.—A municipality is not estopped from levying a tax on certain property by the fact that it had omitted to assess such property in previous years.

4. INJUNCTION AGAINST COLLECTING TAXES.†—An injunction will not be granted to restrain the collection of a tax merely because of an inaccuracy on the assessment roll in the name of the owner, as, for example, the use of "Hibernian Benevolent Society" for "Portland Hibernian Benevolent Society": *Welch* v. *Clatsop County*, 24 Or. 457, cited and approved.

APPEAL from Multnomah: E. D. SHATTUCK, Judge.

The Portland Hibernian Benevolent Society, a corporation organized under the statute providing for the incorporation of churches, religious, benevolent, literary, and charitable institutions, brought this suit to restrain the sheriff of Multnomah County from enforcing the collection of taxes levied upon its property for state and county purposes for the year eighteen hundred and ninety-two, claiming that such property is exempt from taxation under the constitution and laws of the state. From the agreed statement of facts it appears that plaintiff was incorporated in eighteen hundred and seventy-three. Its constitution declares that "The objects of this society shall be charity and benevolence, for the purpose of contributing a weekly allowance for sickness, and the means of defraying the expenses consequent upon the death of a member, and to contribute for the above-named purposes such

* With the case of *Book Agents of the Methodist Episcopal Church South* v. *Hinton* (Tenn.), 19 L. R. A. 289, is an extended note collecting and classifying a large number of authorities on the effect on the right to exemption from taxation of using the property of a religious, charitable, or educational institution for secular business or for revenue. See also the case of *American Sunday School Union* v. *Taylor* (Pa.), 23 L. R. A. 695.—REPORTER.

† The right to an injunction to prevent collecting illegal taxes is the subject of an extensive note to *Odlin* v. *Woodruff* (Fla.), 22 L. R. A. 699.—REPORTER.

sums as a majority of the members may be pleased to contribute." It is further provided by its constitution and bylaws that "every Irishman, or the son of an Irishman, or a son of a member of the society," between the ages of eighteen and forty-five years, "of good moral character, possessed of reputable means of support, and free from all infirmities that might render him burdensome to the society," and a resident of the City of Portland for sixty days preceding his application, may, upon first being duly elected, "become a member thereof by signing the constitution and paying an initiation fee of five dollars." Every person who has been a member of the society for six months, and whose name is on the "list of active members," is entitled, in case of sickness, "to receive such sum as the society may direct, not to exceed seven dollars per week, for three months in succession," provided he furnishes a doctor's certificate that through sickness he is confined to his bed, and that he has not been instrumental in causing his sickness. In addition to this allowance, the society may extend benevolence to sick members as it may deem necessary, to be decided by a two thirds' vote of the members present at any regular meeting. On the death of a member in good standing a sum of money not less than twenty-five dollars nor more than seventy-five dollars is to be paid for funeral expenses, and his widow or orphans receive twenty-five dollars, and, if need be, in three months thereafter, a like sum. Upon the death of his wife, a member is entitled to receive the sum of forty dollars for funeral expenses. If there is no money in the treasury for sick or funeral expenses when required, the board of directors is authorized to levy a special tax on the members for that purpose, and no other. It is provided that no money shall be drawn from the treasury for any but benevolent purposes, and none of the income or revenue of the society is to be used for any purpose other than as set out in the constitution, except for the payment of principal and interest on its indebtedness, and the purchase and improvement of real estate. Provision is also made for the appointment of a committee of three members, whose duty it shall be, when notified of the illness of a member, to visit him as often as convenient, and report from time to time to the board of managers the condition of the member, lest sick dues might be drawn from the treasury contrary to the constitution. The property assessed consists of lot one, block one hundred and seventy-seven, in the City of Portland, upon which is erected a three-story brick building, the lower story of which is rented for stores, the second story for offices, (except one room which is occupied by the plaintiff,) and the third story for a public hall, the revenue derived from such rental being exclusively devoted to the objects and purposes of the society. Upon these facts the court below found that plaintiff was a charitable institution within the meaning of the exemption law, and that the property in question was actually occupied by the plaintiff for the purposes for which it was incorporated, although the greater part of the building was leased to sundry persons to be used for purposes wholly unconnected with the society, and entered a decree enjoining the collection of the tax. From this decree the defendant appeals.   REVERSED.

For appellant there was an oral argument by *Mr. John H. Hall,* and a brief by *Mr. Hall* and *Mr. Wilson T. Hume,* district attorney, to this effect.

Plaintiff is not a charitable institution within the meaning of section 1, article IX of the constitution of Oregon, or of subdivision 3 of section 2732 of Hill's Code. A charitable institution within the meaning of the law is held to mean a public charity—one whose benefits are extended to needy persons generally without regard to their relation to the members of the society or to the fees paid: 2 Am. and Eng. Ency. of Law, 174; *City of Bangor* v. *Rising Virtue Lodge, Number Ten, Free and Accepted Masons*, 73 Me. 429 (40 Am. Rep. 369); *Morning Star Lodge* v. *Hayship*, 23 Ohio St. 144; *Gorman* v. *Russell*, 14 Cal. 535; *Donohugh's Appeal*, 86 Pa. St. 306; *Delaware County Institute of Science* v. *Delaware County*, 94 Pa. St. 163; *State* v. *City of Indianapolis*, 69 Ind. 375 (35 Am. Rep. 223); *Babb* v. *Reed*, 5 Rawle (Pa.), 158 (28 Am. Dec. 650).

Plaintiff admits in the pleadings that it is the owner of the property assessed; that the assessment does not exceed the value thereof, and that plaintiff occupies but one room in the large three-story brick building which constitutes the improvements thereon, and also admit by their stipulation that the remainder of the building is rented out for stores, offices, and public halls; that the proceeds arising therefrom are turned into its treasury and used for the benefit of the members only. It also appears from article II of the constitution in evidence that only "Irishmen, or sons of Irishmen, of good moral character, free from all infirmities that might render them burdensome to the society, and possessed of some known reputable means of support," are eligible to become members and share in its benevolence, and even he must be balloted upon, and, if elected, must pay an initiation fee of five dollars, and if taken sick must wait six months ere he

can obtain relief from the society. This is merely a
plan of insurance or a species of mutual benefit societies wherein the member, while in good health and possessed of worldly goods, seeks to provide himself
against reverses and adversities that may befall him
in after life, by, in common with others, providing a
fund, through initiation fees, dues, etc., upon which to
draw when the chilling blasts of penury, coupled with
disease and old age, assail him. But this cannot interest those who were so unfortunate as not to be born
an "Irishman, or a son of an Irishman," because they
are excluded from entering this society of benevolence
and participating in its bounty, and might sit upon
the steps of plaintiff's massive three-story brick building "crying for bread" and would "receive a stone,"
for by the constitution of the plaintiff no charity could
be disbursed to them and they would have to seek alms
elsewhere. Plaintiff does not even represent one entire class of persons; in the first place they must be
Irishmen or sons of Irishmen, and even were a person
fortunate enough to be in one of these categories, he
must still be able-bodied and able to earn his living,
and also must be a capitalist to some extent and satisfy the plaintiff that he is not likely to be in need of
charity. And though he possess all these, he must
still run the gauntlet of being rejected if five members of plaintiff's society should blackball him. So it
appears that not only are the poor and needy, the
lame, the halt, the sick, and the blind excluded, but
also the unpopular among their brethren are also
forbidden to enter and enjoy the benevolence of plaintiff. This is not charity within the meaning of our
constitution. This does not relieve the public of the
burden of caring for the needy poor, which is the consideration upon which charitable societies are exempted

from taxation; that the state is relieved from the burden and expense of caring for the needy poor within
her borders by virtue of these benevolent societies taking them in hand and supplying their wants and ne-
cessities. But in order that a society may be deemed
charitable it must be a public charity; that is, must
extend charity to all upon the same conditions, or all
of a certain class, as all of the needy poor of a city
or town or county, or to all of a sex or color, etc.
These are the only kinds of classes that are recognized by the courts. The Odd Fellows, Masons,
Knights of Pythias, and many other secret organiza-
tions are charitable to their members, but this is not a
charity within the meaning of the word as used in the
constitution. Their doors are closed against all the
world except their own members, whom they choose
by ballot, and no good reason can be given why they
should be exempted from bearing their proportion of
the public burden, instead of compelling their fellow
man to assume a heavier burden and higher tax than
he would have to bear were they not exempted.

We also contend that where a portion of a building is used for commercial purposes, that is, rented or
leased to other parties for gain, although the entire
proceeds may be used for the purposes for which the
society was organized, it cannot be exempted from
taxation as property devoted to a charitable use: *Trustees of Methodist Episcopal Church* v. *Ellis,* 38 Ind. 3; *Orr* v.
Baker, 4 Ind. 86; *American Sunday School Union* v. *Taylor,*
161 Penn. 307 (23 L. R. A. 695); *Pierce* v. *Cambridge,*
2 Cush. (Mass.), 611; *Proprietors of the South Congregational
Meeting-house in Lowell* v. *City of Lowell,* 1 Metc. 538; *Old
South Society* v. *Boston,* 127 Mass. 378; *County Commissioners of Frederick County* v. *Sisters of Charity of St. Joseph,*
48 Md. 34; *The Appeal Tax Court of Baltimore City* v. *The*

Grand Lodge of Ancient Free and Accepted Masons of Mary-land, 50 Md. 421; *The Appeal Tax Court of Baltimore City* v. *St. Peter's Academy*, 50 Md. 321; *Wyman* v. *City of St. Louis*, 17 Mo. 335; *Young Men's Christian Association of New York* v. *Mayor of New York*, 113 N. Y. 187; *The Connecticut Spiritualist Camp-meeting Association* v. *The Town of East Lyme*, 54 Conn. 152; *Cincinnati College* v. *State*, 19 Ohio, 113.

If your honorable court should determine that plaintiff's corporation is a charitable institution within the meaning of the law, we still most earnestly contend that it is not exempted from taxation by the laws of the state. The history of the exemption law (section 2732, Hill's Code,) under which plaintiff claims, is, that it was passed in exactly the same form as it now stands in eighteen hundred and fifty-four by the territorial legislature, (see section 4, title I, chapter I, page 431, Statutes of Oregon of 1855,) which legislature was working under the organic laws of Oregon of eighteen hundred and forty-five, which placed no limitations upon the legislature in exempting property from taxation. Said section reads as follows: "Section 4. The following property shall be exempt from taxation   *   *   *.   The personal property of all literary, benevolent, charitable, and scientific institutions, incorporated within this territory, and such real estate belonging to such institutions as shall be actually occupied for the purposes for which they were incorporated." In eighteen hundred and fifty-nine the present constitution of the state was adopted by the people of the state, which contains the following clause relating to the power of the legislature in the exemption of property from taxation: "Section 1, article IX. The legislative assembly shall provide by law for such uniform and equal rate

of assessment and taxation as shall secure a just valuation for taxation of all property, both real and personal, excepting such only for municipal, educational,
literary, scientific, religious, or charitable purposes as
may be specially exempted by law." In the compilation of the laws of Oregon in eighteen hundred and
sixty-four, Hon. M. P. Deady copied the act of eighteen hundred and fifty-four, above quoted, *verbatim,* with
the exception that without apparent authority he eliminated the word "territory" and substituted the word
"state" therefor. See section 4, title I, chapter LIII,
General Laws of Oregon, 1845–1864. The same act
was again copied into the statutes of eighteen hundred and seventy-two, and again in Hill's Code in
eighteen hundred and eighty-seven.

Our contention is: that the terms of the section of
the constitution above cited require that in order that
a charitable or religious society may be exempted from
taxation in this state it must apply to the sovereign,
or taxing power, *i. e.* the legislature, and obtain the
passage of a special act exempting it alone from taxation. This was the evident intention of the framers
of the constitution, and was inserted to correct a then
existing evil. The legislative assembly of eighteen
hundred and fifty-four had already passed a general
act exempting such institutions from taxation, which
is the same law that is in force now, never having
been reënacted or amended in any way, and it was to
remedy this that the above clause of the constitution
was framed. If the framers of the constitution had intended that the therein enumerated institutions should
be exempted by a general law such as was then in
force, then the word "specially" has no office or meaning in the clause, for, as the court will observe, if the
word "specially" is eliminated therefrom, then the con-

struction which counsel for respondent claims should be put upon this section would be the only logical one; but in construing statutes, and particularly a constitution, every word should be given an office and a meaning. They are not presumed to have been inserted for mere euphony, and must be presumed to have been employed in their natural and ordinary meaning: Cooley's Constitutional Limitations (4th ed.), 71–72; *District Township of the City of Dubuque* v. *City of Dubuque*, 7 Iowa, 275.

As before stated, the present law, unchanged, was in force at the time of the meeting of the constitutional convention and had been tried for three years, and the framers thereof, perceiving the evil and abuse that was sure to grow out of the then existing system, wisely set about to remedy the evil by requiring the societies, benevolent or otherwise, to apply to the legislative assembly for their exemption. Under our statute there is no person to whom the people have delegated the right or authority to say what is or what is not a charitable society. The assessor may assume it, but he does so without authority of law. It seems very clear to us that the evil was plain, and the remedy provided by the constitution was the proper one, and time has amply justified the fears of the constitutional framers, for in Multnomah County alone there is exempted each year by the assessor over two million dollars' worth of property belonging to these various churches and societies, which entirely escape the burden of taxation. There cannot be any question that these churches and other societies cannot claim as exempt property which they rent out for stores and other purposes, as in the case here, at bar, although they may use the proceeds to advance the purposes of the society. Subdivision 4 of section 27: 2, Hill's Code, expressly provides that the property of churches so used shall be taxed. Then by what process of reasoning can plaintiff contend that an exclusive and limited mutual benefit society can construct great brick buildings in the business centers of the City of Portland, rent the same for stores, saloons, etc., and then refuse to pay their portion of the public burden? The churches, to whom this is denied, do have the merit of offering salvation to every penitent sinner and ask all to come and enjoy the benefit of religious services, without regard to "race, color, or previous condition of servitude."

It is contended that plaintiff corporation is not properly assessed upon the tax roll for the reason that a part of its corporate title has been omitted; that is, the word "Portland" is omitted from the corporate name on said roll, and therefore the assessment is void for the reason that the property is not assessed to the "owner thereof." An error in listing the tax does not destroy the lien nor relieve the owner from paying them. Persons who own land are chargeable with knowledge that it is liable to taxation, and if they neglect to pay what they know it is their duty to pay, they cannot escape liability on the ground of some error or inaccuracy in naming the owner: *Eads v. Retherford,* 114 Ind. 273 (5 Am. St. Rep. 611); *Noble* v. *City of Indianapolis,* 16 Ind. 506.

There is a distinction between the cases of where a tax collector is attempting to sell and convey the title of property in case of an assessment under the wrong name and a case where a party comes in and asks to be relieved from paying any tax upon his property for the reason of some informality in the manner of assessment; while in the former case it is presumed that had the property been assessed to him in his proper name he would have paid the taxes, and consequently it would be unjust either to add additional costs to the tax or to deprive him of his property for the nonpayment of it; but in the latter case he comes into court admitting that he owns the identical property assessed and knowing it to be subject to taxation, and that properly and equitably it should bear its just proportion of the public burden, and asks the court not only to relieve him of the additional costs and expenses, but also to relieve him of the entire tax which is justly due and owing to the government. Our contention is that plaintiff must, before it can maintain this suit, pay or offer to pay the tax that it concedes is justly due, regardless of any mere informality in the assessment, for "he who seeks equity must first do equity." Plaintiff concedes that it is the owner of lot one in block one hundred and seventy-seven, in the City of Portland, Multnomah County, Oregon; that the tax thereon has not been paid, and unless they are exempted from taxation by virtue of being a benevolent society, before they can enjoin the collection of this tax, they must pay or offer to pay the amount of taxes which was assessed against said property: *Dundee Trust Investment Company* v. *Parrish,* 24 Fed. 197; *Welch* v. *Clatsop County,* 24 Or. 457 (33 Pac. 934); *National Bank* v. *Kimball,* 103 U. S. 733; *Albuquerque Bank* v. *Persea,* 147 U. S. 87; *Hunburg* v. *Palmer,* 7 Sawy. 355.

For respondents there was a brief by *Messrs. Gearin, Silvestone, Murphy and Brodie,* and an oral argument by *Mr. John M. Gearin,* to this effect.

The plaintiff is clearly a charitable institution and as such exempt from taxation under article IX, section

1 of the state constitution, as carried out by section 2732 of the Code. A charity has been often defined, and, for illustration, we append a few definitions: "A charity is a gift to a general public use, which extends to the rich as well as to the poor. * * * All property held for public purposes is held as a charitable use in the legal sense of the term charity": *Perin* v. *Carey,* 65 U. S. (24 How.), 465. Again, the supreme court of Massachusetts, in *Jackson* v. *Phillips,* 14 Allen, 556, says: "A charity, in the legal sense, may be more fully defined as a gift to be applied consistently with existing laws for the benefit of an indefinite number of persons, either by bringing their minds or hearts under the influence of education or religion, by relieving their bodies from disease, suffering, or constraint, by assisting them to establish themselves in life, or by erecting or maintaining public buildings or works or otherwise lessening the burdens of government. It is immaterial whether the purpose is called charitable in the gift itself, if it is so described as to show that it is charitable in its nature." Viewed in the light of these definitions, the articles of incorporation of plaintiff clearly describe a charitable association. The second section of the articles of incorporation reads: "The objects of this society shall be the exercise of benevolence and charity, namely, to relieve the distressed, support the afflicted, attend upon the sick, bury the dead, and create a fund out of and with which such kindly and humane service may be performed." The bylaws, too, show that plaintiff is carrying out these objects, and in order the more effectively to accomplish this the building in question was erected by it. It is no answer to this to say that the beneficiaries of the charity at present must be

members of the society or their widows. No charity
can be universal and be effective. To be practical in
its workings and benefits its scope must be limited to
the field capable of being covered with the funds at
its command. And so this plaintiff for the present restricts its benefits to its members and their immediate
dependents — its available funds not permitting it to
practically extend its charity further. But its constitution does not restrict it to this. It may broaden its
field of charitable endeavor as its means increase, and
to enable it so to do and thereby become a general
and public benefit, it asks to be relieved from the burden of taxation. It makes nothing itself, nor do its
members — "it is free from the stain or taint of every
consideration that is personal, private, or selfish."

The only question that is worthy of any consideration is whether the land is actually occupied for the
purposes for which the society was incorporated. In
determining this question an examination of paragraph 4 of section 2732, Hill's Code, becomes pertinent. The exception in paragraph 4, "but any part
of any building, being a house of public worship,
which shall be kept or used as a store or shop, or
for any other purpose, except for public worship or
for schools, shall be taxed," etc., indicates by implication at least, and certainly clearly enough, that such
exception was not contemplated to apply to the property described in. paragraph 3; if the legislature intended to say that any property which was owned by
a charitable institution which was occupied as a store
or shop, but the income from which went into the
fund to be used for charitable purposes, should not
be exempt from taxation, they would have said so.
Their failure to say so in paragraph 3, and so pro-
nouncedly expressing it in paragraph 4 immediately

following, indicates that the exception‑was only to apply to paragraph 4, and was not intended to be considered with reference to paragraph 3. The phrase "actually occupied" must be construed in a reasonable light; the actual occupancy for a charitable purpose might reasonably be a constructive occupancy by a tenant, the rent derived from which occupancy went to carry on the business of the society and accom‑ plish the charity intended by it. The refinement of reasoning which distinguishes between the actual oc‑ cupation by the society itself, and the use of the pro‑ ceeds, where the occupation is constructive, should not have any weight in a court of equity, when the de‑ mand made by the society is not for its own advan‑ tage, but for the benefit of its beneficiaries.

Even if there could be any question as to whether plaintiff is a charitable institution, or whether it was in the actual occupation of this property, the state is now estopped from raising them, for during a long series of years the county assessors have uniformly omitted to assess this property. This is a contempo‑ raneous construction of the statute that ought to have great weight, and, if continued for a long time, will have the effect of positive law: *Westbrook* v. *Miller,* 56 Mich. 151; *Scanlan* v. *Childs,* 33 Wis. 666; *United States* v. *Union Pacific Railroad Company,* 37 Fed. 555.

The assessment is void for the mistake in the name of the owner on the assessment roll.. The corporate name of the plaintiff is "Portland Hibernian Benevo‑ lent Society," while the assessment is against "Hiber‑ nian Benevolent Society." Section 2770, Hill's Code, requires the assessor to set down in separate columns * * * the names of all the taxable persons in his county. Under the application of this very section by our home courts the assessment is void: *Marx* v. *Han‑*

thorn, 30 Fed. 584; S. C. 148 U. S. 172; *Dowell* v. *City of Portland,* 13 Or. 248.   See also *State* v. *Stoss,* 87 Ala. 119 (6 So. 309); *People* v. *Whipple,* 47 Cal. 592; *Hawthorne* v. *East Portland,* 13 Or. 271; *Dunn* v. *Winston,* 31 Miss. 135; *Abbott* v. *Mindenbaum,* 42 Me. 162; *Hume* v. *Wainscott,* 46 Mo. 145; *People* v. *Castro,* 39 Cal. 65; *Heanelman* v. *Steiner.* 38 Cal. 175; *Briddleman* v. *Brooks,* 28 Cal. 72; *Kelsy* v. *Abbott,* 13 Cal. 609; *Yanda* v. *Whalen,* 9 Texas, 408; *Hamilton* v. *Fond du Lac,* 25 Wis. 486; *Mayer* v. *Trubee,* 22 Atl. 424; Cooley on Taxation, 277, 278 (90 Cal. 444).   Applying the law announced in the foregoing decisions to the present case, one cannot escape the conclusion that here there has been no assessment.   Under the heading of "Name of taxpayer," we find the name of "Hibernian Benev. Society," and nothing else.   This is not the name of plaintiff.   Granting to the word "Benev." all that can be claimed for it—that it must be read "Benevolent," we have then, as the name of taxpayer, "Hibernian Benevolent Society."   This does not describe plaintiff, whose corporate name is "Portland Hibernian Benevolent Society."   A corporation can have but one name.   It acts by its corporate name alone.   Not only is this name "Hibernian Benevolent Society" not the name of plaintiff, but it is misleading. No one would ever find it looking through the indices for the "Portland Hibernian Benevolent Society." The name "Portland" is an essential part of plaintiff's corporate name.   It identifies it, as the names "Northern," "Southern," "Union," "Canadian," etc., designate the different Pacific railroads by these names.   It would not be claimed that an assessment of property to the "Pacific Railway" would be a good assessment of the property of the "Southern Pacific Railway."   There may be many "Hibernian Benevolent" societies as there are many Pacific rail-

ways, and an assessment to be valid must specify
which particular one is intended.

Opinion by MR. CHIEF JUSTICE BEAN.

Article IX, section 1 of the state constitution directs
that "The legislative assembly shall provide by law
for uniform and equal rate of assessment and taxation;
and shall prescribe such regulations as shall secure a
just valuation for taxation of all property, both real
and personal, excepting such only for municipal, educational, literary, scientific, religious, or charitable purposes as may be specially exempted by law." Under
this provision no property can be relieved from taxation except such as may be in use for some of the
purposes enumerated therein, and then only to the extent specially permitted by legislative enactment. The
constitution itself does not exempt any property from
taxation, and it authorizes the legislature to do so
"only for municipal, educational, literary, scientific,
religious, or charitable purposes." It follows, then,
that before property can be exempted from taxation
it must not only be used for some of the purposes
specified in the constitution, but the exemption must
be specially authorized by law. Now, the statute which
undertakes to exempt property from taxation, and by
which the questions presented in this case must be
solved, was passed by the territorial legislature in
eighteen hundred and fifty-four, and, so far as not inconsistent with the constitution, was continued in force
by section 7, article XVIII of that instrument, and is
now section 2732 of Hill's Code. By subdivision 3 of
this section it is provided that "The personal property of all literary, benevolent, charitable, and scientific institutions, incorporated within this state, and

such real estate belonging to such institutions as shall
be actually occupied for the purposes for which they
were incorporated," shall be exempt from taxation.
Under these constitutional and statutory provisions it
is manifest that real property, to be exempt from taxation, must belong to some incorporated literary, benevolent, charitable, or scientific institution, and must be
actually occupied for literary, benevolent, charitable,
or scientific purposes.

1. The contention for the defendant is that the
real property upon which the tax in question was laid
is not exempt from taxation for the reason, *first,* that
plaintiff is not a charitable institution within the meaning of the law, because its benefits are confined to its
own members and their families; and, *second,* that the
property assessed is not actually occupied for the purposes for which it was incorporated. Upon the first
point the argument of his counsel is that a charitable
institution, within the meaning of the exemption law,
is one whose benefits are extended to the public generally, or some indefinite portion thereof, without regard to the relation the recipient may bear to the
members of the particular organization or society, or
to the fees or dues paid. But the principal authorities
relied upon by him in support of this position were
determinations of controversies arising under constitutional or legislative enactments exempting from taxation property belonging to institutions devoted to
"purely public charity," which it is held does not include charitable institutions whose benevolence is confined to their own members or persons having some
particular relationship to such members: *Philadelphia* v.
Masonic Home of Pennsylvania, 160 Pa. St. 572 (23 L. R. A.
545, 28 Atl. 954, 40 Am. St. Rep. 736); *Swift's Execu-*

tors v. *Beneficial Society of Easton,* 73 Pa. St. 362; *Delaware County Institute of Science* v. *Delaware County,* 94 Pa. St. 163; *Donohugh's Appeal,* 86 Pa. St. 306; *Mitchell* v. *Treasurer of Franklin County,* 25 Ohio St. 144; *Babb* v. *Reed,* 5 Rawle, 150; *Burd Orphan Asylum* v. *School District of Upper Darby,* 90 Pa. St. 21; *County of Hennepin* v. *Brotherhood of Gethsemane,* 27 Minn. 460 (38 Am. Rep. 298, 8 N. W. 595). But under constitutional or legislative provisions, which, like ours, provide for the exemption of certain property belonging to "charitable institutions," and used for charitable purposes, it is believed that such an institution is entitled to the benefit of the exemption, although its benefactions are confined to its own members or their families. Thus, in *City of Indianapolis* v. *Grand Master,* 25 Ind. 518, it is held that an institution which extends charity to its own members only is a charitable institution within the meaning of the law exempting such institutions from taxation, the court saying: "The third paragraph of the answer presents the question whether that is a charitable institution, in the sense of the statute, which confines its benefactions to those who have become members of the order, having paid the fees commonly required for that purpose? We think that this question must be answered in the affirmative. It is not essential to charity that it shall be universal. That an institution limits the dispensation of its blessings to one sex, or to the inhabitants of a particular city or district, or to the membership of a particular religious or secular organization, does not, we think, deprive it either in legal or popular apprehension of the character of a charitable institution. If that only be charity which relieves human want, without discriminating among those who need relief, then, indeed, it is a rarer virtue than has been supposed. And if one organization may confine itself to a sex, or church, or city, why not to a given fraternity? So narrow a definition of charity as the third paragraph presupposes is not, that we are aware of, ever attached to it, and we are not at liberty to circumscribe the effect of the statute, and defeat its intention, by affixing to its terms an unusually limited meaning." So also in *City of Petersburg* v. *Petersburg Benevolent Mechanics' Association,* 78 Va. 431, it was held that an association which applies its revenues to the payment of current expenses, and to the relief of its indigent members and the families of such as have died in need, was a charitable institution. "These are charitable purposes," says the court, "and the relief afforded is none the less charity because confined to members of the association and families of deceased members. It is not essential to charity that it shall be universal." And, again, in *Book Agents of the Methodist Episcopal Church South* v. *Hinton,* 92 Tenn. 188, (19 L. R. A. 289, 21 S. W. 321,) it was held that a corporation created as an arm or agency of the Methodist Church and charged with the duty of manufacturing and distributing books, periodicals, etc., in the interest and under the auspices of the church, and thereby raising a fund with which to support its worn-out preachers and their families, is a religious and charitable institution within the meaning of the provision of the constitution exempting such institutions from taxation. From an examination of this question, and all the authorites within our reach bearing upon it, we take the result to be that an institution organized for benevolent and charitable purposes, free from any element of private or corporate gain, and which devotes its entire revenue to the payment of current expenses and the relief of the poor and needy, is a charitable institution within the meaning of the law, although it may confine its benefits primarily to its own members and their families.

2. But whether the plaintiff is such an institution or not, we are clear the property in question is not exempt from taxation, for the reason that it is not actually occupied for charitable purposes. Subdivision 3 of section 2732, Hill's Code, under which the exemption is claimed, exempts only such real property belonging to incorporated literary, benevolent, charitable, or scientific institutions as shall be actually occupied for the purposes for which they were incorporated. It does not exempt from taxation the enumerated institutions as such, or real estate simply because it belongs to such institutions, or even because it is used for literary, scientific, charitable, or benevolent purposes, but it expressly confines the right of exemption to such real estate only belonging to them as shall be actually occupied in a particular manner and for a specified purpose, and this right, therefore, clearly cannot be extended to property occupied and used for other and different purposes, although the revenue derived from its use is devoted exclusively to the objects for which the institution was established. It is the actual occupancy of the property which determines its right to exemption, and not the use made of its proceeds. The plain and obvious meaning of the statute is that only the real estate actually occupied and in use by these different institutions for the purposes for which they were organized, shall be exempt from taxation. While so occupied and used, it does not come in competition with the property of other owners, and the purpose for which it is used was supposed by the legislature to be a sufficient benefit to

the public to justify its exemption from the burdens
of taxation imposed upon other property. But when
such property is used for the purpose of accumulating
money, the law imposes upon it the same burden of
taxation as it imposes upon other property similarly
situated. The statute does not undertake to discrimi-
nate between the uses which different societies or individuals will make of the proceeds of their business,
and determine for that reason that one shall be taxed
and the other not. It deals with the property as it
finds it, and not with what may be done with its proceeds in the future. Upon this question the authorities are practically unanimous under similar statutory
provisions: *City of Indianapolis* v. *Grand Master*, 25 Ind.
518; *Presbyterian Theological Seminary* v. *People*, 101 Ill. 578;
Washburn College v. *Commissioners of Shawnee County*, 8 Kan.
344; *Detroit Young Men's Society* v. *Mayor of Detroit*, 3 Mich.
172; *Cincinnati College* v. *State*, 19 Ohio, 110; *Cleveland
Library Association* v. *Pelton*, 36 Ohio St. 253; *First Methodist Episcopal Church* v. *City of Chicago*, 26 Ill. 482; *City of
New Orleans* v. *St. Patrick's Hall Association*, 28 La. Ann.
512; *City of New Orleans* v. *St. Anna's Asylum*, 31 La. Ann.
293; *Mayor of Baltimore* v. *Grand Lodge*, 60 Md. 280; *County
Commissioners of Frederick County* v. *Sisters of Charity of St.
Joseph*, 48 Md. 34; *Appeal Tax Court* v. *Grand Lodge*, 50
Md. 429; *Redemptorists* v. *County Commissioners of Howard
County*, 50 Md. 449; *Salem Lyceum* v. *City of Salem*, 154
Mass. 15 (27 N. E. 672); *Chapel of the Good Shepherd* v.
Boston, 120 Mass. 212; *Mulroy* v. *Churchman*, 52 Iowa, 238
(3 N. W. 72); *Orr* v. *Baker*, 4 Ind. 86; *Trustees of Phil-
lips' Exeter Academy* v. *Exeter*, 58 N. H. 306 (42 Am. Rep.
589); *Morris* v. *Lone Star Chapter*, 68 Texas, 698 (5 S. W.
519); *Proprietors of the South Congregational Meeting-house in
Lowell* v. *City of Lowell*, 1 Metc. (Mass.), 538; *Wyman* v.
City of St. Louis, 17 Mo. 336; *State* v. *Ross*, 24 N. J. Law,

498; *Massenburg* v. *Grand Lodge,* 81 Ga. 212 (7 S. E. 636); *Fort Des Moines Lodge,* v. *County of Polk,* 56 Iowa, 34 (8 N. W. 687). See also notes to *City of Petersburg* v. *Petersburg Benevolent Mechanics' Association,* 8 Am. and Eng. Corp. Cas. 488, and *Book Agents of the Methodist Episcopal Church South* v. *Hinton,* 92 Tenn. 188 (19 L. R. A. 289, 21 S. W. 321).

It is so manifestly just that all property shall bear its due proportion of the expenses of government that laws granting exemption from taxation are always strictly construed, and before such exemption can be admitted, the intent of the legislature to confer it must be clear beyond a reasonable doubt. Thus, it is held that laws exempting from taxation "houses of religious worship," or "buildings erected and used for religious worship," or "property used for religious purposes," etc., do not exempt a parsonage erected by a religious society for the use of its minister, although occupied by him free of rent and built on grounds which would otherwise be exempt: *State* v. *Axtell,* 41 N. J. Law, 117; *County of Hennepin* v. *Grace,* 27 Minn. 503 (8 N. W. 761); *Ramsey County* v. *Church of the Good Shepherd,* 45 Minn. 229 (11 L. R. A. 175, 47 N. W. 783); *Third Congregational Society* v. *Springfield,* 147 Mass. 396 (18 N. E. 68); *Wardens of St. Mark's* v. *Mayor of Brunswick,* 78 Ga. 541 (3 S. E. 561); *Gerke* v. *Purcell,* 25 Ohio St. 229; *Trustees of the Methodist Episcopal Church* v. *Ellis,* 38 Ind. 3; *Vail* v. *Beach,* 10 Kan. 214. And a building belonging to the Young Men's Christian Association, which contains above the basement, in which are the gymnasium, bowling-alley, and bathroom, twenty-two rooms, only one of which is devoted to public worship, was held not exempt under a law exempting "every building used exclusively for public worship": *Young Men's Christian Association of New York* v. *Mayor of*

New York, 113 N. Y. 187 (21 N. E. 86). The constitution
of this state requires an equal and uniform rate of
assessment and taxation of all property, excepting
"such only for municipal, educational, literary, scientific, religious, or charitable purposes as may be specially exempted by law." Taxation is, therefore, the
rule: exemption, the exception; and nothing can be
held to be exempt by implication. It is only such
property used for the purposes specified in the constitution as the legislature may specially exempt which
can escape taxation. Exemption is not a matter of
right, but a pure matter of grace; and every person
or corporation claiming that his or its property, or
any part thereof, is exempt must be able to show some
clear constitutional or legislative provision to that
effect. The legislature in its wisdom has provided
that of the real property belonging to literary, benevolent, charitable, or scientific institutions incorporated
within this state, such only shall be exempt from
taxation as shall be actually occupied for the purposes for which they were incorporated, and under all
the rules for the construction of exemption laws this
cannot be held to include real property which is occupied for other purposes, although the revenues received therefrom may be used for the purposes of the
corporation. Some of the authorities cited go to the
extent of holding that when a portion only of a building belonging to such an institution is occupied for
the purposes for which it was incorporated, and the
remainder is occupied by tenants paying rent, the entire building is liable to taxation, but the general
tenor of the authorities, and no doubt the better rule,
is that in such cases the assessor, in estimating the
value of the property, should make a proper allowance for the portion of the building occupied by the

society, so that the tax levied will be laid only upon the value of that which is not exempt, though the property may be assessed as a whole.

3. It is insisted by the plaintiff that the state is estopped from levying the tax in question for the reason that, while it has owned the property assessed since eighteen hundred and seventy-seven, no attempt was made to assess it until the year eighteen hundred and ninety, and that, relying upon that fact, it borrowed in that year thirty-three thousand dollars on a mortgage, to enable it to erect the building now on the premises, and stipulated and agreed to pay the taxes on such mortgage. But the neglect or omission of the proper officers to assess the property cannot control the duty imposed by law upon their successors, or affect the legal construction of the statute under which its exemption from taxation is claimed: *Vicksburg Railroad Company* v. *Dennis*, 116 U. S. 665 (6 Sup. Ct. 625). The case of *State* v. *Addison*, 2 S. C. 499, relied upon by plaintiff, is not in point. That was a proceeding to enforce a municipal tax. The city had by ordinance in seventeen hundred and ninety-three exempted all and every religious and charitable society from the payment of any city tax, and the city council for more than three quarters of a century had included the relators as among the societies thus exempted, and the court held that the action of the city council for so long a time would be received as the proper interpretation of their own enactment so long as it remained in force.

4. Again, it is claimed that because the name appearing on the assessment roll as the owner of the property is "Hibernian Benevolent Society," and not

the "Portland Benevolent Hibernian Society,"—the real owner,—the assessment is void, and should be enjoined. We understand the rule to be that a court of equity will not interfere by injunction to restrain the collection of a tax merely because of the alleged illegality or irregularity appearing upon the face of the assessment, but will leave the party to his remedy at law: 1 High on Injunctions, § 491; *Odlin* v. *Woodruff*, 31 Fla. 160 (22 L. R. A. 699 and note, 12 So. 227). "In view of the authorities," says LORD, C. J., "the considerations which influence a court of equity to restrain the collection of a tax are confined to cases where the tax itself is not authorized, or, if it is, that such tax is assessed upon property not subject to taxation, or that the persons imposing it were without authority in the premises, or that they have proceeded fraudulently": *Welch* v. *Clatsop County*, 24 Or. 457 (33 Pac. 934). It follows that the decree of the court below must be reversed and the complaint dismissed.

REVERSED.

Decided November 18, 1895.

SPRINKLE *v.* WALLACE.
[42 Pac. 487.]

ASSIGNMENT FOR CREDITORS—JURISDICTION OF EQUITY.—An assignor for creditors who has compounded and settled with his creditors cannot maintain a suit in equity against his assignee to compel a final accounting, but must proceed in the assignment matter for the accomplishment of such purpose. Sections 3173–3187, Hill's Code, prescribe a complete procedure for the administration and settlement of assigned estates, and must be considered a substitute for the equity power to compel the execution and performance of a trust in such matters.

Appeal from Gilliam: W. L. BRADSHAW, Judge.

This is in effect a suit for an accounting. On the thirty-first day of March, eighteen hundred and eighty-eight, D. S. Sprinkle made a general assignment of all his property for the benefit of his creditors to L. R. Dawson, under the general assignment laws of the state, which trust was accepted by the assignee, who qualified and took possession of the property, and proceeded with the administration of the insolvent's estate. About January fourth, eighteen hundred and eighty-nine, Dawson, to enable the plaintiff to procure funds with which to settle with his creditors, turned over to him, through one J. H. Misner, nearly if not quite all the property of the estate, except lots six and eleven in block twelve in the town of Arlington, Gilliam County, Oregon, and in the month following plaintiff succeeded in compromising with and being released by all his creditors. He claims in this present suit that on said fourth day of January Dawson promised and agreed to turn over to and account to him for all the property, both real and personal, of whatsoever nature, that came into his hands as assignee by virtue of the assignment, but that he has failed and still fails and refuses to account for and turn over to him a considerable portion of the personal property, and wholly fails and neglects to reconvey lots six and eleven. Upon these allegations plaintiff prays an accounting, and for a decree for such balance as may be found due, and for a reconveyance of the real property. The defendant, who is Dawson's executor, demurred to the complaint, and, upon his demurrer being overruled, answered, setting up a release from plaintiff after a full and fair settlement; and, further, that defendant had filed his final report in the matter of the assignment at the first term of court after said settlement, asking, among other things, an order of the court for authority to retransfer said real property to plaintiff. Plaintiff having obtained a decree in his favor upon these issues, the defendant appeals.   REVERSED.

For appellant there was a brief by *Messrs. Milton W. Smith* and *Cox, Cotton, Teal and Minor,* and an oral argument by *Messrs. Smith* and *Wirt Minor.*

For respondent there was a brief and an oral argument by *Messrs. J. A. Brown* and *Alfred S. Bennett.*

Opinion by MR. JUSTICE WOLVERTON.

It will be seen that this suit is in no way connected with, but is separate and distinct from, the assignment proceeding. It was instituted for the purpose of requiring a settlement and an accounting by the assignee touching the assigned estate, and of obtaining a decree directing the disposition of such portion or balance of the estate as may yet be found in his custody and under his control. The question to be determined here is whether a person, after having made a general assignment for the benefit of all his creditors under the general assignment laws of the state, and after having compounded and settled with his creditors, can maintain a suit in equity against his assignee to compel a final accounting, or must he proceed in the assignment matter still pending for the accomplishment of that purpose? Upon the one hand it is contended that this suit comes within the purview of well recognized equitable cognizance — that of compelling the execution and due performance of a trust; while upon the other it is claimed that the plaintiff should have sought his relief in the assignment matter, that the general assignment act and the acts amendatory thereof contain ample provisions for the administration and settlement of the estates of insolvents, and that the proceedings thereby adopted are exclusive of any other for directing and requiring the execution and performance of the trust imposed under a general assignment for the benefit of creditors. It is undoubtedly true that a common-law assignment, whether with preferences or for the benefit of all creditors alike, created a trust, and that the power to compel the due observance and execution thereof was peculiarly and exclusively of equitable cognizance, and statutes regulating the manner and prescribing the conditions upon which assignments may be made do not change the rule nor curtail nor limit equitable jurisdiction touching the administration of trusts thus created. Nor is the equitable jurisdiction disturbed by statutory enactments which merely create and prescribe a new procedure for the administration and settlement of insolvent estates. In such cases the equitable dominion will continue, not as affording an exclusive but as a concurrent remedy. If, however, the statutory regulations contain negative words or other language expressly taking away the preëxisting jurisdiction, or if, upon a fair and reasonable interpretation of the whole scope of such regulations, the necessary intendment is to displace such jurisdiction, then the statutory proceedings become exclusive: 1 Pomeroy on Equity, §§ 279, 281.

With these observations in view, we will now examine the statutory enactments governing general assignments for the benefit of creditors, and determine their effect. The act entitled "An act to secure creditors a just division of the estates of debtors who convey to assignees for the benefit of creditors," was passed October eighteenth, eighteen hundred and seventy-eight, and amended February twenty-fourth, eighteen hundred and eighty-five, and, as amended, is contained in Hill's Code, §§ 3173–3187, inclusive. Section 3173 provides that "no general assignment of property by an insolvent, or in contemplation of insolvency, for the benefit of creditors, shall be valid unless it be made for the benefit of all his creditors in proportion to the amount of their respective claims. And such assignment shall have the effect to dissolve any and all attachments on which judgment shall not have been taken at the date of such assignment." When judgment is recovered, however, in the action wherein the attachment is thus discharged it is to be deemed presented, and shall share *pro rata* with other claims. By section 3174 the assent of creditors is presumed. Section 3175 provides the manner of making the assignment, and when creditors are not satisfied with the assignee named by the assignor, it prescribes the manner of selecting an assignee in his stead. Should the creditors be unable to make such selection by the method prescribed, the judge of the circuit court in which the matter is pending is authorized to appoint. When a new assignee is thus selected or appointed it is made the duty of the assignee named by the debtor to assign and convey to him all the property conveyed or assigned by the debtor, and such assignee "shall possess all the powers and be subject to all the duties imposed by this act as fully to all intents and purposes as though named in the debtor's assignment." Section 3176 provides that "the assignee shall also forthwith file with the clerk of the circuit court of the county where such assignment will be recorded a true and full inventory and valuation of said estate, under oath, as far as the same has come to his knowledge, and shall then and there enter into bonds to the State of Oregon, for the use of the creditors, in double

the amount of the inventory and valuation, with two
or more sufficient sureties, to be approved by said
clerk, for the faithful performance of said trust; and
the assignee may thereupon proceed to perform any
duties necessary to carry into effect the intention of
said assignment." Sections 3177, 3178, 3179, and 3180,
provide for giving notice to creditors, the filing of a
report at the end of three months, giving a full and
true list of all creditors proving their claims, and the
settlement and adjudication of such claims. Section
3181 provides that "the assignee shall at all times be
subject to the order of the court or judge, and the
said court or judge may, by citation and attachment,
compel the assignee from time to time to file reports
of his proceedings, and of the situation and condition
of the trust, and to proceed in the faithful execution
of the duties required by this act." By section 3182
the court or judge is empowered to compel the appearance in person of the debtor forthwith, or at the
next term, to answer under oath touching the "amount
and situation of his estate, and the names of the creditors, and amount due each, with their places of residence, and may compel the delivery to the assignee
of any property or estate embraced in the assignment," and section 3183 requires the assignee to file
with the clerk of the court an inventory and valuation of such additional property as may come into his
hands. Section 3184 provides that debts to become
due may be exhibited as well as those matured,
and that such claims as are not exhibited within the
term of three months after publication of notice shall
not participate in dividends until after payment in
full of claims presented within such period and allowed. Section 3185 defines the power and authority
of the assignee. Section 3186 provides that "in case

any assignee shall die before the closing of his trust, or in case any assignee shall fail or neglect, for a period of thirty days after the making of any assignment, to file an inventory and valuation, and give bonds as required by this act, the circuit court or the judge thereof of the county where such assignment may be recorded, on application of any person interested, shall appoint some person to execute the trust embraced in such assignment; and such person, on giving the bond, with sureties, as required above of the assignee, shall possess all the powers conferred on such assignee, and shall be subject to all the duties hereby imposed, as fully as though named in the assignment; and in case any surety shall be discovered insufficient, or on complaint before the court or judge it should be made to appear that any assignee is guilty of wasting or misapplying the trust estate, said court or judge may direct and require additional security, and may remove such assignee and appoint another instead; and such person so appointed, on giving bonds, shall have full power to execute such duties, and demand and sue for all estate in the hands of the person removed, and to demand and recover the amount and value of all moneys and property or estate so wasted and misapplied, which he may neglect or refuse to make satisfaction for, from such person and his sureties." Section 3187 empowers the court or judge thereof, upon the allowance of the final account of the assignee,—when it appears that the assignor has been guilty of no fraud, and that not less than fifty per cent. of the amount of indebtedness over and above the expenses of the assignment has been realized from his estate,—to make an order discharging the assignor from any further liability on account of any indebtedness existing against him prior to the making of such assignment.

The provisions of the assignment law are thus fully set forth that its full scope and bearing may be com-prehended. It is plain that it provides a complete system for the supervision, administration, and settle-ment of the estates of insolvents who assign for the benefit of their creditors. Indeed, the act is closely allied to an insolvent or bankrupt law, if in reality it is not such a law. It provides that when the amount realized from all the assigned property is sufficient to pay at least fifty per cent. of the indebtedness under a fair assignment, the assignor shall, upon final settle-ment of the estate, be thenceforth discharged of all further liability on account of any indebtedness exist-ing against him prior to the assignment. In this respect, at least, it may be said to be a qualified bankrupt law; but whether it may be classed as an insolvent or bankrupt law or not it is not necessary for us to determine at this time. The assignment is entirely voluntary. Through no act of insolvency on the debtor's part can he be coerced into a distribution of his assets among his creditors; in this respect it bears no resemblance to an insolvent law. As before stated, the right to make a general assignment for the benefit of creditors existed at common law, but the debtor could assign with preferences. The statute circumscribes this right, and no general assignment is now valid unless made for the benefit of all credi-tors alike. The assignment must be in writing, duly acknowledged as conveyances of real estate, and re-corded. Thus executed, and free from fraud, it divests the assignor of his estate, and thenceforth the law directs its administration. The conditions which the deed of assignment may prescribe becomes unimportant, as the law specifically fixes the conditions which shall attach to every general assignment, and the settlement of the assigned estate must proceed in accord therewith. The procedure prescribed partakes of an equitable character, and the trust created is purely of equitable cognizance. The effect and final result of the statutory administration and settlement of the insolvent estate does not materially differ from that which equity would effect, except in one very essential and important particular, namely, the assignor may be discharged of all indebtedness existing prior to the date of the assignment. This result could not be accomplished under the general rules of equitable jurisprudence. They afford no primary power or authority to discharge a debtor of his obligations, whether fifty per cent. thereof is paid out of the estate or not. But, upon a final settlement in the assignment proceedings, if the estate has been made to realize fifty per cent. of the assignor's indebtedness, the circuit court, or the judge thereof, may by an order discharge the assignor from liability on account of any indebtedness existing prior to the assignment. This is a direct benefit to the assignor contemplated by the statute, and whoever makes a general assignment will be presumed to have contemplated a discharge from prior liabilities in the event his estate is made to realize fifty per cent. of his indebtedness. Aside from this feature of the assignment law, the circuit court, or judge thereof, is clothed by its provisions with all needful power and authority to require of the assignee the faithful observance and execution of the duties of his trust. He may be compelled by citation and attachment to file reports of his proceedings from time to time, and in due time to make final settlement of the assigned estate. In case of the

assignee's death, the court or judge thereof is empowered to appoint his successor; and in case a surety
shall be discovered insufficient, or if it should be made
to appear that the assignee is .guilty of wasting or
misapplying the trust estate, the court may remove
him, and appoint another in his stead, and such person so appointed may execute the duties as fully and
to all intents and purposes as his predecessor, and
may recover from his predecessor and his sureties
the value of any property so wasted or misapplied.

It would seem from these provisions, and others
that might be referred to, that the circuit court or the
judge thereof possesses ample power to compel the
due and faithful observance by the assignee of the duties of his trust, and a full and just settlement of the
estate by him, and that the statute within itself prescribes a complete procedure for the administration
and settlement of assigned estates. Considering this
circumstance, and in view of the power given the court
or the judge thereof to discharge the debtor from pre-
existing liabilities, we believe the necessary intendment
of the legislature was to take away the ordinary equity
jurisdiction touching the administration, settlement,
and distribution of assigned estates, and that the procedure prescribed by statute is exclusive. This seems
to us to be a proper conclusion upon reason and principle. But we are not without authority for so holding. The courts of New Jersey, Wisconsin, and Illinois, under assignment acts which contain no feature
whatever allying them to an insolvent or bankrupt
law, have held that the statutory procedure is exclusive. See *Hoagland* v. *See,* 40 N. J. Eq. 470 (3 Atl. 513);
Lawson v. *Stacy,* 82 Wis. 303 (51 N. W. 961 and 52 N. W.
306); *Freydendall* v. *Baldwin,* 103 Ill. 329; *Hanchett* v. *Wa-
terbury,* 115 Ill. 220 (32 N. E. 194); *Preston* v. *Spaulding,*

120 Ill. 231 (10 N. E. 903); *Colburn* v. *Shay,* 17 Ill. App.
292. In the latter case BAILEY, J., speaking for the
court, says: "The rule seems to be well settled that
the jurisdiction of the county court over an assignee,
and over the funds placed in his hands by the assign
ment, is exclusive." As bearing on this question see
also *Rumsey* v. *Town,* 20 Fed. 562, and *Clark* v. *Stanton,*
24 Minn. 240. We have been unable to find any case
holding otherwise under a statute like ours. If the
plaintiff could sustain this suit regardless of the statutory procedure, and compel a final accounting and settlement by the assignee, the creditors could accomplish the same purpose by an ordinary suit in equity,
and thus deprive the circuit court, or the judge thereof
acting in the assignment matter, of the opportunity
if not the power of making the requisite order discharging the debtor from preëxisting liabilities, and
thus defeat one of the purposes of the statute. We
think the plaintiff should have proceeded in the assignment matter to the final adjustment and settlement
of the assigned estate. The final account was filed in
due time, and if the assignee was seeking to take advantage of any settlement in turning over to him the
property of the estate, or any part thereof, he had
ample opportunity of surcharging the account for
fraud or mistake, and trying out all the issues that
are here made. The complaint should be dismissed,
and it is so ordered.   REVERSED.

SCHOOL DISTRICT NUMBER TWO *v.* LAMBERT.

[42 Pac. 221.]

1. **POWER OF COUNTY SUPERINTENDENT TO APPORTION SCHOOL FUNDS—CODE, §§ 2590-2626.**— Hill's Code, § 2626, as amended by Laws, 1893, p. 25, provides that when the limits of any city are changed the limits of the school district therein shall be deemed to have been changed so as to conform to the new limits of the city. Section 2590, subdivision 4, as amended by Laws, 1889, p. 116, provides that when changes are made in any school-district boundaries the boards of directors of all the districts concerned, shall make an equitable division of the assets and liabilities, etc. *Held*, that the county superintendent alone has no right to make a division of assets of the district divided by Laws, 1895, p. 442, changing the boundaries of the City of Portland, as that was the duty of the boards of directors.

2. **MANDAMUS TO COMPEL APPORTIONMENT OF SCHOOL FUNDS.**— Hill's Code, § 2590, subdivision 4, as amended by Laws, 1889, p. 116, provides that funds arising from the five-mill county school tax or the irreducible state school fund shall be divided in proportion to the number of persons between the ages of four and twenty years who are actual residents of the district at the time of a division thereof. *Held*, that mandamus will not lie to compel a county treasurer to pay the amount apportioned to a new school district, formed by division of an old one, where the alternative writ fails to show the number of children in both districts, and it does not appear that the number of children in the new district were originally enrolled and enumerated in the original district.

3. **MINISTERIAL ACT OF COUNTY SCHOOL SUPERINTENDENT.**—Where a new school district has been set off from an old district, and the county school superintendent draws on the county treasurer an order in favor of the new district for a share of the irreducible school fund, his act is ministerial only, and the county treasurer is not precluded from questioning the right of such county superintendent to issue the order.

APPEAL from Multnomah: E. D. SHATTUCK, Judge.

This is a mandamus proceeding by School District Number Two of Multnomah County to compel the treasurer of that county to pay an order drawn upon him by the county school superintendent in favor of the clerk of said district. The facts are that on May twenty-fourth, eighteen hundred and ninety-five, the legislative assembly, by an act which took effect on that day, changed the boundaries of the City of Portland so that a part of the territory formerly within the city limits was excluded therefrom, and, by operation of law, the boundaries of school district number one were also altered to conform to the amended limits of the city. Three days after said act took effect the county superintendent established a new school district, which he designated as number two, the boundaries of which included all the territory cut off from district number one, and some uninhabited and unorganized territory adjoining thereto. On the sixth day of the succeeding month school district number two was duly organized, and L. B. Chapman, having been elected clerk thereof, notified the county superintendent that the number of persons between the ages of four and twenty years who were actual residents of said district at the time of the division was one hundred and fifty, whereupon that officer, after apportioning the school funds in the county treasury among the several school districts of his county, drew an order for school district number two on the county treasurer for the sum of nine hundred and thirty dollars in favor of Chapman, who, being refused payment thereof upon demand, sued out an alternative writ of mandamus requiring the defendant to pay said order or show the cause of his omission to do so. The defendant, for his return, after denying the material averments of the writ, alleged that there were no funds which, under the law, could be apportioned by the school superintendent to school district number two, and no funds in his hands out of which he could pay the order in question; that the fund intended to be reached by said order was a portion of the school funds which should have been apportioned to school district number one; that on March thirteenth, eighteen hundred and ninety-five, the clerk of the latter district, pursuant to law, filed in the office of the county superintendent the annual census report, containing the names and ages of all children over four and under twenty years of age residing therein, from which it appeared that the number of such persons was nineteen thousand four hundred and seventy-one; that, without warrant of law, and in the absence of any census of the children of school age residing in district number two, the county superintendent, under the pretense that there were one hundred and fifty such children residing therein, illegally attempted to award to said district nine hundred and thirty dollars out of the school fund of district number one, which district notified him that he would be held personally responsible if he paid upon said order any part of the fund to which it was entitled; and that school district number two was not entitled to any part of the school fund in his hands.   These averments were, by stipulation of the parties, deemed denied, and the court, upon the issues thus made, and an agreed statement of facts, found for plaintiff as to the facts, and, as conclusions of law, that school district number two was entitled to the money apportioned to it by the county superintendent, and that it was entitled to a peremptory writ of mandamus compelling the defendant to pay the same to its clerk, and judgment having been rendered according to these findings the defendant appeals.   REVERSED.

For appellants there was a brief by *Messrs. George, Gregory and Duniway,* with an oral argument by *Mr. Melvin C. George.*

For respondent there was a brief by *Messrs. Williams, Wood and Linthicum,* with an oral argument by *Mr. George H. Williams.*

Opinion by MR. JUSTICE MOORE.

It is contended by the defendant that, the boundaries of the City of Portland having been changed and a portion of the territory cut off, the school district boundaries which were identical with those of the city were changed to the same extent by operation of law; that when a public corporation is divided by a legislative act, which makes no provision for the distribution of the assets and liabilities between the sections of the territory thus separated, courts are powerless to adjust the equities or to award such distribution; and that, conceding school district number one was divided for "school purposes," within the meaning of the statute, the school superintendent has no authority to divide the school fund between the respective districts until their school boards have made an equitable division of the assets and liabilities, or a board of arbitration, in case of disagreement, has adjusted the matter; while the plaintiff insists that under the general provisions of the statute the county superintendent has such authority, and that it is made his duty to divide the school fund between the districts created out of the original territory.

1. The legislative assembly on October twenty-sixth, eighteen hundred and eighty-two, passed an act which has been incorporated in Hill's Code of Oregon

as sections 2625 to 2646, inclusive.   The first two sections of this act, as amended, (Laws, 1893, p. 25,) provide (section 2625): "Whenever the population of any
city or incorporated town shall exceed four thousand
inhabitants, as shown by any census of the state or
of the United States, all school districts or parts of
school districts within the limits of said city shall
constitute one school district, and the boundaries and
limits of such school district shall conform to the limits and boundaries and shall be the same as the limits
and boundaries of said incorporated city or town; *provided,* that in all cases when any part of any school
district shall be included in any such incorporated
city or town, and a part thereof shall not be included
within the boundaries of said city or town, at the time
this act shall take effect, such parts of such school
districts as lie without the boundaries of such city or
town shall continue to be a part of such school district." "2626. When the limits or boundaries of
any incorporated city or town containing four thousand inhabitants or more, which has been by this act
constituted a school district, are changed according to
law, then the boundaries and limits of the school district therein shall be deemed to have been changed
also so as to conform to the new limits and boundaries of such incorporated city or town."   The act of
February twenty-third, eighteen hundred and ninety-
five, (Laws, 1895, p. 442,) amendatory of the charter of
the City of Portland, changed the boundaries thereof,
and cut off a portion of the territory formerly within
its limits, and, when it took effect, on May twenty-
fourth of that year, under the provisions of section
2626, it *ipso facto* changed the boundaries of school
district number one.

Section 2590 of Hill's Code, as amended in eighteen hundred and eighty-nine, (Laws, 1889, p. 116,) provides that, "The duties of the superintendent shall be as follows: 1. He shall lay off his county into convenient school districts, and may also make alterations and changes in the same when petitioned so to do, in the manner hereinafter specified; and he shall make a record showing the boundaries and numbers of all the districts in his county so established and altered. 2. He shall, when he establishes a new district, immediately notify, in writing, some taxable inhabitant of such district, giving in such notice the number and boundaries thereof; and when he makes alterations he shall immediately, in the manner aforesaid, notify the directors of all the districts concerned. 3. He may establish new districts, when not already laid off, on petition of three legal voters of each proposed new district, but shall not make any changes in the districts of his county unless petitioned so to do by a majority of the legal voters of each district concerned in the change." 4. "When changes are made in district boundaries as heretofore set forth, or when any district shall be divided into two or more parts for school purposes, the existing board of directors and clerk shall continue to act for both or all the new districts or parts of districts until such districts or parts of districts shall have been regularly organized by the election of directors and clerks as hereinafter set forth in sections 30, 31, 32, and 33, title IV of the school law. The respective boards of directors of all the districts concerned shall, immediately after such organization, make an equitable division of the then existing assets and liabilities between the old and the new districts, or between the districts already existing and affected by such change; and in case of failure to agree within ten days from the time of such organization, the matter shall be decided by a board of disinterested arbitrators chosen by the directors of the several districts concerned. The arbitrators' decision in the premises shall be final. The said board of arbitrators shall consist of three members, of whom the county superintendent shall be a member, and *ex officio* chairman. Each member of the board of arbitrators shall be entitled to the sum of two dollars, net, per day, for each day's service while sitting in their official capacity, and the expenses thus occurring shall be equally apportioned among the several districts interested. Assets shall include all school property and moneys belonging to the districts at the time of the division. Liabilities shall include all debts for which the district, in its corporate capacity, is liable at the time of the division. In determining the assets, school property shall be estimated at its present cash value. The assets and liabilities shall be divided separately between the districts, in proportion to the last assessed value of the property, real and personal, and the district retaining the real property shall pay to the other district or districts concerned such sum or sums as shall be determined in accordance with the prior provisions of this section; *provided,* that all funds arising (and that shall arise during the current year in which such division is made) from the five-mill county school tax or the irreducible state school fund shall be divided in proportion to the number of persons between the ages of four and twenty years who are actual residents of the district at the time of the division."

This amendment having been made after the passage of section 2626, the question is suggested whether the latter section is wholly superseded thereby. The various sections of the statute in relation to the management of the public schools constitute a system which should be construed, if possible, *in pari materia;* but where the last statute is complete in itself, and intended to prescribe the only rule to be observed, it will not be modified by the displaced legislation, as laws *in pari materia:* Sutherland on Statutory Construction, § 286. An examination of sections 2625 and 2626 of the Code shows the manifest intention of the legislature to take from the county superintendeut all authority to alter the boundaries of school districts organized within incorporated cities containing four thousand inhabitants, and to reserve such power to itself. It also appears from subdivision 5 of section 2631, which is part of the act of October twenty-sixth, eighteen hundred and eighty-two, that it is made the duty of the board of directors of school districts organized within incorporated cities of four thousand inhabitants to create a board of examiners for the purpose of examining all persons who may be employed to teach therein, and, although the county superintendent, whose duty it is to examine applicants for and to grant certificates to all persons employed to teach in his county, is made *ex officio* chairman thereof, it nevertheless shows an intention on the part of the legislative assembly to take from that officer much of his supervisory authority over city schools. It is therefore evident that the act of October twenty-sixth, eighteen hundred and eighty-two, took from the county superintendent all authority to change the boundaries of any district created by such act, and that it made no provision for the division of its property in case of a change in its boundaries by the legislature, and such must be the law unless changed by subdivision 4 of section 2590. This subdivision pro-

vides that "When changes are made in district boundaries as heretofore set forth," (meaning thereby such
changes as are made by the county superintendent
upon the petition of a majority of the legal voters of
each district concerned therein, as prescribed in subdivision 3,) "or when any district shall be divided into
two or more parts for schools purposes," the boards of
directors shall make an equitable division of the assets
and liabilities, etc. There are only two methods by
which the boundaries of organized school districts can
be changed, *first,* by the county superintendent directly
upon the petition of a majority of the legal voters of
each district concerned in such change; and, *second,* by
an act of the legislative assembly changing the boundaries of an incorporated city, and thereby changing
indirectly the boundaries of the school district therein.
Assuming without deciding that the primary object of
the legislative act changing the boundaries of the city
was to subserve the interests of the corporation, but,
as the effect was to change the boundaries of the
school district also, and as the amendment of section
2590 was made after the passage of the act of October twenty-sixth, eighteen hundred and eighty-two, it
must be presumed that the legislative assembly was
cognizant of and referred to the prior act in the system of school laws, and that by making use of the
phrase, "or when any district shall be divided into
two or more parts for school purposes," that body
meant a division by either of such methods; any other
construction would render the phrase superfluous and
meaningless. In view of this construction can the
county superintendent apportion the school fund of a
district which has been divided by a legislative act
without an adjustment of the fund by the boards of

directors of the districts interested therein, or by a
board of arbitrators in case of disagreement?

The latter clause of subdivision 4 of section 2590
provides that the five-mill county school tax and the
irreducible state school fund shall be divided in proportion to the number of persons between the ages of
four and twenty years who are actual residents of the
district at the time of the division of such funds.
That subdivision also prescribes the mode which is to
be pursued by the boards of directors in the division
of the assets and liabilities of the divided school district, and, upon their failure to agree upon an equitable division thereof, it further provides for the appointment of a board of arbitrators, of which the
county superintendent, by right of his office, is constituted a member, and the chairman thereof. The
statute, having prescribed the persons who should
make this equitable division, impliedly excludes all
others from taking any part therein, and this being
so, by what legal right can the county superintendent
make the division except as a member of the board
of arbitrators? But, assuming that this fund is no
part of the assets of a district until it has been apportioned to and received by it, and that the latter
clause of subdivision 4 sanctions an apportionment of
the particular fund by that officer, it will be observed
that such subdivision also provides that the division
shall be made in proportion to the number of persons
between the ages of four and twenty years who are
actual residents of the district at the time it is made.
This provision, fairly interpreted, evidently means that
the fund to be divided must bear the same proportion
to the amount awarded to the new district that the
whole number of persons of school age in the original
district bears to the number of such persons in the

territory cut off from it. The district was divided
May twenty-fourth, eighteen hundred and ninety-five,
when the act of the legislative assembly went into effect, and, though the territory cut off by the act was
not organized until the sixth day of the succeeding
month, when a board of school directors and clerk
were elected therein, the board of directors and clerk
of district number one, by express provision of the
statute, continue to act for the new district until its
organization: Section 2590, subdivision 4, Hill's Code.

2. The records show that there were one hundred
and fifty persons of school age in district number two
at the time of the division, but it does not appear how
many persons of that age there were in school district number one at that time. The statute requires
the clerk of each school district to enroll annually,
for school purposes, all persons in his district over
four and under twenty years of age, and, when completed so as to show the names and ages of such persons, to submit the enrollment made, under oath, to
the directors and citizens of the district at the regular
annual meeting in March for necessary correction,
and, after being corrected, to retain the same in his
office, and file a copy thereof with the county superintendent not later than the fifteenth of that month:
Code, section 2619, subdivision 5. The school clerk of
district number one, in pursuance of this provision,
made, and on March thirteenth, eighteen hundred and
ninety-five, filed in the office of the county superintendent his annual census report, from which it appears that there were at that time nineteen thousand
four hundred and seventy-one persons of school age
in the district; but, assuming that the census thus
made is presumed to show the number of persons in

the district at all times during the school year in which it was prepared,—and this presumption is reasonable, since there is no authority for taking another census,—it does not appear that any of the one hundred and fifty persons residing in district number two were enrolled in or that their names were found upon the annual census of school district number one. The rule is well settled that in mandamus proceedings the alternative writ, which is in the nature of a complaint, must show a clear right to the performance of the public duty which is sought to be enforced: Merrill on Mandamus, § 255; Wood on Mandamus, 17; Moses on Mandamus, 206. It is another rule equally well settled that it is unnecessary to allege in a pleading any facts the existence of which the law will presume (Bliss on Code Pleading, 3d ed., § 175); and, since the law presumes that official duty has been regularly performed, (subdivision 15, § 776, Hill's Code,) it was unnecessary to allege any facts showing the method by which the county superintendent arrived at the conclusion that there were one hundred and fifty persons of school age in district number two. While these facts need not be averred in the alternative writ by reason of presumption, yet such presumption is not conclusive, and, the defendant's return having tendered an issue challenging the right of the clerk of school district number two to make the report, the issue presented became one of fact, to establish which the burden was cast upon the defendant (*National Bank* v. *Harold*, 74 Cal. 603, 5 Am. St. Rep. 576, 16 Pac. 507); and, the agreed statement of facts showing a want of compliance with the terms of the statute, the clear right to the performance of the public duty has not been established.

It may be conceded that a school district has no

vested right to the money arising from the levy of the county school tax, or interest on the irreducible state school fund, until the money has been segregated and apportioned to the district; but it has an inchoate right to the funds, and by mandamus may compel a division thereof by apportionment based upon the annual census of the school clerk. The right to this fund is not in the child, though a per capita division is made for his benefit; for, if it were so, it would follow that the child, by removing from the district at any time within the year after he was enrolled, and before the fund had been expended, could take his portion thereof with him to another district in the county; and if he could do that, he could on the same reasoning take it to any district in the state. True, he may remove to another district, and thus increase the number of school children therein entitled to the school fund under another census, but, except in case the district is divided, no part of the fund which the district received in consequence of his residence can be diverted to the use of another district on account of such removal; and if all the children moved out of the school district after the annual census had been taken, but before the fund received in consequence of their enumeration had been expended in their educa-tion, the money thus received would have to be re-turned to the county treasury for reapportionment (Section 2608, Hill's Code); thus showing that the right is not in the child but in the district as an agent of the state in trust for his education. When a dis-trict has been divided, and the duty of educating a part of the school children has been cast upon another district, fair dealing demands an equitable division of this fund, and our statute has prescribed the method. No provision is made for taking another census as the basis of this division, and hence it is fair to presume, since the clerk is required to state the name and age of each child in his annual enrollment, that the number so found shall be deemed the number actually residing in his district at all times during the ensuing school year, and upon a division of the district the number of children in each part would be easy of ascertainment from an inspection of the clerk's census roll on file in his office. It is also fair to presume that the county superintendent is authorized to divide the fund apportioned to a district upon receiving the statement of the number of school children in each part after a division, from the boards of directors, or, upon their failure to agree, from the board of arbitrators, and to apportion the school fund to the respective districts, not upon a new enrollment, but upon the basis of the old, in accordance with the directors' agreement or the arbitration; but, in the absence of such a settlement by or in behalf of the districts, we fail to find any authority in the statute by which the school superintendent could divide this fund.

3. Counsel for the respondent contends in his argument that, the county superintendent having drawn an order which was payable out of a particular fund, the apportionment of which was solely within his power, it is the duty of the county treasurer upon whom the order is drawn to pay it on presentation, and that he is precluded from questioning the right of the county superintendent to issue the order, except in a direct proceeding to review his action, even though he may have erred in his construction of the law. The rule of law contended for is not applicable unless the county superintendent in drawing the order was exercising judicial and not ministerial functions:

Hill's Code, § 585; *People* v. *Bush*, 40 Cal. 344; *Thompson* v.
Multnomah County, 2 Or. 34. "As a general rule," says
Mr. Throop in his work on Public Officers, § 552, "judicial and quasi judicial acts are conclusive, except when
a method of reviewing the same is given by statute;
and then they are conclusive for every purpose, except for the purpose of such a review." Where the
law authorizes a person to hear and determine issues
between parties, the granting or refusal of the relief
demanded therein is a judicial act; but where a power
vests in judgment or discretion, so that it is of a judicial nature or character, but does not involve the exercise of the functions of a judge, or is conferred
upon an officer having no authority of a judicial character, the expression used is generally "quasi judicial,"
so that where, in the exercise of a power, an officer is
vested with a discretion, his act is regarded as quasi
judicial: Throop on Public Officers, § 553; *United States*
v. *Arredondo*, 31 U. S. (6 Pet.), 689; *United States* v. *California and Oregon Lumber Company*, 148 U. S. 31 (13 Sup.
Ct. 458). But if an officer or board, vested by law
with a discretion, act in excess of the power conferred, and audit a claim which is not legally chargeable against the corporation for which he or it acts,
the treasurer thereof may refuse to pay an order
drawn upon him as evidence of the amount so
awarded: Throop on Public Officers, § 554. "If the
demand for which the warrant is drawn," says NOR-
TON, J., in *Keller* v. *Hyde*, 20 Cal. 593, "was not legally
chargeable against the county, the treasurer may show
this fact in answer to a demand for a mandate to compel him to pay it. The party asking the mandate
must be entitled to the money as against the county,
of which the treasurer is only the disbursing agent,
or the mandate will be refused." If the person doing

an act is a ministerial officer only, and not vested by
law with a discretion to grant or deny the subject
matter demanded, his act is not conclusive, and he
must show in justification that he has acted within the
provisions of the statute conferring the power, and if
he has not done so, he is liable to the person specially
injured thereby: Mechem on Public Officers, § 664;
Flournoy v. *City of Jeffersonville,* 17 Ind. 129 (79 Am. Dec.
468); *Robinson* v. *Chamberlain,* 34 N. Y. 389 (90 Am. Dec.
713); while judicial and quasi judicial officers are not
liable to private action for acts within their jurisdiction: Mechem on Public Officers, § 619. "The duty is
ministerial," says Clopton, J., in *Grider* v. *Tally,* 77 Ala.
422 (54 Am. Rep. 65), "when the law exacting its discharge prescribes and defines the time, mode, and occasion of its performance with such certainty that
nothing remains for judgment or discretion. Official
action, the result of performing a certain and specific
duty arising from designated facts, is a ministerial
act." The statute prescribes the time and manner of
making the apportionment with such certainty that
nothing remains for the judgment or discretion of the
county superintendent, (subdivision 5, § 2500, Hill's
Code,) and hence that officer in drawing the order in
question was performing a ministerial duty only. This
order being presumably regular upon its face, the
county treasurer would have incurred no personal liability if he had paid it without notice of facts sufficient
to put an ordinarily prudent treasurer upon inquiry
which if diligently prosecuted would lead to a discovery of the illegality of the claim upon which the order
was founded: *Los Angeles County* v. *Lankershim,* 100 Cal.
525 (35 Pac. 153, 556); but, having received such information, and being notified that he would be held personally liable, it was the duty of the county treasurer,

if he had any reasonable doubt upon the subject, to contest the payment. It follows that the judgment must be reversed, and the cause remanded with instructions to deny the peremptory writ, and it is so ordered.   REVERSED.

Argued October 23; decided November 11, 1895.

STATE *v.* KELLY.

[42 Pac. 217.]

1. COMPETENCY OF JURORS — CODE, § 187.—A juror who testifies that from reading newspaper reports of the case he had formed and expressed some opinion, but that his opinion was not fixed, and would not influence his verdict, is competent: *State* v. *Ingram*, 23 Or. 434, and *State* v. *Brown*, 28 Or. 147, approved and followed.

2. EXCLUSION OF JURY — CONFESSIONS.— Whether the jury shall be excluded pending the preliminary examination as to the admissibility of a confession is within the discretion of the trial court: *State* v. *Shaffer*, 23 Or. 555, cited and approved.

APPEAL from Multnomah: T. A. STEPHENS, Judge.

The defendant, Joseph Kelly, (more familiarly known in the criminal records as "Bunco" Kelly,) was jointly indicted with X. N. Steeves, an attorney of this court, on a charge of murdering George W. Sayres, and, having been convicted of the crime of murder in the second degree, brings this appeal, assigning as error the decision of the court overruling his challenge to certain jurors for actual bias, and its refusal to exclude the jury from the courtroom during the preliminary hearing before the court to determine the admissibility of an alleged confession offered in evidence by the prosecution.

For appellant there was a brief and an oral argument by *Messrs. John F. Caples* and *John Ditchburn.*

28 OR.—15.

For the state there was a brief by *Messrs. Cicero M. Idleman,* attorney-general, and *Wilson T. Hume,* district attorney, with an oral argument by *Mr. Hume.*

Opinion by MR. CHIEF JUSTICE BEAN.

1.   Upon the examination of the jurors challenged on their *voir dire* each of them testified that he had read what purported to be the facts of the case in the newspapers; that from such reading and what he heard he had formed and expressed some opinion upon the merits, but that it was not fixed, and would not influence his verdict if taken as a juror.   Under these circumstances there was no reversible error in overruling the challenge.   This question has been so often and thoroughly examined by the court that it is unnecessary to do more at this time than refer to the opinions in the following cases: *State* v. *Tom,* 8 Or. 177; *Kumli* v. *Southern Pacific Company,* 21 Or. 505 (28 Pac. 637); *State* v. *Ingram,* 23 Or. 434 (31 Pac. 1049); *State* v. *Brown,* 28 Or. 147 (41 Pac. 1042).

2.   The next point made by the defendant is that the court erred in overruling his motion to exclude the jury from the courtroom during the preliminary hearing before the court as to the competency of a certain alleged confession which the court, after the hearing, refused to admit in evidence because it was obtained by undue influence and improper inducements held out to the defendant by those in authority.   This is a new question here, but we understand the practice in the trial courts has generally been to conduct such examinations in the presence of the jury, and, in our opinion, the question as to whether it shall be so conducted or otherwise should be left to the sound discretion of such courts.   The competency and admis-

sibility of confessions, like other testimony, is for the court to determine; but, when admitted, their weight and credibility is for the jury alone, and hence it is necessary that the jury should be put in possession of all the circumstances surrounding the making of an alleged confession to enable them to intelligibly determine the weight and credibility to which it is entitled. A confession, to be admitted, must have been freely and voluntarily made. When offered in evidence the question whether it was so made is to be decided primarily by the presiding judge, but his decision is not conclusive upon the jury as to the weight or credibility to be given to such evidence. If, upon the whole testimony, they believe it was not the free and voluntary act of the defendant, they have a right to exclude it entirely in their consideration of the case. Therefore, if the preliminary examination is not held in the presence of the jury, and the court admits the confession in evidence, the whole testimony as to the circumstances under which it was made must be gone over again before the jury. And whether this course should be pursued or the preliminary examination had in the presence of the jury in the first instance may be safely intrusted to the sound discretion of the trial court. Cases may arise, it is true, in which the ends of justice might be best served by conducting the examination without the hearing of the jury, but the necessity for such precaution must be left to the enlightened discretion of the presiding judge to determine.

The argument that if the preliminary hearing is had in the presence of the jury they will ordinarily learn the nature of the confession and be influenced thereby in arriving at a verdict, although the court may refuse to admit it in evidence, is based upon an

unwarranted assumption of the ignorance and incompetency .of the jury. During such an examination
they are but silent spectators, who necessarily understand that out of its results something may or may
not come before them as evidence, and that until the
court rules the question is for its consideration and
not for theirs. In the judgment of the law juries are
deemed capable of that amount of discrimination; it
would be impossible to conduct a jury trial on any
other principle. In this as in most other cases where
evidence is offered and objected to it is generally impossible for the court to determine its admissiblity
without the objection itself, the argument of counsel.
or the offer to prove, disclosing to some extent at
least its nature; and the law assumes that jurors are
competent to disregard whatever is heard at such a
time, but not admitted as evidence for their consideration. Experience has shown such to be the case, and
upon this assumption the law proceeds. The defendant cites in support of his position *Hall* v. *State*, 65 Ga.
36, *Ellis* v. *State*, 65 Miss. 44 (7 Am. St. Rep. 634, 3 So.
188), and *Carter* v. *State*, 37 Texas, 362. In the Georgia
case what is said upon this question is mere *dictum*,
and the writer of the opinion failed to note a previous decision of the same court (*Holsenbake* v. *State*, 45
Ga. 43,) where the point was directly made and ruled
to the contrary. And in the subsequent cases of *Woolfolk* v. *State*, 81 Ga. 551, (8 S. E. 724,) and *Fletcher* v.
State, 90 Ga. 468, (17 S. E. 100,) the court took occasion to so explain the Hall case, and to announce what
we conceive to be the true rule,—that it is within the
discretion of the trial court to say whether the jury
shall remain or retire while such preliminary testimony is being taken. In *Fletcher* -v. *State*, 90 Ga. 468,
(17 S. E. 100,) Mr. Chief Justice BECKLEY said:

"Touching the practice of retiring the jury, the strict letter of *Hall* v. *State,* 65 Ga. 36, is not good law. Though approved arguendo in *McDonald* v. *State,* 72 Ga. 55, it has since been toned down in Woolfolk's case, 81 Ga. 564, 565, (3 S. E. 724,) and the true rule announced to be that the question whether the jury shall be retired or not is one resting in the sound discretion of the court. In the Mississippi and Texas cases the judgments were reversed upon other points, and the question as to the proper practice in conducting the preliminary examination to determine the admissibility of confessions seems not to have been necessary to a decision in either instance. We have been unable to find that the question has arisen in any of the other states except Ohio, Alabama, and Nebraska, and in these the courts have held that the propriety of conducting the examination in or out of the presence of the jury must be left to the sound discretion of the trial court: *Lefevre* v. *State,* 50 Ohio St. 584 (35 N. E. 52); *Mose* (*a slave*) v. *State,* 36 Ala. 211; *Shepherd* v. *State,* 31 Neb. 389 (47 N. W. 1118). In this state the rule prevails that such inquiry as to the admissibility of dying declarations may be conducted in the hearing or presence of the jury, or otherwise, as the discretion of the court may dictate, (*State* v. *Shaffer,* 23 Or. 555, 32 Pac. 545,) and no good reason can be suggested why a different practice should prevail as to confessions. There being no error in the record, the judgment is affirmed.

AFFIRMED.

Argued October 7; decided November 11, 1895.

CONNELL v. McLOUGHLIN.

[42 Pac. 218.]

1. SOURCE OF AGENT'S AUTHORITY.—The existence of an agent's authority depends upon the intention of the principal, and is purely a question of fact: *Glenn* v. *Savage*, 14 Or. 567, cited and approved.

2. QUESTION FOR JURY.—If on a trial there is any dispute regarding the facts, or if there may reasonably be a difference of opinion as to the deductions therefrom, the matter should be submitted to the jury: *Hedin* v. *Suburban Railway Company*, 26 Or. 155, cited and approved.

3. PROOF OF AGENCY.—The authority of an agent cannot be proved by the alleged agent's own statements or acts, unless it be also shown that the principal knowingly acquiesced therein.

4. POWER OF AGENT TO EXECUTE NOTE.—An agent authorized to manage and dispose of a sash and door manufacturing plant has no authority to execute a note in the name of his principal in payment for lumber, it not appearing when the lumber was purchased, or that it was used or intended for the benefit of the principal.

5. PRESUMPTION FROM SUPPRESSED EVIDENCE—AGENCY.—Where the authority of an alleged agent to execute a note, in an action thereon against the principal, is in issue, the failure of the agent, who was an unwilling witness, to produce his power of attorney, does not of itself raise a presumption that he was authorized to execute the note.

APPEAL from Multnomah: HARTWELL HURLEY, Judge.

This is an action by Samuel Connell against Martha E. McLoughlin to recover upon a promissory note alleged to have been executed by an agent of the defendant. The facts are that one E. McLoughlin, being the lessee of certain premises in the City of Portland, owned a building thereon in which he operated a sash and door factory under the firm name and style of the Portland Door and Lumber Company; that on June seventh, eighteen hundred and ninety-three, for the expressed consideration of seven thousand dollars, he executed a bill of sale to his mother, the defendant, in which he assigned all his right, title, and interest in and to said building, and also transferred to her all the machinery, tools, and furniture therein, together with the stock of merchandise and material on hand, which bill of sale was duly recorded on the day succeeding its execution; that McLoughlin took a power of attorney from his mother authorizing him to dispose of the property so transferred to her, and continued to operate the factory for her under the same firm name; that one E S. Bryant having furnished to said firm for use in the factory lumber and materials of the reasonable value of four hundred and fifty-two dollars and twenty-one cents, McLoughlin, on June seventh of that year, as evidence of the amount due Bryant, executed to him a promissory note, payable in three months, and signed the same "Portland Door and Lumber Company, per E. McLoughlin, Manager"; that Bryant, in consideration of three hundred dollars to be paid to him, if the amount due thereon could be collected from the defendant, assigned it before maturity to the plaintiff, who alleged in his complaint the necessary facts to show that he was the owner and holder thereof.   The defendant denied the material allegations of the complaint, and upon a trial of the issues thus joined the plaintiff introduced his evidence and rested, whereupon the defendant moved the court for a nonsuit, which, being denied, a verdict was rendered for the plaintiff, and from the judgment thereon the defendant appeals.   REVERSED.

For appellant there was a brief by *Messrs. Davis, Gantenbien and Veasie,* and an oral argument by *Mr. Arthur L. Veasie.*

For respondent there was a brief and an oral argument by *Mr. Albert Abraham.*

Opinion by MR. JUSTICE MOORE.

1. It is contended that the plaintiff failed to introduce any evidence tending to show McLoughlin's authority to execute the note for the defendant, and that the court therefore erred in denying the motion for a nonsuit. The existence of an agent's authority depends upon the intention of his principal, and is purely a question of fact: *Glenn* v. *Savage,* 14 Or. 567 (13 Pac. 442).

2. If there be any dispute as to the fact in issue, it is clearly a question for the jury; or, if there be no dispute as to the facts, but there may reasonably be a difference of opinion as to the inferences and conclusions deducible therefrom, it is the province of the jury to determine the question: *Goshorn* v. *Smith,* 92 Pa. St. 435; *Herbert* v. *Dufur,* 23 Or. 462 (32 Pac. 302); *Hedin* v. *Suburban Railway Company,* 26 Or. 155 (37 Pac. 540). The witness Bryant testified that when he accepted the note he supposed McLoughlin was a member of the Portland Door and Lumber Company, and that he did not know the defendant, nor ever heard of her, while McLoughlin testified that his power of attorney only authorized him to dispose of the property, stock, and material, and that he had no direct authority from his mother to execute the note. Assuming that a conclusion could be based upon a want of proof, and that it might reasonably be inferred that, while the power of attorney did not authorize McLoughlin to execute notes for his mother, he acquired such authority by some other means, and that, although the power to do so was not directly conferred, it was clearly implied, such an inference would not authorize the court to submit the question to the

jury, for the inference so deduced could not be of greater weight than a positive declaration by McLoughlin that he had authority to execute notes for his mother, in the absence of any proof that she knowingly acquiesced in such statements, if made by him.

3. The rule is well established that the authority of an agent cannot be proved by his own statements that he is such, in the absence of evidence that the principal knowingly acquiesced in such declarations: *Graves* v. *Horton,* 38 Minn. 66 (35 N. W. 568); *Hatch* v. *Squires,* 11 Mich. 185; *Streeter* v. *Poor,* 4 Kan. 412; *St. Louis Railway Company* v. *Kinman,* 49 Kan. 627 (31 Pac. 126). The authority of one person to act for another rests upon the intention of the principal to be bound by the acts and contracts of his agent. In controversies between the principal and his agent this intention may be proved by the written commission conferring the power, or by acts or declarations of the principal in acknowledgment of the agent's authority; while in actions between the principal and third persons, growing out of their contracts with his agent, the intention of the principal may be proved in the same manner as in controversies between him and his agent, and in addition thereto it may be inferred from apparent authority, by proving that the principal knowingly permitted the agent to assume, or that he held the agent out to the public as possessing the necessary power, and hence the validity of a contract made with an agent and the right of action founded on its breach grows out of the intention of the principal to be bound by the act of his agent. A principal is bound by whatever his agent may lawfully do within the scope of the power conferred, and, upon the theory that

where a right is conferred the power is also granted without which the right itself cannot exist, this scope includes whatever the agent may necessarily do in the performance of the particular act expressly author- ized: *Law* v. *Stokes,* 32 N. J. Law, 249 (90 Am. Dec. 665). "The authority of an agent," says ANDREWS, J., in *Walsh* v. *Hartford Fire Insurance Company,* 73 N. Y. 5, "is not only that conferred upon him by his commission, but also, as to third persons, that which he is held out as possessing. The principal is often bound by the act of his agent in excess or abuse of his actual au- thority, but this is only true between the principal and third persons, who, believing and having a right to believe that the agent was acting within and not exceeding his authority, would sustain loss if the act was not considered that of the principal." The prin- ciple announced in this case carries the doctrine of lia- bility to the very verge, and proceeds upon the estop- pel of the principal, founded upon the familiar theory that where one of two innocent persons must suffer from the act of a third, he who first trusted such third person and placed in his hands the power which en- abled him to do the act or permitted him to commit the wrong, must bear the loss. But before the appli- cation of this rule of law can be invoked, two import- ant facts must be clearly established, *first,* the principal must have held the agent out to the public in other instances as possessing sufficient authority to embrace the particular act in question, or knowingly acquiesced in the agent's assertions of the requisite authority; and, *second,* the party dealing with such agent must have had reason to believe, and must have believed, that the agent possessed the necessary authority. These two facts must always be established to render the principal liable for the act of his agent in excess or abuse of his authority, for any person dealing with an agent does so at his peril, and the burden falls upon him to show that the agent possessed the necessary authority: *Anderson* v. *Kissam,* 35 Fed. 699. When Bryant accepted the note he supposed McLoughlin was a member of the firm, and, as such, had authority to execute it; and at that time, never having heard of nor known the defendant, he had no reason to believe nor did he believe, from any knowledge derived from her acts, that she was holding her son out to the public as possessing authority to execute notes for her: and it having been assigned by Bryant to Connell as trustee for him, the plaintiff's right of action cannot be superior to that of his assignor; and hence it follows that if the defendant is liable at all it must be in consequence of the express power delegated to the agent: *Bickford* v. *Menier,* 107 N. Y. 490 (14 N. E. 438).

4. No evidence of an express grant of power from the defendant to her son to execute notes for her was introduced at the trial, but the authority to do so is sought to be inferred from the proof of other facts which show that McLoughlin, after the bill of sale was executed, continued to operate the factory for his mother, who furnished him money for that purpose; that he paid off some of the debts of the old firm with merchandise which was transferred to the defendant, and offered to pay Bryant in the same manner; and that he procured from other factories building material which he shipped to patrons of the Portland Door and Lumber Company and thereby made profits in which his mother had no interest. Conceding that McLoughlin had authority from his mother to do the acts established by the evidence, can it be inferred from the proof of such acts that she also

gave him power to execute notes for her? "When the authority to execute or indorse a negotiable instrument," says Mr. Daniels in his work on Negotiable Instruments, (4th ed. § 292,) "is sought to be deduced from an agency to do certain other acts, it must be made to appear affirmatively that the signing or indorsement of such an instrument was within the general objects and purposes of the authority which was actually conferred. And in interpreting the authority of the agent, it is to be strictly construed." An agent employed to make purchases cannot give a negotiable note on which his principal will be liable: *Brown* v. *Parker*, 7 Allen, 337; *Taber* v. *Cannon*, 8 Metc. (Mass.), 456; *Webber* v. *Williams College*, 23 Pick. 302. An agent employed to manage a store has no authority in consequence of such agency to make or indorse notes in the name of his principal: *Smith* v. *Gibson*, 6 Blackf. 369. "The power of binding by promissory negotiable notes," says HUBBARD, J., in *Paige* v. *Stone*, 10 Metc. (Mass.), 160, "can be conferred only by the direct authority of the party to be bound, with the single exception where, by necessary implication, the duties to be performed cannot be discharged without the exercise of such a power. To facilitate the business of note-making, and thus affect the interest and estates of third persons to an indefinite amount, is not within the object and intent of the law regulating the common duties of principal and agent; neither is the power to be implied because occasionally an instance occurs in which a note, so made, should in equity be paid." It has been held that an agent's authority to execute negotiable paper will be implied when a note has been given for goods or material necessary to the transaction of the principal's business, (*Odeorne* v. *Marcy*, 13 Mass. 177,) but in such cases, in order to hold the

principal liable, it must appear that the purchases
were made for his benefit or authorized by him: *Smith
v. Gibson,* 6 Blackf. 369. In the case at bar the evidence does not show whether Bryant furnished the
materials constituting the consideration for the note
before or after the bill of sale was executed, or that
they were for the use or benefit of the defendant or
authorized by her. It follows that McLoughlin, as
manager of the sash and door factory, did not have
power to bind his principal by the execution of the
note, nor can such authority be inferred from the
proof of facts by which it is sought to be established.

5. Counsel for respondent contends that McLoughlin, as a witness for the plaintiff, was unwilling and
hostile, and that, having failed to produce the power
of attorney from his mother, it must be presumed that
if the instrument had been in evidence it would have
established his authority to execute the note. The
bill of exceptions does not show that any previous demand had been made to produce the power of attorney, and this witness testified that it had been at one
time in his possession, but that he did not know where
it was or to whom he had delivered it; and that it did
not contain such authority. Had the plaintiff made a
prima facie case from the production of other evidence,
sufficient by itself to support the judgment. the failure
to produce the power of attorney would raise a presumption that it contained the necessary authority;
but this presumption does not relieve the plaintiff altogether from the burden of proving his case. Had
other evidence of the contents of the power of attorney been introduced, from which it appeared that sufficient authority had been delegated to warrant the
execution of the note,—assuming that McLoughlin

stood in the relation of an adverse party at the trial,—
the presumption invoked might be indulged: Lawson
on Evidence, 137; 2 Wharton on Evidence, § 1268; *The
Life and Fire Insurance Company* v. *Mechanic Fire Insurance
Company,* 7 Wend. 31; *Thayer* v. *Middlesex Mutual Fire Insurance Company,* 10 Pick. 326; *Gage* v. *Parmelee,* 87 Ill.
329; *Diel* v. *Missouri Pacific Railway Company,* 37 Mo. App.
454. A careful examination of the evidence introduced leads us to believe that it failed to show any
authority on the part of the agent to execute the note
for his principal, and that the court erred in denying
the motion for a nonsuit, for which reason the judgment is reversed and a new trial ordered.

REVERSED.

Argued October 14; decided December 2, 1895.

TYLER *v.* STATE.

[42 Pac. 518.]

RECORD OF JUSTICE'S COURT—TESTIMONY—WRIT OF REVIEW—CODE, §§ 587-
2054.—The testimony of witnesses in criminal trials before a justice
of the peace is not part of the "record" in such cases, (Hill's Code,
§ 2054,) and hence is not part of the "certified copy of the record"
that a justice attaches to a writ of review as his answer: Code, § 587

APPEAL from Multnomah: E. D. SHATTUCK, Judge.

This is a proceeding to review the judgment of a
justice's court. The record shows that a verified complaint was filed in the office of the justice of the
peace of South Portland District, Multnomah County,
charging Alfred Tyler with the crime of defacing a
building not his own, and, a warrant being issued
thereon, he was arrested and taken before the justice,
who read the complaint to him, to which he entered
a plea of not guilty. The issue being thus joined, a
trial was had, at which Tyler, after the state had introduced its evidence and rested, moved the court to

dismiss the action and discharge him, but the court overruled the motion, found him guilty as charged, and imposed upon him a fine of ten dollars. Thereupon he filed in the circuit court of said county his petition. in which he purported to set out the substance of the evidence given at the trial by the witnesses for the state. alleging as errors of law the overruling of said motion, and the imposition of the fine, and praying that a writ might issue to review the judgment of the justice's court. A writ of review having been issued and directed to the justice, that officer returned it to the circuit court with a certified copy of the record annexed thereto, and also made the following certificate: "In response to the allegations as to the evidence rendered on the trial of the above entitled action, contained in the petition of Alfred Tyler for a writ of review, I have to state that the evidence given at the trial, or any part thereof, is not part of the record of this court; that the evidence was not written out or in any manner preserved. nor was any request made by defendant or his attorney to extend or preserve the evidence, or make the evidence a part of the record; that to the best of my recollection the testimony set out in the petition of Alfred Tyler is not a full or correct statement of the testimony introduced by the state on said trial; that I have no means of certifying to the evidence rendered at such trial." On the return of the writ, Tyler moved the court for an order requiring the justice to make a more full and complete return thereto, by stating and certifying to the evidence taken before him, which motion having been overruled. the writ was dismissed, and the judgment of the justice's court affirmed, and from the judgment so rendered he appeals.   AFFIRMED.

For appellant there was a brief and an oral argument by *Mr. Sidney Dell.*

For the state there was a brief by *Messrs. George E. Chamberlain,* attorney-general, and *Wilson T. Hume,* district attorney, and an oral argument by *Mr. John H. Hall.*

PER CURIAM. It is contended by the plaintiff that there was an entire absence of proof in the justice's court of the commission by him of the crime charged, and hence the finding of that court that he was guilty thereof is erroneous as a matter of law. The statute. in substance, provides that the writ of review shall be directed to the court whose decision is sought to be reviewed, requiring it to return said writ to the circuit court with a certified copy of the record in question annexed thereto: Hill's Code, § 587. Section 2054 provides that "the records and files of a justice's court are the docket and all papers and process filed in or returned to such court, concerning or belonging to any proceeding authorized to be had or taken therein, or before the justice of the peace who holds such court." The statute nowhere requires the justice to reduce the testimony of witnesses to writing in criminal trials before him as such justice, and hence the evidence taken in a justice's court on the trial of a criminal action is no part of the record. In *Becker* v. *Malheur County,* 24 Or. 217, (33 Pac. 543,) the plaintiff sought to review an order of the board of equalization in the matter of correcting his assessment. The record did not contain the evidence on which the order was founded, but it was held that it must be presumed to have been sufficient to authorize the board to make the order, and the writ was dismissed. BEAN, J., in deciding the case, says: "It thus appears that the only

question on this appeal is whether the proceedings of
a board of equalization, after it has acquired jurisdiction of the taxpayer, will be set aside and annulled on
writ of review because the record does not contain
the evidence on which its findings of fact were based.
There is no provision of law, of which we are aware,
making it the duty of the board to reduce to writing
or preserve the evidence before it in the matter of
the equalization of taxes, and, although it is an inferior tribunal, every presumption exists in favor of the
regularity of its proceedings after it has once acquired jurisdiction." In the case at bar, the evidence
taken at the trial being no part of the record, it
must be presumed to have been sufficient to warrant
the conviction; and as the writ of review brings up
from an inferior court only the record upon which
the court issuing the writ tries the question of jurisdiction and errors affecting the proceedings, (*Road Com
pany* v. *Douglas County,* 5 Or. 406; S. C. 6 Or. 300; *Barton*
v. *La Grande,* 17 Or. 577, 22 Pac. 111; *Smith* v. *City of
Portland,* 25 Or. 297, 35 Pac. 665,) and it appearing
from such record that the justice's court had jurisdiction of both the party to and subject-matter of the
action, it follows that the circuit court committed no
error in dismissing the writ, and hence the judgment
is affirmed.   AFFIRMED.

Argued October 24; decided December 2, 1895.

BIXBY *v.* CHURCH.

[42 Pac. 613.]

STATUTE OF FRAUDS—PROMISE TO PAY DEBT OF ANOTHER.—Where plaintiff performed work for one who contracted with defendants to do it, and, after the work was completed, defendants orally promised to pay therefor, plaintiff cannot recover, though such promise was unconditional.

APPEAL from Multnomah: E. D. SHATTUCK, Judge.

This is an action by Mathias Bixby against Charles P. Church and Joseph Gaston to recover for work and labor alleged to have been performed by the plaintiff for the defendants between the first day of June, eighteen hundred and ninety-two, and the first day of November of the same year. The complaint avers that between the dates named the plaintiff hauled and transported for the defendants, at their special instance and request, thirty-one tons and four hundred pounds of merchandise, at the agreed and stipulated price of six dollars per ton, amounting in the aggregate to the sum of one hundred and eighty-seven dollars and twenty-five cents, no part of which has been paid, except the sum of one hundred dollars. The answer is a specific denial of all the allegations of the complaint. The trial in the court below resulted in the plaintiff recovering judgment for the amount demanded in the complaint, and defendants appeal.

REVERSED.

For appellant there was a brief and an oral argument by *Mr. William H. Adams.*

For respondent there was a brief and an oral argument by *Mr. C. S. Hannum.*

Opinion by MR. CHIEF JUSTICE BEAN.

From the bill of exceptions it appears that at the time the services were rendered defendants were engaged in getting out and marketing logs in the vicinity of Coal Creek, in the State of Washington, and had a contract with one Walter Neish to furnish and deliver logs to them at such place at a stipulated price per thousand, and that the hauling in question was a part of the labor necessary to be done by Neish in performing his contract with the defendants. There was evidence given on the trial from which the jury could have found either (1) that plaintiff was employed by defendants, and that the work was performed for them and on their sole credit, as alleged in the complaint; or, (2) that plaintiff was employed by and rendered the services for Neish, and that defendants agreed to pay him, upon the order of Neish, if they should have funds in their hands belonging to Neish at the time the order should be presented, and not otherwise; or, (3) that the work was performed for Neish, and that defendants verbally agreed to pay therefor in case Neish did not; or, (4) that plaintiff's contract was made with and services rendered to Neish alone, and that after the contract had been completed he gave plaintiff an order on the defendants for the amount sued for, which, upon presentation, they verbally agreed to pay. As applicable to the third and fourth theories of the case suggested, the defendants at the proper time requested the court to instruct the jury, *first,* that if defendants agreed merely to pay Neish's debt in case he did not do so, the verdict must be for them, because the agreement is void under the statute of frauds; and, *second,* that if the contract was made with Neish, and the work per-

formed for him and not the defendants, plaintiff can
not recover, even though defendants afterwards agreed
to pay Neish's debt, because such agreement was not
in writing. That these instructions correctly state the
law as applicable to this case, is not questioned, but
it is claimed that they were given in substance in the
general charge which is made a part of the bill of
exceptions, and consists of three separate instructions,
as follows: "There is some evidence tending to show
that the agreement between the parties was that
Church and Gaston would pay, upon the order of Mr.
Neish, any surplus Neish might have in their hands.
They aver there has been no surplus in their hands,
consequently they have nothing to pay. If that is the
fact about it, your verdict should be for the defendants. There is some evidence still further tending to
show they were sureties; that they undertook to guar-
antee Neish's debt. The plaintiff cannot recover on
that theory of the case, because in such case the undertaking of a man who promises to pay another
man's debt must be in writing; not only in writing,
but must express the consideration. A man cannot be
compelled to pay another's debt unless his promise is
in writing. There is other evidence tending to show
that Church and Gaston undertook to pay absolutely
this demand. You will examine the whole testimony
and determine how the fact was, and if they undertook absolutely to pay, they are bound by that undertaking, and your verdict should be for the plaintiff;
but that is a matter you must decide from the testimony in the case."

These instructions, which are all that were given
by the court, contain no reference to the effect and
validity of a verbal promise of the defendants to pay
made after the work had been performed, in case the

jury should find that it was performed under a contract with Neish and not the defendants. The liability of the defendants is made to depend solely on
whether their promise was conditional or absolute.
The effect of the instructions as given is that if the
defendants' promise was conditional, because made
either to pay out of a particular fund, and such fund
did not exist, or to pay as surety for Neish in case
he did not, plaintiff could not recover, but if the promise was absolute, that is, to pay at all events, the defendants would be liable without reference to whether
it was a promise to pay the debt of another or not.
Now, there was evidence tending to show, and the defendants claimed the fact to be, that plaintiff was
hired by Neish, and rendered the services for him, and
that, if they ever agreed to pay therefor, it was by a
verbal promise made after the work had been performed. Although the jury might have found for the
defendants on this contention, they were necessarily
required, under the instruction of the court, to find a
verdict in favor of the plaintiff if they found the
promise to have been absolute and unconditional, although not in writing. If the defendants hired the
plaintiff to do the work, as he claims in his complaint,
they, of course, would be liable as original promisors;
but if, on the other hand, the work was done under a
contract with Neish, and for him, and the only promise
of defendants to plaintiff was a verbal one, made after
it had been performed, they would not be liable, however absolute their promise may have been, because
such an agreement is within the statute of frauds and
void. There was evidence tending to support this
theory of the case, and defendants were clearly entitled to have it submitted to the jury by proper instructions, and because an instruction to that effect

was not given, although requested, the case must be reversed and a new trial ordered. There are several other assignments of error in the record, but we have not deemed it important to examine them at this time.

REVERSED.

Argued October 30; decided December 9, 1895.

NORTH PACIFIC LUMBER CO. *v.* LANG.
[42 Pac. 799.]

1. NECESSARY ALLEGATIONS FOR A BILL OF INTERPLEADER.—A bill of interpleader must show that two or more persons have presented claims against complainant for the same thing; that complainant has no beneficial interest in the thing claimed; and that he cannot determine without hazard to himself to which of the several claimants the thing belongs; and that there is no collusion with any of the defendants.

2. PRACTICE ON PRESENTING BILL OF INTERPLEADER.— The orderly practice upon the interposition of a bill of interpleader is to determine whether the interpleader will lie or not, and, if it will, to discharge the plaintiff with his costs, upon bringing the money or thing in dispute into court; and the suit should thereafter proceed upon issues joined between the defendants. The making up of these issues may be accomplished in whatever way seems best adapted to secure an orderly and intelligible presentation of the rights of the contending parties.

3. WHAT DEFENDANTS MAY INTERPLEAD.— One of the essential requisites of a bill of interpleader is a showing of a privity of some sort between the defendants, and that the various claims are of the same nature and character. Thus, a holder of a certain fund which is the purchase price of sundry saw logs, cannot oblige various claimants of such fund to interplead with other persons who are setting up claims against the holder of the fund for unliquidated damages—one of such classes being for claims arising *ex contractu* and the other for claims arising *ex delicto;* one set of claims being against the fund, and the other set being against the holder of the fund.

4. CONFLICT OF LAWS—JURISDICTION TO ENFORCE LAWS OF ANOTHER STATE.—It would seem that a statutory lien of one state ought to be enforced in the court of another state having jurisdiction of the subject matter and parties, unless there is a prescribed procedure for its enforcement which attaches as a part of the liability, or unless its enforcement would be against good morals or natural justice, or prej-

udicial to the general interests of the citizens of the forum, under the general principles discussed in *Aldrich* v. *Anchor Coal Company*, 24 Or. 32, but this point is not decided.

6. ENFORCEMENT OF LIENS OF ANOTHER STATE.—Where the statute of Washington provided that a lien on saw logs should not be binding for more than twelve months, unless a civil action should be brought within that time to enforce such lien, and a suit was commenced in Washington in due time, but the logs where thereafter removed to Oregon before a decree was entered, a suit cannot be maintained in Oregon after the twelve months have expired, for the property having been beyond the jurisdiction of the Washington court when the decree was entered, the lien was not fixed thereby, even conceding that the lien can be enforced in Oregon.

APPEAL from Multnomah: HARTWELL HURLEY, Judge.

About March first, eighteen hundred and ninety-three, one Matti Makarainin, at plaintiff's instance, sold and delivered to it certain saw logs of the reasonable value of some three hundred and thirty-one dollars, from which the sum of two dollars and seventy cents was to be deducted as scaling charges, leaving a balance due from plaintiff of about three hundred and twenty-eight dollars, which Makarainin assigned two days thereafter to Eli Maketa, and he to defendant Lang and Company on the seventh of the same month. After the sale Makarainin gave to the defendant Matthieson an order upon plaintiff for forty dollars, which was accepted subject to the ascertainment of the balance due Makarainin, prior, as Matthieson claims, to the assignment. On the twenty-first day of March, eighteen hundred and ninety-three, M. P. Callender caused the moneys due from plaintiff to be attached to secure in part a claim of some three thousand four hundred and ninety-two dollars against Makarainin. The defendants Lang and Company, as the holders of the Makarainin claim, having, on June first, eighteen hundred and ninety-three, commenced

an action against plaintiff in the Circuit Court of the
State of Oregon for Multnomah County to recover the
said sum of three hundred and twenty-eight dollars
and sixty-one cents, the plaintiff, on the third day of
October, eighteen hundred and ninety-three, and before
its time to answer or otherwise plead had expired,
filed a bill of interpleader setting forth the foregoing
facts, and further alleging "That defendants C. O.
Bergman and John Linkman also claim said sum of
money * * * under and by virtue of a certain
judgment by them heretofore obtained against said
Makarainin, and claimed by them to be duly levied
upon said saw logs so sold to plaintiff, and upon said
sum of three hundred and twenty-eight dollars and
sixty-one cents now remaining in the hands of plaintiff." A motion to make the bill more definite and
certain having been overruled, the defendant Callender
was, by consent, defaulted, and the other defendants
filed answers and cross-complaints. Separate demurrers were interposed by Lang and Company and Matthieson to each of the answers and cross-complaints
of Bergman and Linkman, which demurrers were sustained December fourth, eighteen hundred and ninety-
three, and failing to plead further default, was entered
against them on the fifteenth day of February, eighteen hundred and ninety-four, and at the same time
the court further decreed "That said defendants John
Linkman and C. O. Bergman and each of them are
not entitled to any of the money interpleaded by the
plaintiff and deposited in this court, and that the
other parties herein, or the claim or claims of those
which shall hereafter be found to be entitled thereto,
are declared to be prior to the claim of either of said
defendants C. O. Bergman and John Linkman." On
February twenty-third, eighteen hundred and ninety-

four, the court, with the consent of Lang and Company and Matthieson, entered a decree declaring the costs of litigation a first lien on the fund, and directing plaintiff to pay Matthieson forty dollars, and the balance remaining of said fund to Lang and Company. On February twenty-fourth Bergman moved the court for default and judgment against plaintiff upon the ground that it had failed to answer or reply to his answer and cross-complaint, and at the same time Bergman and Linkman moved the court to set aside and vacate the orders of December fourth, eighteen hundred and ninety-three, and February fifteenth, eighteen hundred and ninety-four, and for a rehearing upon the demurrers of Matthieson and Lang and Company. On March sixteenth, eighteen hundred and ninety-four, the court set aside the decree of February twenty-third, but refused to disturb the previous orders and decrees, or to give judgment by default against plaintiff. On March twenty-ninth Lang and Company moved for a decree in their favor upon the pleadings, and at the same time plaintiff demurred to the answers and cross-complaints of Bergman and Linkman. The motion was overruled and the demurrers sustained, whereupon Bergman and Linkman were granted leave to file amended answers and cross-complaints, which they did April twenty-seventh, eighteen hundred and ninety-four. To these plaintiff interposed a motion (but it does not clearly appear from the record whether it was to strike out part of or all the denials because not proper amendments of the original answers), together with demurrers to the new matter for the reason that it does not state facts sufficient to constitute a defense to the suit, which were sustained June sixteenth, eighteen hundred and ninety-four, and thereupon the court decreed that a proper case for interpleader had been shown; that plaintiff should not be taxed with the costs, and should be allowed five dollars as attorney's fees; that Matthie son has a first lien upon the fund for forty dollars; and that Lang and Company have a valid claim for the balance; but that the costs and said five dollars attorney's fees be paid first out of the said fund.

From this decree C. O. Bergman and John Linkman appeal. Bergman, by his amended answer and cross-complaint, in effect denies only the allegations of the complaint relating to the defendants, Matthieson, Lang and Company, and Callender, and then proceeding sets up affirmatively the acquirement of certain loggers' liens upon said logs by himself and certain other persons under and by virtue of the laws of the State of Washington, all which had been duly assigned to him in Lewis County in said state; that on October twenty-seventh, eighteen hundred and ninety-two, and within twelve months after said liens were filed, he commenced a suit in the superior court of said Lewis County to foreclose said liens, and thereafter, on March tenth, eighteen hundred and ninety-three, obtained a decree for two thousand eight hundred and fifty-five dollars and seventy-five cents, and for the foreclosure of said liens, which remains wholly unsatisfied; that the plaintiff, without his consent, and with full knowledge of his rights and equities, and of the fact that said claims of lien on said logs had been filed and suit begun to foreclose the same, eloigned, removed, and transported eighty-nine thousand nine hundred and seventy-five feet of said logs, being the same logs mentioned in the complaint, to Portland, in the State of Oregon, about the first day of March, eighteen hundred and ninety-three, and thereafter sawed the same into lumber, thereby rendering identification uncertain and difficult, of all which the other defendants had full notice and knowledge. The prayer is that the claims of the other defendants, except Linkman, be declared void as to him, that plaintiff's complaint be dismissed, and that said plaintiff be decreed to pay him (the said Bergman) the full sum of three hundred and thirty-one dollars and thirty-one cents to be divided *pro rata* between him and Linkman according to their several demands, and for such other relief as may seem meet in equity. The answer and cross-complaint of Linkman is of like import.

MODIFIED.

For appellants Bergman and Linkman there was a brief by *Messrs. Reynolds and Stewart* and *Milton W. Smith,* and an oral argument by *Mr. David Stewart.*

For respondent North Pacific Lumber Company there was a brief and an oral argument by *Mr. Thomas N. Strong.*

For respondents Lang and Company there was a brief by *Messrs. Cox, Cotton, Teal and Minor,* and an oral argument by *Mr. Joseph N. Teal.*

Opinion by MR. JUSTICE WOLVERTON.

1. It is not attempted by the foregoing statement to set forth or take note of all papers filed or all orders of the court, but the endeavor has been to state sufficient of the record to enable this opinion to be understood. The record is encumbered with many papers which were perhaps unnecessary, and might have been omitted if the ordinary practice attending a bill of interpleader had been pursued. The complaint or

bill of interpleader filed by plaintiff seems on its face to state sufficient for the purposes of the suit. Such a bill will lie where two or more persons claim the same thing or debt or duty from the complainant by different or separate interests, and he does not know to which of the claimants he ought of right to deliver the thing in his custody or render the debt or duty, and by reason thereof is in fear of damage or hurt from some of them; or, as defined by Lord Cottenham, "It is where the plaintiff says, 'I have a fund in my possession in which I claim no personal interest, and in which you, the defendants, set up conflicting claims. Pay me my costs, and I will bring the money into court'": Beach on Modern Equity Practice, § 114; *Hoggart* v. *Cutts,* Craig and P. 204; *Wing* v. *Spaulding,* 64 Vt. 83 (23 Atl. 615). The allegations such a bill should contain are, in purport, (1) that two or more persons have preferred claims against the complainant; (2) that they claim the same thing; (3) that the complainant has no beneficial interest in the thing claimed; and (4) that he cannot determine without hazard to himself to which of the several defendants the thing belongs: *Atkinson* v. *Manks,* 1 Cowp. 703. Under the old equity practice it was usual to annex to the bill an affidavit of the plaintiff showing that there was no collusion between him and any of the defendants: Beach on Modern Equity Practice, § 145; but it is perhaps sufficient under our practice that the fact appear by appropriate allegations in the complaint: *Jerome* v. *Jerome,* 5 Conn. 352, and *Nash* v. *Smith,* 6 Conn. 421.

2. The more orderly practice seems to be to first determine whether the interpleader will lie or not. If not, it is unnecessary to go further; but if it will, then

the plaintiff should be discharged from liability, with his costs, upon bringing the money or thing in dispute into court, and the suit should thereafter proceed upon issues properly joined between the defendants. The plaintiff cannot claim relief against any of the defendants, but only that he be protected against the claims of all, and when he has shown sufficient to entitle him to this he is entitled to his interpleader, which fact being determined by the order of the court, he is thenceforth out of the suit: *St. Louis Life Insurance Company* v. *Alliance Mutual Life Insurance Company*, 23 Minn. 7; *Cullen* v. *Dawson*, 24 Minn. 66; *First National Bank* v. *West River Railway Company*, 46 Vt. 633; 2 Beach on Modern Equity Practice, § 637. If, however, at the hearing on the bill, it is made to appear that the defendants have by their several answers clearly and sufficiently presented the proper issues as between themselves, and that such issues are ripe for adjudication, the court may at the time it determines the question of interpleader upon the complaint and issues thereto tendered, also decide the questions at issue between the several defendants, and dispose of the case finally. But whichever course is adopted, the question as to whether the interpleader will lie is always preliminary to a trial of the issues between the defendants, as without the establishment of this fact the defendants can have no contention as between themselves upon the record: 2 Beach on Equity Practice, § 638; *Cullen* v. *Dawson*, 24 Minn. 66; *Farley* v. *Blood*, 30 N. H. 354; *Kirtland* v. *Moore*, 40 N. J. Eq. 106 (2 Atl. 269); *Hall* v. *Baldwin*, 45 N. J. Eq. 858 (18 Atl. 976). It seems there is no settled practice as to the mode of proceeding after it is ascertained that the bill of interpleader will lie: *City Bank* v. *Bangs*, 2 Paige Ch. 570. VAN FLEET, Vice Chancellor, in *Kirtland* v. *Moore*, says.

touching the case as among the defendants: "The
court may then adopt such course as may seem best
under the circumstances; as by directing that issues
shall be raised by appropriate pleadings, or that an
action at law shall be brought, or that such other
course shall be taken as may seem best suited to the
nature of the case." See *Angell* v. *Hadden,* 16 Ves. Jr.
202. In *City Bank* v. *Bangs,* 2 Paige Ch. 570, the case
was referred to a master, and, as so many conflicting
claims were involved, the court directed that any one
of the parties should be allowed to file before the
master a statement under. oath in the nature of a bill
of discovery, which statement all the other defendants
should be required to answer under oath. And so it
appears competent, for the purpose of determining
what are the issues as between and among the defendants, for the court to adopt any course or method of
pleading which may seem appropriate or best suited
for raising such issues, and, when once raised or settled, the court will pursue the prevailing equitable
practice in trying them. Thus, it will appear that the
orders of the court defaulting the defendants Bergman and Linkman, and declaring that the claims of
Matthieson and Lang and Company were prior and
superior to theirs, before determining whether the bill
of interpleader could be properly entertained, were
premature. See *First National Bank* v. *West River Railway
Company,* 46 Vt. 633. Bergman and Linkman were con
testing the right of plaintiff to proceed under its bill
of interpleader, and until this contest was settled no
issues as among the defendants could be determined.

The main discussion at the trial was directed to
the question as to whether the defendants Bergman
and Linkman had such an interest in the fund in the
hands of the plaintiff as would warrant the court in

directing it to be paid to them regardless of the order in which the court may have proceeded. It is
difficult to say from the answers and cross-complaints
of Bergman and Linkman just what they intended to
accomplish thereby, whether to defeat the interpleader,
and thereby to terminate the proceeding; or whether, if
unsuccessful in this, they intended by their cross-bills
to establish their right to the fund as between themselves and the other defendants; and, if this latter,
whether they designed to establish their right thereto
under the right of action accorded by the statute of
Washington against any person rendering difficult, uncertain, or impossible of identification any logs covered
by the statutory lien, or by virtue of the lien itself.
Their denials, which are mainly upon want of knowledge or information sufficient to form a belief, reach
only·the allegations of the complaint showing that
claims had been preferred by the other defendants
against the fund in the hands of plaintiff. It is admitted that plaintiff has such fund, and that it owes
for the saw logs in the identical amount. It is further
admitted that plaintiff is unable to determine as to
whom it ought to pay the fund without hazard to
itself, that it claims no beneficial interest therein, and
that there is no collusion between it and any of the
defendants. They, themselves, are claiming the fund
beyond question; but they have stated their whole
case upon the record by affirmative allegations, and
whether styled a further and separate defense or a
cross-complaint, or whether designed to defeat the
plaintiff's bill or to establish their right to the fund,
makes but little difference for the purposes of this inquiry. The defendants Matthieson and Lang and Company have by their answers each admitted that they
have laid claim to this fund, and by cross-complaints

have set up their respective demands. Does this record present a case ripe for final determination? The
only apparent obstacle in the way is the issue of fact
raised by the answers of Bergman and Linkman
touching the question as to whether the other defendants had preferred claims against the plaintiff for the
fund in its hands, but, as the other defendants have
tendered no issue in this regard, and as Bergman and
Linkman have not made the point nor. insisted upon
it here, we feel warranted in assuming that they have
intentionally waived it.

3. We are now to determine whether, upon the
face of Bergman's and Linkman's separate defenses or
cross-complaints, they have shown a right to the fund,
or are interested therein. If they have, the case
ought to go back for a completion of the issues between them and the other defendants, and a trial upon
such as may be tendered, but if they have not shown
such right or interest, it ought now to be finally disposed of. At the time the liens of Bergman and
Linkman upon the logs in question were filed in the
State of Washington, there existed, and still exists, in
this state a similar law providing for the acquirement
of a statutory lien upon logs. Indeed, the law of this
state was taken from the Washington statute, with but
few modifications or changes. The Washington statute
contains a provision as follows: "Any person who
shall injure, impair, or destroy, or who shall render
difficult, uncertain, or impossible of identification, any
saw logs, * * * upon which there is a lien as
herein provided, without the express consent of the
person entitled to such lien, shall be liable to the lien-
holder for the damages to the amount secured by his
lien, which may be recovered by a civil action against

such person": Hill's Statutes of Washington, § 1694.
It has been held by this court that where a statute
creates a liability, unless it has prescribed a procedure for its enforcement, which attaches as a part of
the liability, it can be enforced in any court having
jurisdiction of the subject matter and the parties. In
this respect it is similar to the common law right or
liability, and may be enforced without regard to territorial limitations: *Aldrich* v. *Anchor Coal Company*, 24
Or. 32 (41 Am. St. Rep. 831, 32 Pac. 756). The rule
applies to actions arising *ex delicto* as well as to those
arising *ex contractu.* In *Burns* v. *Grand Rapids Railroad
Company*, 113 Ind. 172, (15 N. E. 230,) an action instituted for negligently causing the death of a person,
MITCHELL, C. J., states the rule thus: "A civil right
of action acquired under the laws of the state where
the injury is inflicted, or a civil liability incurred in
one state, may be enforced in any other in which the
party in fault may be found, according to the course
of procedure in the latter state," citing a long list of
authorities. And it is not even necessary that the law
of the state where the right of action accrued and the
laws of the forum where it is sought to be enforced
should both give the same right of action: *Herrick* v.
Minneapolis Railway Company. 31 Minn. 11 (47 Am. Rep.
771, 16 N. W. 413). Such actions arising *ex delicto* are
transitory in their character, and ought not to be circumscribed by locality as to their enforcement, as
otherwise justice might often be defeated. To justify
the courts of one state in refusing to enforce such a
right of action given by another it must be upon the
ground that its enforcement would be against good
morals or natural justice, or that for some good reason it would be prejudicial to the general interests of
the citizens of the state or the forum. Although there

are some cases opposed to this view, it appears to
be sustained by the great weight of authority. See
Dennick v. *Railroad,* 103 U. S. 11; *Boyce* v. *Wabash Railway Company,* 63 Iowa, 70 (50 Am. Rep. 730, 18 N. W.
673); *Knight* v. *West Jersey Railroad Company,* 108 Pa. St.
250 (56 Am. Rep. 200); *Chicago and St. Louis Railway
Company* v. *Doyle,* 8 Am. and Eng. R. R. Cas. 171, and
Leonard v. *Columbia Steam Navigation Company,* 84 N. Y. 48
(38 Am. Rep. 491). So it would seem from the answers that Bergman and Linkman each has a right of
action within this state against the plaintiff for damages in taking these logs away and rendering them
impossible of identification. But the action sounds in
tort; it is one arising *ex delicto,* and it does not appear
to be one in which the tort could be waived and a
civil action substituted. In this view of the matter
the plaintiff is not a stakeholder as to Bergman and
Linkman, as they have no claim upon it for this fund.
Their claim is by independent title, without privity
of estate, title, or contract, as it pertains to the fund.
It is one for unliquidated damages only, arising from
a tort.

One of the essential requisites to equitable relief
by bill of interpleader is that all the adverse titles of
the respective claimants must be connected or dependent, or one derived from the other, or from a common
source. There must be privity of some sort between
all the parties, such as privity of estate, title, or contract, and the claims should be of the same nature
and character. In cases of adverse independent titles
or demands, actions to determine the rights of liti-
gants must be directed against the party holding the
property, and he must defend as best he can at law.
The primordial element which forms the basis of correlative demands being absent, there can be no con-

tention among the claimants; neither can say to the other, "I have a better right or title than you," but each may be able to say, "I have just cause for complaint against him who would have us litigate only among ourselves." Thus, where the only relation which the plaintiff sustains to the defendants is that he is the debtor of one of them, he cannot invoke the aid of an interpleader: *Third National Bank* v. *Skillings Iumler Company,* 132 Mass. 410. So an agent or bailee cannot maintain a bill of interpleader where a person deposits with him money or property, not as a stakeholder, but as such agent or bailee, and the thing deposited is claimed by a third party: 2 Story on Equity Jurisprudence, §§ 816–817. Where one claimant seeks a certain rent from the tenant in possession, and the other unliquidated damages for use and occupation, they cannot be required to interplead: *Johnson* v. *Atkinson,* 3 Anstr. 798; *Dodd* v. *Bellows,* 29 N. J. Eq. 127. In *National Life Insurance Company* v. *Pingrey,* 141 Mass. 411, (6 N. E. 93,) the company had issued a policy of insurance on the life of F. A. P., payable to E. H. P., but subsequently allowed F. A. P. to surrender the policy without the consent of E. H. P., and thereupon issued a new policy to F. A. P., payable to C. L. P. On the death of F. A. P. it was held that the company could not interplead E. H. P. and C. L. P. The court say: "By issuing these two policies the plaintiff has exposed itself to both of these claims, and must meet them as best it may. The difficulty of maintaining a bill of interpleader is not technical, but fundamental. In this form of proceeding we can not inquire whether the plaintiff has incurred a double liability. That result is possible. The plaintiff ought to be in a position to be heard upon the question; but, on a bill of interpleader, which assumes that the plaintiff is merely a stakeholder, the plaintiff cannot be heard: *Houghton* v. *Kendall*, 7 Allen, 72. A plaintiff can not have an order that the defendants interplead, when one important question to be tried is whether, by reason of his own act, he is under a liability to each of them." See, also, *Bechtel* v. *Sheafer*, 117 Pa. St. 555 (11 Atl. 889); 1 Beach on Modern Equity Practice, § 147, and Pomeroy's Equity, §§ 1320–1324. So it is in the case at bar. Plaintiff has upon the face of these cross-complaints incurred an independent liability to the defendants Bergman and Linkman sounding in damages for a tortious act. With the transaction from which the liability arose the other defendants are not in privity, their interest being in the fund; and the converse is also true, Bergman and Linkman are not in privity in title or interest as it pertains to the fund.

4. The next question is, can they establish their right to the fund through their statutory lien upon equitable grounds? It is claimed that, as the laws of Oregon provide for the acquirement by laborers upon saw logs of a like statutory lien, and for a like enforcement thereof, that the lien could as well be enforced in Oregon as in Washington, and, if as against the logs, it could as well against the fund which represents the logs. There is much force in this position, as it has been shown that an action will lie for damages, (*Aldrich* v. *Anchor Coal Company*, 24 Or. 32; 41 Am. St. Rep. 831, 32 Pac. 756,) by a parity of reasoning why not a suit to foreclose the lien, in the absence of any special statutory procedure devised as a part of the remedy. It would seem to be in accord with a just comity between the states where the rights of citizens of the state in which the remedy is in-

voked are not impaired or intrenched upon. But it is not necessary for us to decide this question, because the lien seems to have been lost by failure to invoke the remedy in season, even admitting the proposition to be tenable.

5. The Washington statute provides that the lien shall not bind the logs for a longer period than twelve months, unless a civil action shall be brought in a competent court to enforce the lien within that time: Hill's Statutes of Washington, § 1688. Now, the lien was filed October first, eighteen hundred and ninety-two, and no suit was instituted here within the twelve months. If this suit would suffice for that purpose, it came too late, as it was commenced October third, eighteen hundred and ninety-three. True, a suit was instituted in time in the Washington court, but the logs were removed without its jurisdiction before a decree was entered, and by reason thereof the lien was not fixed by its action. We know of no rule by which the lien would be continued by the commencement of the suit in Washington unless the court retained jurisdiction of the property to fix the lien upon it by a valid decree. This it did not do, and hence no lien can now be established here, even under appellant's contention. The effect of Bergman's and Linkman's further defenses or cross-complaints is to bar the interpleader, and the complaint must be dismissed as to them, as they ought not to be enjoined from proceeding at law; but as to the other defendants the bill is properly filed. In other respects the decree of the court below is in accordance with the facts, and a decree will be entered here in accordance with this opinion.   MODIFIED.

Argued August 1; decided December 9, 1895.

STATE *v.* STEARNS.

[42 Pac. 615.]

EMBEZZLEMENT—INDICTMENT—ALLEGATION OF OWNERSHIP.—In a prosecution under Hill's Code, § 1770, providing for the punishment of any agent of any corporation who "shall embezzle or fraudulently convert to his own use * * * any money * * * of another * * * which shall come into his possession * * * by virtue of his employment," an indictment alleging that defendant, as agent of an insurance company, received for the company money as premiums for insurance, which he failed to pay over or account for, is insufficient for failure to allege that the money received was in fact the money of the company.

APPEAL from Columbia: THOS. A. McBRIDE, Judge.

This is an appeal by L. M. Stearns from a judgment of imprisonment in the penitentiary for the crime of embezzlement. At the beginning of the trial he objected to the introduction of any evidence on the ground that the indictment did not state a crime, because it did not aver the ownership of the property alleged to have been embezzled, nor its value. The charging part of the indictment, so far as material to the questions presented for our determination, is as follows: "The said L. M. Stearns on the first day of August, eighteen hundred and ninety-three, in the County of Columbia and State of Oregon, being then and there a duly qualified solicitor and agent of the State Insurance Company * * * authorized and empowered * * * to solicit business for said company, and to receive the premiums therefor in said Columbia County, Oregon; * * * by virtue of said agency, received for premiums for insurance for said company, from divers persons in Columbia County, Oregon, the sum of one hundred and four dollars and fifteen cents * * * lawful money of the United States of America, consisting of gold and silver coins of the United States of America and United States currency, the particular denominations of said money being now not known to this grand jury, and did afterwards * * * without the consent of said * * * company, feloniously embezzle * * * and fraudulently convert said sum of one hundred and four dollars and fifteen cents to his * * * own use, and did then and there fail and neglect and still fails and neglects to account for said money or any part thereof to said State Insurance Company, according to the nature of his trust, contrary to the statute, etc.

For appellant there was a brief and an oral argument by *Mr. Clarence Cole.*

For the state there was a brief and an oral argument by *Messrs. Cicero M. Idleman,* attorney-general, and *W. N. Barrett,* district attorney.

Opinion by MR. CHIEF JUSTICE BEAN.

This indictment was found under section 1770 of the statute which provides that "If any * * * agent * * * of any incorporation, shall embezzle or fraudulently convert to his own use * * * any money * * * of another, which may be the subject of larceny, and which shall have come into his possession or be under his care, by virtue of such employment, * * * shall be deemed guilty of larceny, and, upon conviction thereof, shall be punished accordingly."

To sustain a conviction under this statute, it is clear the property charged to have been embezzled or fraudulently converted must be the property of another than the person indicted, and that fact must be alleged in the indictment. Now, the indictment here does not aver the ownership of the money alleged to have been embezzled in direct terms or by necessary inference. It is true it alleges that as agent of the State Insurance Company the defendant received for premiums for insurance for the company from divers persons certain sums of money, which he failed to pay over or account for according to the nature of his trust, but this is not an allegation that the money so received was in fact the property of the company. For aught that appears in the indictment it may have been understood between the defendant and the company that the specific money received by him for insurance was not to be turned over to the company, but that he was authorized and expected to mingle and mix it with his own, and it should thus become a matter of account between him and his principal. If such was the case he could not be punished criminally for failing to pay over the balance due the company, however morally wrong it may have been. The object of the statute was not to provide punishment for a mere breach of a contract, but to remedy a defect in the common law which did not provide for the punishment criminally of a servant or agent who came lawfully into the possession of money or property of his principal, and feloniously converted it to his own use. Prior to the statute it was held that, since a larceny must include a trespass or a taking and carrying away of the property stolen, a servant who came rightfully into possession of the property of his master and embezzled or converted it to his own use could not, in general, be punished criminally. It was to avoid this difficulty and defect in the criminal law that embezzlement was declared a crime equal in degree to larceny, with the same penalty attached to its commission. But the same title and right to the possession of the identical property must exist in embezzlement as in larceny. It has consequently been held that where a servant receiving money has a right to mingle it with his own, being answerable for the balance, an indictment for embezzlement does not lie for the failure to pay over according to his contract: *People* v. *Howe*, 2 Thomp. and C. 833; *Commonwealth* v. *Stearns*, 2 Metc. (Mass.), 343; *Commonwealth* v. *Libbey*, 11 Metc. (Mass.), 64 (45 Am. Dec. 185); *Miller* v. *State*, 16 Neb. 179. The indictment in this case does not negative the ownership in the defendant, or allege that the money said to have been embezzled was the property of some person other than the defendant, and consequently does not state a crime. For this reason the judgment must be reversed, and it is so ordered.   REVERSED.

Argued November 18; decided December 23, 1895.

WILLIS *v.* HOLMES.

[42 Pac. 989.]

1. JUDGMENT ON THE PLEADINGS — PRACTICE — VERDICT.—A judgment will not be rendered on the pleadings where they present an issue of fact, although the party upon whom the burden of proof rests refuses to introduce any evidence; the remedy in such a case is to move the court to direct a verdict.

2. PAYMENT AS A DEFENSE — BURDEN OF PROOF — GARNISHEE.—The burden of proving payment is always on the party pleading that defense, and this is the rule applicable to proceedings against a garnishee who admits an indebtedness to the defendant a short time before the service of the garnishment, but claims to have paid the debt before receiving the writ.

3. EVIDENCE — DECLARATIONS OF DEBTOR.— Payment by a garnishee of his debt to defendant cannot be proven against plaintiff by statements of defendant made after service of the garnishment.

28 OR.—19.

APPEAL from Douglas: J. C. FULLERTON, Judge.

This is a garnishment proceeding by P. L. Willis against M. B. Holmes and G. A. Smith, garnishee. On or prior to September sixth, eighteen hundred and ninety-three, the plaintiff commenced an action against Holmes to recover money, and caused a writ of attachment to be issued and served upon Smith, with notice that all money due from him to Holmes was thereby garnished. Subsequently, and on December third, eighteen hundred and ninety-three, he recovered a judgment against Holmes for the sum of one thousand two hundred and seventy dollars and thirty cents, and forty-nine dollars and eighty cents costs and disbursements. Smith's answer to the garnishment being unsatisfactory to plaintiff, he thereupon filed and served upon him written allegations in the nature of a complaint and interrogatories, wherein it is alleged: "That on the sixth day of September, eighteen hundred and ninety-three, the date of the service of the attachment on said garnishee, George A. Smith, he was justly indebted to the defendant M. B. Holmes in the sum of six thousand five hundred dollars — one thousand six hundred dollars for land sold and conveyed by the defendant to said garnishee, and four thousand nine hundred dollars for promissory notes payable to said M. B. Holmes, and by him sold and conveyed to the said George A. Smith garnishee." The garnishee answered, denying that at the date of the service of the garnishment he was indebted to Holmes in the sum of one thousand six hundred dollars or any other sum for land sold and conveyed, or four thousand nine hundred dollars or any other sum for promissory notes sold to him by Holmes, or that he was justly or at all indebted to Holmes in the sum of six thousand five hundred dollars, or any other sum of money whatever. For a further and separate defense he alleged that, on August fifteenth, eighteen hundred and ninety-three, he purchased from Holmes three promissory notes of the face value in the aggregate of four thousand two hundred and fifteen dollars and fifty cents, and on August eighteenth, eighteen hundred and ninety-three, one promissory note of the face value of five hundred dollars—which notes are each particularly described in the answer—and that on the last mentioned day he purchased of Holmes two tracts of land at the aggregate price and value of one thousand six hundred dollars; that the promissory notes and land were sold to him by Holmes at the agreed price of five thousand five hundred dollars; that such purchase price was wholly paid by him on the said eighteenth day of August, eighteen hundred and ninety-three, and prior to the service of garnishment, and that such sales and purchases are the identical transactions referred to and set out in the plaintiff's allegation or complaint. To this a reply was filed denying the payment as alleged in the answer, and admitting all the other allegations. Upon the issues thus joined a trial was had before a jury, which resulted in a verdict in favor of the garnishee, and from the judgment which followed the plaintiff appeals.

REVERSED.

For appellant there was a brief by *Messrs. William R. Willis, A. M. Crawford,* and *Guy G. Willis,* with an oral argument by *Mr. William R. Willis.*

For respondent there was a brief and an oral argument by *Mr. J. W. Hamilton.*

Opinion by MR. CHIEF JUSTICE BEAN.

1. The record discloses that after the jury had been impanelled and the case stated by counsel, the plaintiff claimed that, as the only issue in the case was one of payment, the burden of proof was on the garnishee, and that he should, therefore, submit his evidence first, which he declined and refused to do, whereupon the plaintiff moved for judgment on the pleadings, which was denied, and such ruling is assigned as error. The motion, under the circumstances, was properly overruled. There was an issue of fact presented by the pleadings for determination, and, while it remained undisposed of, no judgment could have been entered on such motion. If, as the case then stood, and the plaintiff now contends, he was entitled to a verdict, he should have moved the court to direct the jury to return a verdict in his favor, and not for a judgment on the pleadings.

2. As the court instructed the jury that the burden of proof was on the plaintiff to show that the garnishee had not, prior to the service of the garnishment, paid for the property purchased from Holmes, it is proper to consider that question here. The allegations of the parties take the place and perform the office of pleadings in an ordinary action at law, (*Smith* v. *Conrad,* 23 Or. 206, 31 Pac. 398,) and, as we understand them, present but one issue of fact, and that is whether the garnishee had, prior to the garnishment, paid Holmes for the property which he admits to have purchased. The answer of the garnishee not only admits all the allegations of the complaint, except the indebtedness, but affirmatively alleges that a short time before the service of garnishment he purchased of the defendant in the action the lands and notes mentioned in the complaint, at the agreed and

stipulated price of five thousand five hundred dollars, but alleges that he had wholly paid for the same prior to such time. The reply denied the allegation of payment, and thus raised the only issue of fact in the case. Upon this issue the burden of proof was clearly with the garnishee. The rule is well settled that when a defendant admits a cause of action set out in the complaint, and relies upon the defense of payment, the burden of proof is upon him to establish that fact: 2 Greenleaf on Evidence, § 516; *Curtis* v. *Perry*, 33 Neb. 519 (50 N. W. 426); *Wolffe* v. *Nall*, 62 Ala. 24; *Conselyea* v. *Swift*, 103 N. Y. 604 (9 N. E. 489); *Bradley* v. *Harwi*, 43 Kan. 314 (23 Pac. 566). And this is the rule applicable to the proceedings against a garnishee who by his answer admits that he was indebted to the defendant a short time before the service of process of garnishment upon him, but claims that the debt was paid and discharged before that time. As is said in Waples on Attachments, (p. 377,) "The *onus* is upon him (the garnishee) when the plaintiff has taken issue upon the answer, after the admission that he held such funds at a period immediately, or within a few weeks or even months, preceding the service of the writ." See also Drake on Attachments, § 674; *Barker* v. *Osborne*, 71 Me. 69. It was contended at the argument that, under the form of the allegations in this proceeding, the defense of payment could have been proven under a general denial, but this contention raises a question of pleadings not necessary to be considered at this time, for, even if the fact of payment could be shown under the general issue, it would not change the rule as to the burden of proof. Mr. Greenleaf says, in the section cited, that in some instances the defense of payment may be made under the general issue, and in others it must be specially pleaded, but,

"in either case, the burden of proof is on the defendant, who must prove the payment of money, or something accepted in its stead, made to the plaintiff or to
some person authorized in his behalf to receive it."
We think, therefore, that the court below erred in
holding that the burden of proof was on the plaintiff,
and in so instructing the jury.

3.   The objection to the testimony of the witnesses
Walcott, Bryant, and Hume should have been sustained.
That of the two former was to the effect that in November, eighteen hundred and ninety-three, Holmes,
the judgment debtor and defendant in the action,
stated to them that the garnishee had paid him for
the notes and land mentioned in the pleadings. This
statement was made after the service of the garnishment, and was, therefore, incompetent evidence against
the plaintiff to show the fact of payment: Drake on
Attachments, § 655; *Warren* v. *Moore,* 52 Ga. 562. The
testimony of Hume, if otherwise competent, was too
remote and uncertain to afford any legitimate inference that the garnishee had on hand at the date of
the payment alleged in the answer the money with
which to make such payment. The judgment of the
court below is reversed, and a new trial ordered.

                                        REVERSED.

THORNTON *v.* KRIMBEL.

[42 Pac. 995.]

1. REFORMATION OF WRITTEN INSTRUMENTS — EQUITY.— In order to justify the interposition of a court of equity to reform a written instrument for an alleged mistake of fact, it must be distinctly alleged and conclusively proved that the mistake was mutual, or that it was the mistake of one party superinduced by the fraud or some inequitable conduct of the other.*

2. CROSS-APPEAL.— A party to a judgment or decree who has not appealed is presumed to be satisfied, and cann   '; the appellate tribunal to modify or reverse the decision of i .. .. 'r court.

APPEAL from Multnomah: LOYAL B. STEARNS, Judge.

This is a suit to reform a contract and bond, and to recover damages for an alleged breach of the con-tract. The facts are, that on March twenty-fourth, eighteen hundred and ninety-three, the defendant Krimbel entered into an agreement with the plaintiff, by the terms of which he undertook to furnish the material and erect and finish a dwelling-house for her, in conformity with the plans and specifications thereof; and it was also provided that the contractor should protect the building from liens, and that a bond should be given for the faithful performance of the terms and conditions of said agreement. The agreement having been reduced to writing, was signed by each of the defendants, but not by the plaintiff, and a joint and several bond, in which Krimbel was designated as principal, and —— and —— as sureties, was signed by the defendants Meyer and Ward only. A lien

*The following Oregon cases require the complaint to also show that the mistake did not arise from the gross negligence of the plaintiff: *Lewis* v. *Lewis,* 5 Or. 169; *Foster* v. *Schmeer,* 15 Or. 363; *Hyland* v. *Hyland,* 19 Or. 51; *Meier* v. *Kelly,* 20 Or. 86; *Osborn* v. *Ketchum,* 25 Or. 352. — REPORTER.

having been filed against the property, the plaintiff, claiming the building had not been completed, commenced this suit, and, in substance, alleges that it was the intention of the parties that she should sign said contract, but through inadvertence she had omitted to do so, and that she offered to sign the same; that it was also their intention that said bond should be executed by Krimbel as principal, and that Meyer and Ward should be named therein as sureties, but through mistake Krimbel failed to sign it, and the names of the sureties were omitted from the body of the bond; that by mistake Krimbel was wrongly described in the contract and bond as "Kimbel"; and, having alleged several breaches of the contract, and the damages resulting therefrom, she prayed a decree reforming said contract and bond, and a recovery of her damages. The defendants, separately answering, after denying the material allegations of the complaint, allege facts tending to constitute an estoppel, and pray that the suit be dismissed. The replies having put in issue the allegations of new matter contained in the several answers, a trial was had, resulting in a decree reforming the contract and bond, awarding Krimbel fifty-six dollars and thirty cents due on the contract, and requiring the plaintiff and Krimbel each to pay one half the costs, and from this decree the plaintiff appeals.   AFFIRMED.

For appellant there was an oral argument and a brief by *Mr. Richard H. Thornton* to this effect.

Error is apparent on a mere perusal of the abstract in this case. The main issues have been ignored, and it is impossible to tell on what basis of fact or of law the decree is framed. The court

granted the defendant Krimbel affirmative relief for
which he did not pray. He asked for no compensation; but the court awarded him fifty-six dollars and
thirty cents. How this amount was ascertained is an
insoluble puzzle. The decree in this case should be
affirmed as to the reformation of the bond, and as to
the perpetual injunction of the action in the justice's
court. It should be reversed as to the payment to
Krimbel by appellant of fifty-six dollars and thirty
cents. It should be amended by awarding compensation to the appellant in the sum of one thousand three
hundred and thirty-two dollars, with interest from
June sixth, eighteen hundred and ninety-four, for
which sum execution should issue against the property of either or all of the respondents, to wit, one
hundred and forty-nine dollars and fifty cents in respect of Burks' lien, five hundred and fifty dollars in
respect of bad painting, and six hundred and thirty-
two dollars and fifty cents at the least, in respect of
noncompletion and vacancy of the house; and by
awarding compensation to the appellant in the sum of
six hundred and fifty-seven dollars and forty-five
cents, with interest from same date, in respect of
overpayment, for which sum execution should issue
against the property of the respondent Krimbel alone.
The costs should be charged to the respondents, the
appellant not having been in fault. Let us then break
forth into singing —

> Jacob Krimbel, Joseph Burke,
> Why should you your contracts shirk?
> Jacob Krimbel, Joseph Burke,
> Try to do some honest work.
> Children burnt will fear the fire:
> Ward *videlicet* and Meyer.

For respondent there was a brief and an oral argument by *Mr. Robert C. Wright.*

PER CURIAM. 1. It is contended by the plaintiff that the court erred in several particulars, which errors are assigned as grounds for a modification of the decree, while the defendants contend that the complaint does not state facts sufficient to constitute a cause of suit, and that the evidence is not sufficient to warrant a reformation of the contract and bond. The rule is well settled that in order to justify the interposition of a court of equity to reform a written instrument for an alleged mistake of fact, it must be distinctly alleged and conclusively proved that the mistake was mutual to both parties, or that it was the mistake of one party superinduced by the fraud or some inequitable conduct of the other: *Fahie* v. *Pressey,* 2 Or. 23 (80 Am. Dec. 401); *Everts* v. *Steger,* 5 Or. 147; *Lewis* v. *Lewis,* 5 Or. 169; *Foster* v. *Schmeer,* 15 Or. 363 (15 Pac. 625); *Hyland* v. *Hyland,* 19 Or. 51 (23 Pac. 811); *Kleinsorge* v. *Rohse,* 25 Or. 51 (34 Pac. 874). There is no evidence of plaintiff's intention to sign the contract, or of Krimbel's intention to sign the bond; and for all that appears he may never have intended to sign it, and, if so, the absence of his signature would not be in consequence of any mistake on his part. It has been repeatedly held that a court of equity will not reform a written instrument upon the ground of mistake, unless the mistake be established by clear and satisfactory evidence: *Shively* v. *Welch,* 2 Or. 288; *Stevens* v. *Murtin,* 6 Or. 193; *Remillard* v. *Prescott,* 8 Or. 37; *Epstein* v. *State Insurance Company,* 21 Or. 179 (27 Pac. 1045).

2. The defendants not having taken a cross-appeal it must be presumed that they were satisfied with the

decree, and cannot now be heard to complain of a
failure to allege or prove the existence of a mutual
mistake, and hence it follows that the decree is affirmed.   AFFIRMED.

Argued November 7; decided December 30, 1895.

GREGOIRE *v.* ROURKE.

[42 Pac. 996.]

1. ACTION BY ASSIGNEE OF CHOSE IN ACTION—CONSIDERATION.— An assignee of a chose in action in Oregon may maintain an action
thereon in his own name, although he paid no consideration therefor: *Dawson* v. *Pogue*, 18 Or. 94, approved and followed.

2. PLEADING ASSIGNMENT OF CHOSE—SURPLUSAGE.— It is not incumbent
upon an assignee of a chose in action to show that he paid a consideration therefor, because the complaint avers a sale as well as an
assignment to him, for the allegation in regard to the sale may be
rejected as surplusage.

APPEAL from Marion: GEORGE H. BURNETT, Judge.

This is an action to recover an alleged balance of
an account. The plaintiff alleges that on September
eighth, eighteen hundred and ninety-one, E. S. Gregoire and himself were copartners in business under
the firm name of E. S. Gregoire and Son, at which
time said firm sold and delivered to the defendants a
quantity of wheat of the value of two thousand nine
hundred and ninety-seven dollars and sixty cents; that
the defendants paid on account thereof two thousand
eight hundred and twenty-two dollars and sixty cents,
leaving a balance of one hundred and seventy-five
dollars due thereon; that said firm sold and assigned
the account to him; and that he is the owner and
holder thereof and entitled to the moneys due thereon
for which he prays judgment. The defendants having denied the material allegations of the complaint,

and the assignment to plaintiff, alleged payment of the amount demanded.   A reply having put in issue the allegations of new matter contained in the answer, a trial was had, at which the plaintiff as a witness in his own behalf testified that the said sum of one hundred and seventy-five dollars was due from the defendants as alleged in his complaint; that his partner died since the assignment; and admitted upon cross-examination that it was made without consideration. Thereupon the court, in substance, instructed the jury that the plaintiff, having alleged a sale and assignment, could not recover as surviving partner nor as assignee unless the claim had been assigned by said firm to him for a valuable consideration; to the giving of which, so far as it relates to the necessity for the payment of a valuable consideration to support the assignment, the plaintiff excepted, and the exception was allowed.   The jury having rendered a verdict for the defendants, the court gave judgment thereon, from which the plaintiff appeals, and assigns as error the giving of said instruction, the overruling of a motion for a new trial, and the entry of said judgment.   REVERSED.

For plaintiff there was a brief and an oral argument by *Mr. John A. Carson.*

For respondents there was a brief by *Messrs. Tilmon Ford, John C. Leasure,* and *Bailey and Balleray,* with an oral argument by *Mr. Ford.*

Opinion by MR. JUSTICE MOORE.

1.   The plaintiff contends that it was unnecessary to allege or prove a valuable consideration for the assignment, and that the want thereof should not bar

his recovery. There is some conflict of authority upon the question presented, but we think the weight of it is in favor of the legal proposition for which the plaintiff contends, and that the right of recovery depends, not upon what may have been paid for the assignment, but whether the plaintiff is the real party in interest. The courts entertaining views different from this proceed upon the theory that, the assignee having paid nothing for the assignment, the donor may change his mind, and withhold from the object of his liberality the contemplated benefit. The weight of authority seems to be that in an action by an assignee of a chose in action, the defendant may controvert the allegation of ownership, and prove that the plaintiff is not the real party in interest. If, however, the assignment is actually made, he cannot question it upon the ground that there was no consideration paid therefor: 1 Beach on Modern Equity Jurisprudence, § 345; *Stone* v. *Frost,* 61 N. Y. 614; *Warder* v. *Jack,*✔ 82 Iowa, 435 (48 N. W. 729); *Wolff* v. *Matthews,* 39 Mo. App. 376; *Pugh* v. *Miller,* 126 Ind. 189 (25 N. E. 1040); ✔*Norris* v. *Hall,* 18 Me. 332; *Arthur* v. *Brooks,* 14 Barb. 533; *Richardson* v. *Mead,* 27 Barb. 178; *Beach* v. *Raymond,* 2 E. D. Smith, 496; *Miles* v. *Fox,* 4 E. D. Smith, 220; *Whittaker* v. *County of Johnson,* 10 Iowa, 161. But, whatever the rule may be elsewhere, it has been settled in this state that the title to a chose in action passes by assignment, that the assignee is authorized to bring an action thereon; and that it is immaterial whether he paid any consideration therefor: *Dawson* v. *Pogue,* 18 Or. 94 (6 L. R. A. 176, 22 Pac. 637).

2. The plaintiff alleged facts showing the existence of a demand against the defendants which had been assigned to him, and hence his complaint shows

that he is the real party in interest, and has a *prima facie* right of action. It is true he alleged that the claim had been sold to him, which implies a payment or promise as a consideration therefor, but as his right of action is founded upon the fact, and not the consideration, of the assignment, it was unnecessary to prove that he had paid any consideration therefor, and hence the allegation that the claim was sold to him was surplusage and should have been disregarded: Bliss on Code Pleading, § 215; *Hoyt* v. *Seeley*, 18 Conn. 352; *Bean* v. *Simpson*, 16 Me. 49; *Grubb* v. *Mahoning Navigation Company*, 14 Pa. St. 302; *Lyons* v. *Merrick*, 105 Mass. 71. The instruction complained of is erroneous, but the rule is well settled that a judgment will not be reversed for that reason unless it appears probable that the jury was misled thereby: 2 Thompson on Trials, § 2401; *Salmon* v. *Olds*, 9 Or. 488. In the case at bar there can be no doubt that the jury was misled by the instruction excepted to, and hence the judgment must be reversed and a new trial ordered.   REVERSED.

Decided December 23, 1895.

NICKLIN *v.* ROBERTSON.

[42 Pac. 993.]

1. VACATING JUDGMENT FOR MISTAKE OR SURPRISE—CODE, § 102.—Under Hill's Code, § 102, providing that the court "may at any time within one year after notice thereof relieve a party from a judgment taken against him through his mistake or excusable neglect," it is not sufficient that the motion be made within a year after notice, but it must be heard and determined within that time.

2. COSTS—CODE, § 554—DISCRETION OF COURT.—The discretion regarding the payment of costs in an equity proceeding conferred by section 554, Hill's Code, extends only to who shall pay them, and once that discretion has been exercised by the court, it is subject to review only for abuse, and the decision ought to be as binding on the lower court as on the appellate court, and cannot be changed.

3. COMPUTATION OF TIME—CODE, §§ 519, 556, 557.—The time provided by sections 556 and 557, Hill's Code, for filing cost bills and objections thereto, should be computed by excluding the first day, and also the last day where it falls on Sunday: Code, § 519.

4. DUTY OF CLERK IN TAXING COSTS.—Where no objections are filed to a statement of costs, the clerk has no discretion in allowing the items therein contained.

5. AFFIDAVIT—CORRECTING JUDGMENT UNDER SECTION 102, HILL'S CODE.— A motion under Hill's Code, § 102, for relief from a portion of a decree on the ground that it was included therein through the mistake, inadvertence, surprise, or excusable neglect of the movant, is ineffectual unless the affidavits submitted therewith show the existence of one of such grounds.

6. CORRECTING JUDGMENT FOR CLERICAL MISTAKE.— A judgment cannot be altered after the close of the term at which it was rendered, for a clerical misprision, where the mistake is not apparent on the record, and must be made out upon affidavits and evidence *aliunde.*

APPEAL from Multnomah: LOYAL B. STEARNS, Judge.

This is a motion to correct a decree in the case of S. C. Nicklin against W. E. Robertson and others, so as to relieve the plaintiff from the taxation of disbursements claimed to have been taxed against her through her excusable neglect. The facts are that on September twenty-nineth, eighteen hundred and ninety-one, the circuit court dismissed the suit, and decreed that the defendants recover of the plaintiff their costs and disbursements. On the sixth day thereafter the defendant filed with the clerk a verified statement of their disbursements, which, *inter alia,* contained the following items:—

C. W. Burrage, witness, 90 days and 8,146 miles
    traveled ....$ 449 60
W. H. Burrage, 4 days' attendance as witness
    and 808 miles traveled 86 80
D. W. Taylor, expert services and 8 days' at-
    tendance 54 50

No objections thereto having been made within the time prescribed by law, the clerk taxed the costs and disbursements claimed in the statement to the plaintiff, and entered the amount thereof in the decree. On March twenty-sixth, eighteen hundred and ninety-two, the plaintiff, having filed affidavits showing that she had no notice of the filing of said statement, moved the court to disallow and strike out the foregoing items thereof for the reason that they were illegal, and that the statement had not been filed within five days from the entry of the decree; but no order thereon having been made, the plaintiff on June sixteenth, eighteen hundred and ninety-four, by leave of court, filed objections to these items, and submitted affidavits tending to show that her neglect to present such objections at an earlier date was excusable. On September twentieth, of the same year, the clerk, in passing upon said objections, retaxed these items as follows:

C. W. Burrage, 1 day, 1 mile....................$ 2 10
W. H. Burrage, 1 day, 1 mile...................   2 10
D. W. Taylor, 3 days, 1 mile...................   6 10

Thereupon the defendants moved the court to retax their said disbursements, and, upon said motion being submitted, the court found the facts to be that C. W. Burrage resided at Canyon City, Colorado, at the time of the trial; that he appeared as a witness without the issuance of an order of the court requiring his attendance, and in doing so it was not necessary for him to travel more than one mile or to attend more than one day; that W. H. Burrage was at Portland, Oregon, and only attended as a witness one day and traveled one mile; and that D. W. Taylor attended said trial three days, and traveled one mile; and upon these findings affirmed the decision of the clerk, and on September twenty-first, eighteen hundred and ninety-four, decreed a modification of the disbursements in accordance therewith, from which the defendants appeal.

REVERSED.

For appellants there was a brief and oral argument by *Mr. William H. Adams.*

For respondent there was a brief by *Messrs. McDougall, Spencer and Jones,* and an oral argument by *Mr. Charles Jones McDougall.*

Opinion by MR. JUSTICE MOORE.

1. It is contended by the defendants that no order modifying the original decree having been made within a year after the plaintiff had notice of the taxation of the disbursements, the court was powerless, after the expiration of that time, to grant the relief sought. It must be conceded that a large portion of the disbursements claimed by the defendants is illegal, and hence the only question involved is the power of the court to retax them. The statute, so far as it applies to the case at bar, provides that the court may "in its discretion, and upon such terms as may be just, at any time within one year after notice thereof, relieve a party from a judgment, order, or other proceeding taken against him through his mistake, inadvertence, surprise, or excusable neglect": Hill's Code, § 102. At the common law no judgment could be amended after the term at which it was entered, except for clerical errors appearing in the record, and then only when there was to be found in some minute of the trial, a memorandum of what actually transpired from which the judgment might be corrected: *Albers* v.

Whitney, 1 Story, 310 (Fed. Cas. No. 137); *Ætna Life Insurance Company* v. *McCormick,* 20 Wis. 279. A statute conferring power to modify a judgment or decree after the term at which it was rendered, being in derogation of the common law, is to be strictly construed; and hence a party, if he could be relieved from a proceeding taken against him through his inadvertence, surprise, or excusable neglect, must apply therefor and obtain a decision thereon within the time prescribed by the statute, or his laches will preclude the court from thereafter amending the record: *Woolley* v. *Woolley,* 12 Ind. 663; *Gerish* v. *Johnson,* 5 Minn. 23; *Knox* v. *Clifford,* 41 Wis. 459; *Flanders* v. *Sherman,* 18 Wis. 575. In the case last cited COLE, J., in construing a statute identical with the one above quoted, says: "But, unless the motion is made within a year from the time the party has notice of the erroneous order or judgment, the court cannot relieve under this statute. It must be made within a year, as the power of the court to grant the relief is expressly limited to that period. After the lapse of that time the court cannot relieve a party from an order or judgment against him through his 'mistake,' 'inadvertence,' 'surprise,' or 'excusable neglect.'" In *Woolley* v. *Woolley,* 12 Ind. 663, one of the parties to a judgment, on the day prior to the expiration of a year from its rendition, under the provisions of a similar statute, applied to the court to set it aside, which the court did on the day after the year had expired. An appeal having been taken from the judgment thus rendered, it was reversed and PERKINS, J., in rendering the decision, says: "Under the section upon which the present suit is founded, the court could not set aside the judgment after the expiration of the year." In *Gerish* v. *Johnson,* 5 Minn. 23, the court, interpreting a similar statute, says: "It by no means follows that because a party may make such a motion within the year, that he has always a year to make it in. He is in each instance bound to make the motion with diligence, and show the existence of some of the causes specified in the statute." "The period," says COLE, J., in *Knox* v. *Clifford*, 41 Wis. 459, "within which the discretion is to be exercised is expressly limited to a year after notice of the judgment; and this time cannot be enlarged or extended by merely giving notice of the motion to vacate the judgment. The party is required to act, and must bring his motion to a hearing, within the year, or the power to relieve under the statute is gone. This provision goes upon the only reasonable assumption that a year affords an ample opportunity for a party to obtain relief if he is diligent." These authorities conclusively show that the statute limits the power to one year after notice of the "judgment, order, or proceeding," and that the expiration of that time leaves the court without authority to set aside or modify its decision for any of the causes enumerated in the section quoted. The plaintiff must have had notice of the taxation of these disbursements on March twenty-sixth, eighteen hundred and ninety-two, at which time she moved the court to disallow them, and more than one year from that time having expired before a modification thereof was decreed, it follows that the court, under the provisions of the statute, had no power to alter the original decree.

2. The plaintiff insists, however, (1) that the allowance of costs in equity rests in the sound discretion of the trial court, which will not be reviewed on appeal except for an abuse thereof; and (2) that the taxation of the disbursements of which she complains

results from the misprision of the clerk, and that the
court possesses at all times the inherent power to
correct such errors. It must be observed that the
discretion referred to by plaintiff does not extend to
the amount of costs and disbursements to be recovered,—but only as to who shall pay them: Hill's
Code, § 554. In the case at bar the court exercised
its discretion at the time it decreed that the defendants recover of the plaintiff their costs and disbursements, and it is this exercise of it that will not be
reviewed except for abuse: *Lovejoy* v. *Chapman*, 23 Or.
571 (32 Pac. 687); *Cole* v. *Logan*, 24 Or. 304 (33 Pac.
658). One of the objects in procuring a judgment or
decree is to put at rest forever the issue litigated,
but if the trial court could, even in matters within its
discretion, change at pleasure its solemn conclusions,
judgments might remain open in all matters relating
to an exercise of this right, and become subject to be
changed at any time in favor of either party who
could show a better reason therefor. When the trial
court has not abused its discretion in the exercise
thereof, its conclusion will not be reviewed in this
court, and such conclusion, when announced, ought to
be as binding upon the court rendering it as it is
upon this court.

3. The statute authorizes the clerk to allow and
tax, as a matter of course, the disbursements claimed
by a party upon his filing a verified statement thereof
within five days from the entry of a judgment or
decree given in his favor, unless the adverse party,
within two days from the time allowed to file the
statement, shall file objections thereto. The statement
may also be filed at any time after five days, but in
such case a copy thereof must be served upon the

adverse party, who is given two days from the service thereof to file objections thereto, and in either case the clerk must pass upon and may allow or reject any or all items to which objections have been made: Hill's Code, §§ 556, 557. It will be observed that judgment was entered September twenty-ninth,— and, excluding the first day from the computation, the five days would expire October fourth, but that day being Sunday must also be excluded, and the statement having been filed on the day following, was within the five-day limit: Hill's Code, § 519.

4. No objections having been filed to the cost bill within the time prescribed by law, the clerk had no discretion in the allowance of the items contained in the statement.

5. The affidavits submitted with the motion on March twenty-sixth, eighteen hundred and ninety-two, did not show that the disbursements had been taxed against the plaintiff through her mistake, inadvertence, surprise, or excusable neglect, and even if it be conceded that a motion filed within one year from the notice thereof authorized the court, after the expiration of that period, to relieve a party from a judgment taken against him under such circumstances, the motion filed would be ineffectual for that purpose.

6. The power of a court, at any time after the entry of a judgment, to correct the misprision of a clerk or other officer of the court, when it can be done by reference to some memorandum of the trial, made at the hearing thereof by the court, or from the pleadings on file or proceedings had therein must be conceded (1 Black on Judgments, § 155; 1 Freeman on Judgments, § 71); but when the mistake is not appar-

ent on the record, and must be made out upon affidavits and evidence *aliunde,* then there remains nothing
to amend by, and the court is powerless to alter the
judgment after the close of the term at which it was
rendered: *Albers* v. *Whitney,* 1 Story, 310 (Fed. Cas. No.
137). The amount of the items claimed in the verified statement is nine hundred and five dollars, which
sum the clerk entered in the decree, and it appearing
that the evidence relied upon to correct the record
consisted of affidavits which were insufficient for that
purpose, it follows that the decree appealed from must
be reversed, and the motion to correct the original
decree overruled.   REVERSED.

NEPPACH *v.* JONES.

[39 Pac. 999; 42 Pac. 519.]

1. RES JUDICATA.—To make a matter *res judicata* there must be identity
   of persons and parties in both causes, and it must be an identity of
   real parties who have interests to be affected by the decision. This
   identity is not destroyed by joining as additional parties in the second cause persons who were not parties to the former litigation, and
   who have no interest in the subject matter.

2. DISMISSING APPEAL—RULES OF COURT—ABSTRACT.—An appeal to the
   supreme court will not be dismissed because the abstract does not
   contain a formal statement of errors as required by the last paragraph of Rule 9 of the supreme court, (24 Or. 600,) where the appeal is from a decree on the pleadings, and it sufficiently appears
   that the alleged error upon which the appellant intends to rely is the
   action of the trial court in sustaining the respondent's motion for
   the decree.

3. DISMISSING APPEAL FOR FAILURE TO FILE BRIEF—RULES OF COURT.—
   The rules of practice in the supreme court regarding abstracts and
   briefs were intended to facilitate business, and it is intended that they
   shall be substantially complied with; yet, if, through excusable neglect or oversight, some requirement has been omitted, the court may,
   on a proper showing, excuse the party in fault, as where a brief has
   not been filed in time through the delay of the printer.

APPEAL from Multnomah: LOYAL B. STEARNS, Judge.

For appellant there was a brief and an oral argument by *Mr. Horace B. Nicholas.*

For respondent there was a brief and an oral argument by *Mr. Ira Jones.*

Decided December 2, 1895.
[42 Pac. 799.]

ON THE MERITS.

PER CURIAM. 1. This is a suit in equity to set aside certain conveyances of real property which plaintiff claims are fraudulent and void as to him. A case involving the same matters in controversy between the plaintiff herein and the defendant J. H. Jones was heretofore tried and finally determined by this court adversely to the plaintiff who is the appellant here: *Neppach* v. *Jones,* 20 Or. 491 (23 Am. St. Rep. 145). The plaintiff attempts to avoid the effect of the decision in that case by joining other defendants with J. H. Jones, to wit, Justice Jones, E. K. Jones, and Ira Jones, and by supplementing the complaint with some further allegations intended to excuse the plaintiff's laches in bringing the suit, which are wholly insufficient for the purpose. From the answer it appears that Justice Jones died in the year eighteen hundred and ninety, which is not denied. And from the reply it appears that defendants Ira Jones and E. K. Jones have no interest whatever in the subject of litigation. The gravamen of appellant's contention now is that the two causes of action are not the same because the parties defendant are different, but by his own pleadings he has shown that J. H. Jones, the defendant in the former suit, is the only real party defendant here, and that the other defendants named have no interest in the subject matter. To make a matter *res judicata* there must be identity of persons and parties: 21 Am. and Eng. Ency. of Law, 227. But they must be real parties having interests to be affected by the litigation. Combining entire strangers to the subject matter of the suit with real parties does not destroy this identity so that *res judicata* cannot be invoked. The decision of *Neppach* v. *Jones*, 20 Or. 491, is therefore decisive of this case, and hence the decree of the court below will be affirmed.   AFFIRMED.

Decided December 3, 1894.

[39 Pac. 999.]

ON MOTION TO DISMISS APPEAL.

PER CURIAM. The respondents move for an affirmance of the decree in this case, because (1) appellant's abstract is not in the form required by Rule 9 of this court; and (2) his brief was not served as required by Rule 6; while the appellant asks to be relieved from his default.

2. The abstract is in the form required by the rules, except that it does not contain a formal statement of errors. The appeal is from a decree given on the pleadings, and, although the abstract is defective, as claimed, it does nevertheless sufficiently appear therefrom that the alleged error upon which the appellant intends to rely is the action of the trial court in sustaining the defendants' motion for a decree on the pleadings, and it therefore accomplishes the purpose intended by the rules, and is a substantial compliance therewith.

8. The brief was not served until two days after the expiration of the time allowed by Rule 6, but from the affidavit of counsel for appellant in support of his motion it satisfactorily appears that the failure to serve his brief in time is due to the neglect and delay of the printer, and not to any fault of the appellant. For this reason his motion should be allowed. While the court expects and will require counsel to substantially observe the rules in the preparation and service of abstracts and briefs, yet if, through excusable neglect, the service is not made in time, the court may relieve the party in default, on a proper showing, from the consequences thereof. The rules were designed and intended to facilitate the business and simplify the practice, and are not so arbitrary or inflexible as to work an injustice, or prevent a hearing in this court, when the failure to comply therewith is owing to the excusable neglect of the party. The motion for an affirmance must be overruled, and appellant's motion to be relieved from his default in not serving his brief within time allowed; the respondents to have twenty days from this date in which to serve and file their brief.

Argued November 13; decided December 9, 1895; rehearing denied.

EGAN *v.* WESTCHESTER INSURANCE CO.
[42 Pac. 611.]

INSURANCE—CONDITIONS OF POLICY—WAIVER BY AGENT.—Where a fire insurance policy provides that no officer or agent shall have power to waive any of its conditions, except by writing, and that no privilege affecting the insurance shall be claimed by the assured unless so written, a parol waiver of any of the provisions of the policy by the agent from whom the insurance was obtained, after it has been accepted by the assured, is a nullity:[*] *Weidert* v. *State Insurance Company*, 19 Or. 261, cited and approved.

[*]With the case of *Smith* v. *Niagara Fire Insurance Company*, 1 L. R. A. 219, will be found a note collating the authorities on the question of how the terms and

This is an action upon a fire insurance policy issued by the defendant on the seventeenth day of March, eighteen hundred and ninety-three, covering loss or damage by fire to the personal property therein described for the term of one year. The contract of insurance was made and the policy issued by one Hart, general agent of the defendant, residing in Portland, who was empowered to make such contracts and issue policies furnished in blank by the company to be countersigned by him, to renew the same, and to assent to transfers and assignments thereof within the territory covered by his agency. The policy in question is known as the "New York Standard Policy", and is in the form and contains the printed conditions usual in such policies, among which are the following: "This entire policy, unless otherwise provided by agreement indorsed hereon or added hereto, shall be void * * * if the subject of insurance be personal property and be or become encumbered by chattel mortgage. * * * No suit or action on this policy for the recovery of any claim shall be sustainable in any court of law or equity until after full compliance by the insured with all of the foregoing requirements, nor unless commenced within twelve months next after the fire." By the concluding clause it is provided that "No officer, agent, or other representative of this company shall have power to waive any provision or condition of this policy except such as by the terms of this policy may be the subject of agreement indorsed hereon or added hereto, and as to such provisions and conditions, no officer, agent, or representa-

conditions of a policy may be waived where the policy has itself provided the mode of such waiver. There is also an additional note on the same subject attached to *Lamberton* v. *Connecticut Fire Insurance Company*, 1 L. R. A. 222. See, further, the following annotated cases: *Weidert* v. *State Insurance Company*. 20 Am. St. Rep. at page 826; *Carey* v. *German-American Insurance Company* at page 911.—REPORTER.

tive shall have such power or be deemed or held to
have waived such provisions or conditions, unless such
waiver, if any, shall be written upon or attached
hereto, nor shall any privilege or permission affecting
the insurance under this policy exist or be claimed by
the insured unless so written or attached." Some two
or three months after the policy had been issued and
delivered, and before the fire, which occurred in August, eighteen hundred and ninety-four, a chattel mortgage was placed on the property with the oral consent
of Hart, but no indorsement to that effect was ever
made upon the policy, nor was the company advised
of the arrangement. It is admitted that unless the
stipulation in regard to the effect of placing a chattel
mortgage on the property was waived, the incum-
brance rendered the policy void, so that the right of
plaintiff to recover depends upon whether the agent
Hart had authority to bind the company by an oral
consent or agreement to waive or modify the stipulations and conditions of the policy in this respect. The
policy was issued to one Opsal, who, after the fire, assigned all his rights to the plaintiff B. F. Eagan. He
recovered a judgment for the amount of the policy,
and defendant appealed.   REVERSED.

For appellant there was a brief by *Messrs. Cox, Cotton,
Teal and Minor*, and an oral argument by *Mr. Lewis B. Cox*.

For respondent there was a brief by *Messrs. Charles H.
Carey*, and *McDougall, Spencer and Jones*, with oral arguments by *Mr. Carey* and *Mr. Schuyler C. Spencer*.

Opinion by MR. CHIEF JUSTICE BEAN.

There is a class of cases which holds that where
a person is authorized by an insurance company to

make a contract of insurance, he thereby becomes invested with authority to modify or waive the printed
stipulations in the policy as to the condition of the
property or other facts then existing. This doctrine
proceeds on the theory that the contract or knowledge
of the agent, within the scope of his real or apparent
authority, is the contract or knowledge of his principal, and to that extent modifies or suspends the
printed terms of the policy, which is prepared for
general use, without reference to the particular case,
contains numerous complex conditions and stipulations,
and is generally not delivered to the insured until
after the contract is closed. In such case it would
certainly not be consonant with fair dealing to permit
an insurer to escape liability because of some stipulation in the policy, which it knew from the very
threshold of the transaction, through the agent who
made the contract, was not in accordance with the
agreement between it and the assured, or to allow it
to take advantage of some cause of forfeiture which
it knew, at the time the contract was closed, would
invalidate the policy from the time of its inception,
and thus render it of no more use to the assured than
so much waste paper. There is another class of cases
which holds that a parol waiver of the conditions of an
insurance policy by a general agent is binding on the
company, although the policy may provide that such
waiver can be made only in writing indorsed thereon,
if the insured, dealing with the agent, has no notice
of a limitation upon his authority to bind the company. But neither of these rules has any bearing
on the question here presented. The policy in this
case was issued and delivered long prior to the date
of the alleged waiver, and contained on its face notice
of the limitation on the power of the agents of the

company. The plaintiff had accepted the contract,
with all its limitations and conditions, and, in the absence of fraud, is conclusively presumed to have
known that by its express terms the authority of the
agents of defendant to waive or change it was limited and circumscribed. He was informed by the insurer, through the policy itself, that no agent, by
virtue of a general appointment, had authority to
change the contract in any other way than by writing indorsed thereon, and, therefore, in dealing with
Hart, he did so with knowledge of the limitation upon
his authority to bind the company.

After a contract of insurance is complete, the policy delivered and accepted, it becomes binding upon
the parties the same as any other valid contract, and
its plain and unambiguous provisions must be interpreted by the same rules. If, therefore, it contains a
limitation upon the power and authority of an agent
to subsequently waive its stipulations or change its
terms, such provision is necessarily notice to the assured that for such purpose the power of the agent of
the company is limited, whatever his authority may be
in other respects. No rule is better settled than that
where a limitation on the power of an agent is brought
home to the person dealing with him, such person
relies upon any act in excess of such limited authority at his peril; and hence, when an insurance company limits the power of its agent, and notice of such
limitation is brought home to the person dealing with
him, it is not bound by any act done by the agent in
contravention of such notice: Wood on Insurance, § 107;
Weidert v. State Insurance Company, 19 Or. 261 (20 Am.
St. Rep. 809, 24 Pac. 242). Now, in this case the policy expressly provides that no officer or agent or
other representative of the company shall have power

to waive any provision or condition of the policy except by a writing upon or attached thereto, and that no privilege or permission affecting the insurance under the policy shall exist or be claimed by the assured unless so written or attached, and, therefore, the limitation upon the authority of Hart was in effect written on the face of the policy. This stipulation is not illegal, or against public policy, and the statement that no agent has authority to waive or change the terms or conditions of the policy unless in writing is notice to the assured of that fact.

The relation of agency, it is true, is the result of the contract between the agent and his principal, and the power of the agent must be determined by his real or apparent authority, as gathered from facts in the case, and a declaration in an insurance policy to the effect that no agent has authority to change or modify its terms or conditions, except in a specified manner, would not preclude the assured from showing, as a matter of fact, if he could, that the defendant did invest the agent with such authority. But where the policy itself, issued and delivered by an agent, informs the assured that for certain purposes no officer, agent, or representative of the company has authority to bind it except in a specified manner, it contains notice to him that the authority of the agent so issuing the policy is limited, and this limitation and restriction is binding upon the assured unless he can show that such power has been enlarged in some way. Mr. Hart was the general agent of the company, and, unless his powers were expressly limited, and the assured had notice of such limitation, it would perhaps be presumed from the nature of his agency that he had power to modify or waive the terms of the policy, because, as general agent, he stood in the place of and represented the company, and could do whatever it could lawfully do. But in this case the policy contained upon its face a restriction upon his powers, which the assured must be held, in law, to have known. His apparent authority was limited by a recital in the body of the policy, assented to by the assured as a part thereof, and possessing the same binding force as any other provision of the contract. There was no evidence given or offered tending to show that Hart's power had been in any way enlarged, or that he had authority to modify or change the contract as originally made. And if it is to be enforced according to the principles governing other contracts under similar circumstances, we see no escape from the conclusion that Hart's parol waiver of terms of the policy is not binding on the company. We must, therefore, hold that, after an insurance policy containing the provisions of the one before us has been delivered and accepted by the insured, a parol waiver of such provisions, or any of them, by the agent from whom the insurance was obtained, merely by virtue of such agency, is a nullity. This seems to be the result and logic of the adjudged cases where the same or similar provisions of insurance policies have come before the courts for consideration: *Walsh* v. *Hartford Fire Insurance Company,* 73 N. Y. 5; *Quinlan* v. *Providence Insurance Company,* 133 N. Y. 356 (28 Am. St. Rep. 645, 31 N. E. 31); *O'Brien* v. *Prescott Insurance Company,* 134 N. Y. 28 (31 N. E. 265); *Moore* v. *Hanover Fire Insurance Company,* 141 N. Y. 219 (36 N. E. 191); *Baumgartel* v. *Providence Insurance Company,* 136 N. Y. 547 (32 N. E. 990); *Hankins* v. *Rockford Insurance Company,* 70 Wis. 1 (35 N. W. 34); *Knudson* v. *Hekla Fire Insurance Company,* 75 Wis. 198 (43 N. W. 954); *Carey* v. *German-American Insurance Company,* 84 Wis. 80 (36 Am. St. Rep. 907, 54 N. W. 18); *Cleaver*

v. *Traders' Insurance Company,* 65 Mich. 527 (8 Am. St.
Rep. 908, 32 N. W. 660); *Gould* v. *Dwelling-house Insurance
Company,* 90 Mich. 302 (51 N. W. 455); *Sprague* v. *Western
Home Insurance Company,* 49 Mo. App. 423; *Smith* v. *Niagara
Fire Insurance Company,* 60 Vt. 682 (1 L. R. A. 216, 15
Atl. 353, 6 Am. St. Rep. 144); *German Insurance Company*
v. *Heiduk,* 30 Neb. 288 (27 Am. St. Rep. 402, 46 N. W.
481). The judgment is therefore reversed, and the
cause remanded, with directions to sustain the motion
for a nonsuit.   REVERSED.

Argued December 18; decided December 30, 1895.

STATE *v.* THOMPSON.
[42 Pac. 1002]

1. LARCENY BY BAILEE — INDICTMENT — CODE, §§ 1771, 1800. — An indictment charging that defendant, being "the bailee and trustee" of a note, the property of another, embezzled and converted it to his own use, charges larceny by a bailee; the word "trustee" not affecting its validity, or charging conversion by a trustee.

2. VARIANCE. — The identity of a note offered in evidence with one described in substance and legal effect in an indictment being unquestionable, a variance of two days in the date thereof is immaterial.

3. APPOINTMENT OF GUARDIAN — COLLATERAL ATTACK. — On a prosecution for larceny by a bailee, even if proof of demand on defendant was necessary, — the undisputed evidence showing an actual conversion and fraudulent application of a note and its proceeds to defendant's use, contrary to the terms of the bailment, — objection could not be made to the regularity of the appointment of the guardian who made the demand, the court making the appointment having jurisdiction of the subject-matter and the parties.

4. EVIDENCE OF VALUE OF STOLEN NOTE. — Evidence that a note was negotiable, and at the time of its conversion by defendant was not due, and that the latter sold it for its face value, is sufficient proof of value to sustain a conviction of larceny thereof by defendant as bailee.

5. EVIDENCE OF OWNERSHIP — LARCENY BY BAILEE. — In an indictment for larceny of a note by a bailee the averment of ownership in a certain person is established by proof that such person had become liable on the note and had paid it, and was entitled to possession thereof at the time of the alleged larceny.

APPEAL from Multnomah: T. A. STEPHENS, Judge.

The defendant C. C. Thompson, an attorney at law, was tried and convicted of the crime of larceny by bailee of a promissory note that had been intrusted to him in his professional capacity. From a sentence of one year in the penitentiary he appeals, assigning error in overruling a demurrer to the indictment, and in the admission of testimony.   AFFIRMED.

For appellant there was a brief and an oral argument by *Mr. Benjamin P. Welch.*

For the state there was a brief and an oral argument by *Messrs. Cicero M. Idleman,* attorney general, and *Wilson T. Hume,* district attorney.

Opinion by MR. CHIEF JUSTICE BEAN.

The undisputed facts in the case are that in June, eighteen hundred and ninety-four, application was made to the County Court of Clackamas County for the appointment of a guardian for one E. W. Cressy, who was old, and feeble in mind and body, and incapable of taking care of himself. At this time Cressy, who was the owner of considerable property, was in possession of a certain promissory note in his favor for three hundred and seventy-five dollars, dated February sixteenth, eighteen hundred and eighty-nine, executed by F. F. Jancke and secured by a mortgage, but which had in fact been paid by one Broetje, who had purchased from Jancke the mortgaged premises, and, as a part of the consideration therefor, had assumed and agreed to pay the note in question, and for that purpose had become a party thereto. Soon after the

application for the appointment of a guardian, and the
service of a citation upon him, Cressy suddenly disap-
peared from his usual place of abode, leaving among
his effects several promissory notes and mortgages,
among the number being the note above referred to,
upon which this prosecution was based. On the fourteenth of June, and after the disappearance of Cressy,
a son of the proprietor of the house where he had
been staying, acting upon the advice of a neighboring
justice of the peace, delivered these notes and mortgages for safe keeping to the defendant, who was, or
claimed to be, attorney for Cressy, and took his receipt therefor as such attorney. A few days afterwards one Hungerford, who was appointed guardian of
the person and estate of Cressy by the Clackamas
County Court, demanded of the defendant possession of
the notes and mortgages which had been so delivered
to him, but without avail. Defendant, being thereupon
cited by the county court to appear and answer concerning the property which had been intrusted to him,
denied having possession of the same, and claimed
that he had redelivered it to Cressy; but in November
following he demanded payment of the note in question from Broetje, and was informed by him that it
had been paid to Cressy, who failed to surrender it because, as he said, it had been lost. Thereafter, the defendant, notwithstanding his knowledge of such payment and the appointment of a guardian for Cressy,
procured his indorsement on the note, which was not
yet due, and sold it for about its face value, and appropriated the money to his own use. After the sale of
the note he was again required by the county court,
on petition of the guardian, to appear and answer concerning the same, which he did, and upon examination
said he did not know what had become of the note;

that he left it lying on his office desk, and it disap-
peared in some manner unknown to him, and he did
not know where it then was; that he never received
anything for it, directly or indirectly, and knew nothing concerning it. Subsequently, on the trial of an
action against Broetje by the purchaser of the note,
defendant, who was a witness, testified that he had
loaned Cressy some money on the note, and had an
interest in it to that extent. There can be no possible
doubt of defendant's guilt on the facts, and unless the
record discloses some error affecting a substantial
right, the judgment should be affirmed. We shall,
therefore, proceed to notice briefly the alleged errors.

1. The charging part of the indictment is as follows: "The said C. C. Thompson * * * was the
bailee and trustee of a certain promissory note
dated ——, signed ——, and for the sum of ——, and
being such bailee as aforesaid, did then and there
feloniously embezzle and unlawfully and wrongfully
convert the said promissory note to his own use, and
did feloniously fail, neglect, and refuse to keep and
account for the same according to the nature of his
trust; said promissory note theretofore having been
delivered and intrusted to him and under his care and
control as such bailee and trustee, contrary to the
statutes" * * *. It is claimed that this charges not
only larceny by bailee under section 1771, Hill's Code*,
but that the use of the word "trustee" makes it charge

---

*Section 1771 reads thus: "If any bailee, with or without hire, shall em-
bezzle, or wrongfully convert to his own use, or shall secret with intent to convert to his own use, or shall fail, neglect, or refuse to deliver, keep, or account
for, according to the nature of his trust, any money or property of another delivered or intrusted to his care or control, and which may be the subject of larceny, such bailee, upon conviction thereof, shall be deemed guilty of larceny,
and punished accordingly."

also conversion by trustee, under section 1800.* The objection to the indictment is untenable. It is in the language of the statute, and does not charge more than one crime. The word "trustee," as used therein, does not affect its validity, or charge a crime under section 1800 of the Code.

2. The variance between the note offered in evidence and the one described in the indictment was not material; they were identically the same except a difference of two days in the date. "The strictness of the ancient rule as to the variance between the proof and the indictment," says EARL, J., "has been much relaxed in modern times. Variances are regarded as material because they may mislead a prisoner in making his defense, and because they may expose him to the danger of being again put in jeopardy for the same offense": *Harris* v. *People*, 64 N. Y. 148. The variance in this case could present no such difficulty. The indictment does not undertake to set out the note according to its tenor, but only in substance and legal effect, and the difference of two days in the date alone could not have misled the defendant in making his defense, and will not expose him to the danger of again being put in jeopardy for the same offense. The identity of the note described in the indictment with the one offered in evidence is unquestionable, and the judgment in this case will protect the defendant from another prosecution for the same offense, and this is all the law requires: *Donovan's Appeal*, 41 Conn. 500.

3. The objection to the regularity of the proceedings of the county court of Clackamas County in ap-

---

* Section 1800 reads as follows: "If any person, being the trustee of any property for the benefit of another, or for any public or charitable use, shall, with intent to defraud, by any means convert the same," etc.

pointing a guardian for Cressy is without merit in this case. The only object of the proof of such ap-pointment was to show a legal demand upon the de-fendant for the possession of the note in question. The county court had jurisdiction of the subject mat-ter and the parties, and it is immaterial for the pur-poses of this case whether the proceedings in the appointment of the guardian were regular or irregu-lar. It made an appointment and issued letters of guardianship to Hungerford, who duly demanded the note of the defendant in order that it might be de-livered to Broetje the owner, and this would no doubt have been sufficient to establish the conversion, if proof of demand was necessary, which may be well doubted, as the undisputed evidence shows an actual conversion and fraudulent application of the note and its proceeds to the defendant's own use, contrary to the terms of the bailment: *State* v. *New,* 22 Minn. 76; *Commonwealth* v. *Hussey,* 111 Mass. 482.

4. It is also claimed that the state failed to prove that the note was of any value, or that it was the property of Broetje, as alleged in the indictment. The note was negotiable, and, at the time of its conver-sion by the defendant, not due, and the fact that he was able to and did sell and dispose of it for its face is sufficient proof of its value.

5. Broetje having paid Cressy and thus discharged his obligation, was entitled to possession of the note, and was therefore the owner within the averments of the indictment.

There are several other assignments of error dis-cussed in defendant's brief, but they proceed on the mistaken theory that the same rules as to the indict-ment and proof prevail in prosecutions for larceny by

bailee and for embezzlement under the statute of this
state, and therefore require no further consideration.
A careful examination of this record has failed to disclose any error affecting a substantial right, and the
judgment must therefore be affirmed.

AFFIRMED.

OSBORN *v.* LOGUS.

[37 Pac. 456; 38 Pac. 190; 42 Pac. 997.]

1. ADVERSE PARTIES IN MECHANICS' LIEN CASES — CODE, § 537. — In mechanic's lien cases all the lien claimants are "adverse" to each other,
within the meaning of section 537, Hill's Code, and must be served
with the notice of appeal: *The Victorian*, 24 Or. 121, approved and
followed.

2. SERVICE OF NOTICE OF APPEAL — CODE, § 537. — The question of who are
"adverse parties" necessary to be served with the notice of appeal
must be determined by the conditions existing when the appeal is
taken, and all who are then "adverse" must be served: *Moody* v. *Miller*, 24 Or. 179, approved and followed.

3. MECHANICS' LIEN CASES — ADVERSE PARTIES. — In a mechanics' lien case
the contractor is not an "adverse party" and need not be served
with the notice of appeal, where he has not been served with summons and has not appeared, though named in the pleadings as a
defendant.

4. RIGHT TO SECOND APPEAL. — An attempt to take an appeal, which in
consequence of an irregularity is not perfected, does not take away
the right to another appeal.

5. MECHANICS' LIENS — PARTIES — PLEADING — CODE, §§ 67, 71. — In a mechanic's lien foreclosure the contractor is not an absolutely indispensable party — he ought to be brought in if he can be served, but the
suit can proceed without him, though, of course, if he is not served
he is not bound by the result. Not being an indispensable party, the
objection of defect of parties must be made by demurrer or answer,
otherwise it will be deemed waived: Code, §§ 67, 71.

6. VARIANCE — MECHANICS' LIENS — NAME OF CONTRACTOR. — A difference
between the name of the firms of contractors as alleged in the complaint for the foreclosure of a mechanics' lien, and as disclosed by
the contract, does not constitute a fatal variance where there is no
question as to the identity of the two firms, and it is clearly apparent that the owner, who alone is contesting the lien, has not been
misled in any respect by the difference.

7. NOTICE OF LIEN — NAME OF PERSON OBTAINING MATERIALS — CODE,
§ 3673. — The naming in a claim of lien, in good faith, of the parties

to whom material was furnished as "J. W. Holm and Brother," while the contract between the owner and contractor was signed "C. N. Holmes and Company," is immaterial, it not appearing that the owner was misled.

8. LIEN NOTICE—CONTRACTUAL RELATION BETWEEN CLAIMANT AND PROP-ERTY-OWNER—CODE, §§ 3669, 3673.—A claim of lien for material or labor furnished a contractor filed under section 3673 of Hill's Code, requiring the claim to contain a true statement of the demand, with the name of the owner or reputed owner, and that of the person by whom the claimant was employed, or to whom he furnished the materials, need not state the contractual relations existing between the claimant and the owner, as the relation is in effect established by section 3669, which provides that the contractor shall be held the agent of the owner for the purposes of the act: *Rankin* v. *Malarkey,* 23 Or. 593; *Curtis* v. *Sestanovich,* 26 Or. 107; *Willamette Manufacturing Company* v. *McLeod,* 27 Or. 272, overruled on this point.

APPEAL from Multnomah: LOYAL B. STEARNS, Judge.

For appellant there was a brief by *Messrs. Snow and McCamant,* with oral arguments by *Mr. Wallace McCamant.*

For respondent there was a brief by *Messrs. Hume and Hall* and *Charles H. Carey,* with oral arguments by *Messrs. Charles H. Carey* and *John H. Hall.*

Decided July 30, 1894.
[37 Pac. 456.]

ON FIRST MOTION TO DISMISS APPEAL.

PER CURIAM. 1. This is a motion to dismiss an appeal. A decree having been rendered dismissing plaintiff's complaint in a suit to foreclose a mechanic's lien, wherein like liens of other claimants upon the same property were foreclosed, the plaintiff attempted to appeal by serving the notice thereof upon the owner of such property only. Appeals are taken by causing a notice to be served upon the adverse party, and filing the original, with proof of service indorsed thereon, with the clerk: Hill's Code, § 537. An adverse party is one whose interest in relation to the judgment or decree appealed from is in conflict with the modification or reversal sought by the appeal: *The Victorian*, 24 Or. 121 (32 Pac. 1040). If the decree should be reversed, and one entered here foreclosing plaintiff's alleged lien, the interests of the other lien claimants would necessarily be in conflict with such decree, in case the property sought to be charged with the lien was upon a sale thereof insufficient to pay the whole amount decreed against it: Hill's Code, § 3677. In such case they would be compelled to share *pro rata* with the plaintiff, and hence the other lien claimants were or might thus become adverse parties.

2. But in order to show that the other claimants would not in fact be affected by such a decree, the appellant filed affidavits, and a copy of the decree with marginal indorsements thereon, from which it appears that the amounts awarded to the several lien claim- ants have been paid. The proofs, however, are silent as to when these payments were made, except as to one of them, the acknowledgment of which was en- tered on the margin of the decree after the notice of appeal was served. Jurisdiction must be determined from the conditions existing when the appeal was taken and could be acquired in this case only by serv- ice of the notice of appeal upon all the adverse par- ties: *Hamilton* v. *Blair*, 23 Or. 64 (31 Pac. 197); *Moody* v. *Miller*, 24 Or. 179 (33 Pac. 402); and plaintiff having failed to serve the other lien claimants with such no- tice the appeal must be dismissed.

                                        DISMISSED.

Decided November 19, 1894.

[38 Pac. 190.]

ON SECOND MOTION TO DISMISS APPEAL.

PER CURIAM. A former appeal, or attempted appeal, in this case, having been dismissed for want of service upon all the adverse parties, the plaintiff has taken and perfected another appeal, which the defendant now moves to dismiss on the grounds (1) that Messrs. Holm and Brother, the contractors to whom plaintiff furnished the material for which the lien is claimed, were not served with notice of the appeal; and (2) that plaintiff's right to an appeal has been exhausted.

3. The contractors to whom plaintiff furnished the material referred to in the complaint, although named as defendants therein, were not served with summons and did not appear in the court below, nor have they been served with the notice of appeal. The contention for defendants is that they are adverse parties within the meaning of the statute. An adverse party is defined by this court to be one "whose interest in relation to the judgment or decree appealed from is in conflict with the modification or reversal sought by the appeal": *The Victorian*, 24 Or. 121 (32 Pac. 1040). Within this rule, the contractors are clearly not adverse parties to this appeal, indeed they are not parties to the decree appealed from at all, and cannot therefore be in any way affected by the modification or reversal thereof.

4. Where an appellant has taken and perfected an appeal his right is exhausted, and he cannot after-

28 Or.—22.

wards take another in the same cause, but where he merely attempts to appeal but in consequence of some irregularity the appeal is not perfected the right to appeal still remains: *McCarty* v. *Wintler*, 17 Or. 391; *Nestuoca Wagon Road Company* v. *Landingham*, 24 Or. 439. An appeal is taken by serving a notice thereof on the adverse party, and filing the original with proof of service indorsed thereon, and when, on account of a failure to comply with this provision of the statute, the former appeal was dismissed, it did not operate as an abandonment of the appeal, or affect the plaintiff's right to take another. The motion to dismiss must therefore be overruled.   OVERRULED.

Decided December 23, 1895.
[42 Pac. 997.]

ON THE MERITS.

Opinion by MR. JUSTICE WOLVERTON.

This is a suit by T. F. Osborn to foreclose a mechanics' lien brought to enforce payment for stone furnished for use in a building under construction by defendant Logus. The decree was against plaintiff in the court below, and he appeals. The facts sufficiently appear further on in the opinion for a full understanding of the points decided.

5. A peculiarity about this proceeding is that, according to the recital in the claim of lien, the stone was furnished to "J. W. Holm and Brother," while the complaint alleges that it was furnished to "J. O. and C. N. Holm," partners as "J. O. Holm and Brother." The original contract with Charles Logus, the owner, purports to be executed by "C. N. Holmes

and Company." It is contended by Logus that this
admixture of both individual and firm names is fatal
to the proceeding upon two grounds: *first,* the statute
having made the contractor the agent of the owner, it
is insufficient to state that the materials were furnished to "J. W. or J. O. Holm and Brother," when the
only agent who had any authority to bind the owner
was "C. N. Holmes and Company"; and, *second,* that the
contractors "C. N. Holmes and Company," being necessary parties, should have been made defendants, and
that the suit cannot proceed without them. That it is
unnecessary under the statute that a judgment against
the contractor should precede or be had. concurrently
with the decree of foreclosure against the property is
settled by *Ainslie* v. *Kohn,* 16 Or. 374 (19 Pac. 97); but
here the objection goes to the nonjoinder of "C. N.
Holmes and Company," who it is claimed must be
made parties, or else the suit must abate. Ordinarily,
the objection arising from a defect of parties should
be taken by demurrer if it appears upon the face of
the complaint, otherwise by answer, and if by neither,
it is to be deemed waived: Sections 67, 70, and 71, Hill's
Code; *Cohen* v. *Utterheimer,* 13 Or. 224 (10 Pac. 20). Unless the statute touching the foreclosure of mechanics'
liens absolutely requires the presence of the contractor
as a party litigant before the suit can proceed, there
is no reason why the ordinary rule should not prevail
here. For the purposes of the mechanics' lien act the
contractor is held to be the agent of the owner. As
touching suits under the act, section 3677 provides
that "suits to enforce the liens created by this act
shall be brought in the circuit courts, and the pleadings, process, practice, and other proceedings shall be
the same as in other cases. * * * All persons personally liable, and all lienholders whose claims have

been filed for record under the provisions of section
3673, shall, and all other persons interested in the matter in controversy, or in the property sought to be
charged with the lien may, be made parties; but such
as are not made parties shall not be bound by such
proceedings." Section 3679 provides, among other
things, that "in all cases where a lien shall be filed
under this act for work done or materials furnished to
any contractor, he shall defend any action brought
thereupon at his own expense; and during the pendency of such action, the owner may withhold from the
contractor the amount of money for which such lien
is filed; and in case of judgment against the owner or
his property upon the lien, the said owner shall be
entitled to deduct from any amount due or about to
become due by him to the contractor the amount of
such judgment and costs; and, if the amount of such
judgment and costs shall exceed the amount due by
him to the contractor, or if the owner shall have settled with the contractor in full, he shall be entitled
to recover from the contractor any amount so paid
by him, the said owner, in excess of the contract
price, and for which the contractor was originally the
party liable." The contractor being the agent of the
owner, his acts may be said to be the acts of the
owner, thereby establishing a privity, for the purpose
of the lien, between the owner and the subcontractors,
material men, and laborers; so that a direct relationship exists between the owner and the subcontractor,
and it is not necessary that the contractor be present
in the proceeding to supply a link to complete and
establish such relationship.

Regarding section 3677 it is contended that the
words "shall" and "may," when used therein with
reference to parties to the suit, are used in contradis-

tinction to each other, and that therefore the word
"shall" becomes mandatory, and should be interpreted
to mean "must." The use of both words in the same
provision may afford a very forcible indication of the
intention of the legislature (Sutherland on Statutory
Construction, § 462); but the mere circumstance of
such use does not alone determine their proper signification. That must yet be determined as the legislative meaning of other words are determined, and by
like rules of interpretation. The section at the out-
set declares that the "pleadings, process, practice, and
all other proceedings shall be the same as in other
cases," and in the latter clause "the proceedings
* * * shall be as nearly as possible made to conform to the proceedings of a foreclosure of a mortgage lien upon real property." From these clauses it
becomes apparent that the legislature intended to conform the practice and procedure in the foreclosure
of mechanics' liens to the practice and procedure "in
other cases," or as nearly as possible in the "foreclosure of a mortgage lien upon real property."
Now, it is well understood what is meant by necessary and what by proper parties in ordinary cases,
or in a suit to foreclose a mortgage upon real estate.
"A necessary party is one whose presence before
the court is indispensable to the rendering of a judgment which shall have any effect upon the property;
without whom the court might properly refuse to proceed, because its decree would be practically nuga-
tory": 2 Jones on Mortgages, § 1394. Such a person,
in this sense, is the owner of the equity of redemption. Subsequent incumbrancers are also regarded as
necessary parties, because a perfect title could not be
given under the decree and sale; but the presence of
such incumbrancers is not indispensable to the decree

of foreclosure, it may be given and rendered without them, but such as are not made parties are not cut off or bound by the decree. See 2 Jones on Mortgages, § 1394. Section 415, Hill's Code, regulating suits for the foreclosure of real estate mortgages, provides that "Any person having a lien subsequent to the plaintiff * * * shall be made a defendant in the suit, and any person having a prior lien may be made defendant at the option of the plaintiff, or by the order of the court when deemed necessary." No one will contend, under this statute, that without the presence of a subsequent lienor as a party defendant, the suit could not proceed.* The decree without him is not binding so far as he is concerned. But a purchaser under such a decree may insist upon a redemption by the lienor not made a party, failing in which such lienor will be thenceforth barred of all interest in the premises: *Sellwood* v. *Gray*, 11 Or. 534 (5 Pac. 196). A person having a prior lien, but not a necessary party in either sense, may be brought in by order of the court. Now the result of all this is that the owner of the equity of redemption is an indispensable party, and without him the suit cannot proceed. Subsequent lienors are considered necessary parties, but their absence from the record does not perforce of that fact render the proceeding a nullity; but interested parties may require that they be brought in for their protection, and proper parties may be brought in if deemed necessary. Section 3677 should be construed in the light of this practice. The owner, of course, is an indispensable party, and his absence would be fatal to the proceeding; a decree without him would be a nullity.

---

*For an example of such a proceeding see *Morrell* v. *Miller*, 28 Or. post, where one Fowler, a subsequent mortgagee, was not a party.—REPORTER.

Persons personally liable and all lienholders are necessary parties in the sense that interested parties may require that they be brought in, so that the whole controversy may be concluded by one proceeding. This, however, should be taken with a word of explanation. If persons only personally liable have absconded, or are nonresidents and beyond the jurisdiction of the court, so that a valid personal judgment cannot be obtained against them, the statute not having provided for substituted service, the proceeding will not abate by reason of the fact that they cannot be brought in. The object of the statute was to give an effective remedy against the property, and the legislature did not intend to put it within the power of any person to defeat it. Hence the absence beyond the jurisdiction of the court of one personally liable cannot defeat the lien. "All other persons interested in the matter in controversy" may be brought in if deemed necessary. One salient circumstance which reenforces this construction of said section is that the owner comes under the category of parties whom the statute says may be made parties, but he is undoubtedly an indispensable party, and no valid decree could be established without him. The intention of the statute was to designate such parties as are necessary and proper for a complete determination of matters pertaining and incident to the foreclosure of the lien, and no particular importance should be given to the auxiliaries "shall" and "may," except perhaps to distinguish between necessary and proper parties. But it is claimed that the provisions of section 3679 requiring the contractor to defend any suit brought to enforce the lien is in itself a stronger reason why the suit should not proceed without his presence as a party litigant. In construing a similar statute, ADAMS, J., in

Horstkotte v. *Menier,* 50 Mo. 160, makes the following
pertinent observations, which are alike applicable here:
"When an owner of property contracts with a responsible party to furnish all materials and erect for him a
building, under this section he has the right to look
to such contractor for protection against all liens by
material men and subcontractors. That, to my mind,
was the evident intention of the legislature. If the
original contractor was not made a party, he would
not be bound by the judgment; whereas, if he was
a party, he would be estopped from disputing the
amount of recovery as between himself and the owner.
* * * What we now hold is that the original contractor ought to be brought before the court as a codefendant, for the purpose of protecting his own rights
and those of the owner. But if he is not brought before the court at the proper time, the judgment will
not for this omission be irregular or void. The objection should have been taken by the owner by demurrer
or answer. If he fails to demur when the defect appears on the petition, or fails to set up the nonjoinder by answer, when it does not appear on the face of
the petition, he will be presumed to have waived the
objection: Wagner's Statutes, 1014, 1015, §§ 6, 10. The
defect of parties cannot be reached by way of instruction." Nor can it be reached when mooted here or at
the trial for the first time.

6. This opinion has proceeded thus far upon the
assumption that "J. O. Holm and Brother" were not
the contractors, and hence that the contractors were
not made parties at all. The case can be no stronger
if they were wrongly named as defendants. We will
now recur to the first contention, as this disposes of
the second. The contract with the owner having been

executed under the firm name of "C. N. Holmes and Company," is it sufficient to state in the complaint that the materials were furnished to J. O. and C. N. Holm, partners doing business under the firm name of "J. O. Holm and Brother," contractors for the furnishing of materials and erection of the building? It appears from the testimony that there were two parties interested as contractors for the stonework of the building erected for Logus. One of these parties styled himself "C. N. Holmes," as is shown by his orders placed with Osborn for stone, and the other styled himself "J. O. Holm," as is shown by his indorsement upon a certificate issued by Stranahan and Dupay, the architects, to "C. N. Holmes and Company," and directed to Charles Logus, August ninth, eighteen hundred and ninety-two. It further appears that these two parties were brothers, although their surnames are not the same. The written contract with Logus for the stonework is subscribed "C. N. Holmes and Company." F. L. Logan, who was looking after Logus' interests during the construction of the building, and was a witness in his behalf, says "J. O. Holm" was the "Company" of "C. N. Holmes and Company," and that he had heard one of them speak of the other as his brother. This and other testimony leaves no doubt that these parties were associated in business for the purposes of this contract at least, but there is no evidence of a general copartnership existing between them. One of the parties has styled the firm "C. N. Holmes and Company." Other parties dealt with these persons with reference to the same contract for stonework under different firm names. Reifschneider and Kenner dealt with them as "Holmes Brothers," Nottingham and Company, as "Holm Brothers," and the plaintiff as "J. W. Holm

and Brother"; so that it is very difficult to determine
by what firm name the association of these brothers
for this particular venture should be styled or designated. But, however this may all be, it is clearly apparent that defendant Logus, who alone is contesting
this appeal, has not been misled to his injury in any
respect by the allegations in the complaint touching
these parties or their firm name, and we are therefore
not inclined to hold that there is such a disagreement
between the proofs and the allegations as to constitute
a variance fatal to plaintiff's case.

7. Closely connected with this objection is another, which goes to the sufficiency of the claim of
lien set out in the complaint, because of the fact that
the parties to whom the stone was furnished are
therein named as "J. W. Holm and Brother." Here,
again, it is not apparent that the defendant Logus
has been misled to his injury, which is a strong circumstance going to the maintenance of the lien. In
Putnam v. *Ross*, 46 Mo. 337, the contractors were named
in the claim of lien as Ross and Shane, whereas Ross
alone, the former partner of Shane, was the contractor. Shane had no interest in the transaction.
The court, in discussing that branch of the case, said:
"The plaintiffs * * * failed to state with precision
who was their debtor, giving the name of a business
firm, instead of the name of the party who had been
the senior member of that firm. He gave the name of
his real debtor, but erroneously coupled with it the
name of a third party who was not liable. Were
the defendants misled to their injury by this mistake?
If so, they ought not to suffer in consequence of the
plaintiff's inadvertence. But there is no probability
that they were harmed by the error. At all events,

it is not to be so presumed in the absence of evidence. If the error wrought the defendants any harm, it cannot be difficult for them to show it; but they aver nothing and prove nothing in that direction. Their objections rest on purely technical and over-critical grounds." So in *Tibbetts* v. *Moore*, 23 Cal. 203, a notice which stated that materials had been furnished to "Moore and Company" was held sufficient, although they were in fact furnished to Moore alone. See, also, *Steinmann* v. *Strimple*, 29 Mo. App. 485, and *Jewell* v. *McKay*, 82 Cal. 144 (23 Pac. 139). The name "J. W. Holm and Brother" was evidently placed in the claim of lien in good faith by Osborn. The account was kept with the contractors under that name. The plaintiff, testifying as to the firm name, says: "I started furnishing them lime on the building. I had the name J. N. Holm. Jim, as he was called, when I was writing the firm name, said, 'That is not right; it should be J. W. Holm,' and I said, 'What is the name of the firm?' and he said, 'J. W. Holm and Brother.' He corrected me at the time, right there." And J. W. Moore, who was in the employ of Osborn, testified in substance that both these brothers gave them the firm name as "J. W. Holm and Brother." The name thus given went upon Mr. Osborn's books and into the claim of lien. The lien claimant having acted in entire good faith in filing his lien, it ought to be clearly manifest that parties have been misled to their injury before a slight misnomer of the contractors' firm name should be allowed to defeat the lien. The last objection is not well taken.

8. It is next contended by defendant that the claim of lien does not state the contractual relations existing between the claimant and the owner, and is,

therefore, void. The claim of lien is in the following language, omitting the verification: "Know all men by these presents: that T. F. Osborn is entitled to a lien on the following described premises, by virtue of an express contract heretofore made with J. W. Holm and Brother for the furnishing of materials to be used in the erection of a certain hotel building, constructed and being upon the following described land, to wit: The southeast quarter of block one hundred and one, in the original townsite of East Portland, being at the northwest corner of East Fifth and East Washington Streets, in the City of Portland. The said materials were furnished to said J. W. Holm and Brother. That Charles Logus is the reputed owner of said land and building, and that J. F. Stranahan is architect of said building. That the contract and reasonable price of such materials so furnished was the sum of one thousand one hundred and eighty-two and thirty-four hundredths dollars lawful money of the United States. That the sum of one thousand and ninety-five and nine hundredths dollars is due, said claim and account being hereinafter specifically stated. Said materials were stone used in said building. That it is the intention of the said T. F. Osborn to hold a lien upon the premises hereinbefore described, and that it his intention to claim and hold such lien, not only upon the said buildings, erections, and superstructures, but also upon the land upon which the same are constructed, together with a convenient space around the same as may be required for the convenient use and occupation thereof. That the following is a true and correct statement of the account and demand due the claimant herein, after deducting all just credits and offsets:—

"For materials furnished June 24th to August
    12, 1892 ....$ 1,182 84

"DEDUCTIONS.

"Cash paid July 28th.................$31 10
"Cash paid August 2d............... 56 15

    "Total amount of deductions..... $87 25

"Balance now due................... $ 1,095 09

"That thirty days have not elapsed since the completion of the said building or since the said materials were furnished.   T. F. OSBORN."

The view we have taken of this question requires a review to some extent of some former decisions of this court wherein it has received consideration: *Rankin* v. *Malarkey,* 23 Or. 593, (32 Pac. 620, 34 Pac. 816,) is the first case touching upon the subject. It was there held that "the statement should show a *prima facie* right of lien. It, therefore, must connect the claimant with the owner of the lot or building against which it is sought to enforce the lien, either by showing that the claimant contracted with the owner or his agent, or that he furnished materials to one who was erecting a building under a contract, or with the owner's consent." Citing Jones on Liens, § 1392, and *Anderson* v. *Knudson,* 33 Minn. 172. But, upon a rehearing, the case was disposed of upon entirely different grounds, thus rendering the question immaterial in determining the controversy. In *Curtis* v. *Sestanovich,* 26 Or. 107, (37 Pac. 67,) the next case in which the question was discussed, it was held that "the contractual relation existing between the owner of the building and the person having charge of the construction thereof should be stated in the notice, when the labor has been done

or the materials have been furnished at the instance
of any other person than the owner," citing *Warren v.
Quade*, 3 Wash. St. 750, (29 Pac. 827,) and *Heald v. Hod-
ler*, 5 Wash. St. 677, (32 Pac. 723,) in addition to the
authorities cited in *Rankin* v. *Malarkey*. This case appears to have been concurred in by the full bench.
But here the claim of lien met the objection upon its
face, and it was still unnecessary to a final disposition
of the case to decide the question as a legal proposition. The next and last case is *Willamette Lumbering
Company* v. *McLeod*, 27 Or. 272 (40 Pac. 93). Here the
same question was made, but the claim of lien itself
again answered the objection, and it was so held.
However, the opinion of the court does not announce
as a proposition of law that such contractual relation
should be so stated. BEAN, C. J., dissented from this
opinion in so far as it assumed that the claim of lien
must upon its face show the contractual relation. The
writer hereof was of the same opinion, but did not
formally dissent, because there was no discussion or
holding upon the question except to declare that the
lien was sufficient to meet the objection. These are
all the cases which touch upon the subject, and it is
not believed the question has become *stare decisis* by
reason thereof. We will, therefore, consider it as one
of first impression.

Section 3669 of Hill's Code provides that any person furnishing material to be used in the construction,
alteration, etc., of any building, etc., shall have a lien
upon the same for labor done or material furnished
"at the instance" of the owner of the building or his
agent; "and every contractor, subcontractor, architect,
builder, or person having charge of the construction,
alteration, or repair, in whole or in part, of any building or other improvement as aforesaid, shall be held

to be the agent of the owner for the purposes of this act." Section 3673 prescribes the manner of perfecting the lien, and the requisites of the claim of lien itself. It must contain "a true statement of his demand, after deducting all just credits and offsets, with the name of the owner, or reputed owner, if known, and also the name of the person by whom he was employed, or to whom he furnished the materials, and also a description of the property to be charged with said lien, sufficient for identification." The claim should substantially state everything required by the statute before it can become effective as a lien: *Rankin* v. *Malarkey,* 23 Or. 597 (32 Pac. 620, 34 Pac. 816); *Gordon* v. *Deal,* 23 Or. 155 (31 Pac. 287); *Pilz* v. *Killingsworth,* 20 Or. 435 (26 Pac. 305); *Allen* v. *Rowe,* 19 Or. 190 (23 Pac. 901). By section 3669 the lien law may be invoked when the labor is performed or the materials are furnished to be used in the building at the instance of the owner or his agent, and it is enacted that the contractor or other person named in the statute shall be held to be the agent of the owner. So that furnishing materials to the contractor is, in effect, furnishing them to the owner; in other words, the material man is dealing with the owner through his agent. This must necessarily be so if we give to the rules of law touching principal and agent their ordinary signification in this connection, and there exists no reason why we should not: *Cross* v. *Tscharnig,* 27 Or. 49 (39 Pac. 540). Here then the statute itself has established a direct contractual relation between the material man and the owner. This being so it aids us very materially in the construction of that clause of section 3673 which prescribes what the claim of lien shall contain. Among other things, it shall contain "the name of the person * * * to whom he furnished the materials." If the person named in the claim of lien is the contractor, or one of either of the other classes of individuals designated, then the owner's agent is named, and this appears to be all that is required by the statute. There is nothing in this language, nor is there anything in the section to which it belongs, which requires that the contractual relations existing between the lien claimant and the owner shall be stated. A literal or even a liberal construction of the section standing alone can by no stretch of the rules of interpretation embrace such a requirement. But if this section is construed *in pari materia* with section 3669, as it ought to be, then the statutory intendment would seem to be against the interpretation contended for, since we have seen the statute itself has established the contractual relations, and the claim of lien could hardly be made stronger by containing a reiteration of what the law itself has established, and we believe that it was not intended by the legislature that such relations should be stated therein. The object of the statute is to provide a ready and available means whereby contractors, sub-contractors, and material men may secure themselves for labor done or materials furnished in the construction and repair of buildings and other structures, and at the same time to furnish the owner with reasonable notice so that he may deal with contractors to whom he is personally liable accordingly. Whether the person for whom the labor is done or to whom the materials are furnished was an agent under the statute, or had authority to bind the owner, and entitle the laborer or material man to a lien, is a matter of pleading and proof at the trial. As sustaining this interpretation see *Lumber Company* v. *Gottschalk,* 81 Cal. 641; *Hurlbert* v. *New Ulm Basket Works,* 47 Minn. 81 (49

N. W. 521); *Post* v. *Miles*, 34 Pac. 586; *Hauptman* v. *Catlin*, 20 N. Y. 247, which are decisions construing similar statutes. Jones on Liens, asserts a contrary doctrine. He says, in effect, that the statement should show a *prima facie* right of lien, and therefore must connect the claimant with the owner by showing that the claimant contracted with the owner or his agent, or that he furnished materials or labor to one who was erecting a building or other improvement under such a contract, or with the owner's consent. The citations in support of the text would indicate however that the doctrine here announced was the outgrowth of the earlier Minnesota cases which were based upon a statute containing a form that might be used in perfecting the lien. MITCHELL, J., in *Keller* v. *Houlihan*, 32 Minn. 486, (21 N. W. 729,) says: "An examination of this form will show that it required a statement (in brief, and not with the fulness, perhaps, required in a pleading) of every fact necessary to entitle the party to the lien which he claimed, including that of a contract with the owner." Citing *Clark* v. *Schatz*, 24 Minn. 300. And these cases were followed in *Anderson* v. *Knudson*, 33 Minn. 132. But the court in *Hurlbert* v. *New Ulm Basket Works*, 47 Minn. 81, holding under a statute which had dispensed with the form, declares: "It was competent for the legislature to dispense with the necessity of embracing such a statement in the lien notice, as it did do when, in prescribing particularly what the notice should contain, it did not include any provision as to a statement of the contract relations of the lien claimant with the owner of the property." So that Jones on Liens has lost much of its weight as an authority in point. *Warren* v. *Quade*, 3 Wash. St. 750, and *Heald* v. *Hodder*, 5 Wash. St. 677, are, however, strong authorities in support of the doctrine as laid down by Jones on Liens, and cannot well be distinguished from the case at bar, but the reasoning upon which they are based does not so well satisfy us as that employed in the cases above cited from California, Minnesota, and New Mexico. We are constrained to hold, therefore, that plaintiff's claim of lien is valid and sufficient, and the decree will be reversed, and one entered here that the lien be foreclosed and the property sold to satisfy the plaintiff's claim and interest, together with one hundred and twenty-five dollars attorney's fees and the further sum of four dollars, the expense of recording the lien.

REVERSED.

Argued April 16; decided November 4, 1895; rehearing denied.

NICKUM *v.* GASTON.

[42 Pac. 130.]

1. **ESTOPPEL — PAYMENT OF TAXES BEFORE SALE.**—One in possession of land is not estopped by lapse of time from defeating a tax title by showing that the taxes for which the land was sold were in fact paid before sale.

2. **EVIDENCE TO SHOW PAYMENT OF TAX.**—Parol or other competent evidence is admissible to show payment of a tax to defeat a tax title based on a subsequent sale for the alleged nonpayment of such tax.

3. **ALTERED WRITING AS EVIDENCE — CODE, § 788.**—Where it is shown, even after an instrument has been admitted over objection of the other party, that the alteration appearing therein was not made after the execution thereof, section 788 of Hill's Code, providing that the party shall account for an alteration made after the execution of the instrument, does not apply.

4. **WHO MAY PAY TAXES.**—The payment of a tax on land by a person claiming an interest therein, and its acceptance by the proper collecting officer, precludes a sale for the tax, whether the claim of interest was well founded or not.

5. **EVIDENCE OF PAYMENT OF TAX — QUESTION FOR JURY.**—Defendant's statement that she had paid the tax levied on land before the sale

thereof, together with a receipt indicating that she had done so, was sufficient evidence to require the court to submit to the jury the question whether the tax really had been paid.

6. JUDGMENT AS AN ESTOPPEL.— A judgment roll in a former action showing judgment in favor of a person claiming under a tax title, accompanied with evidence that said action was brought at the request of defendant against said person, will not estop defendant from defeating said title by showing that the taxes for which the land was sold were paid by defendant before the sale, where it did not appear that the question of payment of said taxes was raised in said former action.

APPEAL from Multnomah: E. D. SHATTUCK, Judge.

This action was commenced in October, eighteen hundred and ninety-one, by J. M. Nickum against Tiny Gaston to recover possession of the northeast quarter of section twenty, township one south, range two east, in Multnomah County. It has been in this court before on appeal from a judgment awarding the land to plaintiff: *Nickum* v. *Gaston,* 24 Or. 391. On a second trial the verdict and judgment were for defendant, and we now have the case on plaintiff's appeal. The record is voluminous, and contains many assignments of error, but it is thought unnecessary to encumber the opinion with an extensive statement of the facts or the numerous errors assigned and relied upon for a reversal of the judgment, as the result, in our opinion, must depend upon the solution of the questions presented by one branch of the case. The pleadings are in the usual form for such actions. Plaintiff alleges title and right of possession. This the answer denies, and, as a further defense, the defendant pleads title within herself, and sets up the statute of limitations as a bar to plaintiff's action, which defense is controverted by plaintiff's reply. The contested questions thus presented are two-fold: *first,* was plaintiff the owner of the legal title? and, *second,* if so, was his right of action barred as claimed? The question of adverse pos-session was, of course, unimportant in the absence of proof that plaintiff was the holder of the legal title, for he must recover, if at all, upon the strength of his own title, and not upon the weakness of that of his adversary. To maintain the issues on his part, and prove his title, the plaintiff gave in evidence a tax deed from the sheriff of Multnomah County to one George W. Brown, dated July first, eighteen hundred and seventy-three, and recorded July fifth, eighteen hundred and seventy-three, purporting to convey to Brown the property in controversy under a sale for delinquent taxes levied upon it for the year eighteen hundred and seventy, and other conveyances showing a complete chain of title from Brown to himself. To defeat the title thus established the defendant under-took to show—*first,* that before the sale to Brown she paid the taxes for which the land was sold; and, *second,* that she and her predecessors in interest had been in the adverse possession of the land for more than ten years prior to the commencement of the action. These two questions, among others, were submitted to the jury for special findings, and were both determined in favor of the defendant, and a general verdict rendered in her favor.   REVERSED.

For appellant there was a brief by *Messrs. Dolph, Mallory and Simon,* and *Mitchell, Tanner and Mitchell,* with oral arguments by *Messrs. Albert H. Tanner* and *Joseph Simon.*

For respondent there were briefs and oral arguments by *Messrs. Parish L. Willis* and *Seneca Smith.*

Opinion by MR. CHIEF JUSTICE BEAN.

Unless the record shows error affecting the question whether in fact Miss Gaston paid the taxes on this land before it was sold, the judgment must be affirmed, although the court may have erred in other respects. Plaintiff's title rested wholly upon the tax deed to Brown, and if there was competent evidence given on the trial from which the jury found that the tax had been paid prior to the sale, and there was no error in admitting testimony on this question, or in instructing the jury in relation thereto, the judgment cannot be disturbed; for, if the taxes had been paid prior to the sale, plaintiff's title necessarily failed, and therefore the other questions in the case are immaterial. When taxes are once paid, the lien of the state therefor is discharged, and a subsequent sale of the land for such taxes, as Mr. Black says, "is without color of authority and void. In other words, actual delinquency is a condition precedent to the right to sell any realty under a tax assessment." So that, if defendant had paid the taxes under which the sale was made, the lien was discharged, and the purchaser at the tax sale obtained no title by his purchase, and, of course, could convey none to his grantees: Hill's Code, § 2843; Black on Tax Titles, § 156; 2 Blackwell on Tax Titles, § 821; Cooley on Taxation, 450. We proceed, then, to examine the alleged errors in the record relating to this question. The defendant, to show that she had paid the taxes for eighteen hundred and seventy, gave in evidence the tax roll for that year, from which it appeared that the fractional southeast quarter of section twenty was assessed to her, and the northeast quarter thereof, being the property in controversy, to unknown owners. She also gave oral evidence tending to show that at the date of the assessment she did not own or claim to own the property assessed in

her name, but did claim to own the said northeast
quarter, which was assessed to unknown owners, and
that she owned no other land in that section. She
then called Joseph Gaston as a witness, who related
his connection with the matter in issue as follows: "I
am the father and agent of the defendant; prior to
eighteen hundred and seventy I purchased the land in
controversy of Hiram Smith for my daughter. I paid
the tax on the land for the year eighteen hundred
and seventy to the sheriff of Multnomah County. I
went to the sheriff's office as usual to pay the taxes
that were owing. That is all the taxes I owed on the
land in question. I found the land assessed to my
daughter, as it had been agreed between me and Mr.
Smith before; that was the first year it had been assessed to my daughter. I paid the taxes when we got
the receipt. It had been paid before by Mr. Smith; it
was assessed in his name. Mr. Smith had come to me
with his receipt; I had to pay the money over to him.
I have the receipt which I took for the taxes for
eighteen hundred and seventy." The witness then
produced a receipt signed by the sheriff of Multnomah County, dated January thirtieth, eighteen hundred
and seventy-one, which purports on its face to be for
the taxes assessed on the land in controversy for the
year eighteen hundred and seventy, which was offered
in evidence. To the admission of this receipt the
plaintiff objected upon the ground that it was immaterial and irrelevant, and because it appeared upon its
face to have been altered or mutilated, and such alteration had not been explained. The alteration, if any,
was made by erasing some letter, and inserting the
letter N in the description of the property in the
margin of the receipt. The objection was overruled
by the court, and the receipt was admitted in evidence,

to which the plaintiff excepted. The witness Gaston was then asked to state what, if anything, he knew about the supposed alteration in the receipt, and replied: "I do not recollect anything definite about that. It evidently had been a mistake of some sort, and at the time of making the receipt it was corrected; I know the receipt has never been altered since I received it. It has been laid away in an old iron box of papers for over twenty-two years. Before the last trial, I took a search through all my papers to find tax receipts to this land, and I found this receipt. I did not notice then that there had been any alteration in it; I did not notice that until the morning of the trial. We were examining it, and I saw the alteration in the receipt. I knew the proper description of the land independent of what might appear on the assessor's books. Am satisfied that I did not look at the assessment roll at the time I paid the taxes. Did not have the land assessed myself—did not have it put in the books." This and all evidence in respect to the payment of the tax for eighteen hundred and seventy was admitted over the objection and exception of the plaintiff.

1. It is claimed that the right to show that the tax was paid before the sale was barred by lapse of time. We are unable to concur in this position. It is admitted that defendant has been in the possession and enjoyment of the land in controversy at least since the spring of eighteen hundred and eighty-two, claiming title. Under such circumstances she certainly could safely rest upon her possession until her title was assailed by some one claiming under the tax deed, and then show, if the facts were with her, that it was void because the tax had in fact been paid.

No presumption can be built up in aid of the tax title by the delay of the holder in asserting his claim, nor can such delay deprive the owner of the property who is in possession of the right to question the validity of the deed when it is sought to establish title under it. That one who claims to have title to property by a tax deed may lie by, without asserting it, a sufficient length of time to estop the owner in possession from proving, when his title is attacked, that the tax was in fact paid prior to the sale, is a doctrine so manifestly unsound that time need not be wasted in attempting to make it appear more so.

2. There is nothing in the position that the payment of the tax could not be shown by parol. The payment may be proved by any competent evidence sufficient to satisfy the jury: Black on Tax Titles, § 159; Blackwell on Tax Titles, § 834; Cooley on Taxation, 452; *Adams* v. *Beale,* 19 Iowa, 61; *Hammond* v. *Hannin,* 21 Mich. 374 (40 Am. Rep. 490); *Davis* v. *Hare,* 32 Ark. 386; *McDonough* v. *Jefferson County,* 79 Texas, 535 (15 S. W. 490). Nor is the taxpayer responsible for the errors or mistakes of the sheriff or taxing officer, or the manner in which he keeps his records or accounts. If, in fact, he pays the tax, the demands of the government are discharged; it no longer has the right to sell his property, and it is immaterial whether a subsequent sale transpires through the mistake of the officer, or in positive disregard of the fact of payment. In either case the purchaser takes no title: Black on Tax Titles, § 162; Blackwell on Tax Titles, §§ 830, 831.

3. It is claimed the tax receipt admitted in evidence was not competent because it had been altered or changed. The statute, section 788 of Hill's Code,

provides that "The party producing a writing as genuine which has been altered, or appears to have been altered, after its execution or making, in a part material to the question in dispute, shall account for the appearance or alteration," etc. Now, it does not appear that the receipt had been altered or changed after its execution or delivery to the taxpayer. Indeed, the only evidence on that subject is the evidence of Gaston, who said he did not recollect anything definite about it, but it was evidently a mistake of some sort, and at the time of making the receipt it was corrected, but "I know the receipt has never been altered since I received it." True, this evidence was given after the receipt was formally admitted, but it was sufficient to cure the objection to its admission on account of its appearance. Its value as evidence, therefore, became a question for the jury.

4. It is next claimed that the defendant did not show sufficient interest in the property to entitle her to pay the tax. The evidence shows that she claimed to have some interest, but, whether this claim was well-founded or not, the right of the state to sell the land ceased when the tax was paid by her and accepted by the proper collecting officer. The power of sale is limited to coercing payment of the tax, and as soon as it is paid the power ceases, and it is generally held to be immaterial by whom the payment was made, if it was in fact accepted by the officers authorized to collect it: Blackwell on Tax Titles, § 826; Black on Tax Titles, § 161; Cooley on Taxation, 450; *Iowa Railroad Land Company* v. *Guthrie*, 53 Iowa, 386 (5 N. W. 519).

5. It is also claimed that the evidence was insufficient to support the finding that the tax had been

paid. The weight and sufficiency of the evidence was
for the jury and not the court. In our opinion it
tended to show that the defendant had paid the tax
prior to the sale. Gaston so testified, and the receipt
produced by him so indicated. As we have already
said, the defendant is not bound by the condition of
the assessment roll or the fact that the sheriff may
have applied the money paid by her to the payment
of the tax assessed against other property: Blackwell
on Tax Titles, § 831. The ultimate fact to be determined in the case was whether the defendant actually
paid the tax upon the property in controversy. If so,
the right to sell ceased, and the purchaser took no
title. This was a question for the jury under the evidence, and we think was properly submitted to them.

6. To defeat defendant's right to show that the
tax had been paid, plaintiff offered in evidence. as an
estoppel, a judgment rendered in favor of James A.
Bennett, and Laura Bennett, the successors of Brown,
who was the purchaser at the tax sale, adjudging them
to be the owners in fee simple of the property in controversy, rendered in an action brought by one Han-
nah M. Smith to recover possession thereof, in which
action the Bennetts set up the tax title to Brown as a
defense, accompanied with an offer to show that the
action was instituted at the request of defendant.
This evidence was, we think, properly excluded, if for
no other reason because it does not appear, and no
offer was made to show, that the question of payment
of the tax was submitted to or passed upon by the
court, or became at all material to the determination
of the case. For aught that appears the plaintiff in
that action may have failed because of the weakness
of her own title, and the defendants may not have

been called upon to make a defense, and so the validity of the tax deed not be called in question. These are all the alleged errors in the record affecting the question concerning the payment of the tax, and, having concluded that none of them are well taken, we are constrained to affirm the judgment, and it is so ordered.   AFFIRMED.

Argued July 80; decided October 28, 1895.

STATE *v.* SCOTT.
[42 Pac. 1.]

CORROBORATION OF ACCOMPLICE—CODE, § 1371.—Under section 1371, Hill's Code, which provides that "a conviction cannot be had upon the testimony of an accomplice, unless he be corroborated by such other evidence as tends to connect the defendant with the commission of the crime, and the corroboration is not sufficient if it merely show the commission of the crime or the circumstances of the commission," the admissions and confession of the woman with whom defendant is charged with having committed adultery are not sufficiently corroborated to sustain a conviction where the corroborating evidence goes merely to show that there was an opportunity to commit the act, but does not show an adulterous mind in either party, or any circumstance from which adultery might be inferred.

APPEAL from Lane: J. C. FULLERTON, Judge.

The defendant, Duncan Scott, an unmarried man, having been indicted, tried, and convicted of the crime of adultery, committed in Lane County with one Louisa Babb, wife of A. J. Babb, was sentenced to imprisonment in the penitentiary for the term of one year. From this judgment the defendant appeals, and assigns as error the denial by the court of his request that it instruct the jury to find a verdict of acquittal.

REVERSED. ·

For appellant there was an oral argument by *Messrs. George B. and George A. Dorris.*

For the state there was an oral argument by Mr. *Cicero M. Idleman,* attorney-general.

Opinion by MR. JUSTICE MOORE.

It is disclosed by the bill of exceptions that Louisa Babb, the person with whom the adultery is claimed to have been committed, testified, as a witness for the state, over the defendant's objection, that, on July twelfth, eighteen hundred and ninety-four, concluding to abandon her husband, she engaged one Sid Horn to come to her house after her clothing, which he did on the following day; that she left her home in his company about eleven o'clock in the forenoon, and, after going a short distance met, without any previous agreement, the defendant, whom she did not like, or look upon as her friend; that, not desiring to be seen by others, she remained in the woods with the defendant until about nine o'clock that evening, during which time she had sexual intercouse with him; that while in his company they ate a lunch consisting of pickles, cheese, cold beef, and bread; that at the time last mentioned she went to Sid Horn's house, and in an hour or more thereafter the defendant called there, but soon went away; that, on the following morning at about two o'clock she left Eugene on the train for Portland to seek work and to visit the coast; that, on entering a car, she saw the defendant who told her to go into another car, which she found on entering to be the smoking car; that, on arriving at Portland, the defendant ordered a cab, and she was conveyed to a hotel, where that night she occupied the same bed and had sexual intercourse with him. The following evidence was also offered and admitted over the defendant's objection, as tending to corroborate the testimony of Mrs. Babb: E. H. How testified that on July thirteenth, eighteen hundred and ninety-four, he was engaged in the business of keeping a restaurant at Eugene, and at eight o'clock in the morning of that day he put up a lunch for the defendant, consisting of sandwiches, pickles, cheese, and cake. Sid Horn testified that about nine o'clock in the forenoon of the same day the defendant came to his house, and invited him to go fishing but he declined the invitation; that he did not tell the defendant anything about his agreement to go after Mrs. Babb's clothing, or that she intended to leave her husband; that the defendant went with him in the direction of Mrs. Babb's house, but remained at the river fishing while the witness went to the house after Mrs. Babb's clothing; that about eleven o'clock, having obtained the clothing, he returned in company with Mrs. Babb to the place where he left the defendant; that Mrs. Babb, not desiring to go to the witness' house until evening, remained with the defendant; that about four o'clock in the afternoon of that day he and his wife, Lillian Horn, saw the defendant and Mrs. Babb together in the woods; and that the defendant on the morning of July fourteenth left Eugene to go to Vancouver, Washington, to get some horses he owned. Lillian Horn testified that she saw Mrs. Babb and the defendant together in the woods at about four o'clock in the afternoon of July thirteenth; and, also, that the defendant called at her house and saw Mrs. Babb about ten or eleven o'clock that night, but soon went away. T. G. Hendricks testified that on the morning of July fourteenth, eighteen hundred and ninety-four, he went on the train from Eugene to Portland; that, as he entered the car at Eugene, he saw the defendant seated therein, and also saw Mrs. Babb enter the car with a valise, and heard some one, but could not say who, tell her to go into another car. A. G. Mathews testified that he saw Mrs. Babb enter the smoking car of the train at Eugene on July fourteenth, and told her she ought to go into another car.

In view of this evidence, it is contended that Louisa Babb, if her testimony is to be believed, was an accomplice; that her admissions and confession have not been corroborated upon the material issue, and that the court erred in refusing to give the instruction requested. "At common law," says STRAHAN, J., in *State* v. *Jarvis,* 18 Or. 360, (23 Pac. 251,) "and in the absence of any statute governing the subject, it was the practice of judges to tell juries that they might legally convict on the evidence of an accomplice alone, if they thought they could safely rely on his testimony; but, at the same time, to advise them never to act on the evidence of an accomplice unless he be confirmed as to the particular person who was charged with the offense: 1 Wharton on Criminal Law, § 785. And Baron Parke said that it had always been his practice to tell the jury not to convict the prisoner unless the evidence of the accomplice be confirmed, not only as to the circumstances of the crime, but also as to the person of the prisoner": 1 Wharton on Criminal Law, § 787, and authorities there cited. "It," says GRAY, C. J., in *Commonwealth* v. *Holmes,* 127 Mass. 424, (34 Am. Rep. 391,) "has always been held that a jury might, if they saw fit, convict on the uncorroborated testimony of an accomplice. Lord HALE, Lord HOLT, and Lord MANSFIELD treated the question of his credibility as one wholly for the determination of the jury, without any precise rule as to the weight to be given to his testimony." But, whatever the rule may have been at common law, the statute now provides that "A conviction cannot be had upon the testimony of an accomplice, unless he be corroborated by such other evidence as tends to connect the defendant with the commission of the crime, and the corroboration is not sufficient if it merely show the commission of the crime or the cir-cumstances of the commission": Hill's Code, § 1371. Louisa Babb's admission of her participation in the alleged commission of the crime makes her an accomplice, and hence the corroborative evidence necessary to convict the defendant must be such as tends to prove adulterous acts on his part: Hill's Code, § 680. In *Commonwealth* v. *Bosworth,* 22 Pick. 399, MORTON, J., in commenting upon evidence in corroboration of the testimony of an accomplice, says: "The mode of cor-roboration seems to be less certain. It is perfectly clear that it need not extend to the whole testimony; but, it being shown that the accomplice has testified truly in some particulars, the jury may infer that he has in others. But what amounts to corroboration? We think the rule is that the corroborative evidence must relate to some portion of the testimony which is material to the issue. To prove that an accomplice had told the truth in relation to irrelevant and imma-terial matters, which were known to everybody, would have no tendency to confirm his testimony involving the guilt of the party on trial. If this were the case, every witness, not incompetent for the want of under-standing, could always furnish the materials for cor-roboration of his own testimony. If he could state where he was born, where he had resided, in whose custody he had been, or in what jail or what room in the jail he had been confined, he might easily get con-firmation of all these particulars. But these circum-stances, having no necessary connection with the guilt of the defendant, the proof of the correctness of the statement in relation to them would not conduce to prove that a statement of the guilt of the defendant was true."

In *State* v. *Odell,* 8 Or. 30, one William George, an accomplice, testified that he and the defendant waited outside while another person went into the building and brought out the property described in the indictment. The testimony of other witnesses tended to prove that the defendant was in the town in which the theft was committed about the time of the commission of the alleged crime, and that a sack of flour was missed from the place where the larceny was alleged to have been committed, but it was there held that such evidence did not tend to connect the defendant with the commission of the crime. In *State* v. *Townsend,* 19 Or. 213, (23 Pac. 968,) an accomplice testified that he and the defendant stole a cow, which they drove from the pasture of the owner, and, in pursuance of a previous agreement, delivered to other persons at Pendleton, at which place she was butchered. The corroborative evidence was the testimony of a witness who said that on January fourteenth, eighteen hundred and eighty-nine, at about eight o'clock in the evening, the accomplice left the house at which the witness was then staying, which was between four and five miles from Pendleton, and a short distance from the pasture from which the cow was stolen; that a little later the accomplice returned in company with the defendant, whom he introduced under an assumed name; that the defendant and accomplice together, soon thereafter left the house, and the next day he heard the cow was missing. The owner of the cow also testified that she was stolen from his pasture on the night of January fourteenth, eighteen hundred and eighty-nine. The state having rested, the counsel for the defendant moved for a nonsuit on the ground that there was not sufficient evidence of the defendant's guilt to be submitted to the jury. LORD, J., commenting upon the facts as elicited from the corroborative evidence, says: "They show that the defendant was not only in the vicinity when the crime was committed, but that he was there under a false name, and at night, and under circumstances not likely to occur without concert between him and his accomplice in furtherance of some common enterprise. In such case it can hardly be said that the facts do not tend in some degree to connect the defendant with the commission of the crime."

If there was any other evidence of the adulterous act, or of facts from which it could be inferred, and it was sought to prove the defendant guilty of it, the proof of the opportunity and the corroborating evidence of circumstances surrounding it might possibly, under the rule thus announced, be held sufficient to warrant a conviction. But in that case the crime was susceptible of proof by the person who lost the animal, while in the case at bar the only evidence of the commission of the crime is the testimony of the accomplice herself. "What appears to be required," says Roscoe in his work on Criminal Evidence, (Vol. 1, *133,) "is that there shall be some fact deposed to, independently altogether of the evidence of the accomplice, which, taken by itself, leads to the inference, not only that a crime has been committed, but ˑthat the prisoner is implicated in it." Tested by this rule, we are unable to discover any evidence, aside from Mrs. Babb's, which, taken by itself, leads to the inference that a crime even has been committed. There was no agreement existing between Mrs. Babb and the defendant to meet on that occasion, nor is there any evidence to show a previous familiarity between them, from which the evidence of the defendant's guilt can be inferred. Mere proof of an opportunity to commit adultery is insufficient to convict a person of that crime, unless there be proof also of an adulterous mind on the part of both parties; and to prove this state of mind circumstantial evidence is admissible to show a purpose or inclination to commit the act: Bishop on Statutory Crimes, § 679. Mrs. Babb's desire to avoid her husband, and to seek seclusion, may have been to her mind a sufficient reason for not wishing to visit Horn's house in the day time. So, too, the defendant's purpose to catch fish must be presumed to have been an honest one. Because he and Mrs. Babb met on the banks of the river, in the woods even, ate a lunch together, and were seen by others, does not necessarily or inferentially, in the absence of evidence of an adulterous mind, prove that they committed the crime of adultery; nor does the corroborating evidence even tend to show the commission of a crime, or any circumstance from which its commission can be inferred. The evidence shows that the defendant went to Portland on the same train with Mrs. Babb, but that in making the journey he had, at least, another purpose, which was to get his horses from Vancouver, Washington, while Mrs. Babb went to obtain work, and to visit the coast. If there was any corroborating evidence of adulterous intercourse between them at Portland, or if the place to which she went was a brothel, and it was proven that the defendant met her there, it might have been sufficient to infer the commission of the offense at the time and place alleged in the indictment (Bishop on Statutory Crimes, § 682); but the evidence of Mrs. Babb as to their conduct in that city is not corroborated by any circumstance except that she and the defendant were seen on the same train at Eugene. From an examination of all the testimony in support of Mrs. Babb's statements we conclude that it does not corroborate the material issue, or present facts from which the commission of the crime can reasonably be inferred, and hence, under the statute, was insufficient to support the conviction, and the court erred in refusing to give the instruction requested, for which reason the judgment is reversed and a new trial ordered.   REVERSED.

Decided March 23, 1896; rehearing denied.

BENNETT *v.* MINOTT.

[39 Pac. 997; 44 Pac. 283.]

1. SERVICE OF NOTICE OF APPEAL — PRESUMPTION. — Where nothing appears in the record to show the residence of respondent's attorney it will be presumed that he resides in the county where the trial was had, (*Roy* v. *Horsley*, 6 Or. 270, approved and followed,) and that his admission of service of a notice of appeal was there made.

2. ADVERSE PARTIES — SERVICE OF NOTICE OF APPEAL. — The grantor in a conveyance of property claimed to be fraudulent as to creditors is not a necessary party to a suit to set aside such conveyance, and, as his interest cannot be affected by the result, he is not an "adverse party," and the notice of appeal need not be served on him: *The Victorian*, 24 Or. 141, cited.

3. PLEADING — WAIVER OF OBJECTIONS. — An objection to a complaint for uncertainty or indefiniteness comes too late after judgment.

4. CREDITOR'S BILL — JUDGMENT NOT NECESSARY. — A creditor need not reduce his claim to judgment before filing a creditor's bill to reach assets of his debtor which have been transferred in fraud of creditors, a lien by attachment being sufficient: *Dawson* v. *Sims*, 14 Or. 561, approved and followed.

5. CREDITOR'S BILL — FRAUDULENT TRANSFER. — Where a debtor, for the purpose of hindering and delaying creditors, organizes a corporation and transfers to it all his assets, he himself being the owner of practically all the corporate stock, and continuing the business the same after as before the incorporation, using the proceeds for his own ben-

efit, equity will set aside such transfer at the instance of creditors, notwithstanding the incorporation is valid, and the corporate stock subscribed by the debtor is subject to sale under execution. Under such circumstances a court of equity will look beyond the legal forms, and decide the case on the rights of the parties.

APPEAL from Coos: J. C. FULLERTON, Judge.

This is a proceeding by Sandford Bennett in the nature of a creditor's bill to subjéct to the payment of his claim certain property alleged to have been trans- ferred by the defendant T. S. Minott to his codefend- ants the Coos Bay Hardware Company, a corporation, and to Lizzie H. Minott, for the purpose of hindering, delaying,˙ and defrauding creditors. From the plead- ings and evidence it appears that from the first day of August, eighteen hundred and ninety, to the eleventh day of June, eighteen hundred and ninety-two, Minott was engaged in the hardware business at Marshfield, in this state, and during that time became largely in- debted to plaintiff and his assignors, and to defendants Hexter, May and Company, D. M. Osborne and Com- pany, and other wholesale merchants, for goods sold and delivered to him. While being pressed by his creditors, he, on the latter date, caused the formation of said corporation; with a nominal capital of thirty thousand dollars, divided into three hundred shares of the par value of one hundred dollars each, of which he subscribed for one hundred and twenty shares, his wife for forty, and his attorney and a friend for one each. The corporation was subsequently organized, and Minott was elected president, general manager, and treasurer, under a contract to serve for one year at a salary of one hundred and fifty dollars per month. He thereupon assigned and transferred to the corporation his business and stock of hardware, which

was substantially all the property he owned not ex
empt from execution, at a valuation of about twelve
thousand dollars, in payment for the shares of stock
subscribed by him.   In this transaction he acted both
for himself as an individual and for the corporation of
which he was president, general manager, and treasurer, and substantially the owner.   About thirty days
after the formation of the corporation he assigned and
transferred to his wife, the defendant Lizzie H. Minott,
all his shares in the corporation, except nine, in payment of a debt he claimed to owe her.   He thereafter
proceeded to do business substantially as before, but
under the name of the corporation, selling and disposing of the goods, and applying the proceeds thereof
to his own individual use.   His creditors being unable
to effect a satisfactory settlement with him, the defendants Hexter, May and Company, in August, eighteen hundred and ninety-two, attached a part of the
stock of goods transferred by Minott to the hardware
company, and on September sixth another part was
attached by the defendants D. M. Osborne and Company, each of whom afterwards recovered judgment
against Minott, containing an order of sale of the attached property.   On September twenty-second, eighteen hundred and ninety-two, Baker and Hamilton duly
recovered a judgment against him for two hundred
and thirty-one dollars and ninety-five cents, upon
which an execution was subsequently issued and returned *nulla bona.*   On October twenty-second, plaintiff,
for himself and as assignee of a large number of the
other creditors, commenced an action and had the entire stock of goods in the possession of the hardware
company attached as the property of Minott.   Based
upon said attachment and the judgment in favor of
Baker and Hamilton, which was duly assigned to him,

the plaintiff instituted this suit to set aside the transfer of the stock of goods from Minott to the hardware
company, and to subject it to the payment of his demands, together with two lots in Dean's Addition to
Marshfield, which had previously been purchased by
Minott, and upon his direction conveyed to his wife.
A receiver was appointed, and the merchandise sold
by him under the order of the court, and the proceeds
thereof now await distribution. The case was afterwards tried, and a decree rendered adjudging the sale
of the stock of goods by Minott to the corporation to
be void as to creditors, but holding that there was no
fraud as to plaintiff in the matter of the purchase of
the lots in Dean's Addition, and decreeing that the
money in the hands of the receiver be applied,—*first,*
to satisfy the costs and expenses of the suit; *second,* to
the discharge of the judgments of Hexter, May and
Company and D. M. Osborne and Company; *third,* to
the satisfaction of the judgment recovered by the
plaintiff in the action wherein he caused said goods to
be attached; and, *fourth,* to the payment of the judgments in favor of the Bridge and Beach Manufacturing Company and Baker and Hamilton. From this decree the hardware company and the plaintiff both appeal, but Minott and his wife are not made parties.

AFFIRMED.

For appellant there was a brief and an oral argument by *Mr. William R. Willis.*

For respondents there were briefs by *Messrs. Cox,
Cotton, Teal and Minor, J. W. Bennett,* and *D. L. Watson,* with
oral arguments by *Messrs. Bennett* and *Wirt Minor.*

ON MOTION TO DISMISS APPEAL.

[39 Pac. 997.]

PER CURIAM. The notice of appeal was filed August thirtieth, eighteen hundred and ninety-four, and the proof of service indorsed thereon is as follows: "Due service and receipt of a copy hereof admitted after filing this twenty-eighth day of August, eighteen hundred and ninety-four. J. W. Bennett, attorney for plaintiff." It is contended (1) that the indorsement does not show the place of service; and (2) that T. S. Minott and Lizzie H. Minott are adverse and therefore necessary parties to the appeal.

1. The service of a notice of appeal may be made either upon the party or upon his attorney of record residing in the county where the trial was had; but when the attorney resides outside of such county the service can be made only upon the adverse party: *Lindley* v. *Wallis,* 2 Or. 203; *Rees* v. *Rees,* 7 Or. 78; *Lewis and Dryden Printing Company* v. *Reeves,* 26 Or. 445 (38 Pac. 622). The proof of service of a notice of appeal may be made by the sheriff of the county, (Hill's Code, §§ 54, 527,) or by the written admission of the adverse party, but in case of service by the latter method, the admission must state the time and place of service, (Code, § 61,) which must be indorsed on the notice when filed, or the appeal is not perfected: *Briney* v. *Starr,* 6 Or. 207. The admission of the service of a summons must show the time and place of service, otherwise no advantage could be taken of the defendant's default in failing to answer. But the place of service of a notice of appeal is, in general, not required to be specifically set forth, although it is otherwise as to time: Elliott on Appellate Procedure, § 179. The transcript shows that J. W. Bennett was the attorney

for the plaintiff in the trial of the suit in Coos County, and nothing appearing to the contrary, it will be presumed that he was a resident of the county in which he appeared as counsel, (*Roy* v. *Horsley*, 6 Or. 270,) and that he acknowledged service of the notice of appeal where the papers show the venue to be laid: Elliott on Appellate Procedure, § 179. The place of service not having been stated, it will, therefore, be presumed to have been in Coos County.

2. The defendants, T. S. Minott and Lizzie H. Minott, though proper were not necessary parties to the suit. Neither of them has any interest either legal or equitable in the property, and neither could be prejudiced by the decree which the plaintiff seeks to obtain: *Blanc* v. *Paymaster Mining Company*, 95 Cal. 524 (29 Am. St. Rep. 149, 30 Pac. 765); *Fox* v. *Moyer*, 54 N. Y. 130; *Potter* v. *Phillips*, 44 Iowa, 353; *Coffey* v. *Norwood*, 81 Ala. 512 (8 So. 199); *United States* v. *Church of Latter-Day Saints*, 5 Utah, 538 (18 Pac. 35); *Bailey* v. *Inglee*, 2 Paige, 278; *Pfister* v. *Dascey*, 65 Cal. 403 (4 Pac. 893). In a suit to set aside a deed alleged to have been fraudulently executed the plaintiff may, though not necessary, elect to make the grantors thereof parties, and having done so a demurrer will not lie for misjoinder: *Pfister* v. *Dascey*, 65 Cal. 403 (4 Pac. 893). The defendants T. S. Minott and Lizzie H. Minott not being necessary parties their interests cannot be adverse to or in conflict with those of the appellant: *The Victorian,* 24 Or. 121 (41 Am. St. Rep. 838, 32 Pac. 1040). As between them and the Coos Bay Hardware Company, the transfer of the stock of goods was complete, and none but their creditors could question the transaction. It follows that the motion to dismiss the appeal must be denied, and it is so ordered.

OVERRULED.

ON THE MERITS.
[44 Pac. 283.]

Opinion by MR. CHIEF JUSTICE BEAN.

In behalf of plaintiff it is contended that the two lots in Dean's Addition were purchased by the defendant Minott and deeded to his wife for the purpose of hindering, delaying, and defrauding creditors, but it appears that the purchase was made before any of the debts involved in this suit were contracted, and, there being no evidence to show that Minott had the property deeded to his wife for the purpose of hindering, delaying, or defrauding his subsequent creditors, the decree of the court below in that respect must be affirmed.

3. It is contended in behalf of the hardware company that the complaint in this suit is insufficient because it does not allege the name of the court in which plaintiff's said action was brought, nor that the indebtedness upon which it is based was due and payable, but this objection comes too late after judgment. No such question was made in the court below. The allegation of the complaint is, in substance, that on the twenty-second day of October, eighteen hundred and ninety-two, the plaintiff commenced an action against the defendant Minott to recover the sum of three thousand eight hundred and eighty-four dollars and sixty-two cents, interest, costs, and disbursements, and caused the entire stock of hardware, tools, implements, stoves, tinware, iron, steel, merchandise, and personal property of every description, transferred by the defendant Minott to the hardware company, to be duly attached by the sheriff of Coos County. This al-

legation of the complaint was denied by the answer, and the judgment roll in the action was admitted in evidence without objection, and it is now too late to raise the question as to the sufficiency of the complaint in this respect.

4. It is also contended that plaintiff had no standing to institute a suit of this character until his action in which the attachment was issued ripened into a judgment, and an execution thereon was returned unsatisfied. On the question as to whether a creditor must reduce his claims to judgment before he can maintain a creditor's bill to reach assets of his debtor which have been transferred for the purpose of defrauding creditors, the authorities are not harmonious, but in this state it may be regarded as settled that a lien by attachment is sufficient for that purpose: *Dawson* v. *Sims,* 14 Or. 561 (13 Pac. 506). But the suit is not grounded alone upon an attachment lien, but also upon the Baker and Hamilton judgment, assigned to plaintiff, upon which an execution was issued and returned unsatisfied, and under all the authorities this is sufficient to enable plaintiff to maintain the suit.

5. It is next claimed that the complaint fails to allege that the hardware company knew of or participated in Minott's fraudulent scheme, but this contention is equally without merit. The complaint avers that Minott formed the corporation for the purpose and with the intent of hindering, delaying, and defrauding his creditors, and that ever since its formation he has had full charge and management of its business, and has used it for the purpose of enabling him to carry on his business, and to cheat and defraud his creditors, and that at all times since its organiza-

tion it has fraudulently transacted business and purchased goods in its own name, but for the use and
benefit of Minott, and in furtherance of his fraudulent
scheme, and that the stockholders "were fully aware
of the objects and purposes for which the same was
formed, and for which its powers were exercised." In
other words, the effect of the allegations is that Minott
was the corporation and the corporation was Minott,
and that it was organized and used by him as a means
of hindering and delaying his creditors. Under such
circumstances a court of equity will look through and
beyond the legal forms in which the transaction was
clothed, and, if its real object and purpose was to hinder and delay creditors, will declare the sale and transfer void as to them, and no rule of law which regards
a corporation as an artificial person, separate and independent of its shareholders, can stand in the way
of such a result. It is next claimed that this suit can
not be maintained because the complaint and evidence
shows that the corporation was regularly and legally
organized, and that Minott received in exchange for
his goods their value in stock of the corporation, and,
therefore, it is argued, had as much property subject
to execution and sale by his creditors after as before
the transfer. But the conclusion is inevitable from the
evidence that the corporation was organized by Minott
as a means of hindering and delaying pressing creditors in the collection of their claims, and therefore the
transfer by him of the stock of goods to it was void
as to creditors, and they are entitled to be protected
against such a scheme by a court of equity. Under
the proofs in this case it is apparent that Minott was
in fact the corporation and the corporation was Minott.
He caused it to be formed, was the president, general
manager, and treasurer, and owned practically all the

subscribed stock at the time the pretended transfer was made. He made the contract therefor between himself as an individual and the corporation, acting for both parties, and conducted the business practically the same after as before the incorporation, using the proceeds for his own benefit. Under these circumstances, although the corporation was organized in due form of law and has a valid corporate existence, the legal rules which regard it as an entity distinct from the real parties in interest, and its stock as property subject to sale under execution, must go down in this attempt to consummate a fraud by legal forms. Equity is not bound by the rules of law in this respect, when such rules will permit fraud to triumph. "In equity," says Mr. Morawetz, "the conception of the corporate entity is used merely as a formula for working out the rights and equities of the real parties in interest; while at law this figurative conception takes the shape of a dogma, and is often applied rigorously without regard to its true purpose and meaning. In equity the relationship between the shareholders is recognized whenever this becomes necessary to the attainment of justice": Morawetz on Corporations, § 227; *Chicago and Grand Trunk Railway Company* v. *Miller*, 51 N. W. 982; *Des Moines Gas Company* v. *West*, 50 Iowa, 16; *Booth* v. *Bunce*, 33 N. Y. 139.

The contention is also made that at the time of the formation of the corporation and the transfer by Minott of his stock in the concern to his wife about a month later, he was justly indebted to her in about the sum of ten thousand dollars, and that such transfer was made in good faith in payment thereof. If this be true, it is not apparent how it can benefit the hardware company on this appeal. Mrs. Minott has not appealed, and the only question between the hardware company and the plaintiff is the validity of the sale and transfer by Minott of his stock of hardware to the corporation. If this sale was valid and made in good faith the plaintiff must fail in this suit without regard to the disposition Minott may have made of his stock in the corporation. But, on the other hand, if it was made, as we think the evidence clearly shows it to have been, for the purpose of hindering and delaying creditors, then it is void as to them, and no subsequent disposition by Minott of his stock or interest in the corporation could give validity to the transaction. The existence of the corporation or the ownership of the stock can in no way be affected by the result of this suit. Whatever the result, the corporation survives, and Mrs. Minott will have the stock she claims to have purchased from her husband. Its value, it is true, will be largely reduced if not practically destroyed, but this result comes, not because of the want of good faith in the sale and purchase of the stock by her from her husband, but on account of a previous fraudulent transaction between the corporation itself and Minott. Under these circumstances we do not regard it important to determine whether Minott was or was not indebted to his wife at the time he transferred the stock in the hardware company to her, because we regard the transaction by which the hardware company claims to have become the owner of the stock of merchandise owned by Minott at the time he contracted the debts upon which this proceeding is based as having been consummated for the purpose of hindering, delaying, and defrauding creditors, and must be declared void as to them.

The only remaining question in this case is one of priority between the plaintiff and defendants Hexter, May and Company, and D. M. Osborne and Company.

Some question is made as to the execution of the writs of attachment in the actions brought by these defendants against Minott, but there seems to have been a substantial compliance with the statute in attaching the property under said writs, and in our opinion the order of distribution made by the court below ought not to be disturbed. It follows that the decree must be affirmed, and it is so ordered.   AFFIRMED.

Decided January 13, 1896.

PEARSON *v.* DRYDEN.

[43 Pac. 166.]

1. INSTRUCTIONS TO JURY — ABSTRACT PROPOSITIONS.— Abstract propositions of law, not applicable to the facts of the case in hand, are misleading and mischievous, and to present such in an instruction to a jury is reversible error*: *Bowen* v. *Clarke*, 22 Or. 566, approved and followed.

2. EJECTMENT — STATUTE OF LIMITATIONS — ADVERSE POSSESSION.— The title of a person who has been in adverse possession of land for more than the statutory period, entering under a survey which both he and the adjoining proprietor believed to be correct, cannot be affected by a subsequent survey showing that the division line had not been correctly located by the first survey: *Joy* v. *Stump*, 14 Or. 361, cited and approved.

APPEAL from Multnomah: E. D. SHATTUCK, Judge.

For appellant there was a brief by *Messrs. Edward Mendenhall, Elbert J. Mendenhall,* and *Watson, Beekman and Watson,* with an oral argument by *Mr. Edward Mendenhall.*

*This proposition is announced and fully sustained in the following cases: *Shattuck* v *Smith,* 5 Or. 125; *Glaze* v. *Whitley,* 5 Or. 165; *Morris* v. *Perkins,* 6 Or. 350; *Rosendorf* v *Baker,* 8 Or. 241; *Hayden* v. *Long,* 8 Or. 244, *Willis* v. *Oregon Railway and Navigation Company,* 11 Or. 257; *Marx* v. *Schwartz,* 14 Or. 178; *Breon* v. *Heacle,* 14 Or. 494; *Glenn* v *Savage,* 14 Or. 567; *Roberts* v. *Parrish,* 17 Or. 583; *Woodward* v. *Oregon Railway and Navigation Company,* 18 Or. 289; *Langford* v. *Jones,* 18 Or. 308; *Larsen* v. *Oregon Railway and Navigation Company,* 19 Or. 241; *Bailey* v. *Davis,* 19 Or. 217; *Rowland* v. *McCown,* 20 Or. 538; *Buchtel* v. *Evans,* 21 Or. 309; *Bowen* v. *Clarke,* 22 Or. 566; *Hislop* v. *Moldenhauer,* 23 Or. 119; *Coos Bay Railroad Company* v. *Sigtis,* 26 Or. 393.— REPORTER.

For respondent there was a brief by *Messrs. C. S. Hannum* and *Joseph W. Ivey*, with an oral argument by *Mr. Hannum*.

Opinion by MR. CHIEF JUSTICE BEAN.

This is an action by Samuel Pearson to recover the possession of real property from William H. Dryden. The complaint is in the usual form, alleging title and right to possession in plaintiff, and a wrongful withholding by the defendant. The answer denies the allegations of the complaint, and sets up title by adverse possession in the defendant, which is denied by the reply. From the pleadings and evidence it appears that plaintiff and defendant have been the owners of adjoining tracts of land in Multnomah County for many years; that in eighteen hundred and seventy-seven, at plaintiff's request, Mr. Burrage, the then county surveyor, surveyed out and marked a line between the premises of the respective parties for a division line; that immediately thereafter a fence was built along such line by the parties, which has been maintained ever since as a division fence; that each party occupied, cultivated, and improved his respective lands up to the fence, claiming to own to the line so marked, without objection from the other until eighteen hundred and ninety, when another line was run by Hurlburt, the then county surveyor, differing from that formerly run by Burrage, whereupon the plaintiff, for the first time, claimed to own the land between the two lines which had been enclosed and occupied by the defendant, and subsequently brought this action to recover possession thereof. There was a judgment for plaintiff and defendant appeals.   REVERSED.

1. On the trial, the court, among other things, charged the jury that "The answer sets up title by adverse possession, that is, open, notorious, and adverse possession for a period of ten years consecutively. You have heard the evidence concerning that matter. It is a general rule, however, that a possession that begins by consent, which has its inception by license, can never ripen into adverse title until such possession has returned to the party from whom the license comes, and then commences anew."

It is contended by the defendant that, although this instruction may be correct as an abstract proposition of law, the court erred in giving it in this case, because it has no application to any issue therein, and in this we think he is correct. There was no question of license in the case. It was admitted by plaintiff all through the trial that defendant was and had been in the exclusive, undisputed possession of the tract in dispute from the time of the Burrage survey in eighteen hundred and seventy-seven up to eighteen hundred and ninety, when the Hurlburt survey was made, under the belief of both parties that it belonged to him. The only witnesses in regard to the circumstances under which the possession was taken were the plaintiff and defendant, and neither of them testified to anything from which a license could in any way be inferred, but they both testified that defendant entered into and took possession of the land in controversy as his own. It has been repeatedly held by this court that abstract propositions of law, not applicable to the facts in evidence, are misleading and mischievous, however correct in themselves, because they necessarily tend to draw the minds of the jury away from the real facts in the case to something which they may conceive to exist, although not found in the evidence. The authorities on this question aro collated by the late Chief Justice STRAHAN in *B....en* v. *Clarke*, 22 Or. 566 (30 Pac. 430). The instruction complained of had a tendency to mislead the jury by leaving them to infer that, in the opinion of the court, the the acquiescence of plaintiff in defendant's occupancy up to the Burrage line might be considered as a mere license, when the undisputed evidence showed to the contrary. For this reason, we think it was error to give it.

2. The court refused the defendant's request to instruct the jury that if he had been in the adverse possession of the property in dispute from eighteen hundred and seventy-seven up to the date of the Hurlburt survey in eighteen hundred and ninety, such survey could not affect in any manner his title thus acquired, and this, in our opinion, was also error. If defendant had been in the adverse possession of the land for more than ten years prior to the Hurlburt survey, his possession had ripened into a title (*Joy* v. *Stump*, 14 Or. 361, 12 Pac. 929,) which could not be affected in any way by such survey. It was peculiarly important to defendant that an instruction to this effect should have been given, because much prominence was given in the evidence and charge of the court to the testimony tending to show that the Burrage survey was incorrect. Indeed, the court began its charge to the jury by saying that "the controversy here has arisen out of conflicting surveys," and then proceeds to instruct them very carefully as to the rules by which they should be governed in determining the effect of the several surveys, and in doing so intimated very strongly, if it did not state in so many words, that

the Hurlburt survey was the more reliable. It was therefore easy for the jury to imagine that the Hurlburt survey, if correct, was conclusive upon the title, and to overlook the effect of defendant's adverse possession. The real question in the case as disclosed by the record before us does not seem to be so much a controversy about conflicting surveys as one of adverse possession, and while the court in its general charge seems to have instructed the jury quite fully upon this question, yet we think the defendant was entitled to the instruction requested as to the effect of the Hurlburt survey upon his adverse possession. if the jury should find that he had been so in possession. It follows that the judgment must be reversed, and a new trial ordered.   REVERSED.

Argued November 5, 1895; decided January 13, 1896.

MORRELL *v.* MILLER.
[43 Pac. 490.]

1. FRAUDULENT CONVEYANCE.— M., being civilly as well as criminally liable for shooting plaintiff, deeded to L., his attorney, at a time when it was apprehended plaintiff would die from the effects of the shooting, his real estate, worth five thousand dollars, and gave him a bill of sale of his personalty, worth five hundred and eighty-five dollars, which together constituted all his property; they executing a secret declaration of trust, whereby, in consideration of the conveyances, L. agreed to defend M. in all suits or actions which might be brought against him, and to dispose of the remainder of the property as he and M. should agree. Thereafter it was agreed that the fees of L should be one thousand dollars. C. and A. were then engaged to assist in the defense of the criminal matters, each to receive one thousand dollars therefor. C., desiring security on the land, and being unwilling to take a mortgage from M., and L. being unwilling to give security himself thereon, because of the trust agreement, M. gave a second deed to L. to cut out the trust as to the land; it being understood that L. should give a mortgage to C., which he did, and that A. should be paid out of the land, there being no understanding that M. should have any interest in the land. Thereafter L. conveyed the land to A., who had notice of all the circumstances.

subject to the mortgage to C., for a recited consideration of two thousand dollars. *Held*, that while the second deed to L. would be considered an absolute conveyance, as between him and M., and not void as to creditors, it was attended with such suspicious circumstances that it would be permitted to stand, as against creditors, only as security for the attorneys' fees.

2. CONSTRUCTIVE NOTICE OF FRAUD.— Where one attorney employs another attorney for his client, and tells him that his client will pay each of them a fee of one thousand dollars, and then conveys to the second attorney, subject to a mortgage of one thousand dollars given to secure the fee of a third attorney, for a recited consideration of two thousand dollars, land worth five thousand dollars, which the client had conveyed to the first attorney with an understanding that the second attorney should be paid out of it, the second attorney will be chargeable with notice of the nature of the first attorney's title, and take it subject to the rights of the client's creditors, that the conveyance to the first attorney be treated only as security for the ees of the attorneys.

3. FRAUD.— A transfer of property by a prisoner under indictment to pay counsel fees, which, though large, are not extortionate, is not void as to creditors, unless made for the purpose of rendering the property inaccessible to them.

4. LIABILITY OF GRANTEE IN FRAUDULENT CONVEYANCE.— Defendant, to whom plaintiff's debtor conveyed his personal property in secret trust for himself, is liable for the value thereof to plaintiff so far as he puts it beyond plaintiff's reach after he instituted his suit to set aside the conveyance as in fraud of creditors.

5. SUBROGATION.— A debtor made conveyances of land and personalty which, as against plaintiff, his creditor, were fraudulent as to the personalty, and, as to the land, amounted only to a mortgage. *Held*, that the grantee having used the personalty in paying off a prior lien on the land, after plaintiff commenced action to set aside the conveyance of personalty, plaintiff would be subrogated to such lien.

APPEAL from Multnomah: LOYAL B. STEARNS, Judge.

This is a suit to set aside certain conveyances and mortgages as being in fraud of creditors. The facts out of which it arose are briefly as follows: On November ninth, eighteen hundred and ninety-two, Joseph Miller shot and seriously wounded the plaintiff, Otto Morrell, for which offense Miller was arrested the same day, and on the fifteenth of December the grand

jury of Multnomah County returned three indictments
against him for offenses growing out of said shooting.
Afterwards, about April twenty-first, eighteen hundred
and ninety-three, Miller was convicted on all three of
the indictments and sentenced to serve a term in the
penitentiary.   On December tenth, eighteen hundred
and ninety-two, the plaintiff began a civil action in the
Circuit Court of Multnomah County against Miller to
recover damages on account of said shooting, and on
May third, eighteen hundred and ninety-three, obtained
judgment for ten thousand dollars and costs, taxed at
thirty-six dollars and fifty cents.   On November eighteenth, eighteen hundred and ninety-two, Miller conveyed to the defendant Charles F. Lord, by deed of
geneial warranty, in consideration of "one dollar and
other valuable consideration," two ten-acre tracts of
land situate in Multnomah County, and certain ease
ments appurtenant thereto, by any bill of sale conveyed to Lord certain personal property, consisting in
the main of a certificate of deposit for three hundred
dollars and a promissory note of two hundred and
eighty-two dollars and sixty cents.   The deed and bill
of sale cover all the property that Miller had.   On
November twenty-fifth the following declaration of
trust was executed by Lord and Miller, showing the
purposes of the deed and bill of sale, to wit: "This is
to certify that for and in consideration of a certain
warranty deed and bill of sale, placed upon record in
the recorder's office of Multnomah County upon the
twenty-third day of November, A. D., one thousand
eight hundred and ninety-two, wherein Joseph Miller
is grantor and Charles F. Lord is grantee, and of a
certificate of deposit for three hundred dollars, and of
a certain promissory note for two hundred and eighty-
two dollars and sixty cents, sold, delivered, and in-

dorsed by said Miller to said Lord, for one dollar and other valuable consideration, the said Lord agrees to defend the said Miller in all or any suits or actions which may be brought against said Miller, and to make disposition of such remainder of said property as said Lord and Miller shall agree." On December ninth Miller, for the purpose of securing to the firm of McGinn, Sears and Simon their fee of one thousand dollars then agreed upon for defending him in said criminal matters, executed and delivered to the defendant H. E. McGinn a mortgage upon the land described in the deed to Lord, but, this security not being satisfactory to the firm, Miller afterwards, upon the same day, executed to Charles F. Lord another deed of general warranty, covering the same premises, which recites a consideration of two thousand dollars, and thereupon Lord executed and delivered to N. D. Simon his note for one thousand dollars, and mortgage upon said premises to secure the same. Both the mortgage to McGinn and the one to Simon were made to secure the same liability. During the course of these negotiations the defendant Mays was employed as counsel to assist in Miller's defense. On December sixteenth, Lord, by deed of general warranty, excepting only the mortgage to Simon, conveyed the premises to Mays, the deed reciting a consideration of two thousand dollars; and on April twenty-sixth, eighteen hundred and ninety-three, Mays and wife mortgaged the property for one thousand eight hundred dollars to the defendant W. H. Fowler. This suit was instituted May twentieth, eighteen hundred and ninety-three, and plaintiff seeks thereby to have all these conveyances and mortgages set aside. Fowler, although made a party to the suit, was not served and did not appear in person or otherwise.

The decree being in part adverse to the defendants
Lord and Mays, they come to this court by separate
appeals; but Lord filed no brief, and did not appear
either in person or by attorney at the argument of the
cause. The plaintiff took a cross-appeal as to Lord
and Mays only.   MODIFIED.

For F. P. Mays there was a brief by *Messrs. Cox,
Cotton, Teal and Minor*, with an oral argument by *Mr.
William W. Cotton.*

For H. E. McGinn and N. D. Simon there was a
brief and an oral argument by *Mr. Alfred F. Sears, Jr.*

For Otto Morrell there was a brief and an oral
argument by *Messrs. James R. Stoddard* and *Edward Byars
Watson.*

Opinion by MR. JUSTICE WOLVERTON.

1. The first question made here, and upon which
the main controversy hinges, is upon the finding of
the court below: "That both said deeds of conveyance
from Miller to Lord, and Lord's deed of conveyance
to Mays, were intended by all the parties to convey
the legal title to said property in trust for said Miller; and that said legal title was taken under said
conveyance and held in trust for said Miller, and the
same is now held in trust for said Miller by said
Mays." It is claimed this finding is not supported by
the evidence. Let us examine first the testimony
touching the execution of the Miller deeds. The declaration of trust, which is signed by both Lord and
Miller, clearly establishes the nature of the first deed
to Lord. The effect of the bill of sale and that deed,
when construed in connection with the declaration,

was to impress the property therein described, in the hands of Lord, with a trust for certain purposes,— *first,* to pay said Lord for his services "in all or any suits or actions which may be brought against said Miller," and, *second,* "to make disposition of such remainder of said property as said Lord and Miller shall agree." At the date of this transaction there had been no understanding or agreement with Miller as to the amount of Lord's fees for the services agreed to be performed. Now, as to the subsequent deed. Lord testifies that "afterwards he (Miller) made the statement to me that he was willing to pay me as much as he would pay Mr. McGinn; as much as he had talked of paying Mr. McGinn. I then asked him what that was, not knowing definitely at the time, and he told me a thousand dollars. Then I asked him, in case we engaged Mr. Mays as an attorney to assist in the trial of the cases, said I presumed he would expect to receive the same amount as he had agreed to pay myself, which he assented to. And, I think, on that day— that I should judge to be the twenty-third or twenty-fourth of November; in that neighborhood—he authorized me to employ Mr. Mays, and I did so; informing Mr. Mays that Mr. Miller had agreed, as with me, to pay the sum of one thousand dollars. One thousand dollars to Mr. Mays, and one thousand to myself—one thousand to each—and we were to look after him in all the cases, either civil or criminal, and also after his own matters. * * * After these arrangements were made, and I had this understanding with Mr. Miller, and had employed Mr. Mays, some time along the first of December—possibly the first week—Mr. Miller told me he desired to engage further counsel; and that he had talked with Mr. McGinn, and he thought McGinn would probably act as one of his counsel in

his cases, as well as myself and Mr. Mays. Some time,
I think about the eighth, possibly, of December, eighteen hundred and ninety-two, Mr. Miller told me he
had engaged Mr. McGinn at the same figure, that is
he had agreed to give him the same amount that he
was to pay Mr. Mays and myself, and he desired me
to make out a mortgage to Mr. McGinn to secure his
fee. I told him then that I did not desire to give a
mortgage upon the property in the condition in which
I held it, because I simply held the property as a
mortgagee, and not in fee. He said he would see Mr.
Simon about that, but Mr. Simon wanted a mortgage,
and I should have to give him one. I think the next
day, anyway the ninth of December, I came to the
courthouse, and Mr. Miller said Mr. Simon had been
there, and was waiting for me upstairs, if I recall. I
talked with Mr. Miller, and he stated that he wanted
me to give the mortgage to McGinn that day, and Mr.
Simon was waiting upstairs, and would see me about it.
I came upstairs and Mr. Simon—by the way, before
coming upstairs I spoke to him again about making
the deed; that I did not care to give it in the present
shape in which the property was. He says, 'Well, I
will sign a deed and you can then give a mortgage.'
I came upstairs, and the deed was drawn up. * * *
The second deed was an absolute deed to the property. I came upstairs, and I think Mr. Simon and I
met in the law library, and the deed was drawn up
there. Mr. Simon went below, and came back, and returned with the deed properly signed and witnessed.
* * * The mortgage was then drawn up in the law
library, I think, and I signed the mortgage and executed it, and also the promissory note for one thousand dollars, after the deed had been made by Mr.
Miller to myself absolutely deeding the property to

me. * * * In the afternoon, when I went down to the jail, Miller informed me that Simon was waiting for me above to draw up the absolute deed to the property. I then explained to him that the agreement which had been entered into between us only related to the first deed, and would be inoperative so far as the second deed was concerned, and that he would either destroy the instrument or hand it back to me. I don't recollect whether he said he had destroyed it, or that he would hand it to me the next morning, but it was understood between us that he should either return it or destroy it, and I presumed, until I had been otherwise informed, that it had been destroyed. * * * There was no understanding or agreement between Mr. Miller and myself subsequently, or at the time of making the second deed, that he should have any interest whatever in the real property, the personal matter remaining as it was in the beginning. * * * He deeded the property to me absolutely, for the purpose of securing my fees and of paying other counsel who had been retained by him in the case." Question—"For the purpose of securing your fees or paying your fees?" Answer—"Well, of paying my fees. * * * The amount was understood thoroughly by Mr. Miller that you (Mays) was to receive for your services in the cases which came up the sum of one thousand dollars, and that sum and fee should be paid out of the property." On cross-examination the following testimony was elicited: Question—"Now, the only reason you give for changing this deed, which enables you to hold the title in trust for Miller, of the twenty-third of November, eighteen hundred and ninety-two, to what you say was an absolute deed on the ninth of December, eighteen hundred and

28 OR.—24.

ninety-two, was the requirement on the part of Mc-
Ginn, Sears and Simon that they should have a mortgage on the property to secure their fee of a thousand dollars? That was the only reason for it."
Answer—"That is the only reason there was for it;
yes, sir." Question—"And so you informed Miller of
that fact that you wanted an absolute deed because
McGinn, Sears and Simon wanted a mortgage, and he
thereupon gave you this absolute deed?" Answer—
"Yes, sir." Question—"And that is all there was of
it?" Answer—"And that is all there was of it."

In this connection Simon's testimony shows that the
McGinn mortgage was given in the morning. This not
being satisfactory, because the legal title was in Miller, it was arranged that Miller should execute to Lord
a second deed, and then that Lord should execute a
mortgage to Simon, and this was accordingly done the
same day, Lord executing the note for one thousand
dollars, which the mortgage was given to secure, Simon writing out the second deed himself. Lord admits that he realized five hundred and eighty-five dollars and sixty cents out of the personal property
which he had acquired under the bill of sale. From
this testimony we are to deduce the object and purpose of the second deed, it being substantially all that
was offered bearing upon the subject, except as the
testimony adduced touching the value of the land may
affect it. The court below found from the testimony
of a multitude of witnesses called upon that question
that its value at the time these deeds and mortgages
were executed was five thousand dollars, and this finding we are not inclined to disturb. Miller was not
called as a witness. A corollary contention is that,
whatever might have been the effect of the first deed
to Lord, the second was intended by the parties *to be*

and was in fact an absolute deed, and was given for
the purpose of cutting out any trust in favor of Miller. It was evidently intended that the legal title
should pass by the second deed, if it still rested with
Miller at the time of its execution, as its purpose was
to so invest Lord with such title as that he could execute a valid mortgage upon the premises to Simon.
Lord says Miller deeded the property absolutely for
the purpose of securing his fees, and paying other
counsel who had been retained, but afterwards declared the purpose was not to secure but to pay his
fees. Subsequently, but in the same connection, he
says that it was thoroughly understood that Mays' fee
should be paid out of the property. Upon cross-examination he testifies that the only reason he had for
taking another deed was to enable him to mortgage
the property to secure McGinn, Sears and Simon, he believing that the former deed was in effect but a mortgage, and that he was therefore without authority to
execute the desired mortgage. And yet he says "there
was no understanding between myself and Miller subsequently, or at the time of making the second deed,
that he (Miller) should have any interest whatever in
the real property, the personal matter remaining as it
was in the beginning." This testimony is somewhat
indefinite and unsatisfactory, and does not disclose a
transaction wherein all the terms and conditions were
distinctly understood and defined. Especially is this
true as it concerns the consideration to support the
deed. But it may be now asserted as a rule of law
that where a deed is perfectly executed, and is intended to operate at once, no trust will result merely
from the want of consideration, unless the attendant
circumstances show that it was not intended the
grantee should take beneficially: 10 Am. and Eng.

Ency. of Law, 56; *Philbrook* v. *Delano,* 29 Me. 410. If the consideration is inadequate, the rule would undoubtedly apply with equal force.

The "attendant circumstances" in the case at bar, other than those related may be briefly stated. Miller was under arrest for a grave offense, then thought to be more serious than it afterwards proved to be, he being apprehensive that Morrell would die of the wound received at his hands. He had incurred a civil liability to Morrell because of the assault made upon him, and had previously transferred all his property, of the aggregate value of five thousand five hundred and eighty-five dollars and sixty cents, to Lord, for the purpose of securing his fees for service as an attorney, with a declaration of trust that the balance should be disposed of as he and Lord should agree. At the time of the execution of these deeds Morrell was a creditor of Miller under *Philbrick* v. *O'Connor,* 15 Or. 15 (13 Pac. 612). This being so, the plaintiff claims that the latter deed was fraudulent as to him, as well as the first. There are some attendant *indicia* of fraud, such as the transfer of all Miller's property of such considerable value to Lord; the declaration of a secret trust in connection therewith; and the inadequacy of consideration for the second deed. But, upon the other hand, Miller was deeply interested. He was in the toils of the law, charged with a grave offense, and his object was to extricate himself therefrom. The purpose of making such use of his property as to secure able counsel to conduct his defense, and to attend to other apprehended litigation, was perfectly legitimate. His right to be heard by counsel is a constitutional right, and he should be permitted, unless hindered by legal process, the free and untrammeled use of his property to obtain legal assistance, otherwise constitutional privileges would be invaded. Upon the whole, we believe the second deed was intended to bo and operated as an absolute conveyance of the title to said premises, and we are unable to say from the evidence that it is fraudulent and void as to creditors. But the transaction is attended with such suspicions circumstances that we ought not to permit the conveyance to stand, except as security for such liability as Miller legitimately incurred to meet the expenses of impending litigation, under the doctrine laid down by Chancellor KENT in *Boyd* v. *Sugden*, 1 Johns. Ch. 47·': "When a deed is sought to be set aside as voluntary and fraudulent against creditors, and there is not sufficient evidence of fraud to induce the court to avoid it absolutely, but there are suspicious ·circumstances as to the adequacy of consideration and fairness of the transaction, the court will not set aside the conveyance altogether, but permit it to stand for the sum already paid." This doctrine has been followed in *Crawford* v. *Beard*, 12 Or. 447, (8 Pac. 537,) and *P'il'ri.* v. *O'Connor*, 15 Or. 15, (13 Pac. 612;) and applied by DEADY, J., in *United States* v. *Griswold*, 7 Sawy. 308 (8 Fed. 496); yet the application of this doctrine here must depend upon whether Mays afterwards purchased the premises in good faith, for a valuable consideration, and without notice of the infirmities of title; as, if he did so purchase, he cannot be deprived of the benefits secured by his deed from Lord.

2. Without going into the evidence upon this subject, it is sufficient to say that because of the fact that Lord arranged with Miller for the amount, manner of payment, and security of Mays' fee, and considering the nature of Lord's and Mays' employment, we have concluded that Mays is chargeable with constructive

notice, at least, of the nature of the title which Lord possessed, and therefore took subject to whatever claim plaintiff may have had upon the premises.

3. As to the fees which Lord and Mays were to receive for their services in the defense of Miller in the criminal and civil actions in which he became involved, while they were large and ordinarily would, perhaps, be deemed excessive, yet we cannot say that they were extortionate and unconscionable. There is no doubt that the evidence of Lord and Mays, against which there is no contradiction, establishes an express contract with Miller, whereby he agreed to pay each of them a thousand dollars for their services. At the time this agreement was entered into it was thought that Miller would ultimately be charged with murder in the first degree, but, as it turned out, his victim survived and three indictments were returned against him, one for an assault with intent to kill, and two for assault with a dangerous weapon. A trial was had upon two of these indictments; in one there was a mistrial, and a second trial was had. As to the third, Miller pleaded guilty. Mays and Lord appeared and assisted in the defense at each of those trials. Prior thereto they, in connection with the firm of McGinn, Sears and Simon, instituted a *habeas corpus* proceeding for the purpose of having the defendant admitted to bail, in which they were successful, and subsequently defended Miller at the trial of the civil action instituted against him to recover twenty thousand dollars' damages, in which the judgment for ten thousand dollars was secured which forms the basis of this suit. There being no evidence that these fees were purposely fixed at the amounts specified for the purpose of covering up Miller's property to render it inacces-

sible to his creditors, we cannot say that because of the large amount thereof the contract supporting them is void and ought to be disregarded.

4. This suit comprehends two funds, and the fairness of the transaction by which Lord acquired them; one consisting of real property, the status of which we have determined, and the other of personal property. out of which Lord realized five hundred and eighty-five dollars and sixty cents. The greater portion of this latter fund he had in his hands at the date of the commencement of this suit, so that he could not deal with it so as to change its legal status to the detriment of plaintiff's rights during the pendency thereof. There is no doubt, under Lord's own showing, that he acquired and held this personal property in secret trust for Miller. The declaration of trust establishes the fact. This fund should not be blended or confused with the real property, as it is separate and distinct therefrom. Lord had expended some of it at the request of Miller, which may be regarded as legitimate, prior to the commencement of this suit. The exact amount we are unable to definitely determine, but it is within bounds to conclude that he had in his hands at that time at least five hundred dollars, for which amount plaintiff should have a decree against him, as well as for his costs in the court below.

5. At the time of the institution of this suit the state had a judgment against Miller for costs in the criminal proceedings for five hundred and nineteen dollars, which it is admitted by all concerned was a first lien upon the real property. In part satisfaction of this lien, Lord paid in June, eighteen hundred and ninety-three, through Mays, two hundred and forty-

seven dollars out of the fund arising from the personal property. An execution having been issued at the instance of the state, Mays, for the purpose of protecting his own lien, paid the balance of this judgment, amounting to two hundred and seventy-two dollars. As to these respective amounts plaintiff and Mays ought to be subrogated to the rights of the state. Aside from this Mays paid twenty-two dollars and forty-five cents taxes upon the premises, which ought to be repaid. With the Fowler mortgage we have nothing to do, as he was not served and made no appearance. Not having a day in court his rights cannot be determined in this suit. In view of these considerations, the decree will be that the sale and assignment of personal property by Miller to Lord be set aside, and that plaintiff have a personal judgment against Lord for five hundred dollars, and his costs in the court below; that the real property be sold, and the proceeds arising therefrom be applied, *first,* to the payment of two hundred and forty-seven dollars to plaintiff; *second,* to the payment of two hundred and seventy-two dollars to Mays, and the further sum of twenty-two dollars and forty-five cents taxes; *third,* to the payment of Simon's mortgage; *fourth,* to the payment of one thousand dollars to Mays; *fifth,* to the payment of two hundred and fifty-three dollars to plaintiff, and his said costs below; *sixth,* to the payment of one thousand dollars to Lord, and the balance, if any remain, to the satisfaction of plaintiff's judgment. Lord ought to have credit upon plaintiff's decree against him until satisfied for such sums as plaintiff may receive from the proceeds of the real property. Appellant Mays will have a decree here for his costs and disbursements upon the appeal.

MODIFIED.

Decided June 10, 1896.

ON MOTION TO RECALL MANDATE.

PER CURIAM. This is a motion by respondent McGinn, Sears and Simon for an order recalling the mandate heretofore issued in this cause. The relief sought thereby seems to be to have the decree so modified as to relieve N. D. Simon and Henry E. Mc-Ginn from the requirement to cancel their mortgages, and to have the mandate withheld until the defendant Fowler can be barred of whatever interest he may have in the premises by a foreclosure of Simon's mortgage. The effect of the decree is to declare the deed to the real property in the hands of Mays an equitable mortgage to secure his reimbursement for certain moneys advanced in discharge of prior liens, and to secure him in the payment of certain fees to which he is entitled for services in the defense of Miller, subject, however, to the prior mortgage from Lord to Simon for one thousand dollars and interest. It also determines the priority of all liens of the parties to the suit except Fowler's. Fowler not having been served and not having appeared in the suit, no decree could be entered affecting his interest whatever it may be. The real property was ordered sold, and the proceeds applied in payment of the liens in the order of their ascertained priority, and that the parties to the appeal be barred and foreclosed of all right or interest therein. Although the suit was instituted for the purpose of having certain conveyances and mortgages set aside, which it is claimed were fraudulent and void as to plaintiff, and subjecting the premises to the payment of his judgment, the result was in effect a foreclosure of all liens of the parties served affecting such premises. And it would seem that a purchaser at the sale would be subrogated to the interests of prior lien claimants with like effect as if the suit had been the usual foreclosure proceeding: 24 Am. and Eng. Ency. of Law, 261; *Sellwood* v. *Gray*, 11 Or. 534; *Watson* v. *Dundee Mortgage Company*, 12 Or. 474; *Brobst* v. *Brock*, 77 U. S. (10 Wall.), 519. For reasons stated herein, as well as in our opinion in the main case, we cannot now give relief against Fowler in this proceeding. Following the language of the entry below to which no objection had been offered, it was, among other things, ordered and decreed here, "that the respondents H. E. McGinn and N. D. Simon do within twenty days from the entry of this decree in the court below release or cancel their said respective mortgages on said real property on the records of said county." It is now desired that this language be stricken from the decree. While we think such order unnecessary yet it would seem to be mere harmless surplusage and we cannot see how it can have any greater effect than the order which follows that each and all the parties be barred and foreclosed of all rights or interests in the real property and every portion thereof." Aside from this it is a doubtful proposition whether this court can recall a mandate and alter or amend a decree after the expiration of the term in which it is rendered and entered. MOTION DENIED.

Decided January 27, 1896.

WILLIS v. LANCE.

[43 Pac. 487; 384.]

1. CROSS-EXAMINATION.—Defendant in an action for injury from fire alleged to have been kindled by him cannot be cross-examined as to a custom to back-fire for the purpose of proving his negligence, where, on his direct examination, he has neither admitted that he set the fire nor testified to any custom.

2. INSTRUCTIONS TO JURY—VALUE OF EXPERT EVIDENCE.—Where witnesses who were present at a fire testified that the wind was from a certain direction, and an officer from the weather bureau, which was several miles distant, testifies that the automatic register, which was located in an elevated position, free from obstruction, showed the wind to have blown from another direction, it was not error for the court to state to the jury "that when a man comes before you, and says that the direction of the wind at a certain time was from such a quarter, so many miles away, and was blowing at the rate of so many miles per hour, irrespective of hills or forests, you will take into consideration your own experience, and the experience of other witnesses who have testified, whether that instrument is to be believed, under such circumstances and at such a distance, or whether your own experience and the testimony of the witnesses are worth anything. Consult your own experience, as well as the report made by the officer." This is only instructing the jury to apply to conflicting testimony the test of their own judgment and experience, which they certainly ought to do.

3. DISCRETION OF COURT—FILING COST BILL—CODE, § 557.—It is within the discretion of the court to extend the time for filing an amended verified statement of costs where the application to extend is made within the five days allowed to file the statement.

4. STATEMENT OF ITEMS IN COST BILL—CODE, § 557.—A verified statement under Hill's Code, § 557, showing the materiality and necessity of each item of costs objected to need not show the materiality of the testimony of witnesses whose fees are taxed, where it states that they necessarily attended court and were sworn and examined as witnesses at the trial, for their testimony must have been material or it would not have been received.

5. COSTS—FINDINGS BY COURT—CODE, § 557.—A party having objected to certain items of a cost bill, the court, upon motion to retax costs, should make separate findings as to each item objected to: *Thomas v. Thomas*, 24 Or. 251, approved and followed.

APPEAL from Multnomah: E. D. SHATTUCK, Judge.

This is an action by Willis Brothers against O. H. Lance to recover damages resulting from the alleged wilful and negligent conduct of the defendant. The facts are that on September fifth, eighteen hundred and ninety-two, the plaintiffs were the owners of a quantity of cord wood cut from and remaining on a tract of land that was bounded on the east by the defendant's land and that of one Mrs. Chase, the latter tract joining the defendant's premises on the north. On said date a fire swept across Mrs. Chase's land to the plaintiff's and burned a portion of their wood, and threatened the destruction of it all, necessitating the employment of men and teams* in removing it from the region of the fire. The plaintiffs allege, in substance, that the defendant wilfully and negligently kindled the fire on his premises and Mrs. Chase's land, from which it spread to their tract and destroyed four hundred and eight cords of wood, of the value of eight hundred and sixteen dollars; that by reason of the defendant's negligence they were compelled to and did pay out one hundred and ninety-eight dollars in the employment of men and teams to remove and protect their said cord wood, and pray judgment for one thousand and fourteen dollars. The answer having put in issue the allegations of the complaint, a trial was had, resulting in a judgment in favor of the defendant, from which the plaintiffs appeal, assigning as errors the rejection of testimony, and the giving of certain instructions to the jury.   AFFIRMED.

For appellants there was a brief and an oral argument by *Mr. Frederick L. Keenan.*

For respondent there were briefs and oral arguments by *Messrs. John F. Caples* and *Greenbury W. Allen.*

Opinion by MR. JUSTICE MOORE.

1. The defendant, having been called as a witness
in his own behalf, testified, in substance, that between
twelve and one o'clock in the afternoon of the day in
question he discovered a fire that had been burning
in the timber approaching his premises near the
northeast corner, the same being the southeast corner
of Mrs. Chase's land; that the wind was then blowing
quite a gale from the northeast, and the fire was
driven thereby upon Mrs. Chase's land near the southeast corner; that he raked away the briers and twigs
at his north line to keep the fence from burning.
Upon cross-examination an objection was interposed
to the following question: "Is it not customary, if one
wants to save his property, to back-fire?" and, the
objection being sustained, the plaintiff saved an exception. It is contended that the question was competent
as tending to prove the defendant's negligence and
want of due care, and that the refusal to permit the
witness to answer it was a restriction of the right of
cross-examination. No direct evidence that the defendant kindled the fire was introduced at the trial,
and his testimony showed that he raked away the
briers and twigs from the fence only to protect it
from destruction. How, then, could the question become material, except upon the assumption that the
defendant owed a duty to the plaintiffs of protecting
their property. If he neglected to "back-fire" along
the line of his fence, in consequence of which it was
destroyed, the loss would fall upon him, and not upon
the plaintiffs. Had he testified that he kindled a fire
to protect his property, there might have been just
reason for allowing him to prove the existence of
such an urgent necessity as would have warranted

and excused his act, but the right to kindle the fire
under such circumstances would not be founded in
any custom, but upon necessity. If the defendant, ap-
prehending the destruction of his property, had "back-
fired," and, through his carelessness, the fire so kindled
by him had escaped and destroyed the plaintiffs' property, proof that the fire was set in conformity with a
custom or usage long established would not excuse his
negligence: 16 Am. and Eng. Ency. of Law, 462. Evidence of a custom or usage is admissible to explain,
but not to contradict, the terms of a contract silent
as to details or ambiguous as to incidents and conditions: *Holmes* v. *Whitaker*, 23 Or. 319 (31 Pac. 705); *Governor* v. *Withers*, 5 Va. 24 (50 Am. Dec. 95). The plaintiffs' action being founded in tort precludes the defendant from proving the existence of any custom or
usage to excuse his alleged negligence, and, this being
so, by what right could the plaintiffs insist upon proving a custom for the purpose of establishing the defendant's liability? As we view the question, assuming
that the question could have been proven in this manner and by one witness, the object sought by asking
it was to show that when one's fence is endangered
by fire it is customary to avert the threatened injury
by "back-firing," and, as the danger to the defendant's
property was imminent, an inference might be invoked
that he kindled the fire which wrought the plaintiffs'
injury. If proof of such a custom were permissible,
the burden of establishing it was cast upon the plaintiffs; and the defendant, in his direct examination, not
having admitted that he kindled the fire, or testified
concerning any custom, what right of cross-examination was restricted by the court's refusal to permit
the witness to answer the question? It is true the
right of cross-examination is a valuable one, tending

to explain the testimony given in chief and to establish truth, but it should be confined to matters stated in the direct examination or properly connected therewith: Hill's Code, § 837. The question not being germane to the issue, nor proper cross-examination, the court committed no error in refusing to permit the witness to answer it.

2. At the trial the plaintiffs sought to show that the defendant kindled the fire complained of, while the defendant undertook to prove that it had been raging in the timber for some time, and on the day in question was driven by force of the wind across Mrs. Chace's land to the plaintiffs' tract, destroying their wood and causing the injury. The plaintiffs' premises being situate west of Mrs. Chase's, the direction and force of the wind became important factors in determining the origin of the plaintiffs' loss. The testimony of the defendant and seven witnesses called in his behalf tended to show the facts he undertook to prove, and that the wind was blowing from the northeast. W. S. Blandford, being called as a witness, testified, in substance, that he was an officer in charge of the United States Weather Bureau at Portland, and had in his possession the records of that office, giving the direction and velocity of the wind for September, eighteen hundred and ninety-two, and, referring thereto, said that on Monday the fifth of said month, the wind was blowing from the north until three o'clock in the morning, at which hour it changed to the east, and continued easterly until eight o'clock in the forenoon, when it changed, veering to the southeast and south until two o'clock in the afternoon, and from the hour last named the wind was blowing from the south until midnight. Referring to the velocity of

the wind on that day, the witness said that from midnight until nine o'clock in the morning it was blowing
from two to six miles per hour; that from the hour
last named until eight o'clock in the evening it was
blowing from nine to fourteen miles per hour, except
between twelve o'clock noon and one o'clock in the
afternoon it was blowing from the south fourteen miles
per hour, and between three and four o'clock in the
afternoon, seven miles per hour. The witness also
said that the record was made by an instrument attached to a wind vane then located on the roof of
the Kamm Building at First and Pine Streets, by
means of which the direction of the wind was printed
on a sheet of paper fastened to a revolving cylinder,
known as an automatic register, that was kept in motion by clockwork. The following question was then
asked the witness by plaintiffs' counsel: "The fact is,
that machine could be relied on against the world, or
a regiment of ordinary people?" to which he answered,
"We would rely upon this, sir, against the city." The
court then asked the following questions: "Suppose
there was a deep canyon running east and west,
and a fire should be built in it, and there was a
strong current of air in the direction of the smoke
and flame to the east, and your observation would say
there was a north wind, would the experience and
observation of those who actually saw it be of any
consequence in comparison with your instrument?"
Answer—"Our instrument would record the actual direction of the wind accurately." Question—"Where?
All over this state?" Answer—"No, sir; we would
say if it blew six miles an hour in this valley (Willamette), it would be the constant direction down the
valley and up." Question—"I am speaking of the
direction, not the velocity." Answer—"Yes, if it was

very light wind, the wind would be liable to change,
I should say, if it was less than six miles an hour."
Whereupon the court, after charging the jury upon
the issues of the case, gave the following instruction:
"There is one matter further that I will mention to
you, and that is part of the testimony offered here is
the record of the weather bureau. That record is not
made by the hand of man; it is made automatically.
It gives the direction and the velocity and the wind
sought to be ascertained by means of machinery, and,
connected with that machinery, these matters, the velocity and the direction of the wind, are recorded.
But that instrument, you will observe, according to
the testimony of the witness, was situated in an elevated position, clear from obstruction, and when a man
comes before you, and says that the direction of the
wind at a certain time was from such a quarter, so
many miles away, and was blowing at the rate of so
many miles per hour, irrespective of hills or mountains
or forests, you will take into consideration your own
experience, and the experience of other witnesses who
have testified here, whether that instrument is to be
believed under such circumstances and at such a distance, or whether your own experience and the testimony of the witnesses are worth anything. Consult
your own experience, as well as the report made by
the officer." An exception to this instruction having
been saved, it is contended that the language there
used was an adverse comment upon expert evidence;
that the court usurped the functions of the jury; that
undue prominence was given to a part of the testimony to the exclusion of other evidence, and that
the record of the weather bureau was not within the
experience of the jurors.

If it be assumed, as the plaintiffs contend, that the
court charged the jury to disregard the testimony of
the officer of the weather bureau, the instruction was
erroneous; or, if it required the jury to determine from
their experience the accuracy of the automatic register used to ascertain the direction and velocity of the
wind, it was equally erroneous; for it must be presumed that such instrument and the record made by
it were matters not within the general knowledge of
mankind, and hence the jury was incompetent to pass
upon the question.   The bill of exceptions does not
show the distance from the weather bureau office to
the scene of the fire, nor how many hills, mountains,
or forests intervened, or that the fire was confined to
a canyon; but, in the absence thereof, it must be presumed that evidence was introduced showing or tending to show the relative positions of the fire and the
office of the weather bureau, together with the geography of the intervening space.   The court did not
attempt to question the veracity of the record made
by the automatic register, so far as it applied to the
location in which the record was made.   There was no
conflict of evidence in relation to the velocity of the
wind between the hours of twelve and one o'clock on
September fifth, eighteen hundred and ninety-two, the
defendant saying it blew quite a gale, while the record
showed that it was blowing at the rate of fourteen
miles per hour.   There is a conflict, however, as to
the direction of the wind at that hour, the defendant
and his witness saying that at the fire it was blowing
from the northeast, while the record shows that at the
City of Portland, several miles distant, it was blowing from the south.   The testimony of the witnesses
who saw the fire and observed the direction of the
wind may have been true, and the contradictory show-

ing of the record made at a different place does not necessarily prove it to be untrue. The question as to the direction of the wind was for the jury to determine from all the evidence submitted. The jury must be presumed to have been composed of intelligent persons, and as such must have known that obstacles, such as hills, mountains, and canyons, would necessarily divert the course of the wind. They may have observed that a great fire would in a slight degree tend to affect its current, and while they, without the aid of a vane, may not have been able to indicate the exact point of the compass from which the wind blew, they could ascertain its general direction. It does not necessarily follow, because the wind was blowing at a certain place from a given direction, that it was blowing at all places from the same quarter. Stations of the weather bureau have been established and are maintained by the government at important points, to observe climatic conditions, and gather and compile useful information, which has become a great aid to agriculture, commerce, and navigation; but the record thus made is not regarded as verity except at the station where taken, and becomes useful to great areas of territory only when compared with observations taken at other stations. By means of the telegraph these comparisons are readily made, from which storm centers are located, and their general direction and the force that impels them noted, enabling the officers of the weather bureau to predict with quite a degree of certainty the "probabilities" of the weather, thereby rendering great benefit to mankind in the saving of lives and property. The court did not attempt to question this record, when applied to the location in which it was made, but submitted it to the jury to say whether, from their experience, it should

outweigh the testimony of numerous witnesses who
saw the fire and observed the direction of the wind.
The experience to which the court referred did not
allude to the operation of the automatic register or to
the record made by it, but to the experience of the
jurors as to wind currents, and particularly when affected by obstacles. This being so, the question is
presented whether jurors could be governed by their
experience in determining the weight of evidence.
Had the fire been in the City of Portland, instead of
several miles away, no one will pretend to say that
the record of the weather bureau was conclusive evidence of the direction of the wind, when contradicted
by the testimony of witnesses. The witnesses may
have been laboring under a mistake, or falsely testified concerning the direction of the wind, yet, if the
jury believed their statements to be true, such testimony would outweigh the report of an automatic register. The jury are the judges of the effect or value
of evidence, except when it is declared by law to be
conclusive, and they are not bound to find in conformity with the declaration of any number of witnesses
which do not produce conviction in their minds,
against a less number or against a presumption or
other evidence satisfying their minds: Hill's Code,
§ 845. If a juror could not consult his experience he
could never reach a conclusion in cases in which the
evidence was conflicting. His experience is or should
be the lamp of reason by which his judgment is controlled, and he may consult and be governed by it in
all cases in which the evidence is conflicting, and not
declared to be conclusive; and the court may properly
instruct the jury that on examining the evidence they
may bring to its consideration in determining the
weight to be given to it such general practical knowl-

edge as they may have upon the subject: *Douglass* v. *Trask,* 77 Me. 85.   We cannot think the instruction complained of violated any rule of law, and hence the judgment is affirmed.   `   AFFIRMED.

ON MOTION TO RETAX COSTS.

This is an appeal from the action of the trial court on a motion for the retaxation of costs in the foregoing case. The facts are that on December eighteenth, eighteen hundred and ninety-three, judgment having been rendered against the plaintiffs for costs and disbursements, defendant on the following day filed a cost bill, containing the names of his witnesses, the number of days each attended, the number of miles traveled, and the fees claimed by the officers of the court, amounting to three hundred and fifty-four dollars and seventy cents. On the twenty-eighth of said month the plaintiffs filed objections to each item contained in the cost bill, and, on January fourth, eighteen hundred and ninety-four, the court having extended the time to that date, the defendant filed an amended verified statement thereof. On being considered by the clerk, that officer allowed and taxed the costs and disbursements at three hundred and twenty-seven dollars and fifty-five cents. The plaintiffs appealed from such taxation to the court, which affirmed the action of the clerk, and retaxed the costs and disbursements at the same amount, from which judgment the plaintiffs appeal, and contend that the trial court erred in extending the time to file the amended verified statement; that such statement is insufficient to support the judgment based thereon; that because the clerk and stenographer did not file an itemized statement of their fees the court was powerless to award any judgment thereon; and that the court failed to make findings upon the separate items of the cost bill objected to by plaintiffs.

3. The statute provides that when objections are made to the claim for costs and disbursements, the party seeking to recover the same may, within five days after said objections are filed, file with the clerk an amended verified statement, showing the materiality and necessity of each item so objected to: Hill's Code, § 557. The objections to the cost bill having been filed on December twenty-eighth, the defendant, on the fifth day thereafter, obtained an order extending the time for filing the amended verified statement to January fourth, on which day such statement was filed. The plaintiffs insist that the court had no authority to extend the time without a showing made for that purpose, and in support thereof cite the case of *Hislop* v. *Moldenhauer,* 24 Or. 106, (32 Pac. 1026,) in which it was held that where no objections to the cost bill had been filed within the two days allowed therefor, it was error to permit such objections to be subsequently made without a showing that the failure to so object within the prescribed time was through the party's mistake, inadvertence, surprise, or excusable neglect. In the case cited, no objections to the cost bill having been made within the time prescribed by law, the judgment had become final, and, the party being in apparent default, the court was powerless to set aside the judgment except upon such a showing. In the case under consideration the defendant was not in default when the order was made extending the time, and, this being so, it was in the discretion of the trial court to enlarge the time: Hill's Code, § 102.

4. The first item of the amended verified statement is as follows: "That the witness J. W. Purcell was necessarily in attendance upon said court on the first trial of said cause as a witness only, and for no other purpose, for two days, and necessarily traveled to and from his home in reaching said court five miles each way, making, as set forth in said original bill, the sum of five dollars." Each item is substantially set forth in the preceding form, and the statement closes with the following: "That each of said witnesses was in attendance upon said court at my request, either by special promise to so attend, or by regular subpœna served upon them respectively, and the testimony of each one of said witnesses was material, and that each was sworn and testified in said action." The plaintiffs insist that this statement fails to show the materiality and necessity of each item thereof. In *Wilson* v. *Salem,* 3 Or. 482, the court, in defining the items of a cost bill, says: "The attendance of a witness is an item, the mileage of that witness is another, the necessity for his attendance a third, and to each the party charged may or may not object." When a witness has attended court by agreement with the prevailing party, or in obedience to the service of a subpœna at his request, but has not been examined or sworn, a just reason exists for requiring a showing of materiality of the testimony expected from the witness in order to recover his fees (*Pugh* v. *Good,* 19 Or. 85, 23 Pac. 827); but when a witness has been sworn and examined, the court must necessarily pass upon his competency and the materiality of his testimony, and, this being so, we fail to see the necessity of an averment even that his testimony was material to the issue. The same court that tried the cause must, upon appeal from the clerk's taxation, retax the costs and disburse.

ments, but it cannot be expected that the court will retry the materiality of the testimony of a witness. A judgment of nonsuit may be given without calling a witness for the defendant, but in such case the prevailing party ought to recover his witness fees upon showing the materiality of their testimony, for the necessity of his witnesses being present is apparent, since he could not know that his motion would be granted until the court passed upon it, or that the plaintiff might not, by leave of the court, cure by amendment the infirmity in his pleading disclosed by the motion. So, too, the prevailing party may, out of an abundance of caution, procure the attendance of witnesses whom he does not call, in which case the materiality and necessity of their testimony become important questions for the consideration of the court upon a motion to retax. When a party, upon objection to his cost bill, states that a given person necessarily attended the court a given number of days as a witness only; that he necessarily traveled a certain number of miles in going from and returning to a given place, and that he was sworn and examined as a witness at the trial, we think he has stated all the law requires, for the necessity having been alleged the materiality is implied from the fact that his testimony was received. Any other rule would require a statement of the substance of the testimony given by the witness, which is not necessary except in case he has not been called.

5. The record does not show that the stenographer or clerk itemized the statement of their fees. The findings of the clerk show that the official reporter performed two and one half days' services at the first trial, and three days at the second, for which he

was allowed fifty-five dollars. The original claim for clerk's fees was thirty-one dollars and five cents, which the clerk taxed at twenty-three dollars and five cents, without enumerating in such taxation the items that constituted the claim. The clerk having given the items of the reporter's fees and reduced his own, it may be inferred therefrom that such statements were filed by these officers. The statute provides that no officer's fees shall be recovered as disbursements unless such officer shall file in said cause an itemized statement of all fees claimed by him therein: Code, § 557. The manifest object of this provision is to bring into the record such facts as will enable the clerk to tax, or the courts, from their inspection, to retax, the fees of its officers. Every party has a right to know the items of disbursements proposed to be taxed against him, and, upon objecting to the cost bill, the fees of officers must be itemized if the prevailing party would seek to recover them. The clerk, in taxing the costs and disbursements, found the number of days' attendance, the number of miles traveled, and the amount due each witness, which, with the fees of the officers, amounted to three hundred and twenty-seven dollars and fifty-five cents. The court, upon the motion to retax, failed to make findings upon each lien objected to, but affirming the findings of the clerk gave judgment for the amount so found. The plaintiffs having objected to each item of the cost bill, the defendant tendered an issue thereon by filing an amended verified statement, thus making each item a separate cause of action, upon which the plaintiffs were entitled to a separate finding of fact and law by the court: Code, § 557; *Thomas* v. *Thomas,* 24 Or. 251 (33 Pac. 565). No findings having been made by the court upon the several items of the amended cost

bill, the judgment is reversed, and the cause remanded
with direction to the court below to make such findings and retax the costs.

AFFIRMED—COSTS RETAXED.

Argued December 3, 1895; decided January 27, 1896; rehearing denied.

BRIGHAM *v.* HIBBARD.

[43 Pac. 383.]

1. SALE—ACCEPTANCE.—Actual acceptance by the buyer is not essential
to a complete sale and transfer of title of goods under a valid contract, where they conform to the contract.

2. PRINCIPAL AND AGENT—IMPLIED AUTHORITY.—A traveling agent and
solicitor of orders has no implied authority to rescind or change a
contract made with him for the purchase of goods, after the receipt
of the goods by the other party.

APPEAL from Multnomah: E. D. SHATTUCK, Judge.

This is an action brought by John W. Brigham, a
manufacturer of boots and shoes in Boston, Massachusetts, to recover for goods sold and delivered to
George L. Hibbard. The defendant admits the delivery of the goods, but denies the sale, claiming that he
gave an order for certain goods, to be manufactured
and shipped from Boston to one Wetmore,—an agent
to solicit orders for plaintiff,—for which he was to
pay five hundred and three dollars, but that the goods
sent did not correspond with the order; that he examined them immediately after their receipt, and, finding that they did not conform to the order, notified
Wetmore, who was in Portland at the time, that he
would not accept the goods; and that by an agreement between him and Wetmore he retained the possession of them, to be sold on plaintiff's account.
Judgment of the court below was in favor of plaintiff,
and defendant appeals.   AFFIRMED.

For appellant there was a brief and an oral argument by *Mr. George G. Gammans.*

For respondent there was a brief and an oral argument by *Mr. Arthur C. Emmons.*

Opionion by MR. CHIEF JUSTICE BEAN.

1. There are numerous assignments of error in the record, but for convenience they may be grouped under two principal heads: *First,* error of the court in ruling, both in admitting testimony and instructing the jury, that if the goods delivered to the defendant were of the kind and quality ordered, plaintiff could recover without proof of an actual acceptance by the defendant; *second,* error in refusing to allow defendant to detail the entire conversation between him and Wetmore at the time, or soon after, the goods were examined. The first assignment of error is based on the contention that in an action for goods sold and delivered the plaintiff must not only prove a sale and delivery, but an actual acceptance by the vendee. We do not so understand the law. When it is sought to give validity to a contract, void under the statute of frauds, there must not only be a delivery but an actual receipt and acceptance of the goods by the buyer: *Caulkins* v. *Hellman,* 47 N. Y. 449 (7 Am. Rep. 461); *Remick* v. *Sanford,* 120 Mass. 309. But where the contract itself is valid, a delivery pursuant to its terms, at the place and in the manner agreed upon, if the goods conform to the contract, will sustain an action for goods sold and delivered, without any formal acceptance by the buyer: *Schneider* v. *Oregon Pacific Railroad Company,* 20 Or. 172 (25 Pac. 391); *Ozark Lumber Company* v. *Chicago Lumber Company,* 51 Mo. App. 555; *Nichols* v. *Morse,* 100 Mass.

523; *Kelsea* v. *Ramsey Manufacturing Company*, 55 N. J. Law, 320 (26 Atl. 907); *Diversy* v. *Kellogg*, 44 Ill. 114 (92 Am. Dec. 152); *Krulder* v. *Ellison*, 47 N. Y. 36 (7 Am. Rep. 402); *Pacific Iron Works* v. *Long Island Railroad Company*, 62 N. Y. 272; Benjamin on Sales (6th ed.), §§ 699, 765; Tiedeman on Sales, § 112. The buyer has a reasonable time after the delivery in which to examine the goods, and, if they are not of a kind and quality ordered, he may then refuse to accept them, and thereby rescind the contract; but this right does not prevent the title from passing nor a recovery by the seller in an action for goods sold and delivered, if in fact they do conform to the terms of the contract: Tiedeman on Sales, § 112.

2. The next assignment of error is not well taken because it does not appear that Wetmore had authority to cancel the contract between plaintiff and defendant, or substitute a new one, or to bind the plaintiff by any agreement in reference to the future disposition of the goods. He was a traveling agent and solicitor of orders for his principal, but such authority did not give him power to rescind or change the contract after the receipt of the goods by defendant: *Diversy* v. *Kellogg*, 44 Ill. 114 (92 Am. Dec. 154); *Stilwell* v. *Mutual Life Insurance Company*, 72 N. Y. 385. In this connection the defendant was permitted to give evidence tending to show that the goods did not conform to the samples and were not of the kind and quality ordered, and that immediately after their receipt he notified Wetmore of that fact, and refused to accept the goods, and the court held, and so instructed the jury, that if the goods were not of the kind and quality ordered, and immediately after the discovery of that fact the defendant tendered them back to

Wetmore, and gave him notice that they were subject to plaintiff's order, such facts would be a sufficient rescission of the contract, and prevent a recovery in this action, and this was as favorable to the defendant as he could reasonably expect under the showing as to Wetmore's authority to bind the plaintiff. The notice to Wetmore by defendant that he declined to accept the goods because they did not conform to the order was perhaps material as part of the *res gestæ*, and as an act on his part explaining and qualifying his conduct in allowing the goods to remain in his store, (*Caulkins* v. *Hellman*, 47 N. Y. 449, 7 Am. Rep. 461,) but it was not within the scope of Wetmore's agency to make a new contract for the plaintiff in reference to such goods. Finding no error in the record, the judgment of the court below must be affirmed.

AFFIRMED.

Argued October 22; decided November 11, 1895.

STATE v. CARR.
[42 Pac. 215.]

1. ACCOMPLICES — QUESTION FOR COURT.—Whether a witness is or is not an accomplice is a question for the court, where the facts in relation thereto are all admitted and no issue thereof is raised by the evidence; but if the evidence is conflicting as to whether a witness is an accomplice, that issue should be ibmitted to the jury under proper instructions.

2. WHO IS AN ACCOMPLICE — CODE, § 1371.— A mature person of ordinary intelligence, who knowingly offers as a bribe to a juror money provided by another for that purpose, becomes an accomplice within the meaning of section 1371, Hill's Code, forbidding a conviction upon the uncorroborated testimony of an accomplice.

APPEAL from Multnomah: T. A. STEPHENS, Judge.

John A. Carr was convicted of the crime of offering to bribe one Thomas Huntington, a juror in a criminal action against Joseph Kelly, (*State* v. *Kelly,* 28 Or. 225,) and from the judgment upon such convic- tion brings this appeal. The verdict was based upon the evidence of Mrs. Huntington, the wife of the juror, who testified, in substance, that on the morning after her husband had been accepted as a juror the defend- ant called at her house, and, after telling her where the jurors boarded, asked her to go there and inter- cede with her husband for Kelly, and told her he would give her fifty dollars if she would do so; that on the afternoon of the same day she called at the restaurant, as requested by the defendant, and had a conversation with her husband, but whether about the case in which he was a juror or some other matter does not appear. The next morning the defendant called, and, when told that her husband ''would have nothing to do with the matter," said "That will end it." A few days later, however, while the trial was still in progress, he accosted her on the street, and asked her, ''How about that affair of Kelly's?" to which she replied, "I don't know." About six o'clock of the same evening, as she was going to see her hus- band on some private business, she met the defendant, who gave her five twenty-dollar gold pieces, and told her to give them to her husband ''to help Kelly.'' She proceeded immediately on her errand, and, meeting her husband on the steps of the courthouse, had a conver- sation with him, during which she held the money in her hand where he could see it. As the result of this conversation she returned the money to the defendant the next morning, and told him ''Mr. Huntington would have nothing to do with it." Two or three days later she again met the defendant on the street, and he put ten dollars in her hand, nothing being said at the time either by the defendant or witness. This

money she retained, and gave to her husband after his
discharge from the jury, and requested him to return
it to the defendant, but he testified on the trial that he
gave it to his boy, who wanted to go fishing. The
court below ruled—whether properly or not we shall
not stop to inquire—that under section 712, Hill's
Code, the witness could not testify as to any conversation between herself and husband, and therefore it is
not very clear from the evidence that she ever complied with the request of the defendant by offering to
her husband the money in question to influence his
verdict, but we shall assume, for the purposes of this
opinion, that she did. This is, in substance, all the
evidence upon which the state relied for a conviction.
At the close of the testimony the defendant moved the
court to direct a verdict of not guilty, on the ground
that Mrs. Huntington was an accomplice, and therefore
no conviction could be had upon her uncorroborated
testimony. The motion was overruled, and the court
submitted the question as to whether she was an accomplice to the jury for their determination, and this
ruling is the principal error relied upon for a reversal
of the judgment.　　　　　　　　　　　　REVERSED.

For appellant there was a brief by *Messrs. Durham,
Platt and Platt, Williams and Williams,* and *Dolph, Nixon and
Dolph,* with oral arguments by *Messrs. George H. Durham,
Joseph N. Dolph,* and *Richard Williams.*

For the state there was an oral argument by *Mr.
Wilson T. Hume,* district attorney, and a brief by *Mr.
Hume* and *Mr. Cicero M. Idleman,* attorney-general, to this
effect.

Wharton on Criminal Evidence, § 440, says "An accomplice is a person who knowingly, voluntarily, and

with common intent with the principal offender unites
in the commission of the crime." This definition is
approved by this court in *State* v. *Roberts*, 15 Or. 197,
and we take it is the law of this state on the subject:
1 Bishop on Criminal Procedure, § 1159. Judged by
this rule Mrs. Huntington was not an accomplice with
Carr; even appellant's counsel makes her an accomplice solely by presumptions of knowledge and intent
on her part.

An innocent elderly lady unacquainted with courts
or law or legal rights, customs, or duties is approached
by a crafty, designing man with a proposition to submit to her husband and she does so and then reports
to this man that her husband would have nothing to
do with his villainous schemes. She is still pursued
by the man placing in her hand the money with a request to give it to her husband a few minutes before
she meets her husband and she again communicates to
her husband what has taken place, and this man who
is gray in sin, a crafty man of the world, engaged
knowingly in trying to save the neck of a murderer
by corrupting the jury, asks this court, as he asked
the trial court, to say that the lady is a person who
knowingly, voluntarily, and with a common intent
united with him in the commission of the crime. The
mere statement of the proposition, in connection with
the evidence in this case, the character of the lady,
her appearance and conduct on the witness stand,
ought to be sufficient answer to appellant's claim, and
satisfy this court of the correctness of the ruling of
the trial court. We do not dispute the proposition
that if Mrs. Huntington is an accomplice that the defendant is entitled to be discharged; we contend
simply that she was an innocent agent. The question
as to whether Mrs. Huntington was or was not an ac-

complice was submitted to the jury as a question of
fact to be decided by them, with proper instructions
of the court to acquit the defendant if they found her
to be an accomplice. We think the court committed
no error in submitting this question to the jury. The
rulings and instructions of the court were evidently
made upon the theory that it was the province of the
jury to determine from the evidence whether Mrs.
Huntington was an accomplice with Carr or was
simply an instrument in his hands, a mouthpiece
through which Carr reached the ear of Huntington,
and the determination of that question by this court
determines all the questions presented by the exceptions of the appellant to the rulings and instructions
of the court. The cases cited by appellant to sustain
his contention are cases where the witness was an admitted accomplice and the errors of the trial courts
consisted in not correctly instructing the jury on the
law affecting corroboration of accomplices' testimony.
In this case the state contended and the jury found
that Mrs. Huntington was not an accomplice and the
evidence in the case sustains the contention.

Opinion by MR. CHIEF JUSTICE BEAN.

1. At common law juries might convict upon the
testimony of an accomplice alone, if it carried conviction to their minds, although it was deemed so unre-
liable that the courts generally advised them not to
do so unless it was corroborated by other evidence.
But the credit to be given to the testimony of such
a witness, and the corroboration necessary to render
it satisfactory, were matters to be considered and determined by the jury, and, if they were fully convinced
thereby, the conviction was legal, though without other

support than the testimony of an accomplice. But in this state the rule has been so changed by statute that the uncorroborated testimony of an accomplice, however satisfactory to a jury, is insufficient to convict. Section 1371 of Hill's Code provides that "A conviction cannot be had upon the testimony of an accomplice, unless he be corroborated by such other evidence as tends to connect the defendant with the commission of the crime, and the corroboration is not sufficient if it merely show the commission of the crime or the circumstances of the commission." This statute absolutely prohibits a conviction in a criminal case upon the uncorroborated testimony of an accomplice, even although the jury may believe such testimony to be entirely true, and that it establishes the defendant's guilt beyond a reasonable doubt. It proceeds upon the theory that experience in the administration of the criminal law has shown the sources of such testimony to be generally so corrupt as to render it unworthy of belief, and that it is therefore better as a matter of public policy to forbid a conviction on the uncorroborated testimony of an accomplice, although the guilty may thereby sometimes escape punishment, than to leave it possible for the conviction of an innocent person on such testimony. Whether this rule of law is wise or unwise is not for us to inquire. It is so written, and must be applied by the court. As said by the late Mr. Justice STRAHAN, in his opinion in the case of *State* v. *Jarvis,* 18 Or. 364, (23 Pac. 251,) "the statute has made corroboration of an accomplice necessary, so that the court has no control over the subject except to apply the statute. The court has no discretion, but is bound to apply the statute, indiscriminately, to all cases wherever an accomplice appears as a witness, and the state's case depends solely upon his uncorroborated testimony. If we were now engaged in making the law, no doubt we would declare a different rule; but the principle is already established and fixed by the authorities, and we could only add to the uncertainty of the law by disregarding them,—a thing which we have no right to do. This point plainly marks the distinction between legislative and judicial power * * *. The legislature might have declared an accomplice incompetent as a witness; but he may be a witness, and the legislature has not said that he shall not be believed if uncorroborated, but that a conviction shall not be had upon his testimony unless there is other evidence tending to prove the defendant's complicity in the offense charged." Now, in the case at bar, it is conceded by the state that there was no testimony whatever given on the trial tending in any way to connect the defendant with the commission of the crime charged, except that of Mrs. Huntington, and her testimony is wholly uncorroborated. If, then, she was an accomplice, within the meaning of the statute, it is plain the evidence was insufficient to convict, however clearly it may have shown the defendant's guilt. The legislature, in its wisdom, has declared that no person shall be convicted of a crime in this state upon the uncorroborated testimony of an accomplice, and upon it and not the courts must rest the responsibility for the consequences. The contention for the defendant is that the trial court should have ruled, as a matter of law, that the witness was an accomplice, and directed an acquittal; while the state claims the question was properly submitted to the jury for their determination. We understand the rule to be that where there is any conflict in the testimony as to whether a witness is or is not an accomplice,

the issue must be submitted to the jury under proper
instructions of the court, but where the facts are all
admitted and no issue thereon is raised by the evidence, it then becomes a question of law for the court
as to the effect of the uncontradicted testimony: *State
v. Roberts,* 15 Or. 187 (13 Pac. 896); *State v. Light,* 17 Or.
358 (21 Pac. 132); *State v. Jarvis,* 18 Or. 360 (23 Pac.
251); *Armstrong v. State,* 33 Texas Crim. Rep. 417 (26
S. W. 829); *Williams v. State,* 33 Texas Crim. Rep. 128
(47 Am. St. Rep. 21, 25 S. W. 629). Here there was
no conflict in the evidence or issue raised thereby as
to the capacity or knowledge of Mrs. Huntington, or
the part she took in the commission of the crime.
Her connection therewith and what she did was admitted, so that the question presented was purely one
of law, and not of fact, and the court erred in submitting it to the jury.

2.   And it seems to us there can be no escape
from the conclusion that on this record Mrs. Huntington
was an accomplice of the defendant. Under all the authorities one who, being of mature years and in possession of his ordinary faculties, knowingly and voluntarily coöperates with or aids and assists another in
the commission of a crime is an accomplice, without
regard to the degree of his guilt: 1 Russell on Crimes,
49; Wharton on Criminal Evidence, § 440; Rice on
Criminal Evidence, § 319; Bishop on Criminal Procedure, § 1159; *Cross v. People,* 47 Ill. 152 (95 Am. Dec. 474).
The term is generally used in discussions involving
the admissibility or weight to be given to the testimony of one *particeps criminis* against his fellow. In
such case the grade of guilt is ordinarily unimportant, and therefore an accomplice is an appropriate
term because it implies nothing as to grade. It is so

used in the statute. It is claimed that the case was
properly submitted to the jury on the theory that
Mrs. Huntington may have been an innocent agent of
the defendant, and therefore not an accomplice, but
there was no issue of that kind made by the testimony. An innocent agent in this sense is one who
does an unlawful act at the solicitation or request of
another, but who, from defect of understanding or
ignorance of the inculpatory facts, incurs no legal
guilt: Bishop on Criminal Law, § 310. Mrs. Huntington was clearly not an agent of this kind. She was
a woman of mature years, in full possession of her
faculties, and, from aught that appears, of ordinary intelligence. She knew the money was handed to her
by the defendant to be given her husband "to help
Kelly," and what part she was expected to take in the
affair. With full knowledge of the purpose to be accomplished, and the use to be made of the money,
she freely and voluntarily undertook to and did aid
and assist in the matter by offering the money to her
husband to corruptly influence his verdict. It may be
true that she was induced by the promise of some
pecuniary reward to herself to participate in the
scheme without fully realizing the enormity of the
offense; but she must have known she was doing
wrong, or at least cannot plead ignorance of the
law as an excuse for her conduct. She knew, or
is conclusively chargeable with knowledge, that the
transaction in which she was engaged was a crime,
and that her coöperation was necessary to its commission. Without her active coöperation it could not
have been committed, because she was the only
means of communication between the defendant and
her husband. No offer to bribe him was made except through her, and, under these circumstances, if

she was not an accomplice the crime charged was not committed. The submission to the jury of the question as to whether Mrs. Huntington was an accomplice was equivalent to allowing them to decide in effect whether the statute should be enforced or suspended as in their judgment would best promote the ends of justice. and, in view of the section above quoted, was an evasion of a duty incumbent upon the court. The statute is binding both on courts and juries, and its provisions cannot be evaded, however wholesome the result might be in a particular case, by submitting to a jury the question as to whether a witness is an accomplice, when no such issue of fact is raised by the testimony. From these conclusions it follows that we have no alternative under the law but to reverse the judgment, and it is so ordered.　　　　　Reversed.

Argued December 4, 1895; decided January 27, 1896.

HUME *v.* KELLY.

[43 Pac. 380.]

1. Parties to Actions on Official Bonds—Code, § 341.—A county is a proper party plaintiff in an action under an official bond of a tax collector, to recover for default in paying over taxes levied and collected for state, county, and school purposes, under Hill's Code, § 341, providing that any person injured by the misconduct of the principal in such bond, may maintain an action thereon in his own name, although the bond runs to the state: *Crook County* v. *Bushnell*, 15 Or. 109, cited and approved.

2. Amending Pleadings by Changing Names of Parties—Code, § 101.—An amendment of the complaint in an action by a district attorney upon an official bond, by adding the county, which is the real party in interest, as plaintiff, is authorized by Hill's Code, § 101, providing that the court may at any time before trial allow a pleading to be amended by changing the name of a party, for such an amendment does not change the cause of action: *Foste* v. *Standard Insurance Company*, 26 Or. 449, cited and approved.

3. AMENDMENTS— OFFICIAL BONDS—CODE, § 342.—Under Hill's Code § 342, before an action can be commenced on an official undertaking by another than the state or corporation in the name of which the undertaking runs, leave must be obtained from the court where the action is triable: *Crook County* v. *Bushnell*, 15 Or. 169, cited and approved.

4. AMENDMENT OF PLEADINGS.—Permission to amend a complaint is properly denied where the amendment if allowed would leave the complaint subject to objections that it was intended to obviate.

APPEAL from Multnomah: E. D. SHATTUCK, Judge.

This action was instituted in the name of Wilson T. Hume, district attorney, to recover upon the official bond of the defendant Penumbra Kelly, given as sheriff and tax collector of Multnomah County, Oregon, with the defendants George B. Markle and E. B. McFarland as sureties. The bond was given to the State of Oregon, in the penal sum of four hundred thousand dollars, conditioned that "if the said Penumbra Kelly shall well and truly and faithfully perform and execute his duties as such tax collector, according to law, and according to the requirements of any law to be hereafter enacted, and pay over to the county treasurer of said county all moneys collected by him as such tax collector for the said year eighteen hundred and ninety-two," then the obligation to become void, otherwise to be and remain in full force and effect. The defendant McFarland moved the court to require the plaintiff to make the complaint more definite and certain, and the defendants Kelly and Markle severally demurred thereto, each assigning substantially the same grounds, namely, *first,* that plaintiff has not legal capacity to sue; *second,* that the complaint does not state facts sufficient to constitute a cause of action; and, *third,* that the plaintiff is not the real party in interest. The motion was overruled, and the demurrers

sustained. Subsequently, the plaintiff moved the court
for leave to amend the complaint by adding the State
of Oregon and County of Multnomah as parties plaintiff in said action, and the defendant Markle moved for
a judgment of dismissal. These motions came on to
heard at the same time, but by consent of the parties
the plaintiff's motion was amended by striking therefrom the State of Oregon as a proposed party, and
upon this state of the record the court disallowed the
former and sustained the latter motion, and thereupon
rendered judgment against plaintiff, dismissing the
complaint with costs, from which judgment plaintiff
appeals.   AFFIRMED.

For appellant there was an oral argument by *Mr.
John H. Hall*, and a brief by *Messrs. Hume* and *Hall*, and
Dolph, Mallory and Simon, to this effect.

The court erred in refusing permission to amend
the complaint by substituting the name of the real
party in interest. It is not denied that the bond set
out in the complaint, and the allegations showing liability of Kelly and the other defendants, state a good
cause of action. The pleading is drawn upon the
theory that the district attorney, as trustee of the
county, was the proper party plaintiff, and that the
county is the *cestui que trust*. It is apparent from the
pleading that Multnomah County is the real party in
interest, and this the demurrer of Markle alleges. The
allegations of the complaint show that the money collected by Kelly was tax money, and belonged to the
county, and that the failure to pay it over according
to his duty, under the law, was the county's loss, and
that Hume, though demanding judgment in the name
of his office, and in the capacity of plaintiff, is in re-

ality demanding the county's money for the county, and as its agent and trustee. There is no dispute that Kelly and the other defendants — his bondsmen — actually owe the money to the county. The question is, had the court authority, under these circumstances, to allow the amendment? This demurrer might be fatal at common law, where forms seemed sometimes a more potential factor in the administration of justice than substance. But our statute has changed this condition and has made substance and not form the chief consideration. Sections 41 and 101 of Hill's Code afford ample authority for allowing this amendment. This statute was enacted to relieve suitors from the effect of the harsh rules of the common law, by enabling courts "in furtherance of justice" to allow amendments to pleadings to that end; and such statutes have always been broadly and not narrowly construed. The following cases show the extent and variety of application of the rule for which we contend: *Harrington* v. *Slade,* 22 Barb. 162; *Stringer* v. *Davis,* 30 Cal. 318; *Henderson* v. *Morris,* 5 Or. 24; *Hexter* v. *Schneider,* 14 Or. 187; *Miller* v. *Gerry,* 30 Iowa, 301; *Adner* v. *Desmukes,* 22 Mo. 101; *Langdon* v. *Shelby,* 75 Mo. 482; *Harris* v. *Plant,* 31 Ala. 689; *Liggett* v. *Ladd,* 23 Or. 26.

It is not claimed that the real character of this proceeding would be changed in the slightest degree if Multnomah County were made plaintiff. Any defense which could be made against the bond with Hume as plaintiff, under the allegations of this complaint, could be made if Multnomah County were plaintiff. In the complaint, as it stands, Multnomah County, is in effect the plaintiff. Hume claims nothing for himself. All that he demands is for Multnomah County. He has used his own name and the name of his office to demand for Multnomah County that which the county,

according to technical rules, should have demanded
itself. Leave to correct this mistake, by making the
record show 'that the county demands its own money
in its own name is all that is sought. It would be
difficult to invent a case where the objection to this
motion could be based upon grounds more absolutely
technical, or where substantial justice could more directly demand that the motion should be allowed.
The cases above cited, based upon statutes substantially similar to our own, settle the question of power,
and since the motion in this case was denied by the
court below upon the ground that it lacked the power
to allow it, and not in the exercise of a discretion, we
think there was error which this court ought to and
will correct.

For respondents there were oral arguments by
Messrs. Zera Snow and *John W. Whalley,* and a brief by
Messrs. Snow and McCamant, and *Whalley, Strahan and Pipes,*
to this effect.

The bond in question running to the state, the
state alone could bring an action at law upon it,
and this action as we claim can only be brought by
the attorney-general under the conditions prescribed
in the act defining his duties: Session Laws of Oregon,
1891, p. 188. The bond itself is executed in attempted
compliance with section 2794, Hill's Code, and being
solely for the benefit of the County of Multnomah
should have run to the latter: Hill's Code, § 2392.

The court did not err in refusing plaintiff the
leave to amend asked for, or in rendering judgment
of dismissal. Amendments will not be allowed where
the effect is to change the cause of action, whether
this change results from a new or distinct cause of

action arising from the allegations in the proposed amendment, or whether it arises by the substitution of one plaintiff for another: *Van De Haar* v. *Van Domseler*, 56 Iowa, 671; *Humphrey* v. *Hughes*, 79 Ky. 487; *Kavanaugh* v. *O'Neil*, 53 Wis. 101; *Stevenson* v. *Mudgett*, 10 N. H. 338 (34 Am. Dec. 158); *Lumpkin* v. *Collier*, 69 Mo. 170; *Carr* v. *Collins*, 27 Ind. 306.

Amendments permitted under section 41 of the Code whereby new parties are added, are allowed only in order to fully determine the cause as between the parties originally brought in. If the plaintiff's right can be determined as between him and the original defendant without the addition of other parties, then amendments cannot be made making additional parties plaintiff or defendant: Pomeroy's Remedies, §§ 418–420; *McMahon* v. *Allen*, 12 How. Pr. 39–45; *Treer* v. *Bryan*, 12 Ind. 343; *Carr* v. *Collins*, 27 Ind. 306.

It is important in considering the question of amendment here to notice who is asking to amend. It is the district attorney alone who on July twenty-third, eighteen hundred and ninety-four, was directed to institute proceedings on the bond in question, by the County Court of Multnomah County. The action is commenced by Mr. Hume in pursuance of such order in his own name: Abstract, page 9. The allegation in the complaint is that the four hundred thousand dollars, the penalty of the bond, is due the State of Oregon. If due the state it cannot be due Multnomah County or Mr. Hume. If due the state, then neither the county nor Hume are parties, for the defendants owe them no duty, no money; in other words, the averment being that it is due to the state excludes any hypothesis that it can be due to others either jointly or severally. The amendment asked for was not to change the averment as to the party to

whom the money was due, but merely to bring in the
state and the county. Would the county or Hume
have had any interests in the controversy, when made
parties, the money being due the state? Is it an abuse
of legal discretion to refuse a proposed amendment,
which, if allowed, would render the complaint demur-
rable for defect or misjoinder of parties? Again, did
not the court properly exercise its discretion in refusing to grant an amendment at the request of a
party who, the court had held, could not sue: who
had no interests; and especially when in the very
motion to make new parties by amendment, it appeared that the party who had no interest and not
the party who had, was seeking the amendment?
Could the court properly exercise a discretion to compel the state of Oregon to come in as a plaintiff in a
case in which the state itself did not ask for it? To
make the state and Multnomah County sue whether or
not the authorities desired to do so? To ask, is, it
seems to us, to answer the questions, and to show that
the court not only did not err, but that it would have
erred had it done otherwise than as it did.

Opinion by MR. JUSTICE WOLVERTON.

1. The corporations and persons entitled to sue
and recover upon official undertakings of the nature
of the one set out herein are appropriately and sufficiently designated by statute. Section 340, Hill's Code,
provides that "The official undertaking or other security of a public officer to the state, or to any county,
city, or other municipal or public corporation of like
character therein, shall be deemed a security to the
state, or to such county, city, town, or other municipal
or public corporation as the case may be, and also,

to all persons severally for the official delinquencies, against which it is intended to provide." Section 341 provides that "When a public officer, by official misconduct or neglect, shall forfeit his official undertaking or other security, or render his sureties therein liable upon such undertaking or other security, any person injured by such misconduct or neglect, or who is by law entitled to the benefit of the security, may maintain an action at law thereon in his own name, against the officer and his sureties, to recover the amount to which he may by reason thereof be entitled." These sections were intended to give a right of action upon the undertaking directly to the real party in interest, whether it be the state, a municipal, or public corporation, or to a private individual. This construction is borne out by reading in connection therewith sections 343 and 344; and, indeed, such is the judicial interpretation thereof. See *Habersham* v. *Sears,* 11 Or. 436 (5 Pac. 208); *Howe* v. *Taylor,* 6 Or. 284; *Crook County* v. *Bushnell,* 15 Or. 169 (13 Pac. 886). Taxes levied for state and county purposes, when collected, belong to the county in which they are levied. The same may also be said of taxes levied for school purposes, until apportioned to the several school districts. The county becomes a debtor to the state to the extent of the state's levy apportioned to such county: *Commissioners of Multnomah County* v. *State,* 1 Or. 359; *State* v. *Baker County,* 24 Or. 141 (33 Pac. 530). The purpose of the action upon the undertaking being to recover for taxes levied for state, county, and school purposes, and collected by the defendant Kelly as tax collector of Multnomah County, that county would be a proper party plaintiff therein although the bond runs in the name of the State of Oregon. Of this there can be no doubt.

2. It is claimed that the court below committed error in disallowing plaintiff's motion for leave to amend the complaint by adding Multnomah County as a party plaintiff, and section 101, Hill's Code, is invoked in support of the contention. It provides that "The court may, at any time before trial, in furtherance of justice, and upon such terms as may be proper, allow any pleading or proceeding to be amended by adding the name of a party or other allegation material to the cause, and in like manner and for like reasons it may, at any time before the cause is submitted, allow such pleading or proceeding to be amended by striking out the name of any party, or by correcting a mistake in the name of a party," etc. It has been settled by this court that under the section quoted from it is within the discretion of the trial court, at any stage of the case before the cause is submitted, to authorize such amendments as may be necessary to make the cause as intended by the original pleading, but not to insert a new and distinct cause of action or defense: *Foste* v. *Standard Insurance Company,* 26 Or. 449 (38 Pac. 617). So that it is not permissible to allow an amendment which would substantially change the cause of action. We understand from the briefs of counsel, and are led to assume, that the court below disallowed the amendment, not in the exercise of its discretion, but solely upon the ground that it believed it had no power to grant the plaintiff leave to so amend. We will therefore consider the question here as one of power in the court, and not as an abuse of its discretion in the premises. If the proposed amendment would substantially change the cause of action, it may be conceded that the court was without power to allow it; and the converse of the proposition may also be conceded. It seems the plaintiff insti-

tuted the action in the exercise of his prerogative functions as the law officer of the state and of the several counties constituting his district, to recover in behalf of Multnomah County; not that he claimed an individual interest in the funds sought to be recovered, but for the reimbursement of the county for funds belonging to it collected by the defendant Kelly, and for which he failed to account. In reality it may be considered as an action brought by the law officer of the county to recover for its use and benefit. In this view of the matter it is not conceived that the cause of action would be in any way changed by allowing the amendment. A general test as to whether a new cause of action would be introduced by a proposed amendment is to inquire if a recovery had upon the original complaint would bar a recovery under the complaint if the amendment was allowed, or if the same evidence would support both, or the same measure of damages is applicable, or both are subject to the same plea: 1 Ency. of Pl. and Pr. 556; *Liggett* v. *Ladd*, 23 Or. 26 (31 Pac. 81); *Lumpkin* v. *Collier*, 69 Mo. 170.

Many cases are to be found establishing the doctrine that the party for whose use the action is brought may be substituted for the nominal plaintiff, where the legal right of action is shown to be in the former. So, where a party sues in his own right, he may, if the facts warrant, amend his complaint so as to make the suit stand in a representative capacity; and conversely, if he sues in a representative capacity, he may be allowed to amend by declaring in his individual capacity; and in neither instance is it considered a substantial change of the cause of action: *Price* v. *Wiley*, 19 Texas, 142; *Martel* v. *Somers*, 26 Texas, 551; *Wilson* v. *First Presbyterian Church*, 56 Ga. 554; *Harris* v.

Plant, 31 Ala. 639; *Montague* v. *King,* 37 Miss. 441; *Wood* v. *Circuit Judge,* 84 Mich. 521 (47 N. W. 1103); *Morford* v. *Dieffenbacher,* 54 Mich. 593 (20 N. W. 600); *Lewis* v. *Austin,* 144 Mass. 383 (11 N. E. 538); *Buckland* v. *Green,* 133 Mass. 421; *Wells* v. *Stomback,* 59 Iowa, 376 (13 N. W. 339). In the last case cited the original petition was entitled "Washington Township, by W. B. Wells, Township Clerk, Kenedy, Lore, and Kingston, Township Trustees," as plaintiff. A demurrer to this petition was sustained upon the ground that plaintiff had no legal capacity to sue. An amended petition was then filed, entitled "W. B. Wells, Clerk of Washington Township, as Plaintiff," and this, under a statute similar to ours, was allowed to stand. In deciding the case, SEEVERS, J., says: "We are asked 'whether the plaintiff, having commenced the suit in the name of Washington Township, could amend the petition making the clerk plaintiff.' In *Township of West Bend* v. *Munch,* 52 Iowa, 132, (2 N. W. 1047,) it was held a township did not have the legal capacity to sue. This being so, it is claimed there was no plaintiff named in the original petition, and, therefore, none could be substituted; that an amended petition could not be filed because there was nothing to amend. But we think, when there is an appearance to the action, and the defendant tests the right of the named plaintiff to maintain the action by a demurrer, and the latter is sustained, the name of the proper parties plaintiff may be substituted in the action by an amended petition, subject of course to an apportionment of the costs, and the right of the defendants to a continuance if taken by surprise. If this is not the rule, the action must abate, and another be brought. This, under the statute, should not be the rule unless substantial justice so demands. The statute in terms provides that the court, in

furtherance of justice, may permit a party to amend
any pleading 'by adding or striking out the name of a
party * * * or by inserting other allegations material to the case, or, when the amendment does not
change substantially the claim or defense, by conform-
ing the pleadings or proceedings to the facts proved':
Code, § 2689. The defendants could make their defense in this action as well as in a new one, and they
could not have been prejudicially affected by the
amendment." So it is here, the defendants could
make their defense, if the amendment was allowed,
as well as now, in so far as it is apparent their defense would not be changed. The complaint, with the
proposed amendment, discloses the same issuable facts
as the one on file, the same evidence would support
both, and the same measure of recovery is applicable.
We think that under these authorities the court had
the power to grant the amendment.

3. But it would appear, notwithstanding, that the
motion was rightly and appropriately disallowed. As
we are advised, one of the grounds for sustaining the
demurrer to the original complaint was that the action was brought by the plaintiff without having obtained leave of the court or judge thereof where the
action is triable as required by section 342, Hill's
Code. At least, the complaint does not show that
such leave had been obtained. The proposed amendment, if allowed, would leave the complaint subject to
the same objection, as the county could not sue upon
the undertaking without having obtained leave for
that purpose, which fact must be alleged: *Crook County*
v. *Bushnell,* 15 Or. 169 (13 Pac. 886).

4. Where the amendment, if allowed, would leave the complaint subject to objections that it was intended to obviate, it is proper to reject it. While courts are always liberal in allowing amendments in furtherance of justice, and that the real object of the dispute may be reached and finally determined, they will not do a vain thing. For these reasons the judgment of the court below will be affirmed.

AFFIRMED.

Argued November 6, 1895; decided January 13, 1896.

STATE *v.* SECURITY SAVINGS COMPANY.
[43 Pac. 160.]

1. FINAL ORDER—APPEAL—CODE, § 535.—An order overruling a demurrer to a bill of discovery, and requiring defendant to answer interrogatories set forth therein is "final" for the purposes of appeal.

2. REQUISITES OF A BILL OF DISCOVERY UNDER SECTION 3143, HILL'S CODE.—In order to sustain a proceeding under section 3143 of Hill's Code, authorizing a bill of discovery, with interrogatories attached, whenever the governor "is informed or has reason to believe" that any bank has any money or other property that has escheated to the state, the bill and interrogatories must be directed to some specific fund alleged to be in the custody of the bank, and must show that the state has a cause of action as to such fund, and, further, that the desired information will aid such action. Under the section cited a general inquisitorial proceeding cannot be maintained.

APPEAL from Multnomah: LOYAL B. STEARNS, Judge.

This is a proceeding brought by the district attorney of the fourth judicial district, by direction of the governor, to ascertain whether the defendant bank has in its possession on deposit or otherwise any funds or other property which has escheated to the state. The information, after averring the official title of the informant, and that it is filed by direction of the governor, alleges, in substance: That the defendant is

a private corporation organized and existing under
the laws of this state, and is now and has been for
four years last past engaged in a general banking
business in the City of Portland; that during such
time divers and sundry depositors in defendant's bank
have, since the date of making their deposit, died intestate, without heirs, leaving sundry and divers amounts
of money and personal property on deposit and in the
custody of defendant which has escheated to the state,
the exact amount thereof, the names of the depositors
and date of deposit being to the informant unknown;
that in order to recover such escheated property for
the use and benefit of the state it is necessary for
the informant to bring and maintain an action at law
against the defendant, and in order to enable him to
do so "it is necessary and proper for plaintiff to learn
from defendant the name of the depositor, the amount
and nature of the deposit, the date of deposit of such
funds and other property as now are in the possession
of the defendant, which have escheated to the state";
that he intends and proposes, as directed by the governor, to commence an action at law pursuant to the
provisions of chapter XXV of the Miscellaneous Laws
of Oregon for the recovery of such escheated funds
and other property "as may be found in the custody
of said defendant bank," but that he is unable to do
so without full discovery from said bank, wherefore he
prays an order of the court directing and requiring
the defendant, its officers and agents, to appear at a
time certain, and answer under oath the information
and the several interrogatories contained therein. The
first, second, third, fourth, sixth, and seventh of such
interrogatories require the defendant to state the
names of all persons depositing or leaving money or
other property with it whose deposits,—whether evi-

.ence by an open account, certificate of deposit, sus-
pense account, or otherwise,—have been dormant or
uncalled for, or upon which no payments have been
made, or against which checks have not been drawn,
for a period of seven years, together with a description
of the property or amount of money standing to the
credit of each of such depositors. The fifth interrogatory requires the defendant to give the names of any
and all depositors whom it knew or believed to have
died prior to August first, eighteen hundred and
ninety-four, (the date of the commencement of this
proceeding,) and against whose accounts no checks had
been drawn on deposits made by any executor, administrator, or other representative, and the amount standing to the credit of each of such depositors. The
eighth requires the defendant to give a list of any
money or property held by it or in its possession at
the time this proceeding was commenced which it
thinks should escheat to the state. And the ninth requires the bank to give the name, date, and amount of
deposit of any and all persons whom the defendant
knew or believed had died intestate without heirs in
this state, and the date of such death as near as it
might know or be informed. The defendant demurred
to the information on the ground that it did not state
facts sufficient to constitute a bill of discovery, or to
entitle the plaintiff to the relief demanded, which demurrer was overruled, and an order entered directing
and requiring the defendant to file on or before a certain date fixed in the decree an answer under oath to
the information and interrogatories, and especially to
answer each and every interrogatory contained in such
information. From this order, or decree, the defendant appeals.   REVERSED.

For appellant there were oral arguments by *Messrs. Joseph Simon* and *Stewart B. Linthicum*, with a brief by *Messrs. Dolph, Mallory and Simon*, and *Williams, Wood and Linthicum*, urging these points.

The principles and doctrines relating to discovery, which have been settled by courts of equity in the past, govern the bill of discovery in this case. In some states, bills of discovery have been abolished by statute; in most, by regulations permitting the parties to testify on their own behalf, and to be called as witnesses by their adversaries, with provisions for compelling the production and inspection of books, documents, etc. Proceedings in relation to much of the ground covered by the bill of discovery have been greatly simplified, and the necessity for a resort to that remedy lessened. It has been decided that where all the grounds upon which a bill of discovery is based have been abolished by statute, the jurisdiction has thereby necessarily terminated; but it has generally been held that these statutory changes have not affected the jurisdiction over discovery, and that the same exists where it has not been expressly abolished: 1 Pomeroy's Equity Jurisprudence, § 193; *Shotwell* v. *Smith*, 20 N. J. Eq. 79. And also that in such cases all the principles of the law of discovery, not modified or abrogated by statute, remain in full force and regulate the action under statutory proceedings: 2 Am. and Eng. Ency. of Law, 210; *Anderson* v. *Bank of British Columbia* (Law Rep.), 2 Ch. Div. 644–658; *Cashin* v. *Cradock* (Law Rep.), 2 Ch. Div. 140–145; *Ingilby* v. *Shafto*, 33 Beavan, 38. It follows conclusively to our minds, and we think the legislature so intended, that the decisions of the courts which have entertained jurisdiction over discovery, and the established principles

apperta'ning thereto, shall apply to and govern the
inquiry under section 3143.

The bill fails to state a case; and does not entitle
the plaintiff to the discovery sought, or any discovery or relief whatever. It must state a *prima facie*
case. No facts are set forth in the bill as justifying
the governor's belief, nor is there any specific statement of any facts either as to whose property it
is claimed has escheated, or that can be otherwise
considered as constituting a foundation for the bill.
Plaintiff has contented itself with the general statement that certain persons have died intestate without
heirs, having money or other personal property in defendants's custody, and propounds certain questions,
the answers to which it is hoped will afford some
foundation for the general allegation and elicit information that may be available in future operations. In
an action at law, or in an ordinary suit in equity, a
demurrer would lie to a complaint embodying the general and meagre statements of the bill in suit, because
no cause of action or suit would be presented thereby.
There would be nothing upon which the court could
predict a judgment or decree. It would seem that the
same observation would apply upon a kindred state of
facts to a bill seeking a discovery, unless such suits
are excepted from the operation of the general rule.
No such exception exists in fact, and there is no good
reason why it should. These fundamental principles
have remained unchanged, and are as binding today as
they have ever been. The rule has been and is, that
the bill must at least present a *prima facie* case. A
prima facie case in this connection imports such a statement of facts as intrinsically shows the existence of a
case, and that the discovery sought is both germane
and proper: 2 Daniel's Chancery Pleading and Prac-

tice, 1556, 1557 (4th ed.); 2 Story's Equity Jurisprudence, § 1493*a* (12th ed.); 1 Pomeroy's Equity Jurisprudence, § 198; *London* v. *Levy,* 8 Vesey, Jr., 404.

The bill in suit states no case whatever. It is clear
from the allegations and interrogations that the hope,
not the certainty, that something would result, was the
animating motive in the institution of the suit. No
action at law may be instituted hereafter, but these
whole proceedings may be fruitless in every way except in subjecting defendant to annoyance and expense. The courts early declared their hostility to
such practices: *Finch* v. *Finch,* 2 Vesey, Sr., 494; 2 Daniel's Chancery Pleading and Practice, 1556 (4th ed.);
2 Story's Equity Jurisprudence, § 1497 (12th ed.); *Leg-
gett* v. *Postley,* 2 Paige Ch. 602. An examination of the
interrogatories will elicit nothing that can be used to
support the allegations of the bill, but will forcibly
emphasize the application of Judge Story's remarks
to this case. Most of the interrogatores are addressed
to finding out the names of all persons who have left
various forms of property with the defendant for
which no demand has been made, and regarding which
no dealings have been had, for seven years, and the
amount and character of such property. The bill
should, perhaps, have stated the grounds of the governor's belief: *Dunlevy* v. *Schwartz,* 17 Ohio St. 640; *Gar-
ner* v. *White,* 23 Ohio St. 192. It should also have set
forth the names of the persons whose property it is
claimed has escheated, and, generally, such facts and
circumstances as would show in a *prima facie* manner
the existence of a right, and the propriety and rele-
vancy of the interrogatories. It is no answer to say
that the bank is named as a defendant; for the bank
is concerned only in so far as it may safely pay over
the money, and it would seem to have no connection

with any subsequent action at law, as under the statute it is required to pay or deposit the money or property into court. We hazard the opinion that no case can be found in the books where the meagre statements of this bill or their equivalent were held to state a case, nor where the general questions asked were held to be material or proper. If such a case exists we have been unable to find it.

For the state there were oral arguments by *Messrs. Cicero M. Idleman*, attorney-general, and *John H. Hall*, deputy district attorney, with a brief by *Messrs. Hall, Wilson T. Hume*, district attorney, and *George E. Chamberlain*, as follows:

The object of the law is inquisitorial for the purpose of discovering funds which should escheat to the state, and is ancillary to section 3137, of the same act, which provides the manner of procedure after discovery is made. The act is mandatory to the governor, commanding him to act upon the information received, or if he from any cause has reason to believe of the existence of escheated funds in a bank; nor is he required to disclose to the district attorney the source of his information nor the reason for his belief, nor is it necessary for the district attorney to set out any other reason for the bringing of the suit, than the directions of the governor. In the case of *People* v. *Hibernia Saving and Loan Society*, reported in 72 Cal. 21, a case similar to the one at bar, the court say: "But we are clear that the person cited cannot avoid examination by merely pleading that he, or it, has no property subject to escheat. The very purpose of the proceeding is the discovery of those things, knowledge of which would render the proceed-

ing unnecessary. It cannot, therefore, have been intended that the state, or attorney-general for the state,
should be compelled to allege and prove the fact, for
the ascertainment of which the proceeding is commenced." It cannot, therefore, he successfully contended in this case, as claimed by appellant, that the
state must designate the particular money or other
property sought, the name of the depositor and of all
persons in interest. Were the state possessed of the
knowledge of those facts, this proceeding would be
wholly unnecessary.

Opinion by MR. CHIEF JUSTICE BEAN.

1. On this appeal two questions have been presented for consideration: *First,* whether the order overruling defendant's demurrer and requiring it to answer
the information and interrogatories as prayed for in
the bill is an appealable order; and, *second,* whether
the information states facts sufficient to constitute a
bill of discovery. The right of appeal is purely statutory, and unless the order from which defendant's
appeal is taken is a final order, judgment, or decree
within the meaning of the statute, the appeal, of
course, cannot be entertained. The law, as we understand it, is that an order or decree is final for the
purposes of an appeal when it determines the rights
of the parties, and no further questions can arise before the court rendering it except such as are necessary to be determined in carrying it into effect:
Freeman on Judgments, § 36; Elliott on Appellate
Procedure, § 90; *St. Louis and Iron Mountain Railroad Com-
lany* v. *Southern Express Company,* 108 U. S. 24 (2 Sup.
Ct. 6). Within this principle we think the present
order or decree is final. The suit was brought for

the sole and only purpose of obtaining from the defendant an answer under oath to the several interrogatories, and for no other relief. The information is a pure bill of discovery in aid of a contemplated action at law, asking no relief; and the only litigated question in the case is the right of the informant to the discovery sought. When, therefore, the demurrer was overruled, and the court held that the plaintiff was entitled to the relief demanded, and ordered and directed the defendant to answer the interrogatories, it effectually determined all the issues in the case, and ended the controversy between the parties so far as it could do so, leaving nothing to be done but to enforce its determination as made. No subsequent question could arise in the case except as to the form or sufficiency of the defendant's answers, and, therefore, in our opinion, it was a final order or decree within the meaning of the statute, and consequently appealable; otherwise the defendant would be without remedy by an appeal, though it should be admitted that the order complained of was in violation of its clear legal rights. If, as contended by the plaintiff, before it can appeal it must comply with the order of the court and answer fully the information and interrogatories, an appeal would be a vain and useless proceeding, for the sole object of the suit would have been accomplished, and defendant's appeal could avail it nothing.

2. In support of the demurrer it is contended that the information is insufficient as a bill of discovery, because it does not aver any facts showing a right of action in favor of the plaintiff and against the defendant in aid of which the discovery is sought, while the contention for plaintiff is that the section of the statute under which it was filed does not contemplate a

common-law bill of discovery, but an inquisitorial proceeding to compel a bank or banking institution to
disclose by answers to interrogatories propounded to
it whether it holds or is in possession of any property
which has escheated or may escheat to the state, in
order that the proper action may be brought in case
escheated property is thus discovered. In a word, the
effect of plaintiff's contention is that the statute is intended to enable the plaintiff to fish for a cause of
action, and not to prove an exisiting case out of its
opponent's mouth, or from documents in its possession, as is the object and purpose of the common-law
bill of discovery. The statute in question provides
that "when the governor is informed, or has reason to
believe, that any bank, banker, or banking institution
in this state now has or holds on deposit, or otherwise, any fund, funds, or other property of any kind
or nature which has escheated to this state, he shall
direct the district attorney in the district where such
bank or banking institution is located to file in the
circuit court an information or bill of discovery, with
proper interrogatories to be answered by the owner,
agent, or manager of such bank or banking institution,
and, upon the filing of such information or bill, the
court shall order and direct, at a time to be desig.
nated in said bill, that said owner, agent, or manager
of such bank or banking institution shall, under oath,
file an answer to said information and interrogatories,
and shall specially answer each and every interroga.
tory contained in such information or bill. If it appears to the court from such answer that said bank,
banker, or banking institution has any property in its
possession which has escheated or may escheat to this
state, it shall direct the said bank, banker, or banking
institution forthwith to bring the same into such court,

and the court shall proceed to dispose of said property as provided elsewhere in this act": Hill's Code, § 3143. Under this statute, whenever the governor is informed or has reason to believe that a bank is in possession of any fund, funds, or other property which has escheated to the state, he is required to direct the proper district attorney to file an information or bill of discovery, with proper interrogatories to be answered by the bank; but, there being no statutory provision as to what the bill shall contain, it seems to us the principles and doctrines governing such proceedings which have long been settled by courts of equity must apply to and determine the sufficiency of the proceedings under the statute.

A bill of discovery has a well known and universally recognized meaning in the law, and, in the absence of anything in the statute to the contrary, it is but fair to presume that the legislature intended to use the term in its generally accepted legal sense. In that sense it is a mere instrument of procedure in aid of relief sought by the party in some other judicial controversy, filed for the sole purpose of proving the plaintiff's case from the defendant's own mouth, or from documents in his possession, and asking no relief in the suit except it may be a temporary stay of the proceedings in another suit to which the discovery relates: Pomeroy's Equity Jurisprudence, § 191. As so construed, the design of the statute is to authorize the governor to direct the district attorney to file an information or bill of discovery whenever he is in possession of facts the averment of which would support such a proceeding, and not otherwise. This is strengthened by the fact that before the governor can direct the proceedings to be commenced he must be informed or have reason to believe that the bank has in its possession some fund or other property which has escheated to the state, and this seems to negative the idea that he may cause a proceeding to be instituted for the purpose of searching for such information, or for some facts upon which to base his belief. The statute does not authorize the information or bill of discovery to be filed at the pleasure of the governor, but only when he is informed that the bank is in possession of escheated property, or when he has knowledge of such facts and circumstances as give him reason to so believe. If he is so informed, he may direct the district attorney to file the proper information without a bill of discovery; but if, from the facts and circumstances within his knowledge, he deems it advisable, he may direct that a bill of discovery, setting out such facts and circumstances, be filed in aid of an action at law about to be brought, and thus require the bank to answer interrogatories concerning the condition, amount, etc., of the particular fund or property which he has reason to believe is in its possession, and has escheated to the state. But, as we read the statute, he has no authority to institute purely inquisitorial proceedings in an endeavor to unearth some possible cause of action, and thus require the bank not only to disclose but to make a public record of the confidential and private relations existing between it and its depositors, without a showing of any kind that the whole proceeding will not be fruitless in every way. Before such a proceeding can be maintained, it should clearly appear that the legislature so intended. We think, therefore, the sufficiency of the bill in this case must be determined by the ordinary rules defining the nature and scope of bills of discovery. Such bills had their origin in the fact that under the inflexible rules of the common law

the parties to an action were incompetent as witnesses,
and no means were provided by which an adverse
party could be compelled to produce documents in his
possession for the use of his opponent on the trial.
For this reason resort was early had, in courts of
equity, to bills of discovery in aid of an action at law
either then pending or about to be commenced, by
which either party could obtain the testimony of his
adversary, or compel the production of documents in
his possession material to his case. And while our
statute has made the parties competent witnesses, and
furnishes a simple, expeditious, and summary means by
which one party may obtain the evidence of another,
or compel the production of documents in his possession, the proceeding by bill of discovery perhaps still
remains, although the necessity for resort to such a
remedy is much lessened. But, if so, the fundamental
principles governing such a bill have remained unchanged, and are as binding today as they have ever
been. Its object is to enable the plaintiff to obtain from
his opponent evidence material to his case, either by
requiring him to answer under oath interrogatories
the answers to which may be used on the trial of the
action at law, or to produce documents in his possession material to plaintiff's case. But it is never suf-
fered to be used to enable him to fish out a case to
bring, or a defense to offer, and the interrogatories
contained in such a bill must be directed to the inquiry as to whether a specific fact is true, and not as
to what are the facts of some supposed case: 62 Law
Times, 146. Consequently it has long been established
that among the essential and indispensible requisites
of such a bill are that it must disclose on its face a
cause of action in favor of the plaintiff in aid of

which it is brought, and that the information sought is material thereto.

In the language of Mr. Daniel, it must state "the matter touching which discovery is sought, the interest of the plaintiff and defendant in the subject, and the facts and circumstances upon which the right of the plaintiff to require the discovery from the defendant is founded": 2 Daniel's Chancery Pleading and Practice (6th Am. ed.), *1557. And Mr. Story says that "If the bill does not show such a case as renders the discovery material to support or defend a suit, it is plainly not a case for the interposition of the court. Therefore, where a plaintiff filed a bill for a discovery merely to support an action, which he alleged by his bill he intended to commence in a court of common law, although by this allegation he brought his case within the jurisdiction of a court of equity to compel a discovery, yet, the court being of the opinion that the case stated by the bill was not such as would support an action at law, a demurrer was allowed. For, unless the plaintiff had a title to recover in an action at law, supposing his case to be true, he had no title to the assistance of a court of equity to obtain from the confession of the defendant evidence of the truth of the case": Story's Equity Pleading, § 319. And by Mr. Pomeroy it is said, "The plaintiff in the discovery suit must show by his averments, at least in a *prima facie* manner, that if he is the plaintiff in the action at law he has a good cause of action, and if he is the defendant, he has a good defense thereto": Pomeroy's Equity Jurisprudence, § 198. And in *Mayor of London* v. *Levy,* 8 Vesey, Jr., 398, Lord Chancellor ELDON, in enforcing the rule that the bill must set forth with reasonable certainty the nature of the action which is brought, or, if not brought, the nature of the claim or right to support which the action is intended to be brought, remarks "That where the bill avers that an action is brought, or, where the necessary effect in law of the case stated by the bill appears to be that the plaintiff has a right to bring an action, he has a right to a discovery to aid that action so alleged to be brought, or which he appears to have a right and an intention to bring, cannot be disputed. But it has never yet been, nor can it be, laid down that you can file a bill, not venturing to state who are the persons against whom the action is to be brought, not stating such circumstances as may enable the court, which must be taken to know the law, and therefore the liabilities of the defendants, to judge, but stating circumstances; and averring, that you have a right to an action against the defendants or some of them." Indeed, to this effect are all the authorities: Story's Equity Jurisprudence, § 1493a; Adams' Equity, 133; 2 Beach's Equity Jurisprudence, § 856; *Bailey* v. *Dean,* 5 Barb. 297; *Newkirk* v. *Willett,* 2 Caine's Cases, 296.

Applying these rules to the case before us, the bill must fail. It does not purport to show that the plaintiff has a cause of action against the defendant, but discloses on its face, both by averment and by the interrogatories, that it is simply searching for one. The averments are that the proposed action cannot be commenced until the plaintiff learns from the defendant "the name of the depositor, the amount and nature of the deposit, and date of deposit of such funds or other property as are now in the possession of the defendant, which have escheated to the state," and that such action is to be "for the recovery of such sums or other property as may be found in the custody of said defendant bank." It is true the information alleges that divers and sundry depositors have since the date of making their deposits died intestate, without heirs, leaving sundry and divers amounts of money on deposit and in custody of the bank, which has escheated to the state. But this does not state a cause of action in favor of the plaintiff and against the defendant. As shown by the other parts of the information, it is but the merest guess, based on no facts whatever, unless it is that the defendant has been in the banking business for four years, and it is barely possible, although nothing appears to render it probable, that some person or persons may have died intestate, without heirs, leaving money or property in possession of the bank. But mere possibilities are not enough to sustain a proceeding of this kind. It must be based upon some tangible and substantial facts. Indeed, the information states no case whatever. It is clear from the allegations and interrogatories that the animating cause which prompted the suit was simply a hope that something would result from the investigation. No action at law could be maintained, so far as the bill discloses, upon the information sought to be obtained by it, unless upon further investigation it should be ascertained that some of the depositors whose names are sought by this suit have died intestate and without heirs. If defendant was required to answer the interrogatories, and should place the plaintiff in possession of all the information sought by the bill, it would still require further investigation and proof to show that the depositors or some of them died intestate and without heirs; so that the bill not only fails to show a cause of action in favor of plaintiff, but the discovery sought, even if obtained, would not furnish facts upon which to base one. It is true it might furnish data which would lead to the discov-

ery of evidence sufficient to support an action by the
state to recover escheated property. But from the
earliest times the courts have with one voice declared
their hostility to such proceedings. "I am not to
compel a discovery to create evidence for some future
case," says Lord ELDON in *Finch* v. *Finch,* 2 Vesey, Sr.,
490, decided in seventeen hundred and fifty-two, and
Judge Story declares that "No discovery will be
compelled except of facts material to the case stated
by the plaintiff, for otherwise he might file a bill and
insist upon a knowledge of facts wholly impertinent
to his case, and thus compel disclosures in which he
had no interest, to gratify his malice or his curiosity
or his spirit of oppression. In such a case his bill
would be most aptly denominated a mere fishing bill":
2 Story's Equity Jurisprudence, § 1497. So universal
is this rule that it is needless to cite further authorities in its support. The information or bill does not
name the person or persons whose property it is
claimed has escheated to the state, nor are the interrogatories directed to an inquiry as to any specific
fact or fund, or the condition of the account of any
particular person or persons, but it is a mere inquisitorial investigation of defendant's business affairs, with
the possibility that such investigation may disclose
the existence of some fund or property, which, upon
further inquiry, the informant may determine has escheated to the state, and for which an action at law
or some other proper proceeding may be instituted.
Whether some such investigation into the affairs of a
bank ought to be made is a question for the legislature, but until it so provides there is no rule of law
of which we are aware that will permit it to be done.
The decree of the court below is reversed, and the
bill dismissed.   DISMISSED.

Argued December 18, 1895; decided January 13, 1896.

STATE *v.* HANSCOM.

[43 Pac. 167.]

1. INDICTMENT—CODE, § 1777—FALSE PRETENSES.—An indictment under Hill's Code, § 1777, for obtaining a signature by false pretenses, alleging that defendant represented to the members of a given firm that he was an agent of a specified corporation, authorized to draw a draft on it for a specified amount, and exhibited to them a false telegram by means of which he procured the firm to indorse a draft for the specified amount, sufficiently shows that the indorsement was obtained for the accommodation of the corporation, and not of the defendant.

2. SECONDARY EVIDENCE—INDICTMENT.—Where an indictment set out the substance of a false telegram used in the commission of a crime which defendant retained, it was proper to admit secondary evidence of the contents of the telegram without giving defendant notice to produce it.

3. CRIMINAL EVIDENCE—FALSE PRETENSES.—Evidence that defendant, charged with obtaining a signature to a draft by false pretenses, received the money on such draft, is admissible to show an implied delivery to him of the draft.

4. FALSE PRETENSES—IMMATERIAL EVIDENCE.—On the trial of one charged with obtaining a signature to a draft by falsely representing that it was for the accommodation of a certain corporation, it is immaterial whether defendant had money due him from the corporation or not.

5. ERRONEOUS INSTRUCTION—FALSE PRETENSES.—An instruction that an agent is not supposed to exceed his authority, and cannot bind his principal if he exceeds his authority, is reversible error on a trial for obtaining a signature to a draft by falsely pretending that it was for the accommodation of the principal, as it gives the impression that defendant would be criminally responsible if he exceeded his authority, however innocently.

APPEAL from Multnomah: T. A. STEPHENS, Judge.

The defendant F. A. Hanscom was indicted, tried, and convicted of the crime of obtaining the signature of another to a writing, the false making whereof would be punishable as forgery, and sentenced to the penitentiary for the term of eighteen months. From

this judgment he appeals, assigning as errors the action of the trial court in overruling his demurrer to
the indictment, admitting incompetent and rejecting
material testimony, refusing to instruct the jury to acquit, and in giving certain instructions. The indictment charges, in substance, that the defendant, with
intent to defraud, represented to the members of the
firm of Woodard, Clarke and Company that he was an
agent of the El Montecito Manufacturing Company, a
corporation existing under the laws of California, and
had authority to draw a draft or bill of exchange
upon it for one hundred and fifty dollars, and exhibited to them a false telegram, purporting to have been
sent from Santa Barbara, California, in the usual
course of business of the telegraph company, to the
defendant at Portland, Oregon, by one W. P. Gould,
president of said corporation, instructing the defendant
to "proceed to Chicago; draw for necessary funds
through Woodard, Clarke and Company," and that, by
means of said false representations and false token, the
defendant, with intent to defraud, obtained the signature of Woodard, Clarke and Company, who, relying
thereon, indorsed their firm name upon a written instrument, of which the following is a copy, to wit:—

"$150.00.   PORTLAND, OREGON, August 26. 1895.
    "At sight pay to the order of Woodard, Clarke and
Company one hundred and fifty dollars, value received,
and charge the same to the account of

                                    "FRANK A. HANSCOM.

    "To El Montecito Manufacturing Company, Santa
Barbara, (Santa Barbara County National Bank,) California."

The indictment then negatives said representations and token, and alleges that the indorsement was obtained contrary to the statute, etc.   REVERSED.

For appellant there was a brief and an oral argument by *Mr. John C. Leasure.*

For the state there were briefs and oral arguments by *Messrs. Cicero M. Idleman,* attorney-general, and *Wilson T. Hume,* district attorney.

Opinion by MR. JUSTICE MOORE.

1. The defendant's first contention proceeds upon the theory that, the bill of exchange having been drawn to the order of Woodard, Clarke and Company, it must be presumed to have been executed by the defendant in payment of his preëxisting debt to them, and that they indorsed it for value, and the failure to allege that Woodard, Clarke and Company indorsed it for the defendant's accommodation renders the indictment fatally defective, wherefore the court erred in overruling his demurrer thereto. In support of this proposition the defendant cites the case of *People* v. *Chapman,* 4 Parker's Crim. Rep. 56, which shows that Chapman executed a promissory note for one thousand dollars, payable to the order of one Boardman, and by falsely representing that he owned a large quantity of barley and oats, and was able to pay every dollar he owed, induced Boardman to indorse it for his accommodation. The defendant having been arraigned upon an indictment which charged the commission of the offense in a manner similar to the indictment in the case at bar, demurred thereto, and it was held, upon appeal, that the failure to allege that the indorsement was obtained for the defendant's accommodation ren-

dered the indictment defective. WELLES, J., in deciding the case, says: "Unless, therefore, it sufficiently
appears by proper averments that the note was made
by the defendant for his own benefit, and that he obtained the indorsement of Boardman with intent afterwards to negotiate it on his own account, and
that Boardman, after indorsing the note, delivered it
to the defendant, and that the defendant received it
for that purpose,—in other words, that it was an accommodation indorsement,—the case made by the indictment is that Boardman, having taken the note in
question, payable to his own order, for a debt due to
himself from the defendant, was induced by the representations set forth, to indorse and deliver it back to
Chapman." The promissory note in that case was
executed by Chapman, and made payable to the order
of Boardman, who, by reason of the false representations, must have relied upon the maker's responsibility
and indorsed the note solely for Chapman's accommodation. There were two parties only to that contract,
and when Boardman delivered the note to Chapman
he knew that the indorsement was made for the
maker's accommodation.

"The theory of a bill of exchange," says Mr.
Daniel, in his work on Negotiable Instruments, § 17,
"is that the bill is an assignment to the payee of a
debt due from the acceptor to the drawer; and it is
undoubtedly true that the payee has a right to suppose that the drawee has funds of the drawer, upon
the faith of which understanding he receives the bill
directing them to be paid to him." It will be presumed that a bill of exchange was given or indorsed
for a sufficient consideration: Hill's Code, § 776, subdivision 21. While a bill of exchange may have been
received by the payee in liquidation of the drawer's

antecedent debt, we cannot think that it should be so
presumed, for the use it subserves is not so much the
payment of a debt as to facilitate exchange and avoid
the transmission of money from one place to another:
1 Daniel on Negotiable Instruments, § 4.   But, conceding that the presumption of the payment of an antecedent debt prevails upon proof of the execution of a
bill of exchange, we think the allegations of the indictment rebut such presumption, and show that the
indorsement of Woodard, Clarke and Company was not
made for the defendant's accommodation.   In the case
at bar there were three parties to the contract, and
the indictment alleges that Woodard, Clarke and Company relied upon the faith of the supposed telegram
and the representations of the defendant, and these
negative any presumption that they indorsed the bill
of exchange for the defendant's accommodation.   They
did not rely upon the defendant's responsibility, but
upon that of the El Montecito Manufacturing Company, for whose accommodation they indorsed the instrument, and delivered it to the defendant, supposing
the contract was entered into with his principal.   The
indictment is based upon an alleged violation of section 1777 of the statute which provides that "If any
person shall, by any false pretenses or by any privy
or false token, and with intent to defraud, obtain, or
attempt to obtain, from any other person, any money
or property whatever, or shall obtain or attempt to
obtain with the like intent the signature of any person to any writing the false making whereof would be
punishable as forgery, such person, upon conviction
thereof, shall be punished," etc.   If an indictment be
direct and certain as to the party charged, and the
crime alleged to have been committed, and states the
particular circumstances of the offense in ordinary and

concise language, and in such a way that a person of
ordinary understanding can know what was intended,
it is sufficient: *People* v. *Saviers*, 14 Cal. 29. In speaking
of the sufficiency of an indictment, SAVAGE, C. J., in
People v. *Herrick*, 13 Wend. 91, says: "It must be remembered, however, that the object of all specification
in indictments is to apprise the defendant of what he
is to meet upon the trial, and that certainty to a common intent is all that can reasonably be required."
Based upon these rules we think the indictment shows
that the indorsement was not obtained for the defendant's accommodation, and sufficiently notified him of
what he was expected to meet upon his trial, and
hence there was no error in overruling the demurrer.

2. It is contended that the court, without notice to
the defendant to produce the original false telegram,
erroneously admitted, over the defendant's objection,
secondary evidence of its contents. The bill of exceptions shows that William F. Woodard, being called
as a witness for the state, testified, in substance, that
on August twenty-sixth, eighteen hundred and ninety-
five, the defendant called at the store of Woodard,
Clarke and Company, and obtained a telegram that had
been delivered at their place of business by a messen-
ger for him; that he opened the message, read it in
the hearing of the witness, and retained it; that the
witness had made an ineffectual attempt to obtain the
dispatch, and did not know what had become of it.
He was then permitted to give from memory, over the
defendant's objection and exception, the language of
the message. When a written instrument is in or
traced to the possession of the opposing party, it is
necessary to give such party notice and a reasonable
time before the trial within which to produce it, be-

fore secondary evidence of its contents can be received; but this rule does not require that notice
should be given to produce documents which are the
subject of the indictment: Wharton's Criminal Evidence (9th ed.), § 212. "It is well settled in criminal
cases," says ELLIOTT, C. J., in *McGinnis* v. *State*, 24 Ind.
509, "that the court cannot compel the defendant to
produce an instrument in writing, in his possession, to
be used in evidence against him, as to do so would be
to compel the defendant to furnish evidence against
himself, which the law prohibits. And it is also evident, where the instrument in writing is the subject
of the prosecution, and is described in the indictment
in such a manner as to give the defendant an advantage on the trial by producing it, that he will do so.
The description of the instrument in the indictment
must be such that it would always serve to notify the
defendant of the nature of the charge against him,
save him from surprise, and enable him to be prepared to produce the writing when it was his interest
to produce it. But when its production would be
likely to work an injury to the defendant by aiding
in his conviction, it could not be expected that he
would produce it in response to the notice. It is,
therefore, difficult to perceive what benefit could result, either to the state or the defendant, from the
giving of such a notice, while to the defendant it is
liable to work a positive injury, by producing an unfavorable impression against him in the minds of the
jury, upon his refusal to produce it after notice." In
the case at bar the gravamen of the charge is the allegation that the defendant, by means of false representations and a false and forged telegram,—the substance of which is set out in the indictment,—and
with intent to defraud, obtained the signature of

Woodard, Clarke and Company to a bill of exchange, a copy of which is also set out therein. The statute makes the offense equivalent to forgery when the instrument to which the signature has been obtained purports to be of or represents value. "This statute," says BRONSON, J., in *People* v. *Galloway*, 17 Wend. 540, in construing the words of a similar section, "like that against forgery, was made to protect men in the enjoyment of their property, and if the instrument obtained can by no possibility prejudice any one in relation to his estate, it will not be an offense within the statute. If the rule were otherwise, a man might be punished criminally for obtaining the signature of another to an idle letter, or any other writing of no importance." The indictment having set out a copy of the bill of exchange, there can be no doubt of the state's right to introduce secondary evidence of its contents, without notice to the defendant, if unable to procure the original. The right to offer secondary evidence in such cases proceeds upon the theory that the indictment having set out a copy of the forged or stolen instrument, the defendant has notice of what he may be expected to meet upon his trial, and hence another notice to produce the writing is unnecessary. The indictment in this case having set out the alleged false telegram, in substance, the defendant was thereby notified of what the state expected to prove. This being so, secondary evidence of its contents, without additional notice, infringed no substantial right of the defendant, while the proof of a notice to produce a written instrument and his failure or refusal to comply therewith might have prejudiced his interests in the minds of the jury. If the indictment, however, had not set out what purported to be a copy of the alleged telegram, notice to the defendant and a reason-

able time before the trial to produce it would have
been necessary before secondary evidence of its contents could have been admitted. The telegram was so
intimately connected with the offense charged in the
indictment, and the execution of the bill of exchange
so dependent upon the alleged false token, that we
think there was no error in admitting secondary evidence of its contents without notice to the defendant
to produce the original.

8. It is contended that the court erred in the admission of evidence tending to show that the defendant, after having obtained the indorsement of the bill
of exchange, secured the money thereon. The evidence of Mr. Woodard shows that he went to the bank
with the defendant, who drew the instrument, and the
witness indorsed the firm name thereon; but he could
not state whether it was delivered to the defendant or
to an officer of the bank, nor whether the money was
paid by him or such officer to the defendant. His
evidence further shows that the defendant received
the money at the bank; that the bill of exchange was
not accepted by the El Montecito Manufacturing Company, but was protested on account thereof, and that
his firm was compelled to repay the bank. The crime
alleged in the indictment is that the defendant, by
means of false representations and a false token, and
with intent to defraud, obtained the signature of Woodard, Clarke and Company to a writing which was or
might become prejudicial in relation to their estate.
In *People* v. *Stone*, 9 Wend. 180, SUTHERLAND, J., in construing a statute similar to section 1777 of our Code,
says: "Under this statute, the offense is complete
when the signature is obtained, if it were obtained by
false pretenses and with a fraudulent intent, although

it may never be used to the prejudice of any person."
This doctrine was affirmed in *People* v. *Genung*, 11 Wend.
18, the court saying: "The offense is complete when
the signature is obtained by false pretenses, with intent to cheat or defraud another. It is not essential
to the offense that actual loss or injury should be sustained." The bill of exchange upon its face expressed
a money value, the false making whereof would have
been forgery, and the crime was therefore committed
if the defendant, with intent to defraud, and by means
of the alleged false token and false representations,
obtained the signature of Mr. Woodard, who, relying
thereon, indorsed the instrument; and hence it is immaterial whether the money was paid to the defendant upon it, except so far as to show a delivery of the
bill of exchange to him. The indictment having stated
that the defendant "obtained" the signature, was equivalent to an allegation that the instrument had been
indorsed and delivered to him, and proof of this allegation was necessary to support a conviction. Mr.
Woodard testified that he indorsed the bill of exchange, and thinks he delivered it to the defendant,
but is not positive about the matter, and cannot state
whether he or the defendant presented it to the bank.
The indorsement which gave a commercial value to
the instrument having been obtained, we think it is
immaterial whether the defendant or Mr. Woodard
presented it to the bank, and the evidence that the defendant obtained the money thereon becomes material
only to show an implied delivery, for if it be conceded
that the bill of exchange was delivered to the bank
by the witness, and that the money drawn thereon
was paid by him to the defendant, it would show that
Woodard was acting in the presence of the defendant
as his agent, and hence the receipt of the money by

the defendant, being a part of the transaction, shows an implied delivery of the instrument. But, as the offense charged consisted in the unlawfully obtaining of a signature to a written instrument representing value which might prejudice the indorsers thereof in respect to their estate, it was certainly immaterial whether they had paid the money back to the bank.

4. It is contended that the court erred in its refusal to allow the witness T. B. Izard, the manager and secretary of the El Montecito Manufacturing Company, to answer any questions tending to show what amount of money, if any, was due the defendant from said corporation at the time the bill of exchange was drawn by him. This witness having been called by the state, stated on cross-examination that the defendant at the time he drew the bill of exchange was in the employ of said corporation as a salesman at a salary of seventy-five dollars per month, whereupon the witness was asked: "On the twenty-sixth of August how much was due him upon salary?" An objection to the question having been sustained, the following was asked: "Was there any money due from El Montecito Manufacturing Company to the defendant, F. A. Hanscom, on the twenty-sixth day of August, eighteen hundred and ninety-five, on the day that this draft was drawn?" to which the court also sustained an objection. These questions could become material only upon the theory that the indorsement was obtained for the defendant's accommodation. If the defendant had represented to Woodard, Clarke and Company that he had money on deposit with or due him from said corporation, and they, relying thereon, had indorsed for his accommodation, the questions asked by defendant's counsel would have been vital;

but the indorsers, by means of the alleged telegram
and the defendant's representations, relied upon the
responsibility of the El Montecito Manufacturing Com·
pany, for whose accommodation they indorsed the in·
strument, and hence we fail to see how evidence of
any money the defendant had on deposit with or due
him.from said corporation could be material.

5.　It is also contended that the court erred in its
instruction, and particularly in answer to a question
from one of the jurors.　After the court had in·
structed the jury upon all the issues pertinent to the
case, one of the jurors asked the following question:
"Could I ask your honor to give us the law in regard
to the responsibility of an employer for the acts of
his agent?　Would that apply in this case?" to which
the court answered: "An agent is not supposed to ex·
ceed his authority.　He cannot bind his company if he
exceeds the instructions that are given him, or the au·
thority vested in him." We think this answer mis
leading for two reasons: 1. The principal is often
bound by the act of his agent in excess or abuse of
his actual authority, but this is only true between the
principal and third persons, who believing and having
a right to believe that the agent was acting within
and not exceeding his authority, would sustain loss if
the act was not considered that of the principal:
Walsh v. *Hartford Fire Insurance Company,* 73 N. Y. 5.
2. It seems to leave the impression that the defendant
would be criminally responsible if he, however inno·
cently, exceeded his authority in the smallest particu·
lar.　This being so we consider the remark of the
court erroneous.

6.　It is insisted that the court erred in overruling
the defendant's motion, made after the state had

rested, to instruct the jury to return a verdict of acquittal. The bill of exceptions contains all the evidence given at the trial, and hence an examination of this question becomes necessary. Evidence was introduced tending to establish all the elements of the offense, but upon the falsity of the alleged telegram it is somewhat obscure. R. L. Brocklett, being called as a witness for the state, testified, in substance, that he was bookkeeper and telegraph operator of the Postal Telegraph Company at its office at Portland, Oregon; that on August twenty-fourth last he, as the operator, received a telegram from Oakland, California, to F. A. Hanscom, which was delivered to Woodard, Clarke and Company, and produced an office copy thereof as follows:—

"Office No. 92.

"OAKLAND, CALIFORNIA, August 24, 1895.

"*To F. A. Hanscom, care of Woodard, Clarke and Company, Portland, Oregon*—Go to Chicago; draw on us funds Woodard, Clarke and Company.

"W. P. GOULD."

The witness Izard testified, in substance, that he knew W. P. Gould, who was the president of the El Montecito Manufacturing Company; that Gould was at Santa Barbara, California, between the twenty-fourth and twenty-seventh of August last; that the Postal Telegraph Company had no office at that city, but the Western Union maintained one there. It is possible that Gould may have been at Oakland, California, on August twenty-fourth, eighteen hundred and ninety-five, and at Santa Barbara between that date and the twenty-seventh of said month, or that he may have ordered some one at Oakland to send the message in his name; but as the state had alleged and relied

upon the defendant's false representations as well as
upon the alleged false token, we think there was no
error in denying the motion.   For the error noted
above the case must be retried.   REVERSED.

Decided December 9, 1895.

HUGHES *v.* CLEMENS.
[42 Pac. 617.]

1. APPEAL FROM JUSTICE COURT—SERVICE OF NOTICE—PRESUMPTION.—It
will be presumed by the appellate court in support of a return of
service of notice of appeal from a judgment of a justice of the peace,
that the attorney for the respondent upon whom the service was
made was a resident of the county, where nothing to the contrary
appears in the transcript on appeal: *Roy* v. *Horsley,* 6 Or. 270; *Bennett*
v. *Minott,* 28 Or. 339, approved and followed.

2. FILING OF TRANSCRIPT ON APPEAL FROM JUSTICE COURT.—A transcript
from a justice's court may be filed with the clerk of the circuit court
immediately after the appeal has been allowed by the justice without
allowing any time for excepting to the sureties on the appeal bond,
or for such sureties to justify if excepted to.

APPEAL from Marion: GEORGE H. BURNETT, Judge.

This is an appeal from the judgment of the circuit
court dismissing an appeal from a judgment rendered
by the recorder of the City of Salem, holding court
as a justice of the peace *ex officio.*   The record shows
that on October fourth, eighteen hundred and ninety-
three, a judgment having been rendered against the
defendant in said justice's court, a notice of appeal
therefrom was served, and filed on the next day, and
an undertaking therefor having been filed on the day
following, the appeal was allowed, and on the ninth
day of that month a transcript of the cause was filed
in the office of the clerk of the circuit court; that
on the date last mentioned the plaintiff filed with the

justice exceptions to the sufficiency of the surety in the undertaking, and on the same day moved the circuit court to dismiss the appeal, assigning as reasons therefor the insufficient service of the notice and premature filing of the transcript. No order on this motion having been made, the defendant, on the following day, by leave of court, withdrew the transcript, returned it to the justice, and on the twenty-third day of the same month served and filed another notice of appeal, together with a new undertaking, and obtained an order allowing the second appeal. On the third day of the succeeding month the transcript was refiled with the clerk of the circuit court, and thereafter the court, on plaintiff's motion, dismissed the appeal, and the defendant appeals. It is contended by the defendant that the first appeal was not perfected, so that in abandoning it he did not preclude himself from a new appeal; and that, having taken the second appeal within the time prescribed by law, the court erred in dismissing it.   AFFIRMED.

For appellant there was a brief by *Messrs. Bonham and Holmes* and *George W. Hollister,* with an oral argument by *Mr. William H. Holmes.*

For respondent there was a brief by *Messrs. George G. Bingham, D'Arcy and Richardson,* and *Seth R. Hammer,* with an oral argument by *Messrs. Bingham* and *Peter H. D'Arcy.*

Opinion by MR. JUSTICE MOORE.

1. The motion to dismiss the original appeal being based on an alleged improper service of the notice renders an examination of the proof of service in-

dorsed thereon important. The return of the officer
who made the service is as follows: "State of Oregon,
County of Marion, *ss.* This is to certify that I served
the within notice of appeal by delivering a true copy
thereof, prepared and certified to by me as marshal of
the City of Salem, Oregon, and *ex officio* constable, to
Seth R. Hammer, one of the attorneys for the respondents; that I served the said notice of appeal on the
said Seth R. Hammer in person and personally within
the city, county, and state aforesaid, on the fifth day
of October, eighteen hundred and ninety-three. Dated
at Salem, Oregon, October fifth, eighteen hundred and
ninety-three. (Signed), H. P. Minto, marshal of the
City of Salem, Oregon, and *ex officio* constable." The
statute requires that the notice shall be served on the
adverse party, but it has been repeatedly held that a
notice of appeal from a judgment rendered by a justice of the peace might be served either upon the adverse party or on the attorney who appeared for him
in the action, if such attorney be a resident of the
county in which the trial was had: *Carr* v. *Hurd,* 3 Or.
160; *Butler* v. *Smith,* 20 Or. 126 (25 Pac. 381); *Lewis Printing Company* v. *Reeves,* 26 Or. 445 (38 Pac. 622). It will
be observed that the proof of service does not show
that Seth R. Hammer, upon whom the notice of appeal
was served, was a resident of Marion County, but the
transcript discloses that he was one of the attorneys
for the plaintiffs at the trial, and, nothing appearing
to the contrary, it will be presumed that he was a resident of the county in which he appeared as counsel:
Roy v. *Horsley,* 6 Or. 270; *Bennett* v. *Minott,* 28 Or. 339
(39 Pac. 997). It is not contended that H. P. Minto, as
marshal of the City of Salem and *ex officio* constable of
that district, was not a proper officer to serve and indorse his certificate thereof on the notice of appeal,

and hence it follows that the original notice was properly served, and the proof thereof sufficient.

2. The most important question presented for consideration is whether the first appeal was perfected when the transcript was withdrawn from the circuit court. This inquiry involves an examination of the statute in relation to the mode of taking and perfecting an appeal from a judgment given in a justice's court. The statute, in general terms, provides that the appeal may be taken within thirty days from the entry of the judgment, by serving a notice thereof on the adverse party, and filing the original, with proof of service indorsed thereon, with the justice, and by giving an undertaking with one or more sureties, who must have the qualifications of bail upon arrest, and, if required by the adverse party, must appear before the justice at a time and place appointed for that purpose, and be examined on oath touching their sufficiency, in such manner as the justice in his discretion may think proper. If required by the adverse party the examination shall be reduced to writing and subscribed by the sureties. When an appeal is taken the justice must allow the same, and make an entry thereof in his docket, and, on or before the first day of the term of the circuit court next following the allowance of the appeal, the appellant must file with the clerk of the appellate court a transcript of the cause, upon the filing of which the appeal is perfected, and thereafter the circuit court has jurisdiction of the cause as if originally commenced therein. When an appeal is dismissed the appellate court must give judgment as it was given in the court below, and against the appellant for costs and disbursements of the appeal; but an appeal cannot be dismissed on the motion of the

respondent, on account of the undertaking therefor being defective, if the appellant, before the determination of the motion to dismiss, will execute a sufficient undertaking, and file the same in the appellate court: Hill's Code, §§ 119, 2117–2129.

The undertaking having been given and the appeal allowed, the transcript was filed with the clerk of the circuit court on the first day of the term of said court next following the allowance of the appeal, thereby transferring the cause to and conferring jurisdiction upon the circuit court, unless the plaintiffs' exception to the sufficiency of the surety rendered the filing at that time premature. In an appeal taken to this court from a judgment or decree rendered in the circuit court, the adverse party is allowed five days after the filing of the undertaking to except to the sufficiency of the sureties therein, and if no exception be taken within that time, his right to except thereto shall be deemed waived; and from the expiration of the time allowed to except to the sureties in the undertaking, or from the justification thereof if excepted to, the appeal shall be deemed perfected: Hill's Code, § 537. But the statute relating to appeals from judgments given in a justice's court does not contain this provision. It provides, however, for the manner of obtaining the justification of sureties in an undertaking on appeal, but does not prescribe the time within which exceptions may be taken by the adverse party to their sufficiency; and, in the absence of such regulation, a reasonable time would doubtless be granted for that purpose, unless the transcript in the mean time had been filed with the clerk of the circuit court. The appeal being perfected by the filing of the transcript, the cause no longer remains in the justice's court, and it would be useless to file in that court exceptions to the sufficiency of the sureties, for the justice would be powerless to secure the transcript for the purpose of obtaining their justification, without the consent of the circuit court. The only injury that could result to an adverse party from this interpretation of the statute would be the possibility of the justice accepting an insufficient undertaking on appeal and granting a stay of proceedings, but the statute has provided a remedy in part for this possible error by providing that the judgment creditor, when the judgment has been given for money in an action on a contract for the payment of money, may give an undertaking and enforce the judgment, notwithstanding the appellant's undertaking for a stay of proceedings: Code, § 2124. So, too, the appellant, by leave of the court, before a motion to dismiss the appeal has been determined, may file a new undertaking, if the original be defective, and by doing so he will protect the adverse party and secure to himself a trial of the action on its merits. The statute not having prescribed the time in which exceptions should be taken to the sufficiency of sureties on an appeal from a justice's court, but having provided that a new undertaking may be given in the circuit court, leads us to believe that a transcript from a justice's court may be filed with the clerk of the circuit court immediately after the appeal has been allowed by the justice. The original appeal having been perfected by the filing of the transcript, the appellant, after abandoning it, could not take another, (*McCarty* v. *Wintler,* 17 Or. 391, 21 Pac. 195; *Nestucca Wagon Road Company* v. *Landingham,* 24 Or. 439, 33 Pac. 983,) but, having done so, there was no error in dismissing the second appeal, and hence it follows that the judgment is affirmed.   AFFIRMED.

Argued November 21, 1895; decided January 13, 1896.

GODFREY *v.* DOUGLAS COUNTY.

[43 Pac. 171.]

1. COURTS—"NEXT TERM" DEFINED—CODE, § 2781—STATUTORY CONSTRUC
TION.— The words "next term" as used in section 2781, Hill's Code,
referring to the time when the county court may complete the work
of the county board of equalization, mean the next session of the
court after the board has adjourned: *Tompkins* v. *Clackamas County*,
11 Or. 364, distinguished. This statute being one relating to the public revenue, it should not be strictly construed.

2. SPECIAL AND GENERAL APPEARANCE—PRESUMPTION.—An appearance by
a party will be presumed to have been general so as to give the court
jurisdiction of the person, where the record fails to show that the
appearance was special.

3. EQUALIZATION OF TAXES—PRESUMPTION.—That alterations are made by
the board of equalization on the assessment roll, upon pages before
and after that on which appears an assessment against a given taxpayer, raises no presumption that the board approved such assessment.

4. EQUALIZATION OF TAXES—PRESUMPTION.—Where an assessment roll
contains a column headed "As Equalized by the County Board," it
will be presumed, where no entry appears in that column opposite
an assessment, that the assessment was not equalized by the county
board.

5. JUDGMENT EQUALIZING AN ASSESSMENT—PRESUMPTION.—Where a taxpayer who has been notified to show cause before a county court
why his assessment should not be increased appeared on the hearing, it will be presumed, on a writ to review a judgment increasing
the assessment, that the judgment was rendered on sufficient evidence, though the record does not show on what it was predicated, or
that it was rendered on any evidence: *Becker* v. *Malheur County*, 24
Or. 217, approved.

APPEAL from Douglas: J. C. FULLERTON, Judge.

This is a special proceeding by O. F. Godfrey,
Peter Hume, and S. C. Flint, partners doing business
under the firm name of the Douglas County Bank,
to have the action of the County Court of Douglas
County in the matter of increasing an assessment re-

viewed by the circuit court. The record shows that on July seventeenth, eighteen hundred and ninety-three, the county court made an order extending the time until the first Monday in October for the county assessor to return the assessment roll; that on September sixth the court met, and continued in regular session until the eleventh of that month, at which time it adjourned to October ninth; that the assessor within the extended time returned the assessment roll, in which the said bank was assessed upon money, notes, and accounts in the sum of six thousand six hundred dollars; that on October second the board of equalization met pursuant to notice, and continued in session until the seventh of that month, during which time the assessments of several persons were examined and altered, but no change was made in that of the bank; that on October seventh the board ordered a reduction of ten per cent. to be made in the assessed value of certain property,—not including money, notes, and accounts,—and delivered the assessment roll to the county court, with its certificate attached thereto, showing that the equalization had not been completed; that on October ninth the court met, pursuant to the adjournment of September eleventh, to complete the equalization, and a notice having been served upon the bank to appear and show cause why its assessment of money, notes, and accounts should not be increased, the court on October twelfth made .the following order: "In the matter of equalization of assessment roll for 1893: Assessment of Douglas County Bank. Now, at this time it is ordered by the court that the assessment of money, notes, and accounts of the Douglas County Bank for the year eighteen hundred and ninety-three be increased to fifteen thousand dollars, S. C. Flint, O. F. Godfrey, and Peter Hume each appearing in person for said bank." It further appears that, the assessment having been increased in pursuance of said order, this proceeding was instituted, and it is alleged that the county court in making said order exceeded its jurisdiction, to the injury of the plaintiff's substantial rights; that the attempted increase of said assessment is unjust and unauthorized by any facts proved before or found by said court; that the assessment roll was not returned until October second, at which time the board of equalization met and approved the assessment of the Douglas County Bank; that the county court thereafter, without legal notice thereof, and in the absence of any certificate that the assessment had not been examined and approved, attempted to act as a board of equalization at an adjournment of the September term of said court; that no evidence whatever was taken or produced before the court upon which it could base an alteration of said assessment, and that its action in so doing was capricious and arbitrary. A writ of review having been issued and served, the county court returned the same with a certified copy of the record, as above recited, from which the circuit court found that the county court had exceeded its jurisdiction in making said order, and rendered a judgment setting it aside, from which the county appeals.

REVERSED.

For appellant there was a brief and an oral argument by *Mr. J. W. Hamilton.*

For respondent there were briefs and oral arguments by *Messrs. William R. Willis* and *A. M. Crawford.*

Opinion by MR. JUSTICE MOORE.

The record presents two questions for consideration: (1) Did the county court have jurisdiction of the subject matter and persons of the interested parties at the time it attempted to increase the assessment; and, if so, (2) Does the record show a judgment unimpeachable upon a direct attack?

1.   The first question suggested requires an examination of the statute prescribing the duties of the assessor, board of equalization, and county court in the matter of returning the assessment roll and equalizing the assessment. The law requires the assessor to assess all the taxable property within his county and return the roll thereof to the county clerk on or before the first Monday in September, (Hill's Code, § 2752,) and it is made the duty of the county judge, county clerk, and assessor, as a board of equalization, to meet on the last Monday in August, and, if necessary, to continue in session one week, for the purpose of examining and correcting the assessment roll and equalizing the assessment: Code. §§ 2760, 2778. And, to guard against the possible contingency of lack of time, the statute provides that the county court shall at its term in September in each year complete the equalization, (Code, § 2782,) but if the assessor is unable to complete the assessment by the last Monday in August the county court may at any regular term thereof, prior to the first Monday of September, extend the time for returning the assessment roll to a day certain, not later than the first Monday in October: Code, §§ 2752, 2777. It is also made the duty of the assessor to give three weeks' public notice of the meeting of the board of equalization prior to the date of returning the roll, (Code, §§ 2760, 2777,) and, if the

board is unable to complete the equalization during
the week in which it is required to meet, it shall be
the duty of the county court "at its next term thereafter sitting to transact county business," to complete
such examination and correction, in the same manner
and with like effect as the board of equalization is required to do: Code, § 2781. The record shows that
the county court, on July seventeenth, eighteen hundred and ninety-three, at a regular term thereof, made
an order extending the time for the return of the assessment roll to the first Monday in October, at which
time, the roll having been returned, the board of
equalization met pursuant to the assessor's notice, and
continued in session one week; but being unable to
complete its labors within that time, the roll was submitted to the county court for final equalization, and
that on October twelfth the court increased the plaintiffs' assessment. The plaintiffs contend that, the
court having at its regular session in September, adjourned to the ninth of October, when it convened on
the latter date its session was a continuation of the
September term, and not its "next term" after the
meeting of the board of equalization, and hence the
county court was at that time powerless to equalize or
correct the assessment roll, and had no authority to
do so until the next regular term after the September
term.

The point for which the plaintiffs contend demands
an examination of the terms of the county court required to be held in Douglas County and a definition
of the word "term" as applied to a session thereof.
The terms of said court, appointed by law, are held
on the first Monday in January, March, May, July,
September, and November, (Hill's Code, § 2335,) and a
term may also be held at such other times as the court

in term or the county judge in vacation may appoint: Code, § 899.   In *Tompkins* v. *Clackamas County*, 11 Or. 364 (4 Pac. 1210), it was held that when the statute referred to the terms of a county court, it meant the regular terms prescribed by law, and not the special terms appointed by the court or judge thereof. This opinion was rendered in the construction of a statute under the authority of which the county court of Clackamas County sought to establish a county road across the plaintiff's premises, and, the proceedings taken being for the purpose of appropriating private property to a public use, the court very properly construed the statute strictly.   The commencement of every term is fixed by statute, and the end by the final adjournment for that term, so that, if it should sit pursuant to an order of adjournment made and entered upon the record in term time, it would not be another session of the court, but a continuation of the statutory term, and this is the case whether the adjournment be from one day to the next or for a longer period (*Bronson* v. *Schulten,* 104 U. S. 410,) and hence it follows that when the county court met on October ninth, pursuant to the adjournment of September eleventh, it was a continuation of the September term, and, if the statute is to be construed strictly, not its next term after the meeting of the board of equalization.

Every citizen owes a duty to the state to bear a just proportion of its burdens, and if the assessor should undervalue his property or omit a part thereof assessable for general taxation, he has no just cause for complaint if a board of equalization or county court adds thereto or increases the value placed upon it by the officer chosen for that purpose. The duty of supporting the state being incumbent upon the cit-

izen in proportion to his taxable property, the right
to equalize the measure of his burden must be in the
state, which, in the interest of the citizen, delegates
this power to the board of equalization, and, if not completed by it within a given time, then to the county
court for final equalization. It is presumed that official duty has been regularly performed, (Hill's Code,
§ 776, subdivision 15,) and, this being so, the list of
property of the citizen returned by the assessor, as
well as the value placed thereon, must be deemed
prima facie correct, and the right of the board or court
to add to the list or alter the value so ascertained
being a delegated power, the measure of such power
must be found in the statute conferring it. This would
require the board or court, if the statute was held to
be mandatory, to alter the assessment at the time and
in the manner only as prescribed by law; but, as we
understand the law, proceedings to equalize assessments of this character are to be construed much
more liberally than an equalization of an assessment
for muncipal purposes: 2 Desty on Taxation, 615. In
the counties of Josephine, Curry, Coos, and Wallowa
no terms of the county court are held after the first
Monday in September until the first Monday in January: Code, § 2335. The county court at its term in
September in each year is required to levy the county,
state, and school taxes, (Code, § 2783,) and if the assessor in either of these counties should be unable to
return his roll on the last Monday in August, and
further time was granted him for that purpose, the
county court could not, to give the statute a strict construction, equalize the assessment until the January
term, if the board of equalization was unable to complete its labors within one week. The result of this
would be that the county court must omit either the

equalization or the levy of taxes, and for this reason
we cannot think that the legislative assembly meant by
"the next term thereafter" the next regular term
after the meeting of the board of equalization. We
are strengthened in this belief from the language of
section 2777, Hill's Code, which provides that the
county court, at any regular term thereof, may extend
the time for the assessor to return his roll, thereby
implying that all other statutory requirements in relation to the assessment, equalization, and levy of taxes
may be complied with at an adjourned term of the
court. The assessment having been made to raise a
public tax, there is no necessity for construing the
statute strictly, and we hold that the language, "at its
next term thereafter sitting to transact county business," means at the next session of the county court
after the meeting of the board of equalization.

2. The court having jurisdiction of the subject
matter, obtained jurisdiction of the persons of the
plaintiffs by their voluntary appearance before it, for
it is a universal rule, which admits of no exception,
that if the court has jurisdiction of the subject matter,
a general appearance gives jurisdiction of the person,
(2 Encyclopedia of Pleading and Practice, 639,) and if
the record fails, as in the case at bar, to show that
the appearance was special, it will be presumed to
have been general: *Deshler* v. *Foster,* Morris (Iowa), *403.

3. The plaintiffs' assessment having been entered on
page 57 of the roll, they contend that it was approved
by the board of equalization, and that this conclusively
appears from the fact that the board altered an assessment entered on page 53 and another on page 114
thereof. This could only be so by indulging the pre-

sumption that the board of equalization began at the
first page of the assessment roll, and continued to ex·
amine and correct the successive entries therein in
regular order, during the week it was in session. The
assessor published a notice of the meeting of the
board of equalization, inviting interested taxpayers to
attend its session for the purpose of having their
assessment corrected; but in appearing in response
thereto it cannot be presumed, or even supposed, that
the persons whose names were entered on the assess·
ment roll appeared before the board of equalization in
the order in which their names were written or ar·
ranged by the assessor, nor does the fact that altera·
tions were made on the roll upon pages before and
after that upon which the assessment of the Douglas
County Bank was entered, show that the board ap·
proved the assessment of the bank.

4. It is contended that the county court could ac·
quire jurisdiction to alter an assessment only by means
of a certificate from the board of equalization that it
had not acted upon or equalized a given assessment,
and no certificate of that character having been is·
sued, the county court had no authority to alter this
assessment. The assessment roll contains a column
for the "Total value of taxable property," in which
the assessor carried out the aggregate value of the sev·
eral classes of property assessed. The next column
to the right is entitled "As equalized by the county
board," and it must be presumed that the board of
equalization entered in this column every assessment it
corrected or equalized, and, no entry of that character
having been made in this column opposite the assess·
ment of the Douglas County Bank, it was apparent to
the county court from the certificate made by the

board of equalization that the plaintiffs' assessment
had not been equalized, and authorized the court to
examine, correct, and equalize the same.

5.   The county court having jurisdiction of the subject matter and of the persons, it only remains to be
seen whether the order complained of is sufficient in
form to withstand a direct attack.   It will be observed
that the judgment contains no recital that it appeared
to the court from any evidence taken before it that
the assessment complained of was incorrect, or that it
should be increased; and the question is presented
whether the entry of a judgment without a statement
that any sum is due, or of any facts upon which it is
predicated, is binding upon the parties affected thereby
except in a collateral proceeding.   Mr. Freeman, in
speaking of the sufficiency of the journal entry of a
judgment, says: "That whatever appears upon its face
to be intended as the entry of a judgment will be regarded as sufficiently formal if it shows, (1) the relief
granted; and (2) that the grant was made by the court
in whose records the entry is written," (Freeman on
Judgments, § 50,) and in another section the same
learned author says: "No particular form is required
in the proceedings of the court to render their order
a judgment.   It is sufficient if it is final, and the party
may be injured": Freeman on Judgments, § 51.   Mr.
Black also says: "It is further to be noted, in connection with matters of form in judgments, that a much
less degree of technicality and formality is required
in the judgments of justices of the peace and other
inferior courts than is exacted in respect to the judgments of courts of record": 1 Black on Judgments,
§ 115.   "The judgment," says WHEELER, J., in *Hamilton* v. *Ward,* 4 Texas, 356, "raises a legal presumption

of the truth of every material averment in the petition or motion, which can only be rebutted by a statement of facts showing the absence of proof." And,
further in the opinion, the same learned justice says:
"It cannot, therefore, be a valid objection to the judgment that it does not recite the facts alleged in the
motion and proved at the trial." If there be any am-
biguity therein the pleadings may be read in connection with the judgment for the purpose of explaining
the uncertainty. The judgment is the final order
predicated upon the prior proceedings which may
always be examined in aid of and to support the judgment: 1 Black on Judgments, § 123.

The plaintiffs, under the provisions of section 2780,
Hill's Code, were served with a written notice which
required them to appear before the county court, to
show why their assessment of money, notes, and accounts should not be increased, and, in obedience
thereto, they personally appeared for that purpose.
This notice is the pleading by which the court obtained jurisdiction of the persons, and may be read in
connection with the order founded thereon for the
purpose of explaining the latter. An examination of
the notice conclusively shows the nature of the inquiry
proposed, and the order of the court based thereon is
equivalent to a finding that the class of property specified in the notice and order was assessed too low, and
for that reason it was the judgment of the court that
the assessment thereof be increased. No board of
equalization can arbitrarily increase the assessment of
a taxpayer, for to do so would be a confiscation of
property; but the pleadings having in effect stated a
cause of action, and an order having been made
thereon, it must be presumed that sufficient evidence
was adduced from which the court concluded that the

assessment should be increased to the amount found
by it. In *Becker* v. *Malheur County*, 24 Or. 217, BEAN, J.,
in speaking of the duties of a board of equalization and
the presumptions indulged in favor of its conclusions,
says: "There is no provision of law of which we are
aware making it the duty of the board to reduce to
writing or preserve the evidence before it in the matter of the equalization of taxes, and, although it is an
inferior tribunal, every presumption exists in favor of
the regularity of its proceedings, after it has once acquired jurisdiction." The judgment of the court an-
nulling the increase in the assessment being erroneous,
the judgment will be reversed and the cause remanded
with instructions to dismiss the writ of review.

REVERSED.

Argued January 20; decided February 10, 1896.

DAY *v.* SCHNIDER.
[43 Pac. 650.]

1. CLOUD ON TITLE—PLEADING—CODE, § 2823.—The averment in a complaint to remove a cloud on title, that defendant claims under a tax
deed, sufficiently shows the apparent validity of the outstanding
title, as a tax deed in Oregon is *prima facie* evidence of title.

2. PLEADING—JOINING SEVERAL CAUSES OF SUIT.—A complaint in a proceeding to remove a cloud on title is not obnoxious to the objection that it improperly unites several causes of suit because it sets
out several reasons why the outstanding title is invalid.

APPEAL from Lane: J. C. FULLERTON, Judge.

This is a suit by Thomas Day against Mike Schnider to remove a cloud upon the title to the northwest
quarter of section twenty-two, township fifteen south,
range one east, in Lane County, created by a tax
deed. The complaint alleges, in substance, that the
plaintiff is the owner and in possession of the real

property in question; that the defendant Schnider claims some right or title thereto adverse to the plaintiff, under a sheriff's tax deed of date February thirteenth, eighteen hundred and ninety-four, which on its face appears to be regular, and recites that said land was levied upon by the sheriff as the property of Frank Burgess for the taxes of eighteen hundred and ninety, amounting to seven dollars and twenty cents, and on the fifth day of February, eighteen hundred and ninety-two, was sold to the defendant for the sum of eighteen dollars and eighty-five cents, being the amount of said taxes and accruing costs. It then proceeds, in six separate and distinct paragraphs, to aver facts which, if true, show the deed to be invalid and a cloud upon plaintiff's title. It further alleges that the plaintiff offered to pay, and tendered to the sheriff of the county, the taxes for the years eighteen hundred and ninety-one, eighteen hundred and ninety-two, and eighteen hundred and ninety-three, but he refused to receive the same or any part thereof, claiming that the taxes for all said years had been paid by the defendant Schnider; that prior to the expiration of two years from the date of the tax sale plaintiff sought to redeem the land, and inquired both of the sheriff and county clerk how much or what sum was required to redeem the same, but that both said officers refused to make or permit redemption to be made, but referred him to the defendant who held the certificate of sale, and who also refused to make or allow redemption thereof to be made, or to say for what sum he would relinquish his claim thereto. That since the execution of the tax deed, and prior to the commencement of this suit, the plaintiff offered and tendered to defendant the entire amount paid by him on account of his purchase, with twenty per cent. per

annum interest on the original purchase price, and ten
per cent. per annum on all other liquidated charges
against said land, for a quitclaim thereto; that he deposited with the clerk of the court fifty dollars from
which the court might reimburse the defendant for
such outlay in case he should be found liable therefor; that any and all payments by defendant for said
premises and subsequent taxes thereon have been voluntary on his part, and not at the request or wish
of plaintiff, but against his wishes and will; that the
reasonable value of said land is one thousand dollars.
A motion and demurrer to the complaint having been
sustained, and plaintiff refusing to plead further, a
decree was entered dismissing the complaint, from
which he appeals.   REVERSED.

For appellant there was a brief and an oral argument by *Mr. A. E. Wheeler.*

For respondent there was a brief by *Messrs. Bilyeu
and Young,* and an oral argument by *Mr. L. Bilyeu.*

Opinion by MR. CHIEF JUSTICE BEAN.

1. The only questions necessary to be determined
on this appeal are the objections to the sufficiency of
the complaint. It is urged by the defendants that the
complaint is defective because it does not sufficiently
show the apparent validity of the tax title claimed by
the defendant Schnider. The general rule in a suit to
remove a cloud from title is that the complaint must
set out the facts which show the apparent validity of
the outstanding title, and also those showing its inva-
lidity, but where, as in this state, the statute declares
a tax deed to be *prima facie* evidence of title, the mere
naming of the instrument and alleging that it is regu-

lar upon its face is sufficient to show its apparent validity: Hill's Code, § 2823; Black on Tax Titles (2d ed.), § 440; *Hibernia Savings Society* v. *Ordway*, 38 Cal. 679.

2. It is next claimed that the motion and demurrer were properly sustained because several causes of suit are improperly united in the complaint. But this contention is without merit. The object and purpose of the suit is to remove a cloud from the plaintiff's title, and the several reasons given in the complaint why the tax deed is invalid do not constitute separate causes of suit. No sufficient reason is suggested by respondent's counsel why the complaint does not state a cause of suit, and none has occurred to us. The decree of the court below will therefore be reversed, and the cause remanded with directions to overrule the motion and demurrer to the complaint, and for such further proceedings as may be proper and right in the premises.   REVERSED.

Argued December 16, 1895; decided February 10, 1896.

JUSTICE *v.* ELWERT.
[43 Pac. 649.]

1. APPEAL—FINDINGS ON CONFLICTING EVIDENCE.—Findings of the trial court on conflicting testimony will not be disturbed on appeal, unless they are clearly against the weight of evidence.

2. MECHANICS' LIENS—COMPLETE PERFORMANCE PREVENTED BY OWNER—WAIVER.—Failure of contractors to complete a building according to contract will not prevent a lien from attaching in their favor for so much of the work as was actually performed according to the contract, where such failure to complete was due to an act of the owner.

APPEAL from Multnomah: LOYAL B. STEARNS, Judge.

This is a suit to foreclose a mechanics' lien. The lien is claimed by virtue of a contract entered into be-

tween plaintiffs, Justice Brothers, and the defendant
J. B. Elwert, by which plaintiffs agreed to furnish the
materials, and do certain painting, graining, and cal-
cimining for Elwert, upon her buildings at Portland,
Oregon, at the agreed price and consideration of two
hundred and eighty-five dollars, to be paid thirty days
after completion of the work. The work was to be
done in accordance with certain specifications, "in a
good, workmanlike, and substantial manner, to the satisfaction and under the direction of the said owner or
superintendent, to be testified by a writing or certificate under the hand of the said contractor." While
engaged in the performance of this contract, plaintiffs
claim that they furnished extra materials and did certain extra work for Elwert, at her instance, of the
agreed value of one hundred and thirty-two dollars.
The claim of lien was filed to secure these two sums,
less sixteen dollars allowed as a credit. The defendant F. E. Beach also seeks to foreclose a lien claimed
upon the same property, to secure payment of the
sum of one hundred and fifty-three dollars and sev-
enty-six cents for paints, oils, and other materials
furnished to Justice Brothers and which were used by
them in and upon the buildings. The defendant's
Elwert's defense to the Justice Brothers' lien is that
they have not performed the conditions of the contract
as required by its stipulations, nor secured the certificate of the contractor or superintendent showing performance of the work to his satisfaction. She denies
absolutely that Justice Brothers did any extra work
at her instance or request, or that she ever agreed to
pay them anything therefor. The plaintiffs do not
claim to have fully performed the contract upon their
part, but insist that the nonperformance was excused
by the acts of defendant Elwert; that they completed

the work under the con'ract, in the main, but that defendant forbade and prevented them from performing entirely. The defense against the Beach claim is confined to the legal question as to whether he is entitled to a lien unless it is established that Justice Brothers performed their contract. The court below, among other things, found that plaintiffs had completed their contract so far as they were permitted by Elwert; that she, without cause, refused to allow a full performance, and that plaintiffs were entitled to the sum of two hundred and fifty dollars for the materials furnished and work done under the contract; that plaintiffs furnished extra material and did extra work, at the request of Elwert, of the value of one hundred and seven dollars, which, with the contract obligation, amounted to three hundred and fifty-seven dollars, against which Elwert was entitled to a credit of eighty-six dollars and twenty cents, leaving a balance of two hundred and seventy-one dollars and eighty cents. The court further found that F. E. Beach furnished plaintiffs materials used in and upon said buildings of the value of one hundred and forty-nine dollars and sixteen cents, which being deducted from plaintiffs' claim, leaves a balance of one hundred and twenty-two dollars and sixty-four cents bearing interest from November twentieth, eighteen hundred and ninety-three. As conclusions of law the court found that plaintiffs have a lien to secure the sum of one hundred and forty-eight dollars, and the defendant Beach a lien for one hundred and seventy-nine dollars and thirty-seven cents, which amounts include interest, attorneys' fees, and costs of filing liens. Upon these findings a decree was entered, and defendant Elwert appeals.   AFFIRMED.

For appellant there was a brief by *Messrs. Watson, Beekman and Watson,* and *Edward Mendenhall,* with oral arguments by *Messrs. Mendenhall* and *Benjamin B. Beekman.*

For respondents Justice there was a brief and an oral argument by *Mr. J. Frank Boothe.*

For respondent Beach there was a brief and an oral argument by *Mr. George G. Gammans.*

Opinion by MR. JUSTICE WOLVERTON.

1. The position of appellant is stated by her attorneys in their brief thus: "Upon their face the notices of lien appear to be sufficient, and we presume no authorities are necessary to support the proposition that in order to entitle plaintiffs to enforce their lien for work under their contract they must have performed its conditions on their part to be performed. * * * We claim that, as a matter of law, plaintiffs are not entitled to any lien, for the reason that they have failed to perform their contract." And "that if the plaintiffs failed to perform their contract, so as to entitle them to recover, then Beach and Company are not entitled to any lien." This pertains to the contract and its fulfillment by plaintiffs, considered aside from the said claim for extra materials and labor. The question thus propounded is a mixed one, consisting of both law and fact. The plaintiffs, however, admit that they have not fully performed, but claim that whatsoever has been left undone by them was excused by the acts of Mrs. Elwert. The court below found that she refused to allow or permit plaintiffs to fully comply with the conditions of the contract, which finding appears to be supported by the testimony, although we find much conflict therein.

But the court having seen the witnesses, heard them testify, and observed their demeanor while upon the stand, its finding ought not to be disturbed, unless clearly against the weight of evidence.

2.   The real question, then, comes to this: Can the lien be maintained without full performance of the contract upon which it is based, where such performance is prevented by the owner, who is a party to the contract?   Regarding this proposition the author of Phillips on Mechanics' Liens, § 138, states the rule as follows: "It is, however, universally true that no loss of lien is occasioned for the work actually performed in accordance with the contract, when the work has been stopped or abandoned in consequence of the default of the owner."   To this rule some of the authorities make an apparent exception in the case of nonpayment of installments by the owner, but it is evidently true that, as to this, the contract stipulations may make the payment of such installments conditions precedent, and thus the nonpayment thereof would become a material default upon the part of the owner.   But where the owner has by positive acts, as in the case at bar, prevented the full performance upon the part of the contractors, there can be no question but they will have a lien for materials furnished and labor performed, so far as they have in good faith proceeded under the contract.   See *Hoₓₑs* v. *Reliance Wire Works Company*, 46 Minn. 47 (48 N. W. 448); *Charnley* v. *Honig*, 74 Wis. 163 (42 N. W. 220); *Smith* v. *Norris*, 120 Mass. 63, and *Merchants' and Mechanics' Savings Bank* v. *Dashiell*, 25 Gratt. 625.   And this rule also has a like application in excusing the plaintiffs from the necessity of procuring the certificate of the architect or superintendent showing a satisfactory compliance

on their part. The court below found that, as far as
plaintiffs were permitted, they had substantially performed, and this finding is warranted by the testimony. Hence plaintiffs were entitled to their lien for
materials furnished and labor performed under the
contract, and it follows that Beach is also entitled to
his lien. All other findings of fact are in substantial
accord with the testimony, and hence the decree of
the court will be affirmed.   AFFIRMED

Argued November 12, 1895; decided January 27, 1896; rehearing denied.

BARBRE *v.* GOODALE.

[38 Pac. 67; 43 Pac. 378.]

1. APPEAL—AMENDING PROOF OF SERVICE.—An imperfect proof of service
   of a notice of appeal may be amended on motion so as to conform to
   the fact: *Dolph* v. *Nickum*, 2 Or. 202, and *Seeley* v. *Sebastian*, 3 Or. 563,
   cited and approved; *Briney* v. *Starr*, 6 Or. 207, and *Henness* v. *Wells*, 16
   Or. 266, distinguished.

2. GENERAL DEMURRER—PLEADING.—A general demurrer to a complaint
   containing several causes of action is properly overruled where any
   one of the causes is well stated.

3. AGENCY—PAROL EVIDENCE TO SHOW REAL PARTIES TO WRITTEN I-
   STRUMENT.—Parol testimony is admissible to show that a contract
   which is not a negotiable instrument, and not required to be under
   seal, although so in fact, executed by and in the name of an agent,
   is the contract of the principal, although the principal is known to
   the other contracting party at the date of its execution.

4. DEGREE OF PROOF—REAL PARTY IN INTEREST.—That plaintiff is the
   real party in interest is not required to be established by higher proof
   than that requisite to establish any other fact in the case.

APPEAL from Lane: J. C. FULLERTON, Judge.

This is an action by J. I. Barbre against J. C.
Goodale to recover upon two separate causes. The
first is upon a written agreement which purports upon

its face to be the agreement of one G. W. Handsaker, of the first part, and J. C. Goodale, of the second part. By its terms, in brief, the first party agrees to cut, haul, bank, and deliver to the second party two million feet of fir logs, and, if certain conditions of the lumber market continued to prevail, an additional one half million feet, at a certain point upon the McKenzie River, in Lane County, at the rate of three dollars per thousand, to be paid by the second party as follows: One dollar per thousand when the logs were cut and banked, and one dollar per thousand when scaled and rolled in the river, and such balance as should be found due between the parties within thirty-one days thereafter. The last clause is as follows: "It is further understood and agreed, and is a part of the consideration of this agreement, that the second party reserves out of and deducts from the balance that may be due the first party, after making said first two payments, any sum or sums that may then be due or to become due to the second party from J. I. Barbre, or for which he is responsible, to pay J. I. Barbre not to exceed one thousand seven hundred dollars, the obligations of which are now created." The contract purports to be under seal. After the plaintiff had cut, hauled, and banked one million four hundred and forty-two thousand feet of logs, and cut in the timber three hundred and eighty-two thousand feet more, and while proceeding with the performance of the contract, the defendant, on March first, eighteen hundred and ninety-two, notified and directed him to discontinue the work, as he would not pay for or take any more of such logs. Whereupon plaintiff commenced this action to recover under the contract for such logs as he had cut and banked, and also for such as he had cut in the timber. The complaint proceeds upon the theory that G. W. Handsaker was Barbre's agent in the execution of said contract, and that it was signed and executed in his name instead of Barbre's by consent of defendant, and hence that Barbre is entitled to sue upon the agreement solely and in his own name. The second cause of action is based upon the sale and delivery by plaintiff to defendant of nine hundred and eighty-seven thousand feet of other logs at three dollars and twenty-five cents per thousand, upon which a balance of four hundred and seventy-two dollars and thirty-four cents is claimed. At the trial plaintiff had a verdict for two hundred and fourteen dollars, and from the judgment entered thereon the defendant appeals.   AFFIRMED.

For appellant there was a brief and an oral argument by *Messrs. L. Bilyeu* and *J. M. Williams.*

For respondent there was a brief and an oral argument by *Messrs. George B. and George A. Dorris.*

ON MOTION TO DISMISS.

PER CURIAM. 1. This is a motion to dismiss the appeal for want of notice. The appellant filed a cross-motion, based upon an affidavit and accompanying papers, from which it appears that within the time allowed by law a notice of appeal was regularly served upon the attorneys for respondent, and the same filed with the clerk of the circuit court, with a certificate of service attached thereto as follows: "State of Oregon, County of Lane, *ss.* I hereby certify that I served the within notice of appeal within said state and county on the second day of April, eighteen hundred and ninety-four, on the within named . defendants George B. Dorris and George A. Dorris

by delivering to them and each of them in person a
true and correct copy of this original notice. J. E.
Noland, sheriff of Lane County, Oregon, George
Croner, deputy." For some reason, not explained, the
paper containing the alleged proof of service became
detached from the original notice, and could not be
found until after the transcript had been filed in this
court, and hence does not appear therein. Although
Messrs. George B. and George A. Dorris were the attorneys for the respondent, and as such could have
been and were in fact served with the notice, the
proof of such service as indorsed or attached to the
notice of appeal when filed is admittedly imperfect.
But under the rule in *Dolph* v. *Nickum,* 2 Or. 202, and
Seeley v. *Sabastian,* 3 Or. 563, it seems to us the appellant should be allowed to amend the return to conform to the fact. The cases of *Briney* v. *Starr,* 6 Or.
207, and *Henness* v. *Wells,* 16 Or. 266, relied upon by
respondent, are to the effect that the proof of service
must accompany and be filed with the notice of appeal, but in neither of these cases was there any
proof or attempted proof of service so filed, and there
was therefore nothing to amend, while in the case at
bar there was an alleged, though imperfect, proof of
service filed with the notice, and hence this case
comes within the rule announced in the two cases
first cited, and not within the cases relied on by the
respondent. We think, therefore, the motion to dismiss the appeal should be overruled, and the cross-
motion to amend allowed.   OVERRULED.

ON THE MERITS.

Opinion by MR. JUSTICE WOLVERTON.

2. A general demurrer was filed to the complaint, but, as it goes to the whole complaint, and one of the separate causes of action is confessedly well set out, the demurrer was properly overruled.

3. At the trial, plaintiff, while a witness in his own behalf, was asked, and permited to answer over the objection of the defendant, the following questions: Question—"How did that clause about the one thou. sand seven hundred dollars, which allows Goodale to deduct from last payment amount due him from Barbre, not to exceed one thousand seven hundred dollars, come to be in the contract?" Answer—"I had been logging for Goodale, and he had paid me about one thousand seven hundred dollars on logs which were claimed by the Oregon and California Railroad Company, and it sued, or threatened to sue, him to recover the value of the logs. If he had to pay the railroad company for the logs, this had to be deducted out of the contract price of those logs." Question—"State what the conversation was at the time of your entering into the contract as to who the true parties to the contract should be." Answer—"Mr. Goodale and I had a conversation about making the contract to get out some logs. I wanted to get out some logs for him, about two million feet. I had the teams and everything neeessary to carry on logging. Mr. Goodale said that he would let me have a contract to get out two million, but did not want to have the contract made in my name; that the railroad company had sued, and he was afraid that if the contract was in my name the company would make trouble, and he said

why not make it in the name of George (meaning
G. W. Handsaker). I told him that I did not want to
bother George. Goodale said that it would not be any
trouble to him, that I could go on and carry on the
contract just the same. I said I could see George
about it, and I did speak to George about it, and he
said so long as he would not be bothered in any way
he would assist me in the matter, and it was agreed
between Mr. Goodale, Mr. Handsaker, and myself that
the contract should be drawn up and signed by G. W.
Handsaker, and that I should carry it out; that it
should be my contract, and not the contract of G. W.
Handsaker, and that Mr. Handsaker should not be
bound by the contract. Under this agreement the contract was drawn up and signed by Mr. Handsaker and
Goodale, and I did the work that was done under it."
This, with other testimony of the same nature, all
elicited over defendant's objection, forms the basis of
the principal grounds of error relied upon for the
reversal of the judgment below.

The question is here presented whether it is competent to show by parol testimony that a contract
executed by and in the name of an agent is the contract of the principal, where the principal was known
to the other contracting party at the date of its execution. There are two opinions touching the question
among American authorities,—the one affirming and
the other denying; but the case is one of first impression here, and we feel constrained to adopt the
rule which may seem the more compatible with the
promotion of justice, and the exaction of honest and
candid transactions between individuals. The English
authorities are agreed that parol evidence is admissible to show that a written contract executed in the
name of an agent is the contract of the principal,

whether he was known or unknown; and the American authorities are a unit so far as the rule is applied to an unknown principal, but disagree where he was known at the time the contract was executed or entered into by the parties. All the authorities, both English and American, concur in holding that, as applied to such contracts executed when the principal was unknown, parol evidence which shows that the agent who made the contract in his own name was acting for the principal does not contradict the writing, but simply explains the transaction; for the effect is not to show that the person appearing to be bound is not bound, but to show that some other person is bound also. And those authorities which deny the application of the rule where the principal was known do not assert or maintain that such parol testimony tends to vary or contradict the written contract, but find support upon the doctrine of estoppel, it being maintained that a party thus dealing with an agent of a known principal elects to rely solely upon the agent's responsibility, and is therefore estopped to proceed against the principal. The underlying principle, therefore, upon which the authorities seem to diverge, is the presumption created by the execution of the contract in the name of the agent, and the acceptance thereof by a party, where the principal is known. Is this presumption conclusive or is it disputable? Without attempting to reconcile the decisions, we believe the better rule to be that the presumption thus created is a disputable one, and that the intention of the party must be gathered from his words, and the various circumstances which surround the transaction, as its practical effect is to promote justice and fair dealing. The principal may have recourse to the same doctrine to bind the party thus entering into contract with his agent. Parol evidence, however, is not admissible to discharge the agent, as the party with whom he has dealt has his election as to whether he will hold him or the principal responsible. This doctrine must be limited to simple contracts, and may not be extended to negotiable instruments and specialties under seal, as they constitute an exception to the rule. As bearing upon these deductions see 1 Am. and Eng. Ency. of Law, 392; *Briggs* v. *Partridge,* 64 N. Y. 362 (21 Am. Rep. 617); *Nicoll* v. *Burk,* 78 N. Y. 583; *New Jersey Steam Navigation Company* v. *Merchants' Bank,* 47 U. S. (6 How.), 380; *Nash* v. *Towne,* 72 U. S. (5 Wall.), 703; *Stowell* v. *Eldred,* 39 Wis. 626; *Chandler* v. *Coe,* 54 N. H. 561; *Ford* v. *Williams,* 62 U. S. (21 How.), 289; *Hunter* v. *Giddings,* 97 Mass. 41 (43 Am. Dec. 54); *Trueman* v. *Loder,* 11 Ad. and E. 589; *Higgins* v. *Senior,* 8 Mees and W. 843; *Calder* v. *Dobell* (Law Rep.), 6 Com. Pleas, 485; Mechem on Agency, §§ 449, 698, 699. If an instrument is valid without a seal, although executed under seal, it is to be treated as written evidence of a simple contract; and the seal adds nothing, except, under our statute, it is made primary evidence of a consideration: *Stowell* v. *Eldred,* 39 Wis. 626; *Byington* v. *Simpson,* 134 Mass. 169 (45 Am. Rep. 314); *Rector of St. David's* v. *Wood,* 24 Or. 404 (34 Pac. 18).

Now, looking to the contract which is the basis of the cause of action under consideration, we find that it was executed in manner and form as requested by the defendant, and to subserve a special purpose peculiar to his own interest, with the express avowal that it should be treated as the contract of plaintiff, although executed in the name of Handsaker the agent. It is further disclosed that both the defendant and the plaintiff afterwards so treated it; the plaintiff proceeding under it, and in obedience with the terms

and conditions thereof in cutting, hauling, and banking
the logs preparatory to delivery, and the defendant by
making payments to him from time to time, sometimes
directly, and sometimes through Handsaker, the agent.
This is ratification, and constitutes a very significent
feature of the inquiry. Aside from this, the contract
discloses upon its face that a part of the consideration
for these logs moved directly from defendant to plaintiff. Under these attendant circumstances, and others
which might be alluded to, we think the court committed no error in admitting the testimony to show
who were the real parties to the contract. as well as
to explain how the clause touching the one thousand
seven hundred dollars came to be placed therein.
The admission of the parol evidence touching this
clause may be upheld as being explanatory of the
consideration which in part supports the contract.

4. The court instructed the jury, among other
things. that "the plaintiff must make out his case by
a preponderance of the evidence; the defendant must
make out his case by a preponderance of the evidence;
that is. each must make out the better case on what
he claims the other owes him," and the defendant requested the court to supplement said instruction with
the following: "But before plaintiff can recover on the
first cause of action set up in his complaint he must
establish that he is the real party in interest by clear
and satisfactory evidence." This request the court refused, and such refusal is assigned as error. We
think the court's action in this regard is not open to
objection. There is nothing in the case to take it out
of the ordinary rule that each party must make out
his case, whenever the burden of proof is cast upon
him, by a preponderance of the testimony. To establish that a party to the action is the real party in

interest requires no higher or superior proof than to establish any other fact in the case. The additional instruction asked would require this and was therefore properly refused.

There are some other questions presented by defendant in his brief and at the argument. These we do not deem it necessary nor profitable to discuss in detail, but suffice it to say we have carefully examined them all, and find no prejudicial error.

AFFIRMED.

Argued December 12, 1895; decided February 8, 1896; rehearing denied.

ARMENT *v.* YAMHILL COUNTY.
[43 Pac. 653.]

1. RULE FOR CONSTRUING CONTRACTS.— Written contracts should be considered from the standpoint of the parties when they were contracting, and be so construed as to give effect to all the provisions, if possible, always prefering that construction which makes the agreement legal rather than one which will make it void: *Hildebrand* v. *Bloodsworth*, 12 Or. 80, approved and followed.

2. CONSTRUCTION OF CONTRACT WITH COUNTY.—A contract with county commissioners for plats and lists of taxable real estate within the county provided that, as a "consideration," fifty dollars was to be paid on their delivery; that in addition thereto the contractors were to receive "for compensation," (1) "An amount equal to the levy of the total tax of eighteen hundred and ninety on all such taxable real estate as shall be found unassessed," etc., and (2) "an amount equal to one half of the levy * * * of the year eighteen hundred and ninety-one," etc., payment "to be made from month to month, as the said tax shall have been collected by the sheriff of said county, and placed to the credit" of the contractors. *Held*, that the additional consideration provided was not for the payment absolutely of amounts equivalent to the designated parts of the levies of eighteen hundred and ninety and eighteen hundred and ninety-one, but for the payment of the designated part of such levies actually collected by the sheriff, payable from month to month, as collected.

APPEAL from Marion: GEORGE H. BURNETT, Judge.

This is an action to recover upon the following contract as modified after the date of its execution by the parties thereto, namely, "This agreement made and entered into this eighth day of January, A. D. one thousand eight hundred and ninety-one, by and between the county commissioners of Yamhill County, State of Oregon, in regular session assembled, parties of the first part, for and in behalf of said County of Yamhill, State of Oregon, and W. T. Shurtleff, J. A. Arment, and Paul A. Ozanne, parties of the second part,—*Witnesseth:* That whereas said parties of the second part have submitted to the commissioners of said county a proposition to furnish said county a list of all the taxable real property lying within its boundaries, and also precinct plats showing the separate tracts and individual ownership thereof, as disclosed by the records of said county; and whereas said proposition of the parties of the second part has this day been accepted, ratified, and approved by said commissioners, for and in behalf of said County of Yamhill, State of Oregon. Now, therefore, be it known that the conditions of this agreement to which we, the parties of the first part, for and in behalf of said county, and we, the parties of the second part, are held and firmly bound, are as follows, to wit: *first,* the said parties of the second part, for and in consideration of the sum of fifty dollars, and in further consideration of the conditions hereinafter mentioned, hereby agree to furnish said county precinct plats of all the taxable real property lying within the boundaries of said county, as at present subdivided into precincts, said precinct plats to show the individual ownership of all the taxable real property lying therein, as disclosed by the records of said county at the date of the delivery thereof; said precinct maps not to include the plat of any town or towns lying therein; *second,* said parties of the second part further agree to furnish

said county with a list or roll of all said taxable real
property lying within said county, and showing the
individual tracts and ownership of the same as disclosed by said precinct plats; said rollbook and indices to same to be furnished by said county; *third,* said
list or roll above mentioned to contain a sufficient
description of the real property therein described
so that tax deeds may readily be drawn from said
descriptions, if found necessary; *fourth,* said precinct
plats and roll to be delivered on or before the first
day of September, eighteen hundred and ninety-one:
fifth, the parties of the second part, in addition to the
consideration first above mentioned, are to receive for
compensation for such services the following, to wit:
first. an amount equal to the levy of the total tax of
eighteen hundred and ninety on all such taxable real
property as shall be found unassessed on or after this
date, whether found by the said parties of the second
part or otherwise, the usual fee allowed the sheriff of
said county for the collection of said tax to be deducted therefrom; *second,* an amount equal to one half
of the levy of the total tax of eighteen hundred and
ninety-one, as made by the County Court of Yamhill
County for county purposes, less one half of the usual
fee allowed the sheriff of said county for the collection of said tax; *third,* the parties of the second part
shall further be entitled to receive an amount equal
to one half of all the collectible taxes in arrears for
the five years preceding the year eighteen hundred
and ninety, upon all such property as shall hereafter
be found unassessed; * * * *sixth,* the asssessment
upon all real property hereafter found unassessed shall
be fairly and equitably made; *seventh,* the fifty dollars
first above mentioned shall be paid to second party
upon the delivery of said precinct plats and assess-

ment roll, and the remaining payments to be made from month to month as the said tax shall have been collected by the sheriff of said county, and placed to the credit of said parties of the second part." On March thirteenth, eighteen hundred and ninety-one, this contract was modified by substituting township for precinct maps. On September fifteenth the time for completing the maps and roll was extended to October first, eighteen hundred and ninety-one, and thereafter clause numbered "third" was stricken out. In other respects the contract sued upon remained as executed.

It appears from the complaint that the plaintiffs found unassessed sixty-five thousand four hundred and seventy-one acres of real property and numerous city and town lots within the county, which the sheriff afterwards assessed for the year eighteen hundred and ninety at two hundred and seventy-nine thousand three hundred and sixty-six dollars. The tax levy for the year named was twenty-two mills on the dollar, which would produce six thousand one hundred and forty-six dollars and five cents. Deducting the sheriff's fees, one hundred and thirty-three dollars and thirty-one cents, there would remain a balance of six thousand and twelve dollars and seventy-four cents. Of this tax so levied the sheriff has collected about one thousand two hundred dollars, the exact amount of which is unknown to plaintiffs. The plaintiffs have been paid out of the general funds of the county two thousand and twenty-two dollars and ninety-four cents, leaving a balance due them on this account of three thousand nine hundred and eighty-nine dollars and eighty cents. The tax levy for county purposes for the year eighteen hundred and ninety-one was four and ninety-eight hundredths mills on the dollar, and the entire levy upon such unassessed lands and town lots was one thousand three hundred and ninety-one dollars and twenty-four cents, one half of which, after deducting the usual fee allowed the sheriff, amounts to six hundred and eighty-eight dollars and sixty-seven cents. Of this three hundred and eighty-five dollars and thirty cents has been paid by the county, leaving a balance due from this source of three hundred and three dollars and thirty-seven cents. It is alleged that about March ——, eighteen hundred and ninety-two, the defendant and said sheriff ceased all further efforts to collect the tax levied upon said assessments, and that Shurtleff had assigned his interest in the contract to plaintiffs. The prayer is for judgment against defendant for four thousand two hundred and ninety-three dollars and seventeen cents, and costs and disbursements. The complaint contains other allegations pertinent to the cause, but the foregoing statement of the facts is sufficient, under the view we take of the contract, to give the reader a proper understanding of the opinion. A demurrer was interposed, which being sustained, judgment was entered dismissing the complaint, from which plaintiffs appeals.   AFFIRMED.

For appellants there was briefs by *Messrs. Irvine and Coshow,* and *Durham, Platt and Platt,* with oral arguments by *Messrs. O. P. Coshow* and *Robert Treat Platt.*

For respondent there was a brief by *Messrs. James McCain,* district attorney, and *Ramsey and Fenton,* with an oral argument by *Mr. W. M. Ramsey.*

Opinion by MR. JUSTICE WOLVERTON.

1. The contract which we are called upon to construe was certainly not drawn by the hand of an adept

in the business, as, without its modification, it would seem the draughtsman had been peculiarly felicitous in stating as much of what was not wanted to be stated as that which was pertinent. Even in its present condition plaintiffs are not claiming under it as its literal interpretation would seem to import. But, like all other contracts in writing, this must be construed by taking it at the four corners and looking through the whole instrument from the identical standpoint of the contracting parties when it was entered into, and that construction must be given it, if possible, which will give effect to all its parts and carry out the obvious intention of the parties, and which will make the contract legal, rather than one that will render it void: *Hildebrand* v. *Bloodsworth*, 12 Or 80 (6 Pac. 233); 2 Parsons on Contracts, 500, 505.

2. The parties differ widely as to the proper interpretation of those provisions of the agreement touching the nature and amount of the additional consideration, and the time and manner of its payment by the county. The plaintiffs contend that the "first," "second," and "third," clauses read in connection the "seventh," determines the measure of the additional consideration to be an amount equal to the levy of the total tax of eighteen hundred and ninety on all such taxable real property as should be found unassessed on or after the date of the contract, plus an amount equal to one half of the levy of the total tax of eighteen hundred and ninety-one for county purposes only, upon such taxable real property, less the usual fee allowed the sheriff for collection, and that in effect the county obligated itself to pay these amounts absolutely, at the expiration of a reasonable time within which to make the collections; in other

words, that the county incurred an absolute liability
by entering into said contract, upon its performance
by plaintiffs, to pay under the "first" clause six thousand and twelve dollars and seventy-four cents, and
under the "second" the sum of six hundred and
eighty-eight dollars and sixty-seven cents, all which
was payable unconditionally at the expiration of a reasonable time within which to collect the sums named
from the taxpayers. Upon the other hand, the defendant claims that the additional consideration which
the plaintiffs were to receive was made conditional,
and depended upon the collection of the taxes designated, that the identical money (taxes) collected
should be placed to the credit of plaintiffs, and paid
to them from month to month, and none other, and
that the liability of defendant is commensurate only
with the amount of such taxes actually collected. So
we are to extract from this contract the nature and
amount of the additional consideration provided for,
and the time and manner of its payment. The nature
and amount of such consideration is the pivotal question, the time and manner of payments are but incidents thereto, yet the provisions of the contract
touching the latter are of vital force in determining
the former. It will be unnecessary to make a critical
analysis of the contract, as the controversy, thus nar-
rowed, must be determined by the effect of a few
controlling elements, considered from the standpoint
of the parties at the time of its execution.

The duties of sheriff as tax collector are well
known. He is in no way subject to the control and
direction of the county court in the exercise of such
duties, and can in no way be affected by its actions
touching the assessment of omitted property and the
collection of taxes, except as its exercise of discre-

tionary powers touching settlements with that officer upon his return of the tax rolls, and at the annual accounting required in July of each year, may incidentally affect him. As tax collector he is not an officer of the court to execute its orders and mandates, but is simply accountable under the statute and upon his official bond, as other officers known to the law. By clause "sixth" the county has stipulated that "the assessment upon all real property hereafter found unassessed shall be fairly and equitably made." Thus far it vouches for the acts of the tax collector, that the assessment when made by him shall be fair and equitable, otherwise it does not undertake that his duties shall be faithfully performed, and especially is it true that the county does not undertake that he shall collect the whole tax to be levied. Taxes of the kind contemplated by the contract, state, county, and school, and especially the county tax, are the funds and property of the county in which they are levied: *Hume* v. *Kelly,* 28 Or. 398 (43 Pac. 380). Now, in the light of these conditions, it was stipulated, in contradistinction to the consideration of fifty dollars, which was to be paid absolutely upon the delivery of the plats and assessment roll, that the parties of the second part are to receive for compensation in addition to the fifty-dollar payment, "first, an amount equal to the levy of the total tax of eighteen hundred and ninety on all such taxable real property as shall be found unassessed * * * the usual fee allowed the sheriff of said county for the collection of said tax to be deducted therefrom"; and "second, an amount equal to one half of the levy," etc., of the year eighteen hundred and ninety one for county purposes, with the same provision as to the "usual fee allowed the sher-

28 OR.—34.

iff." Then comes a stipulation for the payment of
these equivalent amounts, which is "to be made from
month to month as the said tax shall have been collected by the sheriff of said county, and placed to the
credit of said parties of the second part." We think
a reasonable deduction to be drawn from all this is
that the additional consideration which the plaintiffs
were to receive was made contingent and conditional
upon the sheriff making collection of the taxes named,
which should constitute a fund to be set aside by the
county for their benefit, and should be paid to them
from month to month as collected. If the contract
does not mean this, why make and sustain the distinction all the way through between the two kinds of
consideration, and why provide for the collection, setting aside, and payment of a special fund to the plaintiffs? It would have been a simply and easy matter
to have provided directly just what the consideration
should be. Not having done this, it is but a reasonable inference that no absolute consideration was intended, aside from the fifty dollars named. Under this
construction of the contract stipulation, *Noland* v. *Bull*,
24 Or. 479, (23 Pac. 983,) and other authorities of like
tenor relied upon by plaintiffs can have no application.
The doctrine there established is that "where there is
a present indebtedness due absolutely, and the hap-
pening of some future event is fixed for a convenient
time for payment merely, and such future event does
not happen, the debt is payable within a reasonable
time." Here there is no present or absolute indebtedness; indeed, no debt aside from the fifty dollars was
contemplated, but provisions were made looking to the
creation of a fund to be paid to plaintiffs as it accum-
ulated, and to which they were to look solely for compensation, aside from the consideration first named in

the contract. Viewed in the light of this construction
of the agreement, the complaint shows upon its face
that plaintiffs have been paid even more than they
were entitled to, and hence the judgment of the court
below will be affirmed.   AFFIRMED.

Argued December 18, 1895; decided February 8, 1896.

LEICK v. BEERS.
[43 Pac. 658.]

1. NOTICE OF MECHANICS' LIEN—CODE, § 3673.—A claim for a mechanics'
lien reciting that claimant "have, by virtue of a contract heretofore
made with B., * * * in the furnishing sketches, plans, * * *
and superintendence of a certain dwelling-house. The ground on
which said dwelling house was constructed being at the time the
property of said B., who caused said house to be constructed,"—is
insufficient, for failure to state the person to whom the services were
rendered, as required by the Code: *Dillon* v. *Hart*, 25 Or. 49, approved
and followed.

2. COSTS—DISCRETION OF COURT.—It is within the discretion of the trial
court under Hill's Code, § 543, to refuse costs to either party in a
suit in equity: *Lovejoy* v. *Chapman*, 23 Or. 571; *Cole* v. *Logan*, 24 Or.
305, approved and followed.

This is a suit to foreclose a mechanics' lien for the
services of plaintiff as architect in the construction of
a dwelling-house. The plaintiff was employed by and
rendered the services to Mr. and Mrs. C. W. Beers, but
the building was erected upon land owned by the investment company for which Mrs. Beers had a bond
for a deed. Mr. Beers had no interest in the building
or real estate upon which it was erected other than
as husband of the obligee in the bond from the investment company, but he signed the contract for the
erection of the building, and acted in reference thereto
as if he was the owner, and the referee and court
below found that he was the reputed owner thereof.

The lien claim as filed, so far as material to any question presented on this appeal, is as follows: "Know all men by these presents, that C. W. Leick, of the City of Portland, in the County of Multnomah. Oregon, have, by virtue of a contract heretofore made with C. W. Beers, of the County of Multnomah, Oregon, in the furnishing sketches, plans, specifications, details, contract, and superintendence as architect in the construction of a certain dwelling-house. The ground upon which said dwelling-house was constructed being at the time the property of said C. W. Beers, who caused the said house to be constructed, said dwelling-house and land being known and particularly described as follows," etc. There was a decree for defendants, and plaintiff appeals.

AFFIRMED.

For appellant there was an oral argument by *Mr. John H. Woodward.*

For respondent there was an oral argument by *Mr. George H. Williams.*

Opinion by MR. CHIEF JUSTICE BEAN.

1. The court below held the lien insufficient because it states that C. W. Beers was the owner of the property and not the reputed owner thereof, and there is respectable authority to support the ruling: *McElwee* v. *Sandford,* 53 How. Pr. 89; *Malter* v. *Falcon Mining Company,* 2 Pac. 50. But it is unnecessary for us to place our decision upon that ground as the lien is clearly insufficient within *Rankin* v. *Malarkey,* 23 Or. 593, (32 Pac. 620, 34 Pac. 816,) and *Dillon* v. *Hart,* 25 Or. 49 (34 Pac. 817).

2. The refusal of a trial court to allow costs to either party in a suit in equity will not be reviewed here except in case of an abuse of discretion which is not shown in this case: Code, § 543; *Lovejoy* v. *Chapman*, 23 Or. 571 (32 Pac. 687); *Cole* v. *Logan*, 24 Or. 305 (33 Pac. 568). The decree of the court below is affirmed.   AFFIRMED.

<hr>

Decided December 2, 1895; rehearing denied.

WILLAMETTE REAL ESTATE COMPANY *v.* HENDRIX.

[42 Pac. 514.]

1. EXECUTION — COURTS.— In the absence of a statutory provision authorizing an execution to be issued out of the circuit court upon a judgment rendered in the county court, the writ cannot be so issued, and such writ is an absolute nullity.

2. SHERIFF'S DEED AS EVIDENCE — RECITALS.— The recitals in a sheriff's deed of land sold under execution are *prima facie* evidence of the matters recited.

3. VOID JUDGMENT — PUBLICATION OF SUMMONS.— A judgment against a nonresident on service of summons by publication is void, where the record fails to show that the court, prior to the publication, obtained jurisdiction of his property by attachment process.[*]

4. EXTENT TO WHICH A CONFIRMATION CURES INFIRMITIES.— The infirmity of a judgment for want of jurisdiction of the court to render it is not cured by the court's approval of a sheriff's deed of premises sold on an execution thereunder, as a confirmation of an execution sale of real property does not supply defects founded in a want of jurisdiction.

5. ADVERSE POSSESSION.— Claim of ownership of premises, in the absence of occupancy, can never become the foundation of an adverse right.

6. CONSTRUCTIVE POSSESSION.— Entry and occupancy of one of several known lots or tracts conveyed by the same instrument is not constructively an occupancy of all, for the purpose of adverse possession; *Hicklin* v. *McClear*, 18 Or. 126, cited and approved.

[*]The validity of personal judgments rendered upon constructive service of process is the subject of an extensive note to *Moyer* v. *Bucks* (Ind.), 16 L. R. A. 231.—REPORTER.

APPEAL from Washington: T. A. McBRIDE, Judge.

This is a suit by the Willamette Real Estate Company against H. H. Hendrix to quiet the title to lots three, four, five, six, seven, eight, nine, and ten in block twenty-five; lots six, seven, eight, nine, and ten in block twenty-six; blocks thirty-five, thirty-six, and four blocks known as the Courthouse Square, in the town of Cornelius, Oregon. The facts are that on June seventh, eighteen hundred and sixty, the defendant was the owner in fee simple of the following described premises, to wit: "Beginning at a point thirteen and twelve hundredths chains east of the northwest corner of B. Q. Tucker's land claim, in Washington County, Oregon; running thence south forty-five and seventy-five hundredths chains to the base line; thence east thirty chains; thence north forty-five and seventy-five hundredths chains; thence west thirty and sixty hundredths chains to the place of beginning, containing one hundred and forty acres." On the third day of July, eighteen hundred and sixty, the County Court of Washington County, Oregon, rendered judgment in favor of one W. T. Newby against the said defendant, upon his confession, in words and figures as follows, to wit: "In the County Court of the State of Oregon for Washington County. W. T. Newby *versus* H. H. Hendrix--Confession of Judgment. I, H. H. Hendrix, the defendant above named, hereby confess myself indebted to W. T. Newby of Yamhill County, Oregon, in the sum of three hundred and ten dollars, due upon a written contract for the payment of money only. And I hereby further state that the said sum of three hundred and ten dollars is justly due said plaintiff. And I authorize judgment to be entered against me for said sum of three hundred and ten dollars. (Signed) H. H. Hendrix. Dated the seventh day of June, A. D. one thousand eight hundred and sixty. Witnesses: W. D. Hare, Wm. Brown. State of Oregon, County of Washington, *ss.* H. H. Hendrix being duly affirmed, deposes and says that the foregoing confession of judgment is true and correct, and made by him. (Signed) H. H. Hendrix. Subscribed and sworn to before me this seventh day of June, eighteen hundred and sixty. W. D. Hare, Clerk of the County Court." On October twenty-third, eighteen hundred and sixty-one, by consideration of the circuit court of said county, one S. M. Gilmore obtained a judgment against said H. H. Hendrix for eight hundred and ninety dollars and fifty-three cents, in his absence, the service of the summons having been made by publication. On March eighteenth, eighteen hundred and sixty-two, an execution was issued upon the Newby judgment, which recited that: "Whereas on the seventh day of June, eighteen hundred and sixty, by consideration of a confession of judgment in the Circuit Court of the County of Washington in the State of Oregon, W. T. Newby, plaintiff, recovered judgment against H. H. Hendrix, defendant, for the sum of three hundred and sixteen dollars damages and costs, which judgment was enrolled and docketed in the clerk's office of said court on the seventh day of July, eighteen hundred and sixty," and commanded the sheriff of said county to satisfy the same out of the personal property of the defendant, or, if sufficient could not be found, then out of the real property belonging to him in that county. On the same day an execution was also issued on the Gilmore judgment.

The sheriff levied on the real property above described, and other lands of the defendant, under both

writs, and made the following return on the first execution: "Served the within execution by levying upon
the following described real estate (for the want of
personal property) to wit: Lying and being in the
County of Washington, Oregon, and described as follows" (here follows the description of the one hundred and forty-acre tract as above given, and also the
description of another tract known as the H. H. Hendrix Donation Land Claim). "And after duly advertising the same as required by law, as the annexed notice
will show, for sale to the highest bidder, for cash, on
the premises, on Tuesday, the twenty-second day of
April, A. D. one thousand eight hundred and sixty-two,
on which day I proceeded to offer said premises as follows, to wit: The first described piece, and sold the
same to Mrs. Adelia Snelling for the sum of three hundred dollars, she being the highest bidder therefor. I
then proceeded to offer the second described piece, and
sold the same to Mrs. Adelia Snelling for the sum of
one hundred dollars, she being the highest bidder
therefor,—being the sum of four hundred dollars for
the whole of said lands; the interest sold being the
entire interest of said H. H. Hendrix in and to the
same. And I disposed of said proceeds of said sale
as follows: Paid to W. T. Newby the sum of two hundred and eighty-three dollars and seventy-five cents
($283.75), being the principal and interest of this exe-
cution; paid W. D. Hare, clerk, four dollars and seventy-one cents, clerk's fees; paid sheriff's fees, original
costs, seventeen dollars and ten cents; county fee,
three dollars; paid accruing costs, thirty dollars and
fifty-five cents; leaving in my hands the sum of sixty-
three dollars and eighty-five cents to apply on an execution in my hands, issued out of the circuit court in
favor of W. T. Newby, assignee of S. M. Gilmore *versus*

H. H. Hendrix, to pay the costs of the same,—leaving the sum of forty-five dollars and ninety-two cents due on this execution April twenty-second, eighteen hundred and sixty-two. (Signed) R. E. Wiley, Sheriff of Washington County." Said officer indorsed on the second execution the following return: "Served this execution by applying thereon the sum of sixty-three dollars and eighty-five cents, proceeds of the sale of lands, on an execution in favor of W. T. Newby *versus* H. H. Hendrix, upon which this execution was levied by order of plaintiff, and the land advertised. I disposed of the said sums as follows, to wit: Paid clerk's fees, four dollars and sixty-five cents; sheriff's original, seven dollars and sixty-five cents; county, five dollars; advertising, sixteen dollars; paid accruing costs, thirty dollars and fifty cents. (Signed) R. E. Wiley, Sheriff of Washington County." On October twelfth, eighteen hundred and sixty-three, the sheriff executed to the said purchaser, Adelia Snelling, a deed, wherein he recited that the premises therein described had been levied on and sold to her in pursuance of an execution issued out of the circuit court in the case of *Gilmore* v. *Hendrix,* and by virtue of an execution issued out of the county court in the case *Newby* v. *Hendrix.* The following indorsement appears on said deed: "State of Oregon, County of Washington, *ss.* No irregularity in the proceedings concerning the sale within recited appearing, this deed is approved in open court this thirteenth day of October, A. D. one thousand eight hundred and sixty-three. Erasmus D. Shattuck, Judge of the Circuit Court."

Adelia Snelling having died intestate, one Wheelock Simmons was appointed administrator of her estate, who, on July fifteenth, eighteen hundred and sixty-six, in pursuance of an administrator's sale of

the decedant's real property, executed to one Stephen
Sell a deed to the premises so purchased from the
sheriff. On April seventeenth, eighteen hundred and
seventy-one, Sell and wife by deed conveyed the same
premises to one William L. Halsey, who established
and platted the townsite of Cornelius thereon, and,
having dedicated the streets to the public, on September twenty-second of that year filed a plat thereof
for record. On December fifth, eighteen hundred and
seventy-two, Halsey and wife by deed conveyed the
lots and blocks first above described, together with
other lots and blocks in the town of Cornelius, to the
plaintiff, who immediately removed the fences which
inclosed the premises so platted into lots and blocks.
In December, eighteen hundred and ninety-one, the
defendant commenced to inclose the land in controversy, and, refusing to desist when so ordered, this
suit was instituted. The plaintiff alleges in its complaint that it is the owner in fee and in the possession
of the premises, and that it had been in the continued
adverse possession thereof for a period of more than
ten years prior to the commencement of the suit, and
prays that the defendant be required to set forth any
title that he may claim therein; that he be decreed to
have no title to said premises, and that plaintiff has a
valid title thereto. The defendant, after denying the
material allegations of the complaint, alleges that he
is the owner and in possession of the premises, and
sets out the source and muniments of his title; that
the plaintiff is asserting some title thereto, but that
its conveyances and claim based thereon constitute a
cloud on his title which he prays may be removed.
The reply having put in issue the allegations of new
matter contained in the answer, the case was referred
to C. E. Runyon, who took and reported the evidence,

from which the court below found that the equities
were with the defendant, and, having rendered a decree as prayed for in the answer, the plaintiff appeals.

AFFIRMED.

For appellant there was a brief and an oral argument by *Mr. Albert H. Tanner.*

For respondent there were briefs and oral arguments by *Messrs. Thomas H. Tongue* and *S. B. Huston.*

Opinion by MR. JUSTICE MOORE.

1. It is contended by plaintiff that the county
court, being a court of record, and invested with civil
jurisdiction to be defined, limited and regulated by
law, not exceeding the amount of five hundred dollars,
(Constitution of Oregon, Article VII, §§ 1, 12,) was
further invested by an act of the legislative assembly,
approved June fourth, eighteen hundred and fifty-nine,
(Laws, 1859, p. 9,) with authority to enter on the defendant's confession a judgment which should not be
subject to review in a collateral suit.   Conceding without deciding that the county court had such authority,
we will examine the foundation of plaintiff's alleged
title, namely, the judgment, execution, sale, and deed:
McRae v. *Daviner,* 8 Or. 63; *Faull* v. *Cooke,* 19 Or. 455 (20
Am. St. Rep. 836, 26 Pac. 662); *Cloud* v. *El Dorado County,*
12 Cal. 128 (73 Am. Dec. 526); *Clark* v. *Lockwood,* 21 Cal.
220; *Blood* v. *Light,* 38 Cal. 649 (99 Am. Dec. 441).   The
sheriff's return shows that the real property was sold
upon an execution issued out of the circuit court on a
judgment by confession rendered in the county court.
Every court has the inherent right to control its own
process, and, unless authorized by law, no other court
can interfere with such right: *Harris* v. *Cornell,* 80 Ill.

54. There being no statutory provision authorizing the clerk of the circuit court to issue an execution out of that court upon a judgment rendered in the county court, the writ so issued must be regarded as an absolute nullity: 1 Freeman on Executions, § 15; *Chandler* v. *Colcord,* 1 Okl. 260 (32 Pac. 330).

2. The defendant insists that, the Gilmore judgment having been rendered in the circuit court on a service of summons by publication, no jurisdiction of the person was obtained, and, the record introduced in evidence failing to show that the land had been attached so as to render a judgment given in the action *quasi in rem,* no jurisdiction of the subject matter was acquired, and hence the judgment is void; while the plaintiff contends that the court rendering the judgment being one of general jurisdiction, and the record being silent, it must be presumed from the judgment that the court complied with every statutory requirement, and thereby obtained jurisdiction. The sheriff's return indorsed on the execution issued on this judgment discloses that the property was levied upon by virtue thereof, and advertised for sale; but it does not show that any sale was made in obedience to its commands. "While," says BALDWIN, J., in *Cloud* v. *El Dorado County,* 12 Cal. 128, (73 Am. Dec. 526,) "it is undoubtedly the duty of the sheriff to make this return, and while it is important as evidence of a permanent and authentic character that he should do so, the title of the purchaser does not depend upon his performance of this duty. The purchaser has no control over the conduct of the officer in this respect; nor is it just or reasonable that he should be responsible for the remissness or negligence of the sheriff in the discharge of such an office." This doctrine was

affirmed in *Clark* v. *Lockwood*, 21 Cal. 220; *Blood* v. *Light*, 38 Cal. 649, (99 Am. Dec. 441,) and lastly in *Frink* v. *Roe*, 70 Cal. 296 (11 Pac. 820). If the necessary preceding steps have all been properly taken, a sheriff's deed is evidence of title in the grantee, and the recitals therein are *prima facie* evidence of the facts recited: *Dolph* v. *Barney*, 5 Or. 191. "A sale," says Mr. Freeman in his work on Executions, volume 2, § 325, "may be made under several writs. Some of these writs may be valid, and the others void. If either of the writs under which a sale is made is valid, the officer has the power to sell, and consequently the power to convey. If in his deed he recites several writs, some of which are valid and some void, the recital of the void writs may be treated as surplusage, and the deed, being supported by the valid writ, and the power to sell and convey thereby conferred, is as effective as if all the writs were unobjectionable."

3.   The sheriff's deed being *prima facie* evidence of title in plaintiff's grantors, the question is presented whether the judgment rendered in the case of *Gilmore* v. *Hendrix*, upon which the deed must rest for its foundation, is valid, or at least not vulnerable to collateral attack. The judgment in this case is as follows: "S. M. Gilmore *versus* H. H. Hendrix.   And now on this day comes the plaintiff, by M. McBride, his attorney, and the said plaintiff files affidavit of publication of notice of the pendency of this suit, to wit (here insert), in accordance with the order of this court made at the May term thereof, eighteen hundred and sixty-one; and said defendant, being called, comes not, but makes default. It is therefore ordered by the court that the default of the defendant be entered. And it appearing to the court that this suit is founded upon

a promissory note for the payment of money only, and
that there is now due and owing from the said defendant thereon to the said plaintiff the sum of eight
hundred and ninety dollars and fifty-three cents; it is
therefore considered and adjudged by the court that
the plaintiff have and recover off and from said defendant the sum of eight hundred and ninety dollars
and fifty-three cents, together with his costs to be
taxed, and that he have execution therefor." It appears from this record that the defendant was a nonresident of the state, and, not appearing or answering,
the court acquired no jurisdiction to render a judgment *in personam* on the service of a summons by publication; and hence the authority to render the judgment, so as to become *quasi in rem*, must depend on the
court's having obtained jurisdiction of the defendant's
property by some legal process, before any order
could be made authorizing the service of a summons
by publication: *Pennoyer* v. *Neff*, 95 U. S. 714; *Goodale* v.
Coffee, 24 Or. 346 (33 Pac. 990). The statute in force
at the time of the rendition of the judgment contained
ample provisions for and prescribed the mode of attaching the defendant's property to satisfy any judgment which might be rendered against it: Statute 1855,
§ 119, *et seq.* It will be observed that the judgment
contains no recital of the defendant's property being
attached, and no other evidence thereof having been
introduced, can it be presumed that the court obtained
jurisdiction of the subject matter? "The jurisdiction,"
says Mr. Freeman in his work on Judgments, volume
1, § 123, "exercised by courts of record is, in many
cases, dependent upon special statutes conferring an
authority in derogation of the common law, and speci-
fying the manner in which such authority shall be
employed. The decided preponderance of adjudged

cases upon the subject establishes the rule that judgments arising from the exercise of this jurisdiction are to be regarded in no other light, and supported by no other presumptions, than judgments pronounced in courts not of record. The particular state of facts necessary to confer jurisdiction will not be presumed; and if such facts do not appear, the judgment will be treated as void." It is needless to cite further authority in support of this proposition, for the rule has been already settled in this court that whenever a mode of acquiring jurisdiction, not in accordance with the general course of the common law, has been prescribed by statutes, that mode must be strictly followed, and the authority for rendering the judgment in pursuance thereof must affirmatively appear on the face of the record: *Northcut* v. *Lemery,* 8 Or. 316; *Odell* v. *Campbell,* 9 Or. 298. From the failure to prove that the defendant's property had been attached it follows that jurisdiction of the subject matter was not acquired, and the judgment rendered in the case of *Gilmore* v. *Hendrix* is consequently void.

4. The deed recites that the premises were sold on execution issued from the county court, and this, under the authority heretofore cited, is *prima facie* evidence of the fact, but such recital could not prevail here, in the face of a copy of the execution in evidence from which it appears that the writ purports to have been issued from the circuit court. Nor could the court's approval of the sheriff's deed cure the infirmities of the judgment, for a confirmation of an execution sale of real property is a determination of the regularity of the proceedings under the writ only, and supplies all defects except those founded in a want of

jurisdiction: Rorer on Judicial Sales, § 123; *Leinenweber* v. *Brown*, 24 Or. 548 (34 Pac. 475).

5. It is contended that the plaintiff and its predecessors in interest had been in the adverse possession of the premises in controversy, under a claim of ownership, for a period of more than ten years immediately preceding the commencement of this suit. and that, the statute of limitations having run in its favor, the defendant's right of entry was barred. The evidence shows that the one hundred and forty acre tract was inclosed at the time the sheriff's deed was executed, October twelfth, eighteen hundred and sixty-three, and that a portion of the land was cultivated from that time until the plaintiff received its deed. December fifth, eighteen hundred and seventy-two, and removed the fence from that part of the tract embraced in the townsite of Cornelius; that from eighteen hundred and seventy-two to the commencement of this suit the premises in controversy remained open and uninclosed, during which time there was no visible evidence of any claim of ownership on the part of any one; but that the plaintiff appointed persons living at Cornelius to act as its agent, paid the taxes annually assessed on the property most of the time. and sold and conveyed other lots to persons who in some instances erected buildings thereon. From this evidence it is clear that no adverse title had been acquired by plaintiff's predecessors at the time it received its deed. "The legal title," says THAYER, J., in *Swift* v. *Mulkey*, 14 Or. 64 (12 Pac. 76), "draws after it the possession, and a right of entry is not barred, unless there has been a disseisin followed by an actual, open, notorious, and continuous adverse possession for the period of ten years next prior to the

commencement of the action.   To be an adverse possession it must be an occupancy under a claim of ownership, though it need not be under color of title." Adverse possession depends upon the intent of the occupant to claim and hold real property in opposition to all the world, and this intent is to be inferred from proof of the occupancy: *Rowland* v. *Williams,* 23 Or. 515 (32 Pac. 402). It must be admitted that the plaintiff claimed title to the *locus in quo;* but, never having occupied any portion of the premises, its claim of ownership, in the absence of occupancy, can never become the foundation of an adverse right. In *Curtis* v. *La Grande Water Company,* 20 Or. 34 (10 L. R. A. 484, 25 Pac. 373), LORD, J., in commenting upon the character of such occupancy, says: "To effect that result, the possession taken must be open, hostile, and continuous; 'he must unfurl his flag on the land, and keep it flying, so that the owner may see, if he will, that an enemy has invaded his domains, and planted the standard of conquest.'" Tested by this rule there is nothing to show that the plaintiff ever did anything on the land to notify the defendant that it had invaded the premises in dispute.

6.   True, the deed of Halsey and wife described the property as lots and blocks in the town of Cornelius, but adverse possession of it cannot be predicated upon the occupancy of some lot therein by a grantee of the plaintiff.   When the premises consist of several known lots or tracts, and are conveyed by the same instrument, each is distinct, and an entry and occupancy of one under color of title is not constructively an occupancy of all: *Wilson* v. *McEwan,* 7 Or. 87; *Hicklin* v. *McClear,* 18 Or. 126 (22 Pac. 1057); *Stewart*

28 OR.—35.

v. *Harris,* 9 Humph. 714; *Bailey* v. *Carleton,* 12 N. H. 9
(37 Am. Dec. 190); *Denham* v. *Holeman,* 26 Ga. 182 (71
Am. Dec. 198); *Carson* v. *Burnett,* 1 Div. and Bat. L. 546
(30 Am. Dec. 143). Plaintiff not having acquired any
title by its deed, and there being no evidence of its
occupancy of the premises, it follows that the decree
must be affirmed.   AFFIRMED.

Argued December 2, 1895; decided January 27, 1896; rehearing denied.

STATE ex rel. *v.* LORD.*
[43 Pac. 471.]

1. INJUNCTION AT SUIT OF PRIVATE CITIZEN AGAINST PUBLIC OFFICERS.—A
private individual cannot have public officers enjoined from using
public funds unless some personal, civil, or property rights are being
invaded, or, in other words, unless such individual will be himself
injuriously affected by the proposed expenditure: *State* v. *Pennoyer,*
26 Or. 205, approved and followed.

2. INJUNCTION BY STATE AGAINST PUBLIC OFFICERS.—The state, when suing in its corporate capacity for the protection of its property rights,
stands in no different or better position than an individual in respect
to an injunction against public officers: *White* v. *Commissioners of
Multnomah County,* 13 Or. 317; distinguished.

3. ACTION AGAINST PUBLIC OFFICIALS IN MATTERS OF PUBLIC CONCERN.—
In cases of purely public concern affecting the welfare of the whole
people or the state at large the action of a court can be invoked only
by such executive officers of the state as are by law intrusted with
the discharge of such duties.

4. INJUNCTION AGAINST OFFICIAL PERFORMING GOVERNMENTAL DUTIES.†—
The location of a site for a public institution, the purchase of a tract
of land therefor at that place, the employment of an architect to

* This case was originally before the supreme court as *State* v. *Pennoyer,* 26
Or. 205 (25 L. R. A. 862; 37 Pac. 906), before the present governor succeeded Syl-
vester Pennoyer. After reversal the newly installed state officers were substituted
as defendants for those who had retired, and the case proceeded under the present title. The third opinion in the case will be found in 29 Or. ——.—REPORTER.

† For denial of injunction to restrain governmental or political action merely
because unconstitutional, see also *Fletcher* v. *Tuttle,* (Ill.), 25 L. R. A. 143, and
note; *State* v. *Pennoyer* (Or.), 25 L. R. A. 862; *Green* v. *Mills,* (Cir. Ct. App. 4th Cir.),
30 L. R. A. 90. But see also on the other hand *McCullough* v. *Brown,* (S. C.), 23 L.
R. A. 410, and *State* v. *Cunningham,* (Wis.), 17 L. R. A. 145.—REPORTER.

draw plans, etc., for the building, and the letting of contracts therefor by the governor, are matters governmental and executive in their nature, with which the courts cannot interfere by injunction; for it is now settled by a general consensus of authorities that in the execution of duties the performance of which requires the exercise of judgment or discretion, or in political or governmental matters pertaining to and affecting the welfare of the whole people, the executive is not subject to control by the courts. Nor is this rule in anywise changed by the fact that such duties have been delegated to a commission, of which the governor is a member.

5. INFORMATION BY ATTORNEY-GENERAL — PREROGATIVE WRIT.—The mere signature of the attorney-general or other public law officer, in his official capacity, to a complaint or bill shown to be that of a private relator, is not sufficient to impress it with the functions and capacity of an information competent to put in motion the machinery of the courts, whereby they will take cognizance of questions pertaining to the high prerogative powers of the state or affecting the whole people in their sovereign capacity.

6. CONSTITUTIONAL LAW — PRACTICE.—Courts will not pass upon constitutional questions unless they are necessary to the determination of a cause: *Elliott* v. *Oliver*, 22 Or. 47, approved and followed.

7. JURISDICTION OF EQUITY.—A court of equity will not assume to determine the constitutionality of a legislative act unless the case comes within some recognized ground of equity jurisdiction, and presents some actual or threatened infringement of the rights of property on account of such unconstitutional legislation.

APPEAL from Marion: H. H. HEWITT, Judge.

This is a suit to enjoin the defendants William P. Lord, H. R. Kincaid, and Philip Metschan, in their capacity as a state board of commissioners of public buildings, from carrying into effect certain acts of the legislative assembly providing for the construction of a branch asylum in the eastern portion of the state, and appropriating money therefor, because of the alleged unconstitutionality of the portions thereof locating such asylum in eastern Oregon. The amended complaint, omitting the caption and formal parts, alleges: "That the relator herein, A. C. Taylor, in connection with other citizens of the State of Oregon, is

a resident taxpayer within said state, and owns property within said state subject to taxation therein;
that the defendants William P. Lord, H. R. Kincaid,
and Philip Metschan are, in the order in which their
names appear in this amended complaint, the Governor,
Secretary of State, and State Treasurer of the State
of Oregon, and as such constitute the board of commissioners of public buildings for said State of Oregon,
and as such board are bound to expend large sums
of the moneys of plaintiff, to be raised by taxation,
for the purposes hereinafter more fully stated, which
expenditures the plaintiff alleges are unlawful and re
pugnant to the organic law of the State of Oregon,
namely: The members of said board, by virtue of the
powers vested in them as such board, are about to
expend large sums of money belonging to the plaintiff
in the purchase of lands at some point east of the
Cascade Mountains for the purpose of constructing
what is alleged to be a branch asylum in the eastern
portion of said state, as one of the public institutions
of the state, which said acts of the defendants aforesaid they claim to exercise under and by virtue of a
so-called act of the legislative assembly of the said
state purporting to have been passed by said legislature at the seventeenth biennial session thereof,
which said act was filed in the office of the secretary
of state on the twenty-first day of February, eighteen
hundred and ninety-three.

"That of the aforesaid moneys of the plaintiff said
defendants propose to, and, unless restrained by this
honorable court, will, expend of the moneys of the
plaintiff then claimed to have been appropriated, and
also subsequently appropriated by the eighteenth biennial session of said legislature, the sum of one hundred and sixty-five thousand dollars in the construction

of said buildings and fitting the same for use, and for lands on which to erect said buildings.

"That the said defendants, as such board, threaten to and are about to appoint three citizens of the State of Oregon, to be known as supervisors of the work of constructing such buildings, in some of the counties east of the Cascade Mountains, more than three hun- dred miles from the seat of government of said state, which said alleged supervisors are to have charge of the work of constructing such buildings on lands to be purchased and paid for by them of the moneys of the plaintiff, and threaten to and are about to direct said supervisors to expend large sums of money be- longing to the plaintiff aforesaid in advertising for plans and specifications for such buildings, and are about to proceed to construct, in pursuance of said so-called act of said legislature aforesaid, a branch insane asylum and a public institution, together with outbuildings, excavations, and appurtenances thereto, which, in the judgment of said alleged supervisors, may be necessary, under the direction and supervisory control of the defendants hereinbefore named, and are about to expend of moneys of the plaintiff aforesaid the sum of one thousand five hundred dollars to the said so-called supervisors for their alleged services in the construction of said work.

"That the said defendants as such board propose to, and, unless restrained, will, if said buildings are permitted to be constructed and erected, employ a su- perintendent to conduct said institution at a salary of two thousand five hundred dollars per annum, and as- sistant physicians and attendants, all to be allowed the same compensation now fixed by law for like officers and attendants at the state insane asylum at Salem.

"That the said proposed expenditures of the plaintiff's moneys aforesaid, if permitted, would be contrary to law and the constitution of the State of Oregon, in that the said institution is not being constructed at the seat of government of the said state, but more than three hundred miles therefrom; that the expenditures extend to the equipping, furnishing, officering, and maintaining the same, and will greatly increase the burden of taxation, and require the expenditure of one hundred thousand dollars more than would be necessary to expend in the construction of like buildings at the seat of government.

"And the plaintiff further alleges that the annual cost of maintaining the same after it is equipped and ready for use will be fifty thousand dollars per annum more than would be necessary to be expended in maintaining like services for the unfortunate insane of said state, if the same facilities are provided therefor in connection with the institution now in operation at the seat of government.

"That, unless restrained by this honorable court, the defendants will purchase and pay for the lands aforesaid, contract therefor, and build and pay for said building, appoint the supervisors and employ superintendents, physicians, and attendants, upon salaries as aforesaid, all to be paid out of the public funds of the State of Oregon, raised by taxation, thereby greatly increasing plaintiff's burden of taxation, to the great and irreparable injury of plaintiff; that plaintiff has no plain, speedy, or adequate remedy at law for the redress of the grievances herein complained of.

"Wherefore, plaintiff prays that an injunction may issue restraining the defendants and their agents, servants, and attorneys from using the moneys of the plaintiff for any of the purposes which they propose.

as specified in the complaint, and that on final hearing
said injunction be made perpetual, and for such further order or relief as may be meet with equity, and
also for costs and disbursements. James McCain,
district attorney for the third judicial district. H. J.
Bigger and W. H. Holmes, attorneys for plaintiff.

"State of Oregon, County of Marion, *ss.* I, A. C
Taylor, being first duly sworn, say that I am the person commencing the above action as relator for and in
behalf of the State of Oregon; that I have read the
foregoing complaint, and know the contents thereof;
that I believe said complaint to be true. A. C. Taylor. Subscribed and sworn to before me this second
day of March eighteen hundred and ninety-five.
(Seal.) Webster Holmes, Notary Public for Oregon."
The defendants demurred to the complaint upon the
ground that it does not state facts sufficient to constitute a cause of suit, which demurrer was overruled
and the defendants answered. A trial was had upon
the issues thus joined, resulting in a decree in accordance with the prayer of the complaint, from which defendants appeal.   REVERSED.

For appellant there were oral arguments by *Messrs.
William P. Lord, in pro. per.,* and *Julius C. Moreland,* with a
brief by *Messrs. Moreland* and *George G. Bingham,* to this
effect.

An injunction will not lie to control the action or
discretion of the executive. This is an extraordinary
proceeding. The power of the state is invoked to restrain the executive officers of the state from carrying out a plain enactment of the legislature. And
this not because they are invading any private right
of the complainant, but because he alleges such action

would increase in some infinitesimal degree his taxes. The constitution divides the government into three branches, executiye, legislative, and judicial. Each one of these departments is as much bound by the mandates of the constitution as the other. The executive takes as solemn an oath to support the constitution as do the judges. He has quite as much right to interpret the constitution as has any other person. He must interpret the law, and being a coördinate branch of the government, his office created by the same instrument that created this court, his interpretation must be final. The granting of an injunction carries with it the idea of the power to punish for contempt in case of disobedience. While such an occasion will not arise in this case, the decision in this cause will form a precedent, and should be made with this end in view: *People* v. *The Governor,* 29 Mich. 320 (18 Am. Rep. 89); *State* v. *Towns,* 8 Ga. 372; *People* v. *Bissell,* 19 Ill. 233 (68 Am. Dec. 591); *People* v. *Yates,* 40 Ill. 126; *State* v. *Warmoth,* 22 La. Ann. 1 (2 Am. Rep. 712); *Re Dennett,* 32 Me. 508 (54 Am. Dec. 602); *Re Inquiries submitted by Governor,* 58 Mo. 369; *State* v. *The Governor,* 25 N. J. Law, 331; *Jonesboro, Fall Branch, and Blair's Gap Turnpike Company* v. *Brown,* 8 Baxt. 490; *Hawkins* v. *The Governor,* 1 Ark. 570 (33 Am. Dec. 346); *State* v. *Kirkwood,* 14 Iowa, 162.

The president of the United States cannot be restrained by injunction from carrying into effect an act of congress alleged to be unconstitutional, nor will a bill having such a purpose be allowed to be filed: *Mississippi* v. *Johnson,* 71 U. S. (4 Wall.), 475 (18 L. ed. 437.) And it is confidently believed that no case can be found where an executive has ever been enjoined from carrying out a law regularly passed by the legislature.

The court will not grant an injunction, unless the plaintiff proves that he will be damaged. Specula-

tion will not answer the demands of the law: *Gibbs*
v. *Green,* 54 Miss. 612; *Tongue* v. *Gaston,* 10 Or. 328; *State*
v. *Pennoyer,* 26 Or. 205 (25 L. R. A. 862); *Esson* v. *Wat-
tier,* 25 Or. 75.

Contemporaneous construction of a constitutional
provision is always a persuasive authority. When an
act of the legislature has long been recognized as
binding, and when important affairs of the community
affecting individual rights have been transacted in accordance with its provisions, it should not be disturbed, unless it plainly and unequivocally conflicts
with the organic law: *Crawford* v. *Beard,* 12 Or. 452;
Endlich on Interpretation of Statutes, § 527; *Stuart* v.
Laird, 5 U. S. (1 Cranch), 299 (2 L. ed. 115); Cooley on
Constitutional Limitations, pp. 82, 81; *Kelly* v. *Multnomah
County,* 18 Or. 359; *Mitchell* v. *Campbell,* 19 Or. 198; *People*
v. *La Salle County Supervisors,* 100 Ill. 504; *Moers* v. *Reading,* 21 Pa. 188; *Johnson* v. *Joliet and Chicago Railroad Company,* 23 Ill. 207; *People* v. *Dayton,* 55 N. Y. 877; *Rogers* v.
Goodwin, 2 Mass. 478.

For respondent there was an oral argument by *Mr.
H. J. Bigger,* with a brief by *Messrs. Bigger, James McCain,*
district attorney, and *William H. Holmes* urging these
points.

The appellants are acting without authority of
law, and in violation of the constitution of the State
of Oregon, and may be enjoined like other corporate
officers from wasting public funds in doing that which
the law gives them no authority to do, or for proceeding in a manner contrary to that prescribed by
law: *Carman* v. *Woodruff,* 10 Or. 135; *White* v. *Multnomah
County Commissioners,* 3 Or. 317 (57 Am. Rep. 20); *Worm-
ington* v. *Pierce,* 22 Or. 606; *Baker* v. *Payne,* 22 Or. 335;

Rice v. *Smith*, 9 Iowa, 270; *Drake* v. *Phillips*, 40 Ill. 388; *Colton* v. *Hanchett*, 13 Ill. 615; *Webster* v. *Harwinton*, 32 Conn. 131; *Portland and Willamette Valley Railway Company* v. *Portland*, 14 Or. 188 (58 Am. Rep. 299).

The relator need not be the real party, or have any special interest to enforce a public right, but as a voter and citizen he has a general interest in the execution of the law: *State* v. *Ware*, 13 Or. 380. The same rule applies in this case as in an application for mandamus. The relator need show no further interest than that of a citizen interested in having the law enforced or observed, or an unlawful act enjoined: *Pike County Commissioners* v. *People*, 11 Ill. 208; *Hall* v. *People*, 57 Ill. 307; *Glencoe* v. *People*, 78 Ill. 383; *People* v. *Pacheco*, 29 Cal. 212; *Linden* v. *Alameda County Supervisors*, 45 Cal. 7; *Sanger* v. *Kennebec County Commissioners*, 25 Me. 291; *Heffner* v. *Commissioners*, 28 Pa. 108; *People* v. *Regents of University of Michigan*, 4 Mich. 98.

Injunction is the proper, in fact the only, remedy, as the appellants have acted, and purpose and threaten to act, in violation of the constitution and the rights of the people, who have only the remedy of injunction: *State* v. *Judge of Seventh Judicial District Court*, 42 La. Ann. 1104; *Bradley* v. *Powell County Commissioners*, 2 Humph. 428; *Ford* v. *Farmer*, 9 Humph. 157; *Bridgenor* v. *Rodgers*, 1 Coldw. 259; *Marion County* v. *Grundy County*, 5 Sneed, 490; Hilliard on Injunctions, 443; High on Injunctions, §§ 1308, 1319, 1321, 1327.

The inquiry primarily is, is the act sought to be restrained by the injunction one which is purely ministerial; or does it partake of any element of judgment or discretion upon the part of the governor? *Pennoyer* v. *McConnaughy*, 140 U. S. 1 (35 L. ed. 363); *State* v. *Chase*, 5 Ohio St. 528; *Tennessee and Coosa Railroad Company* v. *Moore*, 36 Ala. 371; *Cotton* v. *Ellis*, 7 Jones' L.

545; *State v. Police Jury,* 39 La. Ann. 759; *Groome v. Gwinn,* 43 Md. 572; *Middleton v. Low,* 30 Cal. 597; *Gray v. State,* 72 Ind. 567; *Harpending v. Haight,* 39 Cal. 189 (2 Am. Rep. 432); *Mott v. Pennsylvania Railway Company,* 30 Pa. St. 9 (72 Am. Dec. 664); *State v. Kirkwood,* 14 Iowa, 162; *State v. Blasdel,* 4 Nev. 241; *State v. Whitesides,* 30 S. C. 579 (3 L. R. A. 777); *Greenwood Cemetery Land Company v. Routt,* 17 Colo. 156 (15 L. R. A. 369); Mechem on Public Officers, § 954 *et seq.*; Moses on Mandamus, 80. Counsel for appellants has failed to distinguish between the governor of the state acting in his executive capacity, and his acting in a clerical capacity in the discharge of some duty cast upon him by an act of the legislature: *Pennoyer v. McConnaughy,* 140 U. S. 1 (35 L. ed. 863).

Opinion by MR. JUSTICE WOLVERTON.

1. When this case was here before (*State v. Pennoyer,* 26 Or. 205; 25 L. R. A. 862; 37 Pac. 906), we held that a private individual could not have public officers enjoined from using public funds unless it could be shown that some civil or property rights were being invaded, or, in other words, that the individual was going to get hurt by the transaction. Upon that principle it was decided that he should be required to show that the location and building of the branch asylum in eastern Oregon would be attended with greater cost and expense than if constructed at the capital, thereby increasing the burden of taxation which would be imposed upon him, with others whose duty it is to contribute to the support of the government.

2. It was also held that the state, suing in its corporate capacity for the protection of its property rights, stood in no different or better position in this regard than an individual. This doctrine is supported

by high authority. ALLEN, J., in *People* v. *Canal Board*. 55 N. Y. 395, says: "When the state as plaintiff invokes the aid of a court of equity, it is not exempt from the rules applicable to ordinary suitors; that is, it must establish a case of equitable cognizance, and a right to the peculiar relief demanded." And, as is said by the same eminent jurist in *People* v. *Ingersoll*, 58 N. Y. 14 (17 Am. Rep. 178), "A distinction is to be observed between actions by the people or the state in right of the prerogative incident to sovereignty, and those founded upon some pecuniary interest or proprietary right. The latter are governed by the ordinary rules of law by which rights are determined between individuals." To the same effect is the doctrine announced in *People* v. *Fields*, 58 N. Y. 614. See also 2 High on Injunctions, § 1327. So that we then concluded the plaintiff herein occupied no better or superior position, from a legal standpoint, for enforcing the remedy sought to be invoked than the plaintiff in *Sherman* v. *Bellows*, 24 Or. 553 (34 Pac. 549). From this position we see no sufficient reason for receding, as we believe it to be in sound law, and supported upon reason and authority. It is insisted that the decision in *White* v. *Commissioners*, 13 Or. 317 (58 Am. Rep. 20, 13 Pac. 484), stands in the way of this position, but we do not think so. White had a private interest to subserve in bringing the suit. The increase of the burden of taxation consequent upon maintaining the machinery necessary to secure a registration of voters under the law was sufficient to give him a standing in court to restrain the invasion of a private right: See *Fletcher* v. *Tuttle* and *Blair* v. *Hinrichsen*, 151 Ill. 41 (25 L. R. A. 143; 37 N. E. 683). But the question touching the power of the court to interfere by injunction in restraint of the action of the county commissioners

was not mooted at the hearing, and was not a point
in controversy, although jurisdiction was necessarily
assumed before the ultimate question in the case could
have been decided. So the case is not in point, nor
is it controlling here.

It is stoutly contended that it is shown by the
evidence taken and submitted that the relator will be
damnified by reason of the location and construction
of the branch asylum at the town of Union, under the
rule above established. We have carefully examined
all the testimony found in the record, and are unable
to concur with this view. The whole theory of the
relator, by which he seeks to establish injury, is based
upon the assumption that the legislative and executive
departments of the state will, in the event that the
location and construction of the branch asylum is restrained, provide ways and means for the construction
of such institution upon what is known as the "Cottage Farm," a tract of land now belonging to the
state, and situate some six miles from the capital, and
thereby prevent the necessity of purchasing and acquiring other lands upon which to establish and construct such buildings; that they will utilize in connection therewith certain outbuildings now in use by the
state, and save the expense of constructing other like
buildings; and that, by reason of the proximity of
such location to the present state asylum, they could
dispense with the cost of an additional superintendent,
and some additional physicans and assistants. But
who can say that the legislature would be content to
build the branch asylum at the Cottage Farm, or that
it would see fit to utilize the outbuildings now in use
in connection therewith, or that it would not in any
event provide for the employment of an additional

superintendent, and other physicians and assistants? The matter is of such vital and public concern, and attended with such diverse and dependent circumstances, and so wholly and peculiarly within the province of the legislature to devise the ways and means, that it would be but a conjecture at best to attempt to determine in advance the result of its deliberations in this respect. If the conditions assumed were established, then the question might possibly be capable of demonstration; but where the establishment of these conditions is first left to a body with discretionary powers, the ultimate question for the court to pass upon becomes speculative, and too remote for practical solution and determination. So we are constrained to pass the point without further comment touching the evidence submitted.

3. But it is now contended for the first time that this is a suit by the state in the right of prerogative incident to sovereignty; that it was instituted by the law officer of the state in the interest of the whole people, and being so instituted, the high prerogative powers of government are set in motion, and that the courts of appropriate jurisdiction will take cognizance to control the officers of state from acting in violation of duties imposed upon them by law, and more especially where they sustain trust relations to the whole people,—not in the sense that a public office is a public trust, but as it pertains to the public funds of the people, raised by taxation, and intrusted to their management and control under the laws of the state. Under the common law suit was instituted in behalf of the Crown, or of those who partook of its prerogative, by the attorney-general, who made his complaint to the court purely by way of information. A private

person having cause to complain in a court of equity
proceeded by written statement of his cause, which
was called a "bill in chancery." In all cases of suits
which immediately concerned the rights of the Crown,
its officers proceeded upon their own authority, without the intervention of any other person; but where
the suit did not immediately concern the rights of the
Crown, they generally depended upon the relation of
some person whose name was inserted in the information, and who was called the "relator." It sometimes
happened that the relator had an individual interest in
the matter in dispute, as where he was entitled to
compensation for an injury. In such a case his personal complaint was joined to and incorporated with
the information given to the court by the Crown officer; these together comprised what is known and
termed as "an information and bill." It was the general practice, where suits immediately concerned the
right of the Crown, for the Crown officers to proceed
without a relator; yet by reason of a prerogative of
the Crown not to pay costs to a subject except in
certain cases, sometimes, through the tenderness of
the officers toward the defendant, the interposition of
a relator was required, against whom the costs were
taxed in case it appeared that the suit was improperly
instituted or prosecuted. The introduction of a relator was a mere act of favor on the part of the
Crown and its officers: Story's Equity Pleadings,
(9th ed.) §§ 7, 8; 1 Daniel's Chancery Practice, 2, 3, 7,
11, 12; *State ex rel.* v. *Dayton Railroad Company,* 36 Ohio St.
434; *Attorney-General* v. *Delaware Railroad Company,* 27 N. J.
Eq. 631. In *Attorney-General* v. *Mayor of Dublin,* 1 Bligh,
312, Lord REDESDALE says: "The relator is introduced
properly by the attorney-general, that there may be
some person responsible for the costs of the proceed-

ings, if finally there should be an opinion in the
court that the information has been improperly instituted, or if in the proceedings it should be in any
manner improperly conducted. It is for the benefit of
the subject that the attorney-general in all those proceedings provides persons to be responsible as relators in the information, that the court may award
against them what the court cannot do against him."
So that the relator, where the proceeding immediately
concerned the rights of the Crown, except so far as
to stand sponsor for costs in case the Crown officers
were unsuccessful in the suit, had no personal right
or authority to become a party to the proceeding,
either by relation or otherwise. It was only in cases
where he had some private or individual interest to
subserve, either in conjunction with the rights of the
Crown, or wherein it was the province of the Crown
to protect the rights of its subjects, acquired from it
by grant or otherwise, that he could, as a matter of
right, interpose as a relator through the attorney-
general to set in motion the machinery of the court.
The case stands different in mandamus proceedings.
There a private person may, in behalf of the public,
and without showing any individual or special interest to be subserved, become a relator, and, through
the proper state officer, institute the proceeding. Although the authorities are much divided, it is settled
in this state that "where the question is one of public right, and the object of the mandamus is to procure the enforcement of a public duty, the people are
regarded as the real party, and the relator, at whose
instigation the proceedings are instituted, need not
show that he has any legal or special interest in the
result, it being sufficient to show that he is a citizen,
and as such is interested in the execution of the

law": *State* v. *Ware,* 13 Or. 383 (10 Pac. 885); High on
Extraordinary Legal Remedies, § 431. But in equitable proceedings, where the immediate rights of the
Crown were alone concerned, we have seen that the
attorney-general only could invoke the action of the
courts through tne instrumentality of an information,
and if a relator was made a party, it was at his discretion, that there be some one to stand responsible
for the costs, the relator as of right, having no interest in the proceeding, and no power nor authority to
direct or control the suit in any particular whatever.

The attorney-general could, at common law, by information in chancery, enforce trusts, prevent public
nuisances, and the abuse of trust powers: *People* v. *Mi-
ner,* 2 Lans. 396. His supervision, through equitable
instrumentalities, of public trusts, and his authority to
prevent the abuse of trust powers public in their nature, was apparently the outgrowth of equitable interposition regarding charitable uses. It was formerly
held that it was the source from which the funds
were derived, and not the purpose for which they
were dedicated, that constituted the use charitable:
Attorney-General v. *Heelis,* 2 Sim. and Stu. 77. But subsequently it was settled that the purpose to which the
funds were dedicated was the real criterion by which
the charitable use was to be determined. And this
enlargement of the principle governing charitable
uses extended equitable jurisdiction to public trusts
involving all funds raised by taxation or otherwise
for public purposes: *Attorney-General* v. *Brown,* 1 Swanst.
265; *Attorney-General* v. *Mayor of Dublin,* 1 Bligh (N. S.),
312; *Attorney-General* v. *Eastlake,* 45 Eng. Ch. 218-221. In
the latter case it was declared that the attorney-general was the proper person to represent those who

28 OR.—36.

were interested in having these public funds faithfully
applied to the general and public purposes for which
they were provided and intended. ALLEN, J., in *People*
v. *Ingersoll,* 58 N. Y. 14, says: "It is well settled in
England that, in right of the prerogative of the
Crown, the attorney-general, in his name of office, may
proceed, either by information or bill in equity, to establish and enforce the execution of trusts of property by public corporations, to prevent the misappropriation or misapplication of funds or property raised
or held for public use; and the abuse of power by
the governors of corporations or public officers, or the
exercise of powers not conferred by law, and, generally, to call upon the courts to see that right is done
the subjects of the Crown who are incompetent to act
for themselves. Ordinarily, the remedies sought have
been preventive, but in some cases, as incident to the
preventive and prospective relief, a claim has been
made for retrospective relief, especially when the mis-
appropriated funds could be traced and reclaimed in
specie. The jurisdiction has been sustained upon the
general principles of the right and duty of the court
to grant preventive relief, and the relief actually
granted, if any, in addition and as incident to that,
has depended upon circumstances." But in all cases
the court's action was invoked against faithless trustees to compel a proper execution of the trust, and
the right use of trust funds, at the hands of those
charged with its administration. A breach or violation of public duty enjoined upon those with whom
the trust and the execution thereof is confided or
committed, either actual or threatened or impending,
is at the foundation of every action by the attorney-
general or of the Crown, or the people as sovereign,
and essential to the right of either to maintain, as

well as the right of a court of equity to entertain jurisdiction of, a suit by either touching property or
funds held by public or municipal corporations for
public use. These principles thus established in England have been affirmed to some extent by the courts
of this country and applied in like cases. In *People* v.
Ingersoll, 58 N. Y. 14, it is further said: "Doubtless,
the prerogatives of the Crown, except as affected by
constitutional limitations, exist in the people as sovereign, but to what extent the exercise of this prerogative is committed to the public officials, either by the
legislature or the common law, is a question worthy
of grave consideration, and not to be lightly decided,
and should only be determined when necessary to a
judgment and decision. * * * If there were no other
remedy for a great wrong, and public justice and individual rights were likely to suffer for want of a
prosecutor capable of pursuing the wrongdoer and re-
dressing the wrong, the courts would struggle hard to
find authority for the attorney-general to intervene in
the name of the people." The doctrine is broadly asserted in Missouri, where it is held that it is competent for the state, through its authorized officers, to
proceed in equity in restraint of public corporations
doing acts in violation of the constitution and laws of
the state: *State* v. *Saline County Court*, 51 Mo. 350. But
the case made was for a misappropriation of public
funds in subscriptions to a railroad company, which
funds were to be raised by assessment and taxation
of the people of Saline County. So that the case is
authoritative only upon the power of a court of
equity through its injunctive process to restrain public officers in the misapplication and misappropriation
of public funds, instituted at the instance of the executive or law officers of the state. The decision is,

however, based to a large extent upon a statute providing that "The remedy by writ of injunction or prohibition shall exist in all cases where an injury to real or personal property is threatened, and to prevent the doing of any legal wrong whatever, whenever, in the opinion of the court, an adequate remedy cannot be afforded by an action for damages:" 2 Wagner's Statutes, p. 1032. BLISS, J., in that case admits that he found some difficulty in regard to the question whether injunction would lie at all, but concludes that both upon reason and authority "where the wrong is a public one, suit may be brought in the name of the state, by its proper representative, and that under our statute that representative is the circuit attorney." See also *State ex rel* v. *Dayton Railroad Company*, 36 Ohio St. 434; *State* v. *Curators of State University*, 57 Mo. 178; *State* v. *McLaughlin*, 15 Kan. 228.

The Wisconsin cases, though not authority here, serve to illustrate the question touching sovereignty and prerogative appurtenant thereto, and the use of the extraordinary remedy by injunction, when it is invoked in the service of a sovereign state and in the interest of the whole people, as distinguished from its ordinary use, or coupled with ordinary equitable proceedings. It may be said here that injunction, in itself, is not prerogative or jurisdictional. It was issued in cases where the court had jurisdiction otherwise as preliminary or interlocutory to the final decree, or to give effect and permanency to such a decree. It was remedial and in aid of jurisdiction already attached within the vast range of equitable cognizance. Not so with mandamus, habeas corpus, and quo warranto, they were common law prerogative writs, which "appertain to and are peculiarly the instruments of the sovereign power, acting through its appropriate

department; prerogatives of sovereignty, represented
in England by the king, and in this country by the
people in their corporate character, or in other words,
the state": *Attorney-General* v. *Blossom,* 1 Wis. 278. It has
been said that injunction and mandamus are correlative in their operation; that where one commands the
other forbids; that where there is nonfeasance, mandamus compels the duty, and, where there is malfeas-
ance, injunction will restrain. But this is so in manner only. Injunction is frequently mandatory, and
mandamus sometimes operates as a restraint. Aside
from this, the injunctive writ, not being jurisdictional
but remedial in its operation, a case of well established equitable cognizance must be presented before
its use and adaptation would become appropriate, and
it is not every restraint which may seem beneficial as
a remedy that the writ will enforce. For instance,
some civil or private right must be about to be invaded, or some matter of public trust or concern of
which equity takes cognizance must be deleteriously
involved or affected, before injunction can be brought
into requisition. So that it is apparent that it is not
every case wherein mandamus will command that injunction will, in contrast, restrain. By reason of a provision in the Wisconsin Constitution conferring original
jurisdiction upon the supreme court "to issue writs of
habeas corpus, mandamus, injunction, quo warranto,
certiorari, and other original and remedial writs, and
to hear and determine the same," it has been there
held that injunction is a *quasi* prerogative writ, and
founds jurisdiction as if it were an original writ, whenever a question arises appropriate to its use, which
"should be a question *quod ad statum republicae pertinet,*
one 'affecting the sovereignty of the state, its franchises, or prerogatives, or the liberties of its people'":

Attorney-General v. *Chicago and Northwestern Railway Company,*
35 Wis. 513; *Attorney-General* v. *City of Eau Claire,* 37 Wis.
425; *State* v. *Cunningham,* 81 Wis. 440 (15 L. R. A. 561,
51 N. W. 724). Notwithstanding this constitutional
provision, the earlier cases sought for equitable
grouds in support of the injunctive writ. For instance,
in *Attorney-General* v. *Chicago and Northwestern Railway Company,* 35 Wis. 513, it was argued that courts of equity
have no jurisdiction, at the suit of the attorney-general, to enjoin usurpation, excess, or abuse of corporate franchise. The court, after a careful review of the
authorities both English and American, concluded that
the jurisdiction exists in this country as well as in
England, and says: "The equitable jurisdiction by injunction goes upon the ground of nuisance. As, indeed, any intrusion upon public right is in the realm
of purpresture. The ancient jurisdiction to restrain
nuisance is, perhaps, the most direct ground of the
modern jurisdiction under consideration. And the
former is fully asserted as an American jurisdiction,
as to remedies both by private persons and by the
attorney-general for the public," citing 2 Redfield on
Railways, 307, and 2 Story's Equity, §§ 720, 723. And
so in *Attorney-General* v. *City of Eau Claire,* 37 Wis. 425,
which involved the damming of a public river by the
City of Eau Claire, the court, considering such an encroachment as a purpresture, and within equitable jurisdiction to enjoin, and as it concerned the sovereign
prerogative of the state and the prerogative jurisdiction of the supreme court, declared it to be a fit case
for the exercise of its original jurisdiction by the injunctive writ. But in *State* v. *Cunningham,* 81 Wis. 440,
15 L. R. A. 561, 51 N. W. 724,) which was a later case
involving the constitutionality of the act of apportionment of the state into senatorial and assembly dis-

tricts, the court placed its jurisdiction, as it had intimated might be done in *Attorney-General* v. *Chicago and
Northwestern Railway Company,* upon the single ground
that the constitution had adapted the writ of injunction to prerogative uses.

PINNEY, J., says: "It may well be conceded that
courts of equity would not, by reason of their original
jurisdiction, have authority to interfere by injunction
in a case such as this; but it is to be borne in mind
that the writ of injunction, under our constitution, is
put to prerogative uses of a strictly judicial nature,
as a remedy of a preventive character in case of
threatened public wrong to the soverignty of the
state, and affecting its prerogatives and franchises
and the liberties of the people; their rights being
protected in this court by information in the name of
the state, on relation of the attorney-general." The
learned judge spoke advisedly when he said "it may
well be conceded that courts of equity would not, by
reason of their original jurisdiction, have authority
to interfere by injunction" in such a case, as indeed
there is high authority in support of the concession.
Fletcher v. *Tuttle* and *Blair* v. *Hinrichsen,* 151 Ill. 41, (25
L. R. A. 148, 37 N. E. 683,) are cases involving similar
questions arising out of the passage of an act to apportion the State of Illinois into senatorial districts,
claimed to be unconstitutional and void; but the suits
were instituted by private individuals, and it was
there decided that wherever the established distinc-
tions between equitable and common law jurisdiction
are observed, courts of equity have no authority or
jurisdiction to interpose for the protection of rights
which are merely political, and where no civil or
property right is involved. In all such cases the
remedy, if there is one, must be sought in a court of

law, and the case of *State* v. *Cunningham,* in Wisconsin,
is distinguished. Doctrine of similar import is laid
down by Chief Justice FULLER in *Green* v. *Mills,* 16 Cir.
Ct. App. 516 (69 Fed. 852, 30 L. R. A. 90) a very recent and well considered case. But whatever the true
doctrine might be as to the right use of the injunctive writ in cases involving merely political rights,
the question is not involved here. These cases operate, however, as powerful factors in determining equitable jurisdiction, and fixing the right use of the injunctive writ. Under the Wisconsin Constitution, injunction being held to be a *quasi* prerogative writ, its
operation becomes correlative with the common law
writ of mandamus, and will lie to restrain excess in
the same class of cases that mandamus supplies defect, the use of the one writ or the other in each
case turning solely on the accident of over-action or
shortcoming of the defendant. But not so where the
distinction between the equitable and common law
jurisdiction is still observed, as it is in this state.
Hence, if jurisdiction to issue the injunctive writ is to
be entertained, it must be based upon some well defined equitable grounds to support it. We have seen,
however, that in England the equitable jurisdiction to
enforce trusts, prevent public nuisances, and the
abuse of trust powers, was invoked for prerogative
purposes. Whenever necessary and appropriate injunction was issued in aid of the jurisdiction, and became effective in its exercise. While the writ of injunction is not in itself a prerogative writ, it is put
to prerogative purposes when used in aid of equitable jurisdiction invoked for such purposes. We have
also seen that in this country the jurisdiction and the
writ may be called into requisition for like purposes.
Now, when so called into requsition, in cases appro-

priate for its adoption and use, is there any reason
why the remedy thus invoked is not as effective for
the accomplishment of like high purposes as the
quasi prerogative writ peculiar to the state of Wisconsin under her constitution? We think that none
exists. So, therefore, the lawfully constituted authorities are not without an appropriate remedy in a case
where public officials are proceeding in derogation of
law, in the application and use of public funds,
wherever special injury cannot be predicated. The
sovereign state, the whole people, have a right to see
that the laws are duly executed. In most cases the
common law prerogative writs are appropriate for the
accomplishment of such ends. Whether appropriately
denominated "prerogative" in the states of the Union,
it differs but little, they emanate from a like high
source, pertain to sovereignty, and are adapted to like
uses and purposes. But wherever it is necessary to
prevent the abuse of trust powers, and the misapplication of trust or public funds, the equitable remedy
is likewise appropriate, and likewise emanates from the
like high source, and is attended with equivalent at-
tributes of power. See *People* v. *Ingersoll,* 58 N. Y. 14
and *State* v. *Saline County Court,* 51 Mo. 350. But the
rule and the doctrine upon which it is based has its
limitations. It is not every class of public officers
that may be controlled in any event at the hands of
the judiciary. This will become apparent in the further development of the opinion.

4. We have here to deal with matters not political, but with matters *publici juris,* and with the acts of
public officers touching the administration of public
funds, and affecting the whole people, or the state at

large. And the question comes to this, whether the
governor, the executive officer of the state, can be enjoined while in the discharge of official duties? We
speak of the governor, as it is in effect the acts of the
governor which this proceeding is intended to inter-
dict. True, the act providing for the construction of
a branch asylum at Union, and appropriating funds
therefor, has empowered the board of commissioners
of public buildings of the State of Oregon, consisting
of the governor, secretary of state, and treasurer, to
superintend the construction thereof; but, in the absence of such a commission, it would be the duty of
the governor to see that the law was carried into effect; so that, whether the duty is performed by the
governor, or by a commission named by the legislature, of which he is a constituent part, and empowered
to perform the service, the rules of law touching the
interference of the courts with the performance of
such duty must be the same, whether required to be
performed by the one or the other. The purpose of
the legislature was to construct and equip more com-
modious buildings and apartments for the accommodation of the insane and idiotic of the state. To provide
for and take care of this unfortunate class of individuals, both for their own good and protection, as well
as for the protection and security of all citizens, is a
matter purely of public concern, as it relates to the
welfare of the whole people. The subject is one of
governmental concern only, and relates entirely to the
legislative and governmental departments of state. In
pursuance of this purpose, the acts involved here
were passed and became law by the approval of the
governor. That the legislature had the undoubted
right to determine upon the necessity for such additional buildings, and the amount of funds necessary

for their construction and equipment, as we have said in our former opinion, no one can dispute. Furthermore, it was entirely within its coördinate powers to pass an act locating the branch asylum in the eastern part of the state, and no power vesting in the government could prevent it from so doing, and yet its validity would be determined by the fundamental law, when properly invoked. The governor could prevent its becoming a law by the exercise of the veto power confided to him; but, as above stated, the measure became a law by the approval of the executive. It is the duty of the governor to see that all the laws are faithfully executed, and it is now proposed to execute this law. The judicial department is called upon to prevent its execution. Is it competent for it to interpose in this proceeding, and restrain the executive department of the state? It may well be admitted that if the duty pertained to acts which are merely ministerial in their character, which call for no exercise of judgment or discretion, and do not relate to political or governmental matters, the governor of the state may, at the suit of interested parties, in a proceeding appropriate for the purpose, be compelled at the hands of the judiciary to perform them: *Greenwood Cemetery Land Company* v. *Routt*, 17 Colo. 156 (15 L. R. A. 369, 28 Pac. 1125); *Gaines* v. *Thompson*, 74 U. S. (7 Wall.), 347; Moses on Mandamus, 80; *Enterprise Savings Association* v. *Zumstein*, 15 Cir. Ct. App. 153 (67 Fed 1600); *Board of Liquidation* v. *McComb*, 92 U. S. 541. But if it pertains to duties which require the exercise of judgment or discretion to perform, or to matters political or governmental in their nature, all the authorities agree that the executive is clearly independent of the other coördinate departments of government, and is not subject in any manner to their direct supervis-

ion or control. Chief Justice TANEY, in *Mississippi* v.
Johnson, 71 U. S. (4 Wall.), 498, says: "A ministerial
duty, the performance of which may, in proper cases,
be required of the head of a department, by judicial
process, is one in respect to which nothing is left to
discretion. It is a simple, definite duty, arising under
conditions admitted or proved to exist, and imposed
by law."

This definition of a ministerial duty is concurred in
by Mr. Justice MILLER in *Gaines* v. *Thompson*, 74 U. S.
(7 Wall.), 347. Now, what is the nature of the duties
cast upon the governor by these acts? are they purely
ministerial or do they belong to the domain of governmental affairs? What is he, or the board of which he
is a member required to do? This latter question answered, the former is answered also without the necessity of comment. He shall, within sixty days, locate a
site for a branch insane asylum at some point in one
of the counties named lying in the eastern part of the
state; he shall contract for and purchase a tract of
land at the place selected; he shall hire a competent
architect, who shall, under the direction of the board,
draw plans, prepare specifications, etc. When these
are completed the board shall approve, and thereupon
shall give notice, and in due time let contracts, etc.
In all these prescribed duties there is not a single item
that partakes of a ministerial character. They all
pertain to executive duties, and are wholly and entirely governmental in their nature and purport. The
governor can execute them or not at his will, as they
fall exclusively within his department of government.
To test the question as to whether these enumerated
duties are ministerial or governmental, suppose these
acts of the legislature were entirely free from doubt
touching their constitutional validity, and the governor,

or the board acting in his aid, should refuse to execute the requirements thereof, would this court by a
mandamus proceeding compel him to act? Undoubtedly not, and why? Because the acts required of him
do not fall within the domain of those acts which are
denominated "ministerial." On the contrary, they are
governmental in their nature, pertain to matters *publici
juris,* and affect the welfare of the people at large.
Now, for the sake of the argument, concede that the
law is unconstitutional, and that injunction is an appropriate remedy, and is competent to restrain where
mandamus will compel; could this court with any more
propriety or right interfere with the governmental and
executive acts of the governor? No one will so contend. Chief Justice MARSHALL, in *Marbury* v. *Madison,*
5 U. S. (1 Cranch), 170, says: "It is not by the office
of the person to whom the writ is directed, but the
nature of the thing to be done, that the propriety or
impropriety of issuing a mandamus is to be determined." In *Sutherland* v. *The Governor,* 20 Mich. 283, (18
Am. Rep. 89,) Judge COOLEY says: "In many cases
it is unquestionable that the head of an executive department may be required by judicial process to perform a legal duty, while in other cases, in our judgment, the courts would be entirely without jurisdiction; and, as regards such an officer, we should concede that the nature of the case and of the duty to be
performed must determine the right of the court to
interfere in each particular instance." So that, looking to the nature of the thing to be done and the
duty to be performed by the governor under the requirements of these acts, there can be but one conclusion in respect to them. Whatever else may be said,
they are not ministerial, and hence no judicial process
of the courts can issue to compel or restrain, or in

any manner affect or interfere with, the executive volition of the governor with respect thereto. The mere
fact that a law is alleged to be unconstitutional does
not confer jurisdiction upon courts to interfere with
the acts of the executive officers while proceeding in
pursuance of its requirements: *State of Mississippi* v.
Johnson, 71 U. S. (4 Wall.), 498. True, the board is empowered to make payment upon contracts as the work
progresses, and it is contemplated that such payments
and disbursements shall be made out of the public
funds so appropriated by the legislature, but neither
the governor nor the board can obtain a dollar of such
funds without a warrant from the secretary of state,
by the very terms of the acts themselves. There is
no intimation anywhere that the secretary is about to
or is intending to draw, or contemplating the drawing
of, any warrant against such fund, or any public fund
of the state. Indeed, the secretary of state, acting in
his capacity as such officer, is not a party to the suit.
The judiciary takes cognizance of those proceedings
only, if at all, which operate incidentally as a check
upon a coördinate branch of government. It may, in
a proper case, proceed against an officer engaged in
the discharge of purely ministerial functions, which
may indirectly or incidentally affect the acts of a coördinate branch, and even nullify and render them inoperative; but directly, as against officers acting in a
political, governmental, or discretionary capacity, it
never has and never will, so long as the relative
duties and powers of the coördinate departments are
justly observed: *Gaines* v. *Thompson,* 74 U. S. (7 Wall.),
347.

5. Moreover, it is not fit that these great powers
pertaining to sovereignty, which affect the whole peo-

ple alike, and none less nor more than the rest, should
be invoked by individual citizens, or by a class or
classes, or body corporate, or an aggregation thereof
less than the whole state. State officers should not be
subjected to the annoyance of a suit at the instance
of every individual, when civil or property rights are
not invaded, who might conceive that the laws were
being improperly administered, or that public funds
were not being applied to legitimate public purposes.
State government being divided into three coordinate
branches,—executive, legislative, and judicial,—it is
most essential to the preservation of the autonomy of
government that there be no encroachment of one
branch upon another. And to this end the just limitations of the constitutional powers accorded to either
branch should be nicely defined and jealously guarded.
But sometimes one branch of government, in the discharge of its coördinate functions, oversteps the limit
of its constitutional powers. In such a case one or
both of the other branches of government may operate as a check upon its action. The legislature may
pass an act in disregard of the inhibitions of the constitution. The executive may veto the measure, or,
failing to do so, the judiciary may refuse to recognize
it as controlling. The governor acts upon his own
motion, and by right of high constitutional powers
and privileges reposed in him. The judiciary acts,
not upon its own motion, but only when some suitor
duly authorized by law presents in due form a cause
appropriate for its cognizance. Its machinery may be
set in motion by private suitors, in some form or
another, in all cases where civil or property rights
are being invaded or intrenched upon to their injury
or damage, be the suitor ever so humble or the injury
to be encountered ever so small; but in all cases of

purely public concern, affecting the welfare of the
whole people, or the state at large, the court's action
can only be invoked by such executive officers of state
as are by law intrusted with the discharge of such
duties. The attorney-general was such an officer at
common law. Under the constitution (article VII, section 17) the prosecuting attorneys are made the law
officers of the state and of the counties within their
respective districts. These officers, says WALDO, J.,
in *State* v. *Douglas County Road Company*, 10 Or. 201, are
possessed "with the powers, in the absence of statutory regulation, of the attorney-general at common
law." When the office of attorney-general was created,
it was made the duty of the incumbent to "prosecute
or defend for the state all causes in the supreme
court in which the state is interested": Laws, 1891.
p. 188. Whether his duties and powers in any manner
supersede those of the prosecuting attorneys it is not
now necessary to inquire; but a vital question here is
whether this proceeding has been properly instituted
by the law officer of the state, whether he be a prosecuting attorney or the attorney-general. The pleading, by virtue of which it is contended the court
should take and entertain jurisdiction, may properly
be termed a bill in equity by a private individual, to
wit: A. C. Taylor, the relator. It is verified by him,
and purports to be his bill, and not the information
of the district attorney for the third judicial district,
although signed by that officer. We have seen that
at common law, if a private invidual had an interest
in the proceeding apart from the interest of the government, he might as relator have his bill incorporated with the information of the attorney-general,
which was denominated an "information and bill."
In practice, if it should afterwards appear that the

relator had no interest to be subserved, the bill was dismissed, and the information retained: *Attorney-General* v. *Vivian*, 1 Russel, 236, 237; *State* v. *Cunningham*, 81 Wis. 440 (15 L. R. A. 561, 51 N. W. 724). But do we find here what may be termed an information or bill by the law officer of the state? As such an officer is the only person competent to institute a proceeding of the nature under consideration, the information should show upon its face in no uncertain manner that he is the officer instituting and prosecuting the suit, and the sole person responsible for its inception and main-tenance. The most common form of instituting like proceedings, it seems, has been in the name of the at-torney-general: *Coosaw Mining Company* v. *South Carolina*, 144 U. S. 565 (12 Sup. Ct. 689). Less frequently they are brought in the name of the Crown or the state upon the relation of the attorney-general: *State ex rel.* v. *Hibernian Savings Association*, 8 Or. 396. And, if per-missible at all to bring the suit in the name of the state alone, the complaint or information should show upon its face that the appropriate law officer brings the same for or in behalf of the state. The proceed-ing in either form would fix the responsibility for the maintenance thereof upon that officer, and it is not be-lieved that the mere affixing of his signature in his official capacity to a complaint or bill shown to be the bill of a private relator is sufficient to impress it with the functions and capacity of an information com-petent to put in motion the machinery of the courts, whereby they will take cognizance of questions per-taining to the high prerogative powers of the state, or affecting the whole people in their sovereign capacity: See *State* v. *Saline County Court*, 51 Mo. 350; *Bigelow* v. *Hartford Bridge Company*, 14 Conn. 578 (36 Am. Dec. 502); *State* v. *Anderson*, 5 Kan. 115; *Buck Mountain Coal Company*

v. *Lehigh Coal Company*, 50 Pa. St. 100; *Iroquois County Supervisors* v. *Keady*, 34 Ill. 296; *People* v. *Pacheco*, 29 Cal.
213; *Attorney-General* v. *East India Company*, 11 Sim. 380;
Bobbett v. *State*, 10 Kan. 15; *United States* v. *Throckmorton*,
98 U. S. 70. Having reached these conclusions, the
decree of the court below will be reversed, and the
complaint dismissed.

6.   This leaves the constitutional question still undisposed of, and the fact that we would probably not
declare the acts to be unconstitutional cannot affect or
change our duty in the premises. Courts will not
assume to pass upon a question of that character unless properly before them; and the case at bar, as
presented, not being within our jurisdiction to hear
and determine, it is clearly not within our province to
assume now to decide that question, although of grave
public importance· "As a general rule a court will
not pass upon a constitutional question and decide a
statute to be invalid unless a decision upon that very
point becomes necessary to a determination of the
cause." LORD, J., in *Elliott* v. *Oliver*, 22 Or. 47 (29
Pac. 1). We said when this case was here before
that "this rule arises out of the due respect which
one coördinate branch of the state government entertains towards another. The legislature, in adopting
laws for the government of the people, does so under
its construction of the constitution, and the just presumption always prevails that the business of the legislature is transacted with due regard to the fundamental law by which its acts are limited and governed.
It must be a clear case, therefore, and one in which
the constitutional question is the very *lis mota*, before
courts will assume the responsibility of declaring an
act of the legislative assembly void upon constitu-

tional grounds, and reverse the judgment of a coördinate branch of the state government. The case before us affords a striking illustration of the soundness
of this doctrine. The law complained of was passed
at two succeeding sessions of the legislative assembly,
and received the approval of two executives of the
state. By the last act an expenditure of twenty-five
thousand dollars under the former in the purchase of
a site for the branch asylum is approved, as well as
all other acts of the board in pursuance of its provisions. At the time of the passage and approval of
the latter act, this case was pending in the courts,
which fact was strongly calculated to attract the attention of both the legislative and executive branches
of the state government to the direct point at issue,
and it is but just to assume that the question of its
constitutionality was duly and carefully considered.
Hence, the peculiar gravity of our assuming at this
time to pass upon the constitutional question so ably
and elaborately presented at the hearing. Being in-
hibited by the rule under discussion, we cannot go
into the question.

7.   These conclusions are concurred in by the full
bench, but the majority of the court are of the opinion that such conclusions are susceptible of support
on other grounds, and in this connection I will proceed to state them. The power of a court of equity,
in a proceeding by the attorney-general or district attorney to enjoin the issuance of warrants in payment
for the Eastern Oregon Asylum,—as is heretofore intimated might be done if it be conceded that the act
locating it is in violation of the Contitution,—it is believed, is involved in grave and serious doubt, and
further, the facts in the case do not seem to bring it

within any recognized equity jurisdiction. It is not
claimed, nor can it be, that the objects and purposes
of the acts in question are unconstitutional, or that
the defendants threaten to apply the public funds to
an unconstitutional use, or to waste or dissipate them.
The claim is that the legislature has directed that
the branch asylum shall be located at a place other
than the seat of government, in violation, as plaintiff
claims, of the duty imposed upon it by the Constitution; and this, it is asserted, is sufficient ground upon
which a court of equity should assume jurisdiction.
This is not enough. The construction and location of
public buildings of the character in question is purely
a public governmental question, belonging to the legislative and governmental departments, and affects no
private or property right. Nor do the facts of this
case justify the conclusion, as a matter of law, that it
would be of any pecuniary injury to the state. If the
legislative and executive departments have miscon-
strued the constitution in this regard, their responsibility is to the people. A court of equity cannot, for
that reason alone, assume the right to sit in judgment
on their acts. There is no authority to be found in
the Constitution or statutes of this state for the exercise of such an extraordinary power, nor is it believed
it can be found in the analogies of the common law.
In this state the distinction between common law and
equity as a matter of substance prevails, although
both jurisdictions are invested in the same court:
Ming Yue v. *Coos Bay Railroad Company*, 24 Or. 392 (33
Pac. 641). And, it being well settled that a court of
chancery is conversant only with the maintenance of
property rights, it has no jurisdiction to interfere
with the duties of the other departments of government, except when necessary to the protection of such

rights, and cannot even then interfere with the discretion invested in either of such departments. "The office and jurisdiction of a court of equity," says Mr. Justice GRAY, in *Re Sawyer*, 124 U. S. 210, (8 Sup. Ct. 482,) "unless enlarged by express statute, are limited to the protection of rights of property." And in *Sheridan* v. *Colvin*, 78 Ill. 247, it is said: "It is elementary law that the subject matter of the jurisdiction of the court of chancery is civil property. The court is conversant only with questions of property, and the maintenance of civil rights. Injury to property, whether actual or prospective, is the foundation on which the jurisdiction rests. The court has no jurisdiction in matters merely criminal or merely immoral, which do not affect any right to property. Nor do matters of a political character come within the jurisdiction of the court of chancery. Nor has the court of chancery jurisdiction to interfere with the public duties of any department of government, except under special circumstances, and when necessary for the protection of rights of property." See also *Green* v. *Mills*, 69 Fed. 852, (30 L. R. A. 90, 16 Cir. Ct. App. 516,) and authorities cited by Mr. Justice GRAY in *Re Sawyer*, 124 U. S. 210 (8 Sup. Ct. 482).

The several departments of government are each independent of the other. To the judicial department is intrusted the determination of rights and the enforcement of remedies, and, as an incident to the protection of property, a court of equity has the undoubted right to refuse to recognize as valid a clearly unconstitutional act of the legislature, because the constitution is the paramount law of the land, which every suitor can invoke when an infringement of his rights is threatened under some law in violation thereof. But the mere fact that an act of the legisla-

ture is alleged to be unconstitutional gives it no jurisdiction to determine that question. Its duty is to
determine actual controversies, when properly brought
before it, and not to give opinions upon mooted questions or abstract propositions. Before it can assume
to determine the constitutionality of a legislative act,
the case before it must come within some recognized
ground of equity jurisdiction, and present some actual
or threatened infringement of the rights of property
on account of such unconstitutional legislation. When
the question, as here, is *publici juris* alone, affects no
property rights, and no threatened waste of the public
funds is shown, it may be well doubted whether the
court has any more power to interfere with the duties
of the other departments on the ground that their
acts may be unconstitutional, than it has with their
discretionary powers or duties. The independence of
the different departments in this respect is so complete that, however ill advised the action of the legislature or executive may be, and no matter how gross
an error may be committed, a court of equity is nevertheless powerless to interfere when rights of property are not involved, unless express authority is conferred upon it to do so. The decision of a large class
of public questions must, in the very nature of the
case, be left to the legislative and executive departments, and when the decision is made it must be accepted as correct. Among these is the construction
and location of public buildings, and the presumption
is just as conclusive that in the discharge of this duty
they observe the provisions of the constitution as it
is that the courts properly interpret that instrument
when called upon to do so in discharge of the duty
intrusted to them. It is true that by this rule, practically, public or private interests may sometimes suffer

in either instance, although theoretically there are no
such cases. But, however gross the wrong in fact
committed by the other departments, a court of equity
is powerless to remedy it, unless property rights are
involved, or appeal to the judiciary is given by law.
No greater evil could exist, under our form of government, than the usurpation by the judiciary of powers not intrusted to it. It should therefore refuse,
under all circumstances, to assume jurisdiction in any
case which affects the powers, duties, or prerogatives
of the other departments of government, unless its
right to do so is so clear as to admit of no reasonable doubt. In the opinion of the majority of the
court, this record does not present such a case. No
great public wrong is threatened, nor will public justice or individual rights suffer by the execution of
the law in question. And more, it must be admitted
that the construction sought to be placed upon the
constitution by the plaintiff is at least open to serious question. It has, for almost a quarter of a century, received a practical exposition to the contrary
by the legislative and executive departments, each of
which is as much bound to obey the constitution as
the courts, and to this exposition the courts would be
bound to yield, in a proceeding properly within their
jurisdiction, unless satisfied that it is repugnant to
the plain provisions of the constitution. Indeed, the
very act locating the branch asylum at Union, the
execution of which is now sought to be enjoined, was
passed by the legislature with only three dissenting
votes, while this suit was pending and its constitutional right to enact such a law thereby challenged.
Moreover, it was approved by the present executive,
whose eminent legal attainments and familiarity with
the question, (it having been argued before him in

Sherman v. *Bellows,* 24 Or. 553, 34 Pac. 54°,) justly en-
titles his opinion in the matter to great respect. The
court is bound, therefore, to assume that in the opinion of the legislature and executive there is no constitutional inhibition against the passage of such a
law, and while none of these facts would excuse the
court from assuming jurisdiction, if its right to do so
was clear, nor would the exposition given the constitution by the other departments be absolutely control-
ing upon it when called upon in the discharge of its
duty to construe that instrument, yet they afford a
very persuasive argument why the court should not
struggle to find some grounds, doubtful at best, upon
which it can rest its jurisdiction. Before it could assume the power to question the legality of the action
of the other departments of government in such a
case its right to do so ought to be beyond all possible question, and it ought to be able to place its
jurisdiction upon some well settled ground for equitable interference, which it is believed cannot be done
in this case. Let an order be entered dismissing the
complaint and dissolving the injunction.

REVERSED.

March 2, 1896.

ON REHEARING.

PER CURIAM. Since delivering the opinion in this
case, an elaborate petition for rehearing has been
filed. We have carefully examined it, and, while
some of the points made at the hearing are presented
in a new light and with much force, there is no new
question made not considered by us in the former
opinion. We see no reason for changing the conclusions then reached, hence a rehearing is denied.

REHEARING DENIED.

EDDY v. KINCAID.

[41 Pac. 157.]

1. **CONTEMPORANEOUS CONSTRUCTION OF CONSTITUTION.**—Where a certain
construction has been placed on a constitution by a series of legislative acts, and that construction has been for a long time accepted
by the people and the different departments of government, the
courts will hesitate to depart from it; such a practical exposition is
often of controlling influence:* *Cline* v. *Greenwood*, 10 Or. at page 240,
approved and followed.

2. **LEGISLATIVE POWER TO APPOINT RAILROAD COMMISSIONERS—CONSTITU-
TIONAL LAW—CODE, § 4003.** In view of the fact that the Oregon legislature has from the organization of the state created numerous public
offices and appointed persons to fill them, and that the state constitution contains no express inhibition against the exercise of such
power by the legislature, the court feels bound to now hold that a
section 4003, Hill's Code, which vests in the legislature the power
to appoint railroad commissioners, is constitutional: *Biggs* v. *Mc-
Bride*, 17 Or. 640, and *State* v. *George*, 22 Or. 152, approved and followed.

3. **TENURE OF OFFICE OF RAILROAD COMMISSIONER.**—In view of the provision in article XV, section 1 of the state constitution, that "all
officers shall hold their offices until their successors are elected and
qualified," and the further proviso in the act creating the board of
railroad commissioners that such officers "shall hold their office for
and during the term of two years and until their successors are
elected and qualified as in this act provided," it necessarily follows
that the failure of the legislature to elect a successor to a railroad
commissioner at the expiration of his term of office does not create
a vacancy, and the incumbent is entitled to the emoluments of such
office until his successor is duly elected: *State* v. *Simon*, 20 Or. 365,
approved and followed.

4. **FAILURE OF APPOINTIVE OFFICER TO GIVE BOND.**—The mere failure of
an officer rightfully holding over by virtue of the express provisions
of the law creating the office, to renew his bond, does not of itself
work a forfeiture of the office so as to deprive him of its emoluments.

5. **REPEAL BY IMPLICATION—STATUTORY CONSTRUCTION.**—The Australian
Ballot Law of eighteen hundred and ninety-one, (Laws, 1891, p. 8,)
section 1 of which fixes the date of the general election at which certain named officers and "all other state, district, county, or precinct

---

* In addition to the case cited by the court, the following Oregon cases will
be found in point sustaining the present decision: *Crawford* v. *Beard*, 12 Or. 447
(8 Pac. 537), *Kelly* v. *Multnomah County*, 18 Or. 359 (22 Pac. 1110).—REPORTER.

28 OR.—38.

officers provided by law" shall be elected, does not repeal by implication section 4003 of Hill's Code providing for the election of railroad
commissioners by the legislature, even if it is in conflict with the
Code section, because this section is but a reënactment of a law that
existed long prior to the creation of the board of railroad commissioners.

APPEAL from Marion: H. H. HEWITT, Judge.

This is a proceeding by mandamus to compel Harrison R. Kincaid, who is secretary of state, to draw
a warrant on the state treasurer for the balance of
salary alleged to be due James B. Eddy as railroad
commissioner for the quarter ending March thirty-
first, eighteen hundred and ninety-five. The act creating the board of railroad commissioners provides
that the persons constituting such board shall be
chosen biennially by the legislative assembly, and
"shall hold their offices for and during the term of
two years, and until their successors are elected and
qualified as in this act provided, and if a vacancy occurs by resignation, death, or otherwise, the governor
shall appoint a commissioner to fill such vacancy for
the residue of the term:" Hill's Code § 4003. In compliance with the provisions of this statute, the legislature of eighteen hundred and ninety-three regularly
elected plaintiff as one of the commissioners, and he
immediately thereafter qualified and entered upon the
discharge of his duties, and has continued so to act.
The legislature of eighteen hundred and ninety-five,
although making the necessary appropriation to pay
the salary and expenses of the commissioners, failed
and neglected to choose a successor to plaintiff, and
by reason thereof and the provisions of the law under
which he was chosen he now claims the right to hold
the office and receive its emoluments until a successor
shall be regularly chosen in the manner provided by

law. The defendant, the secretary of state, however, being in doubt as to the plaintiff's right to the office, refuses to draw a warrant in payment of his salary as such commissioner, and suggests as reasons for his refusal: (1) That so much of the act creating the commission as provides for the election of the members thereof by the legislature is unconstitutional and void, and therefore plaintiff was never legally elected to such office; (2) that, if plaintiff was legally elected in eighteen hundred and ninety-three, the failure of the legislature to elect his successor in eighteen hundred and ninety-five created a vacancy in the office, which must be filled by appointment by the governor; (3) if he is in error in both of these positions, he claims that the failure of plaintiff to renew his official bond, *ipso facto*, worked a forfeiture of the office; and (4) that so much of the act as provides for the election of railroad commissioners by the legislature is repealed by implication by the act known as the "Australian Ballot Law." The defendant demurred to the complaint because the facts therein stated did not entitle the plaintiff to any relief, and appealed from the order overruling his demurrer and making the writ peremptory.   AFFIRMED.

For appellant there was an oral argument by *Mr. Frank V. Drake,* and a brief urging these points.*

So much of the acts of the legislative assembly as assumes to confer upon the legislature authority or right to elect the railroad commissioners is un_constitutional,—*first,* because it is opposed to the

---

* The attorney-general did not appear for the secretary of state in this case because he had previously furnished to the governor a written opinion on the very question here involved, in which he expressed the view that the railroad commissioners were lawfully holding over, and that there was no authority for appointing their successors.— REPORTER.

spirit and genius of our institutions. The people of
Oregon originally had, and they have reserved and
retained, the right to nominate and select, by vote, all
their public servants; *second,* by express prohibition,
article III of their constitution, those sovereigns of the
state forbade the exercise of executive or administrative powers by the legislature; *third,* the legislature is
prohibited by the same fundamental law from passing
special laws for the election of state, county, or district officers.   These three subdivisions of our first
point are connected and associated with a general
fundamental principle, namely, that the people of this
country, in organizing their new government, resolved
that they, as sovereigns, would delegate to represen-
tatives specified powers only; that those representa-
tives should be divided into three independent classes,
and that all powers not delegated remained with the
sovereigns, the people. They were jealous and afraid
of solidarity of governmental power in a few hands.
The citizens of the State of Oregon could have elected
to enact laws for their government by direct legislation. They chose the representative form and be-
stowed this power on the legislative assembly. They
conferred on that assembly no other function: Sedgwick on Constitutional and Statutory Law (2d ed.), 132.

Referring specifically to the first subdivision of the
first point, we submit that the express declarations
and reservations in our constitution confines the power
of election to public office to the people, acting in their
politico-executive capacity, viz.: Article I, section 1, all
power is inherent in the people, and all free govern-
ments are founded on their authority. Article II,
section 1, all elections shall be free and equal; section 2, all qualified citizens are entitled to vote at all
elections authorized by law; sections 2, 4, 5, 6, 7, and

8 define the qualifications of electors; section 8, the legislative assembly shall enact laws to support free, unrestrained suffrage of the people (not enact a law by which the legislators may elect); section 14, general elections shall be held on the first Monday of June, biennially; section 17, all qualified electors shall vote in their respective places of residence. So we contend that the constitution inhibits the legislature from attempting to elect any officer of the state, or connected with the state government proper, save that each house, when assembled in session, may elect its own officers, to serve it while in session, as provided in article IV, section 11. No authority appears anywhere in that instrument for the election of any officer in joint session. This high political function belongs to the sovereignty, where, primarily, rested all power, and which may at any time be resumed by the people. This basic principle must not be lost sight of. Further still, the legislature cannot by indirection obstruct or limit the sovereigns in the exercise of the right of suffrage. The right to participate in the selection of public servants or agents is of the highest nature. The citizen has the same transcendent right to express his choice in the selection of judicial, administrative, or executive officers as to declare his preference for a legislative officer. The legislative body has no more power to assume this function of selection than it has to place requirements on the elector beyond those fixed by the constitution: *White* v. *Commissioners,* 13 Or. 317 (57 Am. Rep. 20); *Bourland* v. *Hildreth,* 26 Cal. 215; *Page* v. *Allen,* 58 Pa. St. 338 (48 Am. Dec. 272); *Day* v. *Jones,* 31 Cal. 261.

The legislative assembly has no authority to appropriate the powers usually exercised through the elective franchise. The framers of our constitution,

ex industria, declared against such attempt, not only in
the provisions for elections before quoted, but in the
phraseology and terms adopted in article III. In distributing the powers of government among their rep-
resentatives, they were careful to declare that neither
the legislative or judicial departments should exercise
any of the duties of the executive, including the administrative. Here all power touching the active administration of the government and its laws are
vested in the executive-administrative department.
The people, in the first instance, have the right to select their servants in that department, and in cases of
vacancies, their chief representative in that department may make temporary appointment, until the
sovereigns shall meet again in their constitutional biennial elections. This was the design: this was the
purpose. It is the only means by which the people
can express their choice, or participate in the affairs
of the government of the state, and must so continue,
unless they choose to adopt other systems, or unless
their prerogatives be assumed by a few persons while
temporarily filling the office of legislator, and the
people submit. The election of a state officer does
not involve legislative functions; it is a distinct and
independent prerogative, distinctly administrative in
character: Cooley on Constitutional Limitations (5th
ed.), 105–111; *State v. Hyde,* 121 Ind. 20; *State v. Peele,*
121 Ind. 495; *State v. Gorby,* 122 Ind. 17; Mechem on
Public Officers, §§ 104–107; *State v. Kennon,* 7 Ohio St.
546; *People v. McKee,* 68 N. C. 429; *State v. Denny,* 118 Ind.
457; *City v. State,* 118 Ind. 427; *People v. Bull,* 46 N. Y. 57
(7 Am. Rep. 302); *White v. Commissioners,* 13 Or. 317 (57
Am. Rep. 20); *Taylor v. Commonwealth,* 3 J. J. Marshall,
404; *McGregor v. Baglin,* 19 Iowa, 43; Story on Constitution (5th ed.), Vol. I, §§ 520, 521, 523, and 525.

The legislature is by constitutional inhibition prohibited from passing special or local laws "providing for opening and conducting the election of state, county, or township officers." Plaintiff sues as an incumbent of a public office for the salary of a public office, and claims that he was elected by the legislative assembly assembled at the capitol in the month of February, eighteen hundred and ninety-three, for the term of two years, and until his successor should be elected and qualified. He declares that he is entitled to an annual salary to be paid out of the public treasury by warrants to be drawn thereon by the secretary of state, defendant here. Defendant's contention, in addition to all that has been said before, is that the legislature had no authority to provide for opening or conducting such an election at the capitol, for the special purpose of electing any state officer: Constitution, Art. IV., § 23, ¶ 13; *Morrison* v. *Bachert*, 112 Pa. St. 322; *Maxwell* v. *Tillamook County*, 20 Or. 495, and cases therein cited; *People* v. *Cooper*, 83 Ill. 585; *Page* v. *Allen*, 58 Pa. St. 338 (48 Am. Dec. 272); *State* v. *Herrmann*, 75 Mo. 340; *State* v. *Denny*, 21 N. E. 257, 274; *Davis* v. *Cook*, 84 Ill. 590; *City of Evansville* v. *State*, 21 N. E. 267; *State* v. *The Judges*, 21 Ohio St. 11; *State* v. *Mitchell*, 31 Ohio St. 529; *State* v. *Hammer*, 42 N. J. Law, 435; *State* v. *Boise*, 39 N. E. 64 (40 N. E. 113). This act is special because it provides for an election of one portion of the state's officers by a method different from the election of other state officers. An act which necessarily produces a result forbidden by the constitution cannot be upheld, whatever its form or profession: *People* v. *Cooper*, 83 Ill. 585; *Commonwealth* v. *Patton*, 88 Pa. St. 258; *Couteri* v. *New Brunswick*, 44 N. J. Law, 58; 3 Am. and Eng. Ency. of Law, p. 674.

The genius of our institutions, as now formulated, is crystalized in one central principle, namely, that the people of the state shall, at regular intervals prescribed by law, select their servants to discharge, for limited periods only, high and responsible representative duties. It is the sovereign will, declared by ballot, by which certain citizens of the state are selected and transformed into officers possessing all these varied powers of government. This is a grave and momentous matter in which the sovereign voice alone should be heard. It is the primal and basic principle of our governmental fabric. Choice of public officers is the only means by which the people participate in the administration of our government. This participation is indirect, limited at best, and ought not to be restricted by legislatures acting in excess of their department. The people are sovereigns, and under our system and our constitution they only possess the prerogative of selecting public officers within the state. If the act had provided that the railroad commissioners should be elected by vote of the enrolled militia, or by the members of the trades unions, or by the farmers of the state, or the bankers, or by the various boards of county commissioners assembled at a given time at the seats of their several counties, could such enactment be held to be a compliance with the spirit or terms of our constitution? When the individual members of the legislature declare their vote for an incumbent of a public office in recurring biennial sessions, are they exercising legislative functions? When, ten years hence, members of the legislature vote for railroad commissioners at Salem, will the act constitute a part of the legislation of eighteen hundred and eighty-seven, whereby the office was created? Or, will the act of voting for a commissioner ten years hence be considered as an "amendment" to the acts of eighteen hundred and eighty-seven or eighteen hundred and eighty-nine? The principle for which defendant contends arose in the recent case of *In re Sims,* 87 Pac. 135.

The Australian Ballot Law (Laws, 1891, p. 8,) provided a complete system for the election of all state officers, and supersedes the provisions for the election of certain officers by the legislature. Conformably to the spirit and terms of our constitution before referred to the legislature of the state at its session in eighteen hundred and ninety-one, (Session Laws, 1891, p. 8,) passed an act providing for the election of all state, district, county, and precinct officers provided by law. Section 1 of the act declares that "A general election shall be held in the several election precincts in this state, on the first Monday in June, eighteen hundred and ninety-two, and biennially thereafter, at which there shall be chosen so many of the following officers as are to be elected in such year, namely," (here naming several state officers, including "justices of the supreme court," * * * circuit judges, members of state senate, and other state and county officers,) "and all other state, district, county, and precinct officers provided by law." One only of the justices of the supreme court, and a portion only of the judges of the circuit court were to be elected in that year, hence, the use of the phase in section 1, "So many of the following officers as are to be elected in such year." The election of all classes of officers at regularly recurring general biennial elections was thus provided for. Section 9 of the same act also provides that "all general or special elections hereafter held in this state shall be conducted under

28 OR.—39.

the provisions of this act." And the act thereupon prescribes in detail the time, places, and proceedings for the conduct of all such elections. Section 72 repeals certain specified acts, "and all acts and parts of of acts in conflict with this act." By this act the purpose and letter of the constitution is accomplished and fulfilled. It forms a system harmonious and consistent with the fundamental law. The attempt of the legislature to provide for a special election of a part of the state officers by less than one hundred of the electors of the state, at a place other than as defined in the fundamental law, is not only in conflict with that law, but in conflict with the later legislative act. This general law, governing and controlling all elections in the state, is "an act of the legislature, * * * original in form and complete in itself, exhibiting on its face what the law is to be, its purpose and scope, is valid, notwithstanding it may affect, change, or modify some other law upon the same subject": *Warren* v. *Crosby,* 24 Or. 561, 562; *Little* v. *Cogswell,* 20 Or. 345, and cases there cited. Like the case of *Warren* v. *Crosby,* in 24 Or. the effect of this latest act is to repeal, *pro tanto,* former legislation (special legislation) on a subject common to both. It is the last expression on the subject of election of state officers, and must control. We invoke the rule enforced in the case of *Warren* v. *Crosby,* overruling *State* v. *Wright,* 14 Or. 369, and specially refer to so much of the opinion as appears on pages 568 and 569, 24 Or.: Cooley on Constitutional Limitations, 152. The period of commencement of the term of the railroad commission is not fixed in the act creating that office. The constitution and the statutes, now harmonious, fix the periods of recurring biennial elections in the month of June. The people did not elect any railroad commissioners in eighteen hundred and ninety-four; the legislature did not attempt to elect in eighteen hundred and ninety-five, it had no authority so to do; the governor has made no appointment. Defendant insists that there is no incumbent entitled to a salary. The office is vacant—a house without a tenant.

The act under which petitioner claims his salary, (Laws, 1889, p. 22,) is unconstitutional, as in violation of article IV, sections 20 and 22 of the state constitution. The original act creating the board of railroad commissioners, (Session Laws, 1887, p. 30,) was entitled "An act to create and establish a board of railroad commissioners, and to define and regulate its powers and duties, and to fix the compensation of its members." This act created a board of two persons, to be appointed by the governor, to hold office for the term of four years, and enacted that at the session of the legislature next preceding the expiration of such term, the governor, during such session, should, by and with the advice and consent of the senate, appoint successors, to serve four years. In eighteen hundred and eighty-nine, (Session Laws, 1889, p. 22,) an "amendatory" act was passed under the following title: "An act to amend an act entitled 'An act to create and establish a board of railroad commissioners, and to define and regulate its powers and define its duties, and to fix the compensation of its members,' approved February eighteenth, eighteen hundred and eighty-seven, and being chapter LXXIII of the General Laws of Oregon," as compiled and annotated by William Lair Hill. This last act then purports in terms to amend section 1 of "said act to create and establish a board of railroad commissioners, * * * being section 4002 of the General Laws of Oregon," as compiled by William Lair Hill, so as to read as follows: "Section 4002. There shall be and is hereby established for the State of Oregon a commission * * * to consist of three persons." The last named act then purports to amend section 2 of the original act, "being section 4003 of the general laws" as compiled, so as to read as follows: "Section 4003. Said commissioners * * * shall be chosen biennially by the legislative assembly of the State of Oregon, and shall hold their office for and during the term of two years and until their successors are elected and qualified as in this act provided, and if a vacancy occurs by resignation, death, or otherwise, the governor shall appoint a commissioner to fill such vacancy for the residue of the term." The last act then purports to amend section 6 of the original act, fixing the compensation of the members. Then repeals section 24 of the original act (General Laws, § 4025). Then follows an "emergency clause."

Article IV, section 20 of the constitution, enacts: "Every act shall embrace but one subject, and matters properly connected therewith, which subject shall be expressed in the title. But if any subject shall be embraced in an act which shall not be expressed in the title, such act shall be void only as to so much thereof as shall not be expressed in the title." Section 22 of the same article is as follows: "No act shall ever be revised or amended by mere reference to its title, but the act revised or section amended shall be set forth and published at full length." Defendant calls attention to the fact that neither the above requirements has been observed in the acts referred to, and claims that so much of said acts as relate to election of railroad commissioners is void. In the title to the first act no intimation is given of the subject of appoint-

ment or election to the office. In the title to the last
act no intimation is given of intention to amend or repeal any specific section of the former act, or to provide for an election of commissioners by the legislature of the state. At the time of the passage of these
acts, the general election laws of the state (chapter
XIV, title I, 2 Hill's Compilation, 1170,) then in force,
contained provisions for general elections to be held in
the several election precincts of the state "on the first
Monday in June, eighteen hundred and eighty-six, and
biennially thereafter," for choosing "a governor, (and
the various state, county, and precinct officers,) and all
other state, district, county, and precinct officers provided by law." Then followed, in detail, the methods
of preparing for, opening, conducting, ascertaining, and
declaring the results of such election. All this was in
substantial compliance with the mandates of the constitution. So that the time and methods of election of
the "commissioners" had been fixed by the constitution
and statutes prior to the creation of the board of railroad commissioners, and were in force when both the
original and amendatory acts, creating the office of railroad commissioner, were passed. It follows that the
matter of election of the commissioners was not necessarily or "properly" (using the words of the constitution) connected with the subject of the "act to
create and establish the board, define and regulate its
powers, and fix compensation." It was not essential to
the act, or necessary. The commissioners could have
been elected at the general election and their "term
of office" would have begun, under section 2557, Compiled Laws, then in force (2 Hill's Compilation, 1170).
With the election laws thus in force, no one would
suppose, from reading the title "to create a board,
regulate and define its powers and duties, and fix its

compensation," in the original act, or the title of the amendatory act, that the legislature intended to disregard or repeal the general law touching elections, or to assume the functions of electors, while acting in the capacity of legislators. Applying the test stated in 25 Or. 506, "whether, taking from the title the subject, we can find anything in the bill which cannot be referred to that subject," we submit that the election of·railroad commissioners by the legislators instead of by the people, under the laws then in force, cannot be referred either to "creation of the board," or to "defining and regulating its duties and powers," or to "fixing the compensation" of the members of the board. For these reasons we claim that so much of the act as provides for the election of the board by the members of the legislature is unconstitutional and void. The constitution of Indiana and Texas, in the particulars referred to, are identical with that of Oregon, and some analogous cases from those states, and others, are submitted, namely: *State* v. *Bowers,* 14 Ind. 195; *Igoe* v. *State,* 14 Ind. 239; *Mewherter* v. *Price,* 11 Ind. 199; *City of San Antonio* v. *Gould,* 34 Texas, 49; *Giddings* v. *Antonia,* 47 Texas, 548 (26 Am. Rep. 321); *Smails* v. *White,* 4 Neb. 353; *City of Tecumseh* v. *Phillips,* 5 Neb. 305; *White* v. *City of Lincoln,* 5 Neb. 505; *People* v. *Denaby,* 20 Mich. 349; *Evans* v. *Memphis, etc., Railway,* 56 Ala. 246 (28 Am. Rep. 771); *Beekert* v. *Alleghany City,* 85 Pa. St. 191; *Ryerson* v. *Utley,* 16 Mich. 269.

The pretended term of two years for which plaintiff claims he was elected, expired on the twenty-third day of February, eighteen hundred and ninety-five, at the farthest, that being the date on which the biennial session of the legislature of eighteen hundred and ninety-five adjourned sine die. The legislature did not elect in eighteen hundred and ninety-five.

These conditions were held to create a vacancy in *Frils* v. *Kuhl*, 51 N. J. Law, 191; *People* v. *Reid*, 6 Cal. 288; *People* v. *Baine*, 6 Cal. 519; *People* v. *Miser*, 7 Cal. 519; *People* v. *Langdon*, 8 Cal. 1. See opinion of Justice FIELD in *People* v. *Whitman*, 10 Cal. 39, at page 46 *et seq.*, and in *People* v. *Tilton*, 37 Cal. 614. The case of *People* v. *Reid*, was overruled by a divided court, two out of five judges dissenting. See dissenting opinions. That the express term of two years is a limitation of the tenure of office of the incumbents, and that the qualification or contingency "until successors are elected and qualified" is intended to provide for brief intervals only — interregnums occurring by reason of varying dates in election years rather than a right to hold for two terms. See *County* v. *Bigham*, 10 Iowa, 39, 43; *County* v. *Ring*, 29 Minn. 405; *Chelmsford* v. *Demarest*, 7 Gray, at page 3; *State* v. *Cocke*, 54 Texas, 482 (citing dissenting opinion of FIELD in 10 Cal. 48, and dissenting opinion in *State* v. *Lusk*, 18 Mo. 345, which see, and numerous cases cited under the next succeeding point). Finally, the contentions arising in this case did not arise, nor were they presented or passed upon in *Biggs* v. *McBride*, or *Everding* v. *Simon*, or *State* v. *George*.

One asserting rights to emoluments of office must show, when properly challenged, (1) that he was and continues to be eligible; (2) that he has been duly and legally elected; and (3) that he has qualified as the law requires. The constitution (article V, section 3) requires that "every person elected or appointed to office shall, before entering on the duties thereof, take an oath to support the constitution of the United States, the constitution of Oregon, and an oath of office. Section 4006 of the statutes, in like terms, requires that persons elected as commissioners before entering, etc., must make oath and file it with the sec.

retary of state, and before entering on the discharge of his duties shall also execute a bond with security to be approved by the governor in the sum of ten thousand dollars, and file it with the secretary of state. And section 2551 of the statute declares that a failure or neglect to give or renew official bonds or to deposit oath or bond in the time required by law, shall create a vacancy. The oath required of a railroad commissioner must set forth, among other things, that he will faithfully discharge his duties; that he owns no railway stock or bonds; is not an officer, attorney, agent, or employé of such corporation, and has no pecuniary interest therein: Section 4006. The term of office is two years, and they shall be elected biennially: Section 4003. Biennial elections are held in June, as prescribed by the constitution and the statutes concerning elections. Now, notwithstanding all favorable presumptions, it is quite possible (1) that a person could take that oath in eighteen hundred and ninety-three, and not be able to do so in eighteen hundred and ninety-five; and (2) he might be able to furnish security in the state in the sum of ten thousand dollars in eighteen hundred and ninety-three and fail utterly to do so in eighteen hundred and ninety-five. His sureties may have been responsible in eighteen hundred and ninety-three, and be insolvent in eighteen hundred and ninety-five. The sureties on his bond filed in eighteen hundred and ninety-three are not liable for defaults or omissions for four years. They became surety for one term only — two years. The state has demanded the oath and the bond as security for itself and its citizens, and as a prerequisite to occupancy of the office and payment for services rendered therein. More than two years have elapsed since the petitioner filed his

oath and bond as a railroad commissioner. The legislature in the mean time has convened in regular biennial session and adjourned. No one has been elected
by the people or the legislature to succeed the petitioner. He has not renewed either oath or bond, but
demands a salary. The secretary refuses payment.
Petitioner assumes that, under the circumstances, his
is a continuing term; that it embraced four years, and
that the oath and bond filed by him on February
eighteenth, eighteen hundred and ninety-three, are
efficacious still, and give him title to the office and
salary.

That the legislative intent was to fix the term at
two years is so clearly manifested by the expressed
term of two years, and the provision for biennial elections set forth in the original act, (section 4.03,) and
the subsequent amendatory act of eighteen hundred
and ninety-one, (Session Laws, 1891, § 1, p. 9,) as to be
fairly indisputable. The phrase "and until their successors are elected," etc., is but a common provision
for an interregnum likely to occur between two
"terms." It was not intended to operate as creating
a term of four years. This phraseology has been
under the consideration of the courts in numerous and
some well considered cases, and the weight of reason
and authorities are, we think, decidedly with the position taken by the defense in this case: *County of Wapello*
v. *Bigham,* 10 Iowa, 39; *Mayor* v. *Crowell,* 40 N. J. Law,
207; *Dover* v. *Twombly,* 42 N. H. 59. The bond filed by
petitioner on February eighteenth, eighteen hundred
and ninety-three, under his alleged election by the legislature in eighteen hundred and ninety-three, cannot
be enforced for the present (assumed) "extended"
term. Except for past delinquencies, if any, it is *func-
tus officio.* As to sureties, the rule *strictissimi juris*

always applies. The sureties on executing the bond
were justified in relying upon the expressed term of
two years, and in relying upon the presumption that
the legislature (or the people under the act of eighteen hundred and ninety-one) would elect a successor
to their principal on the bond. The provisions of the
statute were, by operation of law, incorporated into
the terms of their contract as sureties. No recovery
for future delinquencies can be recovered on that bond:
Chelmsford v. *Demarest*, 7 Gray, 1; *Bigelow* v. *Bridges*, 8
Mass. 274; *County of Wapello* v. *Bigham*, 10 Iowa, 39;
Mayor v. *Crowell*, 40 N. J. Law, 207; *Dover* v. *Twombly*, 42
N. H. 59; *State Treasurer* v. *Mann*, 34 Vt. 371 (the authorities are reviewed in this case in a lengthy opinion);
King County v. *Ferry*, 5 Wash. St. 536; *Norridgewock* v. *Hale*,
80 Me. 363; *Jackson* v. *Ring*, 29 Minn. 398; *Welch* v. *Sey-
mour*, 28 Conn. 387; *Harris* v. *Babbitt*, 4 Dillon (Cir. Ct.),
186; *Brown* v. *Lattimor*, 17 Cal. 93; *Winnieshiek County* v.
Maynard, 44 Iowa, 15; *Miller* v. *Stewart*, 9 Wheaton, 681;
United States v. *Kirkpatrick*, 9 Wheaton, 720.

Qualification for office when required by law is a
prerequisite, a condition precedent, to the right of
office: *United States* v. *LeBaron*, 19 U. S. (How.), 73, p. 78;
Jump v. *Spence*, 28 Md. 1; *Thomas* v. *Owens*, 4 Md. 189.
The statute, as before stated, requires an oath of one
first duly elected, which oath must disclose certain
facts. Unless the facts exist in his favor he is disqualified — not eligible. The state demands a good
and sufficient security for the faithful discharge of
duty, and the statute makes this security also a prerequisite. Failure to furnish one or both of these operates as a defeasance — causes a vacancy: Opinion of
Justices, 14 Fla. 277; *State* v. *Cocke*, 54 Texas, 482; *State
ex rel.* v. *Matheny*, 7 Kan. 327; *Rounds* v. *Bangor*, 46 Me.
541 (74 Am. Dec. 469); *Falconer* v. *Shoves*, 37 Ark. 389;

County v. *Bigham,* 10 Iowa, 39; *People* v. *Taylor,* 57 Cal. 620; *Pague* v. *San Francisco,* 3 Cal. 122; Opinion of FIELD, J., in case of *People* v. *Whitman,* 10 Cal. 46, and *People* v. *Reid,* 6 Cal. 288.

Finally, if it be conceded that petitioner is an officer de facto still, it is essential to his claim for a salary that he be an officer de jure. He must show that he is a qualified officer: *Jump* v. *Spence,* 28 Md. 1; *Thomas* v. *Owens,* 4 Md. 48; *State* v. *Cocke,* 54 Texas, 482; *Creighton* v. *Commonwealth,* 83 Ky. 143 (4 Am. St. Rep. 103); *Rounds* v. *Bangor,* 46 Me. 541 (74 Am. Dec. 469); *County* v. *Bingham,* 10 Iowa, 39, and cases before cited; Mechem on Public Officers, § 331. Defendant contends that plaintiff is not entitled to salary or compensation, because he has not furnished the required proof of his eligibility to the office by filing the statutory oath; and because he has not furnished the state the security (bond) required by law. He presents no proof of his election; presents no commission of appointment or election; presents no oath or bond of office.

For respondent there was a brief by *Messrs. Julius C. Moreland,* and *Dolph, Mallory and Simon,* with oral arguments by *Messrs. Moreland* and *Rufus Mallory.*

Opinion by MR. CHIEF JUSTICE BEAN.

It will be observed that this is not a contest between the plaintiff, claiming to hold over after the expiration of his original term, and an appointee of the governor made on the assumption that a vacancy existed in the office. Nor does the case involve the existence of the office itself, but the real question here is, whether the plaintiff shall hold the office and receive its emoluments by virtue of his election in eighteen hundred and ninety-three, or whether it is vacant,

and must be filled by an appointment by the governor?
We proceed to state briefly our views of the objections
made by the secretary of state to the payment of
plaintiff's salary.

1. In view of the former decisions of this court,
and the practical exposition of the constitution from
almost the organization of the state to the present
time, it is in our opinion now too late to question the
right of the legislature to appoint the class of public
officers to which the plaintiff belongs. It is admitted
that there is no direct inhibition in the constitution
against the exercise of such a power by the legislature, and it has been the long continued practice of
that body to create a certain class of public offices,
and to appoint the incumbents thereof. The state
librarian, fish and pilot commissioners, food commissioner, game and fish warden, boatman at Astoria, and
the railroad commissioners have always been elected
by the legislature in joint convention, and the right
to do so has never been questioned except in the case
of *Fox* v. *McBride*, hereafter referred to. We have
thus for a series of years concurrent legislative exposition of the constitution to which the court ought to
yield unless satisfied that it is repugnant to its plain
words. Of course the plain provisions of the constitution cannot be broken down by practical exposition,
but when, as here, such a practice is in violation of
none of its express provisions, such an exposition is a
very persuasive argument, and often of controlling
force. In speaking of the effect of practical exposition, it was said by an able court that "It has always
been regarded by the courts as equivalent to a positive law": *Bruce* v. *Schuyler*, 4 Gilman, 267 (46 Am. Dec.
417). And in *Rogers* v. *Goodwin*, 2 Mass. 477, in giving

a reason for adhering to long continued exposition, it is said: "We cannot shake a principle which in practice has so long and extensively prevailed." Indeed, harmony prevails throughout the whole scope of judicial opinion on this question: *Cline* v. *Greenwood*, 10 Or. 230; *Hovey* v. *State*, 119 Ind. 386 (21 N. E. 890), and authorities there cited. Independently, then, of judicial authority, we should hesitate to declare the act in question unconstitutional because of the practical exposition given to the constitution by the legislature, and acquiesced in by the other departments of government and the people. But we are without authority on the question.

2. In *Biggs* v. *McBride*, 17 Or. 640, (5 L. R. A. 115, 21 Pac. 878,) the right of the legislature to appoint railroad commissioners under the act now before us was called in question, and, while the case might have been decided on another point, it nevertheless received much consideration at the argument, and was one of the principal questions discussed by the court in its opinion, and the conclusion reached presumably met with the approval of the then members of the court. In that case it was contended, as here, that the right to appoint to public office belongs exclusively to the executive, and that the assumption of the legislature to fill the office of railroad commissioner by persons of their own selection is a usurpation by that department of government of powers that are vested by the constitution in the executive. Answering this argument Mr. Justice STRAHAN said: "It was not claimed at the argument that there is any express provision of the constitution which authorizes the governor in direct terms to make the appointment in question, but that it is included in the grant contained in article V,

section 1 of the constitution. That section declares:
'The chief executive power of the state shall be
vested in a governor.' Now, if it could be shown that
the power to appoint all officers which are not expressly made elective by the people is a part of 'the
chief executive power of the state,' the appellant's
contention would be sustained. But no authority
whatever has been cited to sustain this view, nor is
it believed that any exists. On the contrary, the provisions of the fifth article of the constitution, which
relates to the executive department, all seem at variance with this view. The framers of this instrument
evidently designed that no prerogative powers should
be left lurking in any of its provisions. No doubt
they remembered something of the history of the
conflicts with prerogatives in that country from which
we inherited the common law. They therefore defined the powers of the chief executive of the state
so clearly and distinctly that there ought to be no
controversy concerning the method of filling, or, in
some cases, of changing the method of filling, an existing office." And, after referring to the several
offices which have been uniformly filled by appointment by the legislature, the learned judge continued:
"The power exercised by the legislature in the appointment of some of these officers is almost coeval
with the constitution. The power thus exercised has
never been called in question, but has ever been acquiesced in by every department of the government,
and is in itself a contemporaneous construction of the
constitution, which, if the question were doubtful,
might be sufficient to turn the scale in its favor. Under any view, such construction is entitled to great
weight, and could not be lightly regarded." And in
State v. *George,* 22 Or. 152, (29 Am. St. Rep. 586, 29 Pac.

356, 16 L. R. A. 737,) which involved the right of the
legislature to appoint or provide for the appointment
of the bridge commissioners of the City of Portland, by some other authority than the executive, Mr.
Justice LORD said: "Except as limited by constitutional restrictions, it is agreed that the legislature
may exercise all governmental powers. It is the law
making power of the state. While our constitution
separates the powers of government into three distinct departments, and prohibits any of them from
exercising any powers confided to the other, it does
not undertake to declare what shall be considered
legislative, executive, or judicial acts." And he quotes
from WALKER, J., in *People* v. *Morgan,* 90 Ill. 558, that
such "provision declares only in general terms, that
each department of the government shall be confined
to the exercise of the functions of its own department. It does not undertake to define, in any specific
manner, what are legislative, executive, or judicial
powers or acts. Like most other provisions of that
instrument, the terms employed are of the most general and comprehensive character. * * * The executive power in a state is understood to be that
power, wherever lodged, which compels the laws to be
enforced and obeyed. And the instrumentalities employed for that purpose are officers, elected or appointed, who are charged with the enforcement of the
laws. But the power to appoint is by no means an
executive function, unless made so by organic law or
legislative enactment. And in this case it is not so
unless the power is thus conferred." In view of these
judicial expressions by our predecessors, and the long
continued practical exposition of the constitution to
which we have already referred, we feel constrained
to hold the act in question constitutional, although, if

the question was one of first impression, the court, as at present organized, might probably hold otherwise.

3. It is next contended that the failure of the legislature of eighteen hundred and ninety-five to elect plaintiff's successor operated to create a vacancy in the office, and that plaintiff was not entitled to hold over; but it seems to us this question is settled by the express declaration of the constitution of this state and of the law under which he was elected. Section 1 of article XV of the constitution provides that "All officers, except members of the legislative assembly, shall hold their office until their successors are elected and qualified," and the act creating the board of railroad commissioners provides that such officers "shall hold their offices for and during the term of two years and until their successors are elected and qualified as in this act provided." It is thus declared, both in the constitution and the act itself, that the incumbent of the office shall hold until his successor is elected and qualified. The legislature having failed to elect plaintiff's successor, it necessarily follows, if we are to give force and effect to the plain and express provisions of the constitution and the law, that he is entitled to hold the office and to receive its emoluments until such time as his successor shall be duly elected. And to this effect are the authorities under similar provisions of law. *State* v. *Simon,* 20 **Or.** 365 (26 Pac. 170); *Gosman* v. *State,* 106 Ind. 203 (6 N. E. 319); *State* v. *Harrison,* 113 Ind. 435 (3 Am. St. Rep. 663, 16 N. E. 384); *State* v. *Howe,* 25 Ohio St. 588 (18 Am. Rep. 321); *People* v. *Tilton,* 37 Cal. 614; *Badger* v. *United States,* 93 U. S. 599.

4. It is next claimed that the sureties on plaintiff's official bond would not be liable for any breach

thereof occuring after the expiration of the two years'
term provided by law, and that, therefore, his failure
to renew the bond after the expiration of such term
of itself worked a forfeiture of the office.   There is a
line of authorities holding that where one is elected
to an office under a law which provides that he shall
hold the office for a fixed term, and until his successor is elected and qualified, and he is either re-
elected at the expiration of the term, but fails to give
a new bond, or a successor is regularly elected, but
fails to qualify, and he is permitted to hold over, that
the sureties on his bond are not liable for a defalcation occurring after the expiration of the fixed term.
But these authorities seem to proceed generally upon
the theory that his holding over is wrongful, because
his own reëlection or that of his successor, and a failure to qualify, terminated his right to the office, and
created a vacancy which should have been filled by
the proper appointing power: *County of Scott* v. *Ring,* 29
Minn. 398 (13 N. W. 181).   But whatever may be the
true rule in the character of cases above suggested,
"The weight of American authority sustains the
proposition," says Mr. Throop, "that where an officer
holds over rightfully, that is, pursuant to a statute
providing that he shall hold over until his successor
shall be chosen, or shall be chosen and shall qualify;
this constitutes one of the exceptions to the rule that
the liability of the sureties in an official bond does
not extend beyond the principal's term, and that the
sureties are liable for his defaults during the additional time": Throop on Public Officers, § 213.   The
author cites, in support of this position, *Akers* v. *State,*
8 Ind. 484; *Thompson* v. *State,* 37 Miss. 518; *State* v. *Wells,*
8 Nev. 105; *United States* v. *Jameson,* 8 McCrary, 620;

Mayor v. *Horn*, 2 Harr. (Del.), 1ː0; to which may be added *State* v. *Kurtzeborn*, 78 Mo. 98; *State* v. *Daniel*, 6 Jones, (N. C.), 414. It would seem from this rule that, since plaintiff is rightfully holding over by virtue of the express provisions of the law creating the office, and his successor has never been chosen, the sureties on his official bond continue liable, and no new bond is necessary. But, however this may be, it seems to us clear that the mere failure by plaintiff to renew his bond, if it was necessary, did not of itself work a forfeiture of the office, but, under any view, could be nothing more than a ground of forfeiture in a proper proceeding for that purpose. As no such proceeding has been taken, and as there is no law of which we are aware authorizing the secretary of state to declare a public office forfeited, it follows from either view of the question that plaintiff is entitled to the office and its emoluments, notwithstanding the fact that he has failed to renew his official oath or bond.

5. And, finally, it is claimed that so much of the act creating the board of railroad commissioners as provides for the election of such officers by the legislative assembly was repealed by implication by the act of eighteen hundred and ninety-one, known as the "Australian Ballot Law," the first section of which declares "that a general election shall be held in the several election precincts in this state on the first Monday in June, eighteen hundred and ninety-two, and biennially thereafter, at which there shall be chosen so many of the following officers as are to be elected in such year," (naming several state officers, the railroad commissioners, however, not being among the number,) "and all other state, district, county, or pre-

cinct officers provided by law." The contention for
defendant is that the office of railroad commissioner
having been created prior to the passage of this act,
the latter clause of the section quoted repealed by
implication the then existing provisions authorizing
the legislature to elect such commissioners. But a
sufficient answer to this contention is that the section
of the Australian Ballot Law relied upon by the defendant is not a new legislative declaration, but is
merely a reënactment of the provisions of the law as
it existed long prior to the creation of the board of
railroad commissioners, and therefore does not repeal
by implication any provision of that act, even if it is
in conflict therewith: Endlich on Interpretation of
Statutes, § 195. We conclude, therefore, after a careful examination of this case and all the questions involved in it, that the judgment of the court below
was right, and must be affirmed.

AFFIRMED.

Decided September 12, 1895.

ON REHEARING.
[41 Pac. 655.]

Opinion by MR. CHIEF JUSTICE BEAN.

In his petition for a rehearing counsel for the defendant calls attention to the fact that he did not
base his contention as to the effect of the act of
eighteen hundred and ninety-one entirely upon the
first section, but contended at the hearing that sections 9 and 72, as well as section 1, and, in fact, the
whole act indicated an intention to cover the entire
subject of elections, and, in effect, to provide for the
election of all state officers by the people, and is

therefore inconsistent with, and repeals by implication, that portion of the act creating a board of railroad commissioners which provides for the election of its members by the legislature. Repeals by implication are not favored, and it is only when the provisions of the latter act are so repugnant to the former that both cannot stand, or when the latter is clearly intended as a substitute for the former, that such an interpretion is to prevail: Endlich on Interpretation of Statutes, § 210. Now, it cannot be claimed that the act of eighteen hundred and and ninety-one was intended as a substitute for the act creating the railroad commission; nor, in our opinion, is there any conflict between the two acts. The office of railroad commissioner is nowhere mentioned in the act of eighteen hundred and ninety-one, nor does it provide that such officers shall be elected by the people. It begins by declaring that a general election shall be held on the first Monday in June, eighteen hundred and ninety-two, and biennially thereafter, at which time there shall be chosen so many of the following officers "as are to be elected in such year (naming certain officers; the railroad commissioners, however, not being among the number), and all other state, district, county, and precinct officers provided by law." It is thus, by its terms, confined to such officers as are by law to be elected by the people; and, as there is no law providing that the railroad commissioners shall be so elected, it manifestly has no application to them. The act of eighteen hundred and ninety-one was intended, as its title plainly implies, to fix the time for and regulate the manner of conducting state, district, county, and precinct elections; to prescribe the manner of making nominations; the printing and delivery of ballots; and to prevent frauds and punish crimes affecting the right of suffrage. And the section declaring what officers shall be elected in the manner prescribed by the act is only a reenactment of the law as it stood prior to the creation of the board of railroad commissioners. In our opinion, there is nothing, therefore, in the point that the act of eighteen hundred and ninety-one repeals, or is inconsistent with, the law providing for the election of railroad commissioners by the legislature. Counsel also ably and learnedly reargues the question of the constitutionality of the act providing for the election of railroad commissioners by the legislature, but, inasmuch as the points raised were fully considered and determined in the former opinion, a rehearing would be unprofitable. The petition is therefore denied.

REHEARING DENIED.

Argued December 5, 1895; decided February 3, 1896.

BROWER LUMBER COMPANY v. MILLER.

[43 Pac. 659.]

CONTRACTS FOR THE BENEFIT OF THIRD PERSONS.—A provision in a bond of a street contractor to a city that the contractor will pay all money due and to become due for materials used and labor performed in completing his work, does not give to material men and laborers on the improvement any action against the contractor or his bondsmen, for the reason that the contract was made primarily and directly for the benefit of the city, rather than for their benefit, and because there was no fund or property provided in the hands of the promisor on which they could have any equitable claim: *Parker* v. *Jeffrey*, 26 Or. 186, and *Washburn* v. *Interstate Investment Company*, 26 Or. 436, approved and followed.

APPEAL from Multnomah: HARTWELL HURLEY, Judge.

This case is here on appeal from a judgment in proceedings against garnishees. On May fifth, eighteen hundred and ninety-four, the Brower and Thompson Lumber Company commenced an action against Miller and Giddings, and recovered a judgment therein for three hundred and twenty-eight dollars and fifty-nine cents. When the action was commenced a writ of attachment was issued, and Hamilton and Howard were served with garnishee process, to which they first made answer that they were indebted to Miller and Giddings in the sum of two hundred and forty-nine dollars and eighty cents, but afterwards amended their certificate so as to show an indebtedness of sixty-two cents only. The amended certificate being unsatisfactory, the plaintiff had Hamilton and Howard cited to appear before the court, and their answers to the allegations and interrogatories served upon them disclose the status of their indebtedness which it was sought to reach by the garnishment. We state the facts out of which the indebtedness arose from the garnishees' standpoint, as their sufficiency is tested by exceptions which form the basis of the judgment appealed from. It seem that one J. D. Wickliff, having entered into a contract with the City of Portland to make certain street improvements, and to furnish the labor and materials therefor, executed to the city a bond with B. S. Reilly and George W. Bower as sureties, conditioned that he should well and faithfully perform all the stipulations of the contract. On the same day Wickliff, for the consideration of five dollars, assigned the contract to Hamilton and Howard. Concerning these transactions it is alleged: "That although said bond appears to have been given by J. D. Wickliff, said contract had in fact already been assigned to these garnishees; they had succeeded to all the rights and privileges of said Wickliff under said contract, and had assumed all the liabilities and responsibilities there under; that said B. S. Reilly and George W. Bower signed said bond as sureties for these garnishees, and not for said Wickliff"; * * * that at the time said contract was assigned "it was understood and agreed by and between the parties to said assignment that these garnishees shall stand in all respects as the original contractors for said street improvement; that said Wickliff should have no further interest in said contract; that he should be relieved of all liability thereunder; and that all rights and claims thereunder should accrue to these garnishees; and that these garnishees should be responsible for all liabilities or responsibilities arising thereunder." The contract contains the stipulation required by the ordinances of the City of Portland as follows: "That said party of the first part (Wickliff) shall, within ninety days after completion of the work herein agreed to be performed, pay all sums of money due at the completion of said work, or thereafter to become due for materials used in and labor performed on or in connection with said work." Hamilton and Howard let to Miller and Giddings a subcontract for furnishing the nails and labor requisite for carrying out said contract with the city, one half the contract price to be paid in cash, and the other half in city warrants. Miller and Giddings furnished nails and labor of the value of nine hundred eighty-eight dollars and sixty-four cents, all which Hamilton and Howard paid except two hundred and forty-nine and eighty cents. S. D. Powell furnished nails of the value of one hundred and fourteen dollars and eighty cents, at the request of Miller and Giddings, for use in the completion of said contract; Henry Aschenbrenner, John Kruger, and Fred Hyde performed labor for them, for which they claimed fifty-one dollars and forty-six cents, seven dollars and

ninety-nine cents, and thirty-four dollars and three
cents, respectively, and each of said individuals made
demand of Hamilton and Howard for the amount due
him for such nails and labor, and claims a right to
recover against them directly under and by virtue of
the original contract with the City of Portland. Under this state of facts the garnishees claimed that they
were responsible to these several individuals in the
various sums demanded, and not to Miller and Giddings. The court dismissed the proceeding, and rendered judgment against plaintiffs for costs, from which
it appeals.   REVERSED.

For appellant there was a brief and an oral argument by *Mr. Ralph R. Duniway.*

For respondent there was a brief and an oral argument by *Mr. Gustavus C. Moser.*

Opinion by MR. JUSTICE WOLVERTON.

We presume that if Powell, Aschenbrenner, Kruger,
and Hyde each has an action directly against the garnishees upon their several demands, the fact that
such rights of action exist would constitute a good
defense to an action by Miller and Giddings against
the garnishees; and if good against Miller and Giddings, it would also constitute a sufficient defense under the garnishee process. It is intimated, but not
strongly insisted upon, that Wickliff's bond to the city
forms a sufficient basis upon which actions by Powell
and others against the garnishees may be founded.
but this cannot be so, for two reasons, *first,* Hamilton
and Howard are not parties to the bond, and an action
based thereon could not go against them; and, *second,*
it is settled by *Parker* v. *Jeffery,* 26 Or. 186, (37 Pac.

712,) that they have no action upon the bond even as against Wickliff. In that case, which was an action upon a similar bond given in pursuance of the same ordinances, a party had furnished materials directly to the contractor, and it was held that the bond furnished him no remedy. It is stoutly contended, however, that Hamilton and Howard's liability to Powell and others is established by the clause in the contract wherein it is "further stipulated and agreed on behalf of the party of the first part, that said party of the first part shall, within ninety days after tho completion of the work herein agreed to be performed, pay all sums of money due at the completion of said work, or thereafter to become due for materials used in and labor performed on or in connection with said work," upon the doctrine, as asserted generally by some of the authorities, that where a party makes a promise to another for the benefit of a third, the latter may maintain an action upon it, though the consideration did not move from him. Before reaching this question there is another which is involved in some doubt, and that is whether Hamilton and Howard occupy the same position under the contract, with reference to these parties, as Wickliff; but we will pass the latter, and assume that Hamilton and Howard are liable in all respects under the contrct as if they were the original contractors.

It may be premised that the City of Portland was not directly liable to Powell or the other parties asserting demands against the garnishees at the time the contract was entered into, so that the consideration to be paid for the performance of its conditions does not in any way constitute a trust fund in the hands of the contractors for the payment of its obligations; nor can it be said that the contractors have,

for a consideration, undertaken to pay the obligations
of the city. By the very strong current of recent
authority the doctrine contended for by counsel has
been much limited and qualified, and, as was said by
Mr. Justice BROWN, in *Constable* v. *National Steamship
Company*, 154 U. S. 72, (14 Sup. Ct. 1062,) "It is by
no means a universal rule that a person may sue
upon a contract made for his benefit, to which he
was not a party." In *Jefferson* v. *Asch*, 53 Minn. 446,
(25 L. R. A. 257, 55 N. W. 604,) a recent and well
considered case from Minnesota, to which is added an
exhaustive annotation of the authorities by the authors
of that excellent series of reports, the Lawyer's Reports Annotated, Chief Justice GILFILLAN, in tracing
and discussing the limitations to the rule as generally
stated, makes the following deductions from the New
York authorities, to which he gives his sanction as
correct in principle: "To give a third party who may
derive a benefit from the performance of the promise
an action, there must be—*first*, an intent by the
promisee to secure some benefit to the third party;
and, *second*, some privity between the two,—the promisee and party to be benefited,—and some obligation or
duty owing from the former to the latter, which would
give him a legal or equitable claim to the benefit of
the promise, or an equivalent from him personally."
"There must be either a new consideration, or some
prior right or claim against one of the contracting
parties, by which he has a legal interest in the performance of the agreement"; and "there must be some
legal right, founded upon some obligation of the
promisee, in the third party, to adopt and claim the
promise as made for his benefit." Like deductions
are made from the Massachusetts authorities. From
these a further and a more direct and explicit deduc-

tion is discernible, being that which finds support in trust relations, which relations give rise to an implied promise. Such is the result of an investigation of the subject by BEAN, C. J., in *Parker* v. *Jeffery*, 26 Or. 186 (37 Pac. 712). He says: "In nearly if not quite every case coming under our notice in which the action has been sustained, unless on a bond or obligation authorized by law, there has been some property, fund, debt, or thing in the hands of the promisor upon which the plaintiff had some equitable claim, and from which the law, acting upon the relationship of the parties, or the fund, established the privity, implied the promise, and created the duty upon which the action was founded." This deduction is reinforced by the principle established by *Washburn* v. *Interstate Investment Company*, 26 Or. 436, (36 Pac. 533, 38 Pac. 620,) that where the principal contract is executory in its nature, and there is no fund in the hands of the promisor, or debt or obligation due from him, and he has simply obligated himself to pay the debts of another to a third party, who is neither a party to the contract or consideration, no action will lie in favor of such third party against the promisor. For additional authorities bearing upon the question not cited in the two authorities last referred to see *Constable* v. *National Steamship Company*, 154 U. S. 73 (14 Sup. Ct. 1062); *Burton* v. *Larkin*, 36 Kan. 246 (13 Pac. 398); *Anderson* v. *Fitzgerald*, 21 Fed. 294; *Weller* v. *Goble*, 66 Iowa, 113 (23 N. W. 290); *Durnherr* v. *Rau*, 135 N. Y. 219 (32 N. E. 49); *Parlin* v. *Hall*, 2 N. D. 473 (52 N. W. 405); *Morrill* v. *Lane*, 136 Mass. 93.

Now do Hamilton and Howard bring themselves within the purview of the rule thus limited and circumscribed, and show themselves obligated in an actionable capacity to Powell, Aschenbrenner, and oth.

ers? We do not think they do. An effort has been
made to distinguish *Parker* v. *Jeffery* from the case
made by the facts herein stated, but we think the
principle established is alike applicable to the one case
as to the other. The contract with the city is executory in its nature, and it contemplates that the consideration for the intended improvements shall be paid
directly to the contractors when the work is completed, without limitations as to its use by them.
To be sure, they stipulated with the city that they
would within ninety days pay all sums of money due
at the completion of the work, or thereafter to become
due, for materials used and labor performed in connection therewith, which is a wholesome and salutary
provision, required by ordinance, and which inures incidentally and indirectly to the benefit of the material-
men and laborers; yet it would seem the primary object of the stipulation was for the benefit of the city,
as it has exacted a bond in its individual capacity to
insure its faithful performance, together with other
conditions of the contract. Counsel for respondents
invokes in aid of his contention the case of *City of St.
Paul* v. *Butler,* 30 Minn. 459, (16 N. W. 362,) but the case
does not help him. In reality it is an authority the
other way. The contract therein stated provided that
the contractor should "pay all just claims for all labor
performed or materials furnished for or on account of
said contract as aforesaid," but the bond entered into
to secure its faithful performance was given to the
city "for the use of all persons who may do work or
furnish materials" in pursuance of its provisions. The
court expressly held that neither the laborers nor material men had any claim against the contractors by
reason of the contract, but decided that the bond gave
the action upon the like principle as actions are given

under our statute upon official statutory bonds to the
party sustaining an injury. See sections 340 and 341,
Hill's Code of Oregon; *Crook County* v. *Bushnell*, 15 Or.
169 (13 Pac. 836), and *Hume* v. *Kelly*, 28 Or. 398 (43 Pac.
380). So we conclude that the contractors (the garnishees herein) have incurred no greater liability in
this respect under the contract than they have or
would have incurred under the bond had they executed
it instead of Wickliff, the effect of which liability upon
the bond was declared in *Parker* v. *Jeffery,* and the doctrine there enunciated and settled applies with like
vitality and cogency here. It follows from these considerations that the judgment of the court below
should be reversed, and remanded with directions to
enter judgment in favor of plaintiff and against the
garnishees for the sum of two hundred and forty-nine
dollars and eighty cents, and it is so ordered.

REVERSED.

Argued December 19, 1895; decided February 10, 1896.

COMMERCIAL BANK *v.* SHERMAN.

[43 Pac. 658.]

FOREIGN BANKING CORPORATIONS—"TRANSACTING BUSINESS"—CODE, § 3276.
—A foreign banking corporation purchasing a note in the state, but
having no purpose to do any other act in the state, is not "transacting business" in the state within Hill's Code, § 3276, providing that a
foreign banking corporation, "before transacting business" in the
state, must record a power of attorney in each county where it has
"a resident agent," which, so long as the company has "places of
business" in the state, shall be irrevocable: *Bank of British Columbia*
v. *Page,* 6 Or. 431; *Hachney* v. *Leary,* 12 Or. 40, and *Semple* v. *Bank
of British Columbia,* 5 Sawy. 88, distinguished.

APPEAL from Multnomah: E. D. SHATTUCK, Judge.

NOTE.—For an extensive collection of authorities on what constitutes "dealing" or "carrying on business," in a state, with reference to prohibitory statutes,
see notes to the following cases: *State of North Carolina* v. *Ray,* 14 L. R. A. 529;

This is an action by the Commercial Bank of Vancouver, Washington, against D. F. Sherman, as indorser of a promissory note. The facts are that on June twenty-seventh, eighteen hundred and ninety-one, at Portland, Oregon, J. L. Lewis and others made, executed, and delivered to the defendant their negotiable promissory note for nine thousand two hundred and four dollars, and that in August, eighteen hundred and ninety-one, the plaintiff, a banking corporation organized under the laws of the State of Washington, and doing business therein, through its authorized agent purchased the note of the defendant at Portland, and it was at the latter place sold, indorsed, and delivered by defendant to plaintiff, and not being fully paid at maturity this action was commenced to recover the unpaid balance. The defense is that, the note having been sold and transferred to the plaintiff within this state, no action can be maintained against the indorser because the plaintiff corporation had not, at the time of making the contract and purchase of the note, complied with section 3276 of Hill's Code, which provides that a foreign banking corporation "before transacting business in this state, must duly execute and acknowledge a power of attorney, and cause the same to be recorded in the county clerk's office of each county where it has a resident agent, which

Cone Export and Commission Company v. *Poole,* 24 L. R. A. 295; *Milan Milling and Manufacturing Company* v. *Gorton,* 26 L. R. A. 135, and *Florshcim Brothers Dry-goods Company* v. *Lester,* 27 L. R. A. 505. 46 Am. St. Rep. 162 See also *Colorado Iron Works* v. *Sierra Grande Mining Company,* 22 Am. St. Rep. 433.

The question of the validity of contracts made by foreign corporations where they have not complied with the statutory conditions of the right to do business in a state is carefully reviewed in the notes to the following cases: *Edison General Electric Company* v. *Canadian Pacific Navigation Company,* 40 Am. St. Rep. 916, 24 L. R. A. 315; *Dudley* v. *Collier,* 13 Am. St. Rep. 60; *Toledo Tie Company* v. *Thomas,* 25 Am. St. Rep. 931.

With the Colorado case of *Kindel* v. *Beck and Pauli Lithographing Company,* 24 L. R. A. 311, is an interesting discussion of the exclusion of foreign corporations as an interference with interstate commerce.—REPORTER.

power of attorney, so long as such company shall have places of business in the state, shall be irrevocable, except by the substitution of another qualified person for the one mentioned therein as attorney for such company." The plea in abatement having been overruled and judgment entered against the defendant, he appeals.   AFFIRMED.

For appellant there was a brief by *Messrs. Paxton and Beach, Charles H. Carey,* and *J. W. Paddock,* with an oral argument by *Mr. Carey.*

For respondent there was a brief by *Messrs. W. Byron Daniels,* and *Williams, Wood and Linthicum,* with an oral argument by *Mr. George H. Williams.*

Opinion by MR. CHIEF JUSTICE BEAN.

It must be conceded that the contracts of any of the foreign corporations named in the title of the act of eighteen hundred and sixty-four, of which the section referred to is a part, carrying on business here without first having executed and caused to be recorded a power of attorney as required by the statute are void, and no action can be maintained thereon by the corporation: *Bank of British Columbia* v. *Page,* 6 Or. 431; *Hacheny* v. *Leary,* 12 Or. 40 (7 Pac. 329); *In re Comstock,* 3 Sawy. 218 (Fed. Cas. No. 3078); *Semple* v. *Bank of British Columbia,* 5 Sawy. 88 (Fed. Cas. No. 12659). But the record shows that at the time the plaintiff made the contract upon which this action is based it was not carrying on, or proposing to carry on, its corporate business in this state, and, so far as appears, the purchase of the note in question was the only business ever done or contemplated by it here. The single inquiry presented by this record, there-

fore, is whether a foreign banking corporation purchasing a promissory note in this state, and with no
purpose of doing any other act here, is "transacting
business" in the state, within the meaning of the statute. It seems to us this question must be answered
in the negative. In our opinion the statute, when
reasonably construed, was intended to prohibit certain
foreign corporations coming into this state for the
purpose of transacting their ordinary corporate business without first appointing some resident agent
upon whom service of summons could be had in case
of litigation between them and citizens of the state,
and was not designed or intended to prohibit the doing of one single isolated act of business by such a corporation, with no intention apparent to do any other
act or engage in business here. It will be noticed the
statute does not require the power of attorney to be
recorded before "doing any business," but "before
transacting business," and that it shall be filed in
every county where the corporation has "a resident
agent," and shall be irrevocable except by the substitution of another qualified person for the one named
therein so long as the corporation shall have "places
of business" in the state. These provisions would
seem necessarily to indicate that the statute was intended to apply to a corporation whose actual or contemplated business in the state is such as to admit
of its having resident agents or places of business
therein. And to have a resident agent or place of
business it must be carrying on, or intending to carry
on, its ordinary corporate business, for a corporation
doing but a single act of business with no intention
of doing more could not, in the nature of things, be
expected to have a resident agent or place of business. To require a foreign banking corporation to

execute and file the power of attorney required by the statute as a prerequisite to its right to purchase a promissory note or take a mortgage to secure a debt, or to do any other single act of business, when there was no purpose or intention to engage in banking here, would be a very narrow, harsh, and, we think, an unwarranted construction of the statute. The following authorities, although under statutes differing in detail from ours, tend to support this conclusion: Murfree on Foreign Corporations, § 65, *et seq.; Cooper Manufacturing Company* v. *Ferguson,* 113 U. S. 727 (5 Sup. Ct. 739); *Florsheim Brothers Drygoods Company* v. *Lester,* 60 Ark. 120 (46 Am. St. Rep. 102, 27 L. R. A. 505, 29 S. W. 34); *Potter* v. *Bank of Ithaca,* 5 Hill, 490; *Gilchrist* v. *Helena Railway Company,* 47 Fed. 593. There is nothing in the former decisions of this court or of the federal court construing our statute which, in our opinion, conflicts with these views. In *Semple* v. *Bank of British Columbia, In re Comstock,* and *Bank of British Columbia* v. *Page,* the bank was regularly engaged in the transaction of its corporate business in the state. The case of *Hacheny* v. *Leary,* involved the construction of a statute of the then territory of Washington as applied to a contract made in the territory. That statute differed in many respects from the one now before us, and, besides, the case discloses that the corporation had an agent in Washington actually engaged in the business of soliciting and receiving applications for insurance. For these reasons the case is distinguishable from the one under consideration. It follows that the judgment of the court below must be affirmed, and it is so ordered.

AFFIRMED.

28 Or.—41.

Decided February 5, 1896.

GUISEPPE MATASCE *v.* KATE MATASCE.

APPEAL from Lane: J. C. FULLERTON, Judge.

This is a suit for a divorce in which both parties claim affirmative relief, but neither party obtained it, whereupon the plaintiff appealed. The brief for appellant not having been filed within the time limited, the respondent now moves for an order of dismissal, while the appellant files a countermotion for leave to file his brief after the expiration of the time granted by the rules of court.   DISMISSED.

Messrs. W. R. Bilyeu and *Patrick J. Bannon,* for the motion to dismiss.

Messrs. Weatherford and Wyatt, contra.

PER CURIAM. Upon considering this case we have concluded to allow the motion for dismissal, and it is so ordered.   ·   DISMISSED.

Argued July 22; decided October 28, 1895.

STATE *v.* MORGAN.
[42 Pac. 128.]

APPEAL from Multnomah: T. A. STEPHENS, Judge.

Mr. Martin L. Pipes, for appellant.

PER CURIAM. This is an appeal from a judgment upon the conviction of Charles E. Morgan of the crime of embezzlement. The indictment charges, in brief, that the defendant on July second, eighteen

hundred and ninety-four, was the employé of Harry C.
Boyd and E. K. Arnold, partners under the firm name
of Boyd and Arnold, and as such employé and by
means of his employment, received and had in his
possession certain bills, coin, bank checks, bills of exchange, etc., the property of Boyd and Arnold, which
he unlawfully and feloniously converted to his own
use. No brief or argument has been filed by the state,
although the time for filing the same has long since
expired. From an examination of the record and defendant's brief we are of the opinion that under the
evidence the defendant was the agent and employé of
the Hamburg-Bremen Fire Insurance Company, and
that the money alleged to have been converted was
the property of that company, and not of Boyd and
Arnold, as alleged in the indictment. This evidence
entitled the defendant to a verdict, and the court
erred in not instructing the jury to acquit as requested by him. The judgment must therefore be
reversed, and it is so ordered.   REVERSED.

Decided July 22, 1895.

REMILLARD *v.* MULTNOMAH STREET RAIL-
WAY COMPANY.

APPEAL from Multnomah: E. D SHATTUCK, Judge.

Action by Rhoda Remillard to recover damages for
being thrown from a car by its sudden starting while
she was leaving it at a street crossing. Judgment for
plaintiff and defendant appealed. This is now a second
motion to dismiss the appeal and affirm the judgment
because appellant has neither filed a brief nor obtained an extension of time for so doing.

Decided October 29, 1895.

DENNY *v.* THOMPSON.

APPEAL from Multnomah: E. D. SHATTUCK, Judge.

Action by O. N. Denny as receiver of the Portland Savings Bank against David P. Thompson for the possession of certain promissory notes that had been delivered to him to secure him against liability on certain bonds. There was a judgment for plaintiff and defendant appealed.

Messrs. Dolph, Nixon and Dolph, for appellant.

Messrs. Dolph, Mallory and Simon, for respondent.

PER CURIAM. Pursuant to the stipulation of the parties hereto, the appeal in this cause will be dismissed.   DISMISSED.

Argued November 20; decided December 23, 1895.

W. R. WILLIS *v.* G. A. SMITH.
[42 Pac. 990.]

APPEAL from Douglas: J. C. FULLERTON, Judge.

Mr. W. R. Willis, in pro. per., for appellant.

Mr. J. W. Hamilton, for respondent.

Opinion by MR. CHIEF JUSTICE BEAN.

This is a proceeding by garnishment. The pleadings are identical with those in the case of P. L. Willis against the same defendants, 28 Or. 265, except as to the date of the garnishment, and the date and amount of plaintiff's judgment against Holmes. It appears from the record that after a jury had been impanelled to try the cause and both parties had declined to give any evidence, the defendant moved for a nonsuit, and plaintiff for a judgment on the pleadings. Plaintiff's motion was overruled, and the motion for nonsuit allowed, on the theory that the burden of proof was on the plaintiff. For the reasons given in the opinion just filed in the P. L. Willis case, 28 Or. 265, we think the motion for judgment on the pleadings was properly overruled, but the court erred in holding that the burden of proof was on the plaintiff and in granting a nonsuit.　　　　REVERSED.

Argued November 4; decided December 9, 1895.

BIRD *v*. BIRD.
[42 Pac. 616.]

APPEAL from Multnomah: LOYAL B. STEARNS, Judge.

Mr. Raleigh Stott, for respondent.

Mr. Alfred F. Sears, Jr., for appellant.

PER CURIAM. This is a suit for divorce by Lillie Irene Bird against Benjamin M. Bird, and for the custody of a daughter and son of the parties, aged respectively nine and seven years, brought by the wife on the ground of cruel and inhuman treatment. A counterclaim was filed by the husband asking a divorce on the ground of desertion, and for the custody of the children, but the court, having found that the equities were with the plaintiff, decreed her a divorce and awarded the son to her and the daughter to the defendant, and directed the plaintiff to sell at public auction the household furniture and other personal property belonging to the parties, and divide the net proceeds thereof equally with the defendant, from which decree he appeals. The question presented for review is purely one of fact, and having carefully examined the evidence, which we do not deem necessary to quote or comment upon, we deem it sufficient to warrant the conclusion reached by the court. It appears that the defendant, for some time prior to the trial, had been living with his mother, to whom the children became very much attached, and that by order of the court each party had alternately kept these children pending the suit. The daughter being called as a witness for the defendant expressed a wish to remain with her father, and the court so decreed. The children were the wards of the court, which sought their best interests rather than the desire of either party, and, having temporarialy disposed of them with that end in view, we can see no reason for changing the decree which is affirmed.   AFFIRMED.

Argued November 18; decided December 23, 1895.

WILLIS *v.* HOLMES.
[42 Pac. 988.]

This action was brought by W. R. Willis, as administrator of the estate of M. B. Holmes, deceased, to recover from F. W. Holmes the sum of twelve thousand two hundred and thirty dollars as double damages, under section 1125 of Hill's Code. The complaint alleges "That before said administration was granted the defendant did embezzle, alien, and convert to his own use, five thousand five hundred dollars in money, one promissory note, given by James Velzian to said deceased, of the value of three hundred dollars, and one promissory note, given by J. A. Kirkendall to deceased, of the value of three hundred and fifteen dollars, all the property of said deceased, M. B. Holmes, to plaintiff's damage as such administrator in the sum of six thousand one hundred and fifteen dollars." The answer contains a specific denial of all the allegations of the complaint. At the close of plaintiff's testimony the court, on motion, gave the defendant a judgment of nonsuit upon the ground that the plaintiff had failed to prove a cause sufficient to be submitted to the jury, and such ruling is the only assignment of error on this appeal.   AFFIRMED.

APPEAL from Douglas: J. C. FULLERTON, Judge.

For appellant there was a brief by *Messrs. W. R. Willis, in pro. per., A. M. Crawford,* and *Guy G. Willis.*

For respondent there was a brief by *Mr. J. W. Hamilton.*

Opinion by MR. CHIEF JUSTICE BEAN.

In our opinion the testimony was manifestly insufficient to warrant a verdict in favor of the plaintiff. The most that can be claimed for it is that about six months before the death of plaintiff's intestate he received five thousand five hundred dollars for property sold to one Smith, but what disposition he made of it does not appear. At that time he lived alone on a farm some miles from Roseburg, but soon after was taken sick, removed to Smith's house, and thence to Roseburg, where he died in February, eighteen hundred and ninety-four; that during the last two months of his life he was taken care of principally by the defendant, who is his nephew, and the only relative in the state; that during this time he made different statements to the defendant about his money and property, saying that he had been robbed, and that if anything happened to look behind a certain log. A few days before his death, among other rambling and incoherent statements he said, "Floyd," meaning the defendant, "over behind that log you will find something." The evidence further shows that about three weeks before his uncle's death the defendant, in conversation with the plaintiff about his uncle's financial affairs, said he believed that Smith had paid for the property purchased by him, and that his uncle had the money then, for he told him where to look for it after his death, and that he also believed his uncle had the Velzain note, and that the Kirkendall note had not been paid, although the mortgage given to secure it had been satisfied of record. The evidence also shows that defendant made no search for money or property after his uncle's death, and, indeed, there is no testimony that the deceased had any money at the time of his death, or during the time the defendant was caring for him, and there is not a scintilla of evidence in the record to show that defendant received any money or property belonging to his uncle or his estate, or ever saw or knew that he had any. And, furthermore, he was put on the stand by plaintiff, and testified in most positive and unequivocal terms to the contrary. Under these circumstances and this character of testimony the court very properly allowed the motion for a nonsuit.   AFFIRMED.

Argued February 10; decided March 23, 1896.

PELTON v. SISEMORE.
[44 Pac. 286.]

APPEAL from Jackson: W. C. HALE, Judge.

Mr. William M. Colvig, for appellants.

Messrs. Lionel R. Webster and *A. S. Hammond,* for respondent.

PER CURIAM. This is a suit for an accounting by Horace I. Pelton and others against John Sisemore, and the only issues involved in the case are questions of fact. The case comes here on the appeal of plaintiffs from a decree against them. From an examination of the testimony, we are of the opinion that the decree of the court below should be affirmed, and it is so ordered.   AFFIRMED.

Decided December 7, 1895.

EX PARTE CHILDS.

On the twenty-sixth of November, eighteen hundred and ninety-five, Mr. John L. Childs filed with the County Clerk of Josephine County his resignation as an attorney of the Oregon bar, under the provisions of section 1045, Hill's Code, and on December seventh, eighteen hundred and ninety-five, the same was filed with the clerk of the supreme court.
                              RESIGNED.

EX PARTE GARRIGUS.

On September fifth, eighteen hundred and ninety-five, the attorney-general, at the request of the Grievance Committee of the Oregon State Bar Association, filed a complaint in the supreme court charging Lewis C. Garrigus, an attorney duly admitted to practice in eighteen hundred and ninety, with embezzling funds that had been intrusted to him by certain clients, and praying that he be disbarred from practice. It was afterwards discovered that after an investigation by the committee of the Bar Association and before the charges had been filed by the attorney-general, Mr. Garrigus had filed his resignation as an attorney with the clerk of the County Court of Multnomah County. This resignation was forwarded to and filed with the clerk of the supreme court on September sixth, eighteen hundred and ninety-five. Afterwards, on motion of the attorney-general, the complaint was withdrawn.

DISMISSED.

EX PARTE PILKINGTON.

An original application was filed by the attorney-general, at the request of the Grievance Committee of the State Bar Association, praying for the disbarment of Harold Pilkington, an attorney of this court, and showing that said Pilkington had been duly convicted in the Circuit Court of Multnomah County of the crime of embezzlement, and was then undergoing punishment therefor. The defendant appeared and asked an extension of time within which to answer, but before the time had expired he filed with the clerk of the County Court of Multnomah County his resignation as an attorney, under the provisions of section 1045 of Hill's Code. This resignation was filed with the clerk of the supreme court on the twenty-fourth of December, eighteen hundred and ninety-five, whereupon the disbarment proceeding was dismissed.

DISMISSED.

Decided November 18, 1895.

CORBETT *v.* COMMERCIAL NATIONAL BANK.

Action at law by Thomas F. Corbett against the Commercial National Bank to replevin certain title deeds. There was a judgment for defendant and plaintiff appealed. Defendant moves to dismiss for certain irregularities in perfecting the appeal.

DISMISSED.

For the motion, *Messrs. George H. Durham* and *Harrison Gray Platt.*

Contra, Mr. William L. Nutting.

PER CURIAM. The motion is well taken; the appeal cannot be sustained.   DISMISSED.

ROLL OF ATTORNEYS.*

Names of attorneys who have been admitted to practice by the Supreme Court of Oregon between January first, eighteen hundred and eighty-nine, and January first, eighteen hundred and ninety-six, showing the date of admission, and a reference to the record where the same is entered.

Name.	Volume.	Page.	Year.
Abraham, Albert	9	720	1892
Adams, Harry B.	11	21	1895
Adams, Loring K.	9	239	1892
Ailshie, J. F.	9	427	1891
Allen, Harrison	10	553	1894
Ames, William B.	1	179 (Pendleton)	1893
Anderson, Gustave	11	25	1895
Armour, Stuart	10	485	1894
Austin, John L.	1	220 (Pendleton)	1895
Avery, C. W.	9	716	1892
Ayer, John L.	9	845	1891
Bagley, Geo. R.	11	25	1895
Baker, Lydell	9	279	1890
Ballenger, Harry	9	8	1889
Bartlett, Edw. W.	1	1 (Pendleton)	1889
Bartlett, T. Harris	10	181	1893
Bauer, Cecil H.	9	426	1891
Bayne, John	10	181	1893
Beach, Chas. A.	8	460	1891
Beaver, Chas. L.	8	782	1889
Beck, J.	11	25	1895
Beekman, Benjamin B.	8	681	1889
Bell, Robert F.	10	310	1893
Bell, Wells A.	10	485	1894
Bellinger, Victor C.	8	776	1889
Benedict, Edwin E.	10	565	1894
Benson, Patrick H.	10	258	1893
Bergman, M. L.	8	782	1889
Bigger, Henry J.	9	642	1892
Biggs, John W.	10	564	1894
Biggs, M. R.	9	95	1890
Birkhimer, W. A.	8	764	1889
Bishop, B. B.	1	89 (Pendleton)	1891

*It is intended that this list shall supplement the one published in 16th Oregon, and include all who have been admitted to the close of the year eighteen hundred and ninety-five.— REPORTER.

Name.	Volume.	Page.	Year.
Blake, Frank	10	346	1893
Blandford, S. M.	10	184	1893
Bowman, Benton	10	47	1893
Bramley, John G.	9	386	1891
Brattain, Eldon M.	1	71 (Pendleton)	1890
Bretherton, W. W.	1	70 (Pendleton)	1891
Brewster, William L.	9	458	1891
Briggs, E. D.	9	378	1891
Bright, C. J.	9	238	1890
Brink, M. E.	8	777	1889
Brockenbrough, John R.	9	204	1890
Bromley, Van Buren	9	717	1892
Bronaugh Earl C. Jr.	1	66 (Pendleton)	1890
Bronaugh, Jerry E.	10	485	1894
Brooks, William L.	10	305	1893
Brown, Geo. M.	9	456	1891
Brown, John A.	10	61	1893
Brown, Valentine	9	678	1892
Brown, W. M.	10	485	1894
Brownell, D. C.	8	784	1889
Brownell, Geo. C.	9	489	1891
Bruner, Morris E.	10	485	1894
Buck, Reed	10	16	1893
Burnham, Walter R.	9	719	1892
Burtenshaw, L. L.	8	774	1889
Buse, Otto F.	9	720	1892
Butler, Marion A.	1	241 (Pendleton)	1895
Butterfield, Milton G.	9	679	1892
Callison, R. W.	11	25	1895
Cameron, Geo. J.	10	181	1893
Campbell, James U.	10	181	1893
Cannon, A. M.	11	25	1895
Canton, W. J.	9	333	1891
Caples, Jesse R.	10	485	1894
Cardwell, William W.	9	206	1890
Carson, Frederick D.	10	241	1893
Carson, John A.	8	755	1889
Catlin, Robert	10	181	1893
Cattanach, Geo. H.	10	564	1894
Cellars, Geo. B.	11	25	1895
Chance, Chas. H.	9	676	1892
Chapman, T. J.	9	468	1891
Charleston, William S.	1	222 (Pendleton)	1895
Charlton, J. J.	9	456	1891
Childs, John L.	11	107 (Resigned)	1895
Clark, J. C.	9	456	1891
Cleeton, T. J.	10	181	1893
Cleland, Jno. B.	9	312	1890
Cleland, Wm. A.	9	312	1890

Name.	Volume.	Page.	Year.
Cleveland, A. A.	9	46	1889
Cochran, Chas. Edgar	10	537	1894
Cochran, John W.	9	583	1892
Cockerline, H. N.	9	428	1891
Coke, John S., Jr.	10	181	1893
Colby, John L.	11	25	1895
Cole, C. C.	9	458	1891
Colton, W. W.	8	776	1889
Colvig, Geo. W.	8	781	1889
Condit, A. O.	9	456	1891
Condon, Herbert T.	10	526	1894
Conden, J. B.	1	17 (Pendleton)	1889
Cone, Geo. M.	9	348	1891
Connell, William	10	485	1894
Conner, Henry F.	11	62	1895
Connett, A. W.	1	11 (Pendleton)	1889
Conyers, W. H.	11	25	1895
Cooper, W. H.	9	720	1892
Copeland, H. A.	8	701	1889
Copeland, Robert A.	9	615	1892
Coshow, O. P.	9	238	1890
Cotton, William W.	8	776	1889
Cowing, Thos. F.	9	66	1889
Cradelbaugh, John H.	8	652	1889
Crandall, S. B.	9	237	1890
Crosby, Henry T.	10	490	1894
Crowell, Wm. S.	11	171	1895
Cunningham, J. R.	10	485	1894
Curry, Alfred L.	9	221	1890
Curl, L. M.	9	682	1892
Dabney, P. P.	9	493	1891
Dalrymple, C. H.	10	181	1893
Darling, L. W.	1	180 (Pendleton)	1898
Davey, Frank	10	445	1894
Davis, Geo. E.	1	74 (Pendleton)	1891
Davis, James N.	9	368	1891
Davis, Napoleon	10	181	1893
Davis, Wm. M.	9	454	1891
Dawson, John W.	9	715	1892
D'Arcy, Wm. J.	9	720	1892
Denham, Lewis	11	25	1895
Denlinger, Henry	10	485	1894
Dennis, Stephen D.	11	25	1895
Dey, Walter C.	10	181	1893
Dimick, Grant B.	11	25	1895
Dobyns, W. H.	10	485	1894
Dodd, Walter H.	10	181	1893
Dodson, W. D. B.	11	25	1895
Dolph, Chester V.	10	485	1894

Name.	Volume.	Page.	Year.
Delsen, D. P.	10	276	1898
Donaugh, D. M.	8	631	1889
Douglas, B. T.	9	455	1891
Drake, J. Francis	10	485	1894
Driggs, E. F.	10	181	1593
Dunlway, Ralph R.	9	720	1892
Dye, C. H.	9	242	1890
Eastabrook, Frank	9	584	1892
Eaves, David W.	10	554	1594
Eddy, B. L.	10	485	1894
Elkins, Luther	10	485	1894
Ellis, O. G.	9	728	1892
Emmons, E. J.	9	758	1892
Esteb, L. A.	1	36 (Pendleton)	1890
Evans, Pierce	9	581	1892
Ewert, C. C.	1	223 (Pendleton)	1895
Ewing, J. W.	9	220	1890
Fay, John P.	10	166	1893
Fitch, Francis	9	47	1889
Fitzgerald, J. J.	9	720	1892
Flegel, Austin F.	9	677	1892
Fleming, R. J.	10	485	1894
Flood, A. B.	10	392	1894
Flower, J. H.	10	478	1894
Fox, Sydney	1	67 (Pendleton)	1890
Frazier, W. T.	9	616	1892
Fry, Hugh M.	10	488	1894
Gallagher, Andrew E.	8	764	1889
Galloway, William	10	726	1895
Gantenbein, C. U.	9	425	1891
Garland, S. M.	9	255	1890
Garrigus, Lewis C.	9	99 (Resigned)	1890
Gatens, William N.	10	485	1894
Gates, Nathaniel H.	1	200 (Pendleton)	1893
Gebhart, A. E.	9	464	1891
Geisler, Theo J.	9	242	1890
Gest, C. H.	10	133	1893
Glisan, Rodney L.	9	680	1892
Goode, Geo. W.	9	718	1892
Goodell, John	10	746	1895
Gorman, Geo. H.	9	583	1892
Gowan, Walter	10	485	1894
Graham, Reuben P.	1	180 (Pendleton)	1893
Greene, Thos. G	9	678	1892
Greenfield, J. R.	9	676	1892
Gregory, E. R.	9	435	1891
Griffin, Gerald	9	567	1892
Griffith, F. T.	10	564	1894
Griffiths, A. E.	8	640	1889

Name.	Volume.	Page.	Year.
Grimm, Edgar	10	181	1893
Griswold, Norman L.	10	485	1894
Grossman, William	8	773	1889
Groves, A. F.	10	346	1893
Gruber, Samuel H.	9	613	1892
Gullete, H. W.	11	25	1895
Gurley, S. A. D.	10	485	1894
Gwilt, John W.	9	677	1892
Hackett, A. J.	1	4 (Pendleton)	1889
Hailey, Thos G.			1890
Haines, S. H.	9	795	1892
Hale, W. C.	9	226	1890
Haller, John W.	1	220 (Pendleton)	1895
Hamilton, Chas.	10	181	1893
Hand, A. M.	10	153	1893
Hannum, C. S.	8	775	1889
Harbison, Robert	10	244	1893
Hardesty, A. G.	9	109	1890
Hardesty, Elmer	11	25	1895
Harris, Joseph C.	10	485	1894
Harrison, M. C.	10	485	1894
Hart, Geo. B.	11	25	1895
Hart, Julius N.	11	107	1895
Hawley, Willis C.	10	558	1894
Hayes, Geo. W.	1	80 (Pendleton)	1891
Hayter, Oscar	11	107	1895
Hazen, Geo. W.	9	748	1892
Hedges, J. E.	9	683	1892
Hendricks, H. B.	1	180 (Pendleton)	1893
Herrington, Chas R.	10	181	1893
Hicks, Everett	10	173	1893
Hicks, J. C.	9	456	1891
Hill, Geo Henry	10	485	1894
Hill, Leverett A.	9	673	1892
Hindman, W. W.	9	483	1891
Hitchings, J. H.	11	107	1895
Hofer, Ernst	10	167	1893
Hoffman, L. A.	1	220 (Pendleton)	1895
Hoke, B. F.	8	311	1890
Holden, Chas. H.	10	581	1894
Hollister, Geo. W.	10	564	1894
Holgate, H. C.	10	181	1893
Holman, Geo. F.	8	777	1889
Holmes, Webster	10	181	1893
Hosford, J. B.	9	425	1891
Houck, John A.	11	25	1895
Hough, A. C.	10	447	1894
Hovey, A. G., Jr.	9	720	1892

28 Or.—48.

Name.	Volume.	Page.	Year.
Huffer, Frank A.	9	426	1891
Hughes, Carroll E.	11	25	1895
Hughes, J. M.	9	679	1892
Hull, Elmer E.	11	25	1895
Hume, Harry C.	11	95	1895
Humphrey, C. F.	10	541	1894
Humphrey, Geo.	9	839	1891
Huntington, J. B.	1	240 (Pendleton)	1895
Hurgren, Allen A.	10	485	1894
Irwin, G. M.	10	71	1893
Ivey, Joseph William	10	517	1894
Jackson, Wilber L.	9	778	1892
Janney, L. R.	9	719	1892
Jayne, A. A.	9	525	1891
Jeffrey, John A.	10	712	1895
Jewett, Guy R.	10	485	1894
Johns, Jno. M.	1	179 (Pendleton)	1893
Johnson, Daniel B.	11	80	1895
Johnson, George	11	107	1895
Johnson, J. C.	11	25	1895
Johnson, Jasper J.	1	71 (Pendleton)	1890
Johnson, W. H.	9	495	1891
Johnston, A. W.	9	456	1891
Johnston, C. W.	9	253	1890
Jones, W. A. M.	9	678	1892
Joseph, Geo. W. P.	10	181	1893
Jubitz, Raymond	10	485	1894
Kanaga, A. R.	8	640	1889
Kavanaugh, John P.	10	181	1893
Keefer, Miles B.	10	522	1894
Keenan Fred L.	8	778	1889
Kelly, Percy R.	9	683	1892
Kelly, W. Maurice	10	354	1893
Kelsey, F. D.	1	70 (Pendleton)	1890
Kieff, J. W.	9	435	1891
Kilgore, Arthur	9	714	1892
Kindt, Chas. E.	8	785	1889
King, William R.	10	46	1893
Kinsey, George W.	10	564	1894
Knowles, John W.	1	78 (Pendleton)	1891
Kohler, James P.	8	650	1889
Kraemer, Otto J.	11	124	1895
Lachman, L.	11	107	1895
Lafferty, F. S.	9	423	1891
La Force, William M.	9	781	1892
Lake, E. Joel	11	25	1895
Lamson, Roswell B.	10	181	1893
Lawrence Chas. W.	11	25	1895
Lawrence, George, Jr.	11	25	1895

Name.	Volume.	Page.	Year.
Lawrey, John H.	1	179 (Pendleton)	1896
Levens, William S.	1	240 (Pendleton)	1895
Linden, C. C.	9	720	1892
Linkenbach, C.	10	170	1893
Lockwood, Chas. E.	8	786	1889
Logan, John F.	9	676	1892
Long, Ira Milton	11	46	1895
Long, Joel M.	9	733	1892
Lord, Chas. F.	9	545	1891
Lounsbury, Harvey E.	10	485	1894
Lowell, Stephen A.	1	88 (Pendleton)	1891
Lyons, John	11	25	1895
Lyons, Thos. R.	9	720	1892
MacMillan, John	9	435	1891
Macrum, W. S.	11	25	1895
Maddock, Geo. N.	9	720	1892
Malarkey, Daniel J.	9	681	1892
Mallory, Elmer E.	11	25	1895
Mann, John D.	10	564	1894
Margrave, Chas. E.	10	181	1893
Markley, Norman E.	11	25	1895
Marks, J. E.	10	564	1894
Marquam, Thos. A.	11	25	1895
Marsh, Chas. H.	1	139 (Pendleton)	1892
Marsh, Geo. H.	10	181	1893
Martin, Barney S.	10	181	1893
Mason, Samuel R.	10	485	1894
Masters, F. K.	11	25	1895
Matteson, T. C.	10	181	1893
Maulsby, Israel T.	9	179	1890
Maxwell F. M.	10	327	1893
May, William J.	9	717	1892
McBride, Geo. W.	9	130	1890
McCaffrey, J. Carroll	8	649	1889
McCamant, Wallace	9	308	1890
McColloch, Chas. H.	11	25	1895
McCulloch, J. W.	10	485	1894
McCredie, W. W.	9	239	1890
McDevitt, Thos. F. B.	10	564	1894
McDonald, F. A.	8	653	1889
McFadden, A. L.	10	181	1893
McGinn, John L.	10	181	1893
McIntosh, F. Geo.	9	220	1890
McKee, J. T.	9	739	1892
McKim, Maurice	10	181	1893
McLeod, Neil C.	1	221 (Pendleton)	1895
McManus, John K.	1	221 (Pendleton)	1895
McLoney, B. F.	9	572	1892
McNall, S. J.	8	780	1889

Name.	Volume.	Page.	Year.
McNary, John H.	10	485	1894
McNary, Lawrence A.	1	67 (Pendleton)	1893
Mead, James P.	9	72	1890
Medley, John S.	11	107	1895
Meier, Julius L.	11	204	1895
Mendenhall, A. R.	11	107	1895
Mendenhall, Montford	10	485	1894
Menefee, Frank	8	783	1889
Merges, Ernest E.	10	485	1894
Messick, John B.	1	137 (Pendleton)	1892
Metson, W. H.	9	422	1891
Middleton, John H.	10	485	1894
Miller, Alfred D.	10	181	1893
Miller, Elmer E.	1	69 (Pendleton)	1890
Miller, G. M.	8	779	1889
Miller, J. E.	1	2 (Pendleton)	1889
Miller, William	1	140 (Pendleton)	1892
Miller, William L.	10	241	1893
Mills, F. H.	9	221	1890
Mitchell, Hiram E.	9	352	1891
Mitchell, Walter E.	10	485	1894
Montague, R. M.	9	243	1890
Montgomery, Henry M.	10	485	1894
Moon, C. L.	11	107	1895
Moor, C. H.	11	25	1895
Moore, C. A.	9	456	1891
Moore, F. L.	1	68 (Pendleton)	1890
Moore, Virgil	9	682	1892
Morcom, Elisha P.	9	714	1892
Morrill, Ardee H.	10	485	1894
Morrill, Roscoe R.	11	25	1895
Morrison, J. H.	9	459	1891
Moser, Gustavus C.	10	485	1894
Motter, Frank	11	25	1895
Mulkey, Frank M.	9	427	1891
Mullon, J. T.	10	485	1894
Munly, William A.	10	564	1894
Murdoch, Hiram F.	10	497	1894
Murphy, Jas. H.	1	122 (Pendleton)	1892
Napton, H. P.	8	631	1889
Naregan, Norton L.	10	443	1894
Neil, George R.	10	241	1893
Newberry, Sylvester A.	1	200 (Pendleton)	1894
Newport, N. M.	10	181	1893
Nickerson, George S.	10	694	1895
Northrop, L. C.	9	564	1892
Norton, H. D.	10	181	1893
Oatman, John R.	11	25	1895
O'Day, Thomas	9	206	1890

Name.	Volume.	Page.	Year.
O'Donnell, Wm. R.	10	546	1894
Olson, Fred L.	10	485	1894
O'Neil, Mark	9	302	1890
Orr, John S.	9	720	1892
Osborn, F. R.	8	781	1889
O'Shea, Jno.	9	240	1890
Packwood, Wm. H. Jr.	1	200 (Pendleton)	1894
Paddock, H. S.	11	43	1895
Paddock, John W.	8	651	1889
Pague, Bemer S.	10	181	1898
Palmer, A. C.	11	25	1895
Panenberg, Eugene	10	280	1893
Park, Chas. Arthur	10	553	1894
Parke, John S.	10	284	1893
Parker, Irving W.	10	267	1893
Parker, W. H.	8	784	1889
Pattison, J. R.	9	423	1891
Peaslee, Marshall B.	10	93	1893
Peck, W. F.	9	491	1891
Peery, Nash	9	691	1892
Peirsol, Harry Allen	10	354	1894
Perry, Walter S.	9	158	1890
Phelps, Gilbert W.	10	587	1894
Phillipps, J. N.	8	778	1889
Pierce, Walter M.	1	241 (Pendleton)	1895
Pilkington, Harold	8	546 (Resigned)	1888
Platt, Harrison Gray	9	240	1890
Platt, Ralph	11	97	1895
Platt, Robert Treat	9	732	1892
Pogue, M. E.	11	107	1895
Potter, E. O.	1	67 (Pendleton)	1890
Potter, Thad. S.	9	424	1891
Pratt, W. H.	9	235	1890
Prebble, E. B.	9	147	1890
Prim, Chas.	9	424	1891
Pulliam, W. E.	11	25	1895
Quackenbush, A.	9	596	1892
Raley, Frank J.	10	485	1894
Raley, James H.	1	219 (Pendleton)	1895
Ransom, James W.	10	528	1894
Reames, Alfred Evan	10	288	1893
Redfield, Chas. E.	1	205 (Pendleton)	1894
Reed, Charlton A.	8	785	1889
Reeder, L. B.	1	213 (Pendleton)	1895
Reed, Robert R. Jr.	11	107	1895
Relfe, W. S.	9	626	1892
Rhodes, M. D. L.	11	25	1895
Rice, W. J.	9	294	1890
Riddell, Hayward H.	9	684	1892

Name.	Volume.	Page.	Year.
Riddle, Ira B.	10	277	1893
Riley, E. F.	9	614	1892
Rinearson, George O.	10	181	1893
Robb, Bamford A.	9	684	1892
Roberts, L. A.	11	107	1895
Roberts, R. W.	10	435	1894
Robertson, John P.	9	218	1890
Robinson, L. M.	1	11 (Pendleton)	1889
Roblin, Chas. E.	10	181	1893
Robson, Chas. E.	9	278	1890
Ross, James K.	10	836	1893
Rosseter, Frank S.	10	489	1894
Rupel, Chas. T.	9	720	1892
Russell, Geo. T.	8	798	1888
Rutenic, J. Calvin	1	70 (Pendleton)	1890
Ryan, Richard W.	10	545	1894
Sabin, Edward M.	10	284	1893
Savage, L. D.	10	278	1893
Savage, U. G.	10	485	1894
Saxton, Francis M.	1	241 (Pendleton)	1895
Scarborough, William	11	158	1895
Schnabel, Chas. J.	9	427	1891
Schnabel, Joseph W.	10	485	1894
Schulderman, H. J.	11	25	1895
Schutz, Adolph	9	236	1890
Schutz, E.	9	720	1892
Scoular, Robert	9	673	1892
Scott, John H.	11	25	1895
Seabrook, E. B.	11	25	1895
Seaman, A. E.	9	455	1891
Seaver, W. F.	9	181	1890
Selph, E. E.	9	191	1890
Severance, A. W.	9	690	1892
Sewell, Russell E.	9	676	1892
Shambort, Ivan D.	1	50 (Pendleton)	1890
Sheahan, D. W.	1	25 (Pendleton)	1890
Sherman, D. C.	10	485	1894
Shinn, Geo. H.	1	188 (Pendleton)	1892
Short, G. M.	10	564	1894
Showers, C. A.	9	683	1892
Sibley, Joseph E.	9	148	1890
Sims, Chas. B.	10	485	1894
Sinnott. J. F.	11	25	1895
Sinnott, Nicholas J.	1	221 (Pendleton)	1895
Sinnott, W. P.	11	25	1895
Skipworth, Geo. Frank	11	107	1895
Smith, A. M.	9	681	1892
Smith, B. M.	9	456	1891
Smith, F. P.	10	280	1893

Name.	Volume.	Page.	Year.
Smith, Geo. A.	9	564	1892
Smith, Geo. Sanford,	10	181	1893
Smith, Isham N.	9	680	1892
Smith, Jacob B.	1	205 (Pendleton)	1894
Smith, John U.	1	68 (Pendleton)	1890
Smith, Lester P.	11	107	1895
Smith, Robert G.	8	783	1889
Smith, W. D.	10	181	1893
Smith, William	1	2 (Pendleton)	1889
Smith, William H.	9	680	1892
Smith, William K.	8	779	1889
Soliss, Albert N.	10	709	1895
Somers, John M.	9	808	1890
Spencer, Arthur C.	11	25	1895
Spencer, J. J.	9	488	1891
Spencer, Schuyler C.	10	280	1893
Sperry, E. D.	9	240	1890
Spittle, Frank	9	681	1892
Stannislawsky, Henry	9	679	1892
Stevens, Dudley W.	11	25	1895
Stevens, Lenn L.	10	527	1894
Stillman, A. D.	9	456	1891
Story, Henry D.	10	181	1893
Stout, Geo. C.	9	680	1892
Stowe, Edwin S.	10	16	1893
Stowell, Percy E.	10	485	1894
Stratford, J. L.	11	85	1895
Strode, Victor K.*	9	763	1892
Stuart, Dell	9	247	1890
Sweek, Alexander.	8	778	1889
Switzer, H. M.	11	21	1895
Swope, B. F.	10	181	1893
Swope, Geo. W.	10	564	1894
Sydenham, Alvin H.	9	720	1892
Talmage, C. W.	10	695	1895
Tarpley, Louis H.	8	786	1889
Tazwell, George	10	485	1894
Thompson, C. C.	9	454	1891
Thompson, R. W.	9	677	1892
Thorn, James	8	795	1889
Thornton, Thos. G.	10	845	1893
Timms, Eugene D.	10	805	1893
Travis, Henry S.	10	70	1893
True, James N.	9	715	1892
Turner, R. Marvin	1	24 (Pendleton)	1890
Tussing, Amor A.	10	98	1893
Upton, James Monroe	10	352	1893
Van Fridagh, Paul	10	181	1893

*nunc pro tunc for 1881.

Name.	Volume.	Page.	Year.
Vantine, Ashley	10	181	1893
Van Wyck, Sidney McM. Jr.	10	279	1893
Vawter, William I.	9	720	1892
Veasie, Arthur L.	10	181	1893
Vinton, W. T.	9	720	1892
Vreeland, Thaddeus Whitney	10	181	1893
Wade, Edward C.	10	169	1893
Wagner, John P.	9	456	1891
Wagner, T. P.	1	69 (Pendleton)	1880
Wait, Chas. N.	1	68 (Pendleton)	1890
Walker, D. B.	10	275	1893
Walker, William H.	8	780	1889
Wall, John M.	11	25	1895
Ward, E. L. C.	9	313	1890
Ward, L. A.	9	720	1892
Ward, Peter H.	9	503	1891
Warren, M. S.	10	181	1893
Waterous, Thos. C.	9	237	1890
Watson, D. L., Jr.	11	167	1895
Watters, A. W.	9	29	1889
Welch, Benjamin P.	9	241	1890
Wells, Jerome B.	10	181	1893
West, Peter	1	78 (Pendleton)	1891
Wetherby, Geo.	9	572	1892
Wetzel, Jacob P.	9	720	1892
Whalley, John T.	9	548	1891
Wheeler, Albee E.	9	154	1890
Wheeler, R. G.	9	436	1891
White, G. G.	10	885	1894
Whitney, Fred Moore	1	137 (Pendleton)	1892
Wilbur, Ralph W.	10	5	1892
Wilkins, M. O.	11	107	1895
Williams, David D.	1	87 (Pendleton)	1891
Williams, John M.	9	720	1892
Williams, William A.	11	147	1895
Williams, Walter P.	10	558	1894
Willis, Guy G.	9	425	1891
Wilson, A. King	9	682	1892
Wilson, B. F.	1	4 (Pendleton)	1889
Wilson, E. E.	10	181	1893
Wilson, Hollis S.	9	245	1890
Wilson, J. H.	9	720	1892
Wilson, Thos. Edwin	11	25	1895
Wilson, Thos. H.	9	563	1892
Wilson, T. J.	10	181	1893
Winchester, Jason S.	10	485	1894
Winfree, W. H.	9	865	1891
Witten, T. M.	10	485	1894
Wolf, A. Walter	11	25	1895

Name.	Volume.	Page.	Year.
Wright, Geo. E.	9	720	1892
Wright, Marion	9	800	1890
Wright, Robert C.	1	69 (Pendleton)	1890
Wyatt, J. R.	9	288	1890
Yates, J. Fred	10	181	1893
Yates, William E.	9	428	1891
Yerex, Albert E.	10	558	1894
Young, C. D.	9	363	1891
Young, Geo. D.	8	771	1889
Young, J. E.	10	485	1894
Zink, Howard W.	10	415	1894

28 OR.—44.

INDEX.

INDEX.

ADVERSE PARTIES.

Principal is Adverse in Suit on his Bond. See APPEAL, 3.

Grantor in Fraudulent Deed is not Adverse. See APPEAL, 4.

Contractor in Mechanics' Lien Case is not Adverse. See APPEAL, 5.

In Mechanics' Lien Cases all Claimants are Adverse. See APPEAL, 6.

Service of Notice of Appeal on Adverse Parties. See APPEAL, 3, 4, 5, 6.

ADVERSE POSSESSION.

STATUTE OF LIMITATIONS.

1. The title of a person who has been in adverse possession of land for more than the statutory period, entering under a survey which both he and the adjoining proprietor believed to be correct, cannot be affected by a subsequent survey showing that the division line had not been correctly located by the first survey.—*Pearson v. Dryden*, 350.

MERE CLAIM OF OWNERSHIP.

2. Claim of ownership of premises, in the absence of occupancy, can never become the foundation of an adverse right.—*Willamette Real Estate Company v. Hendrix*, 485.

CONSTRUCTIVE POSSESSION.

3. Entry and occupancy of one of several known lots or tracts conveyed by the same instrument is not constructively an occupancy of all, for the purpose of adverse possession.—*Willamette Real Estate Company v. Hendrix*, 485.

AFFIDAVIT.

Requisites of Affidavit to open Judgment or Decree. See JUDGMENTS, 4.

AGENTS AND AGENCY.

SOURCE OF AGENT'S AUTHORITY.

1. The existence of an agent's authority depends upon the intention of the principal, and is purely a question of fact.—*Connell v. McLoughlin*, 230.

PROOF OF AGENCY.

2. The authority of an agent cannot be proved by the alleged agent's own statements or acts, unless it be also shown that the principal knowingly acquiesced therein.—*Connell v. McLoughlin*, 230.

POWER OF AGENT TO EXECUTE NOTE.

3. An agent authorized to manage and dispose of a sash and door manufacturing plant has no authority to execute a note in the name of his principal in payment for lumber, it not appearing when the lumber was purchased, or that it was used or intended for the benefit of the principal.—*Connell v. McLoughlin*, 230.

PRESUMPTION OF AGENCY FROM SUPPRESSED EVIDENCE.

4. Where the authority of an alleged agent to execute a note, in an action thereon against the principal, is in issue, the failure of the agent, who was an unwilling witness, to produce his power of attorney, does not of itself raise a presumption that he was authorized to execute the note.—*Connell v. McLoughlin*, 230.

WAIVER BY AGENT OF TERMS OF INSURANCE POLICY.

5. Where a fire insurance policy provides that no officer or agent shall have power to waive any of its conditions, except by writing, and that no privilege affecting the insurance shall be claimed by the assured unless so written, a parol waiver of any of the provisions of the policy by the agent from whom the insurance was obtained, after it has been accepted by the assured, is a nullity.—*Egan v. West-chester Insurance Company*, 289.

IMPLIED AUTHORITY OF AGENT.

6. A traveling agent and solicitor of orders has no implied authority to rescind or change a contract made with him for the purchase of goods, after the receipt of the goods by the other party.—*Brigham v. Hibbard*, 386.

FALSE PRETENSES BY AGENT.

7. An instruction that an agent is not supposed to exceed his authority, and cannot bind his principal if he exceeds his authority, is reversible error on a trial for obtaining a signature to a draft by falsely pretending that it was for the accommodation of the principal, as it gives the impression that defendant would be criminally responsible if he exceeded his authority, however innocently.—*State v. Hanscom*, 427.

AGENTS AND AGENCY—Concluded.

Parol Evidence to Show Real Parties to Written Instrument.

3. Parol testimony is admissible to show that a contract which is not a negotiable instrument, and not required to be under seal, although so in fact, executed by and in the name of an agent, is the contract of the principal, although the principal is known to the other contracting party at the date of its execution.— *Barbre* v. *Goodale*, 465.

ALLOWANCE TO WIDOW. See Executors.

ALTERED WRITING AS Evidence. See Evidence, 7.

AMENDMENT.

Of Pleadings to Conform to Proofs. See Pleadings, 5.

Discretion of Court in Allowing Amendments. See Pleadings, 8.

Amending by Changing Names of Parties. See Pleadings, 11.

Of Proof of Service of Notice of Appeal. See Appeal, 19.

Useless Amendment will be Refused. See Pleadings, 12.

ANNUAL WORK on Mines Defined. See Mines, 2, 3.

ANSWER. Inconsistent Defenses. See Pleadings, 1.

APPEALABLE ORDER. See Appeal, 16.

APPEAL.

Appeal from Consent Decree.

1. A decree entered at the request of a party, the other party being present and expressly consenting thereto, connot be appealed from by either side. Such a decree will be governed by the provisions of section 536, Hill's Code, although, strictly speaking, it is not a decree given either by confession or for want of an answer.— *Schmidt* v *Oregon Gold Mining Company*, 9.

Accepting Part of a Judgment as a Waiver of Right to Appeal.

2. In actions at law the entire case is either affirmed or reversed, so that an appeal cannot be taken from a part of a judgment, and the balance of it be accepted; thus, where a judgment went for plaintiff for the amount of a note, but the court refused to allow any attorney's fee, the plaintiff cannot accept the money adjudged to him on the note, and then appeal from the refusal to allow the attorney's fee, for if the case is reversed for one purpose it is for all purposes, and the question of the amount due on the note must be tried again.— *Bush* v. *Mitchell*, 92.

Who are Adverse Parties.

3. Where a treasurer and his bondsmen are jointly sued on his official bond, and the former suffers a default, but the sureties make a successful defense on the merits of the case, the treasurer is "an adverse party" within the meaning of section 537 of Hill's Code, and must be served with the notice of appeal, for the decision of the appellate court affects the principal just as it does his sureties.— *Jackson County* v. *Bloomer*, 110.

4. The grantor in a conveyance of property claimed to be fraudulent as to creditors is not a necessary party to a suit to set aside such conveyance, and, as his interest cannot be affected by the result, he is not an "adverse party," and the notice of appeal need not be served on him.— *Bennett* v. *Minott*, 339.

5. In a mechanics' lien case the contractor is not an "adverse party" and need not be served with the notice of appeal, where he has not been served with summons and has not appeared, though named in the pleadings as a defendant.— *Osborn* v. *Logus*, 302.

6. In mechanics' lien cases all the lien claimants are "adverse" to each other, within the meaning of section 537, Hill's Code, and must be served with the notice of appeal.— *Osborn* v. *Logus*, 302.

Costs on Appeal—Discretion of Court.

7. Where a judgment is modified on appeal to the circuit court, the question of costs is in the sound discretion of that court, and its decision will be disturbed only in case of abuse.— *Sugar Pine Lumber Company* v. *Garrett*, 168.

APPEAL — CONCLUDED.

CROSS-APPEAL.

8. A party to a judgment or decree who has not appealed is presumed to be satisfied, and cannot ask the appellate tribunal to modify or reverse the decision of the lower court.— *Thornton* v. *Krimbel*, 271.

ABSTRACT — FORMAL STATEMENT OF ERRORS.

9. An appeal to the supreme court will not be dismissed because the abstract does not contain a formal statement of errors as required by the last paragraph of Rule 9 of the Supreme Court, (24 Or. 600,) where the appeal is from a decree on the pleadings, and it sufficiently appears that the alleged error upon which the appellant intends to rely is the action of the trial court in sustaining the respondent's motion for the decree.— *Neppach* v. *Jones*, 286.

DISMISSING APPEAL FOR FAILURE TO FILE BRIEF.

10. The rules of practice in the supreme court regarding abstracts and briefs were intended to facilitate business, and it is intended that they shall be substantially complied with; yet, if, through excusable neglect or oversight, some requirement has been omitted, the court may, on a proper showing, excuse the party in fault, as where a brief has not been filed in time through the delay of the printer.— *Neppach* v. *Jones*, 286.

DISMISSING APPEAL FOR NOT FILING ABSTRACT.

11. An appeal will be dismissed where appellant fails to serve and file the abstract of the record required by the rules of the court, (Rules 4 and 9, 24 Or. 595-597,) though part of the record has been lost, no effort having been made within a reasonable time to supply the missing papers.— *Close* v. *Close*, 108.

SERVICE OF NOTICE OF APPEAL ON RESPONDENT'S ATTORNEY.

12. Where nothing appears in the record to show the residence of respondent's attorney, it will be presumed that he resides in the county where the trial was had, and that his admission of service of a notice of appeal from the circuit to the supreme court was there made.— *Bennett* v. *Minott*, 339.

13. It will be presumed by the appellate court in support of a return of service of notice of appeal from a judgment of a justice of the peace, that the attorney for the respondent upon whom the service was made was a resident of the county, where nothing to the contrary appears in the transcript on appeal.— *Hughes* v. *Clemens*, 440.

TIME TO DETERMINE WHEN PARTIES ARE ADVERSE.

14. The question of who are "adverse parties" necessary to be served with the notice of appeal must be determined by the conditions existing when the appeal is taken, and all who are then "adverse" must be served.— *Osborn* v. *Logus*, 302.

RIGHT TO SECOND APPEAL.

15. An attempt to take an appeal, which in consequence of an irregularity is not perfected, does not take away the right to another appeal.— *Osborn* v. *Logus*, 302.

FINAL ORDER.

16. An order overruling a demurrer to a bill of discovery, and requiring defendant to answer interrogatories set forth therein is "final" for the purposes of appeal. — *State* v. *Security Savings Company*, 410.

FILING OF TRANSCRIPT ON APPEAL FROM JUSTICE COURT.

17. A transcript from a justice's court may be filed with the clerk of the circuit court immediately after the appeal has been allowed by the justice without allowing any time for excepting to the sureties on the appeal bond, or for such sureties to justify if excepted to.— *Hughes* v. *Clemens*, 440.

FINDINGS ON CONFLICTING EVIDENCE.

18. Findings of the trial court on conflicting testimony will not be disturbed on appeal, unless they are clearly against the weight of evidence.— *Justice* v. *Elwert*, 460.

AMENDING PROOF OF SERVICE.

19. An imperfect proof of service of a notice of appeal may be amended on motion so as to conform to the fact.— *Barbre* v. *Goodale*, 465.

APPEARANCE.

An appearance by a party will be presumed to have been general so as to give the court jurisdiction of the person where the record fails to show that the appearance was special.— *Godfrey* v. *Douglas County*, 446.

APPLICATION TO SET ASIDE DECREE.

Motion must be Granted within one Year. See DECREES, 8.

Affidavit must show some Statutory Ground. See DECREES, 7.

Correcting for Clerical Mistake after Close of Term. See DECREES, 9.

ASSESSMENTS.

Inaccuracy not Ground for an Injunction. See TAXES, 4.

Omitting Assessments does not Estop Present Taxation. See TAXES, 3.

Alteration of Assessment by Board of Equalization. See TAXES, 9, 10, 11.

ASSESSMENT WORK on Mines Defined. See MINES, 3.

ASSIGNEE OF CHOSE IN ACTION.

An assignee of a chose in action in Oregon may maintain an action thereon in his own name, although he paid no consideration therefor.—*Gregoire* v. *Rourke*, 275.

ASSIGNMENT FOR CREDITORS.

An assignor for creditors who has compounded and settled with his creditors cannot maintain a suit in equity against his assignee to compel a final accounting, but must proceed in the assignment matter for the accomplishment of such purpose. ctions 3173-3187, Hill's Code, prescribe a complete procedure for the administration and settlement of assigned estates, and must be considered a substitute for the equity power to compel the execution and performance of a trust in such matters.—*Sprinkle* v. *Wallace*, 198.

ASSIGNMENT OF ERRORS. See APPEAL, 9.

ATTACHMENT AND GARNISHMENT.

TIME WHEN ATTACHMENT LIEN ATTACHES TO CHATTELS.

1. A writ of attachment creates no lien on personal property until it is actually taken into the custody of the officer if it is capable of manual delivery; and when the property is in several parcels so as to require separate and distinct seizures, the lien as to each attaches only as of the time of its actual seizure, and does not relate back to the time of the seizure of the first parcel.—*Maxwell* v. *Bolles*, 1.

PAYMENT AS A DEFENSE BY GARNISHEE.

2. The burden of proving payment is always on the party pleading that defense, and this is the rule applicable to proceedings against a garnishee who admits an indebtedness to the defendant a short time before the services of the garnishment, but claims to have paid the debt before receiving the writ.—*Willis* v. *Holmes*, 265.

ATTACHMENT WILL SUSTAIN CREDITOR'S BILL.

3. A lien by attachment will sustain a creditor's bill without reducing the claim to a judgment.—*Bennett* v *Minott*, 339.

ATTEMPTED APPEAL.

Ineffectual Attempt does not Prevent Subsequent Appeal. See APPEAL, 15.

ATTORNEY AND CLIENT.

PRESUMPTION OF ATTORNEY'S AUTHORITY.

1. The courts must presume, in the absence of a showing to the contrary, that orders and proceedings of attorneys in the conduct of cases are made and conducted under proper authority from their clients, and when it is desired to impeach the acts of attorneys as beyond the terms of their employment, the proper method is to move in the lower court where the facts may be determined by testimony, rather than by an appeal from the objectionable proceeding.—*Schmidt* v. *Oregon Gold Mining Company*, 9.

PRESUMPTION OF RESIDENCE.

2. It will be presumed that an attorney in a case resides in the county where the case was tried, and that his acceptance of service of a notice of appeal was made in such county.—*Bennett* v. *Minott*, 339.

ATTORNEY-GENERAL.

SIGNATURE OF PUBLIC LAW OFFICER TO PRIVATE BILL.

1. The mere signature of the attorney-general or other public law officer, in his official capacity, to a complaint or bill shown to be that of a private relator, is not

28 OR.—45.

610

BURDEN OF PROOF.

ATTORNEY-GENERAL—Concluded.

sufficient to impress it with the functions and capacity of an information competent to put in motion the machinery of the courts, whereby they will take cognizance of questions pertaining to the high prerogative powers of the state or affecting the whole people in their sovereign capacity.—*State ex rel.* v. *Lord*, 499.

ACTION AGAINST PUBLIC OFFICIALS IN MATTERS OF PUBLIC CONCERN.

2. In cases of purely public concern affecting the welfare of the whole people or the state at large the action of a court can be invoked only by such executive officers of the state as are by law intrusted with the discharge of such duties.—*State ex rel.* v. *Lord*, 498.

BANKING CORPORATIONS.

"Transacting Business" Defined. See CORPORATIONS.

BENEFIT OF JUDGMENT.

Accepting Part of Judgment—Right to Appeal. See APPEAL, 2.

BEST AND SECONDARY EVIDENCE. See EVIDENCE, 3; CRIMINAL EVIDENCE, 17.

BILL OF DISCOVERY.

In order to sustain a proceeding under section 3143 of Hill's Code, authorizing a bill of discovery, with interrogatories attached, when the governor "is informed or has reason to believe" that any bank has any money or other property that has escheated to the state, the bill and interrogatories must be directed to some specific fund alleged to be in the custody of the bank, and must show that the state has a cause of action as to such fund, and, further, that the desired information will aid such action. Under the section cited a general inquisitorial proceeding cannot be maintained.—*State* v. *Security Savings Company*, 410.

BILLS AND NOTES.

An agent authorized to manage and dispose of a sash and door manufacturing plant has no authority to execute a note in the name of his principal in payment of for lumber, it not appearing when the lumber was purchased, or that it was used or intended for the benefit of the principal.—*Connell* v. *McLoughlin*, 230.

BOARD OF EQUALIZATION.

ALTERATIONS BY BOARD OF EQUALIZATION.

1. That alterations are made by the board of equalization on the assessment roll, upon pages before and after that on which appears an assessment against a given taxpayer, raises no presumption that the board approved such assessment.—*Godfrey* v. *Douglas County*, 446.

PRESUMPTION OF EQUALIZATION BY BOARD.

2. Where an assessment roll contains a column headed "As Equalized by the County Board," it will be presumed, where no entry appears in that column opposite an assessment, that the assessment was not equalized by the county board.—*Godfrey* v. *Douglas County*, 446.

PRESUMPTION AS TO JUDGMENT EQUALIZING AN ASSESSMENT.

3. When it appears that a board of equalization or a county court has once acquired jurisdiction of the person of the taxpayer whose assessment is equalized it will be presumed that the subsequent proceedings were regular and sufficient to sustain the judgment entered.—*Godfrey* v. *Douglas County*, 446.

BRIEFS.

It is intended the rules regarding the preparation and filing of abstracts and briefs in the supreme court shall be substantially complied with; yet upon sufficient showing a failure may be excused.—*Noppach* v. *Jones*, 286.

BURDEN OF PROOF.

PROVING FORFEITURE OF MINING CLAIM.

1. The burden of proof is always on the party who claims a forfeiture of a mining claim, that being an affirmative defense.—*Bishop* v. *Baisley*, 119.

ON PARTY PLEADING PAYMENT.

2. The burden of proving payment is always on the party pleading that defense, and this is the rule applicable to proceedings against a garnishee who admits an indebtedness to the defendant a short time before the service of the garnishment, but claims to have paid the debt before receiving the writ.—*Willis* v. *Holmes*, 265.

CASES FROM THE OREGON REPORTS that are Cited, Approved, Followed, Distinguished, Criticised, and Overruled in this Volume. See OREGON CASES.

CERTIFCATE.

Road Supervisor's Certificate—Subject of Forgery. See CRIMINAL LAW, 1.

CHARGING JURY.

Instruction as to Applause by Audience. See JURY TRIAL, 4.

Instructions need not be Duplicated. See JURY TRIAL, 6.

Abstract Propositions must not be Given. See JURY TRIAL, 12.

"CHARITABLE INSTITUTIONS."

WHAT CHARITABLE INSTITUTIONS ARE NOT TAXABLE.

1. To constitute a benevolent corporation a "charitable" one within the meaning of article IX, § 1 of the state constitution, and section 2732, Hill's Code, exempting from taxation certain property of "charitable institutions," it is not necessary that its benefits be extended to needy persons generally without regard to the relation the recipient may bear to the society or to dues or fees paid; but it is still "charitable" though it restricts its benefactions to its own members and their families.— *Hibernian Benevolent Society* v. *Kelly*, 173.

PROPERTY OF CHARITABLE INSTITUTIONS EXEMPT FROM TAXATION.

2. Under subdivision 3 of section 2732, Hill's Code, which provides that "such real estate belonging to charitable institutions as shall be actually occupied for the purposes for which they were incorporated" shall be exempt from taxation, a building owned by a charitable institution, only part of which is occupied for the purposes of the institution, is not exempt, though the revenues derived from the use of the remainder of the building are devoted to the objects of the institution, under this section the test of the exemption is the use of the property itself, and not the application of the income derived from it. In such cases the assessor should so value the property that the tax will really be paid by the unexempt part, though the assessment may run against it all.— *Hibernian Benevolent Society* v. *Kelly*, 173.

CHATTELS.

A writ of attachment creates no lien on personal property until it is actually taken into the custody of the officer if it is capable of manual delivery; and when the property is in several parcels so as to require separate and distinct seizures, the lien as to each attaches only as of the time of its actual seizure, and does not relate back to the time of the seizure of the first parcel.— *Maxwell* v. *Bolles*, 1.

CHOSES IN ACTION.

ACTION BY ASSIGNEE OF CHOSE IN ACTION—CONSIDERATION.

1. An assignee of a chose in action in Oregon may maintain an action thereon in his own name, although he paid no consideration therefor.— *Gregoire* v. *Rourke*, 275.

PLEADING ASSIGNMENT OF CHOSE—SURPLUSAGE.

2. It is not incumbent upon an assignee of a chose in action to show that he paid a consideration therefor, because the complaint avers a sale as well as an assignment to him, for the allegation in regard to the sale may be rejected as surplusage.— *Gregoire* v. *Rourke*, 275.

CLERICAL MISTAKE in Judgment.

Vacating after Term has Closed. See JUDGMENTS, 5.

When Mistake is not Apparent. See JUDGMENTS, 5.

CLOUD ON TITLE.

The averment in a complaint to remove a cloud on title, that defendant claims under a tax deed, sufficiently shows the apparent validity of the outstanding title, as a tax deed in Oregon is *prima facie* evidence of title.— *Day* v. *Schnider*, 457.

CODE CITATIONS in this Volume. See STATUTES OF OREGON.

COLLATERAL ATTACK.

On a prosecution for larceny by a bailee, even if proof of demand on defendant was necessary,—the undisputed evidence showing an actual conversion and fraudulent application of a note and its proceeds to defendant's use, contrary to the terms of the bailment,—objection could not be made to the regularity of the appointment of the guardian who made the demand, the court making the appointment having jurisdiction of the subject-matter and the parties.— *State* v. *Thompson*, 296.

CONFESSIONS.

Admissability of— Exclusion of Jury During Preliminary Examination — Discretion of Court. See CRIMINAL LAW, 7.

Corroboration of Confession of Accomplice. See CRIMINAL LAW. 9.

CONFIRMATION OF EXECUTION SALES.

Power of Court to Confirm Irregular Sales. See EXECUTION SALES, 1.

Sale of Real Estate *en masse*— Discretion of Sheriff See EXECUTION SALES, 4.

Extent to which Confirmation Cures Infirmities. See EXECUTION SALES, 6.

CONFLICTING EVIDENCE.

Findings so Based not Usually Disturbed. See EVIDENCE, 10.

CONFLICT OF LAWS.

JURISDICTION TO ENFORCE LAWS OF ANOTHER STATE.

1. It would seem that a statutory lien of one state ought to be enforced in the court of another state having jurisdiction of the subject matter and parties, unless there is a prescribed procedure for its enforcement which attaches as part of the liability, or unless its enforcement would be against good morals or natural justice, or prejudicial to the general interests of the citizens of the forum, under the general principles discussed in *Aldrich* v. *Anchor Coal Company*, 24 Or. 32, but this point is not decided.—*North Pacific Lumber Company* v. *Lang*, 246.

ENFORCEMENT OF LIENS OF ANOTHER STATE.

2. Where the statute of Washington provided that a lien on saw logs should not be binding for more than twelve months, unless a civil action should be brought within that time to enforce such lien, and a suit was commenced in Washington in due time, but the logs where thereafter removed to Oregon before a decree was entered, a suit cannot be maitained in Oregon after the twelve months have expired, for the property having been beyond the jurisdiction of the Washington court when the decree was entered, the lien was not fixed thereby, even conceding that the lien can be enforced in Oregon.—*North Pacific Lumber Company* v. *Lang*, 247.

CONSENT DECREES.

Consent Decrees cannot be Appealed from. See DECREES, 1.

Conditions beyond the Scope of the Pleadings. See DECREES, 2.

Valid if within General Scope of the Case. See DECREES, 3.

CONSIDERATION.

It is not necessary for an assignee of a chose in action to have paid any consideration for the chose to enable him to sue therefor in his own name.—*Gregoire* v. *Rourke*, 275.

CONSTITUTION OF OREGON.

Article VII, section 17, State *ex rel.* v. Lord, 494.

Article IX, section 1, Hibernian Benevolent Society v. Kelly, 173.

Article XV, section 1, Eddy v. Kincaid, 537.

CONSTITUTIONAL LAW.

PRACTICE.

1. Courts will not pass upon constitutional questions unless they are necessary to the determination of a cause.—*State ex rel.* v. Lord, 499.

JURISDICTION OF EQUITY.

2. A court of equity will not assume to determine the constitutionality of a legislative act unless the case comes within some recognized ground of equity jurisdiction, and presents some actual or threatened infringement of the rights of property on account of such unconstitutional legislation.— *State ex rel.* v. Lord, 499.

CONTEMPORANEOUS CONSTRUCTION OF CONSTITUTION.

3. Where a certain construction has been placed on a constitution by a series of legislative acts, and that construction has been for a long time accepted by the people and the different departments of government, the courts will hesitate to depart from it; such a practical exposition is often of controlling influence.— *Eddy* v. *Kincaid*, 537.

CORRECTING JUDGMENT. 613

CONSTITUTIONAL LAW—Concluded.

Legislative Power to Appoint Railroad Commissioners.

4. In view of the fact that the Oregon legislature has from the organization of the state created numerous public offices and appointed persons to fill them, and that the state constitution contains no express inhibition against the exercise of such power by the legislature, the court feels bound to now hold that section 4003, Hill's Code, which vests in the legislature the power to appoint railroad commissioners, is constitutional.— *Eddy* v. *Kincaid*, 537.

Tenure of Office of Railroad Commissioner.

5. In view of the provision in article XV, section 1 of the state constitution, that "all officers shall hold their offices until their successors are elected and qualified," and the further proviso in the act creating the board of railroad commissioners that such officers "shall hold their office for and during the term of two years and until their successors are elected and qualified as in this act provided," it necessarily follows that the failure of the legislature to elect a successor to a railroad commissioner at the expiration of his term of office does not create a vacancy, and the incumbent is entitled to the emoluments of such office until his successor is duly elected.— *Eddy* v. *Kincaid*, 537.

Repeal by Implication—Statutory Construction.

6. The Australian Ballot Law of eighteen hundred and ninety-one, (Laws, 1891, p. 8,) section 1 of which fixes the date of the general election at which certain named officers and "all other state, district, county, or precinct officers provided by law" shall be elected, does not repeal by implication section 4003 of Hill's Code providing for the election of railroad commissioners by the legislature, even if it is in conflict with the Code section, because this section is but a reenactment of a law that existed long prior to the creation of the board of railroad commissioners.— *Eddy* v. *Kincaid*, 537.

CONSTRUCTION.

Of Statute for Raising Revenue. See Statutory Construction.

Of Contracts—General Rule. See Contracts, 1.

CONSTRUCTIVE NOTICE OF FRAUD. See Fraud, 3, 4.

CONSTRUCTIVE POSSESSION. See Adverse Possession, 8.

CONTEMPORANEOUS CONSTRUCTION. See Constitutional Law, 3.

CONTRACTS.

Rule for Construing Contracts.

1. Written contracts should be considered from the standpoint of the parties when they were contracting, and be so construed as to give effect to all the provisions, if possible, always preferring that construction which makes the agreement legal rather than one which will make it void.— *Arment* v. *Yamhill County*, 474.

Construction of Contract with County.

2. A contract with county commissioners provided that the contractors were to receive (1) "An amount equal to the levy of the total tax of eighteen hundred and ninety on all such taxable real estate as shall be found unassessed," etc, and (2) "an amount equal to one half of the levy * * * of the year eighteen hundred and ninety-one," etc., payment "to be made from month to month, as the said tax shall have been collected by the sheriff of said county, and placed to the credit" of the contractors. *Held,* that the contract was not for the payment absolutely of amounts equivalent to the designated parts of the levies of eighteen hundred and ninety and eighteen hundred and ninety-one, but for the payment of the designated part of such levies actually collected by the sheriff, payable from month to month, as collected.— *Arment* v. *Yamhill County*, 474.

Contracts for the Benefit of Third Persons.

3. A provision in a bond of a street contractor to a city that the contractor will pay all money due and to become due for materials used and labor performed in completing his work, does not give to material men and laborers on the improvement any action against the contractor or his bondsmen, for the reason that the contract was made primarily and directly for the benefit of the city, rather than for their benefit, and because there was no fund or property provided in the hands of the promisor on which they could have any equitable claim.— *Brower Lumber Company* v. *Miller*, 565.

CORRECTING JUDGMENT for Clerical Mistake. See Judgments, 5.

CORPORATIONS.

A foreign banking corporation purchasing a note in the state, but having no purpose to do any other act in the state, is not "transacting business" within Hill's Code, § 3276, providing that a foreign banking corporation, "before transacting business" in the state, must record a power of attorney in each county where it has a "resident agent," which, so long as the company has "places of business" in the state, shall be irrevocable.—*Commercial Bank* v. *Sherman*, 573.

CORROBORATION OF Accomplice. See CRIMINAL LAW, 9, 10, 11.

COSTS.

DISCRETION OF COURT ON APPEAL.

1. Where a judgment is modified on appeal to the circuit court, the question of costs is in the sound discretion of that court, and its decision will be disturbed only in case of abuse.—*Sugar Pine Lumbering Company* v. *Garrett*, 168.

DISCRETION OF COURT IN EQUITY CASES.

2. The discretion regarding the payment of costs in an equity proceeding conferred by section 554, Hill's Code, extends only to who shall pay them, and once that discretion has been exercised by the court, it is subject to review only for abuse, and the decision ought to be as binding on the lower court as on the appellate court, and cannot be changed.—*Nicklin* v. *Robertson*, 278.

3. It is within the discretion of the trial court under Hill's Code, § 543, to refuse costs to either party in a suit of equity.—*Leick* v. *Beers*, 483.

COMPUTATION OF TIME.

4. The time provided by sections 556 and 557, Hill's Code, for filing cost bills and objections thereto, should be computed by excluding the first day, and also the last day where it falls on Sunday; Code, § 519.—*Nicklin* v. *Robertson*, 279.

DUTY OF CLERK IN TAXING COSTS.

5. Where no objections are filed to a statement of costs, the clerk has no discretion in allowing the items therein contained.—*Nicklin* v. *Robertson*, 279.

EXTENDING TIME TO FILE COST BILL.

6. It is within the discretion of the court to extend the time for filing an amended verified statement of costs where the application to extend is made within the five days allowed to file the statement.—*Willis* v. *Lance*, 371.

STATEMENT OF ITEMS IN COST BILL.

7. A verified statement under Hill's Code, § 557, showing the materiality and necessity of each item of costs objected to need not show the materiality of the testimony of witnesses whose fees are taxed, where it states that they necessarily attended court and were sworn and examined as witnesses at the trial, for their testimony must have been material or it would not have been received.—*Willis* v. *Lance*, 371.

FINDINGS BY COURT.

8. A party having objected to certain items of a cost bill, the court, upon motion to retax costs, should make separate findings as to each item objected to.—*Willis* v. *Lance*, 371.

COUNTY ROADS.

Time for Filing Remonstrance. See HIGHWAYS, 1.

Vacating by Establishing New Road. See HIGHWAYS, 2, 3.

Court may Disregard Report of Viewers. See HIGHWAYS, 4.

COUNTY SCHOOL SUPERINTENDENT.

Power to Apportion School Funds. See SCHOOLS, 1.

Acts Ministerially in Dividing School Fund. See SCHOOLS, 3.

COURTS.

POWER OF COURTS OVER FINAL DECREES.

1. A court having acquired jurisdiction to enter a final decree undoubtedly possesses the inherent right to subsequently modify both the time and manner of its enforcement, though the essential provisions of final decrees cannot afterward be changed.—*Farmer's Loan Company* v. *Oregon Pacific Railroad Company*, 44.

COURTS—CONCLUDED.

RATIFICATION OF EXECUTION SALE.

2. A court has power to ratify the act of an officer in selling property at a time other than that fixed by a decree, where it might, in the first instance, have ordered a sale on that day.—*Farmer's Loan Company* v. *Oregon Pacific Railroad Company*, 44.

COURT MAY DECLARE WHO IS AN ACCOMPLICE.

3. When all the facts in relation to a witness' connection with a crime are undisputed it is the duty of the court to instruct the jury whether the witness is or is not an accomplice.—*State* v. *Carr*, 389.

"NEXT TERM" DEFINED.

4. The words "next term" as used in section 2781, Hill's Code, referring to the time when the county court may complete the work of the county board of equalization, mean the next session of the court after the board has adjourned.—*Godfrey* v. *Douglas County*, 446.

POWER TO CONTROL EXCUTIONS.

5. Every court has the sole power of controlling its own executions, and, unless by special authority, an execution cannot issue from one court on a judgment entered in another court.—*Willammette Real Estate Company* v. *Hendrix*, 485.

CREDITOR'S BILL.

FRAUDULENT GRANTOR NOT A NECESSARY PARTY.

1. The grantor in a conveyance of property claimed to be fraudulent as to creditors is not a necessary party to a suit to set aside such conveyance as his interest cannot be affected by the result.—*Bennett* v. *Minott*, 339.

JUDGMENT NOT NECESSARY.

2. A creditor need not reduce his claim to judgment before filing a creditor's bill to reach assets of his debtor which have been transferred in fraud of creditors, a lien by attachment being sufficient.—*Bennett* v. *Minott*, 339.

FACTS JUSTIFYING A CREDITOR'S BILL.

3. Where a debtor, for the purpose of hindering and delaying creditors, organizes a corporation and transfers to it all his assets, he himself being the owner of practically all the corporate stock, and continuing the business the same after as before the incorporation, using the proceeds for his own benefit, equity will set aside such transfer at the instance of creditors, notwithstanding the incorporation is valid, and the corporate stock subscribed by the debtor is subject to sale under execution. Under such circumstances a court of equity will look beyond the legal forms, and decide the case on the rights of the parties.—*Bennett* v. *Minott*, 339.

CRIMINAL EVIDENCE. See CRIMINAL LAW, 8, 9, 13, 14, 15, 17, 18, 19, 20.

CRIMINAL LAW.

FORGERY OF ROAD SUPERVISOR'S "CERTIFICATE."

1. An instrument denominated a "time check," purporting to be approved by a road supervisor, and indicating that the person to whom it appears to have been issued had performed certain work on a certain public road, the value thereof being a stated amount, is a "certificate" that may be the subject of forgery, within the meaning of section 1808 of Hill's Code, which denounces the forging of any "certificate" of any public officer, in relation to any matter wherein such certificate may be received as legal evidence, and of section 4085, which requires road supervisors to "certify" to the county court their accounts for labor and material used on the public roads.—*State* v. *Gee*, 100.

DISQUALIFICATION OF GRAND JURORS.

2. Section 947 of Hill's Code, providing that it shall be a sufficient cause of challenge to any juror called "to be sworn in any cause" that he has served as a juror within a year, does not apply to grand jurors, for a "cause" within the meaning of that section is a civil or criminal action at issue and ready for trial in a circuit court, and grand jurors are not required to try such matters.—*State* v. *Brown*, 147.

RES GESTÆ.

3. The remarks and statements made by a defendant as he was hurrying from the scene of his crime, and immediately after its commission, are admissible as part of the res gestæ; as, for example, evidence that defendant ran away from the place of the shooting, with a pistol in his hand, shouting, "I am the toughest son of a bitch that ever struck this town," is competent on the question of malice, for it is closely connected with the principal event, and tends to show the state of the defendant's mind.—*State* v. *Brown*, 148.

CRIMINAL LAW—Continued.

IMPEACHMENT BY GRAND JURY.

4. A witness on trial for murder may be impeached by members of the grand jury as to the testimony given by her before such jury where the proper foundation has been laid.— *State* v. *Brown*, 148.

APPLAUSE BY AUDIENCE.

5. Failure of the court to instruct the jury not to be influenced in their verdict by any applause made by the audience in approval of the remarks of the prosecuting attorney is not cause for reversal, where no such instruction was asked, and the court promptly disapproved such applause.— *State* v. *Brown*, 148.

INSTRUCTION USURPING PROVINCE OF JURY.

6. An instruction on a murder trial that there is evidence "to the effect" or "tending to show" a certain fact, and allowing the jury, if they find it to be a fact, to consider it in determining the degree of defendant's guilt, does not, as being a presentation of facts by the court, violate Hill's Code, §200, prohibiting the court from presenting the facts of a case to the jury, especially where the jury are also instructed that they are the exclusive judges of all the facts in the case as well as the weight of evidence and credibility of the witness.— *State* v. *Brown*, 148.

EXCLUSION OF JURY—CONFESSIONS.

7. Whether the jury shall be excluded pending the preliminary examination as to the admissibility of a confession is within the discretion of the trial court.— *State* v. *Kelly*, 225.

ALLEGATION OF OWNERSHIP OF EMBEZZLED FUNDS.

8. In a prosecution under Hill's Code, §1770, for embezzlement, an indictment alleging that defendant, as agent of an insurance company, received for the company money as premiums for insurance, which he failed to pay over or account for, is insufficient for failure to allege that the money received was in fact the money of the company.— *State* v. *Stearns*, 262.

CORROBORATION OF ACCOMPLICE.

9. Under section 1371, Hill's Code, the admissions and confession of the woman with whom defendant is charged with having committed adultery are not sufficiently corroborated to sustain a conviction where the corroborating evidence goes merely to show that there was an opportunity to commit the act, but does not show an adulterous mind in either party, or any circumstance from which adultery might be inferred.— *State* v. *Scott*, 331.

ACOMPLICE—QUESTION FOR COURT.

10. Whether a witness is or is not an accomplice is a question for the court, where the facts in relation thereto are all admitted and no issue thereon is raised by the evidence; but if the evidence is conflicting as to whether a witness is an accomplice, that issue should be submitted to the jury under proper instructions.— *State* v. *Carr*, 389.

WHO IS AN ACCOMPLICE.

11. A mature person of ordinary intelligence, who knowingly offers as a bribe to a juror money provided by another for that purpose, becomes an accomplice within the meaning of section 1371, Hill's Code, forbidding a conviction upon the uncorroborated testimony of an accomplice.— *State* v. *Carr*, 389.

LARCENY BY BAILEE—INDICTMENT.

12. An indictment charging that defendant, being "the bailee and trustee" of a note, the property of another, embezzled and converted it to his own use, charges larceny by a bailee; the word "trustee" not affecting its validity, or charging conversion by a trustee.— *State* v. *Thompson*, 296.

VARIANCE IN DATE OF NOTE.

13. The identity of a note offered in evidence with one described in substance and legal effect in an indictment being unquestionable, a variance of two days in the date thereof is immaterial.— *State* v. *Thompson*, 296.

EVIDENCE OF VALUE OF STOLEN NOTE.

14. Evidence that a note was negotiable, and at the time of its conversion by defendant was not due, and that the latter sold it for its face value, is sufficient proof of value to sustain a conviction of larceny thereof by defendant as bailee.— *State* v. *Thompson*, 296.

EVIDENCE OF OWNERSHIP OF STOLEN NOTE.

15. In an indictment for larceny of a note by a bailee the averment of ownership in a certain person is established by proof that such person had become liable

CRIMINAL LAW — CONCLUDED.

on the note and had paid it, and was entitled to possession thereof at the time of the alleged larceny.—*State* v. *Thompson*. 296.

INDICTMENT FOR OBTAINING SIGNATURE BY FALSE PRETENSES.

16. An indictment under Hill's Code, § 1777, for obtaining a signature by false pretenses, alleging that defendant represented to the members of a given firm that he was an agent of a specified corporation, authorized to draw a draft on it for a specified amount, and exhibited to them a false telegram by means of which he procured the firm to indorse a draft for the specified amount, sufficiently shows that the indorsement was obtained for the accommodation of the corporation, and not of the defendant.— *State* v. *Hanscom*, 427.

SECONDARY EVIDENCE.

17. Where an indictment set out the substance of a false telegram used in the commission of a crime, which defendant retained, it was proper to admit secondary evidence of the contents of the telegram without giving defendant notice to produce it — *State* v. *Hanscom*, 427.

CRIMINAL EVIDENCE — FALSE PRETENSES.

18. Evidence that defendant, charged with obtaining a signature to a draft by false pretenses, received the money on such draft, is admissible to show an implied delivery to him of the draft.—*State* v. *Hanscom*, 427.

FALSE PRETENSES — IMMATERIAL EVIDENCE.

19. On the trial of one charged with obtaining a signature to a draft by falsely representing that it was for the accommodation of a certain corporation, it is immaterial whether defendant had money due him from the corporation or not.—*State* v. *Hanscom*, 427.

FALSE PRETENSES BY AGENT.

7. An instruction that an agent is not supposed to exceed his authority, and cannot bind his principal if he exceeds his authority, is reversible error on a trial for obtaining a signature to a draft by falsely pretending that it was for the accommodation of the principal, as it gives the impression that defendant would be criminally responsible if he exceeded his authority, however innocently.—*State* v. *Hanscom*, 427.

CROSS APPEAL.

Party not Appealing is Presumably Satisfied. See APPEAL, 8.

CROSS-EXAMINATION.

SCOPE AND CHARACTER.

1. The right of cross-examination is obviously an important one to an opponent, and the practice should be liberal with the purpose of eliciting all the facts in their true light. So, on an issue as to the consideration for a mortgage, the party attacking the instrument is clearly entitled to cross-examine the mortgagee on the facts and the circumstances surrounding its execution and delivery.— *Maxwell* v. *Bolles*, 1.

2. Defendant in an action for injury from fire alleged to have been kindled by him cannot be cross examined as to a custom to back-fire for the purpose of proving his negligence, where, on his direct examination, he has neither admitted that he set the fire nor testified to any custom.— *Willis* v. *Lance*, 371.

DEBTOR AND CREDITOR.

Right of Debtor to Prefer Creditor — Fraud. See FRAUD, 1.

DECREES.

APPEAL FROM CONSENT DECREE.

1. A decree entered at the request of a party, the other party being present and expressly consenting thereto, cannot be appealed from by either side. Such a decree will be governed by the provisions of section 536, Hill's Code, although, strictly speaking, it is not a decree given either by confession or for want of an answer.— *Schmidt* v. *Oregon Gold Mining Company*, 9.

CONDITIONS BEYOND THE SCOPE OF THE PLEADINGS.

2. Where the complaint, in a suit by a trustee to foreclose a mortgage, prays judgment for reasonable attorney fees and for professional services rendered therein, and the parties consent that judgment be rendered in accordance therewith, provisions in the decree that the trustee recover the attorney fees and fees for other professional services in trust for the parties rendering the services are not so entirely

DECREES—CONCLUDED.

without the scope of the pleadings, and the authority of the parties to agree thereto, that the appellate court will declare them void at the instance of the party requesting that such judgment be rendered.—*Schmidt* v. *Oregon Gold Mining Company*, 9.

ISSUES MADE BY THE GENERAL CASE.

3. A judgment or decree entered upon the pleadings or after a contest must fall within the issues made by the pleadings, but consent decrees will be valid and binding if they fall within the general scope of the case.—*Schmidt* v. *Oregon Gold Mining Company*, 9.

HOW FAR A FINAL DECREE MAY BE MODIFIED.

4. Where the original decree for the sale of a railroad in a foreclosure proceeding directed the property to be sold as an entirety, for cash, and that so much of the price "as is not required to be paid in cash may be paid in receiver's certificates." it is not an essential modification to subsequently provide that the sale shall be made for United State gold coin only, for the failure to provide in the original order the proportion of the price to be paid in cash left the provision for the acceptance of receiver's certificates of no effect, and the entire price would have been required in cash under the original decree.—*Farmers' Loan Company* v. *Oregon Pacific Railroad Company*, 44.

5. An order directing that all taxes legally due and owing by a corporation up to a certain date shall be paid out of the purchase money realized from a sale under a prior decree of foreclosure of a trust deed upon the property of the corporation, and that all taxes levied against the property after such date shall be paid by the purchaser, does not alter or vary the essentail parts of the original decree, which made no provision for the payment of taxes, so as to be in excess of the authority of the court, where the purchaser would be bound by law without an order to that effect to pay taxes accruing after that date.—*Farmers' Loan Company* v. *Oregon Pacific Railroad Company*, 44.

POWER OF COURTS OVER FINAL DECREES.

6. A court having acquired jurisdiction to enter a final decree undoubtedly possesses the inherent right to subsequently modify both the time and manner of its enforcement, through the essential provisions of final decrees cannot afterwards be changed.—*Farmers' Loan Company* v. *Oregon Pacific Railroad Company*, 44.

AFFIDAVIT—CORRECTING DECREE UNDER SECTION 102, HILL'S CODE.

7. A motion under Hill's Code, § 102, for relief from a portion of a decree on the ground that it was included therein through the mistake, inadvertence, surprise, or excusable neglect of the movant is ineffectual unless the affidavits submitted therewith show the existence of one of such grounds.—*Nicklin* v. *Robertson*, 279.

TIME WITHIN WHICH DECREE MAY BE VACATED.

8. Under Hill's Code, § 102, providing that the court "may at any time within one year after notice thereof relieve a party from a judgment taken against him through his mistake or excusable neglect," it is not sufficient that the motion be made within a year after notice, but it must be heard and determined within that time.—*Nicklin* v *Robertson*, 278.

CORRECTING DECREE AFTER CLOSE OF TERM.

9. A decree cannot be altered after the close of the term at which it was rendered, for a clerical misprision, where the mistake is not apparent on the record, and must be made out upon affidavits and evidence *aliunde*.—*Nicklin* v. *Robertson*. 279.

DEED of Sheriff is *prima facie* evidence of the matters therein recited.—*Willamette Real Estate Company* v. *Hendrix*, 485.

DEFECT OF PARTIES.

Objection must be made by Demurrer or Answer. See PLEADINGS, 10.

DEFINITIONS. See WORDS AND PHRASES.

DEGREE OF PROOF to show who is Real Party in Interest. See EVIDENCE, 9.

DEMURRER.

A general demurrer to a complaint containing several causes of action is properly overruled where any one of the causes is well stated.—*Barbre* v. *Goodale*, 465.

DEPOSITIONS.

An objection that the certificate to a deposition did not show that the deposition was taken by the person to whom the commission was addressed, nor in the official

DEPOSITIONS — CONCLUDED.

capacity designated therein, must be taken by motion to suppress before the trial is begun, otherwise it will be considered waived under the rule that objections to depositions for defects that may be remedied by retaking cannot be made at the trial.— *Sugar Pine Lumber Company* v. *Garrett*, 168.

DIRECTING VERDICT. See VERDICT.

DISCRETION OF COURT.

AMENDMENT OF PLEADINGS TO CONFORM TO PROOFS.

1. It is not an abuse of discretion by the trial court to permit at the trial an amendment setting up new defenses based on evidence that was objected to when offered, where the case is sent back to the referee to take such additional testimony as may be offered on the new issues.— *Bishop* v. *Baisley*, 119.

ACTUAL BIAS OF JUROR — DISCRETION OF COURT.

2. Under Hill's Code, § 187, providing that the fact that a juror has formed an opinion as to the merits of a case is not sufficient to sustain a challenge unless the court is satisfied from all the circumstances that the juror cannot disregard such opinion and try the case impartially, a clear abuse of discretion in allowing one to act as juror who has stated that he has formed an opinion must be shown to procure a reversal of the judgment on that ground, and in this case the facts set forth do not disclose any such conduct by the trial court.— *State* v. *Brown*, 147.

3. A juror who testifies that from reading newspaper reports of the case he had formed and expressed some opinion, but that his opinion was not fixed, and would not influence his verdict, is competent.— *State* v. *Kelly*, 225.

COSTS ON APPEAL.

4. Where a judgment is modified on appeal to the circuit court, the question of costs is in the sound discretion of that court, and its decision will be disturbed only in case of abuse.— *Sugar Pine Lumber Company* v. *Garrett*, 168.

EXCLUSION OF JURY — CONFESSIONS.

5. It is a matter of discretion with the trial court to conduct the preliminary examination as to the admissibility of a confession without the presence of a jury, or in their presence, as may seem appropriate.— *State* v. *Kelly*, 225.

COSTS IN EQUITY PROCEEDINGS.

6. The discretion regarding the payment of costs in an equity proceeding conferred by section 554, Hill's Code, extends only to who shall pay them, and once that discretion has been exercised by the court, it is subject to review only for abuse, and the decision ought to be as binding on the lower court as on the appellate court, and cannot be changed.— *Nicklin* v. *Robertson*, 278.

7. It is within the discretion of the trial court under Hill's Code, § 543, to refuse costs to either party in a suit in equity.— *Leick* v. *Beers*, 483.

EXTENDING TIME TO FILE COST BILL.

8. It is within the discretion of the court to extend the time for filing an amended verified statement of costs where the application to extend is made within the five days allowed to file the statement.— *Willis* v. *Lance*, 371.

DISMISSING APPEAL.

For Failure to File Brief — Rules of Court. See APPEAL, 10.

For Failure to File Abstract — Rules of Court. See APPEAL, 11.

For Failure to Serve Notice on Adverse Party. See APPEAL, 3, 4, 5, 6.

For not Filing Formal Assignment of Errors in Abstract. See APPEAL, 9.

DISTRICT ATTORNEY.

Effect of Signing Bill of Private Relator. See PREROGATIVE WRIT.

DISQUALIFICATION of Trial and Grand Jurors. See JURY TRIAL, 1, 2, 3.

DOCUMENTS. Notice to Produce — Reasonable Time. See SUNDAY, 1.

EJECTMENT.

Adverse Possession for Statutory Period. See ADVERSE POSSESSION, 1.

EMBEZZLEMENT.

Sufficient Allegation of Ownership of Funds. See CRIMINAL LAW, 8.

EQUALIZATION OF TAXES. See BOARD OF EQUALIZATION.

EQUITY.

JURISDICTION TO ENJOIN TRESPASS ON MINING CLAIM.

1. Equity will interfere by injunction to restrain a continuing trespass on a mining claim by the removal of valuable ores, and to compel an accounting for injuries already inflicted, at the suit of one claiming to be the owner of the realty, though out of possession, where a law action is pending to determine the title, and, if a strong showing is made, the trespass will be enjoined even where no law action has yet been commenced. Ordinarily, the injunction will be only temporary pending the trial of the title, but if the plaintiff presents a *prima facie* possessory title that is not seriously disputed, equity will settle the entire controversy without waiting for any proceeding at law.— *Bishop* v. *Baisley*, 120.

INJUNCTION AGAINST COLLECTING TAXES.

2. An injunction will not be granted to restrain the collection of a tax merely because of an inaccuracy on the assessment roll in the name of the owner, as, for example, the use of "Hibernian Benevolent Society" for "Portland Hibernian Benevolent Society."— *Hibernian Benevolent Society* v. *Kelly*, 174.

POWER TO COMPEL ACCOUNTING BY A GENERAL ASSIGNEE.

3. An assignor for creditors who has compounded and settled with his creditors cannot maintain a suit in equity against his assignee to compel a final accounting, but must proceed in the assignment matter for the accomplishment of such purpose. Sections 3173–3187, Hill's Code, prescribe a complete procedure for the administration and settlement of assigned estates, and must be considered a substitute for the equity power to compel the execution and performance of a trust in such matters.— *Sprinkle* v. *Wallace*, 198.

JURISDICTION TO REFORM WRITTEN INSTRUMENTS.

4. In order to justify the interposition of a court of equity to reform a written instrument for an alleged mistake of fact, it must be distinctly alleged and conclusively proved that the mistake was mutual, or that it was the mistake of one party superinduced by the fraud or some inequitable conduct of the other.— *Thornton* v. *Krimbel*, 271.

DISCRETION OF COURT AS TO COSTS IN EQUITY CASES.

2. The discretion regarding the payment of costs in an equity proceeding conferred by section 554, Hill's Code, extends only to who shall pay them, and once that discretion has been exercised by the court, it is subject to review only for abuse, and the decision ought to be as binding on the lower court as on the appellate court, and cannot be changed.— *Nicklin* v. *Robertson*, 278.

JURISDICTION IN CONSTITUTIONAL QUESTIONS.

6. A court of equity will not assume to determine the constitutionality of a legislative act unless the case comes within some recognized ground of equity jurisdiction, and presents some actual or threatened infringement of the rights of property on account of such unconstitutional legislation.— *State ex rel* v. *Lord*, 458.

ERROR.

Cured by Subsequent Evidence. See HARMLESS ERROR.

Proceedings will be Presumed to have been Regular. See PRESUMPTIONS, 3.

When Formal Assignment of Error is Unnecessary. See RULES OF COURT, 2.

ESCHEAT.

In order to sustain a proceeding under section 3143 of Hill's Code, the bill and interrogatories must be directed to some specific fund alleged to be in the custody of the bank and must show that the state has a cause of action as to such fund, and, further, that the desired information will aid such action. Under the section cited a general inquisitorial proceeding cannot be maintained.— *State* v. *Security Savings Company*, 410.

ESTATES OF DECEDENTS.

Payment of Allowance to Widow. See EXECUTORS.

ESTOPPEL.

ESTOPPEL AGAINST TAXATION.

1. A municipality is not estopped from levying a tax on certain property by the fact that it had omitted to assess such property in previous years.—*Hibernian Benevolent Society* v. *Kelly*, 174.

PAYMENT OF TAXES BEFORE SALE.

2. One in possession of land is not estopped by lapse of time from defeating a tax title by showing that the taxes for which the land was sold were in fact paid before sale.—*Nickum* v. *Gaston*, 322.

JUDGMENT AS AN ESTOPPEL.

3. A judgment roll in a former action showing judgment in favor of a person claiming under a tax title, accompanied with evidence that said action was brought at the request of defendant against said person, will not estop defendant from defeating said title by showing that the taxes for which the land was sold were paid by defendant before the sale, where it did not appear that the question of payment of said taxes was raised in said former action.—*Nickum* v. *Gaston*, 323.

EVIDENCE. For Evidence in Criminal Cases see CRIMINAL LAW.

ERROR CURED BY SUBSEQUENT EVIDENCE.

1. Error in admitting evidence of the contents of an instrument without proof of its loss or destruction is cured by subsequent testimony showing the loss.—*Maxwell* v. *Bolles*, 1.

PRESUMPTION AS TO FOUNDATION FOR IMPEACHING TESTIMONY.

2. The necessary preliminary questions to render an impeaching question proper will be presumed to have been asked and answered where the record does not purport to contain all the evidence.—*State* v. *Brown*, 148.

SECONDARY EVIDENCE.

3. A letter press or other copy of a letter is admissible to prove the contents of the original, where the latter is proven to have been mailed, postage prepaid, directed to the adverse party at his usual postoffice address, and a notice has been given to the latter to produce the original, but he had failed to do so, and there is evidence that such copy is identical with and in every respect an exact copy of the original letter.—*Sugar Pine Lumber Company* v. *Garrett*, 168.

SUPPRESSED EVIDENCE—PRESUMPTION OF AGENCY.

4. Where the authority of an alleged agent to execute a note, in an action thereon against the principal, is in issue, the failure of the agent, who was an unwilling witness, to produce his power of attorney, does not of itself raise a presumption that he was authorized to execute the note.—*Connell* v. *McLoughlin*, 230.

DECLARATIONS OF DEBTOR AS EVIDENCE.

5. Payment by a garnishee of his debt to defendant cannot be proven against plaintiff by statements of defendant made after service of the garnishment.—*Willis* v. *Holmes*, 265.

PAROL EVIDENCE TO SHOW PAYMENT OF TAX.

6. Parol or other competent evidence is admissible to show payment of a tax to defeat a tax title based on a subsequent sale for the alleged nonpayment of such tax.—*Nickum* v. *Gaston*, 322.

ALTERED WRITING AS EVIDENCE.

7. Where it is shown, even after an instrument has been admitted over objection of the other party, that the alteration appearing therein was not made after the execution thereof, section 788 of Hill's Code, providing that the party shall account for an alteration made after the execution of the instrument, does not apply.—*Nickum* v. *Gaston*, 322.

TO SHOW REAL PARTIES TO WRITTEN INSTRUMENT.

8. Parol testimony is admissible to show that a contract which is not a negotiable instrument, and not required to be under seal, although so in fact, executed by and in the name of an agent, is the contract of the principal, although the principal is known to the other contracting party at the date of its execution.—*Barbre* v. *Goodale*, 465.

DEGREE OF PROOF—REAL PARTY IN INTEREST.

9. That plaintiff is the real party in interest is not required to be established by higher proof than that requisite to establish any other fact in the case.—*Barbre* v. *Goodale*, 465.

EVIDENCE — CONCLUDED.

SHERIFF'S DEED AS EVIDENCE OF RECITALS.

10. The recitals in a sheriff's deed of land sold under execution are *prima facie* evidence of the matters recited.— *Willamette Real Estate Company* v. *Hendrix*, 485.

FINDINGS ON CONFLICTING EVIDENCE.

11. Findings of fact of trial courts based on conflicting testimony will not usually be disturbed, unless they are decidedly against the weight of the evidence.— *Justice* v. *Elwert*, 460.

EXCUSABLE NEGLECT as a Reason for Vacating a Judgment.

Time within which Motion must be Decided. See JUDGMENTS, 3.

Requisite of Affidavit Supporting Motion. See JUDGMENTS, 4.

EXECUTION SALES.

RATIFICATION OF EXECUTION SALE.

1. A court has power to ratify the act of an officer in selling property at a time other than that fixed by a decree, where it might, in the first instance, have ordered a sale on that day.— *Farmer's Loan Company* v. *Oregon Pacific Railroad Company*, 44.

INADEQUATE PRICE.

2. An inadequacy sufficient to set aside a public sale of property must be so gross as to shock the conscience, where there are no confidential relations existing between the parties, and no proof of fraud. Within the purview of this general rule the sale of the Oregon Pacific Railroad for one hundred thousand dollars, in December, eighteen hundred and ninety-four, was not a sale for such a grossly inadequate price as to require it to be set aside, so far as appears by the record.— *Farmer's Loan Company* v. *Oregon Pacific Railroad Company*, 44.

WHO ARE "THIRD PERSONS" UNDER EXECUTION SALES.

3. Parties to a decree for the foreclosure of a mortgage, and who are bound thereby, are not "third persons" as to a sale under the decree, within the meaning of Hill's Code, § 292, providing that real property consisting of several lots or parcels shall be sold separately when a portion is claimed by a "third person" who requests that it shall be so sold. Under this section the term "third person" evidently means one who was not a party to the judgment or decree, but who has acquired title to a portion of the judgment debtor's real property subsequent to the rendition of the judgment or decree, and is privy to and bound by it.— *Balfour* v. *Burnett*, 72.

DISCRETION OF SHERIFF IN SELLING REAL ESTATE.

4. Under the terms of section 292, Hill's Code, the sheriff may sell real property on execution in separate parcels or *en masse*, and after confirmation his action will not be reviewed, unless it is shown that he has abused the discretion confided in him.— *Balfour* v. *Burnett*, 73.

COURT FROM WHICH EXECUTION CAN ISSUE.

5. In the absence of a statutory provision authorizing an execution to be issued out of the circuit court upon a judgment rendered in the county court, the writ can not be so issued, and such writ is an absolute nullity.— *Willamette Real Estate Company* v. *Hendrix*, 485.

EXTENT TO WHICH A CONFIRMATION CURES INFIRMITIES.

6. The infirmity of a judgment for want of jurisdiction of the court to render it is not cured by the court's approval of a sheriff's deed of premises sold on an execution thereunder, as a confirmation of an execution sale of real property does not supply defects founded in a want of jurisdiction.— *Willamette Real Estate Company* v. *Hendrix*, 485.

EXECUTORS AND ADMINISTRATORS.

The fact that a widow, prior to the obtaining by executors of an order of court for a monthly allowance, agreed, for a valuable consideration, that it should be in lieu of dower, does not justify the executors in refusing to pay such monthly allowance, except on condition that she receipts for the same as in lieu of dower, where the order contains no provision that it shall be so received.— *Re Dekum's Estate*, 97.

EXPERT TESTIMONY.

A nonexpert witness may properly testify as to whether a person seemed excited or otherwise at a specified time.— *State* v. *Brown*, 148.

FRAUD AND FRAUDULENT CONVEYANCES — Concluded.

Transfer in Payment of Debt.

5. A transfer of property by a prisoner under indictment to pay counsel fees, which, though large, are not extortionate, is not void as to creditors, unless made for the purpose of rendering the property inaccessible to them.— *Morrell* v. *Miller*, 355.

Liability of Grantee in Fraudulent Conveyance.

6. Defendant, to whom plaintiff's debtor conveyed his personal property in secret trust for himself, is liable for the value thereof to plaintiff so far as he puts it beyond plaintiff's reach after he instituted his suit to set aside the conveyance as in fraud of creditors.— *Morrell* v. *Miller*, 355.

Subrogation.

7. A debtor made conveyances of land and personalty, which, as against plaintiff, his creditor, were fraudulent as to the personalty, and, as to the land, amounted only to a mortgage. *Held*, that the grantee having used the personalty in paying off a prior lien on the land, after plaintiff commenced action to set aside the conveyance of personalty, plaintiff would be subrogated to such lien.— *Morrell* v. *Miller*, 355.

GARNISHMENT. See Attachment and Garnishment.

GENERAL APPEARANCE.

Presumption is that Appearance was General. See Appearance.

GENERAL ASSIGNMENT FOR CREDITORS.

Assignment Law Provides Complete Procedure for Settlement of Assigned Estates—Jurisdiction of Equity to Compel Settlement. See Equity, 3.

GRAND JURORS.

Disqualification by Having Served within a Year. See Criminal Law, 2.

Impeachment by Members of Grand Jury. See Criminal Law, 4.

HARMLESS ERROR.

Error in admitting evidence of the contents of an instrument without proof of its loss or destruction is cured by subsequent testimony showing the loss.— *Maxwell* v. *Bolles*, 1.

HIGHWAYS.

Time for Filing Remonstrances.

1. Remonstrances to a petition for the vacation of a county road, which are filed when the report of the viewers is first read, are filed in proper time, under section 4065. Hill's Code, providing that the county court can acquire no jurisdiction prior to the final reading of the report. This is so regardless of what appeals or other proceedings may have occurred—the question is whether the remonstrances were filed before the court acted on the viewer's report.— *Vedder* v. *Marion County*, 77.

Vacating an Old Road by Establishing a New One.

2. The establishment of a new county road upon a petition for the establishment of such road, and also for the vacation of an old road, does not operate to vacate the latter, where the new road does not lie within the termini of the old one, and connects with it only at one end.— *Vedder* v. *Marion County*, 77.

3. A petition for the establishment of a road twenty-nine chains long, and for the vacation of another road connecting with the former at one end and forty-two chains long, and diverging from the former at an angle of more than forty-five degrees, and intersecting the same highway more than thirty chains apart, will be considered as two proceedings,—one for the establishment of a road, and the other for another road,—instead of a proceeding for the alteration of a highway merely.— *Vedder* v. *Marion County*, 77.

Discretion of County Court in Opening Roads—Report of Viewers.

4. A county court has a discretion regarding the opening of roads that is conferred upon it by the express terms of section 4065 of Hill's Code, and, while it cannot open a road over an adverse report of the viewers, it need not follow a favorable report, unless it is satisfied that the proposed road will be of public utility.— *Vedder* v. *Marion County*, 77.

IMPEACHMENT.

Necessary Preliminary Questions—Incomplete Record. See Presumption, 2.

Grand Jurors as Impeaching Witnesses. See Criminal Law, 4.

IMPLIED AUTHORITY OF AGENT. See AGENTS, 3, 6.

INADEQUATE PRICE. Causing Court to Avoid Sale. See EXECUTION SALES, 2.

INADVERTENCE as a Ground for Vacating a Judgment.
Time within which Motion must be Decided. See JUDGMENTS, 3.
Affidavit Supporting Motion to Vacate. See JUDGMENTS, 4.

INCONSISTENT ACTS. Affecting Right of Appeal. See APPEAL, 2.

INCONSISTENT DEFENSES.
Where a defendant denies the execution or delivery of a note, and in a separate defense alleges that the same note was made with a fraudulent intent, the execution - of the note is admitted, for the two statements are utterly inconsistent.—*Maxwell* v. *Bolles*, 1.

INDICTMENT.
Allegation of Ownership of Embezzled Funds. See CRIMINAL LAW, 8.
Word "Trustee" is Immaterial in Larceny by Bailee. See CRIMINAL LAW, 12.
Obtaining Signature by False Pretenses. See CRIMINAL LAW, 16.

INDISPENSABLE PARTIES.
Examples of who are not Indispensable Parties. See PARTIES, 4, 5.

INFERIOR TRIBUNALS.
Presumption of Regularity when Jurisdiction Appears. See PRESUMPTIONS, 11.

INJUNCTIONS.
JURISDICTION OF EQUITY — TRESPASS ON MINING CLAIM.
1. Equity will interfere by injunction to restrain a continuing trespass on a mining claim by the removal of valuable ores, and to compel an accounting for injuries already inflicted, at the suit of one claiming to be the owner of the realty, though out of possession, where a law action is pending to determine the title, and, if a strong showing is made, the trespass will be enjoined even where no law action has yet been commenced. Ordinarily, the injunction will be only temporary pending the trial of the title, but if the plaintiff presents a *prima facie* possessory title that is not seriously disputed, equity will settle the entire controversy without waiting for any proceedings at law.—*Bishop* v. *Baisley*, 120.

INACCURACY OF TAX ROLLS NOT SUFFICIENT.
2. An injunction will not be granted to restrain the collection of a tax merely because of an inaccuracy on the assessment roll in the name of the owner, as, for example, the use of "Hibernian Benevolent Society" for "Portland Hibernian Benevolent Society."— *Hibernian Benevolent Society* v. *Kelly*, 124.

INJUNCTION AT SUIT OF PRIVATE CITIZEN AGAINST PUBLIC OFFICER.
3. A private individual cannot have public officers enjoined from using public funds unless some personal, civil, or property rights are being invaded, or, in other words, unless such individual will be himself injuriously affected by the proposed expenditure.—*State ex rel.* v. *Lord*, 498.

INJUNCTION BY STATE AGAINST PUBLIC OFFICER.
4. The state, when suing in its corporate capacity for the protection of its property rights, stands in no different or better position than an individual in respect to an injunction against public officers.—*State ex rel.* v. *Lord*, 498.

ACTION AGAINST PUBLIC OFFICIALS IN MATTERS OF PUBLIC CONCERN.
5. In cases of purely public concern affecting the welfare of the whole people or the state at large the action of a court can be invoked only by such executive officers of the state as are by law intrusted with the discharge of such duties.—*State ex rel.* v. *Lord*, 498.

INJUNCTION AGAINST OFFICIAL PERFORMING GOVERNMENTAL DUTIES.
6. The location for a site for a public institution, the purchase of a tract of land therefor at that place, the employment of an architect to draw plans, etc., for the building, and the letting of contracts therefor by the governor, are matters governmental and executive in their nature, with which the courts cannot interfere by injunction; for it is now settled by a general consensus of authorities that in the ex-

INJUNCTIONS—CONCLUDED.

ecution of duties the performance of which requires the exercise of judgment or discretion, or in political or governmental matters pertaining to and affecting the welfare of the whole people, the executive is not subject to control by the courts. Nor is this rule in anywise changed by the fact that such duties have been delegated to a commission, of which the governor is a member.—*State ex rel.* v. *Lord*, 498.

INSOLVENTS AND INSOLVENCY.

Preference by Debtor to Relative. See FRAUD, 1.

INSTRUCTIONS TO JURY.

Instructions Specially Desired should be Requested. See JURY TRIAL, 4.

Instructions need not be Duplicated. See JURY TRIAL, 6.

Instruction is Presumed to have been Properly Refused. See PRESUMPTION, 3.

Abstract Propositions must not be given. See JURY TRIAL, 12.

Jury should use their Judgment and Experience. See JURY TRIAL, 13.

INSURANCE,

Where a fire insurance policy provides that no officer or agent shall have power to waive any of its conditions, except by writing, and that no privilege affecting the insurance shall be claimed by the assured unless so written, a parol waiver of any of the provisions of the policy by the agent from whom the insurance was obtained, after it has been accepted by the assured, is a nullity.—*Egan* v. *Westchester Insurance Company*, 289.

INTERPLEADER.

NECESSARY ALLEGATIONS FOR A BILL OF INTERPLEADER.

1. A bill of interpleader must show that two or more persons have presented claims against complainant for the same thing; that complainant has no beneficial interest in the thing claimed; and that he cannot determine without hazard to himself to which of the several claimants the thing belongs; and that there is no collusion with any of the defendants.—*North Pacific Lumber Company* v. *Lang*, 246.

PRACTICE ON PRESENTING BILL OF INTERPLEADER.

2. The orderly practice upon the interposition of a bill of interpleader is to determine whether the interpleader will lie or not, and, if it will, to discharge the plaintiff with his costs, upon bringing the money or thing in dispute into court; and the suit should thereafter proceed upon issues joined between the defendants. The making up of these issues may be accomplished in whatever way seems best adapted to secure an orderly and intelligible presentation of the rights of the contending parties.—*North Pacific Lumber Company* v. *Lang*, 246.

WHAT DEFENDANTS MAY INTERPLEAD.

3. One of the essential requisites of a bill of interpleader is a showing of a privity of some sort between the defendants, and that the various claims are of the same nature and character. Thus, a holder of a certain fund which is the purchase price of sundry saw logs, cannot oblige various claimants of such fund to interplead with other persons who are setting up claims against the holder of the fund for unliquidated damages—one of such classes being for claims arising *ex contractu* and the other for claims arising *ex delicto ;* one set of claims being against the fund, and the other set being against the holder of the fund. — *North Pacific Lumber Company* v. *Lang*, 246.

IRREGULARITIES in Execution Sales.

Confirmation Cures Irregularities. See EXECUTION SALES, 1.

Confirmation does not Confer Jurisdiction. See EXECUTION SALES, 6.

JOINDER of Several Causes of Suit. See PLEADINGS, 14.

JUDGMENTS.

SCOPE OF PLEADINGS.

1. A judgment or decree entered on the pleadings or after a contest must fall within the issues made by the pleadings, but consent decrees will be valid and binding if they fall within the general scope of the case.—*Schmidt* v. *Oregon Gold Mining Company*, 9.

JUDGMENTS—CONCLUDED.

JUDGMENT ON THE PLEADINGS — PRACTICE.

2. A judgment will not be rendered on the pleadings where they present an issue of fact, although the party upon whom the burden of proof rests refuses to introduce any evidence; the remedy in such a case is to move the court to direct a verdict.— *Willis* v. *Holmes,* 265.

TIME FOR VACATING JUDGMENT FOR MISTAKE.

3. Under Hill's Code, § 102, providing that the court "may at any time within one year after notice thereof relieve a party from a judgment taken against him through his mistake or excusable neglect," it is not sufficient that the motion be made within a year after notice, but it must be heard and determined within that time.— *Nicklin* v. *Robertson,* 278.

AFFIDAVIT CORRECTING JUDGMENT UNDER SECTION 102, HILL'S CODE.

4. A motion under Hill's Code, § 102, for relief from a portion of a decree on the ground that it was included therein through the mistake, inadvertence, surprise, or excusable neglect of the movant, is ineffectual unless the affidavits submitted therewith show the existence of one of such grounds.—*Nicklin* v. *Robertson,* 279.

CORRECTING JUDGMENT FOR CLERICAL MISTAKE.

5. A judgment cannot be altered after the close of the term at which it was rendered, for a clerical misprision, where the mistake is not apparent on the record, and must be made out upon affidavits and evidence *aliunde.—Nicklin* v. *Robertson,* 279.

JUDGMENT AS AN ESTOPPEL.

6. A judgment roll in a former action showing judgment in favor of a person claiming under a tax title, accompanied with evidence that said action was brought at the request of defendant against said person, will not estop defendant from defeating said title by showing that the taxes for which the land was sold were paid by defendant before the sale, where it did not appear that the question of payment of said taxes was raised in said former action.—*Nickum* v. *Gaston,* 323.

CREDITOR'S BILL — JUDGMENT NOT NECESSARY.

7. A creditor need not reduce his claim to judgment before filing a creditor's bill to reach assets of his debtor which have been transferred in fraud of creditors, a lien by attachment being sufficient.—*Bennett* v. *Minott,* 339.

PRESUMPTION AS TO JUDGMENT EQUALIZING AN ASSESSMENT.

8. When it appears that a board of equalization or a county court has once acquired jurisdiction of the person of the taxpayer whose assessment is equalized it will be presumed that the subsequent proceedings were regular and sufficient to sustain the judgment entered.—*Godfrey* v. *Douglas County,* 446.

JUDGMENT BY PUBLICATION OF SUMMONS.

9. A judgment against a nonresident on service of summons by publication is void, where the record fails to show that the court, prior to the publication, obtained jurisdiction of his property by attachment process.— *Willamette Real Estate Company* v. *Hendrix,* 485.

JUDICIAL SALES. See EXECUTION SALES.

JURISDICTION.

JURY TRIAL.

DISQUALIFICATION OF GRAND JURORS.

1. Section 947 of Hill's Code, providing that it shall be a sufficient cause of challenge to any juror called "to be sworn in any cause" that he has served as a juror within a year, does not apply to grand jurors, for a "cause" within the meaning of that section is a civil or criminal action at issue and ready for trial in a circuit court, and grand jurors are not required to try such matters.—*State* v. *Brown,* 147.

628 JUSTICES' COURT.

JURY TRIAL—CONCLUDED.

ACTUAL BIAS OF JUROR—DISCRETION OF COURT.

2. Under Hill's Code, § 187, providing that the fact that a juror has formed an opinion as to the merits of a case is not sufficient to sustain a challenge unless the court is satisfied from all the circumstances that the juror cannot disregard such opinion and try the case impartially, a clear abuse of discretion in allowing one to act as juror who has stated that he has formed an opinion must be shown to procure a reversal of the judgment on that ground, and in this case the facts set forth do not disclose any such conduct by the trial court.—*State* v. *Brown*, 147.

3. A juror who testifies that from reading newspaper reports of the case he had formed and expressed some opinion, but that his opinion was not fixed, and would not influence his verdict, is competent.—*State* v. *Kelly*, 225.

FAILURE TO ASK INSTRUCTIONS.

4. Failure of the court to instruct the jury not to be influenced in their verdict by any applause made by the audience in approval of the remarks of the prosecuting attorney is not cause for reversal, where no such instruction was asked, and the court promptly disapproved such applause.—*State* v. *Brown*, 148.

USURPING PROVINCE OF JURY.

5. An instruction on a murder trial that there is evidence "to the effect" or "tending to show" a certain fact, and allowing the jury, if they find it to be a fact, to consider it in determining the degree of defendant's guilt, does not, as being a presentation of facts by the court, violate Hill's Code, § 200, prohibiting the court from presenting the facts of a case to the jury, especially where the jury are also instructed that they are the exclusive judges of all the facts in the case as well as the weight of evidence and credibility of the witnesses.—*State* v. *Brown*, 148.

INSTRUCTIONS NEED NOT BE DUPLICATED.

6. A requested instruction that has been already given in another paragraph need not be given again.—*State* v. *Brown*, 149.

EXCLUSION OF JURY—CONFESSIONS.

7. Whether the jury shall be excluded pending the preliminary examination as to the admissibility of a confession is within the discretion of the trial court.—*State* v. *Kelly*, 225.

QUESTION FOR JURY.

8. If on a trial there is any dispute regarding the facts, or if there may reasonably be a difference of opinion as to the deductions therefrom, the matter should be submitted to the jury.—*Connell* v. *McLoughlin*, 230.

PRACTICE IN DIRECTING VERDICT—JUDGMENT ON PLEADINGS.

9. A judgment will not be rendered on the pleadings when they present an issue of fact, although the party upon whom the burden of proof rests refuses to introduce any evidence; the remedy in such a case is to move the court to direct a verdict.—*Willis* v. *Holmes*, 265.

PAYMENT OF TAX IS QUESTION FOR JURY.

10. Defendant's statement that she had paid the tax levied on land before the sale thereof, together with a receipt indicating that she had done so, was sufficient evidence to require the court to submit to the jury the question whether the tax really had been paid.—*Nickum* v. *Gaston*, 322.

JURY DETERMINES WHO IS AN ACCOMPLICE.

11. Where there is a conflict in the testimony as to whether a witness is an accomplice in a crime that question should be left to the determination of a jury—but it is otherwise when there is no dispute about the facts.—*State* v. *Carr*, 389.

ABSTRACT PROPOSITIONS MUST NOT BE GIVEN.

12. Abstract propositions of law, not applicable to the facts of the case in hand, are misleading and mischievous, and to present such in an instruction to a jury is reversible error.—*Pearson* v. *Dryden*, 850.

JURORS SHOULD USE THEIR JUDGMENT.

13. Where there is a conflict in testimony, and there is a difference between witnesses, the jury may properly be instructed that in arriving at a conclusion they should use their judgment and experience.—*Willis* v. *Lance*, 371.

JUSTICES' COURT.

Presumption of Residence of Respondent's Attorney. See PRESUMPTIONS, 6, 7.

How soon Transcript may be Filed in Circuit Court. See APPEAL, 17.

LARCENY BY BAILEE.

Word "Trustee" is immaterial in the Indictment. See CRIMINAL LAW, 12.

Evidence of Ownership of Stolen Note. See CRIMINAL LAW, 15.

Evidence of Value of Stolen Note. See CRIMINAL LAW, 14.

LEVY of Writ on Chattels.

Lien Attaches at Time of Actual Seizure. See ATTACHMENT, 1.

LIENS.

When Attachment Lien is Impressed on Chattels. See ATTACHMENT, 1.

Enforcement of Liens of Sister States. See CONFLICT OF LAWS, 1, 2.

Mechanics' Liens — Sufficiency of Notice. See MECHANICS' LIENS.

LIMITATION OF ACTIONS.

Adverse Possession as a Defense to Ejectment. See STATUTE OF LIMITATIONS.

MANDAMUS.

Hill's Code, § 2590, subdivision 4, as amended by Laws, 1889, p. 116, provides that funds arising from the five-mill county school tax or the irreducible state school fund shall be divided in proportion to the number of persons between the ages of four and twenty years who are actual residents of the district at the time of a division thereof. *Held*, that mandamus will not lie to compel a county treasurer to pay the amount apportioned to a new school district, formed by division of an old one, where the alternative writ fails to show the number of children in both districts, and it does not appear that the number of children in the new district were originally enrolled and enumerated in the original district.— *School District Number Two* v. *Lambert*, 209

MECHANICS' LIENS.

WHO ARE ADVERSE PARTIES IN MECHANICS' LIEN CASES.

1. In mechanics' lien cases all the lien claimants are "adverse" to each other, within the meaning of section 537, Hill's Code, and must be served with the notice of appeal.— *Osborn* v. *Logus*, 302.

WHEN CONTRACTOR IS NOT AN ADVERSE PARTY.

2. In a mechanics' lien case the contractor is not an "adverse party" and need not be served with the notice of appeal, where he has not been served with summons and has not appeared, though named in the pleadings as a defendant.— *Osborn* v. *Logus*, 302.

CONTRACTOR NOT AN INDISPENSABLE PARTY.

3. In a mechanic's lien foreclosure the contractor is not an absolutely indispensable party — he ought to be brought in if he can be served, but the suit can proceed without him, though, of course, if he is not served he is not bound by the result.— *Osborn* v. *Logus*, 302.

VARIANCE IN NAME OF CONTRACTOR.

4. A difference between the name of the firms of contractors as alleged in the complaint for the foreclosure of a mechanics' lien, and as disclosed by the contract, does not constitute a fatal variance where there is no question as to the identity of the two firms, and it is clearly apparent that the owner, who alone is contesting the lien, has not been misled in any respect by the difference.— *Osborn* v. *Logus*, 302.

NAME OF PERSON OBTAINING MATERIALS.

5. The naming in a claim of lien, in good faith, of the parties to whom material was furnished as "J. W. Holm and Brother," while the contract between the owner and contractor was signed "C. N. Holmes and Company," is immaterial, it not appearing that the owner was misled.— *Osborn* v. *Logus*, 302.

NAME OF PERSON TO WHOM MATERIALS WERE FURNISHED.

6. A claim for a mechanics' lien reciting that claimant "have, by virtue of a contract heretofore made with B. * * * in the furnishing sketches, plans, * * * and superintendence of a certain dwelling-house. The ground on which said dwelling house was constructed being at the time the property of said B. who caused said house to be constructed,"— is insufficient, for failure to state the person to whom the services were rendered, as required by the Code.— *Leick* v. *Beers*, 488.

MECHANICS' LIENS — CONCLUDED.

CONTRACTUAL RELATION BETWEEN CLAIMANT AND PROPERTY-OWNER.

7. A claim of lien for material or labor furnished a contractor filed under section 3673 of Hill's Code, need not state the contractual relations existing between the claimant and the owner, as the relation is in effect established by section 3669, which provides that the contractor shall be held the agent of the owner for the purposes of the act.—*Osborn* v. *Logus*, 303.

COMPLETE PERFORMANCE PREVENTED BY OWNER.

8. Failure of contractors to complete a building according to contract will not prevent a lien from attaching in their favor for so much of the work as was actually performed according to the contract, where such failure to complete was due to an act of the owner —*Justice* v. *Elwert*, 460.

MILEAGE.

A party is entitled to recover mileage for the number of miles actually traveled by each witness within this state.—*Sugar Pine Lumber Company* v. *Garrett*, 168.

MINES AND MINING.

PLEADING FORFEITURE OF MINING CLAIM.

1. The defense of a forfeiture of a mining claim through failure to perform the required work thereon is an affirmative defense, and must be specially pleaded where an opportunity is offered for so doing; and the burden of proof is always on the party claiming the forfeiture.—*Bishop* v *Baisley*, 119.

WHAT IS NOT "WORK AND IMPROVEMENTS" ON A MINE.

2. Picking rock from the walls of a shaft or outcropping of a ledge, in small quantities from day to day, and testing it, in order to find a paying vein, cannot be credited as part of the one hundred dollars' worth of "work and improvements" required by Revised Statutes of United States, § 2324, as amended by Supplement to the Revised Statutes of United States, p 276, to be made by a locator on his claim within one year from the date of his location.—*Bishop* v. *Baisley*, 120.

KIND OF ASSESSMENT WORK REQUIRED.

3. The requirement that a certain amount of labor or improvement shall be done or made on a mining claim each year in order to hold it is for the double purpose of insuring good faith in the claimant, and of requiring him to show a really valuable mine before claiming a patent; from which it follows that the kind of work required by the statute (United States Revised Statutes, § 2324, as amended,) is work tending to develop and exhibit the value of the mine rather than work expended in discovery or preliminary exploration.—*Bishop* v. *Baisley*, 120.

RESUMING WORK ON FORFEITED CLAIM.

4. Where a mining claim has been forfeited by the locator, his afterward going onto the claim with tools, securing samples of the ore, and testing it is not a resumption of work within the meaning of section 2324 of the Revised Statutes of the United States as amended in January, eighteen hundred and eighty, providing that a forfeited or abandoned mining claim may be relocated, provided the original claimant has not "resumed work" before the attempted relocation.—*Bishop* v. *Baisley*, 120.

ENJOINING TRESPASS ON MINING CLAIM.

5. Equity will interfere by injunction to restrain a continuing trespass on a mining claim by the removal of valuable ores, and to compel an accounting for injuries already inflicted, at the suit of one claiming to be the owner of the realty, though out of possession, where a law action is pending to determine the title, and, if a strong showing is made, the trespass will be enjoined even where no law action has yet been commenced. Ordinarily, the injunction will be only temporary pending the trial of the title, but if the plaintiff presents a *prima facie* possessory title that is not seriously disputed, equity will settle the entire controversy without waiting for any proceedings at law.—*Bishop* v. *Baisley*, 120.

MISLEADING INSTRUCTION to Jury. See JURY TRIAL, 12.

MISTAKE as a Ground for Vacating a Judgment.

Time within which Motion must be Heard. See JUDGMENTS, 3.

What Affidavit Supporting Motion must Show. See JUDGMENTS, 4.

Correcting Judgment for Clerical Mistake. See JUDGMENTS, 5.

MODIFICATION OF DECREE.

Power of Courts over Final Decrees. See DECREES, 6.

Extent to which Final Decrees may be Modified. See DECREES, 4-5.

MOTION TO DISMISS APPEAL.

For Failure to File Briefs. See APPEAL, 10.

For Failure to File Abstract. See APPEAL, 10, 11.

For Failure to Serve Notice on Adverse Parties. See APPEAL, 3, 4, 5, 6.

For Failure to Make Statement of Errors. See APPEAL, 9.

Appeal From Consent Decree. See APPEAL, 1.

Accepting Part of Judgment —Waiver of Appeal. See APPEAL, 2.

MOTION FOR JUDGMENT ON PLEADINGS. See PLEADINGS, 16.

MOTION TO SET ASIDE JUDGMENT.

Motion must be Decided within a Year from Judgment. See JUDGMENTS, 8.

MUNICIPAL CORPORATIONS.

A provision in a bond of a street contractor to a city that the contractor will pay all money due and to become due for materials used and labor performed in completing his work, does not give to material men and laborers on the improvement any action against the contractor or his bondsmen, for the reason that the contract was made primarily and directly for the benefit of the city, rather than for their benefit, and because there was no fund or property provided in the hands of the promisor on which they could have any equitable claim.—*Brower Lumber Company v. Miller*, 565.

NAME.

Variance in Name of Contractor. See MECHANICS' LIENS, 4.

NECESSARY PARTIES.

Grantor in Fraudulent Deed not Necessary to Creditor's Bill. See PARTIES, 4.

Contractor not Necessary in Mechanics' Lien Case. See PARTIES, 5.

NEGLECT as a Reason for Vacating Judgment.

Time Limited for Deciding Motion. See JUDGMENTS, 3.

What Affidavit Supporting Motion must Show. See JUDGMENTS, 4.

"NEXT TERM" Of County Court Defined. See WORDS AND PHRASES.

NON-JUDICIAL DAY.

A notice to produce papers at a trial is good though given on a nonjudicial day, and, in the absence of any showing to the contrary, one day's notice may be considered sufficient.—*Sugar Pine Lumber Company v. Garrett*, 168.

NON-RESIDENT.

Judgment without Personal Service or Attachment is Void. See JUDGMENTS, 9.

NOTICE.

To Produce Papers— Reasonable Time. See NON-JUDICIAL DAY.

Of Suspicious Circumstances— Constructive Fraud. See FRAUD, 3, 4.

Of Mechanics' Lien. See MECHANICS' LIENS.

NOTICE OF APPEAL.

Who is an Adverse Party —Service of Notice. See APPEAL, 3, 4, 5, 6.

Service of Notice— Presumption of Residence of Attorney. See APPEAL, 12, 13.

Amending Proof of Service of Notice. See APPEAL, 19.

OBJECTIONS.

For Defect of Proper Parties—Waiver. See WAIVER, 4.

For Indefiniteness or Uncertainty—Waiver. See WAIVER, 8.

632 OREGON CASES.

OBJECTIONS — CONCLUDED.

To Manner of Taking Deposition — Waiver. See WAIVER, 2.

To Confirmation of Execution Sale. See EXECUTION SALES, 1, 2, 4.

To Cost Bill — Computation of Time to File. See COSTS, 4.

To Cost Bill — Extension of Time to File. See COSTS, 6.

OBTAINING SIGNATURE BY FALSE PRETENSES.

Sufficiency of Indictment — Immaterial and Secondary Evidence. See CRIMINAL LAW, 16, 17, 18.

OFFICIAL BONDS.

PARTIES TO ACTIONS ON OFFICIAL BONDS.

1. A county is a proper party plaintiff in an action on an official bond of a tax collector under Hill's Code, § 341.— *Hume* v. *Kelly*, 398.

LEAVE TO SUE ON OFFICIAL BOND.

2. Under Hill's Code, § 342, before an action can be commenced on an official undertaking by another than the state or corporation in the name of which the undertaking runs, leave must be obtained from the court where the action is triable.— *Hume* v. *Kelly*, 399

AMENDING PLEADINGS BY CHANGING NAMES OF PARTIES.

3. An amendment of the complaint in an action by a district attorney upon an official bond, by adding the county, which is the real party in interest, as plaintiff does not change the cause of action — *Hume* v. *Kelly*, 398.

FAILURE OF APPOINTIVE OFFICER TO RENEW BOND.

4. The mere failure of an officer rightfully holding over by virtue of the express provisions of the law creating the office, to renew his bond, does not work a forfeiture of the office so as to deprive him of its emoluments.— *Eddy* v. *Kincaid*, 537.

OREGON CASES Cited, Approved, Followed, Distinguished, Criticised, and Overruled in this volume :—

Ah Doon v Smith, 25 Or. 89, approved and followed, 1.
Ainslie v. Cohen, 16 Or. 374, cited, 307.
Aldrich v Anchor Coal Company, 24 Or. 32, cited, 257.
Allen v. Dunlap, 24 Or. 232, cited. 145.
Allen v. Rowe, 19 Or. 190, cited, 282, 319.

Bank of British Columbia v. Page, 7 Or. 455, cited and approved, 76; distinguished, 573.
Barton v. La Grande, 17 Or. 577, cited, 241.
Bays v. Trulson, 25 Or. 110, approved and followed, 73.
Becker v. Malheur County, 24 Or. 217, cited and approved, 240, 446.
Bennett v. Minott, 28 Or. 339, approved and followed, 440.
Biggs v. McBride, 17 Or. 640, approved and followed, 557.
Bowen v. Clarke, 22 Or. 566, approved and followed, 350.
Briney v. Starr, 6 Or. 207, cited, 343. 465.
Butler v. Smith, 20 Or. 126, cited, 442.

Carr v. Hurd, 3 Or. 160, cited, 442.
Cline v. Greenwood, 10 Or. at p. 240, approved and followed, 537.
Cohen v. Ottenheimer, 23 Or. 224, cited, 307.
Cole v. Logan, 24 Or. 304, cited, 284.
Commissioners of Multnomah County v. State, 1 Or. 359, cited, 405.
Crawford v. Abraham, 2 Or. 167, approved and followed, 168.
Crawford v. Beard, 12 Or. 447, approved, 365.
Cook County v. Bushnell, 15 Or. 169, cited and approved, 398, 573.
Cross v. Tscharnig, 27 Or. 49, cited, 319.
Curtis v. LaGrande Water Company, 20 Or. 34, cited, 497.
Curtis v. Sestanovich, 26 Or. 107, overruled, 303.

Dawson v. Pogue, 18 Or. p. 94, approved and followed. 274.
Dawson v. Simms, 14 Or. 561 approved and followed, 339.
Dillon v. Hart, 25 Or. 49, approved and followed, 483.
Delph v. Barney, 5 Or. 211, cited and approved, 76.
Dolph v. Nickum, 2 Or. 202, cited and approved, 465.
Duffy v. Mix, 24 Or. 265, cited, 146.

Ehrman v. Astoria Railway Company, 26 Or. 377, cited, 97.
Elliott v. Oliver, 22 Or. 47, cited and approved, 530.

Epstein v. State Insurance Company, 21 Or. 179, cited and approved, 274.
Everts v. Stager, 5 Or. 147, cited and approved, 274.

Fable v. Pressey, 2 Or. 23, cited and approved, 274.
Faull v. Cooke, 19 Or. 455, cited, 491.
Fleischner v. Citizen's Invest. Co., 25 Or. 119, cited and approved, 138.
Foster v. Schmeer, 15 Or. 363, cited and approved, 274.
Foste v. Standard Insurance Company, 26 Or. 449, cited and approved, 398.

Glenn v. Savage, 14 Or. 567, cited and approved, 230.
Gordon v. Deal, 23 Or. 155. cited, 319.
Griswold v. Stoughton, 2 Or. 64, cited and approved, 76.

Habersham v. Sears, 11 Or. 436, cited, 405.
Hachney v. Leary, 12 Or. 40, distinguished, 578.
Hamilton v. Blair, 23 Or. 64, cited and approved, 110, 304.
Hedin v. Suburban Railway Company, 26 Or. 155, cited and approved, 230.
Heiple v. Clackamas County, 20 Or. 147, cited, 81.
Henness v. Wells, 16 Or. 266, distinguished, 465.
Herbert v. Dufur, 23 Or 462. cited and followed, 232.
Hicklin v. McClear, 18 Or. 126, cited and approved, 485.
Hildebrand v. Bloodsworth, 12 Or. 80, approved and followed, 474.
Hislop v. Moldenhauer, 24 Or. 106, cited, 382.
Holmes v. Whitaker, 23 Or. 319, cited, 374.
Howe v. Taylor, 6 Or. 284. cited, 405.
Hume v. Kelly, 28 Or. 398, cited, 481.
Hyland v. Hyland, 19 Or. 51, cited and approved, 274.

Inverarity v. Stowell, 10 Or. 261, cited, 96.
In re Comstock, 3 Sawy. 218, cited, 575.

Jolly v. Kyle, 27 Or. 95, cited and approved, 34.
Joy v. Stump, 14 Or. 361, cited and approved, 350.

Kleinsorge v. Rohse, 25 Or. 57, cited and approved, 274.
Kumli v. Southern Pacific Company, 21 Or. 505, cited and approved, 147, 226.

Latimer v. Tillamook County, 22 Or. 291, cited, 80.
Leinenweber v. Brown, 24 Or. 548, approved and followed, 73, 496.
Lewis v. Lewis, 5 Or. 169, cited and approved, 274.
Lewis Printing Company v. Reeves, 26 Or. 445, cited and approved, 442, 345.
Liggett v. Ladd, 23 Or. 26, cited, 487.
Lindley v. Wallis, 2 Or. 203 cited. 343.
Little v. City of Portland 26 Or. 235, cited, 94.
Lovejoy v. Chapman, 23 Or. 571, cited, 284; approved and followed, 453.

McCarty v. Wintler, 17 Or. 391, cited, 306, 445.
McRae v. Daviner, 8 Or. 63, cited, 491.
Mendenhall v. Harrisburg Water Company, 27 Or. 30, distinguished, 119.
Ming Yue v. Coos Bay Railroad Company, 24 Or. 392, cited, 592.
Moody v. Miller, 24 Or 179, cited and approved, 110, 302.
Moore v. Floyd, 4 Or. 260. cited, 97.

Neppach v. Jones, 20 Or. 491, cited, 287.
Nestucca Wagon Road Company v. Landingham, 24 Or. 493, cited, 304, 445.
Nickum v Gaston, 24 Or. 391, cited, 323.
Northcut v. Lemery, 3 Or. 316, cited, 495.

Odell v. Campbell, 9 Or. 298, cited, 495.

Parker v. Jeffery, 26 Or. 186, approved and followed, 565.
Philbrick v. O'Connor, 15 Or. 15, approved, 363.
Pilz v. Killingsworth, 20 Or. 435, cited, 319.
Portland Construction Company v. O'Neil, 24 Or. 54, cited, 92.
Pugh v. Good, 19 Or. 85, cited, 383.

Rader v. Barr, 22 Or 496, approved and followed, 9.
Rankin v. Malarkey, 23 Or. 593, overruled, 303.
Rector of St. David's v. Wood, 24 Or. 404, cited, 472
Rees v. Rees, 7 Or. 78, cited, 343.
Remillard v. Prescott, 8 Or. 37, cited and approved, 274.
Road Company v. Douglas County, 5 Or. 406, cited, 241.
Rowland v. Williams, 23 Or. 515, cited, 497.
Roy v. Horsley, 6 Or. 270, cited, 339, 440.

OREGON PACIFIC RAILROAD.

The sale of the property of this company to Bonner and Hammond for one hundred thousand dollars, in December eighteen hundred and ninety-four, was not made for such a grossly inadequate price as to require a resale, so far as the record shows. —*Farmers' Loan Company* v. *Oregon Pacific Railroad Company*, 44.

PAROL EVIDENCE.

Is Competent to Show Payment of Tax. See EVIDENCE, 6.

To show Real Parties to Written Instrument. See EVIDENCE, 8.

PARTIES.

WHO ARE ADVERSE PARTIES TO AN APPEAL.

1. Where a treasurer and his bondsmen are jointly sued on his official bond, and the former suffers a default, but the sureties make a successful defense on the merits of the case, the treasurer is "an adverse party" within the meaning of section 537 of Hill's Code, and must be served with the notice of appeal, for the decision of the appellate court affects the principal just as it does his sureties.—*Jackson County* v. *Bloomer*, 110.

PARTIES—CONCLUDED.

2. The grantor in a conveyance of property claimed to be fraudulent as to creditors is not a necessary party to a suit to set aside such conveyance, and, as his interest cannot be affected by the result, he is not an "adverse party," and the notice of appeal need not be served on him.—*Bennett* v. *Minott*, 339.

IDENTITY OF REAL PARTIES—RES JUDICATA.

3. To make a matter *res judicata* there must be identity of persons and parties in both causes, and it must be an identity of real parties who have interests to be affected by the decision. This identity is not destroyed by joining as additional parties in the second cause persons who were not parties to the former litigation, and who have no interest in the subject matter.—*Neppach* v. *Jones*, 286.

WHO ARE NOT NECESSARY PARTIES.

4. The grantor in a conveyance of property claimed to be fraudulent as to creditors is not a necessary party to a suit to set aside such conveyance as his interest cannot be affected by the result.—*Bennett* v. *Minott*, 339.

CONTRACTOR IN MECHANICS' LIEN CASES.

5. In a mechanic's lien foreclosure the contractor is not an absolutely indispensable party — he ought to be brought in if he can be served, but the suit can proceed without him, though, of course, if he is not served he is not bound by the result — *Osborn* v. *Logus*, 302.

WAIVER OF DEFECT OF PARTIES.

6. Where one who is a proper though not an indispensable party has been omitted from a case the objection must be taken by either demurrer or answer, as provided by sections 67 and 71 of Hill's Code.—*Osborn* v. *Logus*, 302.

PARTIES TO ACTIONS ON OFFICIAL BONDS.

7. A county is a proper party plaintiff in an action under an official bond of a tax collector, to recover for default in paying over taxes levied and collected, under Hill's Code, § 341, providing that any person injured by the misconduct of the principal in such bond, may maintain an action thereon in his own name, although the bond runs to the state.—*Hume* v. *Kelly*, 398.

REAL PARTIES TO WRITTEN INSTRUMENT MAY BE SHOWN.

8. Parol testimony is admissible to show that a contract which is not a negotiable instrument, and not required to be under seal, although so in fact, executed by and in the name of an agent, is the contract of the principal, although the principal is known to the other contracting party at the date of its execution.—*Barbre* v. *Goodale*, 465.

DEGREE OF PROOF—REAL PARTY IN INTEREST.

9. That plaintiff is the real party in interest is not required to be established by higher proof than that requisite to establish any other fact in the case.—*Barbre* v. *Goodale*, 465.

PLEADINGS.

INCONSISTENT DEFENSES.

1. Where a defendant denies the execution or delivery of a note, and in a separate defense alleges that the same note was made with a fraudulent intent, the execution of the note is admitted, for the two statements are utterly inconsistent.—*Maxwell* v. *Bolles*, 1.

CONSENT DECREE BEYOND THE SCOPE OF THE PLEADINGS.

2. Where the complaint in a suit by a trustee to foreclose the mortgage prays judgment for reasonable attorney fees and for professional services rendered therein, and the parties consent that judgment be rendered in accordance therewith, provisions in the decree that the trustee recover the attorney fees and fees for other professional services in trust for the parties rendering the services are not so entirely without the scope of the pleadings, and the authority of the parties to agree thereto, that the appellate court will declare them void at the instance of the party requesting that such judgment be rendered.—*Schmidt* v. *Oregon Gold Mining Company*, 9.

CONSENT DECREE—ISSUE MADE BY THE PLEADINGS.

3. A judgment or decree entered upon the pleadings or after a contest must fall within the issues made by the pleadings, but consent decrees will be valid and binding if they fall within the general scope of the case.—*Schmidt* v. *Oregon Gold Mining Company*, 9.

PLEADINGS—CONCLUDED.

PLEADING FORFEITURE OF MINING CLAIM.

4. The defense of a forfeiture of a mining claim through failure to perform the required work thereon is an affirmative defense, and must be specially pleaded where an opportunity is offered for so doing; and the burden of proof is always on the party claiming the forfeiture.— *Bishop* v. *Baisley*, 119.

AMENDMENT OF PLEADINGS TO CONFORM TO PROOFS.

5. It is not an abuse of discretion by the trial court to permit at the trial an amendment setting up new defenses based on evidence that was objected to when offered, where the case is sent back to the referee to take such additional testimony as may be offered on the new issues.—*Bishop* v. *Baisley*, 119.

PLEADING FORFEITURE IN TERMS.

6. In pleading under the Code it is only necessary to accurately and concisely state the facts relied upon, and therefore a plea of forfeiture of a mining claim need not aver specially that in consequence of the facts set forth "the claim was forfeited."—*Bishop* v. *Baisley*, 119.

NECESSARY ALLEGATIONS FOR A BILL OF INTERPLEADER.

7. A bill of interpleader must show that two or more persons have presented claims against complainant for the same thing; that complainant has no beneficial interest in the thing claimed; and that he cannot determine without hazard to himself to which of the several claimants the thing belongs; and that there is no collusion with any of the defendants.—*North Pacific Lumber Company* v. *Lang*, 246.

PLEADING ASSIGNMENT OF CHOSE—SURPLUSAGE.

8. It is not incumbent upon an assignee of a chose in action to show that he paid a consideration therefor, because the complaint avers a sale as well as an assignment to him, for the allegation in regard to the sale may be rejected as surplusage.— *Gregoire* v. *Rourke*, 275.

WAIVER OF OBJECTIONS.

9. An objection to a complaint for uncertainty or indefiniteness comes too late, after judgment.—*Bennett* v. *Minott*, 330.

WAIVER OF DEFECT OF PARTIES.

10. The objection that a proper party has been omitted from a proceeding must be taken by demurrer or answer.—*Osborn* v. *Logus*, 302.

AMENDING PLEADINGS BY CHANGING NAMES OF PARTIES.

11. An amendment of the complaint in an action by a district attorney upon an official bond, by adding the county, which is the real party in interest, as plaintiff, is authorized by Hill's Code, § 101, providing that the court may at any time before trial allow a pleading to be amended by changing the name of a party, for such an amendment does not change the cause of action.—*Hume* v. *Kelly*, 398.

USELESS AMENDMENT OF PLEADINGS.

12. Permission to amend a complaint is properly denied where the amendment if allowed would leave the complaint subject to objections that it was intended to obviate.—*Hume* v. *Kelly*, 399.

PLEADING TAX TITLE AS CLOUD.

13. The averment in a complaint to remove a cloud on title, that defendant claims under a tax deed, sufficiently shows the apparent validity of the outstanding title, as a tax deed in Oregon is *prima facie* evidence of title.—*Day* v. *Schnider*, 457.

JOINING SEVERAL CAUSES OF SUIT.

14. A complaint in a proceeding to remove a cloud on title is not obnoxious to the objection that it improperly unites several causes of suit because it sets out several reasons why the outstanding title is invalid.— *Day* v. *Schnider*, 457.

GENERAL DEMURRER—SEVERAL CAUSES OF ACTION.

15. A general demurrer to a complaint containing several causes of action is properly overruled where any one of the causes is well stated.—*Barbre* v. *Goodale*, 465

JUDGMENT ON THE PLEADINGS—PRACTICE.

16. A judgment will not be rendered on the pleadings where they present an issue of fact, although the party upon whom the burden of proof rests refuses to introduce any evidence; the remedy in such a case is to move the court to direct a verdict — *Willis* v. *Holmes*, 265,

POWER OF COURT to Vacate Judgment after Close of Term. See JUDGMENTS, &.

PRACTICE IN CIVIL CASES.

Limit and Character of Cross-Examination. See CROSS-EXAMINATION.

Presumption that Attorney has Authority. See ATTORNEYS, 1.

Attack on Attorney's Acts should be in Trial Court. See ATTORNEYS, 1.

Amending Pleadings to Conform to Facts Proved. See PLEADINGS, 5.

Error by Trial Court will not be Presumed. See PRESUMPTIONS, 8.

Notice to Produce Documents. See NONJUDICIAL DAY.

Procedure on Presenting Bill of Interpleader. See INTERPLEADER, 1, 2, 8.

Judgment on the Pleadings. See VERDICT.

Burden of Proof—Affirmative Defense. See BURDEN OF PROOF.

Allowance of Costs on Appeal. See DISCRETION OF COURT, 4.

Attachment Lien will Sustain Creditor's Bill. See CREDITOR'S BILL.

Reluctance to Determine Constitutional Question. See CONSTITUTIONAL LAW, 1.

Allowance of Costs in Equity Cases. See COSTS, 7.

Extending Time to File Objections to Cost Bill. See COSTS, 8.

Determining Qualification of Trial Juror. See JURY TRIAL, 2, 8.

PRACTICE IN CRIMINAL CASES.

Impeaching by Members of Grand Jury. See CRIMINAL LAW, 4.

Indictment for Embezzlement—Alleging Ownership. See CRIMINAL LAW, 8.

Excluding Jury—Admissibility of Confessions. See CRIMINAL LAW, 7.

Actual Bias of Juror—Discretion of Court. See JURY TRIAL, 2, 3.

PRACTICE IN SUPREME COURT.

Findings of Trial Court—Conflicting Evidence. See EVIDENCE, 10.

PREFERENCES BY INSOLVENT DEBTORS.

In the absence of an intention to hinder, delay, or defraud other creditors, a debtor may prefer a particular creditor to the exclusion of others by transferring his property to him in consideration of his indebtedness; but where such creditor is a relative, or a member of the debtor's family, the transaction will be scrutinized with more than ordinary care.—*Feldman* v. *Nicolai*, 34.

PREROGATIVE WRIT.

The mere signature of the attorney-general or other public law officer, in his official capacity, to a complaint or bill shown to be that of a private relator, is not sufficient to impress it with the functions and capacity of an information competent to put in motion the machinery of the courts, whereby they will take cognizance of questions pertaining to the high prerogative powers of the state or affecting the whole people in their sovereign capacity.—*State ex rel.* v. *Lord*, 499.

PRESUMPTIONS.

OF AUTHORITY IN ATTORNEYS.

1. The courts must presume, in the absence of a showing to the contrary, that orders and proceedings of attorneys in the conduct of cases are made and conducted under proper authority from their clients, and when it is desired to impeach the acts of attorneys as beyond the terms of their employment, the proper method is to move in the lower court where the facts may be determined by testimony, rather than by an appeal from the objectionable proceeding.—*Schmidt* v. *Oregon Gold Mining Com. any*, 9.

IMPEACHING EVIDENCE.

2. The necessary preliminary questions to render an impeaching question proper will be presumed to have been asked and answered where the record does not purport to contain all the evidence.—*State* v. *Brown*, 148.

ERROR NOT PRESUMED.

8. An instruction will be presumed on appeal to have been properly refused where the record does not purport to contain all the evidence.—*State* v. *Brown*, 149.

PRESUMPTION FROM SUPPRESSED EVIDENCE—AGENCY.

4. Where the authority of an alleged agent to execute a note, in an action thereon against the principal, is in issue, the failure of the agent, who was an illi-

PRESUMPTIONS—CONCLUDED.

willing witness, to produce his power of attorney, does not of itself raise a presumption that he was authorized to execute the note.— *Connell* v. *McLoughlin*, 230.

AS TO PARTY NOT APPEALING.

5. A party to a judgment or decree who has not appealed is presumed to be satisfied, and cannot ask the appellate tribunal to modify or reverse the decision of the lower court.— *Thornton* v. *Krimbel*, 271.

PRESUMPTION OF RESIDENCE OF ATTORNEY.

6. Where nothing appears in the record to show the residence of respondent's attorney, it will be presumed that he resides in the county where the trial was had, and that his admission of service of a notice of appeal from the circuit to the supreme court was there made.— *Bennett* v. *Minott*, 339.

7. It will be presumed by the appellate court in support of a return of service of notice of appeal from a judgment of a justice of the peace, that the attorney for the respondent upon whom the service was made was a resident of the county, where nothing to the contrary appears in the transcript on appeal.— *Hughes* v. *Clemens*, 440.

SPECIAL AND GENERAL APPEARANCE.

8. An appearance by a party will be presumed to have been general so as to give the court jurisdiction of the person where the record fails to show that the appearance was special. *Godfrey* v. *Douglas County*, 446.

AS TO ALTERATIONS BY BOARD OF EQUALIZATION.

9. That alterations are made by the board of equalization on the assessment roll, upon pages before and after that on which appears an assessment against a given taxpayer, raises no presumption that the board approved such assessment.— *Godfrey* v. *Douglas County*, 446.

10. Where an assessment roll contains a column headed "As Equalized by the County Board," it will be presumed, where no entry appears in that column opposite an assessment, that the assessment was not equalized by the county board.— *Godfrey* v. *Douglas County*, 446.

CONCERNING JUDGMENT EQUALIZING AN ASSESSMENT.

11. Where a taxpayer who has been notified to show cause before a county court why his assessment should not be increased appeared on the hearing, it will be presumed, on a writ to review a judgment increasing the assessment, that the judgment was rendered on sufficient evidence, though the record does not show on what it was predicated, or that it was rendered on any evidence.— *Godfrey* v. *Douglas County*, 446

PRINCIPAL AND AGENT. See AGENTS.

PRIVATE CITIZEN.

Injunction against Public Official Disbursing Public Funds — Location of Public Building. See INJUNCTIONS, 3, 6.

Cannot Invoke Prerogative Writ. See ATTORNEY-GENERAL, 1.

PROSECUTING ATTORNEY.

Effect of Signature to Bill of Private Relator. See ATTORNEY-GENERAL, 1.

PUBLIC INSTITUTIONS.

Location at Some Place other than the Capital. See INJUNCTIONS, 3, 4, 5 6.

PUBLIC OFFICERS.

Injunctions against Public Officials who are Performing Public Duties Imposed by Law. See INJUNCTIONS, 6.

Legal Effect of Signature of Public Law Officer to Bill of Private Relator. See PREROGATIVE WRIT.

PUBLICATION OF SUMMONS.

Judgment on Publication void without Attachment. See SUMMONS.

QUALIFICATION OF JURORS. See JURY TRIAL, 1, 2, 3.

QUESTION FOR JURY.

Disputed Facts or Inferences. See JURY TRIAL, 8.

RAILROAD COMMISSIONERS.

CONSTITUTIONAL POWER OF LEGISLATURE TO APPOINT.

1. In view of the fact that the Oregon legislature has from the organization of the state created numerous public offices and appointed persons to fill them, and that the state constitution contains no express inhibition against the exercise of such power by the legislature, the court feels bound to now hold that section 4003, Hill's Code, which vests in the legislature the power to appoint railroad commissioners, is constitutional.— *Eddy* v. *Kincaid*, 537.

TENURE OF OFFICE OF RAILROAD COMMISSIONERS.

2. In view of the provision in article XV, section 1 of the state constitution, that "all officers shall hold their offices until their successors are elected and qualified," and the further proviso in the act creating the board of railroad commissioners that such officers "shall hold their office for and during the term of two years and until their successors are elected and qualified as in this act provided," it necessarily follows that the failure of the legislature to elect a successor to a railroad commissioner at the expiration of his term of office does not create a vacancy, and the incumbent is entitled to the emoluments of such office until his successor is duly elected.— *Eddy* v. *Kincaid*, 537.

REAL PARTIES in Interest.

Parol Evidence — Written Instruments. See EVIDENCE, 8.

Decree of Proof Required to show who is. See EVIDENCE, 9.

REAL PROPERTY.

How Sheriff may Sell on Execution. See EXECUTION SALES, 4.

RECITALS in Sheriff's Deed are *prima facie* Evidence of the matters Recited.— *Willamette Real Estate Company* v. *Hendrix*, 485.

"RECORD" OF JUSTICE'S COURT.

The testimony of witnesses in criminal trials before a justice of the peace is not part of the "record" in such cases, (Hill's Code, § 2054,) hence is not part of the "certified copy of the record" that a justice attaches to a writ of review as his answer; Code, § 587.— *Tyler* v. *State*, 238.

REFORMATION OF WRITTEN INSTRUMENTS.

In order to justify the interposition of a court of equity to reform a written instrument for an alleged mistake of fact, it must be distinctly alleged and conclusively proved that the mistake was mutual, or that it was the mistake of one party superinduced by the fraud or some inequitable conduct of the other.— *Thornton* v. *Krimbel*, 271.

RELIEF FROM JUDGMENT on Ground of Inadvertence, Mistake, or Excusable Neglect. See JUDGMENTS, 3, 4, 5.

REMONSTRANCE Against Opening County Road.

Time within which Remonstrance must be Filed. See HIGHWAYS, 1.

REMOVAL OF CLOUD.

Tax Deed is *prima facie* a Cloud. See CLOUD ON TITLE.

REPEAL BY IMPLICATION. See STATUTORY CONSTRUCTION.

REPORTS OF VIEWERS.

County Court not bound by Favorable Report of. See HIGHWAYS, 4.

Court is bound by Unfavorable Report of. See HIGHWAYS, 4.

RES GESTÆ.

The remarks and statements made by a defendant as he was hurrying from the scene of his crime, and immediately after its commission, are admissible as part of the *res gestæ*; as, for example, evidence that defendant ran away from the place of the shooting, with a pistol in his hand, shouting, "I am the toughest son of a bitch that ever struck this town," is competent on the question of malice, for it is closely connected with the principal event, and tends to show the state of the defendant's mind.— *State* v. *Brown*, 148.

RES JUDICATA.

To make a matter *res judicata* there must be identity of persons and parties in both causes, and it must be an identity of real parties who have interests to be affected by the decision. This identity is not destroyed by joining as additional parties in the second cause persons who were not parties to the former litigation, and who have no interest in the subject matter.— *Neppach* v. *Jones*, 286.

RESUMING WORK on Mine. See MINES, 4.

REVIEW, WRIT OF.

"Record" Attached to Writ by Justice as his Answer. See WRIT OF REVIEW.

REVISED STATUTES OF UNITED STATES Cited and Construed in this Volume:

Section 2324, Bishop v. Baisley, 120.

Section 2325, Bishop v. Baisley, 185.

ROADS.

Time for Filing Remonstrance against Opening. See HIGHWAYS, 1.

Vacating by Opening another Road. See HIGHWAYS, 2, 3.

Discretion of County Court in Opening. See HIGHWAYS, 4.

ROAD SUPERVISORS.

Certificate of may be Subject of Forgery. See CRIMINAL LAW, 1.

RULES OF COURT.

DISMISSING APPEAL FOR NOT FILING ABSTRACT.

1. An appeal will be dismissed where appellant fails to serve and file the abstract of the record required by the rules of the court, (Rules 4 and 9, 24 Or. 595-597,) though part of the record has been lost, no effort having been made within a reasonable time to supply the missing papers.— *Close* v. *Close*, 108.

DISMISSING APPEAL—ASSIGNMENT OF ERRORS.

2. An appeal to the supreme court will not be dismissed because the abstract does not contain a formal statement of errors as required by the last paragraph of Rule 9 of the Supreme Court, (24 Or. 600,) where the appeal is from a decree on the pleadings, and it sufficiently appears that the alleged error upon which the appellant intends to rely is the action of the trial court in sustaining the respondent's motion for the decree. — *Neppach* v. *Jones*, 286.

DISMISSING APPEAL FOR FAILURE TO FILE BRIEF.

3. The rules of practice in the supreme court regarding abstracts and briefs were intended to facilitate business, and it is intended that they shall be substantially complied with; yet, if, through excusable neglect or oversight, some requirement has been omitted, the court may, on a proper showing, excuse the party in fault, as where a brief has not been filed in time through the delay of the printer.— *Neppach* v. *Jones*, 286.

SALES.

Actual acceptance by the buyer is not essential to a complete sale and transfer of title of goods under a valid contract, where they conform to the contract.— *Brigham* v. *Hibbard*, 386.

SCHOOLS AND SCHOOL DISTRICTS.

POWER OF COUNTY SUPERINTENDENT TO APPORTION SCHOOL FUNDS.

1. Hill's Code, § 2626, as amended by Laws, 1893, p. 25, provides that when the limits of any city are changed the limits of the school district therein shall be deemed to have been changed so as to conform to the new limits of the city. Section 2590, subdivision 4, as amended by Laws, 1889, p. 116, provides that when changes are made in any school-district boundaries the boards of directors of all the districts concerned, shall make an equitable division of the assets and liabilities, etc. *Held*, that the county superintendent alone has no right to make a division of assets of the district divided by Laws, 1895, p 442, changing the boundaries of the City of Portland, as that was the duty of the boards of directors.— *School District Number Two* v. *Lambert*, 209.

MANDAMUS TO COMPEL APPORTIONMENT OF SCHOOL FUNDS.

2. Hill's Code, § 2590, subdivision 4, as amended by Laws, 1889, p. 116, provides that funds arising from the five-mill county school tax or the irreducible state school

28 OR.—49.

SESSION LAWS.

Laws, 1891, page 118, State *ex rel.* v. Lord 498.

STATUTORY CONSTRUCTION.

1. Section 2781 of Hill's Code being a statute relating to the public revenue is not to be strictly construed.—*Godfrey* v. *Douglas County*, 445.

REPEAL BY IMPLICATION—RAILROAD COMMISSIONERS.

2. The Australian Ballot Law of eighteen hundred and ninety-one, (Laws, 1891, p. 8,) section 1 of which fixes the date of the general election at which certain named officers and "all other state, district, county, or precinct officers provided by law" shall be elected, does not repeal by implication section 4003 of Hill's Code providing for the election of railroad commissioners by the legislature, even if it is in conflict with the Code section, because this section is but a reënactment of a law that existed long prior to the creation of the board of railroad commissioners.—*Eddy* v. *Kincaid*, 537.

STREETS AND HIGHWAYS. See HIGHWAYS.

SUBROGATION.

A debtor made conveyances of land and personalty, which, as against plaintiff, his creditor, were fraudulent as to the personalty, and, as to the land, amounted only to a mortgage. *Held*, that the grantee having used the personalty in paying off a prior lien on the land, after plaintiff commenced action to set aside the conveyance of personalty, plaintiff would be subrogated to such lien.—*Morrell* v. *Miller*, 355.

SUIT TO REMOVE CLOUD.

Tax Deed is *prima facie* a Cloud. See CLOUD ON TITLE.

SUMMONS.

A judgment against a nonresident on service of summons by publication is void, where the record fails to show that the court, prior to the publication, obtained jurisdiction of his property by attachment process.—*Willamette Real Estate Company* v. *Hendrix*, 485.

SUNDAY.

NOTICE TO PRODUCE PAPERS.

1. A notice given on Sunday to produce papers at a trial is as good as though given on a judicial day.—*Sugar Pine Lumber Company* v. *Garrett*, 168.

COMPUTATION OF TIME.

2. The time provided by sections 556 and 557, Hill's Code, for filing cost bills and objections thereto, should be computed by excluding the first day, and also the last day where it falls on Sunday; Code, § 519.—*Nicklin* v. *Robertson*, 279.

SUPREME COURT.

ACCEPTING PART OF A JUDGMENT AS A WAIVER OF RIGHT TO APPEAL.

1. In law actions the entire case is either reversed or affirmed, and appellant cannot take part of his judgment and appeal from the balance.—*Bush* v. *Mitchell*, 92.

FORMAL ASSIGNMENT OF ERRORS IN ABSTRACT,

2. When an appeal is from a decree entered on the pleadings, and it appears that the error relied on is the action of the court in entering the decree, there need not necessarily be a formal assignment of errors in the abstract.—*Neppach* v. *Jones*, 286.

COMPLIANCE WITH PRACTICE RULES.

3. It is intended to enforce a substantial compliance with the rules regarding the filing of briefs and abstracts, but upon sufficient showing omissions and delays may be excused.—*Close* v. *Close*, 106; *Neppach* v. *Jones*, 286.

SURPLUSAGE. See PLEADINGS, 8.

SURPRISE as a Ground for Vacating a Judgment.

Time within which Motion must be Determined. See JUDGMENTS, 3.

What Supporting Affidavit must Show. See JUDGMENTS, 4.

TAXES AND TAXATION.

WHAT IS A "CHARITABLE INSTITUTION"—TAXATION.

1. To constitute a benevolent corporation a "charitable" one within the meaning of article IX, § 1 of the state constitution, and section 2732, Hill's Code, exempting from taxation certain property of "charitable institutions," it is not necessary that its benefits be extended to needy persons generally without regard to the relation the recipient may bear to the society or to dues or fees paid; but it is still "charitable" though it restricts its benefactions to its own members and their families.— *Hibernian Benevolent Society* v. *Kelly*, 173.

WHAT PROPERTY OF CHARITABLE INSTITUTIONS IS EXEMPT FROM TAXES.

2. Under subdivision 3 of section 2732, Hill's Code, which provides that "such real estate belonging to charitable institutions as shall be actually occupied for the purposes for which they were incorporated" shall be exempt from taxation, a building owned by a charitable institution, only part of which is occupied for the purposes of the institution, is not exempt, though the revenues derived from the use of the remainder of the building are devoted to the objects of the institution; under this section the test of the exemption is the use of the property itself, and not the application of the income derived from it. In such cases the assessor should so value the property that the tax will really be paid by the unexempt part, though the assessment may run against it all.— *Hibernian Benevolent Society* v. *Kelly*, 173.

ESTOPPEL AGAINST TAXATION.

3. A municipality is not estopped from levying a tax on certain property by the fact that it had omitted to assess such property in previous years.— *Hibernian Benevolent Society* v. *Kelly*, 174.

INJUNCTION AGAINST TAX—INACCURATE ROLL.

4. An injunction will not be granted to restrain the collection of a tax merely because of an inaccuracy on the assessment roll in the name of the owner, as, for example, the use of "Hibernian Benevolent Society" for "Portland Hibernian Benevolent Society."— *Hibernian Benevolent Society* v. *Kelly*, 174.

ESTOPPEL FROM SHOWING THAT TAXES ARE PAID.

5. One in possession of land is not estopped by lapse of time from defeating a tax title by showing that the taxes for which the land was sold were in fact paid before sale.— *Nickum* v. *Gaston*, 322.

EVIDENCE TO SHOW PAYMENT OF TAX.

6. Parol or other competent evidence is admissible to show payment of a tax to defeat a tax title based on a subsequent sale for the alleged nonpayment of such tax.— *Nickum* v. *Gaston*, 322.

WHO MAY PAY TAXES.

7. The payment of a tax on land by a person claiming an interest therein, and its acceptance by the proper collecting officer, precludes a sale for the tax, whether the claim of interest was well founded or not.— *Nickum* v. *Gaston*, 322.

PAYMENT OF TAX—QUESTION FOR JURY.

8. Defendant's statement that she had paid the tax levied on land before the sale thereof, together with a receipt indicating that she had done so, was sufficient evidence to require the court to submit to the jury the question whether the tax really had been paid.— *Nickum* v. *Gaston*, 322.

ALTERATIONS BY BOARD OF EQUALIZATION.

9. That alterations are made by the board of equalization on the assessment roll, upon pages before and after that on which appears an assessment against a given taxpayer, raises no presumption that the board approved such assessment.— *Godfrey* v. *Douglas County*, 446.

PRESUMPTION OF EQUALIZATION BY BOARD.

10. Where an assessment roll contains a column headed "As Equalized by the County Board," it will be presumed, where no entry appears in that column opposite an assessment, that the assessment was not equalized by the county board.— *Godfrey* v. *Douglas County*, 446.

JUDGMENT EQUALIZING AN ASSESSMENT—PRESUMPTION.

11. Where a taxpayer who has been notified to show cause before a county court why his assessment should not be increased appeared on the hearing, it will be presumed, on a writ to review a judgment increasing the assessment, that the judgment was rendered on sufficient evidence, though the record does not show on what it was predicated, or that it was rendered on any evidence.— *Godfrey* v. *Douglas County*, 446.

TAXING COSTS.

Extending Time to File Cost Bill — Discretion of Court. See COSTS, 6.

Computing Time — Exclude Sundays. See COSTS, 4.

Statement of Items in Cost Bill. See COSTS, 7.

Finding by Court on Items Objected to. See COSTS, 8.

"THIRD PERSONS" Under Section 292, Hill's Code. See WORDS AND PHRASES.

TIME for Filing Cost Bills and Objections. See COSTS, 4, 6.

TRANSACTING BUSINESS in this State within the Meaning of Statutes Regulating Foreign Corporations. See CORPORATIONS.

TRANSCRIPT From Justice Court may be filed in Circuit Court at once upon Allowance of Appeal. See APPEAL, 17.

TRESPASS.

Enjoining Trespass on Mining Claim. See MINES, 5.

TRIAL. See JURY TRIAL.

UNITED STATES STATUTES Cited and Construed in this Volume. See REVISED STATUTES OF THE UNITED STATES.

VACATING JUDGMENT.

Time within which Motion must be Determined. See JUDGMENTS, 3.

Requisite of Supporting Affidavit. See JUDGMENTS, 4.

Clerical Mistake not Apparent. See JUDGMENTS, 5.

VARIANCE.

MECHANICS' LIENS — NAME OF CONTRACTOR.

1. A difference between the name of the firms of contractors as alleged in the complaint for the foreclosure of a mechanics' lien, and as disclosed by the contract, does not constitute a fatal variance where there is no question as to the identity of the two firms, and it is clearly apparent that the owner, who alone is contesting the lien, has not been misled in any respect by the difference.— *Osborn* v. *Logus*, 302.

VARIANCE IN DATE OF STOLEN NOTE.

2. The identity of a note offered in evidence with one described in substance and legal effect in an indictment being unquestionable, a variance of two days in the date thereof is immaterial.— *State* v. *Thompson*, 296.

VERDICT.

A judgment will not be rendered on the pleadings where they present an issue of fact, although the party upon whom the burden of proof rests refuses to introduce any evidence, the remedy in such a case is to move the court to direct a verdict — *Willis* v. *Holmes*, 265.

VIEWERS OF COUNTY ROADS.

Court is bound by Unfavorable Report of. See HIGHWAYS, 4.

Reports — Time for Filing Remonstrances. See HIGHWAYS, 1.

County Court not bound by Favorable Report of. See HIGHWAYS, 4.

VOID EXECUTION. See COURTS, 5.

VOID JUDGMENT. See JUDGMENTS, 9.

WAIVER.

ACCEPTING PART OF A JUDGMENT AS A WAIVER OF RIGHT TO APPEAL.

1. In actions at law the entire case is either affirmed or reversed, so that an appeal cannot be taken from a part of a judgment, and the balance of it be accepted, thus, where a judgment went for plaintiff for the amount of a note, but the court refused to allow any attorney's fee, the plaintiff cannot accept the money adjudged to him on the note, and then appeal from the refusal to allow the attorney's fee, for if the case is reversed for one purpose it is for all purposes, and the question of the amount due on the note must be tried again.— *Bush* v. *Mitchell*, 92.

WAIVER—CONCLUDED.

WAIVER OF OBJECTION TO DEPOSITION.

2. An objection that the certificate to a deposition did not show that the deposition was taken by the person to whom the commission was addressed, nor in the official capacity de-ignated therein, must be taken by motion to suppress before the trial is begun, otherwise it will be considered waived under the rule that objections to depositions for defects that may be remedied by retaking cannot be made at the trial.—*Sugar Pine Lumber Company* v. *Garrett*, 168.

WAIVER OF OBJECTIONS TO PLEADING.

3. An objection to a complaint for uncertainty or indefiniteless comes too late after judgment.—*Bennett* v. *Minott*, 339.

DEFECT OF PARTIES.

4. An objection that a proper party has not been joined in a proceeding must be taken by demurrer or answer, or it will be waived.—*Osborn* v. *Logus*, 302.

WIDOW.

The fact that a widow, prior to the obtaining by executors of an order of court for a monthly allowance, agreed, for a valuable consideration, that it should be in lieu of dower, does not justify the executors in refusing to pay such monthly allowance, except on condition that she receipts for the same as in lieu of dower, where the order contains no provision that it shall be so received.—*Re Dekum's Estate*, 97.

WITNESS.

FOUNDATION FOR IMPEACHMENT.

1. A witness on trial for murder may be impeached by members of the grand jury as to the testimony given by her before such jury where the proper foundation has been laid.—*State* v. *Brown*, 148.

EXPERT WITNESS.

2. A nonexpert witness may properly testify as to whether a person seemed excited or otherwise at a specified time.—*State* v. *Brown*, 148.

MILEAGE FOR WITNESSES.

3. A party is entitled to recover mileage for the number of miles actually traveled by each witness in this state.—*Sugar Pine Lumber Company* v. *Garrett*, 168.

WORDS AND PHRASES.

"ADVERSE 'PARTY."

1. It is now well settled in Oregon that every party to a litigation whose interests in relation to the judgment or decree appealed from is in conflict with the modification or reversal sought by the appeal is an "adverse party" under section 537 of Hill's Code. It is accordingly held that where a principal and his bondsmen are jointly sued on his official bond, and the latter make a successful defense on the merits, the principal is "adverse" to the plaintiff, for his interests are identical with those of his bondsmen.—*Jackson County* v. *B'oomer*, 117.

2. In cases for the enforcement of mechanics's liens all the lien claimants are "adverse" to the property-owner and to each other.—*Osborn* v. *Logus*, 302.

3. In a mechanics' lien case the contractor is not an "adverse party" and need not be served with the notice of appeal, where he has not been served with summons and has not appeared, though named in the pleadings as a defendant.—*Osborn* v. *Logus*, 302.

4. A grantor in a transfer of property that is claimed to be fraudulent as against creditors is not an "adverse party,"—if the conveyance is upheld, the grantee holds the property; if it is set aside, the creditors get what is left, so that the grantor can get nothing either way.—*Bennett* v. *Minott*, 334.

ANNUAL ASSESSMENT WORK.

The kind of work required by the United States Revised Statutes, ? 2324, as amended, is work tending to develope and exhibit the value of the mine rather than work expended in discovery or preliminary exploration.—*Bishop* v. *Baisley*, 120.

"CAUSE."

A "Cause" within the meaning of section 947, subdivision 4, Hill's Code, is a civil or criminal action and ready for trial in a circuit court.—*State* v. *Brown*, 147.

"CERTIFICATE" OF ROAD SUPERVISOR.

An instrument denominated a "time check," purporting to be approved by a road supervisor. and indicating that the person to whom it appears to have been

WORDS AND PHRASES—CONTINUED.

Issued had performed certain work on a certain public road, the value thereof being a stated amount, is a "certificate" that may be the subject of forgery, within the meaning of section 1868 of Hill's Code, which denounces the forging of any "certificate" of any public officer, in relation to any matter wherein such certificate may be received as legal evidence, and of section 4085, which requires road supervisors to "certify" to the county court their accounts for labor and material used on the public roads.—*State* v. *Gee*, 100.

"CERTIFIED COPY OF RECORD." See RECORD.

"CERTIFY."

Under the requirement of section 4085, Hill's Code, that a road supervisor shall direct the expenditure of money in his district, and shall "certify" to the county court his accounts, any intelligible form which indicates with reasonable fullness the amount, nature, and kind of work done or material furnished, with the date, and the name of the person doing or furnishing the same, the value thereof, and the number of the road district, is sufficient.—*State* v. *Gee*, 104, 105.

"CHARITABLE INSTITUTION."

To constitute a benevolent corporation a "charitable" one within the meaning of article IX, section 1 of the state constitution, and section 2732, Hill's Code, exempting from taxation certain property of "charitable institutions," it is not necessary that its benefits be extended to needy persons generally without regard to the relation the recipient may bear to the society or to dues or fees paid; but it is still "charitable" though it restricts its benefactions to its own members and their families.—*Hibernian Benevolent Society* v. *Kelly*, 173.

"CONSENT DECREE."

A "consent decree" is one within the general scope of the case, and entered by agreement of the parties. Strictly speaking it is not a decree given either by confession or for want of an answer, but it is governed by the same rules as to appeal.—*Schmidt* v. *Oregon Gold Mining Company*, 9.

"INDISPENSABLE PARTIES."

See the discussion of this subject in *Osborn* v. *Logus*, pp. 809-311.

The grantor in a conveyance claimed to be fraudulent as to creditors is not an indispensable party to a creditor's bill to set aside the instrument.—*Bennett* v. *Minott*, 839.

"NECESSARY PARTIES."

There is an extended discussion of the meaning of this expression as used in foreclosure proceedings in the case of *Osborn* v. *Logus*, pp. 306, 312.

In a suit to reach assets of an insolvent that have been conveyed to avoid creditors the grantor is not a necessary party.—*Bennett* v. *Minott*, 339.

"NEXT TERM."

The words "next term" as used in section 2781, Hill's Code, referring to the time when the county court may complete the work of the county board of equalization, mean the next session of the court after the board has adjourned.—*Godfrey* v. *Douglas County*, 446.

"PROPER PARTIES."

See the discussion of this subject in *Osborn* v. *Logus*, pp. 308-311.

"RECORD OF JUSTICE" COURT.

The testimony of witnesses in criminal trials before a justice of the peace is not part of the "record" in such cases, (Hill's Code, § 2054,) and hence is not part of the "certified copy of the record" that a justice attaches to a writ of review as his answer: Code, § 587.—*Tyler* v. *State*, 238.

"RESUMED WORK."

Where a mining claim has been forfeited by the locator, his afterward going onto the claim with tools, securing samples of the ore, and testing and essaying it is not a resumption of work, within the meaning of section 2324 of the Revised Statutes of the United States as amended in January, eighteen hundred and eighty, providing that a forfeited or abandoned mining claim may be relocated, provided the original claimant has not "resumed work" before the attempted relocation.—*Bishop* v. *Baisley*, 120.

"TERM" OF COURT.

See the discussion of this subject in *Godfrey* v. *Douglas County*, pp. 450-458.

WORDS AND PHRASES — CONCLUDED.

"THIRD PERSONS."

Parties to a decree for the foreclosure of a mortgage, and who are bound thereby, are not "third persons" as to a sale under the decree, within the meaning of Hill's Code, § 292, providing that real property consisting of several lots or parcels shall be sold separately when a portion is claimed by a "third person" who requests that it shall be so sold. Under this section the term "third person" evidently means one who was not a party to the judgment or decree, but who has acquired title to a portion of the judgment debtor's real property subsequent to the rendition of the judgment or decree, and is privy to and bound by it.—*Balfour* v. *Burnett*, 72.

"TRANSACTING BUSINESS."

A foreign banking corporation purchasing a note in the state, but having no purpose to do any other act in the state, is not "transacting business" in the state within Hill's Code, § 3276, providing that a foreign baking corporation, "before transacting business" in the state, must record a power of attorney in each county where it has "a resident agent," which, so long as the company has "places of business" in the state shall be irrevocable.—*Commercial Bank* v. *Sherman*, 573.

"WORK AND IMPROVEMENTS."

Picking rock from the walls of a shaft or outcropping of a ledge, in small quantities, from day to day, and testing it, in order to find a paying vein, cannot be credited as part of the one hundred dollars' worth of "work and improvements" required by Revised Statutes of United States, § 2324, as amended by supplement to Revised Statutes of United States, p. 276, to be made by a locator on his claim within one year from the date of his location.—*Bishop* v. *Baisley*, 120.

WRIT OF REVIEW.

The testimony of witnesses in criminal trials before a justice of the peace is not part of the "record" in such cases, (Hill's Code, § 2054.) and hence is not part of the "certified copy of the record" that a justice attaches to a writ of review as his answer.—*Tyler* v. *State*, 238.

Ex. £2.13.

Lightning Source UK Ltd.
Milton Keynes UK
UKHW021602110119
335297UK00008B/450/P